Encyclopedia of
School Psychology

Encyclopedia of School Psychology

Edited by

T. Steuart Watson

Miami University
Oxford, Ohio

and

Christopher H. Skinner

University of Tennessee
Knoxville, Tennessee

Kluwer Academic / Plenum Publishers
New York, Boston, Dordrecht, London, Moscow

Library of Congress Cataloging-in-Publication Data

Encyclopedia of school psychology / edited by T. Steuart Watson and Christopher H. Skinner.
   p. cm.
   Includes bibliographical references.
   ISBN 0-306-48480-3
   1. School psychology—Encyclopedias.   2. Child psychology—Encyclopedias.
   3. Educational psychology—Encyclopedias.   I. Watson, T. Steuart.
   II. Skinner, Christopher H.
   LB 1027.55.E52 2004
  370.15′03—dc22

                                    2004049695

ISBN 0-306-48480-3

© 2004 Kluwer Academic/Plenum Publishers
233 Spring Street, New York, New York 10013

http://www.kluweronline.com

10 9 8 7 6 5 4 3 2 1

A C.I.P. record for this book is available from the Library of Congress

Permissions for books published in Europe: permissions@wkap.nl
Permissions for books published in the United States of America: permissions@wkap.com

Printed in the United States of America

Life is often compared to many things: paved roads, journeys, sweet tarts, and baseball games to name a few. In the end, a life lived is the only true measure of a person. It is unique in the radiant joy and intense heartache that it brings to each of us. As the next chapter of life unfolds, I dedicate this book to those who have stood fiercely tall and firm in their support: Tonya, Mackenzie, Tucker, Addison, Dad (Henry), and Mom (Johnnie Marie). God bless each one of you always for your special gifts and contributions.

—TSW

In memory of my father, Carl F. Skinner who passed away as this project was in progress. He loved everything about schools and education.

—CHS

Preface

When approached to edit an encyclopedia of school psychology, we were both excited and concerned. Our excitement stemmed from recognizing that there was a need for an authoritative reference text that would appeal to, and be understood by, a broad audience. Different professions develop their own language and jargon, many of which are abbreviations that allow for more efficient communication among professionals. However, these abbreviations cloud basic communication with those outside the field. With this text and brief entries, our esteemed group of authors has attempted to help readers gain an elementary understanding of this efficient communication and the meaning it conveys.

Despite being a distinct profession for several decades, there remains considerable confusion and lack of knowledge about who school psychologists are, what they do, and the practices and concepts that define our field. This confusion is not limited to lay persons, it also abounds among other professionals. As just one example, a school psychologist was in a meeting recently with individuals representing several professions, one of which was child psychiatry. Upon being introduced as a school psychologist, the psychiatrist replied, "Oh, then you must do guidance counseling." Thus, one of the purposes of this encyclopedia is to assist individuals in acquiring a general understanding of some of the theories, practices, and language associated with the field of school psychology. This is one of the needs that most excited us when we were approached to edit this reference text.

Recognizing the need for an authoritative text also caused us considerable concern. Our concern emanated from the realization that school psychology, as a profession and field, incorporates a breadth of practices and theories and is substantially related to the fields of child clinical psychology, pediatric psychology, special education, education, clinical psychology, applied behavior analysis, developmental psychology, psychopathology, educational psychology, and cognitive psychology,

to name a few. In fact, much of the literature base for the practice of school psychology is derived from these and other fields. Thus, deciding which topics to include and exclude became a rather daunting task. There was always the fear of excluding a topic that someone else would have deemed essential for an encyclopedia of school psychology. Therefore, we used some decision rules for which topics to include. The first rule involved omitting biographies of living persons. There are many current figures whose work and contributions will be well remembered in future encyclopedias and reference works. One of the dangers of including those living is that someone and his/her work will be inadvertently omitted. In addition, it may be some time before the work of current figures is fully recognized for the long-term impact it has on the field. A second rule involved the criterion of representation. Representation in the sense that we realized that not every topic related to school psychology could be reasonably included, so we decided to include those that represent different areas. For instance, it would not be feasible to include every law that has impacted and shaped school psychology. Instead, we chose laws, and other topics, that represent a broad spectrum, within a given area, of the major influences on school psychology. Given the breadth and depth of our field, we found it very difficult to narrow our list of entries. We realize we have made some errors (perhaps many) of omission and inclusion. We will try to do better next time.

The entries in this encyclopedia are organized alphabetically for ease of use and of locating subject matter. Biographical entries are indexed according to the subject's last name (e.g., Skinner, B. F., Watson, John B.). Some entries have multiple "subentries" with different authors. For example, the Reading entry contains an entry on curriculum-based measurement, learning disability, and intervention.

Each entry also contains a bibliography of references that was used by the author(s) as the entry was prepared. Following the bibliography is a list of suggested readings for both professionals and nonprofessionals, where appropriate. Authors were encouraged to include Web sites as additional readings if they were available and germane to the entry. Authors were also instructed to include, within the text of the entry, only a minimal number of citations so as not to interfere with readability and to write in an authoritative but user-friendly tone. Cross references are also included that direct the reader to other entries that provide further clarification on related topics.

A work of this magnitude is the result of the efforts of many. First, our sincere compliments are extended to those who contributed to this volume. Without their expertise and commitment to writing in precise yet understandable language, there would be no encyclopedia. Second, a hearty thank you goes to Mariclaire Cloutier, Publishing Director, Behavioral Sciences, at Kluwer Academic/Plenum Publishers for entrusting us with this most worthy project. Third, for the support and direction provided by Siiri LeLumees, former Child Psychology Editor, at Kluwer Academic/Plenum Publishers and Anna Tobias, who kept us on track and asked all the right questions, we are eternally grateful. And finally, we would like to thank those in advance who will give us constructive feedback on this volume so that future volumes may be improved.

T. STEUART WATSON
CHRISTOPHER H. SKINNER

Aa

Absenteeism

Absenteeism from school may be defined as any legitimate or illegitimate absence from school for school-aged youth (e.g., 5–17 years). Most cases of absence from school are for legitimate or legal reasons, including illness (especially asthma) and extensive medical conditions, religious holidays, important family occasions (e.g., wedding, funeral), poor weather conditions, and special exemptions for attendance at college classes or work-related activities. Other cases of school absenteeism are illegal in nature, and may include situations where parents deliberately keep a child from school, where families are in exigent circumstances (e.g., homeless), or where a child skips school or otherwise refuses to attend school (Kearney, 2001).

The phenomenon whereby youth are kept home from school by their parents is often referred to as school withdrawal. School absenteeism in this fashion may occur for economic reasons (e.g., a need to have the child babysit or work for the family), to comfort parents during a stressful time, to protect the child from potential kidnapping by an estranged spouse or other relative, to protect the child from other perceived or actual threats at school, to assist a parent who has a psychopathological condition (e.g., depression, panic disorder), to punish the child for some wrongdoing, to unnecessarily pursue home schooling, to spite teachers with whom parents disagree, to reduce parental separation anxiety, and/or to sabotage treatment designed to reintroduce a child to school. In other instances, parent-based school withdrawal is based on the need to hide something from school officials, such as effects of maltreatment, malnutrition, a child-based mental disorder, or uncompleted schoolwork.

The phenomenon whereby children miss school on their own for illegitimate reasons refers to school refusal behavior.

School refusal behavior refers to youth who are completely or partially absent from school, those who attempt to refuse school by demonstrating severe morning behavior problems, and youth who attend school under great duress. Partial absence from school often comes in the form of skipped classes (especially physical education and any classes that involve performance before others), missed sections of the day (e.g., all classes after lunch), and tardiness in the morning (Kearney & Silverman, 1996).

Absenteeism from school has been discussed in popular literature for centuries, but first became the focus of educational and psychological study in the late nineteenth to early twentieth centuries. A series of child labor laws enacted in the United Kingdom, United States, and other industrialized nations forced large groups of youth into schools, where naturally some were absent. Absenteeism was initially seen as symptomatic of juvenile delinquency, but today the problem is seen as more complex and as having various etiologies. In addition, absenteeism is often conceptualized as a problem in its own right or as a symptom of certain child mental disorders (e.g., separation anxiety, conduct disorders). The study of absenteeism today is spread among educators, psychologists, criminal justice specialists, sociologists, and physicians (Kearney, 2001).

Overall, approximately 5.5 percent of American children are absent from school on a particular day, although other studies have found absentee rates of 10–20 percent in various areas of the United States and Europe. According to the National Center of Education Statistics (see nces.ed.gov for updates over time), which reports on absenteeism rates for the United States, many 8th-, 10th-, and 12th-graders miss at least 1 day of school in a given 4-week period (i.e., 55 percent, 60 percent, and 72 percent, respectively, in the year 2000). In addition, many of these students miss at least five days of school during this time (i.e., 13.1 percent, 14.1 percent, and 21.4 percent, respectively).

1

According to student report, these absences were primarily due to illness (mean, 44.2 percent), but also to skipping school (mean, 16.9 percent) and unspecified "other reasons" (mean, 38.9 percent). The percentage of children who skip school tends to increase with age.

In addition, many students reportedly cut classes in a given 4-week period (i.e., 11.5, 24.5, and 37.0 percent for 8th-, 10th-, and 12th-graders, respectively). Those who cut three or more classes during this time tended to be seniors (15.8 percent), more so than sophomores (9.3 percent) or eighth graders (4.0 percent). In general, school absenteeism in the United States tends to be higher for inner-city schools (5.7 percent), public schools (5.9 percent), high schools (8.0 percent; large high schools: 9.1 percent), and schools with high percentages of impoverished students (mean, 7.5 percent).

School absenteeism may become extensive in nature and eventually lead to school dropout. According to the National Center for Education Statistics (October, 1999), approximately 5.0 percent of students aged 15–24 years dropped out of grades 10–12 within a previous 12-month period. School dropout rates tend to be higher for females (5.4 percent), Hispanics (7.8 percent), students in low-income families (11.0 percent), and Western areas of the United States (7.1 percent). In addition, risk of school dropout increases with age.

Many problems are associated with extended school absenteeism and school dropout, and these are discussed at greater length in the School Refusal entry. However, general problems associated with these phenomena include delinquency, emotional disturbance, economic and social/marital problems, and greater need for psychological assistance. In general, absenteeism is a significant problem that must be addressed as early as possible.

See also: Anxiety; Bullying; Conduct Disorder; Depression in Children and Adolescents; Pain Syndromes: Recurrent; School Refusal; School Violence Prevention

BIBLIOGRAPHY

Kearney, C. A. (2001). *School refusal behavior in youth: A functional approach to assessment and treatment*. Washington, DC: American Psychological Association.
Kearney, C. A., & Silverman, W. K. (1996). The evolution and reconciliation of taxonomic strategies for school refusal behavior. *Clinical Psychology: Science and Practice, 3*, 339–354.
U.S. Department of Education, National Center for Education Statistics. (2002). *The condition of education, 2002 (NCES 2002-025)*. Washington, DC: U.S. Government Printing Office.

Additional Readings for Nonprofessionals

Kearney, C. A. (2003). *Casebook in child behavior disorders*. Belmont, CA: Wadsworth.

Kearney, C. A., & Albano, A. M. (2000). *When children refuse school: A cognitive-behavioral therapy approach—Parent workbook*. San Antonio, TX: The Psychological Corporation.

Additional Readings for Professionals

Chiland, C., & Young, J. G. (1990). *Why children reject school: Views from seven countries*. New Haven, CT: Yale University Press.
Kearney, C. A., & Albano, A. M. (2000). *When children refuse school: A cognitive-behavioral therapy approach—Therapist guide*. San Antonio, TX: The Psychological Corporation.

CHRISTOPHER A. KEARNEY

Abuse and Maltreatment of Children

Violence against children has existed throughout history in the form of socially condoned infanticide, harsh punishment, abandonment, child prostitution, and the use of children for labor, including slavery and apprenticeships. Although there has been a gradual increase over centuries in society's acknowledgment of children's rights and a few early efforts to protect children from inhumane treatment, such as the 1875 formation of the New York Society for the Prevention of Cruelty to Children, widespread recognition of child maltreatment as a significant social problem primarily occurred during the last half of the twentieth century. This recognition was largely spurred by the publication of medical articles describing children with patterns of fractures and other physical injuries that appeared to have been inflicted by caregivers (Ten Bensel, Rheinberger, & Radbill, 1997), which became known as the "battered child syndrome" (Kempe, Silverman, Steele, Droegemueller, & Silver, 1962). Since that time, laws mandating reporting of child maltreatment cases have been passed, and child protective services agencies (CPS) have been established throughout the United States.

The broader term *child maltreatment* encompasses child physical and sexual abuse, child neglect, and child psychological maltreatment. No universal definitions of the various types of child maltreatment currently exist, making it difficult to compare results of research studies or accurately estimate the prevalence and incidence of different types of child maltreatment. Although definitions may vary considerably across different legal jurisdictions and across different professional disciplines and legal jurisdictions, they generally contain common core elements.

Child physical abuse is generally defined as the nonaccidental physical injury of a child, and includes bruises, fractures, cuts, welts, and other injuries. Child sexual abuse consists of sexual activity with a child for the gratification of another person, and includes oral, vaginal, or anal penetration, sexual touching, exposure, and voyeurism. In contrast to physical and sexual abuse, which involves the commission of abusive acts, child neglect is defined as the failure to provide for the child's basic physical, emotional, medical, mental health, or educational needs. Psychological maltreatment involves acts of commission and omission and is generally defined as a repeated pattern of caregiver behavior that conveys that children are rejected, worthless, unloved, unwanted, or flawed. Psychological maltreatment includes spurning, terrorizing, isolating, corrupting, and denying emotional responsiveness to the child (Myers et al., 2002).

INCIDENCE

In 2000, approximately 3 million reports of suspected child maltreatment were made to CPS agencies in the United States. Of the 879,000 children who were found to be maltreated following investigation, 63 percent experienced neglect, 19 percent experienced physical abuse, 10 percent experienced sexual abuse, and 8 percent were psychologically maltreated. Approximately 1,200 children died because of child maltreatment (U.S. Department of Health and Human Services, Administration on Children, Youth, and Families, 2002). Official CPS data are considered underestimates of the actual occurrence of child maltreatment because many incidents of child maltreatment, particularly less severe incidents, may never be recognized or reported. In addition, children may experience multiple types of child maltreatment, and this is not always reflected in official data.

ETIOLOGY

During the past 35 years, theoretical models regarding the etiology of child maltreatment have evolved from single-factor models (e.g., parental psychiatric disorder; poverty) to more elaborate models that incorporate multiple and interacting factors from various ecological levels, including the individual, family, community, and society. The more recent models attempt to clarify the complexity of individual and environmental influences that may contribute to occurrences of child maltreatment. These models include a variety of risk factors such as stress associated with poverty and other adverse circumstances, distress, family dysfunction and conflict, family isolation, and patterns of cognitive or affective processing that are congruent with the different types of child maltreatment. Although research has improved the knowledge base of child maltreatment risk factors, the causal factors that are necessary and sufficient

for child maltreatment to occur remain undetermined (Myers et al., 2002).

EFFECTS OF CHILD MALTREATMENT

It is clear that children who experience any type of child maltreatment, compared with their nonmaltreated peers, are at greater risk for adverse short- and long-term outcomes. However, considerable diversity in the types of problems attributed to child maltreatment has been observed, suggesting a lack of uniform or universal effects. In addition, a substantial percentage of children who experience maltreatment appear to be resilient and may demonstrate few, if any, known problems. The variation in the type and severity of problems observed in children who have experienced maltreatment suggests that different characteristics of the maltreatment (e.g., severity), child (e.g., coping), or environment (e.g., a supportive adult) may contribute to children's adaptation. Developmental models suggest that the timing and duration of the maltreatment also may play a role, with earlier and chronic maltreatment having greater adverse effects owing to interference with children's ability to complete sequences of developmental tasks (e.g., Myers et al., 2002). Although the following sections focus on the supposed effects of child maltreatment from infancy through adolescence, it is important to remember that many problems appear to persist into adulthood.

Physical Abuse

In addition to physical injuries and fatalities, physical abuse has been associated with left hemisphere neurological impairments that may be associated with impaired language development and limitations in intellectual functioning and academic performance. Compared with nonmaltreated peers, physically abused children are at greater risk for aggressive behavior and cognitive patterns and skills deficits associated with aggressive behavior, such as perceptions of others as hostile and social problem-solving deficits, as well as delinquency, conduct disorder, and substance use. Low self-esteem, depression, and anxiety, including posttraumatic stress disorder (PTSD), have also been documented. Insecure attachments during infancy and difficulties in peer relationships (e.g., social withdrawal, peer rejection) also have been observed (Myers et al., 2002).

Sexual Abuse

Sexual abuse has been associated with interpersonal problems, low self-esteem, depression, and anxiety. Substance abuse, eating disorders, and behavior problems, such as running away, have been documented. Symptoms of PTSD and sexual behavior problems, although not exclusive to sexual abuse, tend to be observed more frequently in sexually abused children than in other maltreated children. A few studies have documented cognitive and school problems in sexually abused children (Myers et al., 2002). However, academic difficulties tend to be less frequently documented in sexually abused children than in other groups of maltreated children, and may be related, at least in part, to symptoms (e.g., difficulties with attention) associated with depression, anxiety, and PTSD.

Neglect

Although less research has been conducted on child neglect than on child physical or sexual abuse, chronic neglect, particularly neglect beginning in infancy and early childhood, may be associated with the most adverse outcomes, including greater numbers of fatalities and significant cognitive and physical developmental delays. Early chronic emotional neglect is related to children's failure to thrive. Language and learning difficulties and academic achievement problems have been documented in children who have experienced neglect. Beginning with insecure attachment in infancy, neglect appears to be related to interpersonal problems, particularly social withdrawal and social inadequacy. In studies comparing children who have experienced no maltreatment, physical abuse, or neglect, neglected children tended to be more aggressive than nonmaltreated children, but less aggressive than their physically abused peers. Other problems observed following neglect have included depression, low self-esteem, substance use, delinquency, and high dropout rates (Hildyard & Wolfe, 2002; Myers et al., 2002).

Psychological Maltreatment

Because of the difficulties in documenting when caregiver behaviors constitute psychological maltreatment, psychological maltreatment as a unique form of child maltreatment has been studied far less than the other types of child maltreatment. Psychological maltreatment also tends to occur with other forms of maltreatment (e.g., verbal abuse accompanies physical abuse; denying emotional responsiveness and emotional neglect are synonymous), and has been thought to account for much, if not most, of the adverse emotional, interpersonal, and behavioral impacts of the other types of maltreatment (Myers et al., 2002).

PRIMARY AND SECONDARY PREVENTION

Primary and secondary prevention efforts are directed at preventing initial occurrences of child maltreatment in the general population and with families determined to be at risk of child maltreatment, respectively. Primary prevention efforts have been directed toward increasing awareness of child maltreatment and changing attitudes and behaviors that may support child maltreatment, but careful research to determine the effectiveness of these efforts has not been conducted. Primary and secondary prevention programs for child physical abuse and child neglect also frequently focus on providing services, such as support, linkage to resources, education, and skill development, to parents. Although some programs, such as nurse home-visiting models, have resulted in positive changes in parental, child, and family functioning, the long-term effectiveness of these programs for preventing child maltreatment, particularly as programs are disseminated to different communities, has yet to be determined (Myers et al., 2002).

In contrast to prevention programs for child physical abuse and neglect, which tend to focus on parents, child sexual abuse prevention programs tend to be focused on improving children's abilities to protect themselves or respond to abuse after it occurs. Programs are frequently school-based and focus on recognition of potential abusers and teaching children safety rules and other concepts (e.g., disclosure, reducing self-blame; Davis & Gidycz, 2000; Myers et al., 2002). A sophisticated analysis of controlled evaluations of these programs suggests that the programs are effective at increasing children's knowledge and skills use in hypothetical abuse situations, particularly when programs consisted of at least four sessions and actively involved children in behavioral rehearsals (Davis & Gidycz, 2000). However, knowledge and skills gains may be small or occur only with respect to specific concepts (Myers et al., 2002). More important, the degree to which children are able to utilize the knowledge and skills in actual abuse situations to prevent abuse has yet to be demonstrated (Davis & Gidycz, 2000).

TERTIARY PREVENTION

Identification and Reporting

A thorough review of child maltreatment indicators is far beyond the scope of this entry, and interested readers should consult more comprehensive texts (e.g., Myers et al., 2002) or seek additional training. In brief, child physical abuse is generally identified through injuries that are unusual in their type (e.g., oddly shaped), location (e.g., back of the hands), severity (e.g., first-degree burns), or frequency (e.g., repeated fractures) for the child's developmental age. Untreated medical or dental conditions, chronic poor hygiene, constant hunger or being underweight, and clothing inappropriate for the weather are indicators of possible neglect. Visible indicators of sexual abuse may not be present or may only be detected through expert medical examinations. Sexual abuse may be discovered through children's disclosures or other suspicious statements or behaviors or through third-party witnessing of the abuse. Identification of psychological maltreatment generally involves evidence of chronic negative parental behaviors directed toward the child, such as swearing or threatening (Myers et al., 2002). Abrupt changes in children's behavior or academic performance, fears, depression, anxiety, and externalizing symptoms may indicate that children are experiencing stress or other adverse circumstances, but are not necessarily specific to child maltreatment.

Although mandated child maltreatment reporting laws vary across legal jurisdictions, reporting laws generally require only a reasonable suspicion or belief that a child has been maltreated prior to reporting. Child protective services then collect evidence to document that maltreatment has or has not occurred. In spite of legal mandates, it is clear that significant percentages of educational, medical, and mental health professionals do not report (Myers et al., 2002). In educational settings, school policies that diffuse responsibility for reporting and a lack of training in identification of child maltreatment, reporting requirements and procedures, and appropriate interventions may contribute to failures to report suspected cases (Berson, 2002).

Assessment and Intervention

After identification of maltreatment, children who are considered to be in danger of future harm may be separated from the person responsible for the abuse by placing the child in foster care or requesting that the abuser leave the home. Interventions are typically conducted with the person who maltreats the child or the child himself/herself. Given the diversity of risk factors families may be experiencing and given variations in children's adjustment following maltreatment, assessment to determine the nature and severity of problems is essential in providing appropriate services.

Child physical abuse and neglect interventions generally involve parent education and training, as well as services specific to other problems identified in the family during assessment (e.g., intimate partner violence, substance abuse). Although long-term research supporting the efficacy of most programs in preventing future occurrences of abuse is limited, promising approaches for improving parental knowledge and skills at the present time include behavioral parent training, abuse-focused family treatment, and ecobehavioral interventions. The most promising interventions for child sexual abuse offenders tend to be cognitive–behavioral in nature (Myers et al., 2002).

A comprehensive child assessment would address the child's educational, psychological, emotional, social, and physical functioning, and services would focus on those domains in which the child was demonstrating problems. For example, learning deficits and academic problems may require special education or other remedial services. Currently, evidence supports the efficacy of abuse-specific treatment and other cognitive–behavioral approaches in addressing psychological and emotional problems (Myers et al., 2002). Finally, it is important that children have environments that are safe and responsive to their needs (Berson, 2002).

See also: Depression in Children and Adolescents; Parenting; Posttraumatic Stress Disorder

BIBLIOGRAPHY

Berson, I. R. (2002). The role of schools in addressing child abuse and neglect. *The APSAC Advisor, 14*(1), 4–6.

Davis, M. K., & Gidycz, C. A. (2000). Child sexual abuse prevention programs: A meta-analysis. *Journal of Clinical Child Psychology, 29*, 257–265.

Hildyard, K. L., & Wolfe, D. A. (2002). Child neglect: Developmental issues and outcomes. *Child Abuse & Neglect, 26*, 679–695.

Kempe, C. H., Silverman, F. N., Steele, B. F., Droegemueller, W., & Silver, H. K. (1962). The battered child syndrome. *Journal of the American Medical Association, 181*, 17–24.

Myers, J. E. B., Berliner, L., Briere, J., Hendrix, C. T., Jenny, C., & Reid, T. A. (Eds.). (2002). *The APSAC handbook on child maltreatment* (2nd ed.). Thousand Oaks, CA: Sage.

Ten Bensel, R. W., Rheinberger, M. M., & Radbill, S. X. (1997). Children in a world of violence: The roots of child maltreatment. In M. E. Helfer, R. S. Kempe, & R. D. Krugman (Eds.), *The battered child* (5th ed., pp. 3–28). Chicago: University of Chicago Press.

U.S. Department of Health and Human Services, Administration on Children, Youth, and Families. (2002, April). *National Child Abuse and Neglect Data System (NCANDS): Summary of key findings from calendar year 2000.* Retrieved August 27, 2002, from http://www.calib.com/nccanch/prevmnth/scope/ncands.cfm

Additional Readings for Nonprofessionals

Couter, G. (1995). *I speak for this child: True stories of a child advocate.* New York: Crown.

Jackson, N. A., & Oates, G. C. (Eds.). (1998). *Violence in intimate relationships: Examining sociological and psychological issues.* Boston: Butterworth-Heinemann.

Additional Readings for Professionals

Helfer, M. E., Kempe, R. S., & Krugman, R. D. (1997). *The battered child* (5th ed.). Chicago: University of Chicago Press.

Kalichman, S. C. (1993). *Mandated reporting of suspected child abuse.* Washington, DC: American Psychological Association.

LINDA ANNE VALLE
JOHN R. LUTZKER

Academic Interventions for Written Language and Grammar

In general, interventions to increase language and grammar performance have incorporated several strategies such as self-monitoring, peer editing, immediate feedback, progress monitoring, and frequent practice. These strategies are incorporated into interventions that target writing productivity across many types of skills, such as writing fluency (i.e., writing speed) and writing accuracy (i.e., specific writing skills). A meta-analysis of writing instruction strategies conducted by Gertsen and Baker (2001) identified three critical components that should be a part of any writing program: instruction in the steps of the writing process (i.e., planning, writing, and revising), instruction in text structuring, and immediate feedback regarding the quality of the written product.

INCREASING WRITING ACCURACY

Planning

Students with writing difficulties spend less time planning and editing their written product (Graham & Harris, 1994). Explicit teaching incorporating modeling, guided use of planning strategies, and feedback should be used to teach students to use their time effectively. Planning sheets, prompt cards, writing checklists, and organization forms are strategies that provide students with a format for planning before they begin writing. (See Englert, Raphael, & Anderson, 1992, for a review of these strategies.)

Peer Editing

The use of peers as educators in the classroom is not a new idea (Greenwood, 1984). Studies by MacArthur, Schwartz, and Graham (1991) found that peer revision had a positive effect on the amount and quality of written performance. Revision skills that should be taught to students are *adding* important or interesting information, *deleting* repetitious or unnecessary information, *paraphrasing* lengthy ideas, and *rearranging* information.

Teaching Specific Writing Skills

Self-Regulated Strategy Development (SRSD) is a well-researched cognitive intervention developed as an instructional strategy to increase success with the writing process (Graham, Harris, & Troia, 2000; Harris & Graham, 1999). This approach to writing instruction focuses not only on writing performance but also on the cognitions and affect that can influence writing skills.

Self-Regulated Strategy Development involves six stages that are considered important as the student progresses through effective writing strategy development. The first stage, Develop Background Knowledge, involves assisting the student to develop necessary preskills that will assist him/her in successful story writing. For example, knowledge on the parts of a story, grammar, and decreasing anxiety will be necessary to increase

the likelihood of successful writing. In the second stage, Initial Conference: Strategy Goals and Significance, students and teachers discuss the importance of one or several writing skills and the student makes a commitment to attempt better writing. At this time, any negative statements toward writing or writing ability can also be discussed. In addition, the teacher and the student discuss the new writing strategy, and how and when to use it. Specific strategies may include mnemonics for remembering the parts of a story, making notes, goal setting, and/or developing an outline. During Modeling of the Strategy, the teacher models the writing process using self-instruction and collaborates with the student on any changes to make the strategy more effective. Next, the student memorizes the writing strategy and any personalized self-statements during Memorization of the Strategy. The fifth stage, Collaborative Practice, requires the student to practice the strategy with teacher feedback. During this time the teacher may introduce self-regulatory strategies such as goal setting, self-recording, and self-assessment. The final stage, Independent Practice, requires students to use the writing strategy independently and covertly. Generalization and maintenance procedures, such as discussing additional situations in which the strategy may be useful, verbal reinforcement contingent on the use of the strategy in new situations, and using the strategy in other classrooms, may be incorporated at any stage to increase the probability that the new writing strategies will be useful.

The strategies involved in SRSD are useful for teaching writing as a whole product or in teaching specific skills necessary to produce a meaningful written product. This process can be continually updated to include new writing strategies and skills. Students progress through SRSD at their own pace and, therefore, instruction is individualized for each student.

INCREASING WRITING FLUENCY

Self-Monitoring

Research has shown that children with difficulty writing struggle to write at length (Deno, Marston, & Mirkin, 1982) and, therefore, tend to produce shorter written products. Research findings indicate that students can increase writing fluency by using the principles of self-monitoring and charting. Moxley, Lutz, Ahlborn, Boley, and Armstrong (1995) asked students to write daily for 15 minutes. Following the free writing time, students counted the number of words written, regardless of spelling, and charted their daily progress in their writing journals. Weekly writing goals in the form of total words written were developed and students earned rewards for meeting their goal. Not only did this intervention increase writing fluency but also increased dialogue quality, sentence complexity, and description of personal experiences.

Van Houten et al. (1974) examined the writing skills of 55 students in second and fifth grades and targeted the number of words written. The intervention consisted of explicit timing, immediate performance feedback, public posting of progress, and instructions to increase their scores. Overall, the participants doubled their writing fluency during the intervention. Van Houten, Hill, and Parsons (1975) replicated this effect and examined writing interventions that included the following components: (a) timing and feedback (i.e., counting total words written); (b) timing, feedback, and public posting; and (c) timing, feedback, public posting, and teacher praise. The combination of timing, feedback, and public posting produced the largest writing fluency gains for all classes.

See also: Group Contingencies; Writing (Written Language)

BIBLIOGRAPHY

Deno, S. L., Marston, D., & Mirkin, P. K. (1982). Valid measurement procedures for continuous evaluation of written expression. *Exceptional Children, 48,* 368–371.

Englert, C. S., Raphael, T. E., & Anderson, L. M. (1992). Socially mediated instruction: Improving students' knowledge and talk about writing. *The Elementary School Journal, 92,* 411–449.

Gersten, R., & Baker, S. (2001). Teaching expressive writing to students with learning disabilities: A meta-analysis. *The Elementary School Journal, 101,* 251–272.

Graham, S., & Harris, K. R. (1994). Implications on constructivism for teaching writing to students with special needs. *Journal of Special Education, 28,* 275–289.

Graham, S., Harris, K. R., & Troia, G. A. (2000). Self-regulated strategy development revisited: Teaching writing strategies to struggling writers. *Topics in Language Disorders, 20*(4), 1–14.

Greenwood, C. R. (1984). Teacher versus peer mediated instruction: An ecobehavioral analysis of achievement outcomes. *Journal of Applied Behavior Analysis, 17,* 521–538.

Harris, K. R., & Graham, S. (1999). Programmatic intervention research: Illustrations from the evolution of self regulated strategy development. *Learning Disability Quarterly, 22,* 251–262.

MacArthur, C. A., Schwartz, S. S., & Graham, S. (1991). Effects of a reciprocal peer revision strategy in special education classrooms. *Learning Disabilities Research & Practice, 6,* 201–210.

Moxley, R. A., Lutz, P. A., Ahlborn, P., Boley, N., & Armstrong, L. (1995). Self recorded word counts of freewriting in grades 1–4. *Education and Treatment of Children, 18,* 138–157.

Van Houten, R., & McKillop, C. (1977). An extension of the effects of the performance feedback system with secondary school students. *Psychology in the Schools, 14,* 480–484.

Van Houten, R., Morrison, E., Jarvis, R., & McDonald, M. (1974). The effects of explicit timing and feedback on compositional response rate in elementary school children. *Journal of Applied Behavior Analysis, 7,* 547–555.

Additional Readings for Professionals

Bradley-Johnson, S., & Lesiak, J. L. (1989). *Problems in written expression: Assessment and remediation.* New York: Guilford.

Graham, S., & Harris, K. R. (2002). *Prevention and intervention for struggling writers.* In M. R. Shinn, H. M. Walker, & G. Stoner (Eds.), *Interventions for academic and behavior problems. II: Preventive and remedial approaches* (pp. 589–610).

Heward, W. L., Heron, T. E., Gardner, R., & Prayzer, R. (1991). Two strategies for improving students writing skills. In G. Stoner, S. Shinn, & H. M. Walker (Eds.), *Interventions for achievement and behavior problems* (pp. 379–398). Bethesda, MD: National Association of School Psychologists, Washington, DC.

Levy, M., & Ransdell, S. (2003). *The science of writing: Theories, methods, individual differences, and applications.* Mahwah, NJ: Erlbaum.

MERILEE MCCURDY

Achenbach System of Empirically Based Assessment (ASEBA): Child Behavior Checklist for Ages 6 to 18

The *Child Behavior Checklist for Ages 6 to 18* (CBCL/6-18) (Achenbach & Rescorla, 2001) is a parent rating form that is part of the Achenbach System of Empirically Based Assessment (ASEBA). The ASEBA is an integrated set of standardized rating forms to assess children's competencies and problems. The ASEBA includes forms to be completed by parents, teachers, and youths themselves, as well as forms for direct observations and clinical interviews with children and adolescents. There are also ASEBA forms for assessing competencies and problems of preschool children and adults. Information obtained from the ASEBA forms can be used in assessment, intervention planning, and outcome evaluation in mental health, school, medical, and social service settings. For school-age children, the ASEBA forms include the CBCL/6-18, Teacher's Report Form (TRF), and Youth Self-Report (YSR).

CBCL/6-18 RATING FORM

The CBCL/6-18 is the original ASEBA instrument upon which other forms have been modeled. The 2001 edition of the CBCL/6-18 is a revision of the Child Behavior Checklist for Ages 4 to 18 (Achenbach, 1991). The CBCL/6-18 is a four-page rating form to be completed by a parent, caregiver, or other person who sees the child in a family-like setting. Page 1 of the CBCL/6-18 requests demographic information about the child (e.g., child's age, child's gender, the respondent's relationship to the child, the parent's type of work, child's grade in school, etc.). Parents then provide descriptive information about the child's involvement in sports, hobbies and activities, social organizations, and jobs and chores. They also rate the child on how much time he/she spends in each activity or sport and how well he/she does each one. On page 2, parents provide information about the child's friendships, relationships with other people, playing and working alone, and performance in academic subjects at school. Parents also rate how well the child plays by himself/herself, how well he/she gets along with others, and how well he/she performs in school academic subjects. Page 2 also contains open-ended items for describing illnesses and disabilities, what concerns the parent most about the child, and the best things about the child.

On pages 3 and 4 of the CBCL/6-18, parents rate the child on 120 problem items. Examples are "Acts too young for age"; "Cries a lot"; "Can't concentrate, can't pay attention for long"; "Gets in many fights"; "Too fearful or anxious"; and "Unhappy, sad, or depressed." In addition to specific problem items, two open-ended items allow parents to add other physical problems without known medical cause and other problems that are not described by specific items listed on the form. Parents rate each problem item for how true it is of the child now or within the past 6 months: 0 = *not true (as far as you know)*; 1 = *somewhat or sometimes true*; 2 = *very true or often true*. Most parents can complete the CBCL/6-18 in about 15 to 20 minutes.

CBCL/6-18 SCORING PROFILE

The CBCL/6-18 is scored on separate profiles for boys and girls ages 6 to 11 and 12 to 18. The scoring profile provides raw scores, *T* scores, and percentiles for Total Competence, three competence scales (Activities, Social, and School), eight syndrome scales, six *DSM*-oriented scales, Internalizing, Externalizing, and Total Problems.

The CBCL/6-18 syndrome scales are: Anxious/Depressed, Withdrawn/Depressed, Somatic Complaints, Social Problems, Thought Problems, Attention Problems, Rule-Breaking Behavior (which replaces the Delinquent Behavior syndrome that was on the 1991 scoring profile), and Aggressive Behavior. The TRF and YSR have similar syndrome scales. The syndrome scales were developed through statistical procedures (factor analyses) that determine which problem items group together to form scales. The word "syndrome" means "things that go together." To develop the 2001 versions of the syndrome scales, statistical analyses were performed on data from CBCL/6-18 forms completed by parents of 4,994 children referred for mental health services.

The *DSM*-oriented scales are Affective Problems, Anxiety Problems, Somatic Problems, Attention Deficit/Hyperactivity Problems, Oppositional Defiant Problems, and Conduct Problems. The TRF and YSR have similar *DSM*-oriented scales. To create the *DSM*-oriented scales, experienced psychiatrists and psychologists rated a list of CBCL/6-18, TRF, and YSR problem items as to whether each item was *not consistent, somewhat consistent*, or *very consistent* with the diagnostic criteria of the *Diagnostic and Statistical Manual of Mental Disorders* (4th ed.) (*DSM-IV*; American Psychiatric Association, 1994). Items that

were rated *very consistent* by at least 14 of 22 raters (64 percent) were selected to form *DSM*-oriented scales. High scores on the *DSM*-oriented scales can alert clinicians to consider whether certain *DSM-IV* diagnoses are appropriate for an individual child. However, this information must be combined with other data to make appropriate *DSM-IV* diagnoses.

The CBCL/6-18 Internalizing scale is the sum of scores for the Anxious/Depressed, Withdrawn/Depressed, and Somatic Complaints syndromes. The CBCL/6-18 Externalizing scale is the sum of scores from the Rule-Breaking Behavior and Aggressive Behavior syndromes. CBCL/6-18 Total Problems is the sum of 0-1-2 scores on all 120 items.

INTERPRETING CBCL/6-18 SCORES

The CBCL/6-18 scoring profile was normed on a U.S. national sample of 1,753 children ages 6 to 18 who had not received professional help for behavioral or emotional problems within the preceding 12 months. The normative sample was representative of the 48 contiguous states, stratified by socioeconomic status (SES), ethnicity, region, and urban–suburban–rural residence. Separate norms are provided for boys and girls for ages 6 to 11 and 12 to 18. The *T* scores and percentiles show how a child scored on each scale compared to the relevant normative sample. Evaluators can use this information to judge whether a child shows fewer competencies and/or more problems than is typical for children of the same gender and age range. Cut points are provided for normal, borderline, and clinical range scores for each scale. This profile perspective highlights strengths and weaknesses in a child's competencies and problems just as high and low subtest scores on intelligence tests highlight patterns of cognitive functioning.

On the CBCL/6-18 Activities, Social, and School scales, *T* scores of 31 to 35 (3rd to 7th percentiles) are considered to be in the borderline range, whereas *T* scores below 31 (<3rd percentile) are in the clinical range. For Total Competence, *T* scores of 37 to 40 (10th to 16th percentiles) are in the borderline range, whereas *T* scores below 37 (<10th percentile) are in the clinical range. For the CBCL/6-18 syndrome and *DSM*-oriented scales, *T* scores of 65 to 69 (93rd to 97th percentiles) are in the borderline range, whereas *T* scores above 69 (>97th percentile) are in the clinical range. For Total Problems, Internalizing, and Externalizing, *T* scores of 60 to 63 (84th to 90th percentiles) are in the borderline range, whereas *T* scores above 63 (>90th percentile) are in the clinical range.

SCORING OPTIONS

The CBCL/6-18 has several scoring options. Hand scoring usually takes about 5 to 15 minutes. Computer scoring is accomplished through modular Windows software, called the Assessment Data Manager (ADM). Traditional CBCL/6-18 forms for handwritten responses require clerical data entry for computer scoring. CBCL/6-18 machine-readable TELEform or OMR bubble forms can be fed into a scanner for computer scoring. Separate software is also available for direct client entry on the computer. Through an ASEBA Web-Link account, users can also use the Internet to obtain CBCL/6-18 forms, transmit data, and obtain computer-scored profiles (www.aseba.org).

COMPUTER-SCORED CROSS-INFORMANT COMPARISONS

In addition to the scoring profiles for each form, the ADM provides comparisons of scores for up to eight different informants who completed the CBCL/6-18, TRF, and/or YSR. These are titled "cross-informant comparisons" on the computer printout. Two pages of the printout provide visual side-by-side comparisons of the 0-1-2 scores for each of the 93 items that are similar across the CBCL/6-18, TRF, and YSR syndrome scales and the 45 items that form the *DSM*-oriented scales. Three other pages of the printout provide cross-informant comparisons of *T* scores for the eight syndrome scales, six *DSM*-oriented scales, and Internalizing, Externalizing, and Total Problems. One additional page provides *Q* correlations that indicate whether agreement between pairs of informants (i.e., parent and teacher, parent and youth, teacher and youth) are *above average*, *average*, or *below average*, compared with samples of similar informant pairs. The cross-informant comparisons can be especially valuable for integrating data from parent reports, teacher reports, and youth self-ratings and for judging the level of agreement about the child's problems.

NARRATIVE REPORTS

The ADM software provides an optional one-page narrative report for the CBCL/6-18, summarizing results on all of the competence and problem scales. The report also lists 0-1-2 scores for 12 critical items that clinicians judged to be especially important for assessment and intervention planning. Examples are "Cruel to animals"; "Physically attacks people"; "Runs away from home"; "Sees things that aren't there"; "Sets fires"; and "Talks about killing self." The narrative report can be imported easily into word processing programs. The narrative reports can save time in writing assessment reports as well as guarantee accuracy of profile interpretation.

See also: ASEBA Youth Self-Report; Attention-Deficit/Hyperactivity Disorder; Conduct Disorder; Oppositional Defiant Disorder

BIBLIOGRAPHY

Achenbach, T. M. (1991). *Manual for the Child Behavior Checklist/4-18 and 1991 profile*. Burlington: University of Vermont, Department of Psychiatry.

Achenbach, T. M., & Rescorla, L. A. (2001). *Manual for the ASEBA School-Age Forms & Profiles*. Burlington: University of Vermont, Research Center for Children, Youth, and Families.

American Psychiatric Association. (1994). *Diagnostic and statistical manual of mental disorders* (4th ed.). Washington, DC: Author.

Additional Readings for Professionals

Achenbach, T. M., & McConaughy, S. H. (1997). *Empirically based assessment of child and adolescent psychopathology: Practical applications* (2nd ed.). Thousand Oaks, CA: Sage.

Achenbach, T. M., & McConaughy, S. H. (2001). *School-based practitioners guide for the Child Behavior Checklist and related forms* (2nd ed.). Burlington: University of Vermont, Research Center for Children, Youth, and Families.

McConaughy, S. H. (2001). The Achenbach System of Empirically Based Assessment. In J. J. W. Andrews, H. L. Janzen, & D. H. Saklofske (Eds.), *Handbook of psychoeducational assessment: Ability, achievement, and behavior in children* (pp. 289–324). San Diego, CA: Academic Press.

McConaughy, S. H., & Ritter, D. (2002). Best practices in multidimensional assessment of emotional and behavioral disorders. In A. Thomas & J. Grimes (Eds.), *Best practices in school psychology IV* (4th ed., pp. 1303–1320). Washington, DC: National Association of School Psychologists.

STEPHANIE H. McCONAUGHY

Achenbach System of Empirically Based Assessment: Semistructured Clinical Interview for Children and Adolescents

The *Semistructured Clinical Interview for Children and Adolescents* (SCICA) (McConaughy & Achenbach, 2001) is a standardized clinical interview for ages 6 to 18. The SCICA was designed as a component of the Achenbach System of Empirically Based Assessment (ASEBA). The ASEBA is an integrated set of standardized rating forms to assess children's competencies and problems. Besides the SCICA, the ASEBA includes forms for obtaining parent reports, teacher reports, youth self-ratings, and direct observations of children in group settings. There are also ASEBA forms for assessing competencies and problems of preschool children and adults. Information obtained from the ASEBA forms can be used in assessment, intervention planning, and outcome evaluation in mental health, school, medical, and social service settings. In addition to the SCICA, the ASEBA forms for school-age children include the *Child Behavior Check-list for Ages 6 to 18* (CBCL/6-18), *Teacher's Report Form* (TRF), and *Youth Self-Report* (YSR) (Achenbach & Rescorla, 2001).

The SCICA includes a protocol of questions and tasks for a clinical interview, standardized rating forms for scoring interviewers' observations and children's self-reported problems, and scoring profiles that are modeled on profiles for other ASEBA forms. The SCICA is designed to sample diverse areas of functioning in ways that are geared to the cognitive and emotional levels of the children and adolescents. Users of the SCICA should have adequate training in clinically interviewing children and using standardized assessment procedures. Administering the SCICA takes approximately 60 to 90 minutes, depending on whether optional sections of the SCICA Protocol Form are included.

SCICA PROTOCOL

The SCICA Protocol is a six-page form that outlines questions and tasks covering nine broad areas: (1) Activities, school, job; (2) Friends; (3) Family relations; (4) Fantasies; (5) Self perception, feelings; (6) Parent/teacher-reported problems; (7) Achievement tests (optional); (8) For ages 6–11: Screen for fine and gross motor abnormalities (optional); and (9) For ages 12–18: Somatic complaints, alcohol, drugs, trouble with the law. The protocol lists instructions and open-ended questions and tasks for interviewing children. (For brevity, the word "children" includes adolescents.) Spaces are also provided for recording observations of children's behavior during the interview and recording notes about children's conversation during the interview. Interviewers can alter the sequence of questions in the first five sections to follow children's natural flow of conversation.

In addition to direct questions, interviewers also ask 6- to 11-year-old children to "draw a picture of your family doing something together." The drawing provides another way that children can depict their family relations and then answer questions about their family. For ages 6 to 11, interviewers have the options of administering brief standardized achievement tests, obtaining a writing sample, and using brief activities to assess gross motor functioning (e.g., having the child hop on alternate feet and play catch). Interviewers can also use play materials while interviewing young children who are reluctant to talk or participate in other tasks. For ages 13 to 18, more structured questions are included to assess somatic complaints, alcohol and drug use, and trouble with the law.

SCICA OBSERVATION AND SELF-REPORT FORMS

After completing the SCICA, interviewers score the child on the SCICA Observation and Self-Report Forms. The Observation Form contains 120 problem items to be scored for ages 6 to 18, plus an open-ended item for scoring other observed problems not covered by more specific items. Many SCICA observation items are similar to problem items on the CBCL/6-18, TRF, and YSR, whereas others are unique to the interview situation. Examples of SCICA observation items are "Acts too young for age"; "Cries"; "Doesn't concentrate or pay attention for long on tasks, questions, topics"; "Doesn't sit still, restless, or hyperactive"; "Too fearful or anxious"; and "Unhappy, sad, or depressed."

The Self-Report Form has 114 items for ages 6 to 18 and 11 additional items for ages 13 to 18, plus one open-ended item for scoring other reported problems. Many SCICA self-report items are similar to those on the CBCL/6-18 and TRF, whereas some are unique to the interview setting. Examples of SCICA self-report items are "Reports arguing or fighting with siblings"; "Reports arguing or verbal altercations (except with siblings)"; "Reports being disobedient at home"; "Reports being unhappy, sad, or depressed"; "Reports difficulty learning"; "Reports feeling nervous or tense"; "Reports physically attacking people, including siblings"; and "Reports temper tantrums or hot temper."

Interviewers score the 120 SCICA observation items, 114 self-report items for ages 6 to 11, and open-ended "other" items on a 4-point scale: $0 = no\ occurrence$; $1 = very\ slight\ or\ ambiguous\ occurrence$; $2 = definite\ occurrence\ with\ mild\ to\ moderate\ intensity\ and\ less\ than\ 3\ minutes'\ duration$; $3 = definite\ occurrence\ with\ severe\ intensity\ or\ 3\ or\ more\ minutes'\ duration$. For the 11 self-report items for ages 12 to 18, interviewers use 4-point scales with different time lines for reports of somatic complaints, alcohol and drug use, and trouble with the law.

SCICA PROFILE/6-18

The 2001 edition of the SCICA scoring profile provides separate scores for ages 6 to 11 and 12 to 18, in contrast to the earlier 1994 profile, which provided scores only for ages 6 to 12. The SCICA Profile/6-18 provides raw scores, clinical T scores, and percentiles for Total Observations, Total Self-Reports, Internalizing, Externalizing, eight syndrome scales, and six *DSM*-oriented scales.

Five SCICA syndrome scales contain problem items that describe observations of children's behavior during the interview. These are Anxious, Withdrawn/Depressed, Language/Motor Problems, Attention Problems, and Self-Control Problems. Three additional SCICA syndrome scales contain items that describe problems reported by children during the interview: Anxious/Depressed, Aggressive/Rule-Breaking, and Somatic Complaints (scored only for ages 12–18). For ages 12 to 18, items on the Aggressive/Rule-Breaking syndrome are also scored on separate Aggressive and Rule-Breaking subscales. The syndrome scales were developed through statistical procedures (factor analyses) that determine which problem items group together to form scales. The word *syndrome* means "things that go together." To develop the 2001 versions of the SCICA syndrome scales, statistical analyses were performed on interviewers' ratings of separate samples of 381 children aged 6 to 11 and 305 children aged 12 to 18. All of the children were referred for mental health or special education services. Items endorsed for fewer than 5 percent of the samples in each age group were excluded from the analyses.

The SCICA *DSM*-oriented scales are Affective Problems, Anxiety Problems, Somatic Problems, Attention Deficit/Hyperactivity Problems, Oppositional Defiant Problems, and Conduct Problems. To create the *DSM*-oriented scales, experienced psychiatrists and psychologists rated a list of CBCL/6-18, TRF, and YSR problem items as to whether each item was *not consistent, somewhat consistent,* or *very consistent* with the diagnostic criteria of the *Diagnostic and Statistical Manual of Mental Disorders* (4th ed.) (*DSM-IV*) (American Psychiatric Association, 1994). Items that were rated *very consistent* by at least 14 of 22 raters (64 percent) were selected to form CBCL/6-18, TRF, and YSR *DSM*-oriented scales. The SCICA *DSM*-oriented scales include items from the SCICA Observation and Self-Report Forms that are comparable to items on the CBCL/6-18, TRF, and YSR *DSM*-oriented scales. High scores on the *DSM*-oriented scales can alert clinicians to consider whether certain *DSM-IV* diagnoses are appropriate for an individual child. However, this information must be combined with other data to make appropriate *DSM-IV* diagnoses.

The SCICA Internalizing score is the sum of scores for the Anxious and Anxious/Depressed syndromes. The SCICA Externalizing score is the sum of scores for the Aggressive/Rule-Breaking, Attention Problems, and Self-Control Problems syndromes. Total Observations is the sum of 0-1-2-3 scores on the 120 observation items, plus other observed problems. Total Self-Reports for ages 6 to 11 is the sum of 0-1-2-3 scores for 114 self-report items, plus other reported problems. Total Self-Reports for ages 12 to 18 is the sum of 0-1-2-3 scores for 125 self-report items, plus other reported problems.

INTERPRETING SCICA SCORES

The SCICA Profile/6-18 provides separate clinical *T* scores and percentiles for ages 6 to 11 and 12 to 18. The clinical *T* scores and percentiles show how a child scored on each scale compared with children in the same age range who were also referred for mental health or special education services. As a general guideline, *T* scores at or above 55 (≥69th percentile) indicate potentially severe problems compared with other clinically referred children. The SCICA scoring profile does not have norms based on samples of nonreferred children, as does the CBCL/6-18, TRF, and YSR. Scores on the SCICA Profile/6-18 are valuable as a quantitative profile of a child's

functioning during a clinical interview. The profile of scores on the various SCICA scales can then be compared to profiles of scores on similar scales of the CBCL/6-18, TRF, and YSR.

SCORING OPTIONS

The SCICA Profile/6-18 can be scored by hand or by computer. For both hand scoring and computer scoring, users need to obtain the paper versions of the SCICA Protocol and SCICA Observation and Self-Report Forms. Hand scoring of the SCICA Observation and Self-Report Forms usually takes 10 to 15 minutes. Hand scoring of the SCICA Profile/6-18 usually requires an additional 10 to 15 minutes. Computer scoring of the SCICA Profile/6-18 is accomplished through the SCICA module of the Assessment Data Manager (ADM) Windows software. Computer software and a videotape are also available for training interviewers in the SCICA scoring procedures.

NARRATIVE REPORTS

The ADM software provides an optional one-page narrative report for the SCICA, which summarizes results on all scales. The report also lists 0-1-2-3 scores for 17 critical items that clinicians judged to be especially important for assessment and intervention planning. Examples are "Reports being cruel to animals"; "Reports physically attacking people, including siblings"; "Reports running away from home"; "Reports seeing things that aren't there during times other than the interview"; "Reports setting fires"; and "Talks about deliberately harming self or attempting suicide." The narrative report can be imported easily into word processing programs. The narrative report can save time in writing assessment reports as well as guarantee accuracy of profile interpretation.

See also: ASEBA Youth Self-Report; Attention-Deficit/Hyperactivity Disorder; Conduct Disorder; Oppositional Defiant Disorder

BIBLIOGRAPHY

Achenbach, T. M., & Rescorla, L. A. (2001). *Manual for the ASEBA School-Age Forms & Profiles.* Burlington: University of Vermont, Research Center for Children, Youth, and Families.

American Psychiatric Association. (1994). *Diagnostic and statistical manual of mental disorders* (4th ed.). Washington, DC: Author.

McConaughy, S. H., & Achenbach, T. M. (2001). *Manual for the Semistructured Clinical Interview for Children and Adolescents* (2nd ed.). Burlington: University of Vermont, Research Center for Children, Youth, and Families.

Additional Readings for Professionals

Achenbach, T. M., & McConaughy, S. H. (2001). *School-based practitioners guide for the Child Behavior Checklist and related forms* (2nd ed.). Burlington: University of Vermont, Research Center for Children, Youth, and Families.

McConaughy, S. H. (2000a). Self-report: Child clinical interviews. In E. S. Shapiro & T. R. Kratochwill (Eds.), *Conducting school-based assessments of child and adolescent behavior* (pp. 170–202). New York: Guilford.

McConaughy, S. H. (2000b). Self-reports: Theory and practice in interviewing children. In E. S. Shapiro & T. R. Kratochwill (Eds.), *Behavioral assessment in schools: Theory, research, and clinical foundations* (pp. 323–352). New York: Guilford.

McConaughy, S. H. (2003). Interviewing children, parents, and teachers. In M. J. Breen & C. R. Fiedler (Eds.), *Behavioral approach to assessment of youth with emotional/behavioral disorders* (2nd ed.). Austin, TX: Pro-Ed.

McConaughy, S. H., & Ritter, D. (2002). Best practices in multidimensional assessment of emotional and behavioral disorders. In A. Thomas & J. Grimes (Eds.), *Best practices in school psychology IV* (4th ed., pp. 1303–1320). Washington, DC: National Association of School Psychologists.

STEPHANIE H. MCCONAUGHY

Achenbach System of Empirically Based Assessment: Youth Self-Report

The *Youth Self-Report* (YSR) (Achenbach & Rescorla, 2001) is a standardized rating form for obtaining youth's self-ratings as part of the Achenbach System of Empirically Based Assessment (ASEBA). The ASEBA is an integrated set of standardized rating forms to assess children's competencies and problems. The ASEBA includes forms to be completed by parents, teachers, and youths themselves, as well as forms for direct observations and clinical interviews with children and adolescents. For school-age children, the ASEBA forms include the Child Behavior Checklist for Ages 6 to 18 (CBCL/6-18), Teacher's Report Form (TRF), and YSR.

YSR RATING FORM

The YSR is a four-page form to be completed by youths ages 11 to 18, as was the previous edition (Achenbach, 1991). The YSR requires a mental age of about 10 years and fifth-grade reading skills. (If reading skills are below fifth-grade, the YSR can be read aloud to the respondent.) Page 1 of the YSR requests demographic information about the youth (e.g., youth's age, youth's gender, the parent's usual type of work, youth's grade in school, youth's work status, etc.). The YSR has most of the same social competence questions as the CBCL/6-18, except

that questions are stated in the second person (i.e., you/your). On page 1 of the YSR, youths provide descriptive information about their involvement in sports, hobbies and activities, social organizations, and jobs and chores. They also rate themselves on how much time they spend in each activity or sport and how well they do each one. On page 2, youths provide information about their friendships, relationships with other people, playing and working alone, and performance in academic subjects at school. They also rate themselves on how well they play alone, how well they get along with others, and how well they perform in their academic school subjects. Unlike the CBCL/6-18, youths are not asked to report on special education services or grade repetition because they may not be willing or able to report such information accurately. Page 2 also contains open-ended items where youths can indicate whether they have any illnesses, disabilities, or handicaps, what concerns they may have about school, other concerns, and best things about themselves.

On pages 3 and 4 of the YSR, youths rate themselves on 105 problem items. All of the YSR problem items are similar to items on the CBCL/6-18, except that they are stated in the first person. Examples are "I act too young for my age"; "I argue a lot"; and "I am nervous or tense." The YSR also includes 16 socially desirable items that enable youths to say something favorable about themselves, such as "I like animals"; "I am pretty honest"; and "I enjoy being with people." The socially desirable items replace CBCL/6-18 problem items considered inappropriate to ask youths. Youths rate each YSR item for how true it is of themselves now or within the past 6 months: 0 = *not true (as far as you know)*; 1 = *somewhat or sometimes true*; 2 = *very true or often true*. Most youths can complete the YSR in about 15 to 20 minutes, unless they choose to take more time to write additional comments about themselves.

YSR SCORING PROFILE

The YSR is scored on separate profiles for boys and girls aged 11 to 18. The scoring profile provides raw scores, *T* scores, and percentiles for Total Competence, two competence scales (Activities and Social), eight syndrome scales, six *DSM*-oriented scales, Internalizing, Externalizing, and Total Problems.

The YSR syndrome scales are comparable to those on the CBCL/6-18 and TRF scoring profiles: Anxious/Depressed, Withdrawn/Depressed, Somatic Complaints, Social Problems, Thought Problems, Attention Problems, Rule-Breaking Behavior (which replaces the Delinquent Behavior syndrome that was on the 1991 scoring profile), and Aggressive Behavior. To develop the 2001 versions of the syndrome scales, statistical analyses (factor analyses) were performed on data from YSRs completed by 2,581 youths referred for mental health or special education services.

The YSR *DSM*-oriented scales are similar to those on the CBCL/6-18 and TRF scoring profiles: Affective Problems, Anxiety Problems, Somatic Problems, Attention-Deficit/Hyperactivity Problems, Oppositional Defiant Problems, and Conduct Problems. To create the *DSM*-oriented scales, experienced psychiatrists and psychologists rated a list of CBCL/6-18, TRF, and YSR problem items as to whether each item was *not consistent, somewhat consistent,* or *very consistent* with the diagnostic criteria of the *Diagnostic and Statistical Manual of Mental Disorders* (4th ed.) (*DSM-IV*) (American Psychiatric Association, 1994). Items that were rated *very consistent* by at least 14 of 22 raters (64 percent) were selected to form *DSM*-oriented scales. High scores on the *DSM*-oriented scales can alert clinicians to consider whether certain *DSM-IV* diagnoses are appropriate for an individual youth. However, this information must be combined with other data to make appropriate *DSM-IV* diagnoses.

The YSR Internalizing scale is the sum of scores for the Anxious/Depressed, Withdrawn/Depressed, and Somatic Complaints syndromes. The YSR Externalizing scale is the sum of scores from the Rule-Breaking Behavior and Aggressive Behavior syndromes. YSR Total Problems is the sum of 0-1-2 scores on all 105 problem items. The 16 socially desirable items are omitted from the YSR Total Problems score.

INTERPRETING YSR SCORES

The YSR scoring profile was normed on a U.S. national sample of 1,057 youths aged 11 to 18 who had not received professional help for behavioral or emotional problems within the preceding 12 months. The normative sample was representative of the 48 contiguous states, stratified by socioeconomic status (SES), ethnicity, region, and urban–suburban–rural residence. Separate norms are provided for boys and girls for the entire age range of 11 to 18. The *T* scores and percentiles show how a youth scored on each scale compared with the normative sample of the same gender. Evaluators can use this information to judge whether a youth shows lower competence and/or more problems than is typical for 11- to 18-year-old boys or girls. Cut points are provided for normal-, borderline-, and clinical-range scores for each scale.

On the YSR Activities and Social scales, *T* scores of 31 to 35 (3rd to 7th percentiles) are considered to be in the borderline range, whereas *T* scores below 31 (<3rd percentile) are in the clinical range. For YSR Total Competence, *T* scores of 37 to 40 (10th to 16th percentiles) are in the borderline range, whereas *T* scores below 37 (<10th percentile) are in the clinical range. For the YSR syndrome and *DSM*-oriented scales, *T* scores of 65 to 69 (93rd to 97th percentiles) are in the borderline range, whereas *T* scores above 69 (>97th percentile) are in the clinical range. For Total Problems, Internalizing, and Externalizing,

T scores of 60 to 63 (84th to 90th percentiles) are in the borderline range, whereas *T* scores above 63 (>90th percentile) are in the clinical range.

SCORING OPTIONS

Like the CBCL/6-18 and TRF, the YSR has several different scoring options. Hand scoring usually takes about 5 to 15 minutes. Computer scoring is accomplished through modular Windows software, called the Assessment Data Manager (ADM). Traditional YSR forms for handwritten responses require clerical data entry for computer scoring. YSR machine-readable TELEform or OMR bubble forms can be fed into a scanner for computer scoring. Separate software is also available for direct client entry on the computer. Through an ASEBA Web-Link account, users can also use the Internet to obtain YSR forms, transmit data, and obtain computer-scored profiles (www.aseba.org).

COMPUTER-SCORED CROSS-INFORMANT COMPARISONS

In addition to the scoring profiles for each form, the ADM provides comparisons of scores for up to eight different informants who completed the CBCL/6-18, TRF, and/or YSR. These are titled "cross-informant comparisons" on the computer printout. Two pages of the printout provide visual side-by-side comparisons of 0-1-2 scores for each of the 93 items that are similar across the CBCL/6-18, TRF, and YSR syndrome scales and the 45 items that form the *DSM*-oriented scales. Three other pages of the printout provide cross-informant comparisons of *T* scores for the eight syndrome scales, six *DSM*-oriented scales, and Internalizing, Externalizing, and Total Problems. One additional page provides *Q* correlations that indicate whether agreement between pairs of informants (i.e., parent and teacher, parent and youth, teacher and youth) are *above average, average,* or *below average,* compared with samples of similar informant pairs. The cross-informant comparisons can be especially valuable for integrating data from parent reports, teacher reports, and youth self-ratings and for judging the level of agreement about the youth's problems.

NARRATIVE REPORTS

The ADM software provides an optional one-page narrative report for the YSR, summarizing results on the competence and problem scales. The report also lists 0-1-2 scores for eight critical items that clinicians judged to be especially important for assessment and intervention planning. Examples are "I physically attack people"; "I run away from home"; "I see things that other people think aren't there"; "I set fires"; and "I think about killing myself." The narrative report can be imported easily into word processing programs. The narrative reports can save time in writing assessment reports as well as guarantee accuracy of profile interpretation.

See also: ASEBA Semistructured Clinical Interview for Children and Adolescents; Attention-Deficit/Hyperactivity Disorder; Conduct Disorder; Oppositional Defiant Disorder

BIBLIOGRAPHY

Achenbach, T. M. (1991). *Manual for the Youth Self-Report and 1991 profile.* Burlington: University of Vermont, Department of Psychiatry.

Achenbach, T. M., & Rescorla, L. A. (2001). *Manual for the ASEBA school-age forms & profiles.* Burlington: University of Vermont, Research Center for Children, Youth, and Families.

American Psychiatric Association. (1994). *Diagnostic and statistical manual of mental disorders* (4th ed.). Washington, DC: Author.

Additional Readings for Professionals

Achenbach, T. M., & McConaughy, S. H. (1997). *Empirically based assessment of child and adolescent psychopathology: Practical applications* (2nd ed.). Thousand Oaks, CA: Sage.

Achenbach, T. M., & McConaughy, S. H. (2001). *School-based practitioners guide for the Child Behavior Checklist and related forms* (2nd ed.). Burlington: University of Vermont, Research Center for Children, Youth, and Families.

McConaughy, S. H. (2001). The Achenbach System of Empirically Based Assessment. In J. J. W. Andrews, H. L. Janzen, & D. H. Saklofske (Eds.), *Handbook of psychoeducational assessment: Ability, achievement, and behavior in children* (pp. 289–324). San Diego, CA: Academic Press.

McConaughy, S. H., & Ritter, D. (2002). Best practices in multidimensional assessment of emotional and behavioral disorders. In A. Thomas & J. Grimes (Eds.), *Best practices in school psychology IV* (4th ed., pp. 1303–1320). Washington, DC: National Association of School Psychologists.

STEPHANIE H. MCCONAUGHY

Adaptive Behavior Assessment

Adaptive behaviors are those skills necessary for everyday functioning. Methods for evaluating adaptive behavior vary according to age, because adaptive skills change over an individual's lifetime. Adaptive behavior is most commonly evaluated when there are questions about an individual's overall functioning and skills. Specifically, adaptive behavior is included as one of the major skill areas requiring documentation for a diagnosis of mental retardation. The *Diagnostic and Statistical Manual of Mental Disorders* (4th ed., text rev.) (*DSM-IV-TR*) is published by the American Psychiatric Association (2000) and includes 11 specific domains of adaptive behavior in its definition of mental retardation. According to the *DSM-IV-TR*, mental retardation is characterized in part by "significant limitations in adaptive functioning in at least two of the following skill areas: communication, self-care, home living, social/interpersonal skill, use of community resources, self-direction, functional academic skills, work, leisure, health, and safety" (American Psychiatric Association, 2000).

Another way of understanding adaptive behavior is the definition adopted by the American Association of Mental Retardation (AAMR). The AAMR wording includes three domains of adaptive skills: conceptual, social, and practical (AAMR, 2002). The AAMR definition is accompanied by five major principles for the assessment and understanding of adaptive behavior (AAMR, 2002):

1. Limitations in present functioning must be considered within the context of community environments typical of the individual's age peers and culture.
2. Valid assessment considers cultural and linguistic diversity as well as differences in communication, sensory, motor, and behavioral factors.
3. Within an individual, limitations often coexist with strengths.
4. An important purpose of describing limitations is to develop a profile of needed supports.
5. With appropriate personalized supports over a sustained period, the life functioning of the person with mental retardation generally will improve.

A major difference between the definitions of adaptive behavior provided by the *DSM-IV-TR* and AAMR is the extent to which adaptive behavior limitations are considered to be lifelong traits. According to the *DSM-IV-TR* definition, adaptive behavior deficits are generally considered to be permanent characteristics of an individual. In comparison, the AAMR definition includes more general ways of describing adaptive behaviors and is accompanied by guiding principle number 5, which specifically states that an individual's adaptive behavior could change over time.

Traditionally, approaches to adaptive behavior assessment have relied heavily on third-party reports. For example, the parent(s), teacher(s), or other caregiver(s) of individuals with adaptive behavior impairments fills out rating scales or are interviewed about an individual's behaviors; this approach to assessment is known as indirect assessment. Indirect adaptive behavior assessments have limitations because those who complete the items may have biased, or inadequate, knowledge about the specific adaptive behaviors being assessed. In response to the limitations of indirect assessment, direct assessment methods for measuring adaptive behavior skills have been developed (Steege, Davin, & Hathaway, 2001). Examples of direct methods include direct observations in everyday settings and analysis of work completed by the individual.

In order for adaptive behavior assessments to be comprehensive, it is recommended that they include at least two, and preferably three, types of data about the individual being assessed. Ideally, a comprehensive adaptive behavior assessment will include information obtained from (a) observations of the individual in real-life, everyday situations, (b) performance of tasks taken from the current program, and (c) interviews and checklists completed by those who work most closely with the individual on a regular basis. It is a good idea to collect information that represents a variety of everyday settings. For example, for a school-age student, observations and task analyses from several different classes, as well as completion of checklists by all current teachers are all necessary in order to obtain a complete picture of current adaptive skills.

The final step in adaptive behavior assessment is to assemble all the collected information to create an adaptive behavior profile. The profile should cover the purpose(s) for assessment, domains of skills assessed, and suggestions for programming and progress monitoring. Taken together, the information contained in the profile can be used to assist in determining the levels of current adaptive behaviors, whether such behaviors lead to eligibility for special services, what additional programming and services are needed, and how progress toward program goals can be monitored on a regular basis.

Although most of the time adaptive behavior assessment is conducted as part of an evaluation for mental retardation, it can be a very useful tool for other types of assessments as well. For example, adaptive behavior assessment methods can be utilized for assessment of any student with social, behavioral, functional life skills issues (Harrison & Boney, 2002).

SUMMARY

Adaptive behaviors are age-appropriate and culturally relevant behaviors that are a part of everyday functioning. Although there are two major ways of thinking about the domains of adaptive behavior, there is agreement that adaptive behaviors are important for participation in the larger society. Assessment of adaptive behavior includes evaluating an individual's skills across several settings and with multiple sources of information to learn whether current behaviors are appropriate for optimal functioning.

See also: *Diagnostic and Statistical Manual of Mental Disorders*

BIBLIOGRAPHY

American Association on Mental Retardation. (2002). *Mental retardation definition, classification, and systems of supports* (10th ed.). Washington, DC: Author.
Steege, M. W., Davin, T., & Hathaway, M. (2002). Reliability and accuracy of a performance-based behavioral recording procedure. *School Psychology Review, 30,* 252–261.

Additional Readings for Nonprofessionals

Kamphaus, R. W., & Frick, P. J. (2002). *Clinical assessment of child and adolescent personality and behavior* (2nd ed.). Boston: Allyn & Bacon.
Salvia, J., & Ysseldyke, J. E. (2001). *Assessment* (8th ed.). Boston: Houghton Mifflin.

Additional Readings for Professionals

Harrison, P. L., & Boney, T. L (2002). Best practices in the assessment of adaptive behavior. In A. Thomas & J. Grimes (Eds.), *Best practices in school psychology-IV* (pp. 1167–1179). Washington, DC: National Association of School Psychologists.
House, A. E. (1999). *DSM-IV diagnosis in the schools.* New York: Guilford.
Sattler, J. M. (2002). *Assessment of children: Behavioral and clinical applications* (4th ed.). San Diego: Sattler.

RACHEL BROWN-CHIDSEY
MARK W. STEEGE

Alternative Education

Any nontraditional arrangement for instruction may be called *alternative education.* Although private schools and home schooling are educational options for some students, the term *alternative education* most often refers to programs provided by school districts for students who are not successful in their neighborhood public schools because of behavior problems. Alternative education students do not necessarily have Individualized Education Plans although special education students who are suspended or expelled must be provided alternative educational services (Individuals with Disabilities Education Act Amendments of 1997, Pub. L. 105–17). The number of districts that also have alternative education programs for general education students who have been expelled or suspended, or who are at risk for dropping out of school, is increasing. "Perhaps the most striking known fact about alternative programs, for at-risk students, is that a *wide range* of alternative program models exist" (Tobin & Sprague, 2002, p. 965). For example, there are mandatory "reform schools" (Hill, 1998) and "second chance" or "turn-around" schools for students with serious disciplinary problems (see Hardy, 2000); charter schools (Manno,

Finn, & Vanourek, 2000) that have a special theme (e.g., social justice, fine arts) that attracts students with similar interests whether or not they have behavioral problems; and within-school programs that provide extra services or different types of programming for a selected group of students, often as a part of dropout prevention efforts (Christenson, Sinclair, Lehr, & Godber, 2001; Tobin & Sprague, 2002).

Issues related to alternative education include (a) funding and logistical problems (Black, 1997; Katsiyannis & Maag, 1998; Katsiyannis & Williams, 1998; Kennedy, 2001; Merchant, 1999; Stewart, 2001) and (b) advantages (Dryfoos, 2002) and disadvantages (Mahoney & Cairns, 1997) for the students in both the traditional and the alternative schools (Clark, 2000). Funding for alternative programs is provided primarily by states and local communities, with occasional help from the federal government, usually in the form of short-term grants, and, increasingly, through partnerships with businesses (e.g., Coca-Cola Valued Youth Program, Seahawk Academy; see Government Accounting Office Report, 2002). The need to make sure that public schools are safe and orderly leads to the exclusion of students who bring weapons or illegal drugs to school, threaten violence, or seriously interfere with others' opportunity to learn. However, from the broader perspective of socializing and educating future members of our society, schools are in a better position than other agencies (e.g., prisons, hospitals) to intervene in the lives of students who are at risk for drug and alcohol addiction, delinquency, unemployment, mental illness, and family problems. As long as neighborhood public schools cannot or will not perform this function, alternative schools will be needed, in spite of concerns about the formation of deviant peer groups in alternative settings and drains on resources that might have been used for whole school reform efforts and improvements in the continuum of special education programs.

Features of effective alternative education programs have been identified (Duke & Griesdorn, 1999; Edwards & Wilson, 2001; Guerin & Denti, 1999; Raywid, 1996, 1998; Tobin & Sprague, 2000a, 2000b, 2002). More research is needed, however, to clarify which aspects are most important and under what circumstances, because the programs come as packages including a variety of components, such as service learning, career exploration, civic education, individualized instruction, opportunities to make choices, clear expectations, and behavioral interventions. The following list highlights key variables frequently reported as important for student outcomes that include improved behavior and academic achievement:

1. Caring adults who provide students with individual attention (Castleberry & Enger, 1998; Hardy, 2000; Lange, 1998)
2. Community agencies' involvement and social services provided (Carpenter-Aeby & Aeby, 2001; Carpenter-Aeby, Salloum, & Aeby, 2001; Dryfoos, 2002)

3. Parental involvement (Carpenter-Aeby & Aeby, 2001)
4. Outdoor education, experiential learning (Monferdini, Maloof, Davis, & Shreve, 2001)
5. Professional technical education (see Tobin & Sprague, 2002)

See also: Antisocial Behavior

BIBLIOGRAPHY

Black, S. (1997, May). One last chance. *The American School Board Journal,* pp. 40–42.

Carpenter-Aeby, T., & Aeby, V. G. (2001). Family–school–community interventions for chronically disruptive students: An evaluation of outcomes in an alternative school. *School Community Journal, 11,* 75–92.

Carpenter-Aeby, T., Salloum, M., & Aeby, V. G. (2001). A process evaluation of school social work services in a disciplinary alternative education program. *Children & Schools, 23,* 171–181.

Castleberry, S. E., & Enger, J. M. (1998). Alternative students' concepts of success. *NASSP Bulletin, 82*(602), 105–111.

Christenson, S. L., Sinclair, M. F., Lehr, C., & Godber, Y. (2001). Promoting successful school completion: Critical conceptual and methodological guidelines. *School Psychology Review, 16,* 468–484.

Clark, C. (2000). Texas charter schools: New choices for Texas families. *Clearing House, 74,* 64–69.

Dryfoos, J. (2002). Full-service community schools: Creating new institutions. *Phi Delta Kappan, 83,* 393–399.

Duke, D. L., & Griesdorn, J. (1999). Considerations in the design of alternative schools. *The Clearing House, 73,* 89.

Edwards, M. A., & Wilson, V. B. (2001). One size doesn't fit all. *School Administrator, 58,* 36–39.

Government Accounting Office Report. (2002, February). *School dropout: Education could play a stronger role in identifying and disseminating promising prevention strategies* (GAO-02-240). Washington, DC: Author.

Guerin, G., & Denti, L. (1999). Alternative education support for youth at-risk. *The Clearing House, 73,* 76.

Hardy, L. (2000). A new way: Troubled kids seek a second chance at this Native American school. *American School Board Journal, 187*(6), 26–27, 30–31.

Hill, D. (1998). Reform school. *Teacher Magazine, 9*(8), 34–35, 38–41.

Kasen, S., Cohen, P., & Brooks, J. S. (1998). Adolescent school experiences and dropout, adolescent pregnancy, and young adult deviant behavior. *Journal of Adolescent Research, 13,* 49–72.

Katsiyannis, A., & Maag, J. W. (1998). Disciplining students with disabilities: Issues and considerations for implementing IDEA '97. *Behavioral Disorders, 23,* 276–289.

Katsiyannis, A., & Williams, B. (1998). A national survey of state initiatives on alternative education. *Remedial and Special Education, 19,* 276–284.

Kennedy, M. (2001, January). Ten top 10 facility design and planning solutions. *American School and University, 73*(5), 30–37.

Lange, C. M. (1998). Characteristics of alternative schools and programs serving at-risk students. *High School Journal, 81,* 183–198.

Mahoney, J. L., & Cairns, R. B. (1997). Do extracurricular activities protect against early school dropout? *Developmental Psychology, 33,* 241–253.

Manno, B. V., Finn, C. E., & Vanourek, G. (2000). Beyond the schoolhouse door: How charter schools are transforming U.S. public education. *Phi Delta Kappan, 8,* 736–744.

Merchant, B. (1999). Now you see it; now you don't: A district's short-lived commitment to an alternative high school for newly arrived immigrants. *Urban Education, 34,* 26–51.

Monferdini, J., Maloof, N., Davis, D., & Shreve, K. (2001). DeKalb alternative school: An atmosphere of caring. *Zip Lines: The Voice for Adventure Education, 43*, 35–38.

Raywid, M. A. (1996). *Taking stock: The movement to create mini-schools, schools-within schools and separate small schools* [Microform]. New York: ERIC Clearinghouse on Urban Education, Institute for Urban and Minority Education.

Raywid, M. A. (1998). Small schools: A reform that works. *Educational Leadership, 55*, 34–39.

Stewart, J. (2001). Preventing violent behavior. *Educational Leadership, 58*, 78–79.

Tobin, T., & Sprague, J. (2000a). Alternative education programs for at-risk youth: Issues, best practices, and recommendations. In H. Walker & M. Epstein (Eds.), *Making schools safer and violence free: Critical issues, solutions, and recommended practices.* Austin, TX: Pro-Ed.

Tobin, T., & Sprague, J. (2000b). Alternative education strategies: Reducing violence in school and community programs. *Journal of Emotional and Behavioral Disorders, 8*, 177–186.

Tobin, T. J., & Sprague, J. R. (2002). Alternative educational programs: Accommodating tertiary level, at-risk students. In M. R. Shinn, G. Stoner, & H. M. Walker (Eds.), *Interventions for academic and behavior problems: Preventive and remedial approaches* (pp. 961–993). Silver Spring, MD: National Association of School Psychologists.

TARY J. TOBIN

American Psychological Association—Division 16 (School Psychology)

In 1945, the American Association of Applied Psychology (AAAP) and the American Psychological Association (APA) merged to form one organization known as the APA. At that time, a division structure was established and the first 19 divisions were recognized as Charter Divisions. Division 16 was one of those Charter Divisions and was initially called the Division of School Psychologists. The name was changed in 1969 to its current title, the Division of School Psychology. The APA currently consists of 53 Divisions.

The Division of School Psychology is composed primarily of doctoral-level scientist-practitioner psychologists with full membership in the Division. Full membership in APA is limited to psychologists who hold the doctoral degree. The Division also includes student members and professional affiliates (specialist degree-level school psychologists). Most members share an interest in practice and/or research with children, youth, families, and the educational system. Division members are employed in public schools, university training programs, private practice, hospitals, clinics, and a variety of other settings.

In the mid 1990s, Division 16, led by Jane Close Conoley and Jan Hughes, developed the archival definition of school psychology. In 1998, the APA-authorized Commission for the Recognition of Specialties and Proficiencies in Psychology (CRSPPP) recommended, and the APA Council of Representatives approved, the following archival definition of the specialty of school psychology.

School Psychology is a general practice and health service provider specialty of professional psychology that is concerned with the science and practice of psychology with children, youth, families; learners of all ages; and the schooling process. The basic education and training of school psychologists prepares them to provide a range of psychological assessment, intervention, prevention, health promotion, and program development and evaluation services, with a special focus on the developmental processes of children and youth within the context of schools, families, and other systems.

School psychologists are prepared to intervene at the individual and system level, and develop, implement, and evaluate preventive programs. In these efforts, they conduct ecologically valid assessments and intervene to promote positive learning environments within which children and youth from diverse backgrounds have equal access to effective educational and psychological services to promote healthy development (APA, 1997).

Division 16 and the APA recognize that the professional preparation for the specialty of school psychology occurs at the doctoral level.

The goal of the Division is the enhancement of the status of children, youth, and adults as learners and productive citizens in schools, families, and communities. Its objectives include (1) the promotion and maintenance of high standards of professional education and training and the expansion of appropriate scientific and scholarly knowledge, (2) the advancement of the practice of psychology in the schools, (3) the support of ethical and social responsibilities and encouragement of minority participation in the specialty, and (4) the advancement of school psychology through publications and conferences.

COMPOSITION OF DIVISION 16

The Division leadership consists of an Executive Committee (EC), with each member serving a 3-year term. The EC is composed of a President; President-Elect; Past President; Secretary; Treasurer; Vice-President of Professional Affairs; Vice-President of Membership; Vice-President of Education, Training, and Scientific Affairs; Vice-President of Publications, Communications, and Convention Affairs; Vice-President of Social and Ethical Responsibility and Ethnic Minority Affairs; and two representatives to the APA Council. In addition, the Student Affiliates in School Psychology (SASP) President, Historian, *School Psychology Quarterly* (*SPQ*) editor, and *The School Psychologist* (*TSP*) editor serve on the EC in an ex-officio capacity. Under each vice-presidency, there are a number of committees and task forces addressing issues relevant to that vice-presidency.

PUBLICATIONS

The Division provides a number of publications and electronic media to members, other professionals, and the general public. *School Psychology Quarterly* is a scholarly journal published quarterly. *SPQ* publishes empirical studies, theoretical analyses, and literature reviews relevant to school psychology. Preference is given to papers that integrate the science and practice of school psychological services in all settings. Established in 1985 as *Professional School Psychology* (*PSP*), the name of the journal was changed in 1990. Editors have included Thomas Kratochwill, Joseph Witt, and Terry Gutkin. The editor-elect for 2004 is Rik Carl D'Amato.

The official newsletter of the Division is *The School Psychologist*. This newsletter is also published quarterly and provides a venue for topical issues related to school psychology and the Division, information of relevance to Division members, and a student section for members of SASP, the Division 16–affiliated student organization.

The Division also sponsors a book series edited by Susan M. Sheridan and Sandra L. Christenson entitled *Applying Psychology to the Schools*. Published by APA books, the goal of the series is to provide school psychologists with suggestions for empirically supported interventions. Authors and titles have included *Collaborative Family–Provider Partnerships in Early Intervention: Intervention and Systems Change* by Susan Epps and Barbara Jackson; *Responding to the Needs of Aggressive Children and Their Parents: A Practitioner's Guide to Parent Training* by Timothy Cavell; *Relationship-Based Interventions Between Teachers and Children: Developmental Systems Perspectives on the Practice of School Psychology* by Robert Pianta; *A Practitioner's Handbook of Health-Related Disorders in Children* edited by LeAdelle Phelps; and *Psychology in Schools and Communities* by Ronda Talley and Candace Sullivan.

In addition, the Division produces *The Conversation Series*, a series of videotaped discussions on topics of professional importance by leaders in the field. Included with the tapes are study guides that contain biographical information on the participants, annotated bibliographies, and study questions. The study guides and the videotapes can be used by trainers, graduate students, school administrators, and practitioners to earn continuing professional development (CPD) credits, as a self-study, and in providing both in-service and pre-service training.

Finally, the Division maintains a Web site (http://www.indiana.edu/~div16/), which can be useful for school psychologists and the general public. This site contains information on the goals and objectives of the Division, publications and conferences, the executive committee, membership information, award recipients and fellows, student affiliates, and links to graduate programs in school psychology.

AWARDS

The Division annually offers a number of awards for outstanding research and service. These include the Lightner Witmer Award, Senior Scientist Award, Jack Bardon Distinguished Service Award, and the Outstanding Dissertation Award. The Lightner Witmer Award, established in 1973, recognizes a school psychologist who has established himself/herself as an outstanding scholar early in his/her career (i.e., within 7 years of receiving degree). The Outstanding Dissertation Award, established in 1993, is presented to a school psychologist whose doctoral dissertation has been judged outstanding and has the potential to contribute to the science and practice of school psychology. The Senior Scientist Award, established in 1993, is awarded to a school psychologist who has maintained a consistent exceptional level of scholarship throughout his/her career. Awardees must be either 20 years removed from their terminal degree or 50 years of age. The Jack Bardon Distinguished Service Award, established in 1970, is presented to experienced school psychologists who, throughout their careers, have demonstrated exceptional programs of service. It is given for accomplishments related to leadership, policy development, research on effective practice, and/or training.

See also: Jack Bardon Distinguished Service Award; Lightner Witmer Award; Senior Scientist Award

BIBLIOGRAPHY

American Psychological Association. (1997, March 5). *Petition for reaffirmation of the specialty of school psychology*. Washington, DC: Author.

Additional Reading for Nonprofessionals

Division of School Psychology Web site http://www.indiana.edu/~div16/

Additional Reading for Professionals

Fagan, T. K., & Wise, P. S. (2000). *School psychology: Past, present, and future* (2nd ed.). Bethesda, MD: National Association of School Psychologists.

STEPHEN G. LITTLE
K. ANGELEQUE AKIN-LITTLE

Americans with Disabilities Act of 1990

Throughout history, human beings have made difficult decisions about how our tribes, communities, or governments should or should not respond to the needs of individuals within those societies. Most often, those decisions are based on the social perception of the availability of resources. For example, in the past, when farming communities experienced times of drought, they relied more upon the physically capable individuals within the group to hunt and gather than when the harvests were abundant. Today, times have not changed as much as we would like to think. When we see the stock markets climbing, neighbors buying new cars, and everybody working (at least those who want to), we recognize the necessity and have the wherewithal to assist those members of our society deemed less capable of meeting their own needs.

Unfortunately, during the "lean" times, not only does our society decide who will not receive assistance, but often justifies those decisions by redefining needy individuals as burdens on society, unwilling to be productive, and basically unworthy of assistance. This activity of predetermining a person's value on the basis of their possessing a characteristic that is not valued by the majority of society is called discrimination.

Discrimination and denial of rights have occurred in all cultures and societies. Many forms of discrimination have targeted people by gender, ethnicity, how much money they earn, and religious or political beliefs, to name a few. Yet, no form of discrimination has so widely and intensely affected people as discrimination against people with disabilities (Percy, 1989).

In response to society's inability to effectively combat discrimination, modern governments have taken the initiative to protect individual citizens as well as attempt to change the social attitudes and values that promote discrimination. These attempts have come in the form of laws. Since the Civil Rights Act of 1964, numerous laws have been enacted that identify groups who need social protection (i.e., women, elderly, and people who have disabilities), define the range of available protection, and provide remedies for failure to comply with the laws.

AN OVERVIEW OF THE AMERICANS WITH DISABILITIES ACT OF 1990

The Americans with Disabilities Act (ADA) of 1990 is the most far-reaching legislation ever passed in the United States where civil rights for persons with disabilities are concerned (Rubin & Roessler, 2001). Based upon Section 504 of the Rehabilitation Act Amendments of 1973, which was the first systemic attempt by the U.S. government to protect the rights of persons with disabilities, the ADA took the antidiscrimination policies and practices out of public, government-operated and subsidized facilities and moved antidiscrimination into all aspects of American society.

The guiding principles of the ADA are inclusion (opportunity) and integration (value). It accomplishes these by guaranteeing accessibility for persons with disabilities to those things that are of critical importance to most of us: employment (Title I); government services including transportation (Title II); public accommodations such as public schools (Title III); telephone communications (Title IV); and other services such as insurance (Title V) (Americans with Disabilities Act, 1990).

HOW IS DISABILITY DEFINED?

Instead of generating a list of disability categories that would qualify persons under the ADA, the act defines disability in *functional terms*. A qualified person with a disability is one who (a) has a physical or mental impairment that substantially limits one or more major life activities; (b) has a record of such impairment; or (c) is regarded as having such an impairment (U.S. Department of Justice, 1991).

The law is very clear that the existence of impairment does not define being disabled unless it substantially limits a major life activity (such as walking or talking) that an average person in the general population can perform with little or no difficulty. In other words, a child diagnosed with juvenile diabetes may or may not be considered disabled depending on the amount of functional limitation the child experiences. This determination must be made on a case-by-case basis. What may be a disabling condition for one may only be impairment for another. Disability can only be determined by looking at the relationship between the impairment a person has and how that limits his/her performance of a public activity.

THE ADA: TITLES I, II, IV, AND V

The ADA provides antidiscrimination protection in five general, yet far-reaching, areas of public life. Title I offers protection in the area of employment—helping people access the employment market during the hiring process (e.g., making applications available to all people, not just those that can walk up a flight of stairs) as well as helping existing employees who have or acquire disabilities keep and maintain their jobs. Title II of the ADA prohibits discrimination of qualified individuals with disabilities by state or local government; any department, agency, or other instrument of a state or local government; and any public transportation authority (other than aircraft or certain rail operations—these operations are covered by other existing laws). In its effort to make all of America accessible, Title IV of the ADA opens the world of mass communication to people who are deaf, hard of hearing, or have speech-related disabilities. This title mandates that telecommunications systems be accessible via relay systems. Title V is labeled *Miscellaneous Provisions* because it covers such diverse topics as State Immunity, Attorney's Fees, Technical Assistance, Coverage of the Congress, and Illegal Use of Drugs.

TITLE III: PUBLIC ACCOMMODATIONS

Title III is one of the most far-reaching provisions of the ADA in that this title prohibits discrimination in public accommodations and services operated by private entities. The terms *private entities* and *public accommodations* contain practically every business, agency, or service in the nation that is not covered elsewhere in this law. Private entity refers to any entity other than a public entity (federal or state funded or operated). The definition of public accommodation covers a vast amount of Americana. This includes any establishment that offers lodging for hire; any establishment serving food or drink; any place of exhibition or entertainment; any place of public gathering; any store, shopping center, or other sales or rental establishment; any service establishment (i.e., laundry, travel service, barber shop, gas station, lawyer, hospital, etc.); any terminal used specifically for public transportation; any place of public display or collection (i.e., museum, library, etc.); any place of public recreation (i.e., park, zoo, etc.); any social service establishment (i.e., day care center, food bank, adoption agency, etc.); any place of exercise or recreation (i.e., golf course, gymnasium, bowling alley, etc.); and last but not least, *any place of education* (i.e., nursery, elementary, secondary, undergraduate, or postgraduate private school).

Entities that are covered by this title include virtually all establishments that serve the public except for private housing facilities and residences, buildings owned by state and local governments (which are covered in Title II), private clubs, and religious organizations (these were excluded because the legislators did not want a potential conflict with the First Amendment's freedom of religion).

According to Burgdorf (1991) Title III prohibits discrimination in the following forms:

1. Denying the participation in or benefit from an opportunity.
2. Affording an opportunity that is not equal to that made available to other individuals.
3. Providing an opportunity that is different or separate, unless such separation or difference is necessary to pro-

vide an individual with a disability an opportunity that is as effective as that provided to others.
4. Providing opportunities that are not in "the most integrated setting appropriate to the needs of the individual."
5. Using standards or methods of administration, directly or through contractual arrangements that have the effect of discrimination on others.
6. Excluding or denying an individual equal treatment because of that person's association or relationship with a person who has a disability.

In addition to prohibiting these forms of discrimination, Title III also addresses five other major public and private practices:

1. Prohibits eligibility criteria for services or goods which screen out persons with disabilities, unless those criteria can be shown necessary for those goods or services.
2. Requires that establishments offering services and products to the public make reasonable modifications to policies, practices, and procedures unless that modification would fundamentally alter the nature of the product or services.
3. Covered entities must furnish auxiliary aids or services, unless doing so would alter the nature of the product, service, facility, etc. or would result in an undue burden.
4. Requires covered entities to remove architectural and communication (that are structural in nature) barriers where their removal is readily achievable.
5. Where barrier removal is not readily achievable, covered entities must still make its goods, services, etc. accessible through alternative methods.

IMPLICATIONS FOR SCHOOL SYSTEMS

One of the first implications that need to be addressed is the distinction between the ADA and previous disability-related laws. The ADA is based on antidiscrimination, not affirmative action. There are no services associated with the ADA, nothing that requires a determination of eligibility. A child is protected from discrimination if he/she is *an otherwise qualified person with a disability.* If nondisabled children receive a public service or access to a public activity, children who have disabilities must (perhaps as a result of readily achievable accommodations) also receive that service or access. For example, your school district offers after-school activities such as music/band. If a student who uses a wheelchair has comparable skill playing the trombone, he/she cannot be denied access to the band unless the activity requires marching and playing at the same time. Even then, the student must be given the opportunity to show how he/she may be able to accomplish the task with reasonable accommodation. What is not required by the ADA in this situation is to change the nature of the band (i.e., do no marching). If the band has been a marching band, there is no obligation to change the activity to accommodate students with disabilities.

A second implication for school systems relates the physical accessibility requirements of the ADA. The ADA (and other previously discussed legislation) requires that all *programs and services* be accessible to students with disabilities. This does not require that all buildings and facilities be modified. Instead, all programs/services offered by the school system must be provided in an accessible environment/building. If a program is housed in a building not accessible to students in wheelchairs, that program must be moved to an accessible location. Another example of accessibility: The school debate team is being transported to a neighboring school for their debate. The school bus is not accessible to students in wheelchairs. The school is required by the ADA not only to provide transportation for the student who uses a wheelchair, but also to ensure that other students ride in the accessible vehicle to enable that student to interact with nondisabled students.

Another, and perhaps more far-reaching, implication for school districts implementing the ADA concerns the state's requirement to provide *free appropriate public education* (Percy, 1989) to all students with disabilities. Although from previous experience it is known that the vast majority of academic accommodations require little or no financial expenditure, school districts are obligated to provide whatever accommodation is deemed necessary to provide the student a free and appropriate public education. For example, in order to ensure that a student who is deaf and who uses sign language has access to lectures and activities in class, the school system must provide sign language interpreters. Yet another dimension of offering free and appropriate public education concerns where that education occurs. The regulations require that educational activities occur in the least restrictive environment—in other words, students with disabilities are not to be isolated from their nondisabled peers unless the school can *demonstrate* that the student's educational program cannot be achieved in the general school setting. The intent of Title III is to ensure equal access to all aspects of public life for all people.

In conclusion, the Americans with Disabilities Act of 1990 went far beyond previous legislation enacted to provide people with disabilities access to public services. Whether in the area of employment (Title I) or mandating nondiscrimination in school programs (Title III), the ADA set a clear and enforceable standard for protecting the rights of people who have disabilities and establishing the groundwork for changing how our society determines the value of its citizens.

See also: Individuals with Disabilities Education Act

BIBLIOGRAPHY

Americans with Disabilities Act of 1990, Pub. L. No. 101-336, 104 Stat. 328 (1991).

Burgdorf, R., Jr. (1991). Equal access to public accommodations. In J. West (Ed.), *The Americans with Disabilities Act: From policy to practice*. New York: Milbank Memorial Fund.

Percy, S. L. (1989). *Disability, civil rights, and public policy: The politics of implementation*. Tuscaloosa: University of Alabama Press.

Rubin, S., & Roessler, R. (2001). *Foundations of the vocational rehabilitation process* (5th ed.). Austin, TX: Pro-Ed.

U.S. Department of Justice. (1991). *Americans with Disabilities Act handbook*. U.S. Department of Justice, Civil Rights Division, Disability Rights Section. Available through DOJ (202-514-0301/voice, or 202-514-0383/TDD).

Charles D. Palmer

Anorexia Nervosa

Anorexia nervosa is an eating disorder that is characterized by a refusal to maintain a minimally normal body weight, an intense fear of fatness, significant disturbance in perceived weight and body shape, and, in postmenarcheal females, amenorrhea (American Psychiatric Association, 1994). In the *Diagnostic and Statistical Manual of Mental Disorders* (4th ed.) (*DSM-IV*) (American Psychiatric Association, 1994), anorexia nervosa is broken down into two subtypes, the restricting type and the binge-eating/purging type. An individual with anorexia nervosa restricting type does not engage in binge-eating or purgative behaviors, such as vomiting or the use of diuretics, whereas an individual with anorexia nervosa binge-eating/purging type regularly engages in binge eating or more probably purgative behavior.

Studies have shown that anorexia nervosa occurs approximately 10 times more often in females than in males, with lifetime prevalence rates ranging between 0.1 and 1 percent (Williamson et al., 2001). Anorexia is found mostly in industrialized, Western cultures, where there is an abundance of food available (Fairburn & Brownell, 2002). The age of onset for anorexia nervosa is typically around mid- to late adolescence, and is associated with a highly variable course and outcome (Raeburn, 2002). Mortality rates range from 6 to 20 percent, commonly the result of starvation, electrolyte imbalance, or suicide. Research studies on the course of anorexia nervosa have shown that approximately 40 percent fully recover, about a third improve, whereas an estimated 20 percent endure a chronic course of illness (Williamson et al., 2001). Some of the medical complications associated with anorexia nervosa include cardiovascular, gastrointestinal, electrolyte, and endocrine abnormalities, osteoporosis, dry skin, loss of hair, intolerance to cold, and lanugo (fine downy hair) growth on the body (Fairburn & Brownell, 2002).

THEORETICAL MODELS OF ETIOLOGY

Many theories have described the etiology, or origins of anorexia nervosa. The cognitive–behavioral theory emphasizes the interaction between personality characteristics (e.g., perfectionism, rigidity, and obsessionality), social modeling (e.g., increasingly thin representations of the ideal female body image in the media), interpersonal pressures (e.g., social comparison, history of teasing, and family environment), and disordered thoughts about body image (Raeburn, 2002). According to this model, it is the intense fear of gaining weight that motivates anorexic behaviors such as food restriction, excessive exercise, and purgative behaviors. Such behaviors are negatively reinforced by subsequent reduction in anxiety or avoidance of stress associated with the fear of weight gain (Williamson et al., 2001). Biological effects of prolonged starvation can lead to binge eating, which in turn can lead to purgative behaviors used to reduce the anxiety caused by binge eating.

According to the psychodynamic and self-psychology models of anorexia nervosa, the extreme methods used to control the individual's biological drive of hunger serve to compensate for perceived feelings of ineffectiveness, lack of control, or identity (Williamson et al., 2001). Other self-psychology models propose that the symptoms of anorexia nervosa serve to replace feelings of emptiness, numbness, tension, or pain within the individual. Psychodynamic theorists often describe anorexia nervosa as a phobic avoidance of an adult, developed female body, and the sexuality that accompanies maturation. It has been suggested that although the avoidance of food may initially serve these functions, in time the initial motivations may be forgotten while the individual continues to use extreme measures to lose weight (Williamson et al., 2001). Psychodynamic theories postulate that individuals with anorexia nervosa develop a sense of security and self-identity with the eating disorder.

The association between personality characteristics and comorbid or co-occurring diagnoses has been a subject of intense study (Williamson et al., 2001). Research has shown that traits of rigidity, obsessionality, perfectionism, and inhibition exist before and after the onset of anorexic symptoms. Genetic influences on the development of anorexia have also been studied. Family studies have shown an increased risk among first-degree relatives with an eating disorder (American Psychiatric Association, 1994). Twin research on individuals with anorexia nervosa has shown a higher rate of concordance between identical twins than fraternal twins.

TREATMENT STRATEGIES

Because of the serious medical consequences and potential mortality associated with anorexia nervosa, an initial step in treatment is to determine the appropriate level of care that is necessary for recovery. The different levels of care can include inpatient hospitalization, partial hospitalization, intensive outpatient treatment, and outpatient treatment (Williamson et al., 1998).

During inpatient treatment, the emphasis is on medical stabilization, establishing regular eating patterns, identifying cognitive distortions and core beliefs about weight and body image, and addressing issues that have contributed to the maintenance of the eating disorder. Partial hospitalization involves attendance at therapy groups and supervised meals throughout the day, while allowing the individual to spend evenings at home. Intensive outpatient and traditional outpatient therapy differs in that the former still attends a selected number of groups at the hospital, and focuses on weight maintenance and relapse prevention skills. In strictly outpatient therapy, the therapist continues to help the individual maintain a healthy weight, address disordered thoughts and dysfunctional eating patterns, and continues with relapse prevention planning.

Dietary interventions include meal planning and nutritional education. Because of the intense fear of weight gain associated with anorexia nervosa, the caloric amounts of meal plans are increased gradually. Behavioral techniques, such as behavioral contracting and gradual exposure to feared foods, are used to modify maladaptive eating patterns, such as starvation and purging. At the inpatient and partial hospitalization levels of care, individuals are supervised during meals, with a time limit and nutritional supplementation for food that is not consumed.

Research has shown that individuals with anorexia nervosa, as well as those with other eating disorders, have a cognitive bias toward information related to food and body image (Williamson et al., 1998). That is, these individuals more readily attend to and recall information related to weight, food, and body size or shape. Cognitive therapy is used to modify this biased cognitive processing, and to teach the anorexic patient how to recognize and challenge their irrational beliefs and distorted thoughts about body image. The cognitive–behavioral approach has been found most effective in treating anorexia nervosa in clinical settings, and is still being investigated in research settings (Fairburn & Brownell, 2002).

For adolescents as well as adults with anorexia nervosa, family therapy can play an important role in the treatment. Because the family is often the individual's primary source of support outside of therapy, education and skills training are vital for relapse prevention (Williamson et al., 1998). The focus of family therapy includes exploring the function of the eating disorder within the family, communication styles, and conflict resolution. Although family therapy with adolescents has been proven effective, it remains secondary to individual treatment for adults diagnosed with anorexia nervosa (Williamson et al., 1998).

Several pharmacological treatments have been found effective for the treatment of eating disorders like bulimia nervosa. However, there have been no controlled medication trials that have shown a significant amount of success or effectiveness in the treatment of anorexia nervosa (Fairburn & Brownell, 2001). When an individual has moderate or severe depression, antidepressants may be considered. However, considering the side effects associated with medication, it is best to preclude their use until medical complications (e.g., very low body weight) associated with anorexia nervosa have been resolved (Fairburn & Brownell, 2001; Williamson et al., 1998). In addition to depression, anorexia nervosa is also commonly comorbid with other *DSM-IV* (American Psychiatric Association, 1994) psychopathology, such as anxiety disorders and personality disorders. The presence of secondary psychopathology may complicate or interfere with treatment, and thus needs to be addressed accordingly.

SUMMARY

Anorexia nervosa is a serious and often chronic disorder that is primarily diagnosed in adolescent females or young women. Although the potential causes for the development of the anorexia remain uncertain, various research models seem to agree that there is no one specific cause, but rather the interaction between different personality, social, biological, and cognitive factors predisposes an individual to the development of anorexia nervosa. There are specific treatment strategies that have proven effective for anorexia nervosa; however, the course and outcome of treatment for anorexia nervosa remains highly variable, with only 50 to 70 percent recovery after extensive and very expensive treatment.

See also: Body Image; Bulimia Nervosa; Family Counseling

BIBLIOGRAPHY

American Psychiatric Association. (1994). *Diagnostic and statistical manual of mental disorders* (4th ed.). Washington, DC: Author.
Fairburn, C. G., & Brownell, K. D. (Eds.). (2002). *Eating disorders and obesity.* New York: Guilford.
Raeburn, S. D. (2002). Women and eating disorders. In S. L. A. Straussner (Ed.), *The handbook of addiction treatment for women* (pp. 127–153). San Francisco: Jossey-Bass/Pfeiffer.
Williamson, D. A., Duchmann, E. G., Barker, S. E., & Bruno, R. M. (1998). Anorexia nervosa. In V. B. Van Hasselt & M. Hersen (Eds.), *Handbook of psychological treatment protocols for children and adolescents* (pp. 413–434). Mahwah, NJ: Erlbaum.
Williamson, D. A., Zucker, N. L., Martin, C. K., & Smeets, M. A. A. (2001). Etiology and management of eating disorders. In P. B. Sutker & H. E. Adams (Eds.), *Comprehensive handbook of psychopathology* (3rd ed., pp. 641–670). New York: Kluwer Academic/Plenum.

Additional Readings for Nonprofessionals

Brumberg, J. J. (1988). *Fasting girls: The emergence of anorexia nervosa as a modern disease.* New York: Plume.
Sacker, I. M., & Zimmer, M. A. (1987). *Dying to be thin: Understanding and defeating anorexia nervosa and bulimia: A practical lifesaving guide.* New York: Warner Books.

Additional Reading for Professionals

American Psychiatric Association. (1993). *Practice guidelines for eating disorders.* Washington, DC: Author.

DONALD A. WILLIAMSON
AMY E. RZEZNIKIEWICZ

Antecedent Analysis

Behavior analysts often describe the occurrence of behavior within a three-term contingency that conveys the interrelation between what happens right before a behavior occurs, the behavior itself, and the consequences that follow the behavior (Sulzer-Azaroff & Mayer, 1991). The stimuli that precede behavior or are present while a behavior occurs are known as *antecedents*. According to Sulzer-Azaroff & Mayer (1991), when a behavior occurs in the presence of certain antecedents and is then reinforced through the consequences that follow, those specific antecedents can come to exert control over the occurrence of that behavior.

To illustrate this relationship, consider the following example within the context of a classroom setting. A girl is presented with a nonpreferred work task. She engages in inappropriate behavior and avoids the task. In this situation, the presentation of the demand and the task materials are the antecedent stimuli that occur prior to the problem behavior. The consequence in this example is the avoidance of the academic task.

Antecedents and consequences each play a role in the occurrence of problem behavior. Manipulating antecedent events can provide information regarding why a behavior might occur. Unlike functional analysis, which manipulates specific antecedent and consequent events to determine the function of a behavior, antecedent manipulation only provides information about what evokes a behavior—not direct information about what reinforces a behavior (Flood & Wilder, 2002). However, research has demonstrated that the manipulation of antecedent variables such as task difficulty, task length, task novelty, presentation of high and low levels of attention, and other curricular variables can lead to the identification of appropriate and successful treatment recommendations (Carr & Newsome, 1985; Carr, Newsome, & Binkoff, 1980; Dunlap et al., 1993; Dunlap, White, Vera, Wilson, & Panacek, 1996; Kern, Childs, Dunlap, Clarke, & Falk, 1994; Taylor, Ekdahl, Romanczyk, & Miller, 1994; Taylor, Sisson, McKelvey, & Trefelner, 1993). Because antecedent manipulation provides such specific information about what triggers a behavior, it is used in a variety of situations during the assessment of problem behavior. Practitioners should exercise caution when inferring functions of problem behavior when using antecedent analyses in the absence of analyses of consequences. However, antecedent analyses can often provide very detailed information about what aspects of an event need to be altered to lower the probability of the occurrence of problem behavior. For example, in the escape condition in a functional analysis, difficult academic materials are presented and a child is prompted through the task. Demonstration of the targeted problem behavior leads to a break from the difficult academic task. A high level of problem behavior in the escape condition suggests that the removal of those task demands (or tasks) reinforces the behavior. What a functional analysis does not reveal is information regarding from which aspects of a task the child is escaping. For instance, is the child escaping the verbal task demands, the visual sight of the materials, the difficulty of the task, the teacher/therapist, the length of the task, the location of the analysis, the subject area from which the tasks were chosen, or some combination of these variables? Antecedent analyses can answer those questions by keeping the consequence (i.e., break from task) constant and manipulating different aspects of the task presentation and the task itself.

Beginning with very broad analyses of variables affecting the occurrence of problem behavior and moving toward very specific aspects of antecedent variables, research has demonstrated the utility of manipulating antecedents. To investigate whether the presence of task demands affects the occurrence of a problem behavior, researchers set up simple comparison conditions in which demands were delivered in one condition and not in the other (Carr et al., 1980; Carr & Newsome, 1985). Because differences in the level of problem behavior occurred in the presence of demands, the researchers hypothesized that the behavior was demonstrated to escape from aversive tasks. They then lessened the aversiveness of the task by incorporating preferred objects and food during the demands that subsequently lowered the problem behavior during the demands.

Carr and Durand (1985) used similar methodology to investigate the effects of attention and task difficulty on childhood problem behavior. Three conditions were used to compare high versus low attention and easy versus difficult tasks. One condition (Easy 33) presented a child with easy tasks and delivered attention during 33 percent of the intervals. The "Easy 100" condition presented the easy tasks while delivering attention during 100 percent of the intervals. In the "Difficult 100" condition, experimenters presented difficult tasks and delivered attention during 100 percent of the intervals. By comparing the level of behavior exhibited in the Easy 33 and the Easy 100 conditions, the experimenters were able to assess the impact of differing levels of attention while holding the difficulty of the task constant. By comparing the level of behavior in the Easy 100 and the Difficult 100 sessions, the experimenters held the level of attention constant and could then assess the relative effects of task difficulty. For two children, problem behavior was highest in the Difficult 100 conditions. For one child, problem behavior was highest in the Easy 33 conditions. For another child, problem behavior was high in both the Difficult 100 and the Easy 33 conditions. These three different patterns of responding suggest control through escaping difficult work, through accessing high levels of attention, and of multiple sources of control, respectively (Carr & Durand, 1985).

More specific classroom variables have been assessed with similar methodologies. That is, by keeping some consequence constant and manipulating some antecedent variables, the differences in the level of a problem behavior can be attributed to the antecedent variable. Dunlap et al. (1993) used this approach to investigate the effects of long- versus short-worksheet assignments, near versus far staff proximity, and choice versus no choice in academic assignments on the problem and appropriate behaviors of children in classroom settings. Childs et al. (1994) investigated five instructional variables thought to affect the problem behavior of one student in a classroom setting. Oral versus written task modality, drill and practice versus problem-solving assignments, short versus long tasks, self-monitoring versus teacher reminders, and the use of a carrel versus not using a carrel during assignments were investigated. As described above, the differences between these different conditions provided information relating to which specific aspects of a demand context were aversive. This led to a detailed intervention plan that incorporated the results of the antecedent analysis.

Although antecedent analyses can be used to identify specific variables that affect problem behavior after a functional analysis (or after functional hypotheses are developed), antecedent manipulations can also be presented within a functional analysis. Mueller, Wilczynski, Moore, Fusilier, and Trahant (2001) manipulated the preference of items used in tangibles conditions and found differential rates of aggression when high versus low preference items were presented and restricted. Again, obtaining more specific information about the variables involved in the occurrence of problem behavior can help researchers, therapists, and practitioners develop more specific recommendations to decrease those behaviors and increase appropriate responding. Antecedent analyses have been successful in revealing the effects of a number of common classroom variables such as the presence or absence of demands and the level of adult attention. Similarly, holding a consequence constant and manipulating an antecedent condition has revealed the effects of many specific curricular and academic variables.

See also: Functional Analysis; Functional Behavioral Assessment; Positive Behavioral Supports

BIBLIOGRAPHY

Carr, E. G., & Durand, V. M. (1985). Reducing behavior problems through functional communication training. *Journal of Applied Behavior Analysis, 18,* 11–126.

Carr, E. G., & Newsome, C. (1985). Demand-related tantrums; Conceptualization and treatment. *Behavior Modification, 9,* 403–426.

Carr, E. G., Newsome, C., & Binkoff, J. A. (1980). Escape as a factor in the aggressive behavior of two retarded children. *Journal of Applied Behavior Analysis, 13,* 101–117.

Dunlap, G., Kern, L., dePerczel, M., Clarke, S., Wilson, D., Childs, K., et al. (1993). Functional analysis of classroom variables for students with emotional and behavioral disorders. *Behavioral Disorders, 18,* 275–291.

Dunlap, G., White, R., Vera, A., Wilson, D., & Panacek, L. (1996). The effects of multi-component, assessment-based curricular modifications on the classroom behavior of children with emotional and behavioral disorders. *Journal of Behavioral Education, 6,* 481–500.

Flood, W. A., & Wilder, D. A. (2002). Antecedent assessment and assessment-based treatment of off-task behavior in a child diagnosed with attention deficit-hyperactivity disorder. *Education and Treatment of Children, 25,* 331–338.

Kern, L., Childs, K. E., Dunlap, G., Clarke, S., & Falk, G. D. (1994). Using assessment-based curricular interventions to improve the classroom behavior of a student with emotional and behavioral challenges. *Journal of Applied Behavior Analysis, 27,* 7–19.

Mueller, M. M., Wilczynski, S. M., Moore, J. W., Fusilier, I., & Trahant, D. (2001). Antecedent manipulations in a tangible condition: The effects of stimulus preference on aggression. *Journal of Applied Behavior Analysis, 34,* 237–240.

Sulzer-Azaroff, B., & Mayer, G. R. (1991). *Behavior analysis for lasting change.* New York: Holt, Rinehart & Winston.

Taylor, J. C., Ekdahl, M. M., Romanczyk, R. G., & Miller, M. L. (1994). Escape behavior in task situations: Task versus social antecedents. *Journal of Autism and Developmental Disorders, 24,* 331–344.

Taylor, J. C., Sisson, L. A., McKelvey, J. L., & Trefelner, M. F. (1993). Situation specificity in attention-seeking problem behavior. *Behavior Modification, 17,* 474–497.

Additional Reading for Professionals and Nonprofessionals

Luiselli, J. K., & Cameron, M. J. (Eds.). (1998). *Antecedent control.* Baltimore: Brooks.

MICHAEL M. MUELLER
TERRY S. FALCOMATA

Antisocial Behavior

The term *antisocial* has several meanings: (a) unfriendly; (b) antagonistic, hostile; (c) detrimental to social order; and (d) a pattern of behavior in which social norms and the rights of others are persistently violated (A–Z Dictionary, 2002). Antisocial individuals have been classified into two types: life-course-persistent and adolescence-limited (Moffitt, 1993). The life-course-persistent individual initiates antisocial behavior early in childhood and continues the rest of his/her life. The adolescent-limited individual does not initiate antisocial behavior until his/her teenage years and does not behave in antisocial ways as an adult. Individuals with early onset of antisocial behavior tend to have low verbal functioning and individuals with adolescence onset tend to report high levels of stress (Aguilar, Sroufe, Egeland, & Carlson, 2000). Brame, Nagin, and Tremblay (2001), however, reported that, for physical aggression, in their large-scale, prospective longitudinal study they found no support for a trajectory of low levels of aggression in childhood followed by high levels in adolescence. Boys with high levels of aggression in childhood were more likely than boys with low levels in childhood to have high levels of aggression in adolescence.

Teacher, peer, and self-report assessments have been used to study antisocial behavior and other characteristics of students with and without disabilities in fourth, fifth, and sixth grades in Chicago and South Carolina (Farmer, Rodkin, Pearl, & Van Acker, 1999; Farmer, Van Acker, Pearl, & Rodkin, 1999). Antisocial behaviors included starting fights, being disruptive, and getting into trouble. Students were grouped according to aggression, popularity, and academic achievement. Although students varied considerably, indicating a need to use functional behavioral assessments, the influence of peers on antisocial behavior was evident in many situations. Students with antisocial behaviors could be found among popular, rejected, and isolated students, indicating that in some situations, peers support aggressive behaviors. Rodkin, Farmer, Pearl, and Van Acker (2000), commenting on this research, state that antisocial boys were popular if they were athletic and/or physically attractive, as long as they were *not* extremely (a) shy, withdrawn, or unfriendly and/or (b) low in academic competence.

Antisocial behavior in children and youth is associated with growing up to be an adult who may be considered to be a psychopath or sociopath who has Antisocial Personality Disorder (ASPD). ASPD is described in *DSM-IV* as a behavior pattern established before age 15 and includes at least three of the following behaviors: (a) repeated criminal acts, (b) deceitfulness, (c) impulsivity, (d) disregard for the safety of others, (e) irresponsibility, and (f) lack of remorse. In the general population, about 3 percent of men and 1 percent of women could be characterized as having ASPD; the percentage would be much higher among prison inmates and residents in alcohol and drug treatment centers (Moeller & Dougherty, 2001).

Antisocial behaviors can be learned by observing others modeling these behaviors and, when reinforced (perhaps inadvertently), are likely to become habitual. Social attention may positively reinforce antisocial behavior, and escaping from unpleasant situations may negatively reinforce it (see Fitzsimmons, 1998). Children and youth who have ADHD and/or can be characterized as conduct disordered are at risk for antisocial behavior, as are their siblings (Faraone, Biederman, Mennin, Russell, & Tsuang, 1998). Talking with a friend about deviant and violent topics is related to violent actions for adolescent males (Dishion, Eddy, Haas, Li, & Spracklen, 1997).

Society has a role to play in the development of antisocial behavior. Children being raised in family situations that involve abuse or neglect, inadequate parenting, extreme poverty, or drug and alcohol problems, are at risk for antisocial behavior (see Walker & Gresham, 1997; Webber, 1997). Lead exposure has been linked to antisocial behavior, perhaps from peeling lead-based paint in the dwellings of low-income families (Lead Exposure, 2002). Lack of touch and human warmth may contribute to antisocial behavior, perhaps mediated by low levels of serotonin (see Embry, 1997). Coercive interactions in families, in which parents and children habitually manage conflict in aversive ways, teach children to use antisocial behaviors (Patterson, Reid, & Dishion, 1992). Children who are physically abused are especially likely to develop chronic patterns of antisocial behavior (Cohen, Brown, & Smailes, 2001). A randomized, control-group study that examined outcomes at age 15 for children who had participated in a 2-year home visitation program indicated that this is an effective way to reduce child abuse and, therefore, antisocial behavior. Nurses made home visits to low-income, new mothers during the prenatal and infancy period. The mediating variable was a reduction in child maltreatment (Eckenrode et al., 2001).

At school, functional behavioral assessment should be used to determine *specific* environmental factors, especially peer-related social structures, that are related to the antisocial behaviors of individual students (see Farmer et al., 1999). Multicomponent interventions are recommended that combine positive behavioral support and social skills instruction for the individual student with systems level interventions (e.g., peer group, classroom, whole school). Farmer, Farmer, and Gut (1999) recommended a functional behavioral assessment to determine the relationships between aggressive behavior and social relationships. They also pointed out that, in addition to individualized interventions, it may be necessary to change classroom environments using methods such as the instructional approach to classroom management described in Langland, Lewis-Palmer, and Sugai (1998) to create normative expectations for prosocial behavior.

A classroom-based intervention to reduce antisocial behavior was compared to a family-based intervention and found to be more effective (Ialongo, Poduska, Werthamer, & Kellam, 2001). However, the authors recommend using both school and family interventions. Hawkins, Catalano, Kosterman, Abbott, and Hill (1999) reported a 6-year follow-up of a comprehensive intervention that involved (a) in-service training for elementary school teachers, (b) parenting classes, and (c) social skills instruction for students. Students who received the full intervention were less likely than controls to report violent delinquent acts, heavy drinking, sexual intercourse, multiple sex partners, and pregnancy or having caused a pregnancy. They were also less likely to have office discipline referrals and more likely than controls to have better academic achievement and to report commitment and attachment to school.

Recommended interventions include *reducing* the use of punishment and providing a range of positive services at all age levels that include primary, secondary, and tertiary prevention efforts (see Fitzsimmons, 1998). An example of a multicomponent, comprehensive intervention following this model was recently reported by Cunningham and Henggeler (2001). In this model, middle schools use universal interventions to address prevention of violence and drug abuse for all students and provide multisystemic therapy (see Henggeler, Schoenwald, Borduin, Rowland, & Cunningham, 1998) for students who are at risk for expulsion from school and involvement with the juvenile justice system.

See also: Abuse and Maltreatment of Children; Attention-Deficit/Hyperactivity Disorder; Conduct Disorder; Functional Behavioral Assessment; Oppositional Defiant Disorder; Parenting; Social Skills Building for

BIBLIOGRAPHY

Agulilar, B., Sroufe, A. L., Egeland, B., & Carlson, E. (2000). Distinguishing the early-onset/persistent and adolescence-onset antisocial behavior types: From birth to 16 years. *Journal of Adolescent Research, 16,* 326–354.

A–Z Dictionary. (2002). Definition of "antisocial." Retrieved August 29, 2002, from http://www.infoplease.com

Brame, B., Nagin, D. S., & Tremblay, R. E. (2001). Developmental trajectories of physical aggression from school entry to late adolescence. *Journal of Child Psychology and Psychiatry, 42*, 503–512.

Cohen, P., Brown, J., & Smailes, E. (2001). Child abuse and neglect and the development of mental disorders in the general population. *Development and Psychopathology, 13*, 981–999.

Cunningham, P. B., & Henggeler, S. W. (2001). Implementation of an empirically based drug and violence prevention and intervention program in public school settings. *Journal of Clinical Child Psychology, 30*, 221–232.

Dishion, T. J., Eddy, J. M., Haas, E., Li, F., & Spracklen, K. (1997). Friendships and violent behavior in adolescence. *Social Development, 6*, 207–225.

Eckenrode, J., Zielinski, D., Smith, E., Marcynyszyn, L., Henderson, C. R., Kitzman, H., et al. (2001). Child maltreatment and the early onset of problem behaviors: Can a program of nurse home visitation break the link? *Development and Psychopathology, 13*, 873–890.

Embry, D. D. (1997). Does your school have a peaceful environment? Using an audit to create a climate for change and resiliency. *Intervention in School and Clinic, 32*, 217–222.

Faraone, S., Biederman, J., Mennin, D., Russell, R., & Tsuang, M. T. (1998). Familial subtypes of attention deficit hyperactivity disorder: A 4-year follow-up study of children from antisocial–ADHD families. *Journal of Child Psychology and Psychiatry, 39*, 1045–1053.

Farmer, T. W., Farmer, E. M., & Gut, D. M. (1999). Implications of social development research for school-based interventions for aggressive youth with EBD. *Journal of Emotional and Behavioral Disorders, 7*, 130–136.

Farmer, T. W., Rodkin, P. C., Pearl, R., & Van Acker, R. (1999). Teacher-assessed behavioral configurations, peer-assessments, and self-concepts of elementary students with mild disabilities. *Journal of Special Education, 33*, 66–80.

Farmer, T. W., Van Acker, R., Pearl, R., & Rodkin, P. C. (1999). Social networks and peer-assessed problem behavior in elementary classrooms: Students with and without disabilities. *Remedial and Special Education, 20*, 244–264.

Fitzsimmons, M. K. (1998). *Violence and aggression in children and youth* [ERIC/OSEP Digest E572]. Reston, VA: ERIC Clearinghouse on Disabilities and Gifted Education. (ED 429 419)

Hawkins, J. D., Catalano, R. F., Kosterman, R., Abbott, R., & Hill, K. G. (1999). Preventing adolescent health-risk behaviors by strengthening protection during childhood. *Archives of Pediatric Adolescent Medicine, 153*, 226–234.

Henggeler, S. W., Schoenwald, S. K., Borduin, C. M., Rowland, M. D., & Cunningham, P. B. (1998). *Multisystemic treatment of antisocial behavior in children and adolescents.* New York: Guilford.

Ialongo, N., Poduska, J., Werthamer, L., & Kellam, S. (2001). The distal impact of two first-grade preventive interventions on conduct problems and disorder in early adolescence. *Journal of Emotional and Behavioral Disorders, 9*, 146–160.

Langland, S., Lewis-Palmer, T., & Sugai, G. (1998). Teaching respect in the classroom: An instructional approach. *Journal of Behavioral Education, 8*, 245–262.

Lead Exposure. (2002). Lead exposure linked to antisocial behavior. Retrieved August 29, 2002, from http://ens.lycos.com

Moeller, G. F., & Dougherty, D. M. (2001). Antisocial personality disorder, alcohol, and aggression. *Alcohol Research and Health: The Journal of the National Institute on Alcohol Abuse and Alcoholism, 25*(1), 5–12.

Moffitt, T. (1993). Adolescence-limited and life-course-persistent antisocial behavior: A developmental taxonomy. *Psychological Review, 100*, 674–701.

Patterson, G., Reid, J., & Dishion, T. (1992). *Antisocial boys.* Eugene, OR: Castilia.

Rodkin, P. C., Farmer, T. W., Pearl, R., & Van Acker, R. (2000). Heterogeneity of popular boys: Antisocial and prosocial configurations. *Developmental Psychology, 36*, 14–24.

Walker, H. M., & Gresham, F. M. (1997). Making schools safer and violence free. *Intervention in School and Clinic, 32*, 199–205.

Webber, J. (1997). Comprehending youth violence: A practicable perspective. *Remedial and Special Education, 18*, 94–105.

GEORGE SUGAI
TARY J. TOBIN
EMMA MARTIN

Anxiety

Many children experience feelings of anxiety from time to time, but, for some, anxiety is overwhelming and causes pain and dysfunctional behavior. A large number of disorders include symptoms of anxiety. Some of these disorders include panic attacks, agoraphobia, panic disorder without agoraphobia, panic disorder with agoraphobia, agoraphobia without history of panic disorder, specific phobia, social phobia, obsessive–compulsive disorder, posttraumatic stress disorder, acute stress disorder, generalized anxiety disorder, anxiety disorder due to a general medical condition, substance-induced anxiety disorder, and anxiety disorder not otherwise specified (American Psychiatric Association, 1994). However, this entry will focus on the more common types of anxiety among children, which include separation anxiety disorder, school phobia, and generalized anxiety disorder.

Separation anxiety disorder is relatively common, affecting 2–4 percent of children and adolescents (Nutt, Bell, Masterson, & Short, 2001). Children who are diagnosed with this disorder exhibit excessive anxiety that is not developmentally appropriate surrounding the separation or anticipation of separations from home or attachment figures (parents, guardians, etc.). The disturbance must last for a minimum of 4 weeks and cause clinically significant impairment in social, academic, or other important areas. Children sometimes experience such extreme anxiety due to separation that they may have panic attacks. When separated from attachment figures, the child may show an extreme need to maintain contact with them (telephone calls) or may constantly need to know where the attachment figures are. Children may express an intense fear of losing the attachment figures or becoming lost themselves and not being able to find the attachment figures. They may become extremely uncomfortable, to the point of misery when separated from home. These children may be reluctant to attend school, to visit friends' homes, or to go places without the attachment figures. These children may also have difficulty going to bed alone and may experience nightmares concerning the loss of attachment figures. These children may also constantly follow parents/guardians while at home and tend to cling to them (American Psychiatric Association, 1994).

The onset of separation anxiety disorder usually occurs after some life stressor (moving to a new school, loss of a pet, death of a relative, etc.). Children diagnosed with this disorder typically come from close-knit families and are not accustomed to being separated from the family. When separated from the family, these children may show signs of withdrawal, indifference, sadness, or difficulty concentrating. Children may fear monsters, burglars, kidnappers, car accidents, or other similar situations that pose a threat to the family. Fears surrounding death and dying are fairly common for these children (American Psychiatric Association, 1994).

Treatment for separation anxiety disorder typically involves behavioral interventions and perhaps psychopharmacological treatments. Behavioral interventions may include graded exposure to the feared situation, or gradual exposure to the feared situation. Also, psychologists will typically work with the parents/guardians to ensure that avoidant behavior is not being reinforced, or supported. A psychopharmacological treatment may include fluoxetine, or Prozac (average dose of 25 mg/day). This drug has been shown to produce a significant improvement in children diagnosed with separation anxiety disorder (Nutt et al., 2001).

School phobia is considered to be a form of separation anxiety disorder. The features of the disorder are the same, but only involve school and school-related activities. School phobia is very common among young children, particularly those in kindergarten or the first grade. The child typically clings to the parent/guardian, and may throw tantrums if forced to enter the school building. Because of the child's intense fear of school, the child often misses school, which then leads to difficulties in academic skills (American Psychiatric Association, 1994).

Treatment for school phobia typically involves teachers and parents/guardians. Parents are encouraged to explain to the child that school attendance is expected, and that they will not be allowed to stay home to avoid school. Teachers are encouraged to provide a warm, nurturing environment for the child so that the child begins to believe that the school is a safe and friendly environment. Usually, school phobia begins to quickly disappear once these factors have been set in place. If problems persist, then parents/guardians and teachers can positively reinforce, or reward, the child for attending school. Another treatment involves requiring attendance of the child for only portions of the day, gradually increasing, until the child stays in school for the entire day.

Generalized anxiety disorder affects approximately 3 percent of children and slightly more adolescents (Nutt et al., 2001). Children with this disorder typically tend to persistently worry about the future, the past, or their personal competence. The feelings of anxiety and worry must persist for a minimum of 6 months for this diagnosis and are usually accompanied by restlessness, fatigue, poor concentration, irritability, muscle tension, or disturbed sleep. Children diagnosed with this disorder experience a great amount of distress owing to feelings of constant worry and experience difficulty controlling the worry. Generalized anxiety disorder may also occur with depressive disorders, dysthymic disorder, other anxiety disorders, or stress (American Psychiatric Association, 1994).

Treatment for generalized anxiety disorder typically utilizes cognitive–behavioral therapy and psychopharmacological treatment. Cognitive–behavioral therapy provides clear focus to the treatment. The two goals for this therapy are to alter inadequate ways of thinking and to help the child meet challenges and opportunities with a calm mind. Some basic cognitive–behavioral techniques are desensitization, behavior modification, rational–emotive therapy, and mindfulness meditation. The goal of desensitization is to reduce feelings of anxiety by eliciting the feeling while the child is in a relaxed state. Behavior modification involves replacing unwanted behavior with a more desirable one by identifying the onset of anxiety, and changing the child's behavior when these feelings arise. Rational–emotive therapy attempts to enable the child to think and act more rationally by identifying irrational beliefs that are causing the anxiety. The goal of mindfulness mediation is for the child to become less anxious of events or thoughts by accepting those thoughts, rather than reacting to them.

Scant research has been conducted on psychopharmacological treatments for childhood generalized anxiety disorder. Benzodiazepines such as alprazolam, or Xanax, can be habit-forming if taken over a prolonged period of time. Some studies, however, have indicated that alprazolam showed no significant improvement in the symptoms of anxiety (Simeon, Ferguson, Knott, 1992). Other studies found fluoxetine (Prozac) and buspirone (Buspar) to be effective in reducing symptoms of anxiety, but more studies need to be conducted on the effects of these drugs in children (Birmaher & Waterman, 1994).

Anxiety can be very frightening for children, as well as parents. The more parents can work with mental health professionals and school personnel to make the child feel less anxious, the quicker the disorder will be resolved. Initial treatment of anxiety typically includes both therapy and psychopharmacological treatment; however, the goal of all therapy is to reduce the amount of medication that a child must use.

See also: Depression in Children and Adolescents; Fears and Phobias; School Refusal

BIBLIOGRAPHY

American Psychiatric Association. (1994). *Diagnostic and statistical manual of mental disorders* (4th ed.). Washington, DC: Author.

Birmaher, B., & Waterman, S. (1994). Fluoxetine for childhood anxiety disorders. *Journal of the American Academy of Child & Adolescent Psychiatry, 33*, 993–999.

Simeon, J. G., Ferguson, H. B., & Knott, V. (1992). Clinical, cognitive and neurophysiological effects of alprazolam in children and adolescents with overanxious and avoidant disorders. *Journal of the American Academy of Child & Adolescent Psychiatry, 31*, 29–33.

Additional Readings for Nonprofessionals

Dacey, J. S., Fiore, L. B., & Ladd, G. T. (2001). *Your anxious child: How parents and teachers can relieve anxiety in children.* New York: Jossey-Bass.

Manassis, K. (1996). *Keys to parenting your anxious child.* Hauppauge, NY: Barron's Educational Series.

Rapee, R. M., Spence, S., Cobham, V., & Wignall, A. (2000). *Helping your anxious child: A step-by-step guide for parents.* Oakland, CA: New Harbinger.

Additional Readings for Professionals

Essau, C. A., & Petermann, F. (2002). *Anxiety disorders in children and adolescents: Epidemiology, risk factors and treatment.* New York: Brunner-Routledge.

Wignall, A., Hudson, J., Rapee, R. M., & Schniering, C. A. (2000). *Treating anxious children and adolescents: An evidence-based approach.* Oakland, CA: New Harbinger.

KIMBERLY R. HALL

Articulation Disorder

Articulation disorder primarily involves the failure to use expected speech sounds that are appropriate for the person's developmental age and dialect. As such, errors are typically observed in the production, representation, and organization of speech sounds associated with letters and words. The most common errors involve substituting one sound for another sound (e.g., teef for teeth) or omitting certain sounds (e.g., ca for cat). According to the American Psychiatric Association (2000), the most frequently misarticulated sounds are for the letters *l, r, s, z, th,* and *ch,* which are usually acquired later in development of speech. In addition, articulation errors range in severity from having very little effect on the person's speech to making it almost impossible to understand his/her speech sounds (i.e., unintelligible). Finally, persons with articulation disorder may also misarticulate sibilants (i.e., high consonant sounds) and have difficulty in selecting and ordering the sounds within syllables and words (e.g., tack for cat).

COMORBID DISORDERS AND ASSOCIATED FEATURES

Articulation disorder can occur during the course of another disorder. When two disorders occur at the same time, the disorders are described as being *comorbid.* Common disorders that occur in conjunction with articulation disorder or increase the probability of experiencing the disorder include hearing impairment due to chronic ear infections, structural deficits in the cleft palate (roof of the mouth), neurological conditions like cerebral palsy, intellectual deficits as seen in mental retardation, and psychosocial problems. Approximately 3 percent of children experience articulation disorder during the preschool years (American Psychiatric Association, 2000).

CULTURAL AND GENDER FEATURES

Before diagnosing an individual with articulation disorder, influences from his/her culture must be taken into account. Variations within a language are referred to as dialects, and these variations are not a basis for diagnosing a child with an articulation or phonological disorder. For example, a person using "black dialect" should not be diagnosed with articulation disorder because many of the speech sounds that may appear to be inappropriate are the result of modeled speech displayed by familiar persons in their culture. Articulation disorder is diagnosed more often in males.

PREVALENCE AND COURSE

Mild forms of articulation disorder are usually not recognized until the child enters preschool or kindergarten. Even in children who are diagnosed with mild forms of the disorder, about three fourths demonstrate normal speech by the age of 6. Approximately 2 percent of students present with moderate to severe articulation disorder during the early elementary school years, with 0.5 percent of students presenting with the disorder by high school (American Psychiatric Association, 2000).

DIFFERENTIAL DIAGNOSIS

Articulation disorder is currently listed as "Phonological Disorder" in the *Diagnostic and Statistical Manual of Mental Disorders* (4th ed., text rev.) (*DSM-IV-TR*) (American Psychiatric Association, 2000) and is listed under the general category of Communication Disorders along with Expressive Language Disorder, Mixed Receptive–Expressive Language Disorder, Stuttering, and Communication Disorder—Not Otherwise Specified (NOS). According to the *DSM-IV-TR*, three criteria must be met for a diagnosis of articulation disorder. Specifically, the criteria include (a) the failure to use developmentally expected speech sounds that are appropriate for developmental age and dialect; (b) speech that causes difficulties in academic, occupational, or social functioning; and (c) articulation problems beyond those typically experienced by persons with mental retardation, speech–motor or sensory deficit, or environmental deprivation. Furthermore, problems associated with speech rhythm or voice are diagnosed as Stuttering or Communication Disorder—NOS and are not included in the diagnosis of articulation disorder.

ASSESSMENT

Screening

Prior to the assessment for an articulation disorder, a brief speech screening is usually completed to determine whether a comprehensive evaluation is warranted. A speech screening is very brief (i.e., 5 to 10 minutes) and aids in determining whether a child potentially exhibits an articulation or phonological disorder. If the child fails the screening by producing articulation errors that interfere with the child's adaptive functioning, then a formal assessment is conducted that includes diagnostic interviews, hearing screening, orofacial examinations, standardized testing, speech samples, and stimulability testing.

Diagnostic Interview

The interview provides information concerning speech and language history (e.g., "Did the child babble and coo as an infant?"), birth history (e.g., "Did the child suffer any complications at birth?"), developmental history (e.g., "Has the child met developmental milestones as expected?"), and medical history (e.g., "Has the child ever been hospitalized?"). Additional questions cover educational history (e.g., "Has the child ever been retained?") and social history (e.g., "How well does the child get along with other peers and adults?").

Hearing Screening

Because hearing loss is a known etiological factor for articulation and phonological disorders, a hearing screening is performed by the speech language pathologist as part of the assessment. Failure of the hearing screening warrants a referral to an audiologist for a comprehensive assessment.

Orofacial Examination

Because adequate structure and function of the speech mechanism is critical for speech sound production, the orofa-

cial examination is an important component of the assessment process. If an articulation disorder is present, the orofacial examination will provide the necessary information to determine whether the disorder is an organic articulation disorder related to structural causes (e.g., cleft palate) or a functional articulation disorder (an articulation disorder with no cause that can be determined during orofacial examination).

Standardized Articulation and Phonological Tests

Some standardized articulation tests utilize single-word responses to assess the child's individual speech sounds at the initial, medial, and final positions of words. Examples of these standardized articulation tests include the *Goldman–Fristoe Test of Articulation* (Goldman & Fristoe, 1986), the *Photo Articulation Test—Revised* (Pendergast, Dickey, Selmar, & Soder, 1969), the *Fisher–Logemann Test of Articulation Competence* (Fisher & Logemann, 1971), and the *Templin–Darley Tests of Articulation* (Templin & Darley, 1969). Other standardized phonological tests provide important diagnostic information for children who display multiple speech sound errors and are highly unintelligible. These tests focus on the patterns of speech sound errors rather than the specific positions of errors within a word. Examples of these tests include the *Bankson–Bernthal Test of Phonology* (Bankson & Bernthal, 1990) and the *Khan–Lewis Phonological Analysis* (Khan & Lewis, 1986).

Speech Sample

A conversational speech sample should be obtained as part of the assessment. Standardized articulation testing will assess individual speech units, but conversational speech samples provide a better picture of the child's speech intelligibility during everyday communication exchanges as well as patterns of speech sound errors.

Stimulability Testing

Stimulability testing may be performed after all other articulation testing has been completed. Stimulability refers to the child's ability to accurately produce an error sound by imitating the clinician's production or by other auditory, tactile, or visual cues. This provides valuable prognostic information, and can help determine target sounds for treatment.

TREATMENT

Treatment for children with articulation problems is usually conducted in school or medical settings by a licensed speech language pathologist. Sessions are typically conducted twice per week for 30 minutes each. The speech language pathologist's training and philosophy will most likely affect his/her choice of treatment approach. However, some general guidelines should be followed regardless of treatment orientation. The clinician often begins by developing a tentative plan of intervention. The target sounds for intervention are selected, along with the sequence of training. In addition, the dismissal criterion is also determined early in intervention development. Finally, plans for generalization and transfer of proper use of speech sounds to more natural environments (e.g., classroom, home, playground) should be developed during the course of treatment. Such efforts are generally facilitated with homework assignments and frequent communication with parents and teachers.

Although there are several methods for treating articulation disorder, the three most common include the traditional, sensorimotor, and multiple-phoneme approaches. The traditional approach to articulation therapy is perhaps the most well-known treatment approach and is primarily associated with Van Riper (Van Riper & Erickson, 1996). This approach focuses on one speech sound error at a time, beginning at the phoneme level, and is generally considered an effective treatment approach. The sensorimotor approach to articulation therapy was developed by McDonald (1968), and begins training at the syllable level of speech. This approach also focuses on specific phonetic contexts to facilitate the correct production of a speech sound. McCabe and Bradley (1975) developed the multiple-phoneme approach on the basis of behavioral principles. Originally, this approach was developed for children with multiple articulation errors associated with cleft palate. This approach provides instruction on several error sounds during each treatment session and is divided into three phases: establishment, transfer, and maintenance. In general, most clinicians typically choose an intervention approach that focuses on one speech sound error at a time, although children with many speech sound errors may benefit from an approach that addresses multiple speech sound errors within one treatment session.

See also: Cleft Lip and Palate; Otitis Media; Stuttering

BIBLIOGRAPHY

American Psychiatric Association. (2000). *Diagnostic and statistical manual of mental disorders* (4th ed., text rev.). Washington, DC: Author.

Bankson, N. W., & Bernthal, J. E. (1990). *Bankson–Bernthal test of phonology.* Chicago: Riverside.

Fisher, H., & Logemann, J. (1971). *The Fisher–Logemann test of articulation competence.* Boston: Houghton Mifflin.

Goldman, R., & Fristoe, M. (1986). *The Goldman–Fristoe test of articulation.* Circle Pines, MN: American Guidance Service.

Khan, L., & Lewis, N. (1986). *Khan–Lewis phonological analysis.* Circle Pines, MN: American Guidance Service.

McCabe, R. B., & Bradley, D. P. (1975). Systemic multiple phonemic approach to articulation therapy. *Acta Symbolica, 6*, 2–18.

McDonald, E. (1968). *Screening deep test of articulation.* Pittsburgh, PA: Stanwix House.

Pendergast, K., Dickey, S., Selmar, J., & Soder, A. (1969). *Photo articulation test.* Danville, IL: Interstate.

Templin, M. C., & Darley, F. L. (1969). *The Templin–Darley tests of articulation.* Iowa City: Bureau of Education Research and Service, University of Iowa.

Van Riper, C., & Erickson, R. (1996). *Speech correction: An introduction to speech pathology and audiology* (9th ed.). Boston: Allyn & Bacon.

Additional Reading for Nonprofessionals

www.asha.org/public/speech

Additional Reading for Professionals

Pena-Brooks, A., & Hedge, M. N. (2000). *Assessment and treatment of articulation and phonological disorders in children.* Austin, TX: Pro-Ed.

THERESA A. DOGGETT

R. ANTHONY DOGGETT

Attention-Deficit/Hyperactivity Disorder

According to the *Diagnostic and Statistical Manual of Mental Disorders* (4th ed.) (*DSM-IV*) (American Psychiatric Association, 2000), Attention-Deficit/Hyperactivity Disorder (ADHD) is characterized by a persistent pattern of inattention and/or hyperactivity–impulsivity. This pattern is more severe than would be expected given an individual's developmental status and gender. ADHD symptoms must be displayed across two or more settings, and they must be present prior to the age of 7 years. Boys with ADHD outnumber girls with this disorder. The ratios range from 2:1 to 5:1 (Barkley, 1998).

Children with ADHD have great difficulties sustaining their attention to tasks. In addition, children with ADHD frequently respond quickly to situations without waiting for complete and adequate instructions (i.e., behave in an impulsive manner). As a result of impulsive behavior, careless errors and taking chances without regard for consequences may occur more often than is expected for a child's age. Similarly, difficulty waiting one's turn, applying the least amount of time and effort to tasks, and blurting out answers are common behaviors of children with ADHD (Barkley, 1998). Children with ADHD may exhibit excessive levels of activity, or hyperactivity, in comparison to typical children of the same age. Children with ADHD often exhibit out-of-seat behavior, fidget, play with objects not related to the task, talk out of turn, or make unusual noises (Barkley, 1998).

As a result of these attentional and behavioral difficulties, children with ADHD often struggle academically (e.g., lower achievement scores, inconsistent work productivity, and lower academic engagement rates), behaviorally (e.g., exhibit defiance and noncompliance), and socially (i.e., develop poor relationships with peers, antisocial acts) into the adolescent and adult years (American Psychiatric Association, 2000; Barkley, 1998; DuPaul & Stoner, 2003).

ASSESSMENT OF ADHD IN THE SCHOOL SETTING

Because of academic and behavioral difficulties encountered in the school setting, school psychologists often are asked to complete assessments to evaluate the presence of ADHD symptoms and their impact on school functioning for a specific child. A school-based assessment approach to evaluation of ADHD is described by DuPaul and Stoner (2003). The described techniques have the greatest empirical support in the research literature. The major components of the evaluation include interviews with the child's parent(s) and teacher(s), parent and teacher completion of questionnaires, and observations of the child's behavior across multiple settings and tasks (Barkley, 1998; DuPaul & Stoner, 2003). Assessment procedures should be used in the context of a problem-solving model similar to the five-stage process described by DuPaul and Stoner (2003). The five stages include screening, multimethod assessment, interpretation of results, intervention design, and treatment evaluation.

Parent and teacher interviews are completed to evaluate the presence or absence of ADHD criteria as specified by the *DSM-IV* (American Psychiatric Association, 2000). Interviews also allow the school psychologist to obtain valuable information regarding historical and/or current factors that may be contributing to or maintaining identified problem behaviors. Questionnaires (i.e., behavior rating scales) are completed by the parent(s) and the teacher(s) to establish the frequency and/or severity of ADHD symptoms in relation to typical children of a similar age level and gender. In addition, the child's behavior is observed on various occasions and across multiple settings (e.g., classroom and playground) to determine the frequency and/or duration of identified problem behaviors. Finally, the school psychologist examines products of the child's behavior to establish whether ADHD-related behaviors impair the child's academic functioning. Examples of examined products may include worksheets, tests, quizzes, and desk organization.

Not only will a comprehensive assessment determine if the child meets the criteria to receive an ADHD diagnosis, but the information will assist in developing a school-based intervention plan for the child. Functional behavioral assessment data are collected to facilitate the design of a contextually sensitive, individualized intervention plan. Furthermore, the intervention plan should be based on the child's needs as targets for remediation, while capitalizing on the child's strengths.

TREATMENT OF ADHD

Behavioral symptoms may contribute to the academic difficulties that children with ADHD experience. Children with ADHD are more likely than children without this disorder to be diagnosed with learning disabilities and may qualify for special education services in a number of ways (e.g., other health impairment; Barkley, 1998; DuPaul & Stoner, 2003). Although some children with ADHD may qualify for special education services, most children with ADHD will not require such services. To facilitate success within the general education classroom, interventions are necessary for children with ADHD within both school and home settings.

Appropriate treatments may include psychotropic medication, interventions targeting behavior, and academic interventions. The combination of behavioral, academic, and medication treatments implemented over time is the ideal school-based intervention approach (DuPaul & Eckert, 1997). In addition, the school psychologist is in a position to consult with parents regarding home-based interventions to promote academic, behavioral, and social gains across settings.

Psychotropic Medication

Stimulant medications are the most commonly used psychotropic drugs to treat the symptoms of ADHD. The most commonly prescribed stimulants are dextroamphetamine (Dexedrine), methylphenidate (Concerta, Metadate, Ritalin), and mixed amphetamine compounds (Adderall). Stimulant medications temporarily alter brain activity thereby increasing attention to effortful tasks and reducing impulsive actions.

According to Barkley (1998), stimulants have been found to improve the behavioral, academic, and social functioning of about 50 to 95 percent of children treated. Alternatively, as many as 20 to 30 percent of treated children may display no positive response or a worsening in behavior in response to stimulant medication (DuPaul, Barkley, & Connor, 1998). Furthermore, children respond idiosyncratically across measures (e.g., behavior and learning), doses, and types of stimulant medications (DuPaul et al., 1998). The side effects of the medication also vary as a function of individual response. Some children may experience initial growth inhibition, reduced appetite, increased heart rate, sleep disturbances, and negative moods (DuPaul et al., 1998). However, the presence and/or magnitude of these side effects also are subject to significant intra- and interindividual variability. Children who do not respond to stimulant medications may be treated with antidepressant (e.g., bupropion) or antihypertensive (e.g., clonidine) compounds; however, the behavioral effects of these drugs are not as pronounced as those obtained with stimulants (Barkley, 1998).

School psychologists and other school personnel need to communicate with parents and physicians to help establish whether medication works for a particular child and to aid in determining the optimal dose (DuPaul & Stoner, 2003). Behavior ratings, classroom observations, and measures of academic performance are important indices of medication response, especially because the behavioral effects of stimulants are most noticeable during the school hours.

Behavioral Interventions

Because the symptoms of ADHD are sensitive to environmental variables, behavioral interventions can have a positive impact. Pfiffner and Barkley (1998) have identified several principles of behavioral interventions for children with ADHD: (a) clear, brief, and visible presentation of rules and instructions; (b) swift and immediate delivery of consequences; (c) frequent delivery of consequences; (d) powerful consequences; (e) highly motivating incentives to reinforce appropriate behavior; (f) variety of reinforcers; and (g) planning ahead by prompting the child to remember rules and consequences prior to entering a situation.

Behavioral interventions can be classified into two general types of strategies: consequence-based and antecedent-oriented. Consequence-based interventions involve the manipulation of environmental events *after* a specific behavior occurs and are reactive. Antecedent-oriented interventions involve altering the environment *before* a specific behavior occurs and are preventative or proactive. A balanced, comprehensive classroom intervention plan is optimal and will include both consequence-based and antecedent-oriented strategies.

Consequence-Based/Contingency Management

The most commonly applied behavioral intervention for children with ADHD is teacher-mediated contingency management (Pfiffner & Barkley, 1998). Functional behavioral assessment data should be used to match contingencies to the function of the target behavior, thereby increasing the likelihood of treatment success.

The most frequently applied form of contingency management, contingent teacher attention, involves teachers giving frequent positive and negative verbal feedback to their students. Teachers often use attention to help students remain on task, while redirecting students who are off task. By strategically attending to appropriate behavior and withdrawing positive teacher attention contingent upon undesirable behavior, a decrease in inappropriate classroom behavior can occur (Pfiffner & Barkley, 1998).

Not all behavior problems of children with ADHD occur in an effort to elicit attention. Therefore, other behavioral strategies may be needed to manage classroom behavior. Reward programs that award special privileges or activities on the basis of attainment of target goals (i.e., token reinforcement) often are applied. These programs may be used for individual children or applied on a classwide basis. According to Pfiffner and Barkley (1998), classwide token reinforcement programs may be particularly effective for children with ADHD. Such programs that target the behavior of all students do not single out the child with ADHD. Classroom token economies involve awarding points or tokens contingent upon specified desirable behaviors. All points earned at the end of a predetermined time (e.g., end of the day, after every hour, or end of the week) may be exchanged for desired activities, tangibles, or privileges.

Response cost, or removing of tokens or points following the display of undesirable behavior, also can be used within a token economy strategy. Children with attentional difficulties may require a reductive procedure like response cost in order to obtain a consistent decrease in inappropriate behavior within the classroom. In order to avoid situations where children earn very few points or token reinforcers, response cost should be used sparingly as teachers also should teach and reinforce alternative appropriate behaviors (Pfiffner & Barkley, 1998).

Another popular consequence-based, reductive intervention strategy is time-out from positive reinforcement (Abramowitz & O'Leary, 1991). Time-out is typically applied when a child exhibits undesirable classroom behavior. As a result, the child is placed within an environment where he/she does not receive positive reinforcement for the inappropriate behavior. Time-out may occur in a nonexclusionary form, where the child remains within the academic situation but ineligible for reinforcement (e.g., tokens, teacher attention, peer attention) for a specified amount of time. Exclusionary time-out involves the child being placed in a designated area outside of the academic situation (e.g., separate area of the classroom or an isolated room within the school building) without reinforcement for a specified amount of time (Barkley, 1998).

Antecedent-Oriented Strategies

Although frequently successful, consequence-based strategies are reactive in nature and do not necessarily improve academic performance (DuPaul & Eckert, 1997). Antecedent-oriented interventions focus on environmental stimuli that precede a behavior of interest, including instructional strategies and the characteristics of tasks presented to the children. More specifically, antecedent conditions can include setting, environmental design (e.g., type of class), the structure of the setting (e.g., daily schedule, class rules), seating arrangements, and characteristics of the task (e.g., amount and type of feedback, stimulation, and response mode; Abramowitz & O'Leary, 1991).

For instance, students with ADHD often have difficulty remaining on task during independent seat work activities and require modifications to the task. These students may not possess the requisite skills for doing the work independently, resulting in frustration, boredom, and off-task behavior. Another problem that may arise during independent seat work is that the students do not know how to obtain help during the activity, again possibly resulting in off-task behavior. A third possible antecedent condition is that too much work is required during independent seat work time. Depending on the particular antecedent, tasks may be modified (a) to be consistent with a child's skill level, (b) to include instructions on how to obtain assistance, or (c) to reduce the amount of work required in a given amount of time.

Another similar consideration is the interest level of the child. According to Reid and Maag (1998), the attention span of children with ADHD is much longer when they are engaged in high-interest activities. For instance, lesson length, format, and difficulty may be manipulated. An additional consideration may be to clarify goals and main points to be covered in a step-by-step presentation, accompanied by modeling, monitoring student understanding, and providing corrective feedback (Reid & Maag, 1998).

In terms of classroom structure, Pfiffner and Barkley (1998) have identified characteristics of the classroom environment that should be considered for children with ADHD: (a) moving the child's desk away from other children and closer to the teacher; (b) placing the child within a physically enclosed classroom; (c) placement within a well-organized, structured, and predictable classroom; (d) frequent use of visual aids; (e) academic tasks that are well-matched to the child's abilities; (f) varying the presentation format and task materials; (g) brief academic assignments presented one at a time; (h) enthusiastic and task-focused delivery of the lessons; (i) interspersing lectures with physical exercise; (j) scheduling of most academic subjects in the morning hours; (k) classroom instructions supplemented with a direct instruction drill of academic skills; and (l) specialized curricula for specific skills deficits.

Cognitive–Behavioral Interventions

Another possible treatment strategy is the application of cognitive–behavioral interventions for children with ADHD. There are two categories of cognitive–behavioral interventions, including self-monitoring/self-reinforcement and self-instruction/problem solving. Self-monitoring involves teaching children to be cognizant of their own behavior, and then rewarding themselves on the basis of observations of their behavior (self-reinforcement). Self-instruction involves teaching children to follow a series of steps when approaching a task. According

to Abramowitz and O'Leary (1991) these steps include repeating the instructions, describing the task, verbalizing how they may attempt the task, thinking about the consequences of the possible approach, deciding how to proceed, actually performing the task, reflecting upon their performance, and evaluating themselves. Unfortunately, cognitive–behavioral interventions have not been very successful in treating ADHD symptoms and related difficulties and are not considered a "first-line" intervention for this disorder (Barkley, 1998).

Academic Interventions

The behavioral problems of ADHD often result in academic difficulties. Because of the symptoms of ADHD and resultant academic performance difficulties, children with ADHD may need adapted instructional environments to promote learning and work completion. Students with ADHD may need more structure, more frequent and salient positive consequences, more consistent negative consequences, and accommodations to assigned work (Pfiffner & Barkley, 1998).

Another approach to intervention design that may be considered is antecedent-oriented programming. By preventing the occurrence of inappropriate behaviors of children with ADHD, academic performance can be targeted for intervention. There are several identified characteristics of classroom instruction that should be optimized via antecedent-oriented strategies to enhance attention span and academic performance of children. These characteristics include high rates of responding and immediate and frequent feedback, along with academic tasks that are within the child's instructional level of learning (Pfiffner & Barkley, 1998).

Empirically supported academic interventions that may promote these characteristics include computer-assisted instruction, task and instructional modifications (e.g., choice making, added structure, and modifying the content of method of the instructional procedures), strategy training (e.g., self-regulation or self-reinforcement), and peer tutoring. Each of these intervention techniques has been found to be successful for children with ADHD. By manipulating the instructional environment, children with ADHD have been found to improve academically and experience a decrease in the occurrence or severity of ADHD symptomatology (DuPaul & Eckert, 1997).

Home-Based Interventions

School psychologists are in an ideal position to consult with parents of children with ADHD regarding home-based interventions targeting behavior and academics. The school psychologist may promote a system of support between the school and the home. This may be facilitated through school–home notes, e-mail or phone contact, or brief face-to-face conversations on a daily or weekly basis (DuPaul & Stoner, 2003).

Use of a contingency contract is a home-based reinforcement program that may strengthen an existing school-based behavior program. A contingency contract specifies the academic performance and classroom behavior that is expected in the school setting. In addition, the contract delineates the privileges that can be earned at home if the child performs/behaves at the expected level. This type of intervention linking school and home is most successful when completed on a daily basis (DuPaul & Stoner, 2003).

Other home-based intervention strategies that have been found to be effective include (a) use of brief, direct commands; (b) positive parent attention in response to appropriate child behavior; (c) earning token reinforcers (e.g., points, poker chips, smiling faces) for appropriate behavior, which may be exchanged for a reward at some specified level of accumulation; (d) time-out or removal from desirable situations to reduce noncompliance or aggression; and (e) discussion with parents about promoting maintenance of improved behavior over time (Barkley, 1998).

CONCLUSIONS

ADHD is a disruptive behavior disorder that begins early in life and is associated with academic, behavioral, and social difficulties that often continue throughout childhood, adolescence, and even into adulthood. School professionals must be aware of the symptoms of this disorder and should play an integral role in identifying students with ADHD and designing effective school-based interventions. At the current time, the combination of behavioral interventions at school and home as well as carefully titrated stimulant medications appears to be the optimal treatment strategy.

See also: Academic Interventions for Written Language and Grammar; Parenting; Time-Out

BIBLIOGRAPHY

Abramowitz, A. J., & O'Leary, S. G. (1991). Behavioral interventions for the classroom: Implications for students with ADHD. *School Psychology Review, 20,* 220–234.

American Psychiatric Association. (2000). *Diagnostic and statistical manual of mental disorders* (4th ed., text rev.). Washington, DC: Author.

Barkley, R. A. (1998). *Attention-Deficit Hyperactivity Disorder: A handbook for diagnosis and treatment* (2nd ed.). New York: Guilford.

DuPaul, G. J., Barkley, R. A., & Conner, D. F. (1998). Stimulants. In R. A. Barkley (Ed.), *Attention Deficit Hyperactivity Disorder: A handbook for diagnosis and treatment* (2nd ed., pp. 510–551). New York: Guilford.

DuPaul, G. J., & Eckert, T. L. (1997). The effects of school-based interventions for Attention Deficit Hyperactivity Disorder: A meta-analysis. *School Psychology Review, 26,* 5–27.

DuPaul, G. J., & Stoner, G. (2003). *ADHD in the schools: Assessment and intervention strategies* (2nd ed.). New York: Guilford.

Pfiffner, L. J., & Barkley, R. A. (1998). Treatment of ADHD in school settings. In R. A. Barkley (Ed.), *Attention-Deficit Hyperactivity Disorder: A handbook for diagnosis and treatment* (2nd ed., pp. 458–490). New York: Guilford.

Reid, R., & Maag, J. W. (1998). Functional assessment: A method for developing classroom-based accommodations and interventions for children with ADHD. *Reading & Writing Quarterly, 14,* 9–42.

Additional Readings for Nonprofessionals

Barkley, R. A. (2000). *Taking charge of ADHD: The complete, authoritative guide for parents.* New York: Guilford.

Power, T. J., Karustis, J. L., & Habboushe, D. F. (2001). *Homework success for children with ADHD: A family–school intervention program.* New York: Guilford.

Additional Readings for Professionals

DuPaul, G. J., Eckert, T. L., & McGoey, K. E. (1997). Interventions for students with Attention-Deficit/Hyperactivity Disorder: One size does not fit all. *School Psychology Review, 26,* 369–381.

MTA Cooperative Group. (1999). Moderators and mediators of treatment response for children with Attention-Deficit/Hyperactivity Disorder. *Archives of General Psychiatry, 56,* 1088–1096.

KRISTI S. LORAH
GEORGE J. DUPAUL

Autism

Portrayals of autism on television or in movies typically reflect a boy who somehow balances "being in his own little world" with some special "brilliance" that astounds everyone who touches his life. This portrait does not accurately reflect most children with autism. Autism is a disorder beginning in early childhood that is characterized by impairments in communication and social interaction, as well as unusual patterns of behavior or interests. Communication difficulties these children face can include failure to speak altogether, echolalia (i.e., repeating the words/statements made by others), speaking in a scripted format, misunderstanding what other people say, and the inability to pretend in play like other children their age. The social problems children with autism experience may involve not sharing their interests or activities with others, failure to develop friendships in the way other children their age do, poor use of nonverbal cues (e.g., pointing, waving), or a lack of responsiveness to the needs or bids for social attention of others. Instead of sharing in typical activities with other children, they are more likely to repetitively show an interest in a small number of items (e.g., only play with the same puzzle or carry a block with them) or parts of objects (e.g., the wheel on a car), repeat a motor mannerism (e.g., hand-flapping, rocking, toe-walking, etc.), or perform a ritual (e.g., constantly clean glasses to the exclusion of all other activities).

In addition to the defining features of autism, there are often many other problem behaviors that may be present. For example, children with autism may have sleep or feeding problems, so they may rest only a few hours per night or refuse to eat many types of foods. They may have difficulties with attention, impulsivity, and hyperactivity that can lead to problems learning new materials. Once they do learn material, they can experience problems using the knowledge or skills in settings other than the one in which they initially learned. A relatively small percentage of children may hurt others or themselves or destroy property. Surprisingly, some of these children become depressed or anxious when they recognize that they are different from others and are unsuccessful in social situations.

Because there is so much variability in the severity of the symptoms of autism, most professionals now think of autism as falling on a spectrum. In fact, a range of disorders (including autism) is often collectively described as Autism Spectrum Disorders (ASD). Autistic Disorder, Asperger's Disorder, Rett's Disorder, Childhood Disintegrative Disorder, and Pervasive Developmental Disorder each fall on the Spectrum. The differences between these disorders are beyond the scope of this entry, so the interested reader is encouraged to read Section 1 in *The Handbook of Autism and Pervasive Developmental Disorders* (1997, 2nd ed.).

Years ago, most people had not heard of, much less encountered, individuals with ASD. The rates of ASD have increased dramatically in recent years. In fact, it is difficult to get an exact figure representing how common ASD are because each new study seems to report that the disorders are more prevalent than the one before. Recent estimates suggest ASD occur in approximately 1 in every 150 people and Autism occurs in around 16.8 in every 10,000 people (Chakrabarti & Fombonne, 2001). Considerable research is now being conducted to determine why the number of people diagnosed with ASD is increasing. Certainly, professionals have become better at identifying children who fall in all ranges of ASD. There is also mounting evidence that the rise in ASD may not be due exclusively to better diagnosis (see Causes below). ASD affects families from every ethnic and socioeconomic group equally. However, boys are much more likely to be diagnosed with the disorder than girls. The reason for this is unknown but may be related to the cause or causes of ASD (see Causes below).

CAUSES

Historically, parents' questions about the causes of ASD were met with wildly inaccurate and cruel speculations that lacked any research support. They were often told ASD was caused by a "refrigerator mother," who was emotionally unavailable and unresponsive. Fortunately, a great deal of research has been conducted since that time and parents are far less likely to contact professionals who profess this cause. Despite the fact that scientists from a variety of professions have dedicated themselves to understanding the causes of ASD, a definitive answer remains unavailable. Multiple studies have, however, associated genetic (Trottier, 1999), neuroanatomical (e.g., macrocephaly; Fombonne, Robe, Claverie, Courty, & Fremolle, 1999), and neurochemical (e.g., elevated levels of serotonin; Whitaker-Azmitia, 2001) abnormalities with ASD. Different studies have produced inconsistent outcomes regarding each of these variables and this hardly represents an exhaustive list of biological variables that have been implicated in ASD. These differences reflect the strong probability that ASD actually has multiple causes. The interested reader is referred to *Autism Spectrum Disorders: A Research Review for Practitioners* (2003), which includes descriptions of various neurobiological explanations throughout the book.

Many environmental variables have also been suggested to moderate or even cause ASD. In many cases, insufficient data are available to support these hypotheses.

For example, many parents worldwide had chosen not to have their children immunized because they feared vaccinations could be the cause of ASD. Several major studies have clearly shown vaccinations were not the cause of ASD. Unfortunately, some parents continue to avoid vaccinations and expose their children to life-threatening illnesses in a misguided effort to avoid ASD.

TREATMENT

In past decades, professionals told parents of children with ASD that there were "no treatment options" and that they should quickly consider institutionalization. Today, fewer parents have to hear these inaccurate and profoundly upsetting reports because more professionals are aware of the staggering improvements many of these children can make when given proper treatment. In fact, nearly half of children with ASD who received intensive behavioral intervention during early childhood made such dramatic improvements that their teachers reported they were "indistinguishable" from same-age peers in first grade (Lovaas, 1987).

The number of research-supported treatment strategies that produce improvements in communication, social interaction, and adaptive and play skills grows every year. Applied behavior analysis is the field that has provided the greatest evidence that such improvements can occur. A wide range of treatment strategies that fall under the umbrella of applied behavior analysis have been published. Structured (e.g., discrete trial training) (Lovaas, 1987; Smith, Eikeseth, Klevstrand, & Lovaas, 1987) and less structured, for example, incidental teaching (Hart & Risley, 1968; Charlop-Christy & Carpenter, 2000), pivotal response training (Koegel & Koegel, 1995), activity schedules (McClannahan & Krantz, 1999), videomodeling (D'Ateno, Mangiapanello, & Taylor, 2003; LeBlanc et al., 2003), and so on have all been useful in increasing functioning in one or more critical domains (e.g., adaptive, communication, social, academic, etc.).

Although there is no drug to cure ASD, drug intervention may be useful in some cases to address specific characteristics associated with ASD. For example, some children can be aggressive, self-injurious, or constantly engage in stereotypic behavior. In conjunction with behavioral intervention, drug treatments for these specific symptoms may be useful if they are closely monitored by a knowledgeable physician. Drug intervention may also be helpful when symptoms of anxiety or depression are present, as may sometimes be the case with children with ASD who are frustrated by unpredictable circumstances or are socially rejected but interested in others.

Untested "treatments" are extraordinarily common for ASD. In the early 1990s, an unsupported intervention called "facilitated communication" became widely popular even though it did not have solid research supporting its use. School systems and families invested tremendous sums of money in technology so they could use facilitated communication because it had such "miraculous" results. Once well-controlled studies were conducted, facilitated communication was shown to be ineffective. All of the money spent on facilitated communication was wasted and families were devastated when they realized they were just seeing what they wanted to see. Unfortunately, it seems as if another fad treatment is offered every month. Families and school systems should be advised to seriously consider where they want to invest their time, money, and energy because each of these valuable resources does have a limited supply.

SUMMARY

ASD are associated with severe impairments in social interaction and unusual and maladaptive patterns of behaving (e.g., repetitive motor movements, rigid adherence to routines, or ritualistic behaviors). More severe cases of ASD (e.g., autism) include serious difficulties with communication. Although these features distinguish ASD from other disorders, many additional symptoms may be present. These symptoms will also require treatment if a child is to meet his or her potential.

A definitive cause for ASD has not been established. Biological causes such as genetic factors, brain anatomy, and neurotransmitters have been clearly implicated in the research conducted to date. Many different environmental causes have been speculated to cause ASD but they lack solid research support at this time. It is, however, completely clear that parents do not cause ASD.

Effective treatment for most individuals with ASD has been identified. Applied behavior analysis treatment strategies such as discrete trial training, incidental teaching, pivotal response training, activity schedules, video modeling, scripting, and so on have been supported by research. In some cases (e.g., self-injury, severe aggression, stereotypy), drug treatment may be considered in conjunction with research-supported techniques. Many ideas for the treatment of ASD that have not received any research support are available; however, these may be dangerous or may waste valuable resources. Families and school systems should be encouraged to avoid these approaches unless they are part of a well-controlled research study.

See also: Self-Injurious Behavior; Stereotypy

BIBLIOGRAPHY

Chakrabarti, S., & Fomboone, E. (2001). Pervasive developmental disorders in preschool children. *Journal of the American Medical Association, 285*, 3093–3099.

Charlop-Christy, M. H., & Carpenter, M. H. (2000). Modified incidental teaching sessions: A procedure for parents to increase spontaneous speech in their children with autism. *Journal of Positive Behavior Interventions, 2*, 98–112.

Cohen, D. J., & Volkmar, F. R. (Eds.). (1997). *Handbook of autism and pervasive developmental disorders* (2nd ed.). New York: Wiley.

D'Ateno, P., Mangiapanello, K., & Taylor, B. (2003). Using video modeling to teach complex play sequences to a preschooler with autism. *Journal of Positive Behavior Interventions, 5*, 5–11.

Fombonne, E., Robe, B., Claverie, J., Courty, S., & Fremolle, J. (1999). Microcephaly and macrocephaly in autism. *Journal of Autism and Developmental Disorders, 29*, 113–119.

Hart, B. M., & Risley, T. R. (1968). Establishing use of descriptive adjectives in the spontaneous speech of disadvantaged preschool children. *Journal of Applied Behavior Analysis, 1*, 109–120.

Koegel, R. L., & Koegel, L. K. (Eds.). (1995). *Teaching children with autism.* Baltimore: Brookes.

LeBlanc, L. A., Coates, A. M., Daneshvar, S., Charlop-Christy, M. H., Morris, C., & Lancaster, B. M. (2003). Using video modeling and reinforcement to teach perspective-taking skills to children with autism. *Journal of Applied Behavior Analysis, 36*, 253–257.

Lovaas, O. I. (1987). Behavioral treatment and normal educational and intellectual functioning young autistic children. *Journal of Consulting and Clinical Psychology, 55*, 3–9.

McClannahan, L. E., & Krantz, P. J. (1999). *Activity schedules for children with autism: Teaching independent behavior.* Bethesda, MD: Woodbine.

Ozonoff, S., Rogers, S. J., & Hendren, R. L. (Eds.). (2003). *Autism spectrum disorders: A research review for practitioners.* Washington, DC: American Psychiatric Publishing.

Smith, T., Eikeseth, S., Klevstrand, M., & Lovaas, O. I. (1997). Intensive behavioral treatment for preschoolers with severe mental retardations and pervasive developmental disorder. *American Journal on Mental Retardation, 102,* 238–249.

Trottier, G. (1999). Etiology of infantile autism: A review of recent advances in genetic and neurobiological research. *Journal of Psychiatry and Neuroscience, 24,* 103–115.

Whitaker-Azmitia, P. M. (2001). Serotonin and brain development: Role in human developmental diseases. *Brain Research Bulletin, 56,* 479–485.

Additional Readings for Professionals and Nonprofessionals

Autism Society of America. (n.d.). Frequently asked questions. Retrieved December 1, 2003, from http://www.autism-society.org/site/PageServer?pagename=FAQ

National Institute of Mental Health. (1997). Autism. Retrieved December 1, 2003, from http://www.nimh.nih.gov/publicat/autism.cfm

SUSAN M. WILCZYNSKI
LORI KRUGER
LAKISHA LEWIS

Awards

See: Jack Bardon Distinguished Service Award; Lightner Witmer Award; Senior Scientist Award

Bb

Bayley Scales of Infant Development—2nd Edition

Several decades ago, Dr. Nancy Bayley conducted longitudinal research on children's development across the first 3 years of life. Under her direction, a meticulous process of data collection served to provide a sample of young children for the initial standardization of the *Bayley Scales of Infant Development* (BSID). Her extensive research emphasized the typical progression of development among young children and the discontinuity of scores between infant mental tests and childhood intelligence. Bayley's data across multiple generations also advanced the understanding of development and interactions between children and mothers, and promoted attention to assessing the "normal" development of young children (Bayley, 1993).

Since the initial publication of the BSID in 1969, research in early childhood has expanded to address the implications of at-risk factors such as prematurity, low birth weight, and exposure to teratogenic substances (e.g., alcohol, nicotine, heroine), on developmental processes. While preserving the characteristics of the original BSID, the *Bayley Scales of Infant Development—2nd Edition* (BSID-II) reflects the change of focus from typical development factors to atypical development factors among researchers and clinicians.

The BSID-II is an early childhood, norm-referenced assessment instrument that evaluates the current level of functioning for young children between 1 and 42 months of age. The instrument, which is individually administered by qualified professionals, assesses developmental domains such as language, cognitive, personal/social, fine motor, and gross motor skills. The assessment of these skills in conjunction with other forms of information collected assists in the diagnosis of developmental delays (Bayley, 1993; Gagnon & Nagle, 2000).

The following three scales comprise the BSID-II: Mental Scale, Motor Scale, and Behavior Rating Scale. The content for the Mental and Motor Scales generally increases in difficulty as the examiner progresses through the assessment items. Starting and ending points for each scale reflect the child's age and performance on individual items. The Mental Developmental Index (MDI) is derived from the raw scores of the Mental Scale whereas the Psychomotor Developmental Index (PDI) is derived from the raw scores of the Motor Scale. The average index score on the MDI and PDI is 100. Scores that are of concern are those that fall below 85 (Mean = 100, Standard Deviation = 15). The Behavior Rating Scale consists of raw scores that are transformed into percentile ranks.

The BSID-II manual offers the norm tables and directions for computation of index scores and percentile ranks in which an individual's performance can be compared to peers his/her own age. The restandardized sample for the BSID-II consisted of 1,700 children aged 1 to 42 months, which matched the U.S. demographic characteristics on age, gender, race/ethnicity, and level of parent education. The BSID-II manual addresses limitations and precautions for interpreting results when adaptations of the assessment or evaluation of a child with severe physical disabilities are made (Bayley, 1993; Fugate, 1998).

The content of the Mental Scale consists of items designed to assess cognitive, language, and social–emotional development. The cognitive development domain assesses short-term and long-term memory, visual preferences, attention, habituation to new stimuli, imitation, problem solving, categorization, and concepts associated with numbers, similarities, and differences. The language development domain reflects the comprehension of communication such as the orientation to sound, eye contact with other individuals and stimuli, and compliance with directions. Language development also consists of vocalizations (i.e., crying, babbling, words), gestures, and comprehension of grammatical rules (i.e., plurals, prepositions). The personal/social developmental domain assesses the child's responsiveness to the social environment. This involves the relationship between the child and caregiver, alertness, affect, temperament, self-comforting skills, adaptability to changes in routine and environment, discrimination between self and others, and reactions to strangers (Bayley, 1993; Fugate, 1998).

The Motor Scale consists of items associated with fine motor and gross motor skills. Fine motor skills include eye–hand coordination activities that involve grasps, isolation of fingers, manipulation of items, extension of hands and fingers, holding a pencil, building a tower of blocks, obtaining small objects from a bottle, and drawing various designs on paper. In contrast, gross motor skills include large-muscle coordination that require several factors, like strength, stamina, muscle tone, postural relations, balance, and body movements. Rolling, crawling, sitting, walking, jumping, kicking, and running are reflective of gross motor development.

The Behavior Rating Scale contains various types of questions (e.g., open-ended, "yes/no," ratings) that address the characteristics of the child's behavior during the assessment. Feedback from the caregiver allows the examiner to determine whether the assessment was a representative sample of the child's daily performance and behavior. The examiner observes the following features of a child throughout the assessment: alertness, cooperation, social engagement, affect (i.e., laughing, fussing), self-comforting skills, activity level, adaptations to changes in environment, interest toward presented objects, persistence, attention, responsiveness to caregiver and examiner, and expressions (i.e., frustration, fearfulness, excitement). Furthermore, the examiner evaluates quality and coordination of motor movements. For example, the control posture and the approach with movements (i.e., slow, spastic, stiff) also affect the child's responses to assessment items.

The BSID-II does not espouse a particular theoretical framework regarding child development. Rather, it incorporates a broad base of research and child development scales into its content. Thus, the BSID-II serves as a vehicle for assessment of infant and toddler development, research on assessment techniques and instruments, and research on early childhood development. Although the BSID-II aims to detect developmental delays among young children, a diagnosis of a delay entails multiple assessments and multiple informants (i.e., caregivers, medical personnel). Even though the designers of the BSID-II assert that interventions can be derived from the assessment instrument, intervention plans require additional observations and analyses so as to sufficiently address the individual needs of children.

See also: Development

BIBLIOGRAPHY

Bayley, N. (1993). *Bayley Scales of Infant Development—2nd edition.* San Antonio, TX: The Psychological Corporation.

Fugate, M. H. (1998). Review of the Bayley Scales of Infant Development—2nd edition. In J. C. Impara, B. S. Plake, & L. L. Murphy (Eds.), *The thirteenth mental measurements yearbook* (pp. 93–95). Lincoln: The University of Nebraska Press.

Gagnon, S. G., & Nagle, R. J. (2000). Comparison of the revised and original versions of the Bayley Scales of Infant Development. *School Psychology International, 21,* 293–305.

Additional Readings for Nonprofessionals

Fugate, M. H. (1998). Review of the Bayley Scales of Infant Development—2nd edition. In J. C. Impara, B. S. Plake, & L. L. Murphy (Eds.), *The thirteenth mental measurements yearbook* (pp. 93–95). Lincoln: The University of Nebraska Press.

Nellis, L., & Brown, D. T. (1994). Review of the Bayley Scales of Infant Development—2nd edition. *Journal of School Psychology, 32,* 201–209.

Additional Reading for Professionals

Chandlee, J., Heathfield, L. T., Salganik, M., Damokosh, A., & Radcliffe, J. (2002). Are we consistent in administrating and scoring the Bayley Scales of Infant Development—II? *Journal of Psychoeducational Assessment, 20,* 183–200.

Lori Chambers Slay

Beery Visual–Motor Integration (The Beery–Buktenica Developmental Test of Visual–Motor Integration—Fifth Edition)

The Beery VMI, formerly known as the Developmental Test of Visual–Motor Integration, is a screening test designed to help determine the extent to which individuals can integrate their visual and motor abilities. The test requires a child aged 2–18 to copy several geometric-form drawings presented in a sequence of increasing difficulty. The fifth edition Beery VMI also has supplemental Visual Perception and Motor Coordination tests intended to help compare an individual's test results with relatively either pure visual or pure motor performances, or both. Visual–motor integration is defined as the degree to which visual perception and finger–hand movements are well coordinated. Perception refers to the ability to interpret visual information, and the motor response refers to the ability to produce images through writing and drawing.

Measuring this kind of skill, broadly referred to as perceptual–motor assessment, has many technical difficulties associated with it. The two biggest problems are with reliability (the degree to which test performance is dependably consistent) and utility (the degree to which skills tested have meaningful diagnostic and instructional implications). Skills such as copying simple and complex shapes or pattern drawings are intuitively consistent with early academic demands. Being able to produce lines, circles, squares, and the like developmentally precedes writing letters and numerals. Being able to perceive such images is an assumed precursor to early reading and writing. Difficulties with motor responses and accurate visual perception are also common among children with learning difficulties. Therefore, it is popular to believe that identifying perceptual–motor difficulties through assessments such as the Beery VMI can serve as early identification of various learning disabilities. Unfortunately, this premise is not supported by research or logic. Performance on the VMI does not even predict handwriting difficulties (Marr & Cermak, 2002). It is possible to not have a learning disability and have perceptual–motor difficulties, and the reverse is as true.

Improving academic skills (i.e., instructional utility) by teaching VMI-related tasks is not supported by research (Salvia & Ysseldyke, 2004). Because of this, teachers and parents should not have children practicing these isolated skills with the hope that it will lead to improved reading or writing skills. The mistaken belief that visual–motor practice will help with academics is encouraged by the publishers of this test, as they have made available separate visual, motor, and visual–motor teaching activities for parents and teachers to use with children. These activities should not divert attention away from genuine reading and handwriting practice. If one keeps in mind that these activities are not diagnostically indicative of learning problems, and that practicing how to copy designs is not preferable to practicing reading or writing or even being read to, then small amounts of time invested in these activities can serve as a resource for providing children with an interesting variety of academic tasks. As Salvia and Ysseldyke pointed out, "The real danger is that reliance on such tests in planning interventions for children may actually lead teachers to assign children to activities that do the children no known good" (p. 538).

BIBLIOGRAPHY

Marr, D., & Cermak, S. (2002). Predicting handwriting performance of early elementary students with the Developmental Test of Visual–Motor Integration. *Perceptual & Motor Skills, 95*, 661–669.

Salvia, J., & Ysseldyke, J. E. (2004). *Assessment in special and inclusive education* (9th ed.). Boston: Houghton Mifflin.

Michael Banner

Behavioral Consultation

Consultation is a term used to describe the interaction between a consultant (typically a school psychologist) and a consultee (typically a teacher), to change the behavior of a client (typically a student). Behavioral Consultation is a specific four-step consultation model where the consultant shares his/her skills with the consultee, who then utilizes those skills to change the behavior of the client.

Consultation in school settings often varies in the type of interactions that occur between the consultant and consultee and by the inclusion of a third party, a client's parent (see entries Direct Behavioral Consultation, Conjoint Behavioral Consultation). Generally, Behavioral Consultation is a model where interactions between consultant and consultee are entirely verbal. Regardless of which behavioral consultation model is used, the core aspects of the process are the same. Typically in each, there are four phases aimed at changing the behavior of the consultee so they can change the behavior of the child.

The first stage of Behavioral Consultation is *problem identification* (Bergan, 1977). This stage of consultation involves an interview with the referring teacher (or other referral person) during which they identify and define the problem behaviors of concern and identify skills versus performance deficits (Kratochwill, Elliott, & Rotto, 1995). It also involves determining the frequency of behavior, identifying the current discipline methods within the classroom, and determining the method and dates for obtaining baseline data. Questions are asked about the antecedents and consequences of behavior, the settings in which behaviors occur, and the general strength of the behavior problems identified (Bergan & Kratochwill, 1990; Gutkin & Curtis, 1999).

The second phase of Behavioral Consultation is the *problem analysis* phase. During this phase, the consultant and consultee again meet to discuss the observations and assessment data in order to develop a treatment plan. Together, they identify reinforcers, select a behavioral goal for intervention success, and determine when the intervention will begin. The consultant and consultee must discuss environmental variables related to the target behavior to determine any potential functional relationships between the target behavior and classroom variables. The treatment plan is developed and the teacher is trained through didactic measures in the procedural aspects of the treatment.

The third stage of Behavioral Consultation is *plan implementation*. During this phase, the consultee implements the behavior plan and collects data on the child's behavior. This is necessary to determine if the treatment is effective or ineffective. The fourth stage of Behavioral Consultation is *treatment evaluation*. During this phase, the consultant and consultee meet again to determine if the treatment was successful. They review data gathered during the consultation process to determine if the treatment goals established during the initial problem identification interview have been met. They also discuss any problems related to implementation and make adjustments as necessary.

Each stage of the Behavioral Consultation process has specific goals and outcomes associated with those goals. This allows the consultant and consultee to evaluate the progress of the process and help establish objectives for continued meetings. Through the use of face-to-face meetings and interviews, direct behavioral observations, and teaching the consultee new skills, the consultant using the Behavior Consultation procedures and sequence can effectively pass on information to school personnel, who may lack certain skills in the assessment and management of childhood behavior problems.

As researchers have continued to investigate the best possible procedures and methods to use during consultation in school settings, some criticism of the Behavior Consultation process have been made. Criticisms have focused on the overreliance of verbal methods to change teacher and, subsequently, student behavior (Witt, 1997). For example, there are several weaknesses of Behavior Consultation that affect its utility and effectiveness. First, Behavior Consultation relies too heavily on verbal interaction to change behavior. According to Witt, the misconception of this model is that talk will actually lead to a change in behavior. In addition, he also noted that what people say and what they do often differ. For instance, if a treatment is failing to change behavior, a consultant might ask a teacher if they are in fact using the intervention as discussed. Research has shown that teachers state that they use interventions with integrity. However, when those statements are compared to observational data produced in those classrooms, actual data suggest that the teachers do not implement interventions as well as they report they do (Robbins & Gutkin, 1994; Wickstrom, Jones, LaFleur, & Witt, 1998). In addition, sometimes teachers respond to questions about children in their classroom on the basis of their own personal motivation to remove a child from their classroom or to get some assistance that they do not necessarily need.

Alternative consultation models to address the above deficits have been used successfully in school settings. One alternative model for consultation is Conjoint Behavioral Consultation, which involves the incorporation of a parent into the consultation process. Although Conjoint Behavioral Consultation has also relied on primarily verbal strategies to affect teacher change, the inclusion of a third party to the consultation process has been shown to bring about positive changes in teacher and student behavior in schools (Sheridan, Eagle, Cowan, & Mickelson, 2001). Direct Behavioral Consultation does not only rely on verbal strategies to change teacher behavior. Instead, more hands-on demonstration, modeling, and observational feedback methods are employed with teachers in the classroom to affect behavior change. Research has clearly demonstrated that more direct methods are superior to verbal strategies when used to teach behavioral procedures to those without extensive behavioral training (Iwata et al., 2000; Moore et al., 2002; Mueller et al., in press). Direct Behavioral Consultation has demonstrated increased procedural integrity of teachers implementing behavioral strategies in a classroom through observational rather than anecdotal data (Mueller, Edwards, & LeBourgeois, 2000).

See also: Conjoint Behavioral Consultation; Direct Behavioral Consultation; Mental Health Consultation

BIBLIOGRAPHY

Bergan, J. R. (1977). *Behavioral consultation.* Columbus, OH: Merrill.

Bergan, J. R., & Kratochwill, T. R. (1990). *Behavioral consultation in applied settings.* New York: Plenum.

Gutkin, T. B., & Curtis, M. J. (1999). School-based consultation theory and practice: The art and science of indirect service delivery. In C. R. Reynolds & T. B. Gutkin (Eds.), *The handbook of school psychology* (2nd ed.). New York: Wiley.

Iwata, B. A., Wallace, M. D., Kahng, S., Lindberg, J. S., Roscoe, E. M., Conners, J., et al. (2000). Skill acquisition in the implementation of functional analysis methodology. *Journal of Applied Behavior Analysis, 33,* 181–194.

Kratochwill, T. R., Elliott, S. N., & Rotto, P. C. (1995). Best practices in school-based behavioral consultation. In A. Thomas & J. Grimes (Eds.), *Best practices in school psychology III.* Washington, DC: NASP.

Moore, J. W., Edwards, R. P., Sterling-Turner, H. E., Riley, J., DuBard, M., & McGeorge, A. (2002). Teacher acquisition of functional analysis methodology. *Journal of Applied Behavior Analysis, 35,* 73–77.

Mueller, M. M., Edwards, R. P., & LeBourgeois, M. (2000). Using direct behavioral consultation to train multiple teachers in effective instruction delivery to increase compliance in the classroom. *Proven Practice: Prevention and Remediation Solutions for Schools, 3,* 3–8.

Mueller, M. M., Piazza, C. C., Moore, J. W., Kelley, M. E., Bethke, S., Pruett, A., et al. (2003). Training parents to implement pediatric feeding protocols. *Journal of Applied Behavior Analysis, 36,* 545–562.

Robbins, J. R., & Gutkin, T. B. (1994). Consultee and client remedial and preventive outcomes following consultation: Some mixed empirical results and directions for future research. *Journal of Educational and Psychological Consultation, 5,* 149–167.

Sheridan, S. M., Eagle, J. W., Cowan, R. J., & Mickelson, W. (2001). The effects of conjoint behavioral consultation: Results of a 4-year investigation. *Journal of School Psychology, 39,* 361–385.

Sheridan, S. M., Kratochwill, T. R., & Bergan, J. R. (1996). *Conjoint behavioral consultation: A procedural manual.* New York: Plenum.

Watson, T. S., & Robinson, S. L. (1996). Direct behavioral consultation: An alternative to traditional behavioral consultation. *School Psychology Quarterly, 11,* 267–278.

Wickstrom, K. F., Jones, K. M., LaFleur, L. H., & Witt, J. C. (1998). An analysis of treatment integrity in school-based behavioral consultation. *School Psychology Quarterly, 13,* 141–154.

Witt, J. C. (1997). Talk is not cheap. *School Psychology Quarterly, 12,* 281–292.

Additional Readings for Professionals and Nonprofessionals

Erchul, W. P., & Martens, B. K. (1997). *School consultation: Conceptual and empirical bases of practice.* New York: Plenum.

Kratchowill, T. R. (1985). Selection of target behaviors in behavioral consultation. *Behavioral Assessment, 7,* 49–61.

Sterling-Turner, H. E., Watson, T. S., & Moore, J. W. (2002). The effects of direct training and treatment integrity on treatment outcomes in school consultation. *School Psychology Quarterly, 17,* 47–77.

MICHAEL M. MUELLER
DANA M. TRAHANT
MELANIE DUBARD

Behavioral Observation: Self-Constructed

Direct behavioral observation is one of the most widely used classroom assessment procedures employed by school psychologists. In a survey of more than 1,000 school psychology practitioners, Wilson and Reschly (1996) found that of the 26 different types of assessment instruments listed across seven different assessment categories, structured observation methods were ranked highest in terms of frequency of use. Overall, practitioners report that they conduct more than 15 behavioral observations of student behavior during the course of a typical month.

GENERAL METHODS OF DIRECT BEHAVIORAL OBSERVATION

Situational Aspects

When observing student behavior within the classroom, school psychology practitioners generally rely on one of two observational techniques. One form, *naturalistic observation,* refers to the observation and recording of behaviors at the time of occurrence in their natural setting, by trained objective observers, using a behavioral description system that requires only a minimal amount of inference by the observers. In particular, naturalistic observation places a premium on obtaining observational data in a typical, day-to-day situation, with strong efforts to minimize any obtrusiveness or reactivity caused by the presence of an observer (Merrell, 1999). A second form of direct behavioral observation, *analogue observation,* uses simulated conditions that are purposively structured and controlled by the observer to reflect how an individual might behave in a real-life, naturalistic situation. In its most typical form, analogue observation involves observing behavior in a simulated or hypothetical situation that is set up to mimic the real-life situation in which the behavior of interest occurs. The direct observation of the behavior is then used to predict the individual's behavior in the natural environment (Hintze, Stoner, & Bull, 2000). Generally speaking, analogue observations either involve the use of enactments, whereby simulated conditions are arranged and the individual's behavior is observed unprompted, or role-plays, where both the situation and the behavior of the individual are controlled. In this instance, behavior is controlled by requesting specific responses (e.g., role-playing introducing yourself to a new acquaintance). Unlike enactments, where the individual's behavior is free to vary, role-play requires the individual to respond in a delineated fashion (Hintze et al., 2000).

Recording Aspects

In addition to the situational aspects of direct behavioral observation, there are a number of considerations in recording what is observed for later analysis. Again, there are two general means by which direct observations of behavior are recorded. The first, *narrative recording* (sometimes also referred to as *descriptive* or *anecdotal recording*), involves the direct observation of an individual's behavior in either a natural or analogue setting, and simply providing a descriptive account or running record of what occurred during the specified time period. The narrative of the behavioral observation varies on a continuum from global descriptions of what occurs (e.g., "Theo was doing a math assignment") to narrow or specific descriptions of what occurs (e.g., "Theo was seated on the edge of his chair with one leg tucked under his buttocks, head and shoulders slouched forward, with his nose approximately 8 inches from his math worksheet, which was oriented diagonally in reference to his desk"). Likewise, the types of inferences that are drawn from this type of observation vary from decidedly subjective high-inference judgments to objective low-inference judgments about what has occurred. In narrating the behavioral observation, *behavioral descriptive statements* relate behaviors as they occur without explanation, whereas *behavioral inferential statements* go beyond describing behaviors and attempt to attach meaning or motivation to the behavior (Sattler, 2002). Because narrative recording is extremely flexible, the procedures are easily used across a wide variety of settings and time periods. A strength of this type of recording is that it guides the observer in hypothesizing about the various behavioral and environmental factors that may be worth further observation and analysis. However, because they lack the specificity that is often required in clinical assessment, narrative recording is generally best used as a precursor to more specific, objective accounts of behavior.

In contrast to narrative recording, *systematic direct observation* refers to the observation of behavior that is explicitly elicited by a predetermined set of environmental stimuli (Hintze, Volpe,

& Shapiro, 2002). In particular, systematic direct observation approaches are distinguished by five characteristics (Salvia & Ysseldyke, 2001). First, the goal of observation is to measure specific behaviors. Second, the behaviors being observed have been operationally defined a priori in a precise manner. Third, observations are conducted under standardized procedures and are highly objective in nature. Fourth, the times and settings for observation are carefully selected and specified. Fifth, scoring and summarizing of data are standardized and do not vary from one observer to another.

Systematic direct observational systems use any one of a number, or a combination, of approaches to record behavior. The more common approaches involve actually counting the number of times a behavior occurs during a specified time period, and/or noting the presence or absence of behavior at specific time intervals of the observational session. Specifically, *frequency* or *event recording* involves counting the number of occurrences of behavior during a specified time period. When the time periods in which the behavior is counted vary, frequencies are converted to rates of behavior per unit of time. For example, an observer may report that a target child raised a hand at an average rate of one time per minute during three separate observations conducted over the course of 3 days, even though the actual duration of each observation period varied. Using rate of behavior allows for comparisons to be made across observational sessions that differ with respect to time. Frequency recording is most useful for observing behaviors that have a discrete beginning and end, and are relatively consistent with respect to the length of time that each behavioral episode occurs for. For example, *noncompliance* might not lend itself well to frequency recording because the beginning and end of the noncompliant episode might be difficult to discern and the length of time that the behavior is present might vary from a few seconds to hours. Moreover, frequency recording is better suited to behaviors that occur at lower rather than higher rates. With high rates of behavior, it is often difficult to record each instance of the behavior as it occurs.

In addition to frequency recording, another very common way of collecting systematic direct-observation data is through the use of *interval recording*. Unlike frequency recording, wherein each instance of a behavior is noted, interval recording divides the observational period into a number of equal intervals and records the presence or absence of specified behaviors at each interval. For example, a 20-minute observation session could be broken down into 120 ten-second intervals. Once the intervals are decided upon, data are generally collected using one of three recording procedures. With *whole-interval recording*, the target behavior is scored as having occurred only when it is present throughout the entire interval. Because the behavior must be present for the entire interval, whole-interval recording lends itself quite well to behaviors that are continuous or intervals that are of short duration. One of the drawbacks of whole-interval recording, however, is that it has the tendency to underestimate the presence of the behavior. For example, if off-task behavior were the target behavior and it was observed for 8 of the 10 seconds during the interval, then the interval would not be scored for the presence of off-task behavior because it did not occur for the entire 10-second interval. In contrast to whole-interval recording, *partial-interval recording* notes an occurrence of a behavior if it occurs during any part of the interval. Partial-interval recording is a good choice for behaviors that occur at a relatively low rate, or behaviors of somewhat inconsistent duration. However, because the interval is scored for any presence of the target behavior, partial-interval recording tends to overestimate the actual occurrence of behavior. Finally, *momentary time-sampling* notes the presence or absence of behavior at only one instant of the interval (e.g., usually the instant that the interval begins). Although perhaps counterintuitive because it is based on the smallest sample of behavior, momentary time-sampling provides the least biased estimate of behavior as it actually occurs. In addition to event and interval recording, other less frequently used recording methods include *duration* (i.e., the actual amount of time that a behavior occurs), *latency* (i.e., the time that it takes for a behavior to be initiated once prompted), and *intensity* (i.e., the amplitude of behavior).

Direct behavioral observation procedures can be used to collect data that are useful for making a variety of psychoeducational decisions and are often included as part of the assessment process. Behavioral observations provide valuable information regarding an individual's behavior in everyday life settings and can serve as a systematic record that can be used in preliminary evaluation, intervention planning and design, the documentation of changes over time, and as part of a multimethod–multisource evaluation that integrates other forms of assessment (e.g., interviews, informant rating scales) and sources (e.g., teachers, parents, children).

See also: Adaptive Behavior Assessment; Curriculum-Based Measurement; Functional Behavioral Assessment

BIBLIOGRAPHY

Hintze, J. M., Stoner, G., & Bull, M. H. (2000). Analogue assessment: Research and practice in evaluating emotional & behavioral problems. In E. S. Shapiro & T. R. Kratochwill (Eds.), *Behavioral assessment in schools: Theory, research, and clinical foundations* (2nd ed., pp. 104–138). New York: Guilford.

Hintze, J. M., Volpe, R. J., & Shapiro, E. S. (2002). Best practices in the systematic direct observation of student behavior. In A. Thomas & J. Grimes (Eds.), *Best practices in school psychology IV* (pp. 993–1006). Bethesda, MD: National Association of School Psychologists.

Merrell, K. W. (1999). *Behavioral, social, and emotional assessment of children & adolescents.* Mahwah, NJ: Erlbaum.

Salvia, J., & Ysseldyke, J. E. (2001). *Assessment* (8th ed.). Boston: Houghton Mifflin.

Sattler, J. M. (2002). *Assessment of children: Behavioral and clinical applications* (4th ed.). San Diego, CA: Author.

Wilson, M. S., & Reschly, D. J. (1996). Assessment in school psychology training and practice. *School Psychology Review, 25*, 9–23.

Additional Reading for Nonprofessionals

Witt, J. C., Daly, E. J., III, & Noell, G. H. (2000). *Functional assessments: A step-by-step guide to solving academic & behavior problems.* Longmont, CO: Sopris West.

Additional Reading for Professionals

Skinner, C. H., Dittmer, K. I., & Howell, L. A. (2000). Direct observation in school settings: Theoretical issues. In E. S. Shapiro & T. R. Kratochwill (Eds.), *Behavioral assessment in schools: Theory, research, and clinical foundations* (2nd ed., pp. 19–45). New York: Guilford.

John M. Hintze

Bender Visual Motor Gestalt Test—Second Edition

In 1938, Lauretta Bender developed a visual–motor Gestalt test that later became known as the Bender-Gestalt. The test consisted of nine figures that are presented one at a time and copied on a blank sheet of paper. The test was used in the assessment of perceptual maturation, neurological impairment, and psychopathology in children and adults. Since its first development, it has undergone numerous scoring and methodological variations as well as imitations. Much of the Bender-Gestalt's appeal comes from its relative ease of use, minimal time investment, and high return of information. Few other tests provide such a wealth of information in such a small amount of time. A testament of the Bender-Gestalt is evidenced by its popularity among psychologists. It has consistently been rated as one of the most frequently used tests among psychologists for more than 30 years (Lubing, Larsen, & Paine, 1971; Rosenberg & Beck, 1986; Tolor & Brannigan, 1980; Watkins, Campbell, Nieberding, & Hallmark, 1995).

The *Bender Visual Motor Gestalt Test—Second Edition* (Bender-Gestalt II) is a revised version of Lauretta Bender's original test. The goal of the revision was to integrate aspects of 60 years of research, scoring, and clinical applications of the original Bender-Gestalt while using the most modern statistical and diagnostic methodology in test development and standards in psychological testing.

The Bender-Gestalt II was designed to measure multiple aspects of visual–motor integration. The Bender-Gestalt II involves copying geometric designs on a blank piece of paper and later recalling the designs from memory. The core of the test includes the original 9 Bender-Gestalt designs. A total of 7 new designs have been added, for a total of 16 designs. Four new designs were added to lower the age range, and 3 new designs were added to raise the age range assessed by the Bender-Gestalt. In addition, new components such as memory recall, perceptual organization, timing procedures, and supplemental tests have been added to increase its clinical utility and to broaden the range of assessment.

The Bender-Gestalt can and has been used for multiple purposes. Indeed, one of its strengths is that it lends itself to a multidimensional interpretation. Since its inception by Bender (1938), many objective scoring systems have been developed that reflect different usages of the test (Brannigan & Brunner, 1996; Hain, 1964; Hutt, 1985; Hutt-Briskin, 1960; Koppitz, 1963; Lacks, 1999; Pascal & Suttell, 1951; Pauker, 1976). Although the multidimensionality of this test may initially seem overwhelming, such diversity in interpretation provides a more complete utilization of test results (Koppitz, 1963). As such, a goal of the revisions was to collect normative information on a variety of scoring and interpretive methods. In addition, new scoring systems were also developed. Examiners have a choice in scoring Bender-Gestalt II performance based on either specific errors, which has traditionally been used, or the accuracy of the drawing. Error-scoring methods examine particular types of errors in performance such as rotation or perseveration. Accuracy measurements are based on the criterion as well as the similarity of the examinee's drawing to the actual design. In addition, a more heuristically accurate method in the form of a rating scale is provided. This variety of scoring systems can be used together or in isolation and tailored to the specific purpose of the assessment. Apart from the typical standard scores, percentiles are available as well. Scores can be used in combination to provide both a peer- and comparison-based score, and a more global score that reflects development over the lifespan.

TARGET AGE RANGE OF USE [SLD1]

The Bender-Gestalt II was normed by a stratified sample of approximately 4,000 individuals ranging in age from 3 to 80+. This represents the most comprehensive set of normative information in the history of the test. The overall sample was based on a comprehensive national sample that was rigorously selected to represent the United States' year 2000 population. The age intervals varied and normative tables with smaller intervals are provided for younger ages because of more developmental change.

COMPARISON WITH PREVIOUS EDITION

Users of the new Bender-Gestalt II will find many similarities with the previous edition and find that many aspects of the previous edition generalize to the second edition. For example, all of the existing Bender-Gestalt designs were preserved in the Bender-Gestalt II. This maintains a familiarity with test items and helps generalize existing scoring and interpretation procedures to the new Bender-Gestalt II. This is particularly important for research and clinical techniques that examine specific types of errors on individual designs.

Selection of the new Bender-Gestalt II features was based on more than 50 years of research on the Bender-Gestalt and its clinical use whereas other features were based on surveys of Bender-Gestalt users. For example, an immediate recall procedure is often incorporated into the assessment procedure by clinicians because of its clinical utility although normative information on memory recall is sparse. Because the memory recall procedure is frequently used by clinicians and research exists to support its validity, it was included into the standardization test administration procedure. Normative information was obtained on the number of designs recalled by age and the accuracy of the recalled designs. The new normative information on memory recall will allow clinicians to use this procedure with confidence. In addition, past research has suggested that the amount of time it takes to complete a Bender-Gestalt design makes it clinically useful. As such, normative data were gathered on the amount of time it took for participants to complete each item.

Other features were based on contemporary methods of test development. For example, new items were added to increase the developmental age range of the Bender-Gestalt. However, there was very little research on the Bender-Gestalt concerning its design characteristics or the quantitative measurement of Gestalt properties or the laws of Pragnantz. However, there is considerable research in item response theory of mathematical models of item difficulty. Such mathematical techniques were useful in selecting the new items. Rasch modeling is a statistical method that evaluates an individual's ability and the difficulty of the item. Rasch analysis was used in both item selection and for norming test performance. Contemporary statistical procedures, such as the Rasch method, provided new possibilities that were not available for the original Bender-Gestalt.

TYPICAL USES

Historically, the Bender-Gestalt has been used for a variety of purposes. Many of these purposes generalize to the Bender-Gestalt II; but by virtue of its new features and methodologies, the Bender-Gestalt II has expanded capabilities, covering different assessment areas.

Warm-Up

The Bender-Gestalt II can be used as a nonthreatening warm-up to more rigorous psychological testing. Indeed, most younger examinees like to draw and will willingly cooperate on the Bender-Gestalt II tasks. Using the Bender-Gestalt II for this purpose helps establish rapport with the examinee. There is a wealth of information that can be obtained just by observing an individual complete the Bender-Gestalt II that is not always quantitatively measured by the objective scoring criteria. A trained clinician can observe many aspects of an individual's personality, response style, attitude, self-concept, frustration, tolerance, and so on, just by observing the examinee's behavior while completing the Bender-Gestalt II. Although these aspects are not always easy to quantitatively verify, they are an important aspect of a comprehensive psychoeducational evaluation.

Perceptual–Motor Development

The Bender-Gestalt II is primarily a test of visual–motor development. Measurement of visual–motor development is helpful in evaluating the possibility of learning disabilities or neurological deficits and aids in developing remediation programs. In addition, two supplemental tests of motor and perception are available that can help differentiate specific problems on the Bender-Gestalt II.

Neuropsychological Screener

Drawing tasks like the Bender-Gestalt II tasks are often referred to as a measure of constructional abilities in neuropsychology as well as visual–motor abilities. Constructional measures are frequently used in neuropsychology as a screener for brain damage. Many studies have found that the Bender-Gestalt is also a good screener for brain damage. Guidelines for brain-damage screening are provided in the manual along with reliability and validity estimates.

Visual Memory

The memory component of the Bender-Gestalt II provides an estimate of an individual's visual memory ability. Multiple validity studies were conducted to determine how this estimate relates to a more comprehensive measurement of visual memory abilities. These studies suggest that the visual memory estimate of the Bender-Gestalt II is a valid and helpful estimate of an individual's visual memory and can be used for screening purposes.

SCORING

The Bender-Gestalt II utilizes the Global Scoring System. This scoring system is an adaptation of Brannigan's Qualitative Scoring System, which has been shown to be highly correlated with criterion-based scoring systems. In addition, this type of scoring system is more similar to Bender's (1938) clinical interpretation method. For this scoring system, each drawn item is rated on a scale of 0 to 4, with 0 being equivalent to scribbles or the complete lack of accuracy and 4 being equivalent to perfect accuracy.

PRACTICAL APPLICATIONS

The Bender-Gestalt II was developed to help clinicians get an estimate of visual–motor ability for children, adolescents, or adults quickly and efficiently. The Bender-Gestalt II can be used to estimate the maturation of visual–motor development and the degree of integration of visual and motor abilities. The Bender-Gestalt II has a low linguistic demand and can be used with individuals with low language ability or those with hearing impairments. In addition, the Bender-Gestalt II can be used to develop hypotheses that are to be further tested by a more comprehensive evaluation.

A wide variety of scores and indices are provided to facilitate the interpretation of a participant's test performance. Clinicians can choose to use a single score of overall development or use more comprehensive scores that include memory, motor, and perception ability.

ORGANIZATION OF THE BENDER-GESTALT II

The Bender-Gestalt II was designed to yield the maximum information in the minimal amount of time. More methods have been developed for using the Bender-Gestalt than any other psychological test. The Bender-Gestalt II attempts to incorporate as many of the historically used methods as possible and provide empirical evidence for their reliability and utility. Ultimately, the methods used for administering and interpreting the results of the Bender-Gestalt II are left to the clinician.

The manual advocates the guidelines of Bender (1938), who suggested both a developmental and a clinical approach to evaluation. To obtain an estimation of developmental level, evaluation is reliant upon normative comparisons. Multiple methods are available for this evaluation. The method chosen is based on clinical judgment, time restraints, and purpose of assessment. Similarly, there are multiple methods for clinical evaluation. Clinical evaluation techniques may also incorporate normative scores, apart from including score comparisons with

clinical populations. In addition, clinical indicators that have been suggested by past research were also included in the standardization of the Bender-Gestalt II. This allows an estimation of base rates or how often these indicators are found in the normal population.

CAUTIONS, ETHICAL CONSIDERATIONS, AND EXAMINER QUALIFICATIONS

In administering the Bender-Gestalt II (or any other psychological measure), the care for the examinee is of the utmost concern. Some examinee, especially in certain clinical groups, may find some drawing on the Bender-Gestalt II very difficult to draw and may become overly frustrated. Efforts should be taken to minimize frustration and emotional distress when taking the test. Clinical judgment should be used in such matters of interpersonal sensitivity.

In addition, all efforts should be made to protect the confidentiality of the examinee as well as the test security and copyright information. Professionals should ensure the confidentiality of both the test results and the test materials in a manner consistent with legal and professional guidelines. Ethical guidelines in the clinician's profession should be consulted for further information guidelines.

Examiner qualifications for the Bender-Gestalt II differ depending on the intended use of the Bender-Gestalt II. In situations where an examiner is only administering the Bender-Gestalt II and will not be making interpretive statements regarding an examiner's performance (e.g., for research or under supervision), examiners should have a thorough knowledge of the administration and scoring procedures of the Bender-Gestalt II. Such information can be obtained from a careful reading of the Bender-Gestalt II administration manual and from sufficient practice. In situations where interpretive statements are made from the examiner's performance, examiners should not only have a thorough knowledge of the administration and scoring procedures of the Bender-Gestalt II, but also have some advanced training in psychology, measurement, and test interpretation. Such proficiency is usually obtained from formal training in education, measurement, and psychology and supervised practicum experience. In addition, these qualifications are not unitary, because different methods involve more or less levels of training in specific areas. As described in the Standards for Educational and Psychological Tests (1999), it is ultimately the user's responsibility to ensure the appropriate use and interpretation of psychological tests. This includes becoming knowledgeable about a test's appropriate use and the populations for which it is suitable. Test users should not attempt to use the Bender-Gestalt II in situations that are outside the range of the user's qualifications.

CAUTIONS

Diagnostic and placement decisions should never be made with a single test score or a single test. Such decisions are best made through the convergence of a number of sources, including school, parent, and consultant evaluations. As such, no single part of the Bender-Gestalt II should solely be relied upon to make diagnostic decisions. In addition, interpretations based on an examinee's performance should be limited in scope to conclusions that have known validity.

See also: Motor-Free Visual Perception Test—Revised

BIBLIOGRAPHY

Bender, L. (1938). A visual–motor gestalt test and its clinical use. *American Orthopsychiatric Association Research Monograph, No. 3.*

Bender, L. (1970). Use of the Visual Motor Gestalt Test in the diagnosis of learning disabilities. *Journal of Special Education, 4,* 29–39.

Brannigan, G. G., & Brunner, N. A. (1996). *The modified version of the Bender-Gestalt Test for preschool & primary school children: Revised.* Clinical Psychology Publishing. Brandon, VT.

Koppitz, E. M. (1963). *The Bender Gestalt Test for young children.* New York: Grune & Stratton.

Lacks, P. (1999). *Bender Gestalt screening for brain dysfunction* (2nd ed.). New York: Wiley.

Pascal, G. R., & Suttell, B. J. (1951). *The Bender Gestalt Test.* New York: Grune & Stratton.

L. Scott Decker
Greg G. Brannigan

Binet, Alfred

Alfred Binet was born on July 11, 1857, in Nice, France. He was the only child of an affluent physician father and an artistically cultured mother. Binet spent the majority of his formative years in Paris under the guidance of his mother. During Binet's childhood education, he achieved academic honors in literary composition and translation. Binet furthered his studies with an introductory law degree in 1878. He expressed dissatisfaction soon after and pursued interests in science and medicine. Eventually, in 1894, he obtained a doctorate in the natural sciences. By then, Binet's career aspirations focused on the newly developed field of psychology (Cunningham, 1997; Fancher, 1998).

Binet initially studied a French publication entitled *Revue Philosophique* that described the progression of psychology in different countries. He conducted sensory experiments on two-point thresholds and submitted his findings to the journal for publication. Although he received harsh criticism for

methodological errors, Binet proceeded to expand his studies in psychology (Cunningham, 1997).

Binet worked as an unpaid research assistant with a famous neurologist, Jean-Martin Charcot, at the Salpetriere Hospital in Paris from 1884 to 1890. He investigated many subjects, including individual case studies, associationistic psychology, attention, fetishes, illusions, and personality changes. Furthermore, Binet and a colleague conducted multiple investigations on hypnosis with the use of large magnets near the participants. Purportedly, magnetic energy rather than suggestions caused changes in behavior during hypnosis. Although the results were published in a book, they received strong reproach regarding their influential behavior toward the participants during the experiments. Binet publicly agreed that erroneous and biased outcomes existed from the experimenters' expectations unintentionally placed upon participants through their verbal and nonverbal behavior. Binet called this phenomena *cholera of psychology* and recognized the importance of its avoidance during the administration of experimental procedures. In later research, however, Binet methodically examined the effects of suggestibility on behavior.

Once Binet left Salpetriere, his two young daughters served as participants in home-based studies that tested reaction time and sensory discrimination. The tasks resembled measures designed by other researchers as indicators of intellectual functioning, including color naming, definition of objects, discrimination between lines, and size differences among coins. Binet observed their responses and attention to the tasks as compared with adults. Binet noted differences in accuracy of responses across the ages and diverse approaches to problem solving between the two girls. Binet continued to explore the complexities of mental process and problem-solving styles among individuals at Sorbonne.

Binet collaborated with Henri Beaunis (1830–1921) at Sorbonne, the first French laboratory in experimental psychology. He served as an unpaid associate in 1889 and later established a journal *L'Annee Psychologique.* With the initial issue published in 1895, the journal chronicled research conducted at the laboratory and included other psychological accounts outside of France. He accomplished several publications and investigations as director of the Sorbonne from 1895 to 1911.

Although Binet's research interests varied across age groups and areas in psychology, he carried on the examination of complex cognitive tasks and distinctive characteristics with various participants. Initially, he conducted case studies among individuals with specialized skills in mathematical calculations, chess, and creative writing. He analyzed their unique strategies through interviews and observations. Binet and Victor Henri (1872–1940) assessed memory skills among children utilizing word lists and sentences from paragraphs. They also evaluated the impact of suggestibility and group pressure among school-age children through the manipulation of multiple variables, including the type of interrogation toward the participants. Binet's research on eyewitness testimony suggested that the manner in which the evaluator interrogated the children affected results on recall accuracy. Eventually, Binet and Henri designed a battery of cognitive and physical tests that attempted to differentiate individuals' skills. This line of research continued with Theodore Simon (1873–1961).

Binet, in 1899, joined a professional society dedicated to educational research and developed another publication entitled the *Bulletin*. Changes in French laws permitted the education of individuals with mental deficiencies. Upon a challenge from the government, Binet partnered with Simon to examine ways in which children could be accurately identified for special education and constructed an instrument for measuring intelligence. They administered 25 items, primarily related to comprehension, to children with varying abilities across schools in France. In 1905 *L'Anne Psychologique* published the initial scale, with normative data for children up to 11 years of age. Revised editions followed in 1908 and 1911, with more test items and broader age ranges. The instrument gained use in France during the 1920s and received recognition abroad, including the United States during World War I. Research on the Binet–Simon scales in the United States produced the Terman–Merrill and Stanford–Binet revisions (Fancher, 1998; Wolf, 1961), including the current Stanford–Binet IV.

Binet proposed that intelligence did not remain stable from birth, but changed and advanced with age. Moreover, he asserted individuals with mental deficiencies could improve their intelligence through training on such skills as attention and memory. He suggested extreme caution in assigning numerical results to the intelligence scale. Individualistic styles of responses remained an important consideration for Binet's work on intelligence scales.

Binet developed a multimethod approach to research by combining data obtained through observations, interviews, and experimental manipulation of variables. Although Binet strongly supported the analysis of individual characteristics, he warned against total reliance upon the quantification of data from intelligence scales and experimental findings. As his research developed, Binet viewed results with caution because of potential fallacies inherent with experiments. Binet's research efforts in psychology gave rise to 13 books and 200 articles. Furthermore, his writings extended to the stage as he cowrote plays related to psychological thrillers. He remained an unpaid director at the Sorbonne until his death, at the age of 54, on October 18, 1911. Alfred Binet's (1857–1911) contributions to the field of psychology extend far beyond the scope of intelligence scales. His quest for knowledge in different areas of psychology led to numerous publications and served as a heuristic for many other researchers and clinicians. Although he received no formal training in psychology and acquired no professorships, his legacy in the profession continues to be recognized (Cunningham, 1997).

See also: Intelligence Quotient (IQ)

BIBLIOGRAPHY

Cunningham, J. L. (1997). Alfred Binet and the quest for testing higher mental functioning. In W. G. Bringmann, H. E. Luck, R. Miller, & C. E. Early (Eds.), *A pictorial history of psychology* (pp. 309–314). Carol Stream, IL: Quintessence.
Fancher, R. E. (1998). Alfred Binet, general psychologist. In G. A. Kimble & M. Wertheimer (Eds.), *Portraits of pioneers in psychology* (Vol. 3, pp. 67–83). Mahwah, NJ: Erlbaum.
Wolf, T. (1961). An individual who made a difference. *American Psychologist, 16*, 245–248.

Additional Reading for Nonprofessionals

Wolf, T. (1982). A new perspective on Alfred Binet: Dramatist of Le Theatre de L'Horreur. *The Psychological Record, 32*, 397–407.

Additional Reading for Professionals

Wolf, T. (1973). *Alfred Binet.* Chicago: University of Chicago Press.

LORI CHAMBERS SLAY

Body Art

To an adolescent, appearance is a means of self-expression. Teenagers use personal effects such as clothes, makeup, and hairstyles to express their individuality. Tattoos and body piercing have also become a common method of communicating individuality for many teenagers. Additional explanations for body art include (a) sense of ownership over body while also a sign of uniqueness, (b) sense of belonging to a particular group, and (c) a form of self-mutilation (Carroll & Anderson, 2002). It is estimated that between 10 and 13 percent of adolescents aged 12 to 18 have tattoos, and the occurrence of body piercing is also on the rise among this age group (Carroll, Riffenburgh, Roberts, & Myhre, 2002). Adolescents view this type of body modification as objects of self-identity and body art, whereas adults consider this type of body modification as deviant behavior. The question for many parents is whether they should view this as a sign of other risk-taking or delinquent behaviors.

The most popular piercing site includes the ear, a location that is often viewed as acceptable by our culture. However, other sites are gaining in popularity, and are not viewed as socially acceptable. These locations include the lips, tongue, navel, nipples, eyebrows, nose, and the genital area. One advantage of piercing over tattooing is the decrease in permanence. Jewelry can be removed, although there is a chance of scarring.

However, research has suggested a greater risk of contracting a sexually transmitted disease when the individual had a genital piercing (Samantha, Tweeten, & Rickman, 1998).

The majority of medical research has focused on health complications and procedural risks because of tattooing and body piercing. There seems to be a low occurrence of health complications for the amount of tattooing and body piercing that is done among youth. Armstrong, Stuppy, and Gabriel (1996) reported that the most common health complications of tattooing and piercing are infection and bleeding. Hepatitis B and C from contaminated needles is the most common long-term concern when receiving a piercing or tattoo. However, branding, a less popular type of body art, is a design on the skin obtained from second- and third-degree burns. Branding has potential for serious health complications such as infection and tissue damage. Because of the severe pain involved and the possible health risk, this type of extreme body art should be monitored closely (Martel & Anderson, 2002).

Carroll et al. (2002) surveyed 484 adolescents, ranging in age from 12 to 22, examining eating behavior, violence, drug abuse, sexual behavior, and suicide and questioning about body art. Results suggested that adolescents with tattoos or body piercings (in areas other than their earlobes) were more likely to engage in risk-taking behaviors such as disordered eating, gateway drug use, sexual activity, hard drug use, and suicide. They were twice as likely to engage in sexual activity and engage in the use of gateway drugs, such as marijuana, alcohol, and cigarettes. Data also indicated that adolescents with body art were 3 times as likely to use hard drugs such as cocaine and methamphetamine. Their findings also suggested that 90 percent of teenagers with tattoos and 72 percent with body piercings had sex within the last 30 days, whereas only 41 percent of adolescents without body modifications had engaged in sexual intercourse. For both genders, the younger the participant when they got their body modifications, the more likely they were to use marijuana, alcohol, and cigarettes.

Although results are mixed, studies have consistently reported that individuals who receive tattoos from an amateur have increased dissatisfaction with the tattoo, a greater likelihood of problem behavior, and decreased academic achievement. Gender differences were also suggested, in that females with body art had an increased occurrence of suicidal thoughts and disordered eating. Females were also more likely to engage in fights if they had a body piercing. Males with tattoos were at higher risk of participating in violent behavior than those with no body art.

Although research suggests that the presence of tattoos and body piercing should not serve as an indicator of problematic behavior, it could effectively serve as a cue that questions need to be asked concerning the adolescent's risk-taking behaviors. In addition, the presence of a tattoo or body piercing should not be considered a certain, overt sign of possible risk-taking behavior. Although adolescents with some type of body art may be at greater risk for experimenting with risk-taking behaviors such as sexual activities and drug use, adolescents without body art still report engaging in problematic behaviors.

In summary, the role of the parent in a child obtaining body art should be in the form of education and involving an adolescent's pediatrician in the process. This effort by the parent could reduce the chances of medical complications. Involving a pediatrician allows the adolescent to obtain anticipatory guidance that may be seen as lecturing coming from the parent.

See also: Antisocial Behavior; Conduct Disorder; Eating Disorders

BIBLIOGRAPHY

Carroll, L., & Anderson, R. (2002). Body piercing, tattooing, self-esteem, and body investment in adolescent girls. *Adolescence, 37*, 627–637.

Carroll, S. T., Riffenburgh, R. H., Roberts, T. A., & Myhre, E. B. (2002). Tattoos and body piercings as indicators of adolescent risk-taking behaviors. *Pediatrics, 109*, 1021–1027.

Samantha, S., Tweeten, M., & Rickman, L. S. (1998). Infectious complications of body piercing. *Clinical Infectious Diseases, 26*, 735.

Martel, S., & Anderson, J. E. (2002). Decorating the "human canvas": Body art and your patients; tattoos and body caught on as teenage, and even preteen, fashion statements. Here's how to help your patients avoid the pitfalls of this form of self-expression. *Contemporary Pediatrics*. Retrieved December 19, 2003 from http://www.findarticles.com/cf_dls/mOBGH/8_19/90869065/print.jhtml

Additional Readings for Nonprofessionals

http://www.med.umich.edu/opm/newspage/2003/bodyart.htm
http://www.vh.org/pediatric/patient/dermatology/tattoo/#TOC

Additional Readings for Professionals

Armstrong, M. L., & McConnell, C. (1994). Tattooing in adolescents, more common than you think: The phenomenon and risks. *Journal of School Nursing, 10*, 22–29.

Stirn, A. (2003). Body piercing: Medical consequences and psychological motivations. *The Lancet, 361*(9364), 1205–1215.

TONYA SARTOR BUTLER

Body Image

The concept of body image has assumed increasing importance in Western society as people have become preoccupied with youth, body shape, and control over personal health. Body image has assumed a significant role clinically with regard to its relationship with eating disorders. There are three other clinical areas besides eating disorders in which body image is relevant: (1) In some neurological conditions, there may be a faulty perception of one's own body, for example, failure to recognize hemiplegia (paralysis of one side of the body) after a stroke. (2) Some people may suffer from a physical disfigurement through illness or surgery, whereby one's bodily self-perception is altered. (3) Another condition, body dysmorphic disorder, involves a preoccupation with a real or imagined defect in appearance concerning a particular area of the individual's body.

The physician Schilder first used the term *body image* in a monograph, *The Image and Appearance of the Human Body*, in 1935. He characterized body image as "the picture of our own body which we form in our mind, that is to say the way in which the body appears to ourselves." Modifications have since been made to his operational definition. Most noteworthy, Slade (1988) expanded the concept of body image by emphasizing the affective domain—the strong reactions that individuals may entertain in response to their own bodies. He stated that it is "the picture we have in our own minds of the size, shape and form of our bodies; and to our feelings concerning these characteristics and our constituent body parts" which is "influenced by a variety of historical, cultural and social, individual and biological factors, which operate over varying time spans."

The development of one's body image is incompletely understood but is thought to derive from multiple sources, from very early in life, when the infant begins to evolve a sense of "me versus not-me." The literature indicates three main contributing areas: (1) perception of interrelational experiences, (2) experience/exposure to the prevailing societal and cultural values, and (3) the development of one's self-concept and its resultant personal evaluations of success and effectiveness.

RELATIONAL INTERACTIONS

The mother, and then the family, are the first sources of social and interpersonal interaction that begins the process of molding the child's sense of self and others. This contributes to one's self-concept, a component of which is body image. These early and often continuous interactions allow individuals to experience, monitor, and influence their evaluation of self and further development of their self-concept. There is research supporting the major role of the family environment in the development of a child's body image. For example, girls' perceptions of troubled family dynamics have been found to be a predictor of later disordered eating behaviors and body image disturbance. Adolescents whose parents were perceived as supportive had lower rates of eating and weight concerns. Relating within an environment that is unpredictable or overly critical heightens a child's sense of rejection and being unworthy. Early childhood is also critical in the transmission of values,

including those involving appearance. In many families, unfortunately, young girls learn to rely on their outward appearance for determining their overall self-worth.

Later in childhood, an individual's peer community provides information and attitudes, and often functions as the main comparison group, from which the individual members evaluate their "position" and act accordingly. Middle and elementary school-aged children have been shown to be affected by peers, especially teasing, in relation to weight, and this has been found to be related to weight concerns and body dissatisfaction. Deviations from what are usual   whether it is in the timing of on set of puberty, height, or other characteristics—provide an opportunity for negative self-evaluation in comparison with one's peers.

SOCIETAL AND CULTURAL ATTITUDES TOWARD THE PORTRAYAL OF THE "IDEAL" AND ITS EFFECTS ON BODY IMAGE

Societal images of beauty change over time. With the speed and degree of media penetration today, these images play a major role in the evolution of one's body image. Advertising first enabled women to compare themselves with others. The interest in self-cultivation evolved in American culture from the early 1900s when appearance came to be viewed as a window on the person. The body has become the site of symbolic work in the projection of a personal image. Culture's dominant belief that the body is malleable and that one can, and should, strive to change the size and form of one's body underlies the increased frequency of eating disorders. Consumerism through advertising implies the possibility that the body can be personally created. The role of media and fashion industries, especially those targeting women and girls, in promoting unrealistic standards of female beauty has been extensively discussed (Garfinkel & Dorian, 1997).

Over the past few decades, media ideals for women have become slimmer while the average woman is becoming bigger. Young girls and women are bombarded with images that often result in negative self-comparison. Individuals who look to society's standards to define a personal concept of ideal beauty may internalize standards to replace the representation of the "ideal self." This may result in the perception of a discrepancy between the real and idealized bodies and increase the possibility of engaging in behaviors to compensate.

Persons who have higher levels of body satisfaction, perhaps because their perception of their body shape is similar to the "media ideal" or for those whose shape and weight are not important determinants of self-worth, may be less influenced by the barrage of media images (Dorian & Garfinkel, 2002). Greater exposure to the media is related to greater inclination to internalize the standard of the media ideal, thus increasing the chance of displaying greater body dissatisfaction, making one more susceptible to engaging in eating-disordered behaviors.

PERCEPTION OF THE SELF AS AN EFFECTIVE INDIVIDUAL

Appearance may influence others' evaluation or treatment of others, which may result in an individual's perception of self to be modified according to the reactions of others. When individuals have a negative self-evaluation in such a body-oriented society, it is not surprising that the body and the dissatisfaction with it become the concretization of one's sense of personal dissatisfaction. If one can be successful at compensatory behaviors (e.g., dieting), it may help buffer the sense of self. These compensatory behaviors might produce changes that are much more attainable, immediately noticeable, and rewarding than such things as increasing the quality of interpersonal relationships. The perceptions of personal achievement are often a function of bodily control, which is especially predominant in a society that is preoccupied and oriented toward the self.

IMPLICATIONS FOR PREVENTION AND TREATMENT OF EATING DISORDERS

Effective treatments for people with eating disorders take into account the problems with body image. It becomes important for the person with an eating disorder to trust that she can become more comfortable in her body and not have "to do" in response to negative feelings. Activities such as dance and yoga are extremely beneficial as adjuncts to treatment. Because a great deal has been learned about the mechanisms involved in the eating disorders, it is possible to develop programs of prevention. It is striking that some programs only change knowledge whereas others have a positive effect on attitudes and behaviors, and yet others make people worse. Programs that are beneficial are interactive rather than didactive and are broad-based rather than focusing on eating and weight alone. These latter programs emphasize self-esteem and its regulation, self-concept, and body awareness. The effectiveness of these programs provides support for the pivotal role that self-esteem and healthy concept formation play in interacting with body image.

See also: Anorexia Nervosa; Bulimia Nervosa

BIBLIOGRAPHY

Dorian, L., & Garfinkel, P. E. (2002). Culture and body image in Western cultures. *Eating and Weight Disorders, 7*, 1–19.

Garfinkel, P. E., & Dorian, B. J. (1997). Factors that may affect future approaches to the eating disorders. *Journal of Eating and Weight Disorders, 2*, 1–16.

Jarry, J. L. (1998). The meaning of body image for women with eating disorders. *Canadian Journal of Psychiatry, 43*, 367–374.

Additional Readings for Nonprofessionals

Dorian, J., & Garfinkel, P. E. (1999). The contributions of epidemiologic studies to the etiology and treatment of the eating disorders. *Psychiatric Annals, 29*, 187–192.

Slade, P. D. (1994). What is body image? *Behaviour Research and Therapy, 32*, 497–502.

Additional Readings for Professionals

Slade, P. D. (1988). Body image in anorexia nervosa. *British Journal of Psychiatry, 153*, 20–22.

Thompson, J. K., Coovert, M. D., & Stormer, S. M. (1999). Body image, social comparison, and eating disturbance: A covariance structure modelling investigation. *International Journal of Eating Disorders, 26*, 43–51.

LEANNE M. FITZGERALD
PAUL E. GARFINKEL

Boredom

The *Oxford English Dictionary* (Simpson & Weiner, 1989) defines *boring* as tedious, wearying, and dull. The verb *to bore* was first used in the middle of the eighteenth century whereas the noun *boredom* dates only from the mid-nineteenth century. Boredom has been attributed to increasing amounts of free time due to technical advancements (Ragheb & Merydith, 2001). Although some authorities claim that boredom is a result of a lack of environmental stimulation, most agree that boredom is temporary and situation-specific (Kelly & Markos, 2001).

Throughout history, boredom has caused a variety of positive and negative behaviors. Sparta's elite in ancient Greece fought boredom by imposing military discipline and engaging in war. In Athens, the elite developed a variety of mental activities to occupy their free time. These activities were the beginning of history, literature, poetry, plays, and other important contributions to the early development of mathematics, astronomy, and the natural sciences (Scitovsky, 2000).

THE IMPACT OF BOREDOM ON CHILDREN AND ADOLESCENTS

Among children and adolescents, boredom has been identified as a contributing factor to substance abuse, smoking, juvenile delinquency, pathological gambling, cutting class, and dropping out of school. In addition, feelings of worry, anger, hatred, aggression, loneliness, life dissatisfaction, and depression have also been linked to boredom (Kelly & Markos, 2001; Ragheb & Merydith, 2001; Scitovsky, 2000).

Students describe school as boring when teachers are burned out, schools are bureaucratic and disrespectful of students' learning preferences, and there is a lack of value placed on student contributions. An oppressive school atmosphere, according to student focus groups, creates the desire for students to cut class and for many students to drop out of school altogether. In addition, students report that boredom occurs when teachers focus a great deal of attention on struggling students, while expecting students who "get it" to wait for new, challenging instruction to occur. The lack of elective choices and engaging extracurricular activities results in school environments that students see as sterile, uninviting, and boring.

ADDRESSING BOREDOM

Boredom in general can result from lack of physical and mental engagement, social isolation and negative mood or feelings, as well as various environmental characteristics (Ragheb & Merydith, 2001). Boredom is related to doing mundane, repetitive tasks that require little cognitive energy. Boredom is reduced when an activity is optimally challenging and there is an interaction with the environment or with oneself. However, interaction with oneself can also lead to maladaptive methods of controlling boredom (e.g., worry, excessive daydreaming; Kelly & Markos, 2001). Social isolation is the absence of others and a lack of friends, intimate or platonic. Often, watching television is the choice replacement for social interaction. Extreme boredom is positively related to depression and/or suicide, where intrinsic enjoyment is related to involvement and interest. Environments lacking change and complexity are associated with boredom; therefore, aesthetics of the environment and variation within the environment are necessary to avoid boredom.

SUMMARY

Boredom has been a common issue to the human race throughout history. With advances in technology, children and adolescents are more prone to socially isolate and develop maladaptive methods for addressing boredom. In schools, the effects of boredom can be devastating (e.g., droppingout and violence). Thus, it is essential that school environments are challenging and adaptable. It also is essential that parents, by becoming active participants in the lives of their children, reduce the need for social isolation. With dedicated attention to creating challenging activities in the social worlds of children and adolescents, boredom can be overcome.

See also: Academic Interventions for Written Language and Grammar; Depression in Children and Adolescents

BIBLIOGRAPHY

Kelly, W. E., & Markos, P. A. (2001). The role of boredom in worry: An empirical investigation with implications for counsellors. *Guidance & Counselling, 16*(3), 81–86.
Ragheb, M. G., & Merydith, S. P. (2001). Development and validation of a multidimensional scale measuring free time boredom. *Leisure Studies, 20*, 41–59.
Scitovsky, T. (2000). The wages of boredom. *NPQ: New Perspectives Quarterly, 17*(2), 45–52.
Simpson, J. A., & Weiner, E. S. C. (Eds.). (1989). *Oxford English dictionary* (2nd ed.). Oxford: Oxford University Press.

Additional Reading for Nonprofessionals

Spacks, P. M. (1995). *Boredom: The literary history of a state of mind*. Chicago: University of Chicago Press.

Additional Reading for Professionals

Fallis, R. K., & Opotow, S. (2003). Are students failing school or are schools failing students? Class cutting in high school. *Journal of Social Issues, 59*, 103–119.

SHELLY F. SHEPERIS
JOSÉ A. VILLALBA

Brazelton Neonatal Behavioral Assessment Scale

In 1975, Dr. T. Berry Brazelton, a clinical professor of pediatrics emeritus at Harvard University Medical School, developed the *Brazelton Neonatal Behavioral Assessment Scale* (NBAS), also known as "the Brazelton." Since its initial development, revisions were completed by Brazelton in 1985 and by Brazelton and Nugent in 1995 (Brazelton & Nugent, 1995). A new assessment instrument, the *Clinical Newborn Behavioral Assessment Scale* (CLNBAS), has been developed for use by clinicians (Nugent & Brazelton, 2001) to assess the sensory, motor, physical, and neurological responses of newborns up to 2 months of age.

The NBAS is used by obstetricians, pediatricians, and pediatric psychologists primarily as a research tool and is composed of 28 behavior and 18 reflex items. The NBAS offers an assessment of the infant's capabilities and his/her progressive regulation and control of the following: autonomic system, motor activities, state of consciousness, and social interactions.

Observations of the infant are used to provide information about the infant's strengths, individuality, adaptive responses, and possible vulnerabilities. The assumption underlying this measure is that newborns' behaviors have meaning: specifically, they cry to get a response, attend to stimuli that are familiar and preferred, and move to avoid aversive stimuli. The parents are then better able to match their caretaking behaviors to meet the infant's needs, thereby promoting a strong parent–infant relationship.

Administration time is 20 to 30 minutes. Training is needed to administer this instrument and to obtain the best performance from the child. Frequently, the infant requires support to exhibit skill in areas such as state regulation. Therefore, training is needed to determine the sequencing of the steps to be taken to assist the professional in providing information to parents about their infant's specific physical needs and behavior style. Behaviors evaluated within the autonomic system include regulation of breathing, temperature, posture, and signs of stress in response to environmental events. Signs of stress include tremors, startle response, color changes, yawning, and closing of the eyes. To evaluate the motor system, observation is conducted to assess the child's ability to inhibit random movements and control activity levels. Assessment of muscle tone, activity level, and reflexes is also performed. Reflexes can be grouped into two categories: survival (seeking nourishment and protection) and postural (provide maintenance of upright posture). Survival reflexes assessed with the NBAS include foot reflexes (withdrawal, plantar grasp, ankle clonus, and Babinski), hand reflexes (withdrawal, hand or palmar grasp), and head, face, and mouth reflexes (rooting, sucking, Moro, tonic neck). Postural reflexes assessed include standing, automatic walking. These reflexes are rated on a 3-point scale for low, medium, and high intensity of response and for asymmetry and absence, and can be considered neurological items.

The underlying premise of the assessment of autonomic and motor behavior is that once the infant gains control over these areas, he/she will be able to focus energy on the next developmental task, which is state regulation. Assessment of these states includes observation of the ability to maintain a state, ability to be consoled, and identification of predominant and liability states. There are six states of consciousness that can be observed in infants: deep sleep, REM (active sleep), drowsy, quiet alert, active alert (including fussing), and crying. Once these areas have been assessed, the infant's social interaction is assessed. This is considered the ultimate task in the young infant's development in that social interaction is an indication of the infant's engagement with his/her environment. Increased regulation of the autonomic, motor, and state systems should be observed as the child matures.

Behavioral items are rated on a 9-point scale, with the midpoint of the scale indicating expected behaviors of a 3-day-old normal infant. These behaviors may be observed or elicited.

Assessment includes evaluation of the child's ability to interact with inanimate objects (e.g., ball, bell) and animate stimuli (e.g., evaluator's or mother's voice and face). Other general behaviors that are assessed include degree of alertness, motor maturity, cuddliness, consolability with intervention, peak of excitement, irritability, startle count, self-quieting activity, hand-to-mouth facility, and number of smiles.

The CLNBAS was developed to accomplish two goals: to provide physicians with an assessment instrument that is quicker to administer than the NBAS and to offer an instrument that focuses on key elements that may assist parents in understanding the infant's behavior. In the assessment using this instrument, the parent is involved in the assessment process and, with only 18 behavioral and reflex items to administer, it requires only a few minutes of a physician's time. This instrument is considered to be a "relationship-building tool" for the physician and family, and for the parent and child (Nugent & Brazelton, 2001).

Both the NBAS and the CLNBAS are assessment tools that may be used by researchers and professionals. It offers a description of a newborn's strengths and challenges (or difficulties) that the child faces in adjusting to the extrauterine environment. These assessment instruments can also be used to assess the presence of asymmetries and delays in the four domains and to note the presence of stress in the infant's environment.

See also: Bayley Scales of Infant Development—2nd Edition

BIBLIOGRAPHY

Brazelton, T. B., & Nugent, J. K. (1995). *The Neonatal Behavioral Assessment Scale*. Cambridge, MA: MacKeith.

Nugent, J. K., & Brazelton, T. B. (2001). *The Clinical Newborn Behavioral Assessment Scale*. Cambridge, MA: MacKeith.

Additional Readings for Nonprofessionals

http://www.naeyc.org (National Association for the Education of Young Children)

http://www.zerotothree.org (Zero to Three: National Center for Infants and Families)

Additional Readings for Professionals

Gitlin-Weiner, K., Sandgund, A., & Schaefer, C. E. (2000). *Play diagnosis and assessment*. New York: Wiley.

Linder, T. W. (1993). *Transdisciplinary play-based assessment: A functional approach to working with young children*. Baltimore: Brookes.

Meisels, S. J., & Fenichel, E. (1996). *New visions for the developmental assessment of infants and young children*. Washington, DC: Zero to Three.

CARLEN HENINGTON

Brief Functional Analysis

In 1982, Iwata, Dorsey, Slifer, Bauman, and Richman created a functional analysis methodology for identifying environmental variables that maintain problem behaviors. Functional analysis consists of manipulating environmental events with the purpose of isolating maintaining factors by using various contrived situations, or "conditions." These conditions traditionally have included tests for a behavior's sensitivity to social attention, escape from tasks or demands, and access to preferred tangible items. Also, alone sessions are often conducted to assess the possibility that problem behavior may be maintained by the arousal or reduction of physical sensations associated with the behavior itself. In addition, a control condition is implemented. The behavior observed during control conditions serves as a comparison with the other test conditions. When using functional analysis, behavior analysts have the ability to formulate effective treatments, because they can, to isolate the factors that maintain problem behaviors and use those variables in the treatment. The information provided by functional analyses allows behavior analysts, school psychologists, and other care providers to create interventions that address those specific maintaining variables.

In settings such as outpatient clinics, classrooms, and any of a number of other contexts in which problem behavior is regularly observed, there may exist certain constraints that limit care providers' ability to carry out some functional analysis methodologies. These constraints may be related to the amount of time available for assessment. Although functional analysis has been demonstrated as effective for assessing problem behaviors, some care providers have found it necessary to modify these methodologies in order to utilize them in their respective settings to address time and other constraints.

To utilize functional analysis in settings that are not conducive to the traditional methodology described by Iwata et al. (1982), a modified version called brief functional analysis was developed. Cooper, Wacker, Sasso, Reimers, and Donn (1990) and Northup et al. (1991) modified the functional analysis methodology described in Iwata et al. (1982) to apply functional analysis to their respective outpatient clinics and abbreviated time limits associated with those settings. Brief functional analysis differs from the methods used with "traditional" functional analysis in several ways. First, fewer test conditions are conducted. Instead of testing all potential reinforcers for a problem behavior (e.g., attention, escape, tangibles, alone, etc.), emphasis is placed on potential reinforcers to test through reports provided by parents, teachers, and other care providers prior to the assessment (Derby et al., 1992). By ruling out variables that have never been associated with the target behavior, fewer conditions need to be tested in the analysis. Second, single data points are collected for each condition instead of the several data points used with traditional functional analysis. Third, conditions containing the highest and lowest rates of problem behavior are repeated to provide additional verification of the information provided in the single data point for each condition. Finally, after the condition containing the highest level of problem behavior has been identified, a contingency reversal is implemented. A contingency reversal allows the behavior analyst to assess problem behavior when an appropriate behavior leads to the reinforcer and the target behavior is on extinction. In other words, the contingency for reinforcement is reversed from the demonstration of the target (problem) behavior to an appropriate behavior leading to reinforcement. If an alternative (appropriate) response can be taught to replace the problem behavior, the motivation to engage in that problem behavior should decrease along with the level of that problem behavior. This additional test also serves as a brief treatment probe. For example, in an attention condition, a therapist delivers attention following the demonstration of a target (problem) behavior. During a contingency reversal for an attention condition, the therapist would deliver attention for an appropriate behavior and not for the targeted problem behavior. It is important to note that communicative responses can serve as the appropriate behavior.

Through ruling out conditions that do not need to be presented, presenting fewer sessions of the conditions that are included in the analysis, and by using a contingency reversal, the maintaining variables of a target behavior can be identified in a fewer number of sessions than with using a traditional approach. Another modification involves the length of the sessions themselves. Often, during brief functional analyses, the individual session durations are as short as 5 minutes in length—much shorter than the 15 minutes described by Iwata et al. (1982).

Although brief functional analyses have been demonstrated as effective in a large number of cases and with a variety of populations, it should not be assumed that they are *more* effective than the traditional methodology (Derby et al., 1992). However, when compared to indirect measures such as checklists and surveys, it is believed that brief functional analyses more effectively identify the maintaining factors for problem behavior (Derby et al., 1992). Limitations of the brief functional analysis model include not presenting a test condition in the analysis that may contain a reinforcer for the target behavior, making decisions on the basis of an initially elevated level of behavior in a condition that does not contain the actual reinforcer for the target behavior, and the potential for inconclusive results if no condition is elevated from the others in the initial series in which they are presented.

See also: Extinction; Functional Analysis; Functional Behavioral Assessment

BIBLIOGRAPHY

Cooper, L. J., Wacker, D. P., Sasso, G. M., Reimers, T. M., & Donn, L. K. (1990). Using parents as therapists to evaluate appropriate behavior of their children: Application to a tertiary diagnostic clinic. *Journal of Applied Behavior Analysis, 23*, 285–296.

Derby, K. M., Wacker, D. P., Sasso, G., Steege, M., Northup, J., Cigrand, K., et al. (1992). Brief functional assessments techniques to evaluate aberrant behavior in an outpatient setting: A summary of 79 cases. *Journal of Applied Behavior Analysis, 25*, 713–721.

Iwata, B. A., Dorsey, M. F., Slifer, K. J., Bauman, K. E., & Richman, G. S. (1994). Toward a functional analysis of self-injury. *Journal of Applied Behavior Analysis, 27*, 197–209.

Northup, J., Wacker, D., Sasso, G., Steege, M., Cigrand, K., Cook, J., et al. (1991). A brief functional analysis of aggressive and alternative behavior in an outclinic setting. *Journal of Applied Behavior Analysis, 24*, 509–522.

MICHAEL M. MUELLER
TERRY S. FALCOMATA

Bulimia Nervosa

Although ravenous overeating has been reported since the Roman Empire, overeating followed by vomiting is an aberrant pattern of behavior that was first recognized as a psychiatric syndrome in 1979 (Russell, 1979). The results of studies conducted since the late 1970s have led to a better understanding and more specific classification of bulimia nervosa, an eating disorder characterized by an excessive concern with body size, binge eating, and inappropriate compensatory behaviors. The most common compensatory behavior used to avoid weight gain after a binge is self-induced vomiting. However, other techniques such as excessive exercise, fasting, laxative use, enemas, and diuretics may be used by themselves or in combination with vomiting (American Psychiatric Association, 1994). People who binge and purge using vomiting, laxative, diuretics, or enemas are classified as bulimia nervosa, purging type. Those who solely use fasting and excessive exercise as compensatory behaviors are classified as bulimia nervosa, nonpurging type. It is estimated that approximately 1–3 percent of adolescent and young adult women have bulimia nervosa at some point in their lifetime (American Psychiatric Association, 1994). Bulimia in males is uncommon, making up approximately 10 percent of all cases.

DEVELOPMENT OF BULIMIA NERVOSA

Many psychosocial factors can contribute to the development of bulimia nervosa. The media's portrayal of an increasingly thin ideal body size, coupled with the increased incidence of this condition in the late twentieth century, suggests that societal influences may promote the adoption of a thin ideal body shape that contributes to the development of bulimia nervosa. Although the environment undoubtedly has opened the door to the pursuit of a thinness-at-all-costs attitude, cognitive factors help explain why some individuals develop eating disorders whereas others do not.

Cognitive theories suggest that in response to body dissatisfaction, many individuals develop biased ways of thinking about their body shape and food. Research has supported this cognitive theory by demonstrating that individuals with eating disorders have attentional, memory, and judgment biases for concepts related to fatness (Williamson, Muller, Reas, & Thaw, 1999). The net result of biased thinking is obsessional thoughts about weight and body size, which motivates restrictive eating. When restrictive eating can no longer be maintained, because of hunger or other factors, overeating or binge eating results. This overeating or binge eating leads to guilt and increased anxiety associated with body size and fear of fatness. To decrease this anxiety, the individual engages in unhealthy compensatory mechanisms, such as self-induced vomiting. The longer the cycle of dietary restriction, binge eating, and vomiting continues, the more difficult it is to break.

Other factors such as depression and stressful life events can also contribute to and may strengthen the cycle of bulimic behaviors. Binge eating may serve as a way to escape negative feelings by consuming pleasurable foods. It is theorized that this escape from negative emotions leads to a loss of inhibitions and consequently to binge eating (Heatherton & Baumeister, 1991).

BULIMIA NERVOSA COMPARED TO OTHER EATING DISORDERS

According to the *Diagnostic and Statistical Manual of Mental Disorders* (4th ed.) (*DSM-IV*), bulimia nervosa has characteristics that distinguish it from anorexia nervosa and binge eating disorder (BED). Anorexia nervosa and bulimia nervosa differ in respect to body weight. The majority of women diagnosed with bulimia nervosa are normal weight and often have regular menses, whereas the diagnosis of anorexia nervosa is characterized by amenorrhea (the absence of menstrual periods) and being 85 percent or less of ideal body weight. BED differs from bulimia nervosa primarily by the lack of compensatory behaviors after a binge. In addition, individuals with BED tend to be obese.

WARNING SIGNS OF BULIMIA NERVOSA

A person can suffer from bulimia nervosa secretly because body weight may remain within a normal range. However, on closer examination most bulimics engage in predictable behaviors or display warning signs of their disorder. Of note is the disappearance of large amounts of food in short periods of time. Empty wrappers and containers of hidden food are often found in rooms or households of bulimics. Bulimics may "go to the bathroom" after eating to purge and may engage in excessive exercise with little regard to weather conditions, time of day, or physical injuries. The commitment to binge eating and compensatory behaviors and/or the depression associated with bulimia nervosa may lead to social isolation or withdrawal from usual activities or relationships. Physical signs of bulimia nervosa include calluses on the back of the hand (from using a finger to repeatedly induce vomiting), swelling of the parotid glands (in the cheek and jaw area), erosion of tooth enamel, and relatively large short-term fluctuations in weight. Medical complications such as heart arrhythmias can occur as a result of mineral imbalances related to vomiting or other compensatory behaviors.

TREATMENT

Research has shown that two methods of psychotherapy, cognitive behavioral therapy (CBT) and interpersonal therapy (IPT), are effective treatments for bulimia nervosa (Fairburn & Brownell, 2002). Most treatment for bulimia nervosa is conducted using outpatient therapy. CBT focuses on modifying disturbed eating behavior and the thoughts associated with body size, dieting, and so on. The behavioral component of CBT includes self-monitoring of what, how much, when, and where food was eaten, along with reports of compensatory behaviors or urges to binge or purge. Another behavioral technique of CBT is exposure with response prevention (ERP) (Williamson et al., 1999). Many bulimics progress to the point of rarely eating without subsequent purging. To prevent this occurrence, ERP can be implemented by having patients consume meals followed by relaxation in an environment that prevents them from being alone and engaging in compensatory behaviors.

The cognitive component of CBT works in conjunction with the behavioral components to help the patient restructure irrational or dysfunctional thoughts, expectancies, and beliefs. The process includes identification of the thoughts, challenging the thoughts, and then restating the thoughts in a more functional and rational manner. CBT is often used as a technique in helping bulimic patients improve body image and decrease their beliefs that self-worth is based on their body size and shape. CBT is commonly integrated with treatment from a registered dietitian. A dietitian can help the patient set up an appropriate meal plan and educate the patient on the concepts of healthy eating.

In contrast to CBT, IPT does not directly focus on eating and weight concerns. Instead, the goal of IPT is to change the social context in which the eating disorder developed and is maintained. Treatment emphasizes improved social functioning through grief management, resolving interpersonal disputes, dealing with role transitions, and improving interpersonal deficits.

Pharmacotherapy is another effective treatment for bulimia nervosa. Studies have shown that monoamine oxidase inhibitors (MAOIs), tricyclic antidepressants (TCAs), and selective serotonin reuptake inhibitors (SSRIs) can decrease bulimic behaviors (Garner & Garfinkel, 1997). However, in recent years, SSRIs are most commonly prescribed because of their efficacy and lack of side effects compared with MAOIs and TCAs. It was once thought that these medications were effective because they improved depression, which in turn led to reduced binge eating and purging. However, recent research has shown that the effectiveness of SSRIs is not due to their impact on depression but instead on their ability to decrease urges to engage in the binge–purge cycle of bulimia.

On average, 8 weeks of antidepressant treatment yields approximately a 70 percent decrease in binge eating and purging, regardless of initial level of depression (Garner & Garfinkel, 1997). Although SSRIs can be an effective short-term treatment, relapse rates after 6 months (without psychotherapy) may be as high as 45 percent. Because of this high relapse rate, medication without psychotherapy is not recommended. Research has shown that CBT is a more effective treatment than medication alone, and adding medication to CBT has modest additional benefits.

If an individual is suspected of having an eating disorder, a medical and psychological evaluation is recommended. As a result of these evaluations, the most effective medical and psychological intervention can be implemented. Bulimic patients should seek treatment in a structured program or participate in psychotherapy that utilizes empirically grounded treatments such as CBT or IPT. Different levels of care are often required for bulimics depending on the severity of the condition (Williamson, Zucker, Martin, & Smeets, 2001). Inpatient hospitalization is appropriate in severe cases, whereas a partial hospitalization or intensive outpatient program is often utilized with patients who are medically stable but still require intensive structure and treatment. Traditional outpatient therapy may be appropriate for individuals who have progressed through more intensive stages of treatment or are just beginning to show signs of developing an eating disorder.

See also: Anorexia Nervosa; Body Image

BIBLIOGRAPHY

American Psychiatric Association. (1994). *Diagnostic and statistical manual of mental disorders* (4th ed.). Washington, DC: Author.
Fairburn, C. G., & Brownell, K. D. (Eds.). (2002). *Eating disorders and obesity* (2nd ed.). New York: Guilford.
Garner, D. M., & Garfinkel, P. E. (Eds.). (1997). *Handbook of treatment for eating disorders* (2nd ed.). New York: Guilford.

Heatherton, T. F., & Baumeister, R. F. (1991). Binge eating as escape from self-awareness. *Psychological Bulletin, 110*, 86–108.

Russell, G. F. M. (1979). Bulimia nervosa: An ominous variant of anorexia nervosa. *Psychological Medicine, 9*, 429–448.

Williamson, D. A., Muller, S. L., Reas, D. L., & Thaw, J. M. (1999). Cognitive bias in eating disorders: Implications for theory and treatment. *Behavior Modification, 23*, 556–577.

Williamson, D. A., Zucker, N. L., Martin, C. K., & Smeets, M. A. M. (2001). Etiology and management of eating disorders. In P. B. Sutker & H. E. Adams (Eds.), *Comprehensive handbook of psychopathology* (3rd ed., pp. 641–667). New York: Academic/Plenum.

Additional Readings for Nonprofessionals

Fairburn, C. G., & Wilson, G. T. (Eds.). (1993). *Binge eating: Nature assessment and treatment.* New York: Guilford.

Siegel, M., Brisman, J., & Weinshel, M. (1997). *Surviving an eating disorder: Strategies for family and friends.* New York: HarperPerennial.

Additional Reading for Professionals

Wilfley, D. E., Dounchis, J. Z., & Welch R. R. (2000). Interpersonal psychotherapy. In K. J. Miller & J. S. Mizes (Eds.), *Comparative treatments for eating disorders* (pp. 129–159). New York: Springer.

Donald A. Williamson
David B. Creel

Bullying

Bullying occurs when an individual or group of individuals repeatedly subjects an individual or group of individuals to negative acts including physical violence, verbal assault, obscene gestures, and intentional exclusion (Olweus, 1993). Bullying by boys typically involves physical aggression (e.g., hitting, pushing), whereas bullying by girls tends to be verbal in nature (e.g., verbal manipulation, spreading rumors). Bullying is most likely to occur in areas where there is little adult supervision and a diminished likelihood of being caught (e.g., school bathroom, bus stop).

There are, in general, two types of bullying: overt and covert. Overt bullies do so in plain view of others and often dare, either directly or implicitly, others to intervene on behalf of the victim. Research on characteristics of overt bullies indicated that they generally have less social skills than bullies who are covert, are loud, obnoxious, and frequently use physical or verbal assault as a means of bullying. Covert bullies, on the other hand, tend to be more socially skilled and are often popular among a larger population of their peers. Adults generally like them as well because of their seeming polite demeanor. For obvious reasons, covert bullying is more difficult to detect, monitor, and treat. Covert bullies tend to use exclusion, rumors, and manipulation as bullying tactics.

BULLIES AND THEIR VICTIMS

Research indicates that bullies tend to come from homes in which corporal punishment is frequently used and the parents use an authoritarian style of parenting. They are typically defiant and ignore school rules. Bullying peaks in grades 6 through 8 but occurs in all grades (Nansel et al., 2001). When considering the various ethnic groups, research has suggested that Hispanics reported bullying others slightly more than Caucasians or African Americans. Other studies have found African Americans to be more aggressive than other ethnic groups. Still other studies have found little to no ethnic differences in either bullying or victimization rates between Asians, Hispanics, Caucasians, or African Americans. Bullying is as likely to occur among children attending small rural schools as children attending medium- to large-size urban or suburban schools. Bullies operate under the premise that others will not intervene with bullying. A recent study seems to confirm the accuracy of this premise, as teachers intervened in only 4 percent of reported bullying incidents (Craig & Pepler, 1997).

Numerous surveys of school-aged children have found that about 20–30 percent of children report being bullied. Boys are more likely than girls to be the victims of bullies. The victims are generally physically smaller than the bully, shy, withdrawn, and have a very small circle of friends. Victims of bullying tend to respond rather passively by either withdrawing or crying. Victims often blame themselves for being bullied and separate from their peer group, resulting in feelings of isolation and loneliness. They often become fearful of the school environment and sometimes bring weapons to school to protect themselves from being bullied, leading to further escalations in violence. Unfortunately, victims of bullies sometimes turn to bullying by finding children younger or smaller than themselves, which perpetuates the cycle of this type of violence in schools.

Peers of those who have been victimized by bullying often blame the victim and sometimes respond with aggression toward the victim, thus compounding the negative effects of the bullying. Victims often report feelings of vengefulness and anger after a bullying incident, feelings that may persist long after the bullying has subsided. In fact, students who have committed heinous acts of violence on school campus (e.g., Jonesboro, AR; Paducah, KY; Pearl, MS) were the victims of repeated bullying from an early age.

COMORBIDITY IN BULLIES AND VICTIMS

Bullying is rarely an isolated problematic behavior. That is, children who engage in bullying are likely having difficulty in other areas as well. For instance, studies have found that bullies are more likely to be "angry" and generally aggressive than their peers who do not bully are. Depression has also been found at high rates, not only in the victims of bullying but in the bullies as well. In fact, those who have been victimized and then engaged in bullying have the highest risk of depression and suicidal ideation. There also appears to be a relationship between elevated levels of anxiety and being victimized by bullies, although this link is not completely understood. For victims with increased anxiety, this might lead to somatic complaints (headache, stomachache), school refusal, higher rates of absenteeism, and other types of school avoidant behavior.

INTERVENTIONS FOR BULLYING

Because of the seriousness and scope of bullying, a number of formal programs have been implemented to reduce bullying in schools. However, there is a frightening lack of research on effective bullying prevention programs. Because of the large number of different antibullying efforts, only those that are most commonly used will be discussed here.

Apart from specific programs, there are a number of common components that should be part of any antibullying package. First and foremost, antibullying efforts should primarily be preventive rather than reactive. Second, the major focus should be on changing the ecology of the school environment as opposed to addressing the behavior of selected individuals. Third, the antibullying effort should be a formal part of the school administrative agenda, with a committee that meets regularly and whose purpose is to reduce/eliminate bullying. Fourth, members of the committee must include students as well as faculty, staff, and parents. Fifth, committee members should receive formal training in antibullying techniques/programs. Sixth, there should be some mechanism in place for bullying to be anonymously reported, to avoid retaliation against reporters of bullying incidents. Seventh, aversive procedures should not be used in response to bullying incidents because they tend to result in increased aggression without decreases in bullying. Eighth, an evaluation should be conducted at least yearly to determine the effectiveness of the antibullying efforts.

Student-Based Problem Solving

Kenney and Watson (1998) were the first to use a student-based problem-solving model to address problems of crime and violence on school campuses. In brief, work groups of students and a teacher were taught to use a four-step problem-solving model to address problems of crime, including bullying, on their school campus. After implementing the program for 1 year, reductions in all types of school crime and bullying, fear of crime among students and teachers, and increased feelings of empowerment were noted. The program was deemed a model program by the Department of Justice, which subsequently initiated a 20 million dollar grant program to replicate the program in schools across the country.

Crime Prevention through Environmental Design (CPTED)

CPTED is a simple concept that has been implemented in communities nationwide and has been largely successful. The idea behind CPTED is to identify those elements in the environment that make bullying "easier" or that provide a "good place to bully" and change them in some meaningful way. For instance, if a far corner of the playground is where a great deal of bullying occurs, then a bench may be installed in that area so that teachers can relax during recess yet provide the adult presence that is known to suppress bullying.

Students against Violence Everywhere (SAVE)

The SAVE program incorporates many of the essential elements of effective programs discussed above. Students are the nucleus of a team that meets regularly to plan for school improvement and to address safety and crime issues on campus. Peer mediators who are trained to deal with student–student conflicts are an integral component of the SAVE program. School resource officers are available not only to enforce laws and provide certain types of crisis intervention, but also to mentor students and participate in rule enforcement. Preliminary evaluations of the SAVE program have provided mostly positive results.

Skillstreaming

Skillstreaming is a package of social skills training techniques and activities that teaches social skills to both bullies and victims, primarily through role-play, modeling, imitation, and feedback. The basis for this type of program is twofold: (1) that victims do not evidence the proper skills that make future bullying incidents less likely and (2) bullies need other, more appropriate skills to use in place of aggression and hostility. This is a well-researched package that has been found to reduce many types of aggressive behavior, including bullying. Although effective for teaching social skills and enabling students to label prosocial behavior, skillstreaming has not been shown to reduce bullying.

Peer-Influenced

A number of different interventions fall under this heading and include peer pressure, peer mentoring, peer mediation, peer pairing, peer empathy, and peer support. The common element in each of these programs is the use of peers to influence the behavior of the bully and to prompt them to engage in more appropriate, less aggressive behaviors. Although these types of programs are extremely popular, there is scant evidence of their effectiveness and is mostly based on teacher perceptions and not direct bullying data.

Target Hardening

Target hardening is extremely popular among school officials and parents. In brief, target hardening refers to such measures as installing security cameras, locking doors and windows, and installing metal detectors. The rationale behind target hardening is that these measures make the target environment one in which it is more difficult or "harder" to commit acts of violence. Although popular, target hardening has not been shown to positively affect violence or bullying and, in fact, may increase fear of the educational environment (Kenney & Watson, 1998).

Many of the antibullying programs suffer from methodological issues ranging from simply not collecting outcome data to poor research design. Given the large numbers of children who report being bullied and the problems caused not only to the victims but also to the bully, the school, and the community, it is important for schools to seriously implement and evaluate antibullying efforts. If antibullying programs are not a part of every school, then teachers, parents, and students themselves should demand a systematic, committed effort aimed at reducing, and eventually eliminating, bullying.

See also: Crisis Intervention; Peer Mediation; Social Skills Building for Adolescents; Social Skills Building for Elementary Children

BIBLIOGRAPHY

Craig, W. M., & Pepler, D. J. (1997). Observations of bullying and victimization in the schoolyard. *Canadian Journal of School Psychology, 13,* 41–59.

Kenney, D. J., & Watson, T. S. (1998). *Crime in the schools: Reducing disorder and disruption using student-based problem-solving.* Washington, DC: Police Executive Research Forum.

Nansel, T. R., Overpeck, M., Pilla, R. S., Ruan, W. J., Simons-Morton, B., & Scheidt, P. (2001). Bullying behaviors among US youth—Prevalence and association with psychosocial adjustment. *Journal of the American Medical Association, 285,* 2094–2100.

Olweus, D. (1993). *Bullying at school: What we know and what we can do.* Cambridge, MA: Blackwell.

Additional Readings for Professionals and Nonprofessionals

Batsche, G. M. (1997). Bullying. In G. G. Bear, K. M. Minke, & A. Thomas (Eds.), *Children's needs. II: Development, problems, and alternatives* (pp. 171–179). Bethesda, MD: National Association of School Psychologists.

Bullying prevention and intervention: Integrating research and evaluation findings [Mini-series]. (2003). *School Psychology Review, 32,* 365–470.

Cohn, A., & Canter, S. (2003). *Bullying: Facts for schools and parents.* Retrieved October 24, 2003, from http://www.naspcenter.org/factsheets/bullying_fs.html

Garrity, C., Jens, K., Porter, W., Sager, N., & Short-Camilli, C. (1994). *Bully-proofing your school.* Longmont, CO: Sopris West.

http://www.nwrel.org/safe (National Resource Center for Safe Schools)

T. STEUART WATSON

Cc

Classwide Peer Tutoring

Classwide Peer Tutoring (CWPT) (Greenwood, Delquadri, & Carta, 1997) is an instructional program designed to involve all students within a single classroom in the repeated practice of academic skills. By providing students with frequent opportunities to accurately practice skills (e.g., spelling words, solving math facts, or reading sentences), students acquire proficiency more readily and thereby increase their learning in less time (Greenwood, Maheady, & Delquadri, 2002). Charles Greenwood and his colleagues developed CWPT in the early 1980s for two reasons: (1) to support the inclusion of students with diverse abilities within the general education classroom and (2) to increase at-risk students' involvement in learning. Greenwood and his colleagues at Juniper Gardens Children's Project in Kansas City, Kansas, had observed that students in local Title I schools participated at low levels during traditional, whole-group instruction (Greenwood et al., 2002). By training students to monitor their peers' practice of skills, CWPT affords students 2 to 3 times the amount of practice typically provided within traditional instruction, maximizing time on task and increasing academic performance (Greenwood et al., 1997).

When used in the elementary classroom, CWPT does not replace instruction; rather, it supports instruction, typically taking the place of independent or small-group practice of basic skills (Greenwood et al., 2002). CWPT is designed to be used with the existing curriculum and, therefore, requires no additional cost. The only requisite materials include a kitchen timer, reproducible student handouts, and overhead transparencies for demonstration purposes during training (Greenwood et al., 1997). Students typically participate in CWPT a minimum of 4 days per week for 30 minutes per day. On the 5th day, mastery of the prior week's content is assessed and the subsequent week's material is introduced (Greenwood et al., 1997).

CWPT is generally implemented within the classroom gradually, beginning with one content area, spelling, and then adding math and finally reading (Greenwood et al., 1997). A list of items to be practiced is identified, typically including 10 to 30 items, of which the class is able to correctly answer less than 50 percent on average when pretested (Arreaga-Mayer, Terry, & Greenwood, 1998). This low percentage ensures adequate opportunity for growth from pretesting to posttesting. The length of the list should allow the lowest performing student to be able to practice each item on the list twice during a 10-minute period (Greenwood et al., 1997).

When using CWPT for spelling or math, the teacher randomly assigns students within the classroom to tutoring pairs weekly. For both spelling and math, the correct answers are provided, allowing tutors to check tutees' responses for accuracy (Greenwood et al., 2002). The students are instructed in the procedures for implementing CWPT in four sessions. During these sessions, the procedures are explained, modeled, and role-played within the classroom (Arreaga-Mayer et al., 1998). Practice includes students' moving to their tutoring partner, tutoring, and reporting points earned. The timer is set for 10 minutes, and one student tutors by providing a word to spell or a math fact to solve. The tutee responds by saying and writing the correct spelling or math response. The tutor immediately evaluates the answer and awards two points for a correct response, similar to points earned for accurately shooting baskets in basketball. If the tutee spells the word incorrectly or provides the wrong answer to the math problem, the tutor immediately corrects the error and encourages the tutee to correct the response by awarding one point for corrected responses. This is similar to points earned in basketball for making a foul shot. To correct an error, the tutor spells the word or provides the correct math response and the tutee writes it correctly three times. The teacher monitors the activity of the tutoring pairs and awards 1 to 5 bonus points to the tutor and tutee for completing their roles competently. The students alternate between roles during the tutoring session, so that each student assumes and benefits from both roles. The timer is then reset for 10 minutes. The teacher's monitoring and awarding of bonus points is essential to ensure that students perform their roles accurately without misrepresenting the number of points they have earned (Greenwood et al., 1997).

The tutoring pairs comprise two teams in the classroom, and these two teams compete for points and peer recognition (e.g., praise, applause; Greenwood et al., 2002). Because both members of the pair are on the same team, they work cooperatively to contribute points to their team, which is in competition with the opposing team (Arreaga-Mayer et al., 1998). The teacher posts individual and team points daily. The points are summed for each team, and the winning team is announced daily and weekly. Both the winning team and the losing team are praised for their efforts (Greenwood et al., 1997). Individual progress is assessed weekly through comparison of pretest to posttest results in spelling and math. If the class obtains an average of 80 percent correct on the posttest, the material is considered mastered (Arreaga-Mayer et al., 1998).

When implementing CWPT with reading, some procedural differences exist. The teacher divides the selected story from the basal text into four equivalent passages to be used during CWPT sessions. The length of the passage should allow the lowest ability reader to be able to read it twice within a 10-minute session (i.e., approximately 100 words; Greenwood et al., 1997, 2002). Students should be able to read 50 to 80 percent of the words correctly at pretest and read 80 percent or more of the words at posttest. Because not every student's reading ability can be assessed weekly, five students are chosen to be assessed (i.e., three students with low reading skills and two students with average skills). Students are asked to read for 1 minute, and both the percentage of words read correctly and percentage of comprehension questions answered correctly are determined (Greenwood et al., 1997).

When assigning pairs for reading, ability matching is generally recommended (Arreaga-Mayer et al., 1998). Thus, students are randomly assigned to partners within the same reading level. For lower ability students, pairing them with higher ability students will ensure that more errors are detected. In addition, by having the higher ability student read first, this student could preview the passage for the lower ability student (Greenwood et al., 1997).

During CWPT with reading, the timer is set for 10 minutes, and students are awarded two points for correctly reading each sentence. Tutors provide immediate feedback regarding the accuracy of their reading. When an error is made, the tutor pronounces the word correctly, and the tutee rereads the entire sentence correctly. One point is awarded for correctly rereading the sentence. After 10 minutes have expired, the timer is reset for 5 minutes, and the tutor asks the tutee questions to assess his/her comprehension of the passage. Two points are awarded for correctly answered questions. At the end of 5 minutes, the roles are reversed and the timer is reset to 10 minutes. The goal of CWPT with reading is to increase students' reading fluency or their ability to read quickly and accurately (Greenwood et al., 1997).

Research has repeatedly demonstrated that CWPT improves the academic performance of elementary through secondary students with and without disabilities, including students with learning disabilities and behavioral disorders, as well as English Language Learners (ELLs) (Arreaga-Mayer et al., 1998; Greenwood et al., 1997). The use of CWPT has also led to decreases in disruptive behaviors and increases in positive social interactions with peers (Greenwood et al., 1997). CWPT has been applied across academic subject areas and target behaviors including oral reading, spelling, mathematics, and social studies (Arreaga-Mayer et al., 1998). A 12-year longitudinal follow-up study of students who participated in CWPT for 4 years indicates that CWPT can help improve long-term educational outcomes for students as indicated by achievement on standardized tests, placement in special education programs, and dropout rates in high school (Arreaga-Mayer et al., 1998).

See also: Group Contingencies; Inclusion

BIBLIOGRAPHY

Arreaga-Mayer, C., Terry, B. J., & Greenwood, C. R. (1998). Classwide peer tutoring. In K. Topping & S. Ehly (Eds.), *Peer-assisted learning* (pp. 105–120). Mahwah, NJ: Erlbaum.

Greenwood, C. R., Delquadri, J. C., & Carta, J. J. (1997). *Together we can! Classwide peer tutoring to improve basic academic skills.* Longmont, CO: Sopris West.

Greenwood, C. R., Maheady, L., & Delquadri (2002). Classwide peer tutoring programs. In M. R. Shinn, H. M. Walker, & G. Stoner (Eds.), *Interventions for achievement and behavior problems II: Preventive and remedial approaches* (pp. 611–650). Bethesda, MD: National Association of School Psychologists.

Additional Reading for Nonprofessionals

Slavin, R. E. (2000). *Educational psychology: Theory and practice* (6th ed.). Boston: Allyn & Bacon.

Additional Readings for Professionals

Greenwood, C. R., Delquadri, J., & Hall, R. V. (1984). Opportunity to respond and student academic performance. In W. L. Heward, T. E. Heron, J. Trap-Porter, & D. S. Hill (Eds.), *Focus on behavior analysis in education* (pp. 58–88). Columbus, OH: Merrill.

Greenwood, C. R., Terry, B., Arreaga-Mayer, C., & Finney, R. (1992). The classwide peer tutoring program: Implementation factors moderating students' achievement. *Journal of Applied Behavior Analysis, 25*, 101–116.

Christine E. Neddenriep

Cleft Lip and Palate

A cleft is a separation or gap in the tissues of the lip and palate. Cleft lip and palate, also known as oral–facial cleft, is estimated to affect 1 in 700 to 900 children, and is currently the fourth most common birth defect (congenital defect). It is possible to have a cleft lip alone, a cleft palate alone, or a combination cleft lip and palate—because the lip and palate develop separately. In addition, the cleft lip and/or palate may present as unilateral (separation above one side of the lip) or bilateral (separation above both sides of the lip). It has been estimated that from 1 to 5 percent of children with cleft lip and/or palate have an associated syndrome, and approximately 150 to 300 syndromes have been identified as accompanying clefting conditions (Edmondson & Reinhartsen, 1998). Identifying associated syndromes or abnormalities is essential to the determination of treatment (Fiorello, Wright, & Mason, 1998).

Cleft lip and palate present more often in males, whereas females appear to be affected more by cleft palate alone (Edmondson & Reinhartsen, 1998). The incidence of cleft lip and palate is reportedly highest among Native Americans compared with other racial groups such as Asians, Caucasians, and African Americans.

DEVELOPMENT OF CLEFT LIP AND PALATE

The lip and palate develop approximately during the 4th and 8th weeks of conception (Edmondson & Reinhartsen, 1998). The formation of these facial features includes the joining of parts that begin as "openings" during the gestation period. Normal fetal development involves the closing of these elements in the 8th to 10th week of pregnancy. It is the failure to close or join during facial development (Speltz, Endriga, Fisher, & Mason, 1997) that results in the separation of the lip, the roof of the mouth, or the soft tissue in the back of the mouth, otherwise known as a cleft (Edmondson & Reinhartsen, 1998).

CAUSES OF CLEFT LIP AND PALATE

The causes of cleft lip and palate are currently attributed to a combination of genetic and environmental factors (Edmondson & Reinhartsen, 1998). It has been suggested that nonhereditary factors such as drugs, infections, and nutritional deficiencies (i.e., folic acid) are possible explanations for the basis of cleft lip and palate (March of Dimes Birth Defects Foundation, 2001). The recurrence rate of clefting in subsequent children varies according to factors such as the number of parents and/or children previously affected and the severity of the cleft (Edmondson & Reinhartsen, 1998).

PROBLEMS AND CONCERNS

The child with cleft lip and palate may have a wide range of problems and concerns, depending on the seriousness of the cleft. Concerns may exist about feeding, oral motor development, speech, dental needs, frequent fluid in the ears and hearing loss, and psychosocial development. There may also be additional problems or concerns related to the presence of associated syndromes affecting the child. Consultation with a genetic specialist will be important in obtaining a diagnosis and information about the associated syndrome.

In the school-age child, cleft lip and palate are often associated with speech and language difficulties and hearing loss. In addition, the child is at risk for language delays and language-based learning disabilities (Richman, Eliason, & Lindgren, 1988). Information on the behavioral effects of cleft lip and palate is more mixed; there may be an increase in internalizing behavior (anxiety, depression, and withdrawal) in girls as they approach adolescence, whereas boys show only slight elevations in internalizing behavior (Richman & Millard, 1997). Externalizing behavior (conduct problems) are more severe for young boys, but decrease as boys get older, whereas girls have significantly more difficulty in early adolescence than same-age girls (Richman & Millard, 1997).

TREATMENT

Children born with cleft lip and/or palate should be evaluated as soon as possible after birth. A transdisciplinary team approach is best because of the wide range of difficulties the child may face. In addition to medical and dental specialists, the team may include a speech/language pathologist, audiologist, social worker, and psychologist.

The parents of a child with cleft lip and/or palate should contact the school system to find out about obtaining appropriate services before the child turns 3. The school will have its own multidisciplinary team, including the school psychologist, speech/language pathologist, teachers, and other professionals as needed. The parent is always a part of this team as well. This team will review any medical information provided, and will conduct any additional evaluations that are needed to establish eligibility for special education services. School treatment should address both the academic and social needs of the child with cleft lip and/or palate, and may include speech/language therapy, hearing-impaired services, learning disabilities services, and individual or group counseling.

BIBLIOGRAPHY

Edmondson, R., & Reinhartsen, D. (1998). The young child with cleft lip and palate: Intervention needs in the first three years. *Infants and Young Children, 11*(2), 12–20.

Fiorello, C. A., Wright, L. B., & Mason, E. J. (1998). Cleft lip and palate. In L. Phelps (Ed.), *Health-related disorders in children and adolescents.* Washington, DC: American Psychological Association.

March of Dimes Birth Defects Foundation. (2001). *Public Health Education Information Sheet: Cleft lip and palate.* Retrieved September 10, 2002, from www.marchofdimes.com

Richman, L. C., Eliason, M. J., & Lindgren, S. D. (1988). Reading disability in children with clefts. *Cleft Palate Journal, 25,* 21–25.

Richman, L. C., & Millard, T. (1997). Brief report: Cleft lip and palate: Longitudinal behavior and relationships of cleft conditions to behavior and achievement. *Journal of Pediatric Psychology, 22,* 487–494.

Speltz, M. L., Endriga, M. C., Fisher, P. A., & Mason, C. A. (1997). Early predictors of attachment in infants with cleft lip and/or palate. *Child Development, 68*(1), 12–25.

Additional Readings for Nonprofessionals

Edmondson, R., & Reinhartsen, D. (1998). The young child with cleft lip and palate: Intervention needs in the first three years. *Infants and Young Children, 11*(2), 12–20.

www.marchofdimes.com

www.widesmiles.org

Additional Readings for Professionals

Edmondson, R., & Reinhartsen, D. (1998). The young child with cleft lip and palate: Intervention needs in the first three years. *Infants and Young Children, 11*(2), 12–20.

Fiorello, C. A., Wright, L. B, & Mason, E. J. (1998). Cleft lip and palate. In L. Phelps (Ed.), *Health-related disorders in children and adolescents.* Washington, DC: American Psychological Association.

Catherine A. Fiorello
Anisha Kurian-Philip

Cognitive Development

School psychologists, teachers, and other school personnel should be aware of the cognitive development of children from birth through various school ages. We need to be able to recognize signs of typical and atypical cognitive development and make recommendations for interventions as necessary.

JEAN PIAGET'S THEORY OF COGNITIVE DEVELOPMENT

Jean Piaget's stage theory is the most comprehensive theory of cognitive development in the field of psychology. This theory is present in practically every developmental textbook on the market in the United States today. Although Piaget began publishing his ideas in the 1920s, they did not begin to have an impact on American researchers until the 1950s. Because his theory was based mostly on systematic observation, it had been viewed as unscientific and scientists were reluctant to adopt it. Much of Piaget's research came from interviewing his own and others' children and probing the children for the reasoning behind their correct and incorrect responses (McDevitt & Ormrod, 2002).

The basis of Piaget's theory of cognitive development is that children learn by mentally organizing stimuli into *schemes* or groups of similar thoughts or actions (McDevitt & Ormrod, 2002). Initially, these schemes are concrete, but as children mature, they become able to create schemes that are increasingly mental and abstract. Children eventually organize schemes into larger systems of mental processes or *operations* (Piaget, 1973). Piaget used the term *operation* synonymously with *logic*, indicating that with age, children begin to think in increasingly logical ways.

Other important Piagetian terms are *assimilation* and *accommodation* (Piaget, 1973). These terms relate to the way we mentally organize new experiences. We assimilate information when we categorize it under our existing schemes. The new information is similar enough to a past experience that we are able to fit into an existing scheme. When we encounter a new experience that is too different to fit into an existing scheme, we must accommodate. Accommodation occurs when we must either alter an existing scheme or create an entirely new scheme within which to categorize the new information. Because assimilation requires less cognitive work, we attempt to assimilate new experiences first. Only when this does not work do we accommodate these experiences. Because accommodation leads to increased categories of information, it is more crucial to learning and cognitive development than is assimilation (McDevitt & Ormrod, 2002).

STAGES OF COGNITIVE DEVELOPMENT

Piaget believed that thinking is qualitatively different at different age levels. He identified four stages of cognitive development, each with defining characteristics or abilities (Piaget, 1973). The first stage is called the *sensorimotor* stage. In this stage, children's schemes are mainly characterized by sensory perceptions and motor actions. The child learns through seeing and moving. A child typically remains in the sensorimotor stage until 2 or 3 years of age.

The second stage of cognitive development is called the *preoperational* stage. A child enters this stage when he begins to exhibit *symbolic thought*. Symbolic thought is the ability to represent and think about objects and events that are not physically present. The benchmark achievement marking the beginning of this stage is *object permanence*. Object permanence is achieved when the child realizes that an object (or person) continues to exist even when it is out of sight. This is evidenced by a child searching for an object after it is hidden from sight. During this stage, children begin to be able to recall past events and to imagine future ones. The preoperational stage is the period when language skills are developing the most rapidly and play is characterized by fantasy and make-believe.

The third of Piaget's stages is the *concrete operational* stage (Piaget, 1973). The ability to *conserve* marks the beginning of this stage. The term *conservation* is used to indicate the realization that if nothing is added or taken away, an amount remains the same regardless of any change in shape or arrangement. One of the most common conservation tasks consists of pouring liquid from a short, wide glass into a tall, thin glass. The child watches the transformation and is then asked in which glass the liquid is greater or lesser. A preoperational child will respond that by moving the liquid to the tall glass, you have made its volume larger. A child performing at the concrete operational stage will respond that even though the shape has changed, the amount of liquid remains constant. This stage typically begins between ages 7 and 11. Although children at this stage have the ability to think logically about tangible objects, they still lack the ability to think logically about hypothetical and abstract notions (Inhelder & Piaget, 1969).

Piaget's final stage of cognitive development is the *formal operational* stage. This stage is characterized by the ability to reason about abstract and hypothetical ideas and ideas that contradict reality. Formal operational thought involves the ability to formulate and test multiple hypotheses and the ability to mentally determine the role of one variable while holding the others constant in one's mind. This stage varies the most across individuals. The age at which people reach this stage varies widely. In fact, some never reach the formal operational stage (Piaget, 1972).

EDUCATIONAL IMPLICATIONS

Piaget's theory of cognitive development has many enduring contributions for the field of school psychology. He gave us the notion that the nature of children's thinking and reasoning changes with age. Piaget's stage theory provides us with general guidelines as to when new abilities are likely to emerge. Recent research stresses, however, that it is the *sequence* of stages that is fixed, not the ages at which children reach them. The ages at which children reach the different stages vary greatly across cultures and individuals. Finally, we learn that children can only benefit from experiences that they can relate to what they have already learned.

Piaget's theory of cognitive development has practical implications for education. These include providing hands-on materials and opportunities for perspective sharing. Educators should be aware of the cognitive abilities of the students they work with and design activities accordingly.

See also: Physical/Motor Development; Social–Emotional Development

BIBLIOGRAPHY

Inhelder, B., & Piaget, J. (1969). *The early growth of logic in the child*. New York: Norton.

McDevitt, T. M., & Ormrod, J. E. (2002). *Child development and education*. Upper Saddle River, NJ: Merrill/Prentice Hall.

Piaget, J. (1972). Intellectual evolution from adolescence to adulthood. *Human Development, 15*, 1–12.

Piaget, J. (1973). *The child and reality: Problems of genetic psychology*. Paris: Editions Denoel.

Additional Reading for Nonprofessionals

Siegal, M. (2003). Cognitive development. In A. Slater & G. Bremner (Eds.), *An introduction to developmental psychology* (pp. 189–210). Malden, MA: Blackwell.

Additional Readings for Professionals

Cobb, P., & Bowers, J. (1999). Cognitive and situated learning perspectives in theory and practice. *Educational Researcher, 28*, 4–15.

Peverly, S. T. (1995). An overview of the potential impact of cognitive psychology on school psychology. *School Psychology Review, 23*, 292–309.

ELIZABETH MCCALLUM
CHRISTOPHER H. SKINNER

Conduct Disorder

Conduct Disorder (CD) is one of the most prevalent childhood disorders and it accounts for more than half of all childhood clinical referrals. It is also one of the most costly childhood disorders, both in terms of economic costs and human suffering. According to the *Diagnostic and Statistical Manual of Mental Disorders* (4th ed.) (*DSM-IV*) (American Psychiatric Association, 1994), the primary characteristic of this disorder is behavior that violates the basic rights of others or age-appropriate societal norms. This includes aggression, property damage, theft, and serious rule violations. The primary features of CD are often accompanied by associated features such as early onset of drug and alcohol use, low self-esteem, school problems, suicidal behavior, and low academic achievement.

DEFINITION

The core characteristic of CD is "repetitive and persistent patterns of behavior in which the basic rights of others or major-appropriate societal norms or rules are violated" and that must cause "clinically significant impairment in social, academic, or occupational functioning" (p. 85, American Psychiatric Association, 1994). CD is a childhood disorder, with age of onset typically being late childhood or early adolescence. Males tend to have an earlier onset relative to females. Earlier onset is associated with more severe symptomatology and poorer outcomes.

Symptoms of CD have been clustered into four subcategories: aggression to people or animals, destruction of property, theft or deceitfulness, and major rule violations. Diagnostic criteria state that 3 of the 15 criteria must be present within the last year, with at least one symptom occurring within the last 6 months (American Psychiatric Association, 1994).

Central to the diagnosis of CD is the clause "repetitive and persistent pattern of behavior." Children demonstrating aggression and major rule violations have been referred to as antisocial, aggressive, delinquent, undercontrolled, disruptive, and psychopathic, all of which must be differentiated from CD. Many children and adolescents often engage in antisocial behavior. These behaviors may include lying, stealing, fighting, setting fires, and running away. Isolated acts of antisocial behavior are developmentally normal, as evidenced by empirical studies of the prevalence of these behaviors in the general population. For example, at age six, 53 percent of children were reported by their mothers to lie, and 20 percent of 5-year-olds were reported by parents to destroy others' things (Achenbach, 1991). CD is differentiated from developmentally "normal" antisocial activity by frequency and intensity, repetitiveness/chronicity, and impairment. In the *DSM-IV*, these factors are operationalized by (1) the number of antisocial acts needed to meet criteria (i.e., three or more), (2) impairment in life activities, and (3) a severity rating (i.e., mild, moderate, and severe).

Delinquency is a legal term used to describe children who have come in contact with the legal system, usually for committing antisocial acts. Although many children with CD are or will become delinquent, most delinquent children would not qualify for a diagnosis of CD. Delinquent and antisocial activity may lead some youth to the attention of the legal system, but such activity may be transitory or short-lived, not indicative of a more persistent and pervasive pattern associated with CD.

The terms *undercontrolled* and *disruptive behaviors* usually refer to a constellation of behaviors that include impulsiveness, inattentiveness, hyperactivity, disobedience, minor rule breaking, aggression, and major violations of societal norms. These labels are more inclusive than CD, as these behaviors also encompass the *DSM* categories of Attention-Deficit/Hyperactivity Disorder (ADHD) and Oppositional Defiant Disorder (ODD).

CD SUBTYPES

Because the core features of CD may manifest in a variety of conceptually unrelated behaviors (e.g., physical or verbal aggression, staying out late, bullying other children, torture of animals), several classification systems that attempt to create more homogeneous groups of CD have been developed. These include age of onset (childhood vs. adolescence onset), undersocialized versus socialized, relational versus direct aggression, covert versus overt antisocial behavior, proactive versus reactive aggression, and psychopathic versus nonpsychopathic aggression (Frick, 1998). Many of these subtypes possess theoretical appeal, although only a few have received solid empirical support (Connor, 2002). The current *DSM-IV* only includes subtypes based on age of onset of the disorder, whereas childhood onset is defined by the presence of at least one criterion behavior being present before the age of 10. Early onset CD is associated with more violent and aggressive behavior, lower academic achievement, solitary (as opposed to group) aggressive and antisocial activity, and comorbid attentional and neurological impairments, and has a significantly poorer prognosis. In contrast, adolescence-onset CD is associated with less frequent violent and aggressive activity and better long-term prognosis of the disorder into adulthood.

PREVALENCE

Between 2 and 16 percent of American youth are diagnosed with CD, making it one of the most frequently diagnosed childhood disorders. More conservative estimates place the prevalence of CD at around 1 to 9 percent. Youth diagnosed with CD are estimated to account for 30–75 percent of psychiatric hospitalizations. Some reports suggest prevalence rates may be higher in urban and lower socioeconomic status (SES) groups. The proportion of males to females diagnosed with CD is about 3–5:1, although this ratio tends to be more equal in adolescence.

DEVELOPMENTAL COURSE AND OUTCOME

CD seems to be a relatively stable condition, and approximately 25–50 percent of children who are diagnosed with CD will continue to show persistent antisocial behavior into adulthood, as indicated by a diagnosis of Antisocial Personality Disorder (APD), which is roughly the adult equivalent of CD. Even for youth with CD who do not meet all criteria for APD as adults, significant social, occupational, and personal impairment is likely. Adults who were diagnosed with CD as children are more likely to engage in criminal behavior, to be alcoholics, to have poorer work performance, and to present with other psychiatric diagnoses.

The developmental precursor to CD is Oppositional Defiant Disorder (ODD), characterized by defiant, disobedient, and hostile behavior. As many as 80–90 percent of children with CD also demonstrate behaviors associated with ODD. The *DSM-IV* states that "because all of the features of ODD are usually present in CD, ODD is not diagnosed if the criteria are met for CD" (p. 93). Several longitudinal studies have reported that over a period of several years, only 25 percent of children diagnosed with ODD have the diagnosis remitted. Of the other 75 percent, 50 percent continued to show behavior characteristic of ODD, whereas another 25 percent progressed into more serious antisocial behavior associated with CD. Furthermore, these patterns of antisocial behavior often persist into adulthood.

COMORBIDITY

CD has a high rate of comorbidity with other disorders. Estimates of the comorbidity of CD with at least one other psychiatric disorder range from 50 to 90 percent. Among the most frequent co-occurring diagnoses are ADHD, substance abuse disorders, learning problems, anxiety disorders, and depressive disorders. Rates of comorbidity for CD and these disorders vary depending on the criteria used to define the disorders, the type of sample investigated (e.g., general population, psychiatric inpatient, outpatient), and the gender characteristics of the sample.

ADHD is the most frequent co-occurring diagnosis in youth with CD. Approximately 30–75 percent of youth with CD are also diagnosed with ADHD. Of all the combinations of the disruptive behavior disorders, comorbid CD + ADHD has the worst prognosis. Individuals with comorbid CD + ADHD exhibit more physical aggression, a greater range of antisocial behavior, higher rates of peer rejection, higher rates of academic

learning problems and learning disabilities, increased drug use, poorer prognosis in adolescence and adulthood, and increased rates of cognitive deficits. These deficits seem to be specific to comorbid CD + ADHD, and do not appear when CD co-occurs with other comorbid conditions. Moreover, the combination of ADHD and CD is considered a possible developmental precursor to psychopathy, a condition characterized by antisocial behavior coupled with a cold, callous, unemotional presentation.

Rates of comorbid substance abuse disorders (SUD) vary as a function of age. In older youth, SUD co-occurs in approximately 50 percent of persons diagnosed with CD. Most studies report a higher proportion of males with CD having co-occurring SUD than of females.

There is accumulating evidence of relatively high rates of comorbidity of CD with internalizing disorders, specifically depression and anxiety. Approximately 40–60 percent of youth diagnosed as conduct disordered have a co-occurring depressive disorder (i.e., major depression or dysthymia), and about 25–50 percent have a co-occurring anxiety disorder (e.g., phobias, generalized anxiety, separation anxiety). Gender dramatically moderates this relationship, with females having approximately twice the rate of comorbid internalizing disorders. Comorbid CD and depression (CD + DEP) appears to be associated with increased risks of suicidal behavior. Children with comorbid CD and anxiety disorder (CD + ANX) seem to exhibit fewer symptoms of aggression and have fewer police arrests for violent offenses, suggesting a suppressing effect of anxiety on the expression of CD.

Historically, there has been a strong link between the disruptive behavior disorders (i.e., ADHD, ODD, and CD) and learning problems (LP). A rather robust finding is that youth with CD demonstrate an IQ deficit of approximately 8 points, which was almost exclusively due to deficits in Verbal (relative to Performance) IQ (Moffitt, 1993). Recent examinations of the relationship between ADHD, CD, and LP have demonstrated that although higher than expected rates of LP occur in children with CD, this relationship was attributed almost exclusively to comorbid attention deficits (i.e., ADHD) for preadolescent children. For adolescents, the relationship is not so clear and the empirical evidence is equivocal. Adolescents with CD also show impaired academic performance and higher rates of LP, although this relationship is not entirely accounted for by comorbid ADHD.

ETIOLOGY

At least three broad explanatory frameworks have received a good deal of attention, including biological factors, familial influences, and sociocognitive variables. No single framework is sufficiently comprehensive to explain the etiology of CD. Rather, biological, familial, and sociocognitive variables most likely interact to influence the development of antisocial behavior patterns.

Aggressive and antisocial behavior have been linked to genetic transmission. Concordance rates among delinquent adolescents are approximately 90 percent for monozygotic twins and 70 percent for dizygotic twins, illustrating a modest genetic effect. Other biological markers have also been associated with aggression, including neuroanatomical, biochemical, and physiological abnormalities. Neuroanatomical deficits have been reported in many studies using neuropsychological assessments (e.g., Halstead-Reitan), implicating frontal lobe dysfunction and deficits in executive control functions; however, many contrary findings exist. Also, using more direct measures (e.g., PET, MRI) it was seen that there is not enough evidence that children with CD have demonstrable and reliable differences in brain anatomy and function.

A number of biochemicals have been implicated in the development of CD, including cortisol and testosterone. In general, although many studies have found associations between levels of brain chemicals and aggression, the relationship is highly inconsistent across studies. The same is true for evidence of neurotransmitter abnormalities. Although there is evidence suggesting that serotonin, dopamine, monoamine oxidase, and norepinephrine may be correlated with aggression, existing studies do not consistently find significant correlations between neurotransmitter levels and CD.

Familial factors that influence the development of CD include ineffective parenting practices, family functioning, family structure, and parental psychopathology. The presence of divorce and marital discord also increases the likelihood of a child receiving a diagnosis of CD. In general, larger family size and being a middle child is associated with a diagnosis of CD. However, the effects of these variables on the development of CD seem to be mediated by other contextual variables, such as parental availability, preexisting aggressive tendencies in children, and psychopathology of parents. Parent–child interactions have moderate to strong relationships with children's antisocial behavior. Low levels of parental involvement, parental supervision, and harsh and inconsistent discipline have been implicated in the development of CD.

Parental psychopathology also has a specific effect on development of childhood conduct problems. For example, parental antisocial personality is strongly related to childhood-onset CD. Children whose parents are alcoholic, engage in criminal behavior, or are diagnosed with APD are much more likely to be diagnosed with CD.

Sociological variables that are related to the development of delinquency include peer associations, SES, and exposure to violence. The influence of deviant peers on the development of aggression and CD is irrefutable. Multiple studies have documented that association with delinquent peers increases the risk for subsequent antisocial behavior, although many variables significantly moderate this effect, including parental monitoring (Handwerk, Field, & Friman, 2000). SES shows a consistent relationship with delinquency; however, these effects interact with other environmental and parental variables (stage of development, parental monitoring). Exposure to domestic and neighborhood violence is also correlated with subsequent aggression.

TREATMENT

Several comprehensive and authoritative reviews of the treatment of CD suggest this particular disorder is one of the more difficult childhood disorders to treat. Some of the more promising and empirically validated approaches include parent training, family therapy, multisystemic therapy, and cognitive–behavioral approaches.

Although the content and methods of training differ significantly between parent training programs, most programs tend to teach parents to (1) differentially attend to their child's positive behaviors, (2) selectively ignore minor to moderate misbehavior, (3) and apply consequences to more serious rule infractions (e.g., time-out, response-cost, etc.). Although the effectiveness of behavioral parent training for families with oppositional and defiant younger children is well established, evidence for the effectiveness of many of these programs for older youth with more chronic and established patterns of antisocial behavior is limited. Although short-term effectiveness of parent training with older, antisocial youths has been documented in several studies, long-term results have been somewhat disappointing.

The effectiveness of family therapy has been evaluated in numerous studies. Several variants of family therapy have been identified as potentially efficacious for treating adolescent CD (e.g., structural family therapy, functional family therapy), although most include elements of communication training, reframing, problem-solving, and negotiation skills. Validated family therapy methods typically include teaching parents elements of behavioral management as well. In a number of studies, family therapy appears to produce significant reductions in aggression and increases in family cohesion that are maintained at long-term follow-up.

MST has received much support as an effective treatment approach for adolescent delinquency and CD. Drawing upon Bronfenbrenner (1979), MST intensively targets multiple systems in the adolescent's life (e.g., family, school, peers, etc.) borrowing interventions from established, evidence-based practice to engage participants embedded within these systems to effect change in the adolescent's life. Several randomized trials have indicated that MST is more effective in reducing delinquency than routine care-as-usual, both short and long term. These effects have also been found to apply not only to delinquency but also to associated conditions such as substance use, school attendance, and family functioning.

Cognitive–behavioral techniques include social skills training, anger management, problem-solving, moral reasoning, and relaxation training. A limited body of research suggests that these techniques may produce modest reductions in antisocial activity and attitudes, although some evidence suggests that multicomponent packages containing many CBT elements may be more effective, especially when combined with parent-management programs.

See also: Antisocial Behavior; Oppositional Defiant Disorder; Parenting

BIBLIOGRAPHY

Achenbach, T. M. (1991). *Manual for the Child Behavior Checklist/4-18 and 1991 profile.* Burlington: University of Vermont, Department of Psychiatry.

American Psychiatric Association. (1994). *Diagnostic and statistical manual of mental disorders* (4th ed.). Washington, DC: Author.

Bronfenbrenner, U. (1979). *The ecology of human development: Experiments by nature and design.* Cambridge, MA: Harvard University Press.

Connor, D. F. (2002). *Aggression and antisocial behavior in children and adolescents: Research & treatment.* New York: Guilford.

Frick, P. J. (1998). *Conduct disorders and severe antisocial behavior.* New York: Plenum.

Handwerk, M. L., Field, C., & Friman, P. C. (2001). The iatrogenic effects of group interventions: Premature extrapolations. *Journal of Behavioral Education, 10,* 223–238.

Moffitt, T. E. (1993). The neuropsychology of conduct disorder. *Development and Psychopathology, 5,* 135–151.

Additional Readings for Nonprofessionals

Kazdin, A. E. (1995). *Conduct disorders in childhood and adolescence* (2nd ed.). Thousand Oaks, CA: Sage.

Patterson, G., & Forgatch, M. (1987). *Parents and adolescents living together: Part 1. The basics.* Eugene, OR: Castilia.

Additional Readings for Professionals

Brosnan, R., & Carr, A. (2000). Adolescent conduct problems. In A. Carr (Ed.), *What works with children and adolescents?: A critical review of psychological interventions with children, adolescents, and their families* (pp. 131–154). Philadelphia: Brunner-Routledge.

Hinshaw, S. P., & Anderson, C. A. (1996). Conduct and oppositional defiant disorders. In E. J. Mash & R. A. Barkley (Eds.), *Child psychopathology* (pp. 113–149). New York: Guilford.

Patterson, G. R. (1982). *Coercive family process: A social learning approach* (Vol. 3). Eugene, OR: Castilia.

MICHAEL L. HANDWERK

Conflict Resolution

Recently, issues related to student violence and aggression have become more relevant in public schools, as education professionals try to balance children's right to an education with the concern for students' safety. Attempting to achieve this balance, however, has resulted in increased stress for teachers and administrators and a perception of an eroding lack of student control in the classroom. Oftentimes, educators are left with few alternatives to counter the problems associated with disruptive school environments. Administrative decisions to deal with inappropriate student behavior are frequently punitive, resulting in student suspension from school, or placement in alternative school settings or special education programs. Few professionals would agree, however, that punitive reactive measures designed to reduce violent, aggressive acts in school teach appropriate behaviors and that they are effective in the long term. Thus, effective program design is crucial in ensuring school safety and creating environments in which students feel empowered and where they have an opportunity to practice prosocial behaviors.

As a response to the need for programs that promote school safety and provide alternatives to adult-directed student discipline strategies, Girard and Koch (1996) note that many educators are implementing school-based prevention programs focused on conflict resolution (CR) and peer mediation (PM). According to Shepherd (1994) PM is the fastest growing response to school violence. Schoolwide interventions such as CR and PM that focus on students' resolving their own conflicts, as well as the conflicts of their peers, suggest a move away from programs that rely on seclusionary methods of behavior control (e.g., school suspension) and movement toward students' managing their own behavior. When students focus on managing their own behavior and the behavior of their peers, teacher and administrator stress can be reduced and their ability to provide a safe environment that is conducive to learning is increased.

CONFLICT RESOLUTION

According to Robinson, Smith, and Daunic (2000), conflict resolution refers to curricula that focus on acknowledging individual differences among people, changing win–lose situations with win–win solutions, using a mediation process to resolve complex conflicts, and applying a theme of cooperation throughout a school community. With a CR curriculum, adults work together with students to positively address social conflict by focusing on developing skills, as compared to merely focusing on the resolution of an immediate situation.

Typically, students view social conflict as situations where there are winners and losers instead of a double-winner scenario. By using a CR curriculum, the win–lose paradigm is countered as an appropriate way of handling conflict, with more appropriate and constructive ways to manage conflict.

As Levy (1989) notes, schoolwide CR programs should be student- rather than adult-centered. Most often discipline programs are adult-centered, where teachers and other education professionals serve as mediators to resolve both student–student conflicts as well as adult–student conflicts. These types of programs that depend solely upon teachers and other adult figures to mediate conflict often fail to teach students appropriate methods for dealing with conflict in the absence of adult supervision. Especially as children get older, they cannot always count on adults to solve their problems. The use of a CR curriculum can teach students communication and problem-solving skills, the mediation process, and, in some instances, peace and nonviolence education.

PEER MEDIATION

For students to effectively resolve their social conflicts, educators should not only teach students to resolve conflict appropriately, they must also provide students with opportunities to practice suitable responses to conflict. Often exposed to less proficient responses to conflict such as violence and aggression on television and possible parental actions such as spousal abuse, arguing, and fighting, students should have multiple opportunities to observe appropriate, positive responses to conflict, as well as opportunities to practice conflict resolution skills in unthreatening environments. When students learn about conflict resolution through a CR curriculum, peer mediation, wherein students act as their own behavior change agents, offers an opportunity for educators to instill students with appropriate conflict resolution skills.

Peer mediation refers to the implementation of specific techniques or skills to facilitate the resolution of a conflict. In PM conferences, disputants sit face to face in the company of a trained peer mediator and present their viewpoints in a supportive environment. During PM, the problem between disputants is defined, solutions are delineated, and the potential outcomes are evaluated. The skills required for effective PM include self-control, communication (including issues related to confidentiality), problem solving, critical thinking, and planning by disputants and mediators. The PM process differs from other programs facilitated by peers, such as peer counselors or peer helpers, because it involves a clearly defined, formal process with distinct roles for each party involved (Levy, 1989). Providing students with the opportunity to mediate their own disputes should help to improve self-esteem and self-control, and lead to a better school climate.

Moreover, student-focused programs such as PM may allow teachers to concentrate on maintaining high levels of instructional time, rather than spending time attending to disputes (Johnson, Johnson, & Dudley, 1992). Johnson et al. state that teachers and administrators spend their time more wisely if they teach students constructive methods and skills for settling their own disputes. When students are involved in settling their own disputes, they often demonstrate an increased ability to benefit from programs that rely on structure, guidance, and reinforcement that is intrinsic as opposed to extrinsic (Robinson et al., 2000).

Benefits of PM may include (a) a more effective method of discipline as compared to expulsion and suspension, (b) seeing conflict as a positive opportunity for learning new skills and interpersonal growth, (c) reduction of school vandalism, absenteeism, and violence, (d) providing students with the necessary skills to solve their own problems, and (e) promotion of mutual understanding of individual differences (Schrumpf, Crawford, & Usadel, 1991). Skills and knowledge acquired in PM programs can enable students to become self-sufficient and successful students and citizens.

AN EXAMPLE OF A CONFLICT RESOLUTION PROGRAM WITH PEER MEDIATION

One example of a validated, evidence-based, theoretically driven program is *Working Together to Resolve Conflict* (Smith, Miller, & Daunic, 1999). *Working Together to Resolve Conflict* includes conflict curriculum and peer mediation training materials designed for schoolwide application in middle schools. Part of a 4-year research effort, the curriculum includes instructional units on understanding conflict, understanding and handling anger, effective communication, and introductory information about the peer mediation process. Role-plays are used throughout the curriculum to allow students to gain basic knowledge about the nature of social conflict and to practice some of the skills for a constructive handling of conflict situations. The last unit on peer mediation describes the formal mediation process that is useful when an individual involved in a dispute is unable or unwilling to resolve a specific conflict on their own.

The *Working Together to Resolve Conflict* program also includes training materials for a small cohort of students in a school to be trained as peer mediators. Preparation to be a mediator requires about 12 hours of intensive training. Students who complete the training successfully are able to engage in the mediation process with minimal adult supervision or intervention by adults. The peer mediation part of the *Working Together to Resolve Conflict* program requires a systematic referral process for students to access peer mediation. Verbal harassment, threats, insulting a family member, or spreading rumors are oftentimes the basis for students seeking peer mediation on their own or for teacher referral. Referral forms, which provide a record of the referring party, conflict location, brief description of the problem, and disputants' names, are available to students and staff in classrooms, central office, or guidance office. Participation in peer mediation is always voluntary. At the conclusion of each mediation, disputants along with their mediators sign an agreement form that includes date, type of conflict, and an agreed-upon solution.

CONCLUSION

Successful and sustained conflict resolution programs are characterized by committed leadership on the part of faculty and administration, consistency of program promotion and follow-up, as well as thoughtful and deliberate selection of peer mediators who may not always be the "best" students. When teachers, students, parents, and administrators embrace the goals of conflict resolution, a schoolwide commitment exists to prevent problem behaviors, promote student problem solving and independence, and provide a safe and peaceful learning environment. Helping students to learn to resolve their own conflicts, instead of relying on a punishment–obedience orientation, gives students a set of positive experiences as they learn to get along with others. Effective conflict resolution programs offer an important step for students to become more self-directed and thus more mature.

See also: Crisis Intervention; Social Skills Building for Adolescents; Social Skills Building for Elementary Children

BIBLIOGRAPHY

Girard, K., & Koch, S. J. (1996). *Conflict resolution in the schools: A manual for educators.* San Francisco: Jossey-Bass.

Johnson, D. W., Johnson, R. T., & Dudley, B. (1992). Effects of peer mediation training on elementary school students. *Mediation Quarterly, 10,* 89–99.

Levy, J. (1989). Conflict resolution in elementary and secondary education. *Mediation Quarterly, 7,* 73–87.

Robinson, T. R., Smith, S. W., & Daunic, A. P. (2000). Middle school students' views on the social validity of peer mediation. *Middle School Journal, 31*(5), 23–29.

Schrumpf, F., Crawford, D., & Usadel, H. C. (1991). *Peer mediation: Conflict resolution in schools.* Champaign, IL: Research Press.

Shepherd, K. K. (1994). Stemming conflict through peer mediation. *School Administrator, 51*(4), 14–17.

Smith, S. W., Miller, M. D., & Daunic, A. P. (1999). *Conflict resolution/peer mediation research project* (Final Report). University of Florida: Department of Special Education, Aggression Research Center.

Additional Readings for Nonprofessionals

Daunic, A. P., Smith, S. W., Robinson, T. R., Miller, M. D., & Landry, K. (2000). Implementing schoolwide conflict resolution and peer mediation programs: Experiences in three middle schools. *Intervention in School & Clinic, 36,* 94–100.

Smith, S. W., & Daunic, A. P. (2002). Using conflict resolution and peer mediation to support positive behavior. In R. Algozzine & P. Kay (Eds.), *Preventing problem behaviors: Handbook of successful prevention strategies* (pp. 142–161). Thousand Oaks, CA: Corwin.

Additional Readings for Professionals

Deutsch, M. (1994). Constructive conflict resolution: Principles, training, and research. *Journal of Social Issues, 50*(1), 13–32.

Smith, S. W., Daunic, A. P., Miller, M. D., & Robinson, T. R. (2002). Conflict resolution and peer mediation in middle schools: Extending the process and outcome knowledge base. *Journal of Social Psychology, 142,* 567–586.

STEPHEN W. SMITH

Conjoint Behavioral Consultation

Conjoint behavioral consultation (CBC) is a structured indirect model of service delivery in which parents, teachers, and support staff work together to address collaboratively the academic, social, and behavioral needs of a student for whom all parties bear some responsibility (Sheridan, Kratochwill, & Bergan, 1996). CBC is based on an ecological model, which emphasizes (a) the interaction between the child and the primary systems in his/her life and (b) increasing collaborative problem solving and decision making across those systems. CBC consists of a 4-stage problem-solving process, which parallels that of behavioral consultation and includes problem identification, problem analysis, plan implementation, and plan evaluation. The primary objectives of CBC are to address the needs of individual students and to enhance the relationships among the systems in the child's life by creating home–school partnerships (Sheridan et al., 1996).

CBC expands on behavioral consultation by involving families and school professionals in collaborative problem solving and highlighting reciprocal interactions between the child and the primary systems in his/her life. Expanding the model to include both schools and families promotes effective resolution of concerns for several reasons. First, numerous individuals with expertise can provide information on conditions surrounding the target behavior. Second, data collection and intervention implementation can be initiated systematically across several settings, thereby enhancing the generalization and maintenance of treatment gains (Sheridan & Kratochwill, 1992).

In addition to addressing the needs of individual students, CBC establishes a framework for enhancing relationships across home and school settings. It can be initiated by teachers who have concerns that permeate school and home, or by a school psychologist who recognizes the need to address referral concerns across home and school settings. The model facilitates relationships by presenting opportunities for parents and teachers to work together, thereby increasing communication and trust across systems. Further, joint problem solving and active decision making is encouraged, resulting in shared responsibility for the concerns and mutual support for educating and socializing children.

The advantages of CBC can be illustrated through a case study involving a 7-year-old girl who was referred for consultation owing to difficulty following instructions. Prior to beginning consultation, the parents and the teacher had a strained relationship because of a series of behavioral problems and negative parent–teacher phone calls. Through the CBC process, an intervention was created that successfully increased compliance across both settings. In addition, a home–school note was implemented, resulting in increased positive communication and collaboration between the teacher and the family.

Research findings demonstrate the effectiveness of CBC. The results of a 4-year study yielded moderate to high positive results across home and school for a variety of concerns, including behavior disorders, learning disabilities, anxiety, and attention-deficit/hyperactivity disorder (ADHD) (Sheridan, Eagle, Cowan, & Mickelson, 2001). In addition to meaningful outcome data, parents and teachers rated CBC as a highly acceptable and the most preferred consultation approach (Freer & Watson, 1999). Because of high levels of effectiveness and acceptability, CBC offers a framework for providing cross-system consultation services in the school.

See also: Direct Behavioral Consultation; Mental Health Consultation

BIBLIOGRAPHY

Freer, P., Watson, T. S. (1999). A comparison of parent and teacher acceptability ratings of behavioral and conjoint behavioral consultation. *School Psychology Review, 28,* 672–684.

Sheridan, S. M., Eagle, J. W., Cowan, R. J., & Mickelson, W. (2001). The effects of conjoint behavioral consultation: Results of a 4-year investigation. *Journal of School Psychology, 39,* 361–385.

Sheridan, S. M., & Kratochwill, T. R. (1992). Behavioral parent–teacher consultation: Conceptual and research considerations. *Journal of School Psychology, 30,* 117–139.

Sheridan, S. M., Kratochwill, T. R., & Bergan, J. R. (1996). *Conjoint behavioral consultation: A procedural manual.* New York: Plenum.

Additional Readings for Nonprofessionals

Canter, A. S., & Carroll, S. A. (Eds.). (1998). *Helping children at home and school: Handouts from your school psychologist.* Bethesda, MD: National Association of School Psychologists.

Christenson, S. L., & Sheridan, S. M. (2001). *Schools and families: Creating essential connections for learning.* New York: Guilford.

Additional Readings for Professionals

Christenson, S. L., & Buerkle, K. (1999). Families as educational partners for children's school success: Suggestions for school psychologists. In C. R. Reynolds & T. B. Gutkin (Eds.), *The handbook of school psychology* (pp. 709–744). New York: Wiley.

Gutkin, T. B., & Curtis, M. J. (1999). School-based consultation theory and practice: The art and science of indirect service delivery model. In C. R. Reynolds & T. B. Gutkin (Eds), *The handbook of school psychology* (pp. 598–637). New York: Wiley.

SHANNON E. DOWD
SUSAN M. SHERIDAN

Consultation

See: Conjoint Behavioral Consultation; Direct Behavioral Consultation; Mental Health Consultation

---

Cooperative Learning

Cooperative learning (CL) describes a set of teaching strategies in which students work together in small groups (typically four students) to master academic content or to complete an academic task (Slavin, 1995). Extensive research has demonstrated that CL can improve academic performance and peer relationships for students across grade levels, content areas, and differing types of schools. Additional benefits include enhanced self-esteem, improved attitudes toward school, and greater acceptance of individual differences among students (Putnam, 1998; Slavin, 1995).

Although many teachers routinely use small group activities within their classrooms, CL procedures employ two essential components that may not be included in typical small group activities. First, CL incorporates a group reward, where either all or none of the group members receives access to a reward. Second, there is individual accountability as each student's learning is assessed and rewards are delivered contingent upon learning of the group, as opposed to completing a group project. Because students are more likely to earn rewards when all members of their group participate and achieve, they are more likely to encourage and support their fellow group members' learning (Slavin, 1995).

Although differing approaches to CL exist, each typically includes the following procedures or characteristics (Putnam, 1998). First, students are assigned to groups composed of members differing across ability level, gender, ethnicity, and social and behavioral skill levels. Having mixed groups ensures that each group reflects the diversity within the classroom and that students enhance each other's learning. Second, each group member helps one another and in turn benefits from the actions of each group member (positive interdependence). Positive interdependence is highest when each member is assigned a specialized task or role within the group. Third, learning is individually assessed for each member (individual accountability). Individual accountability is ensured through individual test taking or other independent assessment procedures. Fourth, students are taught skills to effectively work within a group (cooperative skills). These skills may include listening while others are speaking, taking turns, complimenting others, and/or respectfully disagreeing with others. Fifth, each student has an equal opportunity to contribute to the success of the group by improving upon their previous performance or meeting individual goals. Thus, students of all levels desire to do their best, as their contributions are equally valued within the group. Sixth, students engage in face-to-face interaction, verbally and nonverbally communicating with one another. Finally, an opportunity to reflect upon the performance of the group (e.g., "How well did we interact with one another?") and to set goals for the next group session are incorporated. Group members or teachers can participate in reflection, which may occur at the end of the group session or throughout the session. By reflecting upon the process of working as a group, students can monitor and enhance their use of cooperative skills.

As implemented within the classroom, CL does not take the place of teacher-led instruction. Rather, CL methods are used within both elementary and secondary classrooms in place of independent seat work or individual practice to master basic skills as well as to critically evaluate content and problem-solve solutions (Slavin, 1995). Following teacher presentation, students work within their groups to ensure that each member has mastered the concept presented. Students benefit from both teaching and learning, being able to clarify concepts and to provide explanations in their own words. The teacher actively monitors the groups' activity and assists groups as necessary. Following the completion of group work, individual members are assessed through individual quizzes, tournament participation, or other individual assessment procedures. Individual contributions are assessed, group points summed, and groups are recognized for their performance (Slavin, 1991, 1995).

STUDENT TEAM LEARNING

Development of CL methods and research regarding their effectiveness in classroom settings began in the early 1970s. The Student Team Learning methods developed and researched at Johns Hopkins University (Slavin, 1991, 1995) have been extensively evaluated and found to improve student achievement. Three general methods that can be adapted to most subject areas and grade levels include *Student Teams–Achievement*

Divisions (STAD), *Teams–Games–Tournament* (TGT), and *Jigsaw II* (Slavin, 1991, 1995). A brief description of these methods follows.

Student Teams–Achievement Divisions (STAD)

Students are assigned to four-member teams. Each team is composed of students with different ability levels, gender, ethnicity, and cooperative skill levels. The teacher provides direct instruction regarding the concept to be learned. The students then meet in groups to review the information using study guides or worksheets to rehearse and master the content. Following group practice, the students are then individually tested. Improvement from prior performance is determined and points are assigned on the basis of relative gain. Points are then summed for each team and recognition given for their performance (e.g., certificates, applause).

Teams–Games–Tournament (TGT)

Similar to that in STAD, in TGT students are assigned to four-member, mixed-ability teams, the teacher provides direct instruction, and students study in groups. However, students are assessed differently: students participate in weekly tournaments in which three students from differing teams play academic games at tournament tables. These tournament tables consist of members of equal ability, based on their past performance level. Students earn points on the basis of their performance within the tournament table. For example, the top-scoring student within the tournament table brings back a maximum of 60 points to their group. Thus, the lowest ability student has the opportunity to contribute the same amount as the highest ability student given their performance is equal within their tournament table. Each week, changes in student composition of the tournament tables are made on the basis of past performance in order to maintain equality within the competition. Points are summed on the basis of individual contributions of the team members and recognition is given on the basis of their performance.

Jigsaw II

In Jigsaw II, students participate in four-member, mixed-ability groups, similarly to STAD and TGT. Rather than being directly taught, however, they are given a reading assignment (e.g., a chapter in social studies regarding the Revolutionary War). All members read the assigned material and are designated as "experts" regarding a certain aspect of the reading (e.g., Boston Tea Party, Declaration of Independence, George Washington, and the Minutemen). These individuals meet with members of the other teams who are designated experts on the same topic. The students then discuss that information and return to their respective teams to teach what they have learned to their group members. Similarly to STAD, individual team members participate in an individual assessment covering all the topics. Points are determined on the basis of improvement from previous performance and added to the team total. Teams are recognized on the basis of their performance.

See also: Group Contingencies; Inclusion; Mainstreaming

BIBLIOGRAPHY

Putnam, J. W. (1998). The process of cooperative learning. In J. W. Putnam (Ed.), *Cooperative learning and strategies for inclusion: Celebrating diversity within the classroom* (2nd ed., pp. 17–47). Baltimore: Brookes.
Slavin, R. E. (1991). *Student team learning: A practical guide to cooperative learning* (3rd ed.). Washington, DC: National Education Association.
Slavin, R. E. (1995). *Cooperative learning: Theory, research, and practice* (2nd ed.). Boston: Allyn & Bacon.

Additional Reading for Nonprofessionals

Slavin, R. E. (2000). *Educational psychology: Theory and practice* (6th ed.). Boston: Allyn & Bacon.

Additional Readings for Professionals

Johnson, D. W., & Johnson, R. T. (1994). *Learning together and alone: Cooperative, competitive, and individualistic learning* (4th ed.). Boston: Allyn & Bacon.
Kagan, S. (1992). *Cooperative learning resources for teachers.* San Juan Capistrano, CA: Resources for Teachers.
Slavin, R. E., & Fashola, O. S. (1998). *Show me the evidence! Proven and promising programs for America's schools.* Thousand Oaks, CA: Corwin.

CHRISTINE E. NEDDENRIEP

Coping

Coping consists of complex cognitive and behavioral efforts to manage specific external and internal demands and the possible conflicts between them. Children and adults alike are required to cope with ordinary external demands such as the pressures of school, peers, family, and work, and most are able to do so constructively. Some external demands are extraordinary, however, and require extraordinary coping behaviors. Not all people are able to cope constructively with the threat of incapacitating illness or injury, or actual incapacity or handicap, or with family disruption, loss of a loved one, or prolonged unemployment. The extent to which they cope constructively depends on the severity of the stressful external situation and on their own personal resources (e.g., knowledge, social and intellectual ap-

titudes, personality traits, skills, material assets, and personal convictions and values) and external resources (e.g., the support of family, friends, professionals, and society as a whole). Some resources may be an asset in some situations and a deficit in others. Trusting people is an asset in establishing casual and intimate personal relationships, whereas it is a deficit when a person learns that trust has been violated.

Consider Amy's coping problems. A young adolescent, an only child in the family, she had a trusting relationship with her parents. When they were divorced following vindictive personal and legal altercations, Amy found herself in a quandary because both parents took turns vilifying one another to her. How does she appraise the situation and cope with it? How does she behave toward each parent? How does she handle her anger, feeling of betrayal, depression, sense of loss, and ambivalent feelings about her parents?

An example of unconstructive coping would be to (a) blame herself for the divorce, blame one parent and idolize the other, or blame both; and (b) sink into depression and (c) shut herself off from all interpersonal relationships and new pursuits. An example of constructive coping would be to (a) tell each parent that she intends to remain the loving daughter of each and does not wish to take sides; (b) reassure herself that she is a worthwhile person in no way responsible for her parents' difficulties; (c) maintain positive relationships with age peers and adult relatives; (d) initiate and/or accept challenges in her schoolwork, social activities, and hobbies; and (e) prepare herself to see a counselor or psychotherapist, if and when she feels the need to do so.

Amy's coping agenda is incomplete. She will have to rework her beliefs and assumptions about the world she lives in. She was a trusting child who believed that her parents loved one another as much as they apparently loved her—her parents had constantly reassured her of their mutual love. She realizes that her trust was misplaced and begins to question other basic assumptions about life. Will she be able to trust what others tell her in the future? Will she be able to trust her own judgment about other people? Which beliefs about life will she retain and which will she discard? It will not be easy for her to adjust to the demands of her new life circumstances and to maintain a sense of well-being unless she deals in a positive manner with her shattered belief system, on her own or with the help of a wise confidante or a professional counselor (Janoff-Bulman, 1992).

PROBLEM-CENTERED AND EMOTION-FOCUSED COPING BEHAVIORS

Many people assume that emotions are the deciding factor in coping behavior and that coping consists primarily of an act of will to gain and maintain self-control. This assumption ignores the cognitive and behavioral components of coping and their interaction with the emotions. There are exceptional life circumstances that circumvent cognitive appraisal (e.g., terrorist attack, conflagration) and elicit immediate and impulsive reactions of fight, fright, or flight. These are rare events for most people, however, and once the immediate crisis has passed, coping by cognitive interpretation and concomitant behaviors takes place and provides some degree of control of negative emotions.

Coping behaviors are designed to affect the external situation, to solve the problem at hand to the extent that it is possible to do so. An inexperienced teacher burdened with an unruly group of students might ask other more experienced teachers for advice, and then modify the way she structures her lesson plans or the way she handles breaches of discipline. If the problem-focused coping is effective, then the teacher becomes less emotionally distressed in the course of her work.

Sometimes, it is not possible to change the distressing situation, and one must either learn to live with the situation or leave it altogether. Children cannot leave a disruptive home situation. Some distraught teachers find that they cannot deal effectively with unruly students, are not permitted to transfer them out of their classes, and are not able to resign from their position in the middle of the school year. Children and teachers may cope with their respective difficulties by restructuring the way they interpret their respective predicaments. Children may tell themselves, "Nobody's family is going to change, but I can change the way I feel about them and what I can hope to expect from them." They may elect to attend to the positive features of their relationship with each parent and learn to ignore the negative. They may tell themselves, "This is as good as it gets," and look elsewhere for compensatory gratifying relationships with other adults. Teachers may reassure themselves that they are worthwhile human beings and are adequate, even highly proficient, teachers with students of a different age or cultural background. They may complete the year by exercising damage control, minimizing the psychological distress one might experience in this difficult situation, and take a different teaching assignment the following year. This kind of coping may be called cognition-focused because it does not attempt to change the external situation but rather one's interpretation of it; it may also be called emotion-focused because the interpretations affect one's emotional state (Milgram, 1986).

The appraisals and conclusions cited above for children and teachers serve to decrease or eliminate emotional distress. Different interpretations and conclusions that could be derived from the same experiences will increase emotional distress. Consider how children feel if they conclude, "I can never be happy if my parents are not happy with each other." Consider how teachers might feel if they conclude, "I am an inadequate teacher, I don't have what it takes," or "I always wanted to be a teacher and I find I am a failure even before I begin my teaching career."

Emotion-focused coping may take other forms. Unhappy children may retreat to their room and read novels about children living happier lives than their own. Teachers may go from school to a sports clinic, jog on the track, take a hot shower, and go home feeling relaxed. These are constructive behaviors that serve to alleviate emotional distress. By contrast, some emotion-focused coping behaviors by children or teachers are destructive: children spending most of their time in their room, lost in fantasy episodes from novels or television, or in their own private fantasies; teachers drinking to excess at a bar or at home, or becoming addicted to large doses of antidepressant or anxiety-allaying medications.

The role of emotions in coping is complex. In any given situation emotions are both cause and effect. Emotional distress motivates us to find ways to change the situation that caused the distress or to find ways to reduce the distress. In both cases, if appropriate coping behaviors are applied to the situation, negative emotions are reduced and positive emotions are experienced.

DEFENSE MECHANISMS AND COPING

Some theorists assert that Freud's classical *defense mechanisms* may serve as useful coping strategies under certain conditions. Freud used the term to refer to cognitive and behavioral strategies that people use *without conscious awareness* to deal with *unconscious anxiety*. People in highly stressful situations may follow back on some of these defense mechanisms and use them in a more deliberate *conscious* manner in dealing with *manifest anxiety*, threat, or loss. They may direct their attention away from an unpleasant situation and behave as if the threat does not exist (*denial*), find substitute means to gratify a given motive when the preferred means is not available (*displacement*), gain detachment from a stressful situation by dealing with it in abstract terms (*intellectualization*), and profess and strive to adopt socially acceptable motives for behaviors that were originally driven by less acceptable motives (*rationalization*). In some circumstances these coping strategies may be constructive and consistent with social ethics. On the other hand, two major defense mechanisms when employed in a deliberate manner are problematic. Attributing to others exaggerated intensities of their own personal, socially unacceptable motives (projection) and professing/practicing motives at variance with strong personal underlying motives (*reaction formation*) may well be effective Machiavellian strategies in pursuing one's immediate goals. They exact a price, however, because, apart from experienced personal discomfort, they subvert one's personal integrity and the integrity of one's relations with others (Atkinson, Atkinson, Smith, Bem, & Nolen-Hoeksema, 2000).

COPING: AN EXERCISE IN DECISION MAKING

The ways in which people cope with external and internal demands reflect a deliberate choice, a weighing of possible behaviors, and the selection of one over another. Why some people cope by denying the darkness, others by cursing the darkness, and still others by lighting a candle has to do with many factors. Some have to do with the nature of the problem, others with the resources available to the person, and still others with the values and goals of the person. All of these factors play a role in the coping behaviors that characterize an individual in a given situation as compared with the same individual's coping behavior in another situation, and the coping behavior of still other individuals in comparable situations.

See also: Crisis Intervention; Divorce; Posttraumatic Stress Disorder; Traumatic Incidents

BIBLIOGRAPHY

Atkinson, R. L., Atkinson, R. C., Smith, E. E., Bem, D. J., & Nolen-Hoeksema, S. (2000). *Hilgard's introduction to psychology* (13th ed.). New York: Harcourt Brace.

Janoff-Bulman, R. (1992). *Shattered assumptions: Toward a new psychology of trauma.* New York: The Free Press (Macmillan).

Lazarus, R. S. (1991). *Emotion and adaptation.* New York: Oxford University Press.

Milgram, N. A. (1986). Attributional analysis of war-related stress: Modes of coping and helping. In N. A. Milgram (Ed.), *Stress and coping in time of war: Generalizations from the Israeli experience* (pp. 9–25). New York: Brunner/Mazel.

Additional Reading for Nonprofessionals

Teyber, E. (2001). *Helping children cope with divorce.* New York: Wiley.

Additional Readings for Professionals

Antonovsky, A. (1979). *Health, stress, and coping.* Washington, DC: Jossey-Bass.

La Greca, A. M., Silverman, W. K., Vernberg, E. M., & Roberts, M. C. (Eds.). (2002). *Helping children cope with disasters and terrorism.* Washington, DC: American Psychological Association.

Moos, R. H. (Ed.). (1987). *Coping with life crises: An integrated approach.* New York: Plenum.

NOACH MILGRAM

Corporal Punishment

The legal definition of corporal punishment may vary according to a state's definition of child abuse. Most states define it as punishment that uses physical force. For our purposes here, we will use Straus' (1994) definition: "Corporal punishment is the use of physical force with the intention of causing a child to experience pain but not injury for the purposes of correction or control of the child's behavior" (p. 4).

Corporal punishment is typically associated with spanking, slapping, or paddling a child for misbehavior. It has become the single most controversial child-rearing topic among parents concerning whether it should be used. Many national organizations, such as the American Academy of Pediatricians, the American Counseling Association, the National Committee for the Prevention of Child Abuse, the National Association for the Advancement of Colored People, the National Parents and Teachers Association, the National Education Association, the American Medical Association, and the American Bar Association, have officially denounced its use. The United States is one of the few Western democracies (with the exception of Canada and one state in Australia) where the use of corporal punishment in schools is still allowed. It is, however, becoming increasingly rare. In 1976, this practice was illegal in only 2 states, whereas by 2002, 27 states had outlawed corporal punishment in the schools. What parents do in the home is an entirely different matter. Corporal punishment remains very popular among parents, with 94 percent reporting that they spank their children (Straus, 1994).

WHY IS CORPORAL PUNISHMENT CONTROVERSIAL?

When considering whether to use any type of punishment, two questions arise: (1) "Is it effective (i.e., does the target behavior decrease in frequency)?" and (2) "Is it associated with any positive or negative outcomes?" An excellent source on these questions with regard to corporal punishment is a recent issue of *Psychological Bulletin*, which contains a meta-analysis by Gershoff (2002). In her review, Gershoff concluded that corporal punishment is associated with 11 child behaviors and experiences. Ten of these were negative, including increased aggression and lower levels of moral internalization and mental health. In terms of increased aggression, it appears that children who are corporally punished learn that violence is a legitimate way to deal with problems. Corporal punishment has been associated with increases in anxiety, tension, bedwetting, conduct problems, and depression, and sleeping patterns are disturbed as well. Straus (1994) reported an increased risk of suicide, delinquency, aggressive tendencies, academic difficulties, lower IQ, aberrant sexual behavior, and physical abuse of other children.

The one positive child behavior associated with corporal punishment was immediate compliancy. This means that when children were corporally punished, they stopped misbehaving rather quickly. As with any punishment, for immediate compliancy to occur, corporal punishment has to be administered immediately after the misbehavior occurs. This is where support for corporal punishment falls apart. To avoid allowing the parent's anger to turn corporal punishment into abusive behavior, it is often recommended that the parent take a few seconds to calm down before administering the spanking. However, taking a few seconds is in direct conflict with the contiguity needed for punishment to be effective. Thus, it is practically impossible for a parent to administer corporal punishment in an effective way and yet control for the potential for abuse.

As previously mentioned, Gershoff (2002) found corporal punishment to be associated with decreased moral internalization. This means that the child was less likely to behave appropriately in the absence of corporal punishment. Thus, corporal punishment as a punisher does not seem to be effective because it does not reduce the frequency of the target misbehavior.

WHY DO PARENTS STILL USE CORPORAL PUNISHMENT?

If corporal punishment is not effective and is associated with so many negative outcomes, why do so many parents still use it? Some scholars have suggested that geographic region may be related to support for corporal punishment. A 1989 Harris poll found that only 33 percent of Southerners opposed corporal punishment in the schools compared with 66 percent in the East. In 1986, the states with the highest proportion of students being paddled were Arkansas, Mississippi, Alabama, Tennessee, Florida, Georgia, Oklahoma, Texas, and South Carolina. Moreover, in that same year, 12 Southern states accounted for 80 percent of the paddlings nationally.

Why do more Southerners accept corporal punishment? Wiehe (1989) found that support for corporal punishment was related to biblical literalism. Specifically, the Book of Proverbs is used in advising not to "spare the rod." Flynn (1994) found that conservative Protestants (e.g., Southern Baptists, Assemblies of God, Seventh Day Adventists, Jehovah's Witness) were much more likely to favor spanking than those affiliated with other denominations. Fundamental religious beliefs, strong adherence to tradition, and conservative ideology all seem to contribute to the resistance of Southern community leaders to abolish corporal punishment (Richardson, Wilcox, & Dunne, 1994). In terms of tradition, teachers who were corporally punished by their parents and who had been paddled in school are more

likely to paddle their students more often (Dubanoski, Inaba, & Gerkewicz, 1983).

CHANGING ATTITUDES TOWARD CORPORAL PUNISHMENT

Given that corporal punishment is ineffective and potentially harmful for children, many scholars have pushed for ways to decrease its use. One approach to decreasing spanking in the home is to make it illegal. In 1979, Sweden was the first nation in the world to outlaw corporal punishment. The ban appears to have decreased the use of corporal punishment. As a result of the successful Swedish model, nine European countries (Sweden, Finland, Denmark, Norway, Austria, Cyprus, Croatia, Latvia, and Germany) have made parental corporal punishment illegal.

Passing a law that would make corporal punishment illegal in the United States appears to be a daunting task, given such widespread support. Some researchers have focused on changing persons' attitudes toward corporal punishment to reduce this widespread support. Griffin, Robinson, and Carpenter (2000) had students read about the ineffectiveness and harmfulness of corporal punishment by searching the research literature. They found that students' support for using corporal punishment decreased. Perhaps through similar efforts like this a greater majority of future parents can become educated about the potential dangers of corporal punishment and decide against using it.

See also: Differential Reinforcement; Negative Reinforcement; Positive Reinforcement; Punishment; Time-Out

BIBLIOGRAPHY

Dubanoski, R. A., Inaba, M., & Gerkewicz, R. (1983). Corporal punishment in schools: Myths, problems, and alternatives. *Child Abuse & Neglect, 7*, 271–278.

Flynn, C. P. (1994). Regional differences in attitudes toward corporal punishment. *Journal of Marriage and the Family, 56*, 314–324.

Gershoff, E. T. (2002). Corporal punishment by parents and associated child behaviors and experiences: A meta-analytic and theoretical review. *Psychological Bulletin, 128*, 539–579.

Griffin, M. M., Robinson, D. H., & Carpenter, H. (2000). Changing teacher education students' attitudes toward using corporal punishment in the classroom. *Research in the Schools, 7*, 27–30.

Richardson, R. C., Wilcox, D. J., & Dunne, J. (1994). Corporal punishment in schools: Initial progress in the Bible Belt. *Journal of Humanistic Education and Development, 32*, 173–182.

Straus, M. A. (1994). *Beating the devil out of them: Corporal punishment in American families*. Lexington, KY.

Wiehe, V. R. (1990). Religious influence on parental attitudes toward the use of corporal punishment. *Journal of Family Violence, 5*, 173–186.

Additional Reading for Nonprofessionals

Hyman, I. A. (1990). *Reading, writing, and the hickory stick: The appalling story of physical and psychological abuse in American schools.* Lexington, KY.

Additional Readings for Professionals

Baumrind, D., Larzalere, R. E., & Cowan, P. A. (2002). Ordinary physical punishment: Is it harmful? A comment on Gershoff (2002). *Psychological Bulletin, 128*, 580–589.

Holden, G. W. (2002). Perspectives on the effects of corporal punishment: Comment on Gershoff (2002). *Psychological Bulletin, 128*, 590–595.

DANIEL R. ROBINSON

Counseling

See: Family Counseling; Group Counseling; Individual Counseling; Peer Counseling Programs

Creativity

Over the past 50 years, there has been considerable research on creativity and creative thinking. Although creativity has been defined in various ways, one recent definition by Cropley (1999) focuses on individuals and has specific relevance to this entry. That is, he defined it as "an aspect of thinking, as a personality constellation, and as an interaction between thinking, personal properties, and motivation" (p. 511). Although there is a vast literature on creativity/creative thinking, this brief entry will focus on the development of creativity and learning.

LEARNING

There are two factors that are generally involved in creative learning: cognition and affect. Methods abound that influence creativity/creative thinking; for example, brainstorming, using open-ended questions, idea checklists, attribute listing, goal setting, values clarification, role-playing, and creative problem solving (CPS). These methods, in turn, influence student learning and academic achievement.

ACADEMIC ACHIEVEMENT

Feldhusen and Treffinger (1980) developed 10 recommendations for establishing a classroom climate that is conducive to creative thinking, which, in turn, should influence learning. (See Feldhusen and Treffinger, 1980, p. 32, for a complete list of these recommendations.) Teacher behaviors also influence the attainment of creativity, and, thus, facilitate learning (e.g., methods used, mentoring and modeling creative thinking, and motivational techniques [especially to stimulate intrinsic motivation]). It is interesting that extrinsic motivation has been reported to interfere with creativity (Amabile, 1983). This contradicts the research reported by Epstein and Lapotsky (1999), who found that external reinforcers enhance creativity.

DEVELOPING CREATIVITY

There is also a vast amount of research regarding the development of creativity in schools. It is beyond the scope of this entry to present these in detail. (See Fasko, 2000/2001, p. 320, for a partial listing of this research.) Indirect instruction, for example the inquiry–discovery approach, has been touted as a technique for enhancing creativity. Feldhusen and Treffinger (1980) provided seven suggestions for inquiry–discovery learning, which promotes active learning. (See Fasko, 2000/2001, p. 321, for a list of these suggestions.)

Although extrinsic motivation techniques have been reported to undermine creative thinking (e.g., Amabile, 1983), other behaviorally oriented methods have been demonstrated to stimulate creativity, for example, component-skills training, goal setting, and self-management training (Epstein & Lapotsky, 1999). Self-management training research supports its use in stimulating creativity. In fact, Glover (1980) developed an effective model that includes nine steps for "modifying one's own behavior in which the goal is to emit behavior that is especially fluent, flexible, elaborate, and original" (cited in Epstein & Lapotsky, 1999, pp. 180–181).

TEACHING CREATIVITY

There are many programs available to help teach creativity/creative thinking in students. For example, research supports Renzulli's schoolwide enrichment model (SEM) (Renzulli & Reis, 1985, 1994) because for those students in the program it (a) stimulated creativity and task commitment and (b) enhanced the development of more diverse and complex creative products. In addition, creative thinking can be taught through 25 techniques developed by Sternberg and Williams (1996).

(See Sternberg and Williams, 1996, p. 5, for a complete listing of these techniques.)

IMPLICATIONS FOR PRACTICE

The current emphasis for student-centered teaching and learning relates well with the fostering of creativity and/or creative thinking. Further, there are several effective models and programs available for promoting creativity, which were discussed previously. Obviously, it appears that if educators were attempting to foster creative thinking, then it would behoove them to begin with simple exercises and/or methods that focus on one problem, and then use more sophisticated exercises for more challenging problems. Thus, from the discussion above, it appears that creative thinking skills and creativity can be taught. However, there are many factors (e.g., classroom climate) that can influence the teaching and acquisition of these skills. Hopefully, future research will provide additional information as to how educators can best develop creativity in students, and, in turn, enhance learning.

See also: Gifted and Talented

BIBLIOGRAPHY

Amabile, T. M. (1983). *The social psychology of creativity*. New York: Springer-Verlag.

Cropley, A. J. (1999). Education. In M. A. Runco & S. R. Pritzker (Eds.), *Encyclopedia of creativity* (Vol. 1). San Diego, CA: Academic Press.

Epstein, R., & Lapotsky, G. (1999). Behavioral approaches to creativity. In M. A. Runco & S. R. Pritzker (Eds.), *Encyclopedia of creativity* (Vol. 1). San Diego, CA: Academic Press.

Fasko, D. (2000/2001). Education and creativity. *Creativity Research Journal, 13* (3/4), 317–327.

Feldhusen, J. F., & Treffinger, D. J. (1980). *Creative thinking and problem solving in gifted education*. Dubuque, IA: Kendall/Hunt.

Glover, J. A. (1980). *Become a more creative person*. Englewood Cliffs, NJ: Prentice-Hall.

Renzulli, R. S., & Reis, S. M. (1985). *The schoolwide enrichment model: A comprehensive plan for educational excellence*. Mansfield Center, CT: Creative Learning.

Renzulli, R. S., & Reis, S. M. (1994). Research related to the schoolwide enrichment triad model. *Gifted Child Quarterly, 38*, 7–20.

Sternberg, R. J., & Williams, W. M. (1996). *How to develop student creativity*. Alexandria, VA: Association of Supervision and Curriculum Development.

Additional Readings for Nonprofessionals

Baer, J. (1997). *Creative teachers, creative students*. Boston: Allyn & Bacon.

Csikszentmihalyi, M. (1996). *Creativity: Flow and the psychology of discovery and invention*. New York: Harper Collins.

Additional Readings for Professionals

Runco, M. A., & Pritzker, S. R. (Eds.). (1999). *Encyclopedia of creativity* (Vols. 1, 2). San Diego, CA: Academic Press.

Torrance, E. P. (1966). *The Torrance Tests of Creative Thinking: Norms—Technical manual*. Princeton, NJ: Personnel Press.

DANIEL FASKO, JR.

Crisis Intervention

All schools experience some type of crisis event and administration should critically review how the event was handled, carefully noting what worked and what did not. Schools should anticipate any additional types of crises that might occur and formulate plans to deal with them. School administrators must develop crisis plans at all three of the following levels:

1. *Primary prevention*, consisting of activities devoted to preventing a crisis from occurring. Examples include conflict resolution, gun safety, safe driving, suicide prevention programs, training school personnel in first aid, and CPR.

2. *Secondary intervention*, which includes steps taken in the immediate aftermath of the crisis to minimize effects and escalation. Examples are evacuating students to a safe place away from danger, reopening school as quickly as possible and immediately after a death in the school family.

3. *Tertiary intervention*, which involves providing long-term follow-up assistance to those who have experienced a severe crisis. Examples would be monitoring and supporting the friends of a suicide victim for a year after the suicide and adding support personnel such as counselors.

DEVELOPING CRISIS TEAMS

Each school or district must look at its own resources and then choose one of the following three options as teams are organized:

1. A *building team* in which every member works in the same building. The obvious advantages are that team members are acquainted with each other and the student body, and that they can easily and routinely meet to review crisis plans. This approach works well when a school is large enough to have campus personnel in key positions (e.g., nurse, counselor, psychologist, and security).

2. A *district team* in which all members are employed by the school district but are located in various buildings

throughout the district. This arrangement makes communication and crisis planning more difficult than in a building approach. A counselor or nurse may need to cover several locations, and the psychologist may need to be called from the central office. It is important that the team include a representative from each high school because statistics clearly indicates that high school students are more at risk for violent and accidental deaths.

3. A *combination district and community team* in which some team members are district employees and others (e.g., medical personnel, mental health workers, or police officers) are employed by community agencies. This arrangement is more difficult to organize, but it is essential in many small and rural school districts in order to develop comprehensive plans. A school district should never be in the position of establishing relations with outside agencies *after* a crisis has occurred.

Planning meetings should be scheduled and should include representatives from all the agencies that will be involved. In the past, some schools have been frustrated by a lack of response from community agencies. It is particularly important to exercise caution with outside professionals who contact a school on the day of a crisis and volunteer to help; their credentials and expertise should be examined to ensure that their skills would be useful in the current situation. Ideally, arrangements could be made to locate and interview these professionals before a crisis occurs.

Schools with building crisis teams may need to call for extra assistance from the district or central office. Brock and Poland (2002) have discussed the difference between centralized and on-site teams. In an effort to increase awareness of services offered by centralized or on-site teams, they may consider publicizing their services and establishing credibility. If a campus or administrator is resistant to outside assistance, the team could consider adding a staff member from the resistant campus to the team. Site or building teams are in the best position to work on prevention, and centralized or district teams can assist with intervention after a crisis has occurred.

The purpose of a team is to incorporate sufficient staff to delegate duties, because it is impossible for one administrator to do everything that is needed in the aftermath of a crisis. There are school districts with 20-member teams and 200-page crisis plans. Plans that are so lengthy that school personnel will not review them on a regular basis are virtually useless. The question of team size is an administrative as well as a commonsense issue. Pitcher and Poland (1992) have recommended a team size of five to eight. At a minimum, the team should include the following members to assist the responsible administrator: (1) a medical liaison, (2) a security liaison, (3) a parent liaison, and (4) a counseling liaison. This would result in a team of

five and these liaisons could designate additional school staff members to assist them. The addition of a media liaison and a campus or staff liaison would be useful, but the building principal may prefer to carry out these duties rather than delegate them.

POSSIBLE PREPARATORY ACTIVITIES FOR CRISIS TEAM MEMBERS*

There are a number of practical suggestions for school personnel and crisis team members:

Administrative

- Emergency communication to team members/administration
- Overall evacuation plan
- Lock down signal
- Develop a folder containing important information for police use
- Create a crisis or emergency box
- Develop crisis plans that include after-school activities and summer sessions
- Designate a "reunion" spot for faculty, students, and parents and plans for transporting large groups to that spot
- Procedures for canceling school, early dismissal, using the school as a shelter
- Instructions, and activities, for teachers if regular instruction needs to be suspended
- Establish a policy for funerals or memorial services
- Develop alternative ways to communicate to parents besides the telephone
- Develop procedures to quickly account for students
- Determine alternate ways to transport students home

Staff

- Emergency communication system to warn and inform teachers
- Advance designation of teachers for various duties
- Plan for assembling teachers and disseminating factual information to them
- Instructions for managing troubled students in the classroom
- Establish communication channels for faculty to report threatening situations
- Establish a phone tree that includes janitors, cooks, drivers, etc.

Medical

- Establish emergency communication lines to obtain medical help
- Train staff on CPR and emergency medicine
- Discuss transportation and potential capacities with local hospitals
- Establish a list of staff trained in CPR and emergency medicine
- Order and maintain emergency medical supplies
- Keep track of who required medical treatment and to which facility they were transported
- Have a plan if school nurse is not on campus
- Develop an emergency medical team

Parent

- Emergency communication to parents such as telephone tree, Web site, or e-mails
- Develop a system to make emergency calls or contacts to parents
- Develop a system to utilize parent volunteers after a crisis
- Sample letter to parents
- Setting up/managing parent meeting
- Plans for disseminating factual information to parents
- Designate a nearby site to receive distraught parents

Counseling

- Train counselors in dealing with emotionality
- Designate a "safe room" for talking after the incident (students and staff) or coordinate sending support personnel to affected classrooms
- Discuss with and plan for outside counseling support, both short and long term
- Make advance preparations for "anniversaries" of a tragic event or special remembrance
- Periodically screen and maintain contact with those previously affected by a crisis
- Develop classroom strategies to deal with emotionality

Media

- Contain and establish limits for the media during the event
- Train staff in media issues, "dos and don'ts"
- Clarify district policy about media on campus
- Keep records of media requests and contacts
- Schedule press conferences

Security

- Establish a method whereby police notify schools on dangerous community events
- Establish a method for notifying law enforcement in emergency
- Coordinate plans for students and staff for police operation during an emergency event
- Keep roadways clear so that medical and law enforcement personnel can get to the affected school
- Build positive relationships with students and implement prevention programs

*Used with permission from "Best practices in crisis intervention" in Poland, Pitcher, and Lazarus (2002b).

COPING WITH A DEATH OR TRAGEDY

Poland and McCormick (1999) cited governmental figures that indicate that the number of deaths for young people is at or near an all-time high. The leading causes of death for children are, in order, accident, homicide, and suicide. Annual estimates are that 1 in 1,200 high school students, 1 in 3,000 middle school, and 1 in 4,000 elementary students will die or be killed. This means that all schools must cope with the death of students and sometimes with the death of faculty members and parents as well. Pitcher and Poland (1992) have emphasized that school personnel, especially counselors, need to be aware of the developmental stages of children's understanding of death. We recommend that the principal verify the death and then notify the faculty through either a calling tree or faculty meeting, keeping in mind the importance of giving school personnel the opportunity to work through their own issues about death and loss before having to assist their students. If it is not possible to utilize either of these notification methods, then the teacher should be given a hand-delivered memorandum that includes specific information as well as ideas about how to assist their students. Pitcher and Poland (1992) have developed a tip sheet for teachers in dealing with death, and we recommend an in-service training session designed to empower teachers to help many students by supporting the expression of a range of emotions. Teachers can provide various beneficial classroom activities for expressing emotions such as talking, writing, artwork, music, or activities to assist the family of the deceased. Having students make a list of all the good things and positive memories of the deceased, and preparing students for funeral attendance are additional positive activities. Key risk factors in the impact of death on students are the following:

- Familiarity with the victim
- Previous trauma or loss

- Individual psychopathology
- Family psychopathology
- Concern about family members' safety
- Physical proximity to the tragedy

Children's reaction to a tragedy often fall into these key areas:

- Fears of all sorts
- Regression academically and behaviorally
- Nightmares and sleeping difficulties
- Need to be comforted, reassured, or held frequently
- Easily becoming tearful or angry
- Vulnerability to depression, substance abuse, reckless behavior, and suicide, particularly in adolescents

SUICIDE INTERVENTION

Unfortunately, schools have been placed in the position of managing the aftermath of youth suicide. National interest in youth suicide prevention has escalated as a result of the surgeon general's Call to Action to Prevent Suicide (U.S. Public Health Service, 1999), and national suicide prevention strategies have been developed. The Call to Action stressed three key components: awareness, intervention, and methodology.

Even though it is the third leading cause of death for teenagers, the problem of youth suicide is sometimes overlooked because of the many other problems facing young people today. A recent CDC (Poland & Lieberman, 2002) survey found that 8 percent of high school students had already attempted suicide, 27 percent had seriously contemplated it, and 16 percent had made a plan to commit suicide. Recent research has emphasized that the suicide rate for 10- to 14-year-olds has more than doubled in the last decade.

School administrators have been slow in addressing the problem of youth suicide, and a national grass-roots parent effort is helping schools and communities to increase prevention efforts. One organization that is making a difference is Yellow Ribbon, founded by suicide survivors. Yellow Ribbon's Web site, www.yellowribbon.org, outlines this group's important work. Poland and McCormick (1999) have documented that few schools have training in suicide prevention or a plan in place and cited a growing number of cases in which schools have been subjected to lawsuits after the suicide of a student. The key issue is not whether the school somehow caused the suicide, but whether the school failed to take reasonable steps to prevent it. Schools have a responsibility to have prevention programs in place, to foresee that a student who is threatening suicide is at risk, to take steps to supervise that student, and to obtain psychological help for that student. School personnel must also notify parents whenever they have reason to believe that a student is suicidal.

Elsewhere, Poland and McCormick (2000) have applied Caplan's model to the problem of youth suicide and outlined the roles of the schools as the following:

1. Detection
2. Assessment
3. Parent notification
4. Referral and follow-up

All school personnel who interact with students (including, for example, secretaries, bus drivers, and cafeteria workers) must be taught the warning signs of suicide and must be empowered to follow procedures to alert the appropriate personnel and get assistance for a suicidal student. When school personnel are provided with correct information about the problem, many commonly held misperceptions could be addressed. It must be emphasized that no one should keep a secret about suicidal behavior. School psychologists and counselors are the logical personnel to assess the severity level. It is very important that these personnel receive training on how to interact with suicidal students and what questions to ask.

Poland and Lieberman (2002) have clarified that a key question is not whether the parents should be called (because that is a given), but rather what to say to the parents and how to elicit a supportive reaction from them. Because some parents are occasionally uncooperative and minimize the suicidal ideation or actions from their child, school personnel must be firm in their recommendation that immediate counseling assistance is necessary. Parents have become angry with school personnel during this notification process and have tried to forbid them from interacting with their child again. When parents refuse to get emotional assistance for a suicidal child, a referral should be made to the local child protective services agency. It is absolutely essential that the appropriate school personnel follow up and provide emotional support, regardless of what the parents do or do not do.

Schools must have postvention plans in place for use after a suicide occurs. The American Association of Suicidology (AAS) has published school postvention guidelines that include the following (AAS, 1998):

- Do not dismiss school or encourage funeral attendance during school hours
- Do not hold a large-scale school assembly or dedicate a memorial to the deceased
- Do provide individual and group counseling
- Do verify the facts, and treat the death as a suicide
- Do contact the family of the deceased
- Do emphasize that no one is to blame for the suicide
- Do emphasize that help is available, that suicide is preventable, and that everyone has a role to play in prevention

The AAS postvention guidelines also include the following recommendations that encourage the media not to dramatize the suicide:

- Do not make the suicide front-page news
- Do not print a picture of the deceased
- Avoid details about the method
- Do not report the suicide as the result of simplistic, romantic, or mystic factors
- Do emphasize that there are alternatives to suicide, and publicize where to get assistance

For more information contact AAS at 202-237-2280 or www.suicidology.org about the important guidelines that can help prevent further suicides.

EFFECTS OF NATIONAL TRAGEDIES

Most children in America viewed the extensive and graphic television news coverage of shocking school shootings such as that at Columbine and the 9/11/2001 Attack on America. School officials should anticipate increases in feelings of fear for student safety in their school subsequent to such an event. Usually increases in written or verbal threats of violence, bomb threats, bringing weapons to campus, and rumors of copycat attempts also occur. Because the students are already aware of the developments, such incidents can present a "teachable moment" because students are more open to discussion about the incidents and are more open to constructive input from adults. The following are key points:

- Conduct faculty meetings to prepare for discussion of the tragedy with students.
- Make sure classroom discussions are focused on how to make schools safer rather than on glamorizing the perpetrators.
- Students need to be told specific information about who the perpetrators are believed to be, and they should be cautioned not to blame everyone of a single race or religion.
- The Attack on America especially demonstrated the necessity of classroom discussions on tolerance and diversity so that all Arab Americans and Muslims were not blamed. Explaining facts about Arab Americans and the Islamic faith and emphasizing the many positive contributions that Arab Americans have made at the community and national levels was very beneficial.
- There has been debate about whether or not television coverage of a national tragedy should be viewed in the classroom. Young children should view very little, if any, coverage and it should be emphasized that the tragedy is far away when that is the case. Older students could view the coverage but not constantly, and the most important point is for the teacher to turn off the coverage and lead classroom activities to process the event.
- School personnel must recognize that children of different ages are at different developmental levels, with elementary children in particular needing reassurance of their personal safety. Middle and high school students will have strong opinions about the tragedy, a greater understanding of the finality of death, and will offer concrete suggestions about what needs to be done.
- Students will look to adults to see how they are responding. Adults should remain calm and let students know that they have permission for a range of emotions. They should be given opportunities to express emotions through talking, writing, music, projects, artwork, ceremonies, rituals, and fundraising and memorializing activities.
- Students' questions should be addressed, and they should be told the truth in age-appropriate terms. Adults should avoid overwhelming students with more information than is requested, and they should avoid statements such as, for example, "Our world will never be the same" when referring to the 9/11/2001 Attack on America.
- Let students know that trustworthy adults—the president of the country and other national leaders—are in charge of the situation.
- Provide activities and projects that will enable children to express their emotions. Examples would be collecting money to assist the victims' families and writing letters to rescue workers, government leaders, and families who have lost loved ones.

NATIONAL RESOURCES

The National Association of School Psychologists (NASP) has been very responsive to the needs of schools and communities in the aftermath of school violence. NASP formed the National Emergency Assistance Team (NEAT) in 1996. The specific purposes of the seven-member team are:

- Promote training in crisis intervention
- Provide direct on-site assistance when requested at national-level crises that affect children and schools
- Provide consultation to schools and school psychologists across the country who are faced with a tragedy via telephone and through sending written materials

- Support state school psychology associations as they form state-level crisis teams as have already been done in Florida, Georgia, and California

NEAT has formed partnerships with organizations such as the National Organization for Victim Assistance (NOVA), The U.S. Department of Education, the American Red Cross, Federal Emergency Management Agency, and state emergency response teams. The team is also working with the International School Psychology Association to create an international network and foundation for crisis intervention. To contact NEAT, visit National Association of School Psychologists' Web site at www.naspweb.org/NEAT or call 301-657-0270, ext. 301. This information line provides current team members' names and geographic areas of responsibility. The NASP Web site also lists important links to other organizations providing crisis information.

SUMMARY

Poland and McCormick (2000) outlined the following important crisis lessons for school personnel:

- Recognize that it could happen to you
- What you learn in one crisis situation will help you in the next situation, although no two crisis situations are alike
- Crisis plans must be updated annually and crisis team members must understand their duties
- Everyone must be alert for crises, and crisis intervention is an "inside job" that involves a prepared staff, student body, and community

All schools need a carefully developed crisis plan and a commitment from both staff and students. School administrators need to coordinate their crisis planning efforts with local, state, and national homeland security initiatives and must carefully review the excellent body of literature available on the topic of school crisis.

See also: Coping; Posttraumatic Stress Disorder; School Threats: Legal Aspects; School Violence Prevention; Traumatic Incidents

BIBLIOGRAPHY

American Association of Suicidology. (1998). *Suicide postvention guidelines: Suggestions for dealing with the aftermath of suicide in the schools.* Washington, DC: Author.

Brock, S., & Poland, S. (2002). *School crisis preparedness.* In S. Brock, P. Lazarus, & S. Jimerson (Eds.), *Best practices in school crisis prevention & intervention* (pp. 273–289). Bethesda, MD: National Association of School Psychologists.

Caplan, G. (1964). *Principles of preventative psychiatry.* New York: Basic Books.

Pitcher, G., & Poland, S. (1992). *Crisis intervention in the schools.* New York: Guilford.

Poland, S., & Lieberman, R. (2002). *Best practices in suicide intervention.* In A. Thomas & J. Grimes (Eds.), *Best practices in school psychology* (Vol. 3, pp. 1151–1166). Bethesda, MD: National Association of School Psychologists.

Poland, S., & McCormick, J. (1999). *Coping with crisis: Lessons learned.* Longmont, CO: Sopris West.

Poland, S., & McCormick, J. (2000). *Coping with crisis: Quick reference guide.* Longmont, CO: Sopris West.

Poland, S., Pitcher, G., & Lazarus, P. (2002a). Best practices in crisis intervention & management. In A. Thomas & J. Grimes (Eds.), *Best practices in school psychology* (Vol. 3, pp. 1057–1080). Bethesda, MD: National Association of School Psychologists.

Poland, S., Pitcher, G., & Lazarus, P. (2002b). Best practices in crisis intervention. In A. Thomas & J. Grimes (Eds.), *Best practices in school psychology* (Vol. 4). Bethesda, MD: National Association of School Psychologists.

U.S. Public Health Service. (1999). *The Surgeon General's call to action to prevent suicide.* Washington, DC: Author.

Vossekuil, B., Fein, R., Reddy, M., Borum, R., & Modzeleski, W. (2002). *The final report of the Safe School Initiative: Implications for the prevention of school attacks in the United States.* Washington, DC: U.S. Secret Service & U.S. Department of Education.

Additional Reading for Nonprofessionals

Poland, S., & McCormick, J. (2000). *Coping with crisis: Quick reference guide.* Longmont, CO: Sopris West.

Additional Readings for Professionals

Brock, S., Lazarus, P., & Jimerson, S. (2002). *Best practices in school crisis prevention and intervention.* Bethesda, MD: National Association of School Psychologists.

Poland, S., & McCormick, J. (1999). *Coping with crisis: Lessons learned.* Longmont, CO: Sopris West.

SCOTT POLAND

Crystallized–Fluid Theory of Intelligence

Intelligence means many different things to different people and in different contexts. In some situations, what one might consider as "smart" is producing the conforming or expected solution consistent with social norms, whereas in others, the "smart" answer may be the one no one has thought of before. Intelligence may refer to the individual's overall ability to be successful in a given situation, such as school, or may refer to an individual's ability to adapt to a new situation. Many individuals have argued for multiple intelligences (e.g., Gardner, 1983) or multiple components of intelligence (Carroll, 1993). Two aspects of intelligence that have been considered not only in theoretical discussions of intelligence, but also in the construction of instruments to measure intelligence, are crystallized and fluid intelligence or ability (Cattell, 1992).

Crystallized intelligence generally refers to those abilities that are affected by prior experience or learning. For example, when various tasks measure vocabulary skills, general knowledge, listening skills, and general ability to understand spoken language as well as the ability to communicate effectively with language and have awareness of the grammatical rules of one's language (McGrew & Flanagan, 1998), part of the individual's ability to respond correctly is not only a function of their innate ability but also is a function of the person's exposure to the same type of task or prior learning of the information. At the same time, however, measures of crystallized ability should not be achievement tests; they should not include tasks like reading or math that are curricular bound (Kaufman & Kaufman, 1993). More than "school learning," it is the overall range of the individual's knowledge of the world around them, the language and culture of their world, and the ability to apply this knowledge (McGrew & Flanagan, 1998). For these reasons, the measurement of crystallized ability may be more culture- and native-language-bound than is fluid ability.

In contrast, fluid intelligence generally refers to the ability to engage in strategy use and step-by-step problem solving when faced with a novel situation. Fluid ability is presumed to incorporate those skills under the general heading of "reasoning" that include inferential or inductive reasoning in conjunction with more abstract thinking and problem solving, as well as learning rate (McGrew & Flanagan, 1998). Tasks measuring fluid ability may require the individual to classify or categorize objects, to identify an underlying rule (e.g., what characteristic is important?), to follow a set of sequenced steps while adhering to predetermined rules, and to determine the appropriate strategy for a given situation. Fluid ability is not as heavily affected by exposure, experience, or prior learning as is crystallized ability; it is presumed to be associated with the maturation of the central nervous system (Kaufman & Kaufman, 1993). As such, there is a gradual increase in one's fluid ability that parallels neurological development. Tasks used to measure fluid ability are often nonverbal in nature, thus decreasing the linguistic component that could be compromised by experiential variables. As such, given the presumed biological basis and decreased emphasis on language, fluid ability is viewed as being relatively culture free and applicable across cultures (Cattell, 1992). Also related

to the presumed biological underpinnings, fluid ability may be considered a key indicator of cognitive functions (Stankov, 2000).

Fluid and crystallized ability are both purported to be measured by specific subtests of the myriad measures of intelligence currently available; however, in many instances, tasks tapping crystallized and fluid ability are combined in such a way that measurement of these is mixed with the measurement of other aspects of intelligence (Cattell, 1992). In contrast, the *Kaufman Adolescent and Adult Intelligence Test* (KAIT) (Kaufman & Kaufman, 1993) was developed with the intent of providing a means of measuring crystallized and fluid intelligence. Although initially limited to only crystallized and fluid intelligence in Cattell's early model, it is now understood that other components of intelligence also must be considered (McGrew & Flanagan, 1998). As a result, some researchers have suggested the use of a cross-battery approach to assess fluid–crystallized intelligence and related abilities. The conceptualization of intelligence as based within two broad domains (fluid and crystallized) does not preclude other aspects of intelligence (e.g., memory, visualization, and processing speed), but provides a framework for integrating the various components of intelligence (McGrew & Flanagan, 1998). More recently, additional emphasis is being placed on related aspects of working memory and cognitive speed in conjunction with a better understanding of fluid and crystallized intelligence theory (Stankov, 2000).

See also: *Gf–Gc* Theory of Intelligence; Intelligence Quotient (IQ)

BIBLIOGRAPHY

Carroll, J. B. (1993). *Human cognitive abilities: A survey of factor analytic studies.* Cambridge: Cambridge University Press.

Cattell, R. B. (1992). The relevance of fluid and crystallized intelligence concepts to nature–nurture investigation. *The Mankind Quarterly, XXXII*(4), 359–375.

Gardner, H. (1983). *Frames of mind.* New York: Basic Books.

Kaufman, A. S. & Kaufman, N. L. (1993). *Kaufman Adolescent and Adult Intelligence Test manual.* Circle Pines, MN: American Guidance Service.

McGrew, K. S., & Flanagan, D. P. (1998). *The intelligence test desk reference: Gf–Gc cross battery assessment.* Boston: Allyn & Bacon.

Stankov, L. (2000). The theory of fluid and crystallized intelligence: New findings and recent developments. *Learning and Individual Differences, 13*, 1–3.

Additional Reading for Nonprofessionals

Mackintosh, N. J. (1998). *IQ and human intelligence.* New York: Oxford University Press.

Additional Readings for Professionals

Bates, T. C., & Shieles, A. (2003). Crystallized intelligence as a product of speed and drive for experience: The relationship of inspection time and openness to *g* and *Gc*. *Intelligence, 31*, 275–287.

Conway, A. R. A., Cowan, N., Buntin, M. F., Therriault, D. J., & Minkoff, S. R. B. (2002). A latent variable analysis of working memory capacity, short-term memory capacity, processing speed, and general fluid intelligence. *Intelligence, 30*, 163–183.

Garlick, D. (2002). Understanding the nature of the general factor of intelligence: The role of individual differences in neural plasticity as an explanatory mechanism. *Psychological Review, 109*, 116–136.

Osman, D. C., & Jackson, R. (2002). Inspection time and IQ: Fluid or perceptual aspects of intelligence? *Intelligence, 30*, 119–127.

Primi, R. (2001). Complexity of geometric inductive reasoning tasks: Contribution to the understanding of fluid intelligence. *Intelligence, 30*, 41–70.

CYNTHIA A. RICCIO

Curriculum-Based Measurement

See: Mathematics; Reading; Spelling: Academic Interventions; Writing (Written Language)

Dd

Depression in Children and Adolescents

Depression is one of the most common mental health concerns of adults, but it has long been overlooked with children and adolescents. It has only been since the 1980s that depression in children and adolescents has emerged as an issue at the forefront of professional concern.

Depression is considered to be one of four main "internalizing" types of disorders or syndromes, which also include anxiety, social withdrawal, and physical (somatic) complaints. Internalizing disorders constitute a specific major subtype or domain of emotional and behavioral problems. The term *internalizing* indicates that these problems are developed and maintained to a great extent *within* the individual. This fact makes it difficult to detect symptoms simply through direct observation, and therefore requires a more in-depth assessment of how the individual feels and thinks about himself/herself and his/her environment. It is not uncommon for depression, anxiety, social withdrawal, and physical complaints to occur in unison, and there are many overlapping symptoms. It is also possible for children and adolescents to exhibit both serious conduct problems or hyperactivity (i.e., fighting, stealing, and inattention) and internalizing symptoms at the same time. However, internalizing disorders are considered to be *overcontrolled*, meaning that the individual suffering from the symptoms often attempts to maintain a maladaptively high level of control of his/her emotions, behaviors, and thought processes. Aggressive behavior and other conduct problems, on the other hand, are considered to be *undercontrolled*, meaning that the individual has not developed sufficient strategies for self-regulation of his/her behavior, affect, and cognitions.

The same criteria used for diagnosing depression in adults are used with children, although some of the manifestations of symptoms may differ between children and adults. The primary characteristics of depression are excessive sadness, loss of interest in activities, sleeping problems (either sleeping too much or not enough), slowing of physical movements or in some cases physical agitation, lack of energy, a preoccupation with death or dying, feelings of worthlessness or excessive guilt, and difficulty in thinking, concentrating, or making decisions. One symptom commonly seen in depressed children and adolescents is a failure to make expected weight gains. Two additional symptoms often characterize the presentation of depression in children and adolescents: irritability and physical complaints (i.e., stomach pains, headaches). Not all of these symptoms are necessary for significant depression to exist. The general criterion for a diagnosis of depression is that at least five of these symptoms are present most of the time for the same 2-week period, and at least one of the symptoms is excessive sadness or loss of interest.

It is not entirely certain how many children and adolescents suffer from depression. On the basis of a variety of studies and estimates, a conservative estimate of the percentage of children and adolescents who suffer from the symptoms of depression to an extent that would constitute a disorder or significant problem is 3–6 percent. It is reported that depression is more commonly observed in girls than in boys. This is particularly true after adolescence, when the difference between the sexes becomes apparent, with about twice as many girls than boys experiencing significant symptoms of depression.

To best understand depression, it is often helpful to consider how problems associated with the symptoms of depression develop. There is some evidence that suggests biological influences have been implicated in depression, in terms of abnormalities in neurotransmission (sending and receiving of brain chemicals). Neurotransmitter abnormalities may involve a genetic link in determining how some people are more vulnerable to depression. Another biological influence comes from what researchers have noted about infants whose temperamental characteristics make them easily excitable, highly alert, and very reactive to new and different stimuli. These infants are more likely than other infants to become anxious, shy, and socially withdrawn during childhood when coupled with a learning environment that is likely to play a role in development of depression. Endocrine system (hormone) abnormalities may also play a biological role in vulnerability to depression.

Family factors associated with vulnerability to depression include strained family relationships, conflict, and poor family communication and problem-solving skills. Furthermore, children raised with parents who are themselves depressed may be more likely to experience symptoms of depression because of behaviors, emotional symptoms, and cognitive patterns that are part of the vicious cycle of depression being modeled. Psychological stress or an exposure to highly stressful events, such as death or medical problems, can also influence the risk for depression. Cognitive influences, such as particular styles of thinking about the world and the control one has over one's own life, have been shown to have a major impact on how depression develops. Finally, patterns of behavior such as isolating oneself from friends and family, as well as not doing things that lead to social gains or rewards, can cause and maintain feelings of depression, loneliness, and low self-esteem.

Although there may be several categories of potential causal factors that influence the development of depression, this fact does not necessarily indicate that there is always a specific cause for the depression, nor does identifying the cause necessarily indicate that a specific type of intervention is more desirable. In fact, it is usually hard to identify one specific primary cause of depression, because most sources of influence have an interacting role with other potential sources in a person's life.

A formal assessment for depression can serve several valuable purposes, including access to services, a framework for professionals to communicate and understand the problem, and help in developing an intervention plan that addresses the areas of greatest concern. Assessing depression should be based on an aggregated, comprehensive portrait of the child or adolescent's functioning in different situations. Overall, an assessment strategy is based on using a solution-focused approach that links the problems a particular child or adolescent is exhibiting to the tools for addressing these problems.

The methods of social–emotional assessment for school professionals may include direct observation, behavior rating scales, interviews, records reviews, self-report measures, and projective techniques. Because depression is associated with internal perceptions and states, obtaining the child or adolescent's self-report is usually critical. Assessment information may

also be obtained from the actual child or adolescent, parents, other family members, teachers, school personnel, peers, and community-based informants, all of whom have had opportunities to observe the social and emotional behaviors of the child or adolescent. In many cases, the child or adolescent, parent(s), and teacher are the most reliable and accurate sources of assessment information. Assessment settings refer to where the assessment information is based and include school, home, clinic, playground, and other community settings. Typically, the home and school settings are the primary focus for the assessment information. Given the time constraints and limited resources in school settings, best practices in comprehensive assessment would recommend a minimum of two methods, sources, and settings.

A primary aim of assessment is to link the information obtained from the assessment to an effective intervention plan. The most effective psychosocial interventions for treating depressed children and adolescents that have been documented to date are comprehensive cognitive–behavioral methods of intervention. The cognitive component of these intervention programs focuses on changing the maladaptive thinking style of the depressed person, whereas the behavioral component focuses on increasing positive activities and behaviors that are likely to increase the amount of social and response-contingent reinforcement available to the depressed child or adolescent. Incorporating a psychoeducational plan has also proven to be a very successful component of some treatment programs. In school settings, tailoring an effective treatment program for either one student or a group involves not only selecting an appropriate type of treatment, but also other factors such as the number of sessions that should be scheduled, emphasizing the critical components of the program, and how to establish a therapeutic relationship based on trust and respect.

There are several common key components of psychosocial treatments that appear to be important for successfully helping children and adolescents cope with and overcome depression. One component common in several programs is training in appropriate communication skills. Students are taught how to express their feelings and thoughts to others (peers, therapists, family, etc.) in a clear and understandable manner. Another component is emotional or affective education, where the student is trained to identify and label pleasant and unpleasant emotions, and then identify situations where these specific emotions are likely to occur. The next step of emotional education is to identify and understand the link between these thoughts and situations. Identification of problem or maladaptive cognitive patterns is another component that is usually linked with emotional education. This component addresses automatic negative thoughts, cognitive distortions, maladaptive attribution styles, and irrational thinking. Cognitive-change strategies that challenge negative thoughts and dispute irrational thoughts while focusing on positive thoughts and events are usually included as part of the cognitive–behavioral intervention. Finally, training in life skills such as goal setting, problem solving, negotiation, and conflict resolution, as well as practicing appropriate social skills, are recommended strategies as part of a comprehensive treatment program plan.

In addition to psychosocial interventions for depressed children and adolescents, there have been significant advances in the use of medications for treatment, and the evidence in support of various antidepressant medications as an effective treatment component is increasing. In recent years, a category of medications referred to as selective serotonin reuptake inhibitors (SSRIs) has made a dramatic impact on the treatment of depression and related problems with adults, adolescents, and children. Examples of names of commonly used SSRIs include Prozac, Serotonin, Zoloft, and Celexa. These medications are thought to work by increasing the availability of a particular neurotransmitter, serotonin, which seems to enhance mood states. Other classes of medications are also used in treating depression and related problems. However, most of the research on the use of any of these medications for treating depression has been conducted with adults and older adolescents, and most of the available medications are not specifically approved by the U.S. Food and Drug Administration for use with children.

In sum, depression in children and adolescents has been long overlooked in the education and mental health fields, and it is a source of suffering for many youths and their families. However, there have been important recent advances in assessment, identification, and treatment of depression that have provided clinicians with increasingly effective tools to prevent and treat this problem.

See also: Development

Additional Readings for Nonprofessionals

Cytryn, L., & McKnew, D. (1998). *Growing up sad. Childhood depression and its treatment.* New York: Norton.

Fassler, D. G., & Dumas, L. S. (1998). *"Help me. I'm sad": Recognizing, treating, and preventing childhood and adolescent depression.* New York: Penguin.

Additional Readings for Professionals

Merrell, K. W. (2001). *Helping students overcome depression and anxiety.* New York: Guilford.

Reynolds, W. M., & Johnston, H. F. (1994). *Handbook of depression in children and adolescents.* New York: Plenum.

KENNETH W. MERRELL
DUANE M. ISAVA

Development

See: Sexual Development

Diagnostic and Statistical Manual of Mental Disorders

The *Diagnostic and Statistical Manual of Mental Disorders* (*DSM*) is published by the American Psychiatric Association (APA). The *DSM* is designed to aid clinicians in making diagnoses of mental disorders, facilitating research, and improving communication between clinicians and researchers. The *DSM* offers the official terminology used by psychiatrists, psychologists, social workers, physicians, and other health professionals who work with individuals with mental health issues. The *DSM* is also used to guide health care recordkeeping and to establish categories for epidemiological research into the prevalence and outcomes associated with mental disorders.

HISTORY

The *DSM* was originally published in 1952 in an effort to aid in statistical recordkeeping and to provide guidelines for making diagnoses. Numeric codes presented in the first edition matched codes used in the *International Classification of Diseases* (6th ed.) (*ICD*) (WHO, 1948). The second edition of the *DSM* was released in 1968 and the third edition came 12 years later. The *DSM-III* was followed in 1987 by a minor revision called the *DSM-III-R*. The fourth edition (*DSM-IV*) was released in 1994 and then updated with a text revision 6 years later. Thus, the most current edition is the *DSM-IV-TR* (*Diagnostic and Statistical Manual of Mental Disorders* [4th ed., text rev.], 2000). The most recent editions are regarded as the most empirically based and most reliable classification system yet for addressing mental disorders (Adams, Luscher, & Bernat, 2001).

MULTIAXIAL DIAGNOSIS

The *DSM* requires that diagnosticians include information across five axes. Axis I is used to indicate either clinical disorders or other conditions that may be the primary focus of clinical attention. Axis II lists longstanding diagnoses such as personality disorders or mental retardation. Axis III is used to list medical conditions that may be relevant to understanding or treating the individual's problem. Axis IV provides a checklist for current psychosocial stressors and environmental problems that may affect diagnosis, prognosis, and treatment selection. Finally, Axis V provides a quick summary of the individual's global functioning level.

The multiaxial reporting format is a clear improvement over the former system, where only primary diagnostic categories were recorded. One could easily imagine how important it could be to consider information across these areas of concern when planning treatment for an individual with symptoms of Attention-Deficit/Hyperactivity Disorder (ADHD) who has juvenile-onset diabetes and recently separated parents versus planning treatment for a child with ADHD who has no medical complications and negligible social stressors. These two cases should receive different treatment packages even though the children carry the same primary diagnosis. Thus, the multiaxial format makes it harder for a health care professional to treat a person solely on the basis of an Axis I disorder.

DSM DIAGNOSES AND SCHOOL CONSIDERATIONS

Emotional and behavioral disorders often compromise a student's ability to participate in public education. However, children diagnosed with a mental disorder listed in the *DSM* do not automatically qualify for special education or support services in most states. In fact, federal laws are written so that a diagnosis provided by a single health care provider is not typically enough to determine access to specialized support. In 1997, Congress reauthorized the Individuals with Disabilities Education Act (IDEA) that, among other things, requires multidisciplinary teams to conduct specialized assessments above and beyond diagnostic evaluations for children suspected of having a disability. Many children have received appropriate assessment and treatment options because of this law. Because of a variety of reasons beyond the scope of this entry, children with severe social maladjustment (e.g., conduct disorder) may be excluded from public schools in many states. In practice, children diagnosed with *DSM*'s category of Conduct Disorder often are considered to have severe social maladjustment. Readers should know that there are current lobbying efforts underway by the National Association of School Psychologists (NASP) to address the exclusion of children.

IMPLICATIONS OF DIAGNOSIS

An important implication of receiving a diagnosis is that health professionals will be involved in following the child.

Other benefits may be that a diagnosis may provide children and their families with access to specialized assessment and treatment services, to selected medications approved to treat their disorder, and even to insurance benefits in some cases. Although receiving a diagnosis may provide access to resources, there are several important cautions about labeling effects. The *DSM* offers diagnoses from a classification system for *disorders that people have* rather than the *people* themselves. Nevertheless, the social implications of receiving a diagnosis can be substantial. Many are concerned with labeling effects on the child or people in the child's world. Care must be taken to monitor and discourage the phenomenon known as "self-fulfilling prophecy," where children start behaving in ways consistent with their diagnostic label. For diagnosed children, this can result in lowered standards or reduced efforts in academic and social domains. Staff and parents must be careful that they adjust expectations and alter their own behavior on the basis of the child's individual situation rather than the child's diagnosis. School psychologists will want to be familiar with the educational validity of different diagnostic categories before using the diagnosis to make predictions about the child's prognosis under different conditions.

WHEN SCHOOL PERSONNEL WORK WITH COMMUNITY MENTAL HEALTH PROVIDERS

School psychologists may have to work with mental health professionals from community settings who are unaware of how multidisciplinary teams are required by law to utilize several sources of input in determining an individualized education plan. A local psychiatrist or community mental health clinician may not understand that no single clinician can be the sole determiner of a child's status and may be surprised to find out that his/her diagnosis is not simply accepted by the local school system (Doucette, 2002).

KEY STRENGTHS AND WEAKNESSES OF THE CURRENT *DSM*

The most recent versions of the *DSM* have a couple of key strengths worth noting. First, they have produced the highest reliability ratings (e.g., agreements on diagnoses among professionals) to date. This is good in that the more reliable a category, the more consistently it can be applied across children, settings, and time. Second, the latest revisions have been based on the strong empirical evidence rather than simply expert consensus. Within the childhood disorders, for example, the category of ADHD has received perhaps the most empirical scrutiny. Large-scale, multisite field trials yielded a wealth of data to determine diagnostic features such as symptom lists and symptom cutoff scores. For example, education validity issues were carefully considered in setting the cutoff scores for determining if the Inattention component of the ADHD diagnostic criteria was met. Children meeting six or more *DSM-IV* symptoms of Inattention (using total number reported by a parent and by a teacher) have an extreme risk of academic impairment (McBurnett, 1996).

Despite key strengths, several problems with the *DSM-IV-TR* remain that have a practical impact on children, educators, and health care providers. One issue is that the *DSM* continues to rely on a *categorical* as opposed to a *dimensional* classification approach. A categorical system uses present/absent-based criteria (e.g., "yes/no" to symptom presence, and the individual must exhibit at least six symptoms to qualify for the diagnosis) rather than continuum-based criteria (How severe is the symptom on a scale of 1 to 100?). Although this approach results in increased reliability, it also results in a number of subthreshold cases where individuals with substantial symptomatology are excluded from receiving a diagnosis and therefore may not receive treatment.

Another significant problem is that there are significant comorbidity issues with many of the diagnoses. This is evident with many childhood disorders (e.g., ADHD and other disorders such as Conduct Disorder, Oppositional Defiant Disorders, and Learning Disorders). High levels of comorbidity within a classification system make using the system for treatment selection more problematic. Also, because high levels of comorbidity reduce diagnostic reliability, rules have been added to promote categorical exclusivity. The *DSM* contains many such rules but some critics argue that arbitrarily adding these rules may artificially inflate reliability estimates while not adding to the overall validity of the classification system.

McBurnett (1996) points out that although it is a good thing to have increased emphasis on requiring empirical support to evaluate modifications of *DSM* categories, there has been an uneven amount of research conducted on many disorders quite likely to confront school personnel. For example, a great deal of research has been reported on ADHD but relatively little has been integrated on behalf of the diagnostic categories for Mental Retardation and Learning Disorders.

MAKING THE DIAGNOSIS

The *DSM* does not include explicit guidelines for collecting the information required to make diagnoses. However, several categories that affect school-aged children clearly require input from school personnel familiar with the child's symptoms and level of impairment. For example, ADHD criteria require that symptoms be present in more than one setting (i.e., school and home), so teachers are often asked to supply information on symptoms at school. School psychologists and other personnel should be prepared to facilitate collection of information necessary for health care providers assessing for *DSM* diagnoses.

One word of caution is in order at this point. Just as someone without training in psychoeducational assessment should not attempt to administer an IQ test, someone without training in diagnostic interviewing and the use of assessment instruments will not be able to use the *DSM* in a valid manner. Thus, individuals who have access to a *DSM* should not consider themselves qualified to use it. Structured interviews have been developed, which greatly increase the reliability and validity of diagnostic decision making (McGrath, Handwerk, Armstrong, Lucas, & Friman, in press). These structured interviews are quite detailed and require significant training before they can be used in a valid manner (Schaffer, Fisher, Lucas, Dulcan, & Schwab-Stone, 2000).

OVERALL

The *DSM-IV-TR* (2000) represents a work in progress. The most recent revisions of the *DSM* have been made with perhaps the greatest emphasis on empirical findings in history. Nevertheless, there remains an uneven amount of research conducted across disorders and, unfortunately for school psychologists, relatively little research in the areas of learning disorders and mental retardation. On the plus side, the diagnostic criteria for many disorders (e.g., ADHD) have undergone substantial empirically based revisions and now offer reasonable reliability and improved validity for most disorders (McBurnett, 1996).

The *DSM* should be used by professionals who have had appropriate training in supervised settings. It is not to be used in cookbook fashion by untrained individuals. Professionals and consumers alike will have to understand that although the *DSM* does not lead to treatment selection (and was not designed to do so!), it does facilitate more reliable communication between professionals.

School psychologists will likely find that their training in functional behavioral assessment and psychoeducational testing is much more relevant for assisting the majority of students in their schools. However, all school psychologists should be prepared to help identify appropriate informants when *DSM* diagnoses are sought, and should be especially attentive to coordinating multidisciplinary efforts when outside health professionals providing *DSM* diagnoses are involved. It is likely that school psychologists will be in a unique position to facilitate communication between school personnel familiar with state and federal requirements for assisting students with learning difficulties and health professionals who use the *DSM*.

BIBLIOGRAPHY

Adams, H. E., Luscher, K. A., & Bernat, J. A. (2001). The classification of abnormal behavior: An overview. In H. E. Adams & P. B. Sutker (Eds.), *Comprehensive handbook of psychopathology* (3rd ed., pp. 3–28). New York: Kluwer/Plenum.

American Psychiatric Association. (2000). *Diagnostic and statistical manual of mental disorders* (4th ed., text rev.). Washington, DC: Author.

Doucette, A. (2002). Child and adolescent diagnosis: The need for a model-based approach. In L. E. Beutler & M. L. Malik (Eds.), *Rethinking the DSM: A psychological perspective* (pp. 201–220). Washington, DC: American Psychological Association.

Frances, A. J., Widiger, T. A., & Pincus, H. A. (1989). The development of *DSM-IV*. *Archives of General Psychiatry, 46,* 373–375.

Individuals with Disabilities Education Act. (Pub. L. 105–17), 20 U.S.C. § 1400 (1997).

McBurnett, K. (1996). Development of the *DSM-IV*: Validity and relevance for school psychologists. *School Psychology Review, 25,* 259–263.

McGrath, A. M., Handwerk, M. L., Armstrong, K. J., Lucas, C. P., & Friman, P. C. (2004). The validity of the ADHD section of the Diagnostic Interview Schedule for Children. *Behavior Modification, 28,* 349–374.

National Association of School Psychologists. (March, 2002). *Diagnosis and treatment of attention disorders: Roles for school personnel* (rev. ed.). Retrieved September 16, 2002, from http://www.naspcenter.org/factsheets/add_fs.html

Westen, D., Heim, A. K., Morrison, K., Patterson, M., & Campbell, L. (2002). Simplifying diagnosis using a prototype-matching approach: Implications for the next edition of the *DSM*. In L. E. Beutler & M. L. Malik (Eds.), *Rethinking the DSM: A psychological perspective* (pp. 221–250). Washington, DC: American Psychological Association.

World Health Organization. (1948). *Manual of the international statistical classification of diseases, injuries, and causes of death* (6th ed.). Geneva: Author.

Additional Reading for Nonprofessionals

http://www.nasponline.org (National Association of School Psychologists)

Additional Readings for Professionals

House, A. E. (2002). *DSM-IV diagnosis in the schools (updated 2002).* New York: Guilford.

Schaffer, D., Fisher, M., Lucas, C. P., Dulcan, M. K., & Schwab-Stone, M. E. (2000). NIMH Diagnostic Interview Schedule for Children Version IV (NIMH DISC-IV: Description, differences from previous versions, and reliability of some common diagnoses). *Journal of the American Academy of Child & Adolescent Psychiatry, 39,* 28–38.

KEVIN J. ARMSTRONG

Diana v. State Board of Education

During the 1960s and 1970s, a significant number of educational reforms occurred, particularly with regard to the classification and placement of children in special education. Many changes were sought because minority children were found to be overrepresented in special education, especially in the category of mental retardation. Several court cases were brought against individual states and independent school districts, which resulted in changes in special education practices, including nondiscriminatory assessment, due process, parental involvement, and the placement of children into the least restrictive environment possible. These changes were ultimately integrated into federal laws such as Public Law (Pub. L.) 94–142 (Macmillan, Hendrick, & Watkins, 1988).

Diana v. State Board of Education was a civil, class-action lawsuit filed on behalf of nine Mexican American students living in California who had been placed in classes serving students classified as educable mentally retarded (EMR). Current practice at that time was to classify and place students in special education on the basis of standardized, norm-referenced intelligence test scores (e.g., Stanford–Binet). The suit was filed to prevent the Board of Education from placing children in EMR classes on the basis of the results of standardized intelligence tests. Plaintiffs claimed the intelligence tests used for placement purposes were linguistically biased against students whose primary or first language was not English. In addition, the intelligence tests used were weighted heavily with verbal items and subtests. All subtests had verbal directions, and many subtests required verbal responses from the test taker. Therefore, plaintiffs argued, a disproportionate number of bilingual children were being placed in EMR classes not because they were mentally retarded, but because they performed poorly on intelligence tests that were administered in English (Gatti & Gatti, 1975). As an example, one of the plaintiffs, Diana, was from a predominantly Spanish-speaking family. Her original special education placement in an EMR classroom was made on the basis of an IQ score of 30, which was obtained from an intelligence test administered in English only. When she was reassessed by a bilingual psychologist using the same intelligence test, Diana's obtained IQ score was significantly higher, suggesting that she had been incorrectly placed in the EMR classroom (Jacob-Timm & Hartshorne, 1998).

In 1970, the case was settled and both parties agreed to several stipulations. According to the consent decree, the California State Board of Education was required to conduct all future intelligence testing in a child's native language using interpreters or bilingual psychologists. If this was not possible, then children were to be tested with sections of tests not requiring the use of English in student responses (e.g., performance-related subtests). All Mexican American and Chinese students who were currently in EMR classes were retested in their native languages. Indeed, seven of the nine students named in *Diana* were able to transition back to the general education setting following retesting. In addition, the California school districts were required to make a special effort to help all students who were misplaced by transition into their new educational environments. The school districts also agreed to try to create an intelligence test that would be appropriate for individuals whose native language was not English.

BIBLIOGRAPHY

Gatti, R. D., & Gatti, D. J. (1975). *Encyclopedic dictionary of school law.* New York: Parker.

Jacob-Timm, S., & Hartshorne, T. S. (1998). *Ethics and law for school psychologists* (3rd ed.). New York: Wiley.

Macmillan, D. L., Hendrick, I. G., & Watkins, A. V. (1988). Impact of Diana, Larry P., and Pub. L. 94–142 on minority students. *Exceptional Children, 54,* 426–432.

Additional Readings for Nonprofessionals

http://www.ideapractices.org/
http://www.wrightslaw.com/

Additional Readings for Professionals

Diana v. State Board of Education. Civil Action No. C-70-37 (N. D. Cal. 1970).

Forness, S. R. (1985). Effects of public policy at the state level: California's impact on MR, LD, and ED categories. *Remedial and Special Education, 6*(3), 36–43.

HEATHER E. STERLING-TURNER
MELANIE DUBARD

Differential Reinforcement

Differential reinforcement is a behavioral procedure utilizing two basic behavioral principles: reinforcement and extinction. In differential reinforcement, a desirable behavior is reinforced while undesirable behaviors are not reinforced. As a result, the desirable behavior is strengthened and undesirable behaviors are weakened (Miltenberger, 2001). Differential reinforcement is used when the goal is to increase the frequency (or some other dimension) of a particular behavior relative to other less desirable behaviors. Teachers use differential reinforcement when they provide praise for correct answers but not for incorrect answers in an attempt to strengthen correct responding by their students. Teachers use differential reinforcement when they provide praise or other reinforcers for any form of desirable behavior from their students (using manners, sharing, asking appropriate questions in class, turn taking, completing assignments, etc.), while not providing reinforcers for competing or undesirable behaviors. Differential reinforcement is a component of a number of behavioral acquisition procedures such as shaping, prompting and fading, chaining, and behavioral skills training procedures.

There are three major variations of differential reinforcement: differential reinforcement of alternative behavior, differential reinforcement of other behavior, and differential reinforcement of low rates of behavior (Miltenberger, 2001).

DIFFERENTIAL REINFORCEMENT OF ALTERNATIVE BEHAVIOR (DRA)

The terms *DRA* and *differential reinforcement* are often used synonymously. In DRA a specific desirable behavior is reinforced while undesirable alternative behaviors are not reinforced. DRA is used when a student has a behavioral deficit (a desirable behavior that does not occur often enough) and the teacher wants to increase the frequency of the behavior, or when a student has a behavioral excess (a problem behavior that occurs too frequently) and the teacher wants to decrease the frequency of the behavior. In both cases, the teacher strengthens the desirable behavior by reinforcing its occurrence and weakens the competing or undesirable behavior through extinction.

DRA is an appropriate procedure to use when (a) the desirable behavior is already occurring at least occasionally so that it can be reinforced and (b) you have identified a reinforcer that you can use to strengthen the desirable behavior. If a desirable behavior is not occurring at least occasionally, you must use a procedure such as shaping or prompting to get it to occur so that it can be reinforced.

You can identify a reinforcer to use in a DRA procedure (or other differential reinforcement procedures) in a number of ways: (a) ask the student (or the student's parents) what his/her preferences are, (b) observe the student to identify preferred activities or items to use as reinforcers, (c) observe the student to identify the reinforcer for problem behaviors, and (d) conduct a systematic reinforcer assessment in which you test the effects of a variety of possible reinforcers (e.g., Fisher et al., 1992). When DRA is used to decrease a problem behavior, it is important to conduct a functional assessment of the problem behavior to identify the reinforcer maintaining the behavior. Once you have identified the reinforcer for the problem behavior, you can deliver this reinforcer contingent on the desirable behavior while withholding the reinforcer when the problem behavior occurs (e.g., Durand, Crimmins, Caufield, & Taylor, 1989). In this way, the desirable behavior you are strengthening is functionally equivalent to the problem behavior (produces the same reinforcer). The desirable behavior should take the place of the problem behavior if it produces the reinforcer and the problem behavior no longer produces the reinforcer. For example, if a student's disruptive behavior in the classroom is reinforced by teacher attention (the teacher provides reprimands or extensive discussion following the problem), DRA would involve withholding attention when the student engaged in disruptive behavior (extinction) while providing attention for appropriate behavior such as participation in class activities. Likewise, if a student's problem behavior is reinforced by escape from academic activities (the teacher terminates a task when the problem behavior occurs), DRA would require that the teacher not terminate the task when the problem behavior occurs (extinction) while reinforcing task completion with a break or the delivery of other reinforcers.

DIFFERENTIAL REINFORCEMENT OF OTHER BEHAVIOR (DRO)

DRO is a procedure in which the reinforcer is delivered following an interval of time in which the problem behavior is absent while the reinforcer is withheld following the occurrence of the problem behavior (e.g., Mazaleski, Iwata, Vollmer, Zarcone, & Smith, 1993). In this way, the absence of the problem behavior is reinforced and the problem behavior is extinguished. Although its name would suggest that a reinforcer is contingent on some "other behavior," in fact the reinforcer is contingent on the absence of the problem behavior during consecutive intervals of time. Unlike DRA, which is used to strengthen desirable behavior, DRO is used to decrease undesirable behavior by reinforcing its absence.

The following steps are involved in the use of DRO: (1) Identify the problem behavior to be decreased. (2) Identify the reinforcer to deliver contingent on the absence of the problem behavior. (3) Choose the DRO intervals. The DRO intervals should be short enough initially so that a number of intervals will elapse without an occurrence of the problem behavior and, thus, the reinforcer can be delivered. Over time, the intervals are lengthened as the problem behavior decreases.

To implement DRO, you use a stopwatch or clock to time the intervals and, following each interval in which the problem behavior does not occur, deliver the reinforcer. If the problem behavior occurs in an interval, do not deliver the reinforcer and reset the interval. For example, a 6-year-old girl with mental retardation banged her head on the floor for teacher attention numerous times throughout the day. DRO involved the delivery of attention following every 15 seconds that she did not bang her head. When she did bang her head during an interval, the teacher provided no attention and reset the interval to 15 seconds again. After head banging had decreased to low levels with the 15-second interval, the DRO interval was increased to 30 seconds, then 1 minute, and so on over a period of days and weeks. Eventually, the interval was increased to 30 minutes,

which was manageable for the teacher to implement in the classroom.

DIFFERENTIAL REINFORCEMENT OF LOW RATES OF BEHAVIOR (DRL)

DRL is a procedure in which the reinforcer is delivered when the target behavior occurs at a lower rate relative to its baseline rate of occurrence (e.g., Deitz & Repp, 1973). The goal of DRL is to decrease the rate of a behavior but not necessarily to eliminate it. Therefore, DRL is used when the target behavior is a problem by virtue of its excessive rate of occurrence. There are two variations of DRL: full-session DRL and spaced-responding DRL.

In full-session DRL, the reinforcer is delivered if the target behavior occurs fewer than a specified number of times during the session or observation period. For example, if there is an excessive number of talk outs during a 50-minute junior high school class, the teacher could use a full-session DRL procedure. The teacher would identify a tolerable number of talk outs during the class period and tell the students that if they kept the number below that level for the 50 minutes they could get 5 minutes of extra free time as a reinforcer. When using the full-session DRL procedure, it is important to provide feedback on the number of responses in the session. For example, the teacher could put a tally mark on the board each time there is a talk out and the students could see how close they were getting to the DRL criterion for reinforcement.

In spaced-responding DRL, a reinforcer is delivered for a response only if it is separated from the previous response by a specified interval of time. If the response occurs before the end of the interval, the reinforcer is not delivered and the interval is reset. The goal is to slow down the response rate by requiring that a certain amount of time occur between responses for a reinforcer to be delivered. In full-session DRL, the timing of responses is not important. In spaced-responding DRL, the timing of responses is important. For example, suppose that a student raises her hand so many times during class to answer questions that other students do not get a chance to participate. To use spaced-responding DRL, the teacher could tell the student that after she raises her hand she must wait 5 minutes before she can raise her hand again. If she waits the 5 minutes before raising her hand, the teacher will call on her to answer a question (a reinforcer for the student). If she raises her hand before the 5-minute interval is up, the teacher will not call on her and will reset the interval so that she has to wait another 5 minutes before she can raise her hand and get called on by the teacher.

See also: Extinction; Positive Reinforcement

BIBLIOGRAPHY

Dietz, S. M., & Repp, A. C. (1973). Decreasing classroom misbehavior through the use of DRL schedules of reinforcement. *Journal of Applied Behavior Analysis, 6,* 457–463.

Durand, V. M., Crimmins, D. B., Caufield, M., & Taylor, J. (1989). Reinforcer assessment. I: Using problem behavior to select reinforcers. *Journal of the Association for Persons with Severe Handicaps, 14,* 113–126.

Fisher, W., Piazza, C. C., Bowman, L. G., Hagopian, L. P., Owens, J. C., & Sevin, I. (1992). A comparison of two approaches for identifying reinforcers for persons with severe and profound disabilities. *Journal of Applied Behavior Analysis, 25,* 491–498.

Mazaleski, J. L., Iwata, B. A., Vollmer, T. R., Zarcone, J. R., & Smith, R. G. (1993). Analysis of reinforcement and extinction components of DRO contingencies with self-injury. *Journal of Applied Behavior Analysis, 26,* 143–156.

Miltenberger, R. G. (2001). *Behavior modification: Principles and procedures.* Belmont, CA: Wadsworth.

RAYMOND G. MILTENBERGER

Direct Behavioral Consultation

Direct Behavioral Consultation (DBC), a variant of the Behavioral Consultation (BC) model, was first described by Watson and Robinson (1996). DBC is different from other models of consultation in that the consultees (usually teachers) are taught skills directly for both problem solving and intervention implementation. DBC is based on the premise that, many times, consultees lack the necessary skills to accurately identify and analyze a student's (client's) problem behavior as well as design an appropriate intervention.

In traditional models of consultation, consultees and consultants work through four general phases of problem solving: Problem Identification, Problem Analysis, Treatment Plan Implementation, and Plan Evaluation. These stages typically are conducted through interviews with the consultee in which the consultant must rely on teacher report to characterize and evaluate both problem behavior and treatment outcomes. In contrast, the focus during DBC is to use the consultant's interaction with the client to move through the four stages of problem solving.

In the Problem Identification stage, the consultant and consultee define the problem behavior of interest. Unlike other models of consultation, the consultant usually collects data regarding the problem behavior himself or herself, as opposed to relying on teacher report. The consultant frequently will conduct a functional assessment to determine environmental factors contributing to the problem behavior. In Problem Analysis, the consultant models interpretation of data collected in the Problem Identification stage and develops appropriate treatments to alter client behavior in the desired direction. Although the consultant is responsible for most aspects of treatment planning, the consultant seeks input from the consultee regarding resources (e.g., time, materials, etc.) available in the classroom. In Plan Implementation, the consultant directly trains the consultee to implement the designed intervention with accuracy and consistency. In addition, the consultant continues to collect data on student behavior change and provides ongoing feedback on treatment implementation to the consultee. In Plan Evaluation, the consultee and the consultant evaluate the effects of treatment and make decisions of whether treatment modification is required, the treatment is working as planned and should be continued, or the treatment should be terminated because the problem behavior has been remediated. Throughout each stage of the problem-solving process, the consultant models and instructs the consultee in relevant behaviors (e.g., data collection, data interpretation, etc.) in hopes that the consultee will then be able to use these skills in similar situations in the future.

Although not necessarily unique to DBC, proponents of this model place special emphasis on teacher training in intervention use. Research has shown that the best means by which to train intervention agents is through such procedures as modeling, rehearsal, and performance-based feedback. Research support for the DBC model in the area of teacher training is robust and continues to mount. For instance, Sterling-Turner, Watson, and Moore (2002) compared verbal instructions and direct training methods (rehearsal/feedback) on special education teachers' correct use of interventions (treatment integrity) and subsequent impact on student behavior outcomes. Results showed that indirect, verbal-only training methods did not generally result in high levels of treatment integrity; however, when direct training methods were used, treatment integrity rose to acceptable levels. In addition, when treatments were implemented with high integrity, there were greater changes in student behavior. Watkins-Emonet, Watson, and Shriver (2002) found similar results in their investigation of training methods for teachers working with noncompliant preschoolers. These researchers also found that training in one setting results in the teachers using the same skills in another setting (generalization). This was the first study to measure generalization of treatment effects in consultation. Freeland and Watson (2002) replicated Watkins-Emonet et al. (2002) and found that, after DBC, teachers were more proficient at using praise and were more likely in some cases to generalize their use of label–praise statements to other settings.

A school-based example of the DBC process might be as follows. Leo is referred by his third-grade classroom teacher, Mrs. Borrat, for "disrupting the class and not obeying the teacher." The consultant, Dr. Primm, meets Mrs. Borrat to identify specific behaviors of concern. Upon doing so, Dr. Primm schedules times for classroom observation to (a) confirm the verbal report of behavioral concern and (b) to collect data on the identified behaviors. On the basis of the observation, Dr. Primm may either agree that a behavior problem does exist as stated or meet with the teacher to convey the results of the observation in an attempt to reidentify the correct problem behavior. Dr. Pimm noted in his observations that Leo was typically more disruptive (in this case defined as out of seat, yelling at the teacher, and poking other children with his pencil) when assigned any task that involved reading. Dr. Primm decides that a functional assessment is warranted in this consultation case to identify variables that may be contributing to Leo's disruptive behavior. Specifically, Dr. Primm is interested in determining whether or not the type of academic task (i.e., reading) or other variables such as teacher or peer attention are maintaining Leo's behavior. Therefore, Dr. Primm describes the purposes and procedures of functional assessment to Mrs. Borrat. Working together, they conduct a naturalistic functional assessment and find that reading tasks are reliably associated with disruptive behavior as compared with other variables such as mathematics and other academic tasks. In addition, disruptive behavior was also reliably followed by teacher attention in the form of reprimands, redirection, and academic assistance. As an additional aspect of the Problem Analysis, Dr. Primm models Curriculum-Based Measurement probes for Mrs. Borrat to determine if Leo's current reading skills are commensurate with his teacher's level of instructional materials. Indeed, Leo's reading skills were found to be significantly below that of his peers and his current placement in the reading curriculum. As part of intervention planning, Dr. Primm recommends instructional modification for reading tasks focusing on remediation of deficits. Mrs. Borrat and Dr. Primm also agree to implement a positive-reinforcement-based component whereby Leo is rewarded for completing reading tasks without disruptive behavior. He demonstrates the instructional modification procedures for Mrs. Borrat and then gives her an opportunity to practice using the procedures while he observes so as to provide corrective and reinforcing feedback. Finally, Dr. Primm continues to check on the data by Mrs. Borrat on Leo's problem behavior after the academic intervention was implemented. After a period of 3 weeks, Mrs. Borrat and Dr. Primm review Leo's data for both reading performance and disruptive behavior. Data indicated a dramatic decrease in disruptive behavior as well as a gain in weekly reading test scores. On the basis of these data, Dr. Primm and Mrs. Borrat decide to continue with the intervention but conclude that further meetings are unnecessary at this juncture.

See also: Conjoint Behavioral Consultation; Curriculum-Based Measurement; Functional Behavioral Assessment; Mental Health Consultation; Treatment Integrity

BIBLIOGRAPHY

Freeland, J. T., & Watson, T. S. (2003). *Programming generalization through the use of direct behavioral consultation.* Manuscript submitted for publication.

Sterling-Turner, H. E., Watson, T. S., & Moore, J. W. (2002). Effects of training on treatment integrity and treatment outcomes in school-based consultation. *School Psychology Quarterly, 17,* 47–77.

Watkins-Emonet, C., Watson, T. S., & Shriver, M. D. *Acquisition and generalization of teacher skills following direct behavioral consultation.* Manuscript submitted for publication.

Watson, T. S., & Robinson, S. L. (1996). Direct behavioral consultation: An alternative to traditional behavioral consultation. *School Psychology Quarterly, 11,* 267–278.

Additional Readings for Professionals

Noell, G. H., & Witt, J. C. (1996). A critical re-evaluation of five fundamental assumptions underlying behavioral consultation. *School Psychology Quarterly, 11,* 189–203.

Watson, T. S., Sterling, H. E., & McDade, A. (1997). Demythifying behavioral consultation. *School Psychology Review, 26,* 467–474.

T. STEUART WATSON
HEATHER E. STERLING-TURNER

Discrete Trial Teaching

Discrete trial teaching (DTT) is a method of instruction that includes tight levels of control of the instructional environment, the presentation of teaching materials, and the delivery of reinforcement. DTT is based on principles of applied behavior analysis (ABA), especially the work of B. F. Skinner. According to Skinner, all human behavior, including learning, can be understood and taught through reinforcement of target behaviors. DTT is related to an understanding that learning happens over a series of stages, with lower level skills needed to progress to higher level skills (Rivera & Smith, 1997). Although reinforcement of target behaviors has been identified as a crucial variable in learning, other research has shown that students need to know what the desired behavior is and be able to do the desired behavior at a certain level before rewards will be effective (Rivera & Smith, 1997).

A number of researchers have experimented with the use of teaching methods based on ABA principles. The best known of these is the work of Lovaas and his colleagues (1987), who developed an instructional program for young children with autism that employed discrete trial teaching methods. The DTT methods involved breaking larger behavioral objectives, including language task, into small discrete behaviors that were taught over massed trials under highly controlled conditions. On the basis of the promising results of this and similar research, DTT methods have been used in instructional programs for individuals with moderate to severe disabilities, including autism.

The operational principle in DTT is discrimination training. The learner develops and maintains correct desired behaviors through reinforcement of correct discriminations among objects, words, settings, or people (Miltenberger, 2001). Over time, a basic repertoire of behaviors is built that allows for accurate and appropriate behaviors across a wide variety of settings. A key feature of DTT is the large number of learning trials. These trials are brief, individual opportunities for the learner to give the correct response. Every time the correct response is given, the learner is rewarded. Typically, a large number of trials are offered as a form of "massed practice" so that the learner has many opportunities to be exposed to the educational demands and to be reinforced for correct responding.

Importantly, the learner must have the capacity to engage in the target behavior to be successful on a trial. Thus, DTT emphasizes determining a learner's initial skill levels in the instructional area so that trials are used only for behaviors that the learner can engage in successfully. If discrete trials are held for target behaviors that the learner is unable to do, there will be a low level of reinforcement and the sessions are likely to be ineffective. Once a base rate of responding for known target behaviors is identified, new skills can be taught using DTT as well. The next level of a skill is demonstrated and rehearsed by the teacher with the student. Then, the learner is given multiple trials (opportunities) to do the new skill and reinforced for accurate use of the new skill. In this way DTT is used to link related behaviors together over time with the goal of improved overall daily functioning.

Another key feature of DTT methods is the use of salient reinforcers for all trials. A salient reinforcer is one that is highly desirable for a given learner. For example, Sundberg and Partington (1998) identified edibles and social reinforcement as salient for most learners. If trials are conducted with rewards that the learner dislikes or feels ambivalent about, the sessions are likely to be less effective. In order for DTT to be effective, salient, and person-specific, reinforcers must be identified and used. Over time, the saliency of certain reinforcers may change, for learners and instructors need to be aware of such changes and adjust reinforcers accordingly.

As noted by Sundberg and Partington (1998), DTT has many advantages. It allows for a high number of training trials, can be implemented by staff with minimal training, is easy to run in a classroom setting, target responses are clear, consequences are easy to deliver, student progress is readily observable, curriculum components are preidentified, and it incorporates data collection and progress monitoring of student improvement. In addition, DTT may help to facilitate development of learner behaviors such as attending and stimulus discrimination. At the same time, there are drawbacks to DTT that must be considered. DTT requires specialized procedures and settings, includes mainly teacher-initiated activities, relies on reinforcers that are sometimes not available outside of the trial setting, the tasks include primarily rote responding, and the nonfunctional nature of the training may generate escape or avoidance behaviors.

DTT is one of many teaching strategies that can be used to teach a range of skills and behaviors. Although commonly thought of as a strategy for use with individuals with severe disabilities such as autism, it has also been used in other teaching situations such as teaching athletic skills; teaching academic skills (rewriting spelling words); managing social situations such as rehearsing an important speech; and daily tasks such as baking cookies. All of these are examples of how DTT employs consistent presentation of task-specific stimuli, repeated practice of target behavior, and reinforcement for correct responding as part of instructional methods.

See also: Autism; Positive Reinforcement

BIBLIOGRAPHY

Lovaas, I. (1987). Behavioral treatment and normal educational and intellectual functioning in young autistic children. *Journal of Consulting and Clinical Psychology, 55*, 3–9.

Rivera, D. P., & Smith, D. D. (1997). *Teaching students with learning and behavior problems* (3rd ed.). Boston: Allyn & Bacon.

Sundberg, M. L., & Partington, J. W. (1998). *Teaching language to children with autism or other developmental disabilities.* Pleasant Hill, CA: Behavior Analysts.

Additional Reading for Nonprofessionals

Miltenberger, R. G. (2001). *Behavior modification: Principles and procedures.* Belmont, CA: Wadsworth/Thomson Learning.

Additional Reading for Professionals

Maurice, C., Green, G., & Luce, S. C. (1996). *Behavioral intervention for young children with autism.* Austin, TX: Pro-Ed.

RACHEL BROWN-CHIDSEY
MARK W. STEEGE

Divorce

Divorce is an unfortunate and painful reality in American society. Roughly one half of all marriages end in divorce, a figure that peaked in 1980 and has been slightly decreasing for three decades. Approximately 1 million children each year are affected by divorce and may experience both short- and long-term consequences associated with their parents' disunion. It is not, however, a foregone conclusion that children of divorced parents will necessarily suffer any or all of the adverse consequences of divorce. There are a number of factors that seem to buffer, or make children more resilient to, the pain of traumatic events such as divorce. Divorce is a complicated matter with many issues that are well beyond what can be adequately addressed in this entry. Therefore, this entry will answer some of the most frequently asked questions about divorce.

WHO GETS DIVORCED?

Although divorce affects all cultural groups, the divorce rate among African Americans is higher than that of whites, Hispanics, and Asian Americans. There appear to be two "peak" periods for divorce, one before 7 years of marriage and the other after 20 years of marriage. Thus, some parents choose to divorce while the children are still young and others seem to choose to wait until the children are grown and out of the house. Those who marry young tend to have higher divorce rates than those who wait until they are older.

HOW ARE CHILDREN AFFECTED?

Divorce is not an *event*; it is a *process* that may affect children's lives for relatively long periods of time. Thus, one must consider both the short- and long-term effects on children and when they become adults. The short-term effects have more to do with adjusting to everyday life without one of the parents (usually the father) and the concomitant changes it brings about versus divorce per se.

It is far too simplistic to say that girls are more affected or differently affected by divorce than boys and vice versa. Some studies have suggested that girls are more likely to evidence increased difficulties with anxiety and depression (internalizing problems) whereas boys are more likely to be aggressive or engage in overtly negative behavior (externalizing problems). Other studies have not supported this differentiation between boys and girls. Girls from divorced families tend to begin sexual intercourse at an earlier age than girls from intact families. It has been suggested that boys who live with their unmarried mothers are more vulnerable to the effects of divorce, even up to 6 years after the divorce. Results of other studies tend to show that it is the father's involvement (because most often fathers are noncustodial) that is responsible for either buffering or enhancing the negative effects for both boys and girls. Children whose

fathers are involved, emotionally close, warm, supportive, and psychologically healthy tend to adjust better and evidence less problems than children whose fathers are the opposite. On the academic side, math scores tend to be lower in children whose parents are divorced as compared with children who live with both parents and are slightly less likely to graduate from high school. On a related note, research indicates that male, African American children are the most susceptible to adverse effects, perhaps because African American males are less likely to have contact with their children postdivorce. Even in those situations where children exhibit more problems after the divorce than before, there seems to be a return to "normalcy" after about 2 years.

As adults, children of divorce often have painful memories of divorce and still believe that the divorce affects them in some profound way. For instance, nearly three fourths of adults indicated that they would be different and that their lives would be different in some significant way had their parents not divorced. About half believe that they would be a different person if they had spent more time with their father, worry about events like marriages and graduation where both parents will attend, believe that their childhood was more difficult, and report that they remember missing their father very much. Sadly, about 30 percent wonder if their father loves them.

FACTORS THAT AFFECT CHILDREN'S ADJUSTMENT

One of the primary factors that affects children's adjustment to divorce is parental conflict. In fact, children from divorced families where there is low parental conflict do not differ in psychological adjustment from nondivorced families with low parental conflict. Interestingly, children from families where there is high parental conflict often improve after a divorce. The most common themes in postdivorce parental conflict involve visitation with the noncustodial parent, child support, custody, and discipline. Children who are aware of conflict involving these issues tend to be more affected than children who either are unaware of the conflict or for whom there is no conflict on these issues.

The psychological health of the parents is one of the central factors in determining postdivorce adjustment. Although depression is a common adult response to divorce, it is typically considered a transient psychological state that will abate about 2 years after the divorce. In this context, psychological health refers to more longstanding mental health issues. For instance, a parent who suffered from bipolar disorder before the divorce will still exhibit these behaviors postdivorce, with the divorce perhaps making the symptoms worse. It is not merely the presence of a mental disorder that affects a child's adjustment to divorce; rather it is the degree to which the disorder affects the parent's ability to parent, provide supervision, and foster and develop close emotional relationships with their children.

Another factor strongly affecting adjustment to divorce is the child's diminished contact with the noncustodial parent (usually the father), with as many as 25 percent of fathers having no contact with their children 2–3 years postdivorce. Over time, contact that was once present tends to decrease. Some research has suggested that it is not necessarily the amount of contact the children have with the noncustodial parent but the *quality* of that contact that is more important. Quality may be defined as frequent visits that are relatively conflict free, allow the development of emotional closeness, do not involve psychopathology of the noncustodial parent, and that are supported by the custodial parent. Care must be taken between the parents when providing opportunities and visitation schedules, as research has found that increased contact with the noncustodial parent often increases parental conflict.

Quite obviously, the child's relationship with the custodial parent also affects postdivorce adjustment. It is interesting that the type of parenting best suited for children of divorce is also that which is best suited for all children—firm limits and guidelines for behavior, supportive, warm, emotionally close, not overly indulgent, and reasonable discipline. Often, ineffective parenting that existed prior to the divorce is merely perpetuated and perhaps exacerbated following the divorce, which results in an increase in problem behaviors exhibited by the child. Other times, factors that diminish a custodial parent's quality of parenting may be present, including parental conflict, decreased financial stability and resources, and depression.

PROTECTIVE FACTORS (BUFFERS)

There are at least four factors that help children adjust more rapidly to the pain of divorce and that seem to decrease the intensity of the negative feelings associated with divorce. The first and most important factor is a positive relationship with the custodial parent. The negative effects of divorce are reduced when the relationship between the children and their custodial parent is warm but with firm discipline. The second factor relates to the amount and type of conflict between the parents. When there is little conflict or when conflict is controlled, not accessible to the children, is not hostile, and is resolved satisfactorily, children adjust more rapidly to the divorce. The third factor has to do with economic stability. When there is little to no change in the lifestyle of the custodial parent and the children following the divorce, children tend to cope better with divorce. Conversely, when the lifestyle changes dramatically because the custodial parent does not have the economic

means to support the lifestyle to which they have become accustomed, children find adapting to the divorce more difficult. Obviously, this factor is more important for older children than for those who are so young that they have no basis for comparing pre- and postdivorce lifestyles. The fourth factor involves the relationship with the noncustodial parent. If that relationship is positive and supportive, then children tend to adjust more rapidly and with fewer problems than children whose relationship with the noncustodial parent is strained or nonexistent. This fourth factor does not seem to be as important for predicting psychological adjustment, but is important for reducing painful feelings that may persist into adulthood.

WHAT IS THE BEST CUSTODY/VISITATION ARRANGEMENT?

Custody and visitation are extremely complex and emotionally fraught issues. There is no one best answer and each situation must be carefully reviewed before decisions are made. The information in this section assumes that there is no type of abuse perpetrated by either of the parents. In cases where abuse has been documented and substantiated (vs. merely accused), the issue of custody and visitation is a simple one. Most cases of divorce, fortunately, do not involve issues of abuse. There are two types of custody: (1) physical and (2) legal. Physical custody has to do with where the children reside a majority of the time. Legal custody has to do with who has the responsibility of making decisions on behalf of the child. Either type of custody may be sole or joint. In many instances, parents share legal custody but only one parent has physical custody.

Although the primary legal mandate under which custody decisions are made is in the "best interests of the child," there are no adequate clinical or legal guidelines for determining the child's best interests. However, the Uniform Marriage and Divorce Act set forth five considerations when determining the best interests of the child and include (1) the wishes of the parent(s); (2) the wishes of the child; (3) the relationship of the child with parents, siblings, and significant others; (4) the child's adjustment to home, school, and the community; and (5) the mental and physical health of all parties involved. It is important to mention that most states do not use grounds for divorce (e.g., adultery, irreconcilable differences) as a factor when deciding custody. That is, a parent may have committed adultery but that in no way prevents them from gaining custody of their child. Obviously, in cases where abuse has occurred, different rules and standards apply.

Determining the type of custody situation is not simple. There is evidence to suggest that boys who reside with their father are more well adjusted than children who reside with their mother. Joint physical custody, although potentially more difficult and conflict-provoking, can be made to work if both parties are committed to the arrangement. There is research to support both sole and joint physical custody and that the decision regarding custody must be made on an individual basis with compassion and care for the well-being of the children.

See also: Coping; Stress

BIBLIOGRAPHY

Laumann-Billings, L., & Emery, R. E. (2000). Distress among young adults from divorced families. *Journal of Family Psychology, 13*, 1–12.

Additional Reading for Nonprofessionals

Emery, R. E. (2003). *The truth about children and divorce.* New York: Viking/Penguin.

Additional Reading for Professionals

Schroeder, C. S., & Gordon, B. N. (2002). *Assessment and treatment of childhood problems: A clinician's guide* (2nd ed.). New York: Guilford.

T. STEUART WATSON
RACHEL J. VALLELEY

Doctoral Training Programs in School Psychology

A current listing of doctoral training programs in school psychology that are approved by the National Association of School Psychologists may be found online at http://www.nasponline.org/certification/gradschools.html

Drugs (Psychotropic Medication)

Psychotropic medications are frequently utilized to treat child and adolescent behavioral and emotional problems (Zito et al., 2000). Although a comprehensive review of all medications prescribed for childhood disorders is beyond the scope of this entry, Table 1 lists many of the more commonly prescribed psychotropic drugs.

There are several important caveats to bear in mind when perusing the table. First, the listing of psychotropic medications used to treat child and adolescent behavioral and emotional problems is not comprehensive. Only some of the more frequently prescribed medications are listed. Second, indications for use include those officially recognized by the U.S. Food and Drug Administration (FDA) as well as common off-label uses. Still, many of the medications may have infrequent application beyond the indications listed in the table (e.g., the use of BuSpar for ADHD is rare but not unheard of). And third, the area of psychopharmacology constantly changes, which renders making an up-to-date list nearly impossible.

The effectiveness ratings provided in the table are rather subjective. No formal criteria were used in deriving these ratings. These are simply estimates based on multiple extant published data and comprehensive reviews of empirical knowledge regarding the effectiveness of these classes of drugs for particular child and adolescent disorders. Informal criteria used in deriving these ratings included

5: Multiple randomized clinical trials; multiple open-label trials; high percentage of children and adolescent responders; clearly more effective than placebo/other treatments.

3: Few, if any, randomized clinical trials; multiple open-label trials; and/or moderate–high level of children and adolescent responders; or evidence of effectiveness, though some inconsistent findings across studies.

1: No randomized clinical trials; few open-label trials; and/or low–moderate level of children and adolescent responders; or little evidence of effectiveness, many inconsistent findings across studies.

It is important to bear in mind that lower ratings do not necessarily mean that the drug is ineffective. Rather, a lower rating may either be due to ineffectiveness, lack of data regarding its effectiveness, or both. Data reviewed include only those studies in which children and adolescents were the primary or sole participants. Although the effectiveness of many of these drugs for adult disorders has been established, data regarding the use of many of these medications for children and adolescents are lacking (Riddle et al., 2001).

Listings of side effects are not comprehensive. Side effects listed in the table are those commonly associated with the particular class of drug, including both frequent and rare, but serious, side effects. However, many other side effects can develop for each class of drug listed. It should also be noted that there can be rather dramatic differences in side-effect profiles between drugs in the same drug class (e.g., the SSRIs, Prozac and Paxil).

Readers interested in more detailed descriptions of the effectiveness, side effects, and other characteristics of psychotropic medication for children and adolescents should consult the resources below.

Table 1. Common Psychotropic Medications

Drug class	Common indications	Effectiveness	Side effects
Stimulants			
Ritalin (methylphenidate)	ADHD	+ + + + +	*Common*
Dexadrine (dextroamphetamine)			Insomnia, irritability, appetite suppression, tachycardia, paradoxical
Adderall (dextroamphetamine and amphetamine)			worsening of behavior, gastrointestinal distress
			Uncommon, but serious
Concerta (methylphenidate)			Worsening of tics/Tourette's
Metadate (methylphenidate)			
Antidepressants			
SSRIs	Depression	+ + +	*Common*
Prozac (fluoxetine)	OCD	+ + + +	Gastrointestinal distress, sedation, insomnia, dry mouth, weight loss,
Paxil (paroxetine)	Other anxiety	+ +	abnormal dreams, excess sweating, sexual problems, motor
Zoloft (sertraline)	Bulimia	+ +	restlessness, social disinhibition, headache, dermatitis, tremor,
Celexa (citalopram)	ADHD	+ +	abrupt discontinuation syndrome
Luvox (fluvoxamine)	Tics/Tourette's	+ +	*Rare, serious*
			Suicidal ideation
Tricyclics	Depression	+	*Common*
Tofranil (imipramine)	Enuresis	+ + +	Cardiac, drowsiness, dry mouth, blurred vision, constipation,
Elavil (amitriptyline)	ADHD	+ + +	insomnia/nightmares, incoordination
Anafranil (clomipramine)	OCD	+ + + +	*Rare, serious*
	School/separation anxiety	+ +	Sudden death, hypotension, seizures
Other			
Effexor (venlafaxine)	Depression	+	*Common*
	Generalized anxiety	+	Nervousness, weight loss, sleep problems, constipation, nausea,
Desyrel (trazodone)			excessive sweating, sexual side effects
	Depression	+	*Common*
	Insomnia	+	Drowsiness, dry mouth, dizziness, lightheadedness, nausea/vomiting,
Wellbutrin (bupropion)			sexual side effects
	Depression	+	*Common*
	ADHD	+ +	Agitation, motor restlessness, sleep problems, constipation,
			nausea/vomiting, headache, tremor
			Rare, but serious
			Seizures
Mood Stabilizers			
Lithium	Bipolar	+ +	*Common*
Eskalith, Lithobid, Lithotabs	Severe aggression	+ + +	Thirst, weight gain, frequent urination, headaches, hand tremors,
			nausea, fatigue, acne, gastrointestinal problems
			Rare, serious
			Renal impairments, lithium toxicity (coordination problems,
			vomiting, impaired consciousness, seizures), thyroid impairments
Anticonvulsants	Bipolar	+ +	*Common*
Depakote (valproic acid)	Severe aggression	+ +	Sedation, dizziness, gastrointestinal problems, sedation,
Tegretol (carbamazepine)			irritability/mania, incoordination, double vision/vision problems,
			dermatitis, emotional lability
			Rare, serious
			Hepatic failure, polycystic ovarian disease, agranulocytosis
Anxiolytics			
Benzodiazepines	Anxiety disorders	+ +	*Common*
Xanax (alprazolam)	Insomnia	+	Sedation, cognitive dulling, behavioral disinhibition, potential for
			dependence
Librium (chlordiazepoxide)	Anxiety disorders	+	*Common*
Ativan (lorazepam)			Dizziness, headache, drowsiness, insomnia, nausea
Other			
BuSpar (buspirone HCl)			

(Continued)

Table 1. (*Continued*)

Drug class	Common indications	Effectiveness	Side effects
Antipsychotics[a]			
Atypical	Schizophrenia	+ +	*Common*
Risperdol (rispiridone)	Aggression	+ + +	Sedation, cardiac arrhythmias, weight gain, cognitive dulling,
Zyprexa (olanzapine)	Tics/Tourette's	+ + + +	constipation, hypotension, dizziness, dry mouth, sleep
Clozaril (clozapine)	Bipolar	+ +	disturbances, agitation
Typical			*Rare, serious*
Thorazine (chlorpromazine)			Hepatic toxicity, agranulocytosis, dyskinesias, acute dystonia,
Haldol (haloperidol)			extrapyramidal, akathisia, neuroleptic malignant syndrome
Other/Misc.			
Selective norepinephrine reuptake inhibitor			
Strattera (atomoxetine)	ADHD	+ + + + +	*Common*
			Appetite suppression, headache, gastrointestinal distress, irritability,
			dermatitis, dizziness, fatigue
			Rare, but serious
			Cardiac concerns, blood pressure changes
Alpha-adrenergic agonist	ADHD	+ + +	*Common*
Catapres (clonidine)	Aggression	+ +	Sedation, gastrointestinal upset, headaches, hypo/hypertension,
	Tics/Tourette's	+ +	dizziness
			Rare, but serious
			Cardiac problems, vivid dreams, increased blood glucose, sexual
			dysfunction

Note: See text for description of effectiveness ratings. ADHD: Attention-Deficit/Hyperactivity Disorder; OCD: Obsessive–Compulsive Disorder; Tics/Tourette's: chronic motor/vocal tics and Tourette's Disorder.
[a] The newer, atypical antipsychotics are used to treat the same disorders as the older, typical antipsychotics. Atypical antipsychotics produce the same side effects, though typically the prevalence of side effects, especially those rate but serious side effects, is reduced.

BIBLIOGRAPHY

Zito, J. M., Safer, D. J., dosReis, S., Gardner, J. F., Boles, M., & Lynch, F. (2000). Trends in the prescribing of psychotropic medications to preschooler. *Journal of the American Medical Association, 283*, 1025–1030.

Additional Readings for Nonprofessionals

Dulcan, M. K. (1999). *Helping parents, youth, and teachers understand medications for behavioral and emotional problems.* Washington, DC: American Psychiatric Press.
Wilens, T. E. (1999). *Straight talk about psychiatric medications for kids.* New York: Guilford.

Additional Readings for Professionals

Bezchilibnyk-Butler, K. Z., & Jeffries, J. J. (2000). *Clinical handbook of psychotropic drugs* (10th ed.). Seattle, WA: Hogrefe & Huber.
Green, W. H. (2001). *Child & adolescent clinical psychopharmacology* (3rd ed.). Philadelphia: Lippincott, Williams & Wilkins.
Riddle, M. A., Kastelic, E. A., & Frosch, E. (2001). Pediatric psychopharmacology. *Journal of Child Psychology & Psychiatry, 42*, 73–90.
Rosenberg, D. R., Holttum, J., & Gershon, S. (1994). *Textbook of pharmacotherapy for child & adolescent psychiatric disorders.* New York: Brunner/Mazel.

MICHAEL L. HANDWERK

Dyslexia

The term *dyslexia* refers to a learning disability in reading; dyslexia is the most common type of learning disability according to Sally Shaywitz (1996) of the Yale Center for the Study of Learning and Attention. Dyslexia is a language-based learning disability of biological origin; the most salient characteristic is difficultly decoding single words, usually associated with weaknesses in phonological processing. Persons with dyslexia have problems with decoding despite normal functioning in other cognitive and academic areas. Persons with dyslexia typically have problems with reading, spelling, and writing (Lyon, 1995).

Historically, people thought of dyslexia as a disorder reflected primarily by reversals in reading and spelling and, hence, a visual problem (Shaywitz, 1996). For example, the word *saw* might be misread or incorrectly written as the word *was*. However, recent research has yielded some professional consensus about the disorder. Interest and research in dyslexia increased dramatically in the 1990s, as evidenced by a 1999 article in the nationally popular magazine *Newsweek* (Kantrowitz &

Underwood). There is a growing consensus that "dyslexia reflects a deficiency in the processing of the distinctive linguistic units, called phonemes, that make up all spoken and written words" (Shaywitz, 1996, p. 98). More simply, the key element of dyslexia appears to be deficits in phonological skills. Further, a student's ability to rapidly access names for symbols, sometimes referred to as *processing speed* or *rapid automatic naming ability*, is apparently a second cognitive processing ability that is deficient in some persons with dyslexia (Wolf, 1999). Researchers have referred to the deficits in phonological skills and processing speed as the "double deficit," which predisposes a learner to more difficulty in reading than does either of the deficits alone (Wolf, 1999).

Students with dyslexia tend to have difficulty acquiring beginning reading skills, failing to recognize and remember words they have recently been taught. However, for most, the problem tends to begin earlier with phonemic awareness, which refers to the ability to recognize and manipulate individual units of sound. Because English is a phonetically complex language, persons with phonemic awareness problems are predisposed to have difficulty with phonics, which involves associating letters and groups of letters with sounds and sound patterns. The reversals exhibited by struggling readers and writers tend to be caused more by problems with auditory memory, sequencing, and sound–letter association than by visual perceptual problems (Bell, McCallum, & Cox, in press). Students with dyslexia also tend to be slow and dysfluent when they read. Though effective early intervention improves the ability to decode and recognize words, persons with dyslexia tend to continue to read slowly and laboriously (Shaywitz, 1996).

Studies by Shaywitz and colleagues (1996) indicate there are brain differences in persons with dyslexia. Functional magnetic resonance imaging indicates the brains of persons with dyslexia experience increased activity in the areas associated with speech production, perhaps because they are trying to find alternative ways to process reading information because of inefficient brain pathways. Dyslexia tends to run in families, suggesting a genetic etiology.

DIAGNOSING DYSLEXIA

Researchers tend to agree that early assessment and intervention of dyslexia is critical if persons with dyslexia are to successfully learn to read (Fletcher & Foorman, 1993). However, practical and valid assessment of dyslexia is problematic because current practices in assessment of a reading disability may be inappropriate or insufficient in the diagnosis of dyslexia. Many states in the United States require that a reading disability be diagnosed only if there is a significant difference between intelligence and reading scores. Although Shaywitz (1996) notes, "in

dyslexia, the seemingly invariant relation between intelligence and reading ability breaks down" (p. 98), other experts argue that there is little difference between poor readers in general and those diagnosed with IQ–reading achievement discrepancies (Felton, 1993). In some cases, intelligence test scores are lowered by weaknesses in the abilities related to dyslexia—auditory or phonological processing problems and slow processing. In the most significant cases of dyslexia, a discrepancy may exist. However, in less extreme cases the discrepancy may not be significant.

Because dyslexia may be best characterized as a *pattern* of performance, rather than a *discrepancy* in performance, diagnosis is difficult. Currently there is no single, valid, comprehensive measure of dyslexia that yields measures of all the relevant skills and abilities. However, there is some consensus that diagnosis requires assessment of academic skills (sight word recognition, phonics or word decoding, reading comprehension, and spelling) and cognitive skills (phonemic awareness, rapid automatic naming and/or processing speed, and memory). In addition, some argue that a measure of listening comprehension and/ or general intellectual ability should be assessed to rule out global cognitive impairment as the cause for the reading problem.

TREATING DYSLEXIA

Fortunately, there are a variety of effective teaching techniques for students with dyslexia. The Center for the Study and Treatment of Dyslexia (1999) recommends "explicit instruction in phonological awareness, ample repetition and practice to assure learning to mastery, very small increments in new linguistic concepts, integrated decoding and spelling, and direct systematic teaching of all aspects of the sounds of English" (p. 1). Research suggests that for most children, a balanced approach to reading instruction (i.e., emphasis on both reading for comprehension and basic reading skills) is the most effective. However, students with significant dyslexia patterns may require extra instruction, particularly in basic reading skills and fluency. The Center for the Study and Treatment of Dyslexia and the International Dyslexia Association provide names of reading programs and approaches that have demonstrated effectiveness for hard-to-teach readers. Researchers suggest implementation of phonemic awareness activities in kindergarten and first grade as preventive and early intervention techniques to avoid reading failure. In addition, direct strategies to improve fluency are increasingly being recommended (National Reading Panel, 2000). With appropriate instruction in decoding and fluency, children with dyslexia gain the skills that allow them to read for meaning and pleasure and at a level more commensurate with their other talents and abilities.

See also: Learning Disabilities; Reading: Academic Interventions for Reading Comprehension

BIBLIOGRAPHY

Bell, S. M., McCallum, R. S., & Cox, E. A. (2003). Toward a research-based assessment of dyslexia: Using cognitive measures to predict reading. *Journal of Learning Disabilities, 36,* 505–516.

Center for the Study and Treatment of Dyslexia. (1999). *Interventions in reading, writing and spelling for students with dyslexia* [Brochure]. Murfreesboro, TN: Author.

Felton, R. (1993). Effects of reading instruction on the decoding skills of children with phonological-processing problems. *Journal of Learning Disabilities, 26,* 583–589.

Fletcher, J. M., & Foorman, B. R. (1993). Issues in definition and measurement of learning disabilities: The need for early intervention. In G. R. Lyon (Ed.), *Frames of reference for the assessment of learning disabilities: New views on measurement issues.* Baltimore: Brookes.

Kantrowitz, B., & Underwood, A. (1999, November 22). Dyslexia and the science of reading. *Newsweek,* 72–78.

Lyon, G. R. (1995). Toward a definition of dyslexia. *Annals of Dyslexia, 45,* 3–30.

National Reading Panel. (2000). *Report of the National Reading Panel. Teaching children to read: An evidence-based assessment of the scientific research literature on reading and its implications for instruction.* National Institutes for Child Health and Development. Washington, DC.

Shaywitz, S. (1996, November). Dyslexia. *Scientific American,* pp. 98–104.

Wolf, M. (1999). What time may tell: Towards a new conceptualization of developmental dyslexia. *Annals of Dyslexia, 49,* 3–28.

Additional Readings for Nonprofessionals

www.interdys.org (International Dyslexia Association)
www.mtsu.edu/~dyslexia (Center for Study and Treatment of Dyslexia)
www.nichd.nih.gov (National Institutes of Health)

Additional Reading for Professionals

Annals of Dyslexia, published annually by the International Dyslexia Association.

R. Steve McCallum
Sherry Mee Bell

Ee

Eating Disorders

See: Anorexia Nervosa; Bulimia Nervosa; Obesity

Educational Specialist Training Programs in School Psychology

A current listing of specialist training programs in school psychology that are approved by the National Association of School Psychologists may be found online at http://www.nasponline.org/certification/gradschools.html

Encopresis

Fecal incontinence, or encopresis, occurs when children aged 4 or older void feces in inappropriate places such as clothing at least once monthly for a minimum of 3 months. According to diagnostic criteria, encopresis cannot be the result of medications or a medical condition. Although some children with encopresis will not have previously achieved fecal continence (primary type), encopresis can occur with children who have been toilet trained (secondary type). The subtypes of encopresis indicate if soiling is accompanied by constipation and overflow incontinence (American Psychiatric Association, 2000). Approximately 80–95 percent of all cases of encopresis are characterized by constipation and overflow incontinence and are referred to as retentive encopresis. In retentive encopresis, voiding is involuntary and occurs as a result of constipation and overflow incontinence. Overflow incontinence occurs when fecal matter seeps around impacted feces and leaks into the child's underwear and is frequently detected by the smell of feces or stained underwear.

When constipation and overflow incontinence are absent, voiding is voluntary and sometimes labeled manipulative encopresis. Stool is typically well formed, of normal consistency, and excreted typically in conspicuous locations such as on the floor or on furniture. Children displaying manipulative encopresis often have a history of oppositional and/or defiant behavior (Ondersma & Walker, 1998).

Less than 3 percent of children are diagnosed with encopresis. The average age of diagnosis is approximately 7 years, and boys are more likely to be affected. The majority of encopretic children soil during the day, frequently at school. Soiling occurs at night for 38–58 percent of children, depending upon the study (Fishman, Rappaport, Schonwald, & Nurko, 2003). Most encopretic referrals are made to pediatricians or other primary care physicians and may include complaints that the child is soiling on purpose or that the child is stubborn.

For children with retentive encopresis, bowel movements are infrequent, foul smelling, and are typically characterized by small quantities of poorly formed feces due to constipation. However, some children will occasionally eliminate massive quantities of dark stool if the impaction is dislodged. Overflow incontinence occurs when fecal matter seeps around impacted feces and leaks into the child's underwear and is frequently detected by the smell of feces or stained underwear. Other symptoms of constipation include complaints of abdominal pain, less than three weekly bowel movements, poor appetite and/or weight loss, palpable abdominal mass, and attempts to withhold bowel movements and/or crying or screaming surrounding toileting. The emotional upset associated with constipation is the result of previous painful bowel movements. Children will usually have multiple symptoms of constipation but may present uniquely because of individual differences and developmental abilities.

The most common causes of chronic constipation are diet and lifestyle factors. Specifically, children who consume low-fiber diets and inadequate water are more likely to become constipated. Diminished activity level further compounds the problem. In addition, some children are predisposed to becoming constipated. Thus, the combination of biological predisposition, low fiber and water intake, and inadequate physical exercise often leads to a phenomenon described as "slow-moving bowels." Although rare, other causes of constipation are food allergies, irritable bowel syndrome, abdominal tumors, anal abnormality, severe dehydration, and Hirschsprung disease.

In Hirschsprung disease, the lower portion of the colon lacks sufficient nerves to signal the urge to defecate. Physical anal abnormalities are extremely unusual. However, studies indicate that most encopretic children contract, rather than relax, the external sphincter during attempts to defecate. It is unclear if there is an organic cause of this atypical physiological response of the anal sphincter or if it is a learned behavior.

The second major supported theory regarding the development of encopresis is based on the learning history of encopretic children (Ondersma & Walker, 1998). It is possible that children learn to contract their sphincter during bowel movements that contribute to the development of constipation. These contractions may result from trying to withhold the passage of painful bowel movements. Painful bowel movements resulting in physical and consequent emotional distress are thus avoided through withholding stool. Unfortunately, withholding stool exacerbates constipation as the colon walls stretch and decrease sensitivity to cues, thus increasing the probability of another painful, or even increasingly painful, bowel movements. Other reasons for withholding include entering novel or unsanitary restrooms and the desire to continue a preferred activity such as play.

Although encopresis is not usually the direct result of organic or medical conditions, a thorough physical examination is always the first step in assessment and intervention. The physical exam may include palpation for fecal mass, testing for blood in stool, and a rectal examination. More invasive procedures may be required if potential problems or warning signs are present during the physical and when history is obtained.

In the absence of a more serious illness, purgative therapy in the form of enemas and/or laxatives is provided to clear the impaction caused from constipation. For some children, this physical "clean out" is sufficient to treat encopresis.

However, there are additional simple-to-implement changes that increase therapeutic effectiveness. First, increasing fiber and water consumption is crucial to maintaining regularity once the impaction is removed and to prevent future constipation. Nutritionists and pediatricians can recommend a high-fiber diet tailored to the child if requested. Some foods high in fiber include bran cereals, kidney beans (7.3 grams), whole wheat spaghetti (3.9 grams), green peas (3.6 grams), apples (3.5 grams), dried prunes and strawberries (3 grams), and corn (2.9 grams). Bran cereals vary in fiber content, with some having as much as 13 grams of fiber per serving.

Second, physical exercise and activity should be increased to assist motility. Ironically, constipation often results in lethargy and decreases in activity level which, in turn, contributes to constipation. Thus, ensuring that children have opportunities incorporating running, jumping, skipping, throwing balls, and so on into play is essential in the effective treatment of encopresis. A third lifestyle change is that a physician may recommend regular consumption of stool softeners or laxatives, typically mineral oil, for prolonged periods of time to help prevent constipation.

Next, scheduled toilet sits increase the probability of the child successfully defecating in the toilet. The sits should occur two times daily and last a maximum of 5 minutes. A flat surface such as a stool should be provided so that the child has a flat, firm surface to place both feet on during scheduled sits. Timing toilet sits to occur after meals and exercise further increases the child's successful toileting experience.

Rewarding children for sitting and/or production of bowel movements is crucial. Many children have a lengthy history of punishment associated with encopresis as the result of the inaccurate belief that the inappropriate soiling was under the child's voluntary control. As a result, parents should enthusiastically reward toilet sits and/or eliminating feces in the toilet while being careful not to punish soiling clothes or defecating in other inappropriate places. One easy way to reward children is to create a grab bag containing small treats such as candies, small toys, stickers, or other items of interest to the child. Immediately following the scheduled sit, the child is allowed to pick an item from the grab bag regardless of whether or not a bowel movement was produced.

When soiling occurs during training, children are responsible for cleanup duties including rinsing and laundering soiled clothes, quickly showering to cleanse, and redressing. Parents may provide gentle, occasional verbal reminders or prompts, being careful to refrain from nagging or completing cleanliness tasks for the child. Finally, soiling should not be discussed. Rather, the emphasis remains on the desirable behaviors of sitting on the toilet and production. Although this is often difficult for parents, avoiding discussing soiling removes the potential for punishment and associating bowel movements with aversive or unpleasant conditions.

Instead, children should be gently guided with verbal prompts to rinse or launder the soiled laundry, take a brief shower or bath to quickly clean up, and change into clean clothes. Parents are advised to refrain from nagging the child during the cleanup and from mentioning the soiling incident at any time.

Although encopresis is distressing for children and their families, in most cases there is no underlying medical condition(s) contributing to the problem. Instead, encopresis is considered a behavioral difficulty for most encopretic children. However, collaboration with the child's pediatrician is necessary to first ensure there is no organic pathology before treating for constipation. Once constipation is alleviated, parents can implement simple, yet important, changes into the child's diet and lifestyle that have been found to effectively treat encopresis. Furthermore, consultation with nutritionists and psychologists may further support families dealing with encopresis.

See also: Enuresis; Oppositional Defiant Disorder

BIBLIOGRAPHY

American Psychiatric Association. (2000). *Diagnostic and statistical manual of mental disorders* (4th ed., rev.). Washington, DC: Author.

Fishman, L., Rappaport, L., Schonwald, A., & Nurko, S. (2003). Trends in referral to a single encopresis clinic over 20 years. *Pediatrics, 11,* 604–607.

Ondersma, S. J., & Walker, C. E. (1998). Elimination disorders. In T. H. Ollendick & M. Hersen (Eds.), *Handbook of child psychopathology* (3rd ed., pp. 355–378). New York: Plenum.

Additional Readings for Nonprofessionals

Beard, L. M. (2003). *Salt in your sock and other tried and true home remedies.* New York: Three Rivers.

Schiff, D., & Shelov, S. P. (1997). *Guide to your child's symptoms: Birth through adolescence.* New York: Village Press.

www.encopresis.com (Devoted to discussion of encopresis, causes and solutions, links to related sites)

www.pottymd.com (Provides discussion of potty training, enuresis [wetting], encopresis [soiling])

Additional Readings for Professionals

Crain, E. F., & Gershel, J. C. (2003). *Clinical manual of emergency pediatrics* (4th ed.). New York: McGraw–Hill.

Ondersma, S. J., & Walker, C. E. (1998). Elimination disorders. In T. H. Ollendick & M. Hersen (Eds.), *Handbook of child psychopathology* (3rd ed., pp. 355–378). New York: Plenum.

NANCY FOSTER

Enuresis

Enuresis is the diagnostic term used when a child wets his/her bed or clothes. It is safe to say that enuresis is an age-old problem and has been distressing children and their parents for hundreds, perhaps even thousands, of years. Some of the earliest descriptions of enuresis are found in the Ebers papyrus of 550 B.C. and in the first English language pediatrics manual in a selection entitled "Of Pyssying in the Bedde" (Glicklich, 1951). Bedwetting, or wetting during sleep, is called *nocturnal enuresis*, whereas wetting clothes during the day, or wetting while awake, is called *diurnal enuresis*. In some situations, a child may wet both at night and during the day. In such cases, this is referred to as *mixed enuresis*.

When a child has never been dry, it is referred to as *primary enuresis*. When a child has been dry for at least 6 months and then starts to wet again, it is referred to as *secondary enuresis*. Primary nocturnal enuresis is far more commonly diagnosed than either diurnal or mixed enuresis as it accounts for about 80–90 percent of all cases of enuresis. Friman and Jones (1998) estimated that diurnal and mixed enuresis occurs in about 0.5–2 percent of girls and boys aged 6–7 years old.

To be diagnosed with enuresis, a child must meet several criteria: (1) the wetting must not be due to an illness or medication; (2) the child is past the age of 5 years or, in the case of children with developmental delays, a developmental age of 5 years; and (3) the wetting occurs twice per week for at least 3 months or results in significant distress for the child (American Psychiatric Association, 2000). These criteria were established, in part, to help clinicians and parents differentiate between children with enuresis versus children who have an occasional accident. If all of the above criteria are met, it does not matter if the child is wetting voluntarily or by accident for the behavior to be considered enuresis.

It is extremely important to mention that occasional accidents are very common in children until the age of 5 and should not concern parents or caregivers. It is also not unusual for a child 6 or 7 years of age to have an accident when they are sick, extremely tired, or on medication.

PREVALENCE

Enuresis is more commonly diagnosed in males, as approximately 7 percent of males and 3 percent of females are enuretic at age 5. The percentage of children with enuresis decreases with age as approximately 5 percent of 10-year-olds and 2 percent of children aged 12–14 are enuretic. Spontaneous remission rates (the rate at which children stop wetting without treatment) are about 5–10 percent a year. It is perhaps surprising that 1 percent of the adult population are thought to be enuretic.

Children with developmental delays and disabilities are more likely to be enuretic than children who are experiencing normal development. Children living in institutions, regardless of their developmental or cognitive status, are more likely to be enuretic than children living in traditional home environments. This higher prevalence rate among institutionalized children may be due more to incomplete toilet training than an emotional or physical cause. It has also been suggested that children from lower socioeconomic backgrounds and those from larger families are also more likely to exhibit enuresis, although it is difficult to separate the influence of these factors from cultural beliefs and practices regarding toileting.

ETIOLOGY

Although the exact etiology of enuresis is unclear, there are a number of factors that may be related to urinary incontinence. The first of these factors are medical conditions such as seizure disorders, spina bifida, juvenile diabetes, disorders and structural problems of the bladder and genitourinary system, nervous system disorders, and sickle-cell disease. Children with these conditions often have difficulty achieving and maintaining continence. A second factor that may contribute to enuresis is family history (genetics). Family history is one of the best predictors of enuresis as the majority (75 percent) of enuretic children have at least one first-degree relative who was previously enuretic. In fact, when both parents were enuretic, 77 percent of their children are enuretic as compared to 44 percent when one parent was enuretic and only 15 percent when neither parent was enuretic (Bakwin, 1973). It is unclear if there is indeed a genetic transmission of enuresis or if these high rates among family members are more reflective of toilet training and practices that are passed down from one generation to the next.

A third factor that may be related to nocturnal enuresis is what parents have reported for years, namely, that children who wet the bed sleep more deeply than children who do not. One study showed that children with nocturnal enuresis were 4 to 5 times more difficult to awaken than children who do not wet the bed. That is, they may be sleeping so soundly that they do not respond to the sensation of impending urination by contracting their urinary sphincter to avoid wetting.

A fourth factor that figures predominately in enuresis is broadly called "learning factors." This means that the child has had insufficient training or learning opportunities to control the urinary reflex. In addition, significant emotional or psychological problems may interfere with learning to control urination, but are not direct causes, in and of themselves, of enuresis. Therefore, children with enuresis have simply failed to learn the skills required to voluntarily control their urinary sphincter.

Some popular factors that are linked to enuresis but have not been established through scientific research include the previously mentioned emotional or psychological trauma/problems, sleep disorders, lower bladder capacity, lower levels of antidiuretic hormone, and food allergies.

TREATMENT

The first step in the treatment of enuresis involves a medical examination to rule out a medical/physical cause or the effects of medication as the reason for the enuresis. As mentioned earlier, primary nocturnal enuresis is the most common form of enuresis and interventions have primarily focused on its treatment. Among the various interventions available, the urine alarm has a success rate of approximately 75 percent. Upon urination, an alarm sounds that awakens the child. Eventually, the child learns to contract the urinary sphincter during sleep in order to avoid urinating and, thus, waking up. An incentive program (positive reinforcement), combined with the urine alarm, is the most effective treatment strategy and works for about 85–90 percent of children. Complete urinary continence is usually achieved in about 4 to 6 months. Although about 10 percent of children experience a relapse when the alarm is removed, dryness usually returns quickly either by providing incentives for dry nights and/or reusing the alarm for several days. The primary drawback to using the urine alarm is that parental involvement is required, particularly in the beginning, and may lead to negative interactions between parents and children if they refuse to get out of bed when the alarm sounds.

Responsibility training is often added to the alarm/incentive program. This simply means that the child completes as much of the cleanup associated with wetting as they are capable. For instance, an older child will probably be able to remove and replace their nightclothes, sheets, and wash them without help from parents. Younger children may be able to remove sheets and pajamas but may need assistance in replacing and washing them. This component is not meant to be a punishment for the child who wets and should be completed without a negative interaction between the parents and child.

Although medication is often prescribed by pediatricians and family physicians for treating enuresis (most typically imipramine and desmopressin), their success rate is lower than that of the urine alarm and the relapse rate is much higher (with some drugs, 100 percent, as is the case with desmopressin). In addition, the side effects that are possible with each drug make them generally undesirable, particularly when other interventions are safer and more effective. Having said that, however, desmopressin (DDAVP) may be useful for circumstances where the child needs to be immediately dry at night (camp, sleepovers, etc.) for a limited period of time.

A FINAL WORD OF CAUTION

Although most children develop toileting skills without intervention, a small percentage of children have difficulty achieving urinary continence at an age expected by their parents and some continue wetting after the age of 5. Any type of punishment, including spankings, scolding, shaming, making children sit for extended periods of time on the toilet, or removing toys or privileges, is an ineffective means of teaching children proper toileting skills. Some adults, in frustration over the child's wetting, often inflict serious or fatal harm upon a child. In fact, difficulty in toilet training is one of the leading antecedents for fatal child abuse in America. Thus, professionals and all adults need to be aware of children who are having difficulty achieving urinary continence and assist their parents or caregivers in obtaining professional assistance for this problem.

See also: Differential Reinforcement; Encopresis; Positive Reinforcement

BIBLIOGRAPHY

American Psychiatric Association. (2000). *Diagnostic and statistical manual of mental disorders* (4th ed., text rev.). Washington, DC: Author.

Bakwin, H. (1973). The genetics of enuresis. In I. Kolvin, R. C. MacKeith, & S. R. Meadow (Eds.), *Bladder control and enuresis* (pp. 73–77). Philadelphia: Lippincott.

Friman, P. C., & Jones, K. M. (1998). Elimination disorders in children. In T. S. Watson & F. M. Gresham (Eds.), *Handbook of child behavior therapy* (pp. 239–259). New York: Plenum.

Glicklich, L. B. (1951). An historical account of enuresis. *Pediatrics, 8*, 859–876.

Additional Readings for Professionals and Nonprofessionals

Schroeder, C. S., & Gordon, B. N. (2002). *Assessment and treatment of childhood problems* (2nd ed.). New York: Guilford.

http://www.kidney.org/patients/bw/index.cfm

http://www.wetlessnights.com/

T. STEUART WATSON

Ethical Standards of the National Association of School Psychologists (NASP)

A complete copy of the NASP professional conduct manual may be accessed online at http://www.nasponline.org/pdf/ProfessionalCond.pdf

Ethics: NASP Guidelines

The National Association of School Psychologists (NASP) is the largest professional association of school psychologists in the world. Composed of university instructors, school psychology students, and practicing school psychologists, NASP promotes sound educational and psychological practices that benefit all children. The association has adopted several sets of integrated standards for various aspects of school psychology, including the Principles for Professional Ethics that appear in the NASP Professional Conduct Manual (NASP, 2000). As a part of joining NASP, each member agrees to follow the Principles for Professional Ethics. The information that follows will explain the role of ethical standards in relation to professional practice and examine the content areas of the current principles.

ETHICS IN CONTEXT

Ethics are a set of values that govern behavior. Principles of ethics generally set forth certain rules of competence and expected behavior consistent with the mission (or values) of an organization. School psychology is a helping profession where the central focus is on children encountering some type of difficulty in school. As an organization, NASP advocates for the rights of children and the dignity of all persons, promotes research-based psychological and educational services, and supports provision of professional services of the highest quality. Thus, the NASP Principles for Professional Ethics reflect these values across the many professional roles played by its members. Not only do the principles define minimum competency and expected behaviors, but they also provide a framework to analyze specific situations for ethical ramifications.

All psychologists working in schools or in private (independent) practice are expected to be knowledgeable about ethical principles related to their profession and use them to guide practice. Whether members of an organization or not, school psychologists would be expected to understand and follow the standards set forth either by the American Psychological Association (APA) or NASP. Most school psychologists who belong to a professional organization are NASP members. Those with a doctorate can belong to APA in lieu of, or in addition to, NASP. Both organizations publish their standards and make them available at their Web site. In addition, all university training programs currently approved by NASP require students to complete a course on ethics. Each individual is charged with the responsibility to recognize potential problems and seek clarification by consulting standards and/or a peer, or by accessing other print materials that address professional ethics. In addition, the NASP ethics committee routinely responds to requests for help or clarification from members and the general public. The ethics committee is also required to investigate complaints and determine appropriate remedies when necessary.

CONTENT OF PROFESSIONAL ETHICS

NASP has organized its Principles for Professional Ethics under the following headings: Professional Competency; Professional Relationships; Professional Practices—General Principles; and Professional Practice Settings—Independent Settings. Although the headings facilitate organization of content, specific ethical questions that arise often have elements that overlap or have dimensions covered in different sections. School psychologists may need to review several ethics components to understand which standard(s) to apply in deciding how to proceed.

PROFESSIONAL COMPETENCY

Although the content under Professional Competency is the shortest and has only six principles, this section defines several important areas of competency that form the basis for the remaining standards. A basic foundation is the idea that school psychologists will limit their practice to areas in which they are trained and competent. Even though all school psychologists who successfully complete a training program in their field are competent to practice, there may be certain roles in which they are not competent. For example, school psychology training programs do not generally prepare practitioners as family therapists. Thus, without additional training, a school psychologist could not ethically provide such a service. Another component of being competent is the idea of *maintaining* competency. School psychologists are expected to engage in continuous professional development. They must remain up-to-date on revised materials, learn new behaviors as the profession advances, seek supervision and assistance when the need arises, and build on existing skills.

Another principle covered under Professional Competency is the idea of integrity. School psychologists do not mislead others as to their competence or misrepresent themselves in any way. They recognize situations in which their effectiveness may be compromised by personal problems or conflicts and take appropriate action. Because trust is essential in a helping profession, the school psychologist must follow a strict standard to ensure credibility.

As part of professional competence, school psychologists must use ethical principles in guiding practice. This section makes it incumbent on the professional to know and follow the rules. Ignorance of ethics, as in the law, is not an acceptable defense. Taken together, the principles outlined under Professional Competency are designed to ensure that school psychologists have the skills to perform their jobs.

PROFESSIONAL RELATIONSHIPS

Much of what a school psychologist does can be defined in the context of professional relationships. Whether working with students or parents, consulting with teachers and administrators, or coordinating care with other professionals, school psychologists engage in many behaviors that have ethical dimensions. Beyond general principles governing professional relationships, NASP has further focused in on standards that should be applied to the types of relationships that exist between school psychologists and various groups including students, parents/guardians/surrogates, the community, other professionals, and school psychologist trainees and interns.

Several concepts are present in the general principles governing professional relationships, including the ideas of responsibility, objectivity, advocacy, sensitivity, and communication. School psychologists do not let personal biases or values influence delivery of services. They respect individual differences. Communication is timely and direct. Conflicts are identified, shared with clients, and resolved to the benefit of the client. They also do not use their professional role to exploit clients in any manner, including manipulation, coercion, or sexual relationships.

The area of professional relationships includes the important concept of conflict of interest that the NASP standards address in a section covering dual relationships. School psychologists do not become involved in situations in which they have divided interests. Thus, they do not provide services to family members or to relatives of close personal friends or business associates. School psychologists do not provide private practice services to children who attend schools they serve, nor do they refer such children to private practice partners, or act in any other manner that could be questioned in terms of their personal motives or gain.

One other general idea that is essential to professional relationships is the process to be followed when a school psychologist has concerns about the ethical behavior of others. There are clear steps to be taken in addressing problems with other professionals in a direct, confidential, reasonable manner.

Trust and clarity of communication are the intent of items covering professional relationships with clients. School psychologists attempt to engage students in services by explaining everything at a level that can be easily understood. Use of information obtained about students is treated in a manner that maintains the dignity of the student.

While working with parents or other responsible adults, school psychologists are expected to take steps that ensure understanding and cooperation. Parents have a right to understand proposed services before giving consent, and to be involved in educational decisions about their child. When children initiate a request for service, school psychologists carefully explain the limits of confidentiality and make students aware of the need to gain parent permission for continued service. Information is explained to parents in terms they can understand. Services that are to be delivered by an intern or trainee are clearly identified prior to the parent's giving consent.

The interests of students should be foremost in the interactions of school psychologists with other professionals. Respect of, and cooperation with, outside professionals is expected. Appropriate information is shared in a confidential manner and school-based services are coordinated with community professionals as needed.

PROFESSIONAL PRACTICES—GENERAL

In this section, NASP addresses several areas that are related to the daily functioning of the school psychologist. Advocacy is expanded from other sections to mean actively representing the interests of clients. As part of their service delivery, school psychologists are aware of legal requirements and workplace conditions that affect their job. They actively work to promote policies and practices consistent with ethical principles.

Several standards address principles associated with assessment and intervention services. School psychologists are required to select instruments and techniques that are up-to-date and the most appropriate for the purpose. Research should be used to inform and guide practice. Decisions need to be made on the basis of multiple sources of data. Services should be monitored through data collection and ineffective practices or services should be discontinued in the absence of supporting evidence.

The area of safeguarding and reporting information is often fraught with problems. The school psychologist is charged with responsibility to see that information is only available to authorized individuals. Likewise, parents are entitled to access to all information collected or written about their child. As a best practice, school psychologists should have face-to-face meetings with parents to explain data or reports in terms the parents can easily understand. The school psychologist is responsible for the accuracy of any reports they sign.

NASP principles discourage, but do not prohibit, the use of computer-generated reports. The standards also make the school psychologist responsible for maintaining security of tests that would be rendered useless if available for public inspection. Activities that violate a publisher's copyright, such as duplicating protocols or tests materials, are forbidden. Technology further creates unique challenges for the school psychologist. Confidentiality is difficult to ensure in cases where information is transmitted via fax machines or e-mail. Cell phone conversations may also not be private given the mobility of the user when receiving or making calls.

One other section under Professional Practices governs the behavior of school psychologists who are engaged in research, publication, and presentation. Clients must be made aware of services that are part of research and give consent to participate. School psychologists must follow accepted standards for conducting, reporting, and publishing research outcomes. Items in this section also address protocol for citing the contribution of others to research and publications, and clearly identify falsification of data or plagiarism as unethical behaviors.

PROFESSIONAL PRACTICE SETTINGS—INDEPENDENT PRACTICE

Although most practicing school psychologists work full-time in schools, some are engaged in independent practice. NASP has developed principles to address issues that typically arise in cases where the school psychologist is working in schools and engaged in private practice. These items are intended to help define the relationship between the school psychologist and the school employer, and to provide guidance in defining services and communicating rights to clients. The standards define conditions under which service delivery takes place and describe conditions for advertising or making announcements about available services.

SUMMARY

The Principles of Professional Ethics of the National Association of School Psychologists provides a framework for defining competence and appropriate behavior. As with all ethical standards, few questions will be answered by one specific item in the NASP principles. Although the standards are organized under several convenient headings, readers will typically need to cull through several related items to interpret the ethical elements in a particular situation. In addition to review of the principles, readers with concerns are advised to discuss situations with a school psychologist or to contact a member of the NASP ethics committee. The NASP Principles, information about filing an ethics compliant, and directory listings for the ethics committee can be found on the NASP Web site, which is www.nasponline.org.

BIBLIOGRAPHY

National Association of School Psychologists. (2000). *Principles for professional ethics (revised)*. Bethesda, MD: Author.

Additional Readings for Nonprofessionals

http://www.educationplanet.com (Education Planet: An Education Web Guide)
http://www.nasponline.org/pdf/ProfessionalConduct.pdf
http://www.schoolpsychology.net (School Psychology Resources Online)

Additional Readings for Professionals

Jacob-Timm, S., & Hartshorne, T. S. (1998). *Ethics and law for school psychologists* (3rd ed). New York: Wiley.
Nagy, T. F. (2000). *Ethics in plain English*. Washington, DC: American Psychological Association.

MICHAEL C. FORCADE

Exercise

When people use the term *exercise* in daily conversation, they often assume others understand what they are talking about. However, exercise has a variety of connotations and even conflicting definitions in the physical activity literature (Berger, Pargman, & Weinberg, 2002). This encyclopedia entry clarifies definitions of exercise found in the sport and exercise psychology literature.

Lox, Martin, and Petruzzello (2003) define exercise as "... a form of leisure physical activity ... that is undertaken in order to achieve a particular objective" (p. 4). Defined in this way, exercise is different from household chores or job-related physical movements because it is done for the purpose of reaching a particular goal. These can include reduced stress, improved physical appearance, or increased cardiovascular health. Other researchers (Berger, Pargman, & Weinberg, 2002) begin with the American Heritage Dictionary's (1982) definition of exercise as "... an activity that requires physical or mental exertion, espe-

cially when performed to develop or maintain fitness" (p. 474, as cited in Berger et al., 2002, p. 2). This dictionary definition further emphasizes large-muscle activity, a focus on fitness or health (through activities such as running, swimming, weight training, rock climbing, and aerobic dance) as well as competitive recreational activities like racquetball, tennis, or rugby. In addition, the U.S. Department of Health and Human Services (USDHHS) defines exercise as "... planned and purposeful physical activity ... that often has health, fitness, skill, and competitive foci" (USDHHS, 1996, p. 20, as cited in Berger et al., 2002, p. 2).

Exercise differs from sport in significant ways. For example, sport is traditionally defined as "... institutionalized competitive activities that involve rigorous physical exertion or the use of relatively complex physical skills by participants motivated by internal and external rewards" (Coakley, in press). Therefore, the important criteria for sport are that it (a) is a *physical activity*—it cannot be chess, for example; (b) is *competitive*—it is not just two people throwing a softball to each other; (c) is *an institutional process*—a process through which formal rules and patterns of behavior become standardized over time; and (d) contains two types of motivations—internal and external. Play, on the other hand, involves activity done for its own sake, often spontaneously, with no goal in mind. Scholars have also arranged specific physical activities along a continuum according to exercise intensity, duration, and competitive intensity, including a focus on winning. Play and sport serve each as one end of the continuum, with exercise in the middle (Berger et al., 2002).

Parents and educators can play a major role in encouraging a healthy lifestyle that includes exercise. They can promote the idea that exercise has many psychological, health, and social benefits. For example, it can be used as an adjunct to "talk" therapy to establish optimal mental health. This includes, but is not limited to, enhancing or altering mood, helping treat mental disorders such as depression and anxiety, enhancing confidence and self-concept, and helping children reach their full potential (Berger et al., 2002). Health benefits related to exercise involve reducing stress and lowering cardiovascular disease physical risk factors such as blood pressure, cholesterol, and body fat percentage. There are social benefits as well, including enhanced feelings of control, positive social interactions with others, and opportunities for enjoyment and fun (Weinberg & Gould, 2003). Quality of life—defined as one's "... behavioral functioning ability" or the ability to do "... everyday stuff" (Kaplan, 1994, as cited in Weinberg & Gould, 2003, p. 392)—is also improved in both the short and the long term. This is because those who are physically active, especially beginning at a young age, tend to have better health, more stamina, a greater ability to cope with stress, greater life satisfaction, enjoy school and work more, and are less dependent on others compared with those who do not (Weinberg & Gould, 2003).

See also: Nutrition; Sports

BIBLIOGRAPHY

Berger, B. G., Pargman, D., & Weinberg, R. S. (2002). *Foundations of exercise psychology.* Morgantown, WV: Fitness Information Technology.

Coakley, J. (2004). *Sports in society: Issues & controversies* (8th ed.). New York: McGraw–Hill.

Lox, C. L., Martin, K. A., & Petruzzello, S. J. (2003). *The psychology of exercise: Integrating theory and practice.* Scottsdale, AZ: Holcomb Hathaway.

Weinberg, R. S., & Gould, D. (2003). *Foundations of sport & exercise psychology* (3rd ed.). Champaign, IL: Human Kinetics.

Additional Reading for Nonprofessionals

Prochaska, J. O., Norcross, J. C., & DiClemente, C. C. (1994). *Changing for good: A revolutionary six-stage program for overcoming bad habits and moving your life positively forward.* New York: Avon.

Additional Reading for Professionals

Weinberg, R. S., & Gould, D. (2003). *Foundations of sport & exercise psychology* (3rd ed.). Champaign, IL: Human Kinetics.

Leslee A. Fisher

Extinction

One strategy for decreasing or eliminating problematic behavior is extinction. A technical definition of extinction would include two components: first, reinforcement no longer follows a response; second, a decrease in the response is observed. Therefore, in order to use extinction, one must know what is reinforcing the problematic behavior. For example, if a child's talking out of turn is reinforced by attention from peers and a teacher responded by ignoring, this would not be considered extinction (and likely would not be effective). Alternatively, if the teacher taught the child's classmates to ignore talking out of turn (i.e., not to laugh or otherwise respond when the child talked out of turn), then this would be considered extinction *if* a subsequent decrease in talking out was observed.

TYPES OF EXTINCTION

Extinction can take four forms depending on what is maintaining the targeted behavior. If the behavior is maintained by attention, then extinction would involve no longer delivering attention following the behavior, as in the example above. If the target behavior is maintained by access to preferred items,

then extinction would involve ensuring that the child no longer gained those items when the problem behavior occurred. For example, if a child bullies other children to gain access to their toys, extinction would involve ensuring that the child no longer gained the toys after bullying. If the target behavior is performed in order to escape or avoid a certain task or situation, then extinction would involve making sure that escape never followed the behavior. Consider, for example, a child who is disruptive when asked to complete a task. A common response might be to send the child to time-out. If, however, the child prefers time-out in order to avoid doing the work, then time-out may increase the child's disruptiveness. Extinction would involve having the child continue working on assignments when he/she is disruptive. Finally, the target behavior might be maintained by sensory reinforcement. For example, a child with autism might flap his/her hands because the feel of flapping is reinforcing. In this case, extinction involves blocking the reinforcing effects of hand flapping—something that may be quite difficult to do.

CHARACTERISTICS OF EXTINCTION

There are three characteristics of extinction that should be considered before making a decision to implement extinction as an intervention. They include (1) consideration of the schedule of reinforcement in place prior to treatment, (2) the probability of an extinction burst, and (3) resurgence.

First, the frequency with which a behavior was reinforced (or paid off), prior to intervention may affect how long it takes extinction to cause a decrease in the behavior. If a behavior was reinforced almost every time it occurred, then the use of extinction will cause a more rapid decrease in the behavior. Alternatively, if the behavior was reinforced only occasionally, then extinction likely will take longer to have an effect. Consider, for example, a child who teases his/her classmates when assigned seatwork. The teacher's response to that behavior might be to *occasionally* send the child to the principal's office. In such a scenario, the teasing is sometimes, but not always, reinforced (when sent to the office the child avoids work). If the teacher decides to use extinction—and no longer send the child to the office for teasing—then it may be some period of time before a decrease in the teasing is observed. This occurs because, in the past, the behavior was not reinforced every time it occurs and so treatment (extinction) will not appear any different to the child at first.

A second characteristic of extinction to consider is the likelihood of an extinction burst. Bursting is defined as a temporary increase in the frequency, intensity, or duration of a problem behavior following implementation of extinction. For example, a teacher who uses extinction to decrease a child's crying behavior by ignoring that behavior might initially observe the child to cry harder, longer, or more often than previously. Although the extinction burst is a frequently discussed side effect of extinction, a review of extinction research by Lerman and Iwata (1995) showed that the extinction burst is not frequently observed. They suggested that extinction bursts are less likely to occur when extinction is used in conjunction with a differential reinforcement program. In other words, to decrease the likelihood of an extinction burst, one should make sure that other, more appropriate behaviors are rewarded when a problem behavior is placed on extinction. For example, if teasing maintained by peer attention is placed on extinction, one should make sure the child has other, more appropriate ways to gain attention from peers (e.g., asking them to play, working appropriately on group projects).

A final characteristic of extinction to consider is resurgence. Resurgence refers to the fact that, after extinction has been implemented for some time and problem behavior has rarely if ever occurred, the problem behavior may briefly recur for a period of time. For example, the teacher in the above example may have taught children to ignore a peer's teasing and observed a significant decrease in teasing. Several weeks later, the child may engage in a great deal of teasing "out of the blue." When this occurs, it appears as if the child is "testing" to determine whether the intervention is still in place. So long as extinction continues to be implemented with fidelity (the peers continue to ignore teasing), the resurgence in teasing will be short-lived. If, however, teasing is reinforced at all, it likely will return at full strength. Thus, it is critical that those implementing extinction be aware that resurgence may occur and keep the intervention in place for as long as it is needed.

See also: Differential Reinforcement; Punishment; Time-Out

BIBLIOGRAPHY

Lerman, D. C., & Iwata, B. A. (1995). Prevalence of the extinction burst and its attenuation during treatment. *Journal of Applied Behavior Analysis, 28,* 93–94.

CYNTHIA M. ANDERSON
JODI POLAHA

Ff

Family Counseling

Family counseling evolved as clinicians (Bowen, 1960; Minuchin, 1974) realized that clients who were removed from their home often improved, only to quickly regress when they reentered their family system. Most families seek services for one individual member of the family. It is common in family counseling for this person to be referred to as the "identified patient," or "IP." This language reflects a central tenet of family counseling, that the person who is identified as needing services is considered a symptom bearer of problems within the family. Alhough a family counselor might work initially with the family's conceptualization as the individual as "troubled," he/she is conceptualizing the systemic difficulties and intervening to affect these systemic problems. Family counselors work with both content (what each family member is saying in the session) and process (how family members interact within the session). Fundamental to the systemic approach is the belief that circular causality is more relevant than linear causality. That is, rather than arguing about whether A caused B or B caused A, it is likely more useful to consider how A and B are mutually influential. For example, one person in a relationship may justify an affair by arguing that the partner was not meeting his/her sexual needs whereas the partner argues that he/she did not feel sexually attracted to the partner because of a lack of emotional intimacy. Likely, it is more useful in this case to consider that sex and emotional intimacy are mutually influenced between the couple. A central tenet is that change in any part of the system will influence change throughout the system.

As an example, consider a family in which a 13-year-old child (John) is setting small fires that are potentially dangerous. A counselor working with John might take various approaches to working with John, depending on theoretical orientation, such as setting up a behavioral contract, exploring emotional triggers for the fire-setting behavior, and looking at cognitive processes that lead to the fire-setting behavior. All are viable interventions and have merit. A family counselor, however, might consider structural issues within the family. One hypothesis that might emerge out of the assessment process is that John's father is physically and emotionally disengaged from John, and only becomes involved (albeit angrily) with John when responding to his fire-setting behavior. On the basis of this conceptualization, the family counselor might direct John's father to spend time with John teaching him fire safety. Although the directive is presented to the family as a way to help John (thereby working with their schema of John as "the problem"), the true intent of the intervention is to get John's father more engaged in the father–son subsystem of the family. Moreover, this intervention has the potential paradoxical effect of changing the context of fire setting from antisocial to social, thereby "ruining" the rebelliousness of this act.

MAJOR SYSTEMS THEORIES

Similar to individual counseling, a variety of theoretical approaches to family counseling have emerged and received empirical support for their effectiveness. Among the classic schools of family counseling, some theories emphasize the importance of behavioral change, such as *structural* (Minuchin, 1974), *strategic* (Haley, 1984; Madanes, 1981), and *behavioral* and *cognitive–behavioral family therapy* (Ellis, 2000; Patterson, 1975). Other theories, however, have emphasized the importance of liberating effect, such as *experiential* (Napier & Whitaker, 1978; Satir, 1988) theories, whereas yet others have emphasized the importance of cognitive insight, such as *Bowenian* (Bowen, 1978) and *object relations* (Scharff & Scharff, 1987).

Newer models and theories of family counseling are based on the constructivist notion that clients and family systems play a pivotal role in creating their solutions. Solution-focused family therapy focuses on solutions and competencies, whereas narrative therapy helps families to rewrite the stories that brought them in for family therapy.

See also: Group Counseling; Individual Counseling

BIBLIOGRAPHY

Bowen, M. (1960). A family concept of schizophrenia. In D. Jackson (Ed.), *The etiology of schizophrenia*. New York: Basic Books.

Bowen, M. (1978). *Family therapy and clinical practice*. Northvale, NJ: Jason Aronson.

Ellis, A. (2000). Rational–emotive behavior marriage and family therapy. In A. M. Horne (Ed.), *Family counseling and therapy* (3rd ed., pp. 489–514). Itasca, IL: Peacock.

Haley, J. (1984). *Ordeal therapy*. San Francisco: Jossey-Bass.

Madanes, C. (1981). *Strategic family therapy*. San Francisco: Jossey-Bass.

Minuchin, S. (1974). *Families and family therapy*. Cambridge, MA: Harvard University Press.

Napier, A., & Whitaker, C. A. (1978). *The family crucible*. New York: Harper & Row.

Patterson, G. R. (1975). *Families: Applications of social learning to social life*. Champaign, IL: Research Press.

Satir, V. (1988). *The new peoplemaking*. Mountain View, CA: Science and Behavior Books.

Scharff, D. E., & Scharff, J. S. (1987). *Object relations family therapy*. Northvale, NJ: Jason Aronson.

Additional Reading for Nonprofessionals

Carter, E. A., McGoldrick, M., & Carter, B. (Eds.). (1998). *The expanded family life cycle: Individual, family, and social perspectives* (3rd ed.). Boston: Allyn & Bacon.

Additional Readings for Professionals

Gladding, S. T. (2001). *Family therapy: History, theory, and practice* (3rd ed.). Upper Saddle River, NJ: Prentice-Hall.

Minuchin, S., & Fishman, H. C. (1981). *Family therapy techniques*. Cambridge, MA: Harvard University Press.

Worden, M. (2003). *Family therapy basics* (3rd ed.). Pacific Grove, CA: Brooks/Cole.

CRAIG S. CASHWELL

Fears and Phobias

DEFINITION AND PREVALENCE

Fear can be defined as a discrete, normal emotional response elicited by a specific object, situation, or activity that is perceived as threatening. Feelings of fear are often accompanied by distress, physiological activation ("fight-or-flight" syndrome), and a desire to escape or avoid the feared stimulus (Albano, Causey, & Carter, 2001). Examples of common childhood fears are fear of strangers, fear of dogs, and fear of the dark.

Age-appropriate fears are very common in childhood. A recent study found that 78 percent of children between the ages 7 and 19 reported some level of fear (Schaefer, Watkins, & Burnham, 2003). Age-appropriate fears are fears that are considered developmentally normal at certain ages. Some typical age-appropriate fears include

- 5-year-olds: animals, "bad" people, the dark, separation from caretakers
- 6-year-olds: supernatural beings (e.g., ghosts, monsters, etc.), bodily harm, storms, sleeping alone, separation from caretakers
- 7- to 8-year-olds: supernatural beings, staying alone, bodily harm, extraordinary events (e.g., war, bombings, kidnappings, etc.)
- 9- to 12-year-olds: tests, public speaking, peer bullying, rejection
- 13- to 18-year-olds: social alienation, embarrassment, failure, school performance, death, injury or serious illness, natural or man-made disasters (Albano et al., 2001)

These developmentally normal fears are generally temporary and tend to change in form as the child gets older.

A fear that is irrational, excessive, uncontrollable, and/or occurs beyond an age at which it would be considered age appropriate may be termed a *phobia* (Albano et al., 2001). Under the most recent edition of the *Diagnostic and Statistical Manual of Mental Disorders* (*DSM-IV-TR*), phobias that are associated with extreme emotional distress and avoidance of the object resulting in impairment in a child's daily academic or social functioning may be diagnosed as an anxiety disorder called *Specific Phobia* (American Psychiatric Association, 2000). According to the *DSM-IV-TR*, a Specific Phobia is a fear that is excessive, related to a specific situation or object (such as a fear of dogs or the dark), and triggers a physiological anxiety response (or crying, tantrums, clinging in children). Furthermore, this fear results in avoidance of certain situations or extreme distress, which causes impairment in the child's daily functioning (e.g., normal routine, academic or social functioning) and lasts 6 months or longer.

Therefore, fears and phobias can be conceptualized as occurring along a continuum, with fears being the least severe and a Specific Phobia being the most severe. Thus, phobias are less common than fears, and phobias that warrant a diagnosis of Specific Phobia occur even less often, with a lifetime prevalence rate of 4 to 8.8 percent (American Psychiatric Association, 2000).

EPIDEMIOLOGY

Although fears are common in childhood, the number of fears typically decreases with increasing age. As compared to younger children, only 3 to 4.6 percent of 13- and 15-year-olds report having at least one fear (Poulton, Trainor, Stanton, McGee, & Silva, 1997). In addition, fears and phobias are more common in females than males (American Psychiatric Association, 2000). Research on ethnic differences in fears and phobias in the United States is mixed (Schaefer, Watkins, & Burnham, 2003). Although childhood fears are experienced throughout the world, the object of the fear may differ by culture (American Psychiatric Association, 2000).

ETIOLOGY

The specific causes of fears and phobias are not fully understood. Historically, theorists have highlighted classical conditioning, Mowrer's two-factor theory, and Rachman's information transmission models, yet these theories fail to explain childhood phobias that exist in the absence of any clear environmental cause (Ollendick, King, & Muris, 2002). Currently, experts believe that fears and phobias are the result of multiple converging factors. In a recent review of the research literature, Ollendick and colleagues (2002) identified several factors that they believe together contribute to the development of fears and phobias in children: genetic predisposition, temperamental influences, parental psychopathology, parenting practices, and individual conditioning histories. These studies suggest that many children inherit a genetic predisposition for fearfulness and a fearful and inhibited temperament. Children whose parents have anxiety disorders may have a learning history shaped by parental modeling of anxious and avoidant behaviors, misinterpretation of ambiguous situations as threatening or harmful (maladaptive thoughts), and reinforcement for avoidance of potentially threatening situations. Furthermore, these parents may engage in overprotective parenting practices. Finally, personal conditioning experiences (either direct or indirect), such as observing another child being bitten by a dog, may contribute to the establishment of childhood fears and phobias.

ASSESSMENT

In clinical settings, multimethod, multitrait, and multiinformant assessment techniques are recommended for assessing fears and phobias in children. A combination of diagnostic clinical interviews (Anxiety Disorders Interview Schedule for *DSM-IV*: Child/Parent), clinical rating scales (Child Behavior Checklist, Behavior Assessment System for Children—parent and teacher formats), self-report measures (Fear Survey Schedule for Children—Revised), and direct observation methods are typically used (Albano et al., 2001). An example of a commonly used observational method for assessment of fears and phobias is a behavioral avoidance test (Albano et al., 2001). This test simply measures the proximity with which a child will approach a feared object or the duration they will remain in a phobic situation.

PREVENTION AND TREATMENT

Despite limited understanding of the causes of fears and phobias in children, there is a great deal of evidence regarding effective methods for their prevention and treatment. There are a number of things that parents can do to prevent or lessen their children's fears. If a child's fear becomes extreme and debilitating, parents should seek therapy services from a qualified clinician with training and experience using behavioral and cognitive–behavioral therapy techniques with children. Overall, research indicates that graduated exposure to the feared object or situation is a key feature of most successful treatment efforts.

Ordinarily, parents can help children cope with fears by supporting and encouraging bravery, while gently discouraging avoidance (Kelley, 1995). It is very important for parents to provide children with opportunities for graduated exposure to the feared object or situation. Parents should acknowledge children's feelings of fear while providing accurate yet reassuring information regarding why they need not be afraid (e.g., "I understand you feel scared when it is dark, but you are safe here because monsters are not real."). Parents also can set attainable "bravery" goals and reward children for accomplishing them. Finally, parents can help prevent excessive fears by modeling bravery and positive methods for coping with fears (Kelley, 1995).

For treatment of severe or debilitating fears in a clinical setting, research indicates that the most effective childhood fears/phobias are those centered on behavioral and cognitive–behavioral therapy (CBT) techniques (Ollendick & King, 1998). These methods incorporate graduated exposure to the feared stimulus, modeling of good coping methods, and rewards for completing exposure training.

Empirically supported treatments for childhood fears and phobias can be divided into four categories: Systematic Desensitization (imaginal and in vivo), Modeling (participant, live, and filmed), Contingency Management (reinforced practice), and Cognitive–Behavioral Therapy (self-instruction training). Systematic desensitization involves the presentation of fear-producing stimuli in the presence of other responses that are incompatible with fear, such as relaxation. First, a fear hierarchy is established ranking feared objects from least to most threatening. Then the child progresses through the hierarchy, first being exposed to the least feared objects and gradually progressing to the most feared objects. Fear-producing stimuli can be presented in real life (in vivo) or imagined by the child. Systematic desensitization requires assistance of a therapist trained in this technique. Modeling involves having the child observe another person adaptively coping with exposure to an anxiety-producing situation or event. In participant modeling, the child assists another child, who is not afraid, with the exposure task. In other words, the child who is fearful actually participates in the activity that he/she fears. In filmed modeling, the child observes a film of a person being exposed to the feared stimulus. In live modeling, the child directly observes a person being exposed to the feared stimulus. Reinforced practice involves the gradual exposure of the participant to the fear-inducing object followed by reinforcement. CBT involves techniques to alter a child's maladaptive thoughts. For example, positive phrases may be repeated by the child to help the child change unhelpful thoughts about a fear-evoking stimulus (Ollendick & King, 1998).

Treatments with the best research support are considered "well established" and include participant modeling and reinforced practice. Treatments with good research support are considered "probably efficacious" and include modeling (live and filmed), systematic desensitization (imaginal and in vivo), and CBT (self-instruction training) (Ollendick & King, 1998).

See also: ASEBA Child Behavior Checklist; Anxiety

BIBLIOGRAPHY

Albano, A. M., Causey, D., & Carter, B. D. (2001). Fear and anxiety in children. In C. E. Walker & M. C. Roberts (Eds.), *Handbook of clinical child psychology* (3rd ed., pp. 291–316). New York: Wiley.

American Psychiatric Association. (2000). *Diagnostic and statistical manual of mental disorders* (4th ed., text rev.). Washington, DC: Author.

Kelley, M. L. (1995). *Helping children cope with fear and anxiety.* Unpublished manuscript, Louisiana State University.

Ollendick, T. H., & King, N. J. (1998). Empirically supported treatments for children with phobic and anxiety disorders: Current status. *Journal of Clinical Child Psychology, 27,* 156–167.

Ollendick, T. H., King, N. J., & Muris, P. (2002). Fears and phobias in children: Phenomenology, epidemiology, and aetiology. *Child and Adolescent Mental Health, 7,* 98–106.

Poulton, R., Trainor, P., Stanton, W., McGee, R., & Silva, P. (1997). The (in)stability of adolescent fears. *Behavior Research and Therapy, 35,* 159–163.

Schaefer, B. A., Watkins, M. W., & Burnham, J. J. (2003). Empirical fear profile among American youth. *Behaviour Research and Therapy, 41,* 1093–1103.

Additional Reading for Nonprofessionals

Rapee, R. M., Spence, S., Cobham, V., & Wignall, A. (2000). *Helping your anxious child: A step-by-step guide for parents.* Oakland, CA: New Harbinger.

Additional Readings for Professionals

Achenbach, T. M., & Rescorla, L. A. (2001). *Manual for ASEBA school-age forms & profiles.* Burlington: University of Vermont, Research Center for Children, Youth, & Families.

Kendall, P. C. (2000). *Cognitive–behavioral therapy for anxious children: Therapist manual.* Ardmore, PA: Workbook.

Ollendick, T. H. (1983). Reliability and validity of the revised fear survey schedule for children (FSSC-R). *Behaviour Research and Therapy, 21,* 685–692.

Reynolds, C. R., & Kamphaus, R. W. (1992). *Behavior Assessment System for Children manual.* Circle Pines, MN: American Guidance Services.

Silverman, W. K., & Albano, A. M. (1996). *Anxiety Disorders Interview for DSM-IV—Child/Parent.* Boulder, CO: Graywind.

Silverman, W. K., & Kurtines, W. M. (1996). *Anxiety and phobic disorders: A pragmatic approach.* New York: Plenum.

SARA E. SYTSMA-JORDAN
JACQUELINE BEINE BROWN

Fellows: Division 16 (School Psychology) of the American Psychological Association

Achieving Fellow status in the American Psychological Association is associated with the recognition that the individual has achieved great distinction in his/her field. Nomination for Fellow status is made by Divisions, and APA Bylaws and Association Rules give divisions a great deal of latitude in establishing procedures used to nominate individuals. The Bylaws do state that the minimum standard is "evidence of unusual and outstanding contribution or performance in the field of psychology." Division 16's criteria to be recommended for Fellow status state that individuals must have made contributions in at least one of the following areas:

1. Sustained publication in the field of school psychology documenting empirical research, the development of significant theory or method, or other scholarly pursuits
2. A major role in conceiving, planning, and directing relevant research and training programs
3. Spreading an understanding and application of new knowledge about school psychology through innovations in teaching and/or practice
4. Demonstrating leadership in identifying problems, defining goals, formulating methods, communicating the aims and ideals of the field, and advancing the organizational implementation of its purpose

There are currently 195 living Fellows of Division 16. They are

Richard R. Abidin
Judith L. Alpert
Grace T. Altus
Stephen J. Bagnato
Walter B. Barbe
Allan G. Barclay
James R. Barclay
David W. Barnett
Andres Barona
John R. Bergan
Virginia Berninger
Donald N. Bersoff
Ann E. Boehm
Ruth F. Boland
Bruce A. Bracken
Jeffrey P. Braden
John C. Brantley
Patricia M. Bricklin
Jere E. Brophy
Norman A. Buktenica
Joy P. Burke
Anthony A. Cancelli
William M. Canning
Cindy I. Carlson
James L. Carroll
Eloise B. Cason
Russell N. Cassel
Harvey F. Clarizio
Elaine Clark
Robert C. Colligan
Jane Close Conoley
Frances M. Culbertson
Jack A. Cummings
Michael J. Curtis
Raymond S. Dean
Harold A. Delp
Stephen T. DeMers
Beth Doll
George DuPaul
Raymond A. DiGiuseppe
Helen L. Dunlap
Ron P. Edwards
Byron R. Egeland
Jack Z. Elias
Maurice J. Elias
Victor B. Elkin
Stephen N. Elliot
Colin Elliott
Ann W. Engin
William P. Erchul
Thomas K. Fagan
Frank Farley

Marvin J. Fine
Marian Fish
Dawn Flanagan
Iris G. Fodor
Susan G. Forman
Peter G. Fotiu
Raymond D. Fowler
Joseph L. French
Glydys D. Frith
Douglas H. Fuchs
Gerald B. Fuller
Maribeth Gettinger
Harry B. Gilbert
Annette L. Gillette
David S. Goh
Roland H. Good
Dwight L. Goodwin
Edward F. Gotts
Gloria B. Gottsegen
Frank M. Gresham
Terry B. Gutkin
Rosa A. Hagin
William F. Hall
Patti L. Harrison
Stuart N. Hart
Virginia Smith Harvey
Mary Henning-Stout
Scott Huebner
Jan N. Hughes
Irwin A. M. Hyman
George W. Hynd
Robert J. Illback
John H. Jackson
William R. Jenson
Randy W. Kamphaus
Alan S. Kaufman
Nadeen L. Kaufman
Thomas J. Kehle
Timothy Z. Keith
Harold R. Keller
Warren A. Ketcham
Barbara K. Koegh
Edward R. Knight
Howard M. Knoff
Jack J. Kramer
John Kranzler
Thomas R. Kratochwill
Peter J. Kuriloff
Nadine M. Lambert
Beatrice A. LeCraft
O. Bernard Leibman
Donald A. Leton

Steven G. Little
Stuart M. Losen
Charles A. Maher
Lester Mann
Brian K. Martens
Roy P. Martin
Emanuel J. Mason
W. Mason Mathews
R. Steve McCallum
Paul McDermott
Eugene T. McDonald
Judith S. Mearig
Frederic J. Medway
Ken Merrell
Joel Meyers
Lee Meyerson
John B. Mordock, Jr.
Richard J. Morris
Barbara A. Mowder
Richard Nagle
Jack A. Naglieri
Rosemery O. Nelson-Gray
Raymond C. Norris
Jack I. Novick
Ena Vasquez Nuttal
Thomas D. Oakland
John E. Obrzut
Raymond L. Ownby
Kathleen D. Paget
Steven I. Pfeiffer
LeAdelle Phelps
Beeman N. Phillips
Henry Platt
Thomas Power
David P. Prasse
Norman M. Prentice
Walter B. Pryzwansky
Jean C. Ramage
Arthur L. Rautman
David H. Reilly
Daniel J. Reschly
Cecil R. Reynolds
Maynard C. Reynolds
William M. Reynolds
Mildred T. Richardson
Sylvia A. Rosenfield

Donald K. Routh
Penelope P. Russianoff
Phillip A. Saigh
Jonathan H. Sandoval
Jerome M. Sattler
Winifred S. Scott
J. Kirk Seaton
John T. Seaton
Dorothy D. Sebald
Herbert H. Severson
Trevor E. Sewell
Edward S. Shapiro
Susan Sheridan
Mark R. Shinn
Virginia C. Shipman
Hirsch L. Silverman
Dorothy G. Singer
William A. Sivers, Jr.
Christopher Skinner
Barbara R. Slater
Anne B. Spragins
Phillip M. Stone
George A. W. Stouffer, Jr.
Beth Sulzer-Azaroff
Mark E. Swerdlik
Rhonda C. Talley
Cathy F. Telzrow
Deborah Tharinger
Sigmund Tobias
Gilbert M. Trachtman
Gary R. VandenBos
Wallace A. Verburg
Nancy Waldron
Barbara H. Wasik
Marley Watkins
Richard A. Weinberg
Roger P. Weissberg
David W. Winikur
Robert D. Wirt
Joseph C. Witt
Robert H. Woody
Roland K. Yoshida
Lillian J. Zach
Barry J. Zimmerman
Joseph E. Zins

See also: Jack Bardon Distinguished Service Award; Lightner Witmer Award; Senior Scientist Award

K. Angeleque Akin-Little
Stephen G. Little

Fetal Alcohol Syndrome and Other Alcohol-Related Birth Defects

Alcohol consumption during pregnancy is a known cause of birth defects. The most widely known consequence of drinking alcohol during pregnancy is Fetal Alcohol Syndrome (FAS). A medical professional diagnoses this condition when alcohol consumption during the pregnancy is documented and three criteria are observed in the child: (1) craniofacial abnormalities, (2) restricted growth, and (3) central nervous system dysfunction (Jones, Smith, Ulleland, & Streissguth, 1973). Craniofacial abnormalities refer to a pattern of deviations from the normal structure of the face. Most of us have some abnormalities in one or more of our features; however, children with FAS display a pattern of abnormalities that has only been associated with prenatal alcohol exposure. Restricted growth refers to the shorter stature and slower growth (Day et al., 2002). A variety of factors can be used as evidence of central nervous system dysfunction including microcephaly (an abnormally small head circumference) and mental retardation.

Although FAS is the most widely known consequence of prenatal alcohol exposure, it is only the tip of the iceberg, representing the most severely affected children. In the absence of an FAS diagnosis, we cannot assume that the alcohol-exposed child is unaffected. Even when children do not meet the criteria for FAS, moderate to heavy alcohol exposure is associated with reductions in intelligence, attention difficulties, inhibition deficits, and learning difficulties. To better acknowledge the range of effects observed in exposed children, several new diagnostic categories have been proposed, including partial fetal alcohol syndrome (PFAS), alcohol-related birth defects (ARBD), and alcohol-related neurodevelopmental disorder (ARND) (Institute of Medicine [IOM], 1996). Each of these new diagnostic categories requires documentation of maternal drinking during the pregnancy but does not require all three FAS diagnostic criteria to be present. This is very important because many alcohol-exposed children do not display the characteristic craniofacial abnormalities or growth restriction, but still have significant behavioral or psychological difficulties that affect their ability to succeed within the normal school environment.

Prenatal alcohol exposure affects more individuals than many people realize. Studies suggests that between 1 and 5 out of every 1,000 children born alive in the United States and Western European countries may have FAS (Abel & Sokol, 1991; Sampson et al., 1997). When children with ARND are included, it is estimated that approximately 9 out of every 1,000 live births are affected by prenatal alcohol exposure (Sampson et al., 1997).

Because prenatal alcohol exposure affects the brain, it may affect the child long after birth. Alcohol exposure can affect neurons, the cells in the brain, by (a) increasing cell death, (b) altering the time at which cells are created, and (c) altering cell migration within the brain. These disruptions in normal brain development can lead to a smaller brain, reductions in the size of specific brain regions, and insufficient or incorrectly established connections between different neurons or different areas of the brain (Guerri, 1998). Several areas of the brain seem to be particularly sensitive to the effects of prenatal alcohol exposure, including the corpus callosum, a structure that enables the left and right hemispheres of the brain to communicate with each other, the basal ganglia, and the cerebellum (Mattson et al., 1994).

The damage that prenatal alcohol exposure causes to the developing brain is often displayed through neurobehavioral deficits such as reductions in intelligence and mental retardation. Intelligence has been widely studied in this population, in part because prenatal alcohol exposure is the leading preventable cause of mental retardation. One misperception is that most or all children with FAS have mental retardation. However, research suggests that only 25% of children with FAS have intelligence scores that fall within the mental retardation range (Streissguth, 1997). In fact, intelligence scores for alcohol-affected children vary widely, with reported scores ranging from a low of 20 to a high of at least 120 (Streissguth, Randels, & Smith, 1991). As a result, neither an acknowledgment of alcohol exposure nor a diagnosis of FAS is a good predictor of the future school or life success of a particular alcohol-affected child.

School performance of the alcohol-exposed child can be affected by a variety of other alcohol-related deficits as well as the structure and support that is available to the child within the family unit and the school system. For example, impairments in attention, difficulties in using feedback to change their behavior, and difficulties sequencing activities can cause the child to fail to complete tasks that he/she agreed to complete and appears to know how to complete. This can lead to a cycle of frustration and failure that may be exacerbated when the child's failure is misinterpreted as willful disobedience or laziness, rather than a reflection of his/her underlying disability.

Alcohol-affected children can succeed within the school environment. However, this is most likely to occur when parents and the school system work together to create a highly structured learning environment that is composed of clear, concrete rules and realistic expectations. To reduce the probability of the child experiencing repeated failures, educational strategies should include a system that allows for frequent monitoring of the child's learning in order to identify effective strategies and set realistic goals (Streissguth, 1997).

See also: Learning Disabilities

BIBLIOGRAPHY

Abel, E. L., & Sokol, R. J. (1991). A revised conservative estimate of the incidence of FAS and its economic impact. *Alcoholism: Clinical and Experimental Research, 15,* 514–524.

Day, N. L., Leech, S. L., Richardson, G. A., Cornelius, M. D., Robles, N., & Larkby, C. (2002). Prenatal alcohol exposure predicts continued deficits in offspring size at 14 years of age. *Alcoholism: Clinical and Experimental Research, 26,* 1584–1591.

Guerri, C. (1998). Neuroanatomical and neurophysiological mechanisms involved in central nervous system dysfunctions induced by prenatal alcohol exposure. *Alcoholism: Clinical and Experimental Research, 22,* 304–312.

Institute of Medicine. (1996). *Fetal alcohol syndrome: Diagnosis, epidemiology, prevention, and treatment.* Washington, DC: National Academy Press.

Jones, K. L., Smith, D. W., Ulleland, C. N., & Streissguth, A. P. (1973). Pattern of malformation in offspring of chronic alcoholic mothers. *Lancet, 1,* 1267–1271.

Mattson, S. N., Riley, E. P., Jernigan, T. L., Garcia, A., Kaneko, W. M., Ehlers, C. L., et al. (1994). A decrease in the size of the basal ganglia following prenatal alcohol exposure: A preliminary report. *Neurotoxicology and Teratology, 16,* 283–289.

Sampson, P. D., Streissguth, A. P., Bookstein, F. L., Little, R. E., Clarren, S. K., Dehaene, P., et al. (1997). Incidence of fetal alcohol syndrome and prevalence of alcohol-related neurodevelopmental disorder. *Teratology, 56,* 317–326.

Streissguth, A. (1997). *Fetal alcohol syndrome: A guide for families and communities.* Baltimore: Brookes.

Streissguth, A. P., Randels, S. P., & Smith, D. F. (1991). A test-retest study of intelligence in patients with fetal alcohol syndrome: Implications for care. *Journal of the American Academy of Child and Adolescent Psychiatry, 30,* 584–587.

Additional Readings for Nonprofessionals

Kleinfeld, J., Morse, B., & Wescott, S. (2000). *Fantastic Antone grows up: Adolescents and adults with fetal alcohol syndrome.* Fairbanks: University of Alaska Press.

Streissguth, A. P., & Kanter, J. (1997). *The challenge of fetal alcohol syndrome: Overcoming secondary disabilities.* Seattle: University of Washington Press.

Additional Reading for Professionals

Wass, T. S., Mattson, S. N., & Riley, E. P. (2003). Neuroanatomical and neurobehavioral effects of heavy prenatal alcohol exposure. In J. Brick (Ed.), *Handbook of the medical consequences of alcohol and drug abuse* (pp. 139–170). Binghamton, NY: Haworth.

TARA S. WASS

Functional Analysis

Historically, severe behaviors such as self-injury (head banging, hand biting, face slapping, head punching), severe aggression to others (hitting, biting, kicking, hair pulling), and severe property destruction were once thought to have an organic etiology beyond the reach of behavioral interventions. In the late 1960s and early 1970s, researchers demonstrated that severe problem behavior could be increased and decreased by altering the level of social events, such as attention from adults or avoiding work or academic demands (cf. Berkson & Mason, 1963, 1965; Carr, Newsome, & Binkoff, 1976; Lovass, Freitag, Gold, & Kassorla, 1965; Lovaas & Simmons, 1969). These findings were useful in decreasing problem behavior because it allowed behavior analysts to use the variables in behavioral intervention. However, the use of those interventions was still a guessing game. There was no assessment methodology that would determine which behaviors were more appropriate for interventions that relied on attention versus interventions that used breaks from work. In 1982, Iwata, Dorsey, Slifer, Bauman, and Richman created a methodology to test relevant social variables that led directly to recommendations regarding which social variables would also be useful in intervention.

Functional analysis is an assessment technique used to identify variables that cause problem behaviors to persist. Behavior analysts have demonstrated that certain events that occur immediately prior to problem behavior (antecedents) and certain events that immediately follow problem behavior (consequences) can make behavior more likely to occur. Functional analysis is a methodology in which the environment is manipulated to isolate and present short test conditions containing the antecedents and consequences that are thought to influence problem behavior. The results allow behavior analysts to use those same variables in the planning of interventions to decrease the problem behavior.

In naturally occurring situations, there are several reasons why it is often very difficult to observe a problem behavior and determine which variables are influencing the behavior. First, problem behavior can occur in the presence of several different antecedents and consequences making pinpointing just one impossible. Second, several antecedents or several consequences could be occurring simultaneously, making the independent effects of each indistinguishable. Third, some behaviors occur infrequently and require very lengthy observation periods in order to witness the chain of events that surround the behavior. Finally, any one behavior can serve different functions for the same person. That is, a child might demonstrate aggression because it leads to attention in one situation and because it allows them to escape from work in another situation. The same child could demonstrate aggression and self-injury because both response classes lead to the same social consequences. Because of these complex interactions, observing one situation may not provide information about the behavior in a different setting.

To delineate the effects of different antecedent and consequent events, small situations can be created in order to assess the effects of different variables on a target behavior. Several of these test conditions can be presented in random order so that several variables can be isolated and tested in the same analysis over relatively short periods of time. This test methodology is called functional analysis, and the small test situations a person is exposed to are called functional analysis conditions.

Conditions are created to test whether or not a behavior is sensitive to certain positive reinforcers and certain negative reinforcers. Positive reinforcers that are isolated and presented independently in different conditions include adult attention, peer attention, tangible items, and sensory stimulation. Negative reinforcers that are isolated and presented independently in functional analysis conditions are escape from academic tasks, escape from manual labor/work chore activities, escape from social attention, and escaping sensory situations.

Most functional analyses are analog (Hanley, Iwata, & McCord, 2003). Analog functional analyses occur in a different environment from which the referral was made. For example, if a problem behavior was occurring in a classroom setting, an analog functional analysis would be presented in a separate, isolated room to minimize the amount of outside influence and allow the behavior analysts more experimental control. A behavior analyst would remove the child from class, bring the child to the assessment room, and implement the assessment. Some functional analyses are conducted in classroom settings with teachers trained to implement all the assessment conditions (Moore & Edwards, 2003; Moore, Edwards, Wilczynski, & Olmi, 2001; Moore, Mueller, Dubard, Roberts, & Sterling-Turner, 2002; Mueller, Edwards, & Trahant, in press). This method is believed to increase the ecological validity by keeping more of the environment as similar to the referral environment as possible. There are potential pros and cons to each type of assessment. For analog settings, more experimental control relates to more confidence in outcome because fewer extraneous variables could have influenced the results. The potential downside is that relevant environmental variables from the referral setting might not be included in the analog setting. This limitation might be overcome with sufficient descriptive assessment and observation. The benefits of conducting the analyses in classrooms are many. All relevant variables from the referral environment are included. The teacher, teacher assistant, or paraprofessional can be trained to serve the role of the therapist, peers can be incorporated into the analyses, and other classroom variables such as time of day, location, physical surrounding, along with other sights and sounds from the classroom, can be present during the analysis. The potential downside to classroom-based analyses are the potential for unwanted sources' influence from peers, teachers, or school staff not implementing the assessment accurately, and the potential for disrupting other students when behavior escalates.

Common analog conditions include teacher attention, peer attention, escape, tangibles, alone, and control. Some variations of these have been demonstrated as effective. Each commonly used condition will be described below. The logic of all the conditions is the same even if the variables (potential reinforcers) that are presented as consequences to problem behavior are different. In each condition, some potential reinforcer is presented contingent on the occurrence of a target behavior and withheld at other times.

ATTENTION CONDITION

This is a test of a target behavior's sensitivity to positive reinforcement in the form of verbal attention. The student is given moderately preferred tasks to engage while the teacher remains close but is himself/herself engaged in some activity, typically reading a book. The teacher ignores all behavior except those targeted for analysis. If any instance of the target behavior is demonstrated, verbal attention is delivered. Usually the verbal attention is in the form of a brief reprimand. However, research has shown that longer amounts of attention have been associated with different outcomes when compared with briefer forms of attention. When this condition is used to assess peer attention, the student's peers have to be trained to deliver attention when, and only when, the target behavior is demonstrated. For teacher or peer attention conditions, following the attention, the teacher or peer resumes the activity they were engaged in previously. This is repeated throughout the entire condition. If the student exhibits no target behaviors, no attention would be delivered. If high levels of target behavior were demonstrated, the teacher or peers would deliver a lot of attention.

TANGIBLES CONDITION

This is a test of a target behavior's sensitivity to positive reinforcement in the form of tangible items. The student is given access to a highly preferred item for 1 or 2 minutes prior to the start of the condition. The condition begins with the teacher restricting the item from the child. If the student exhibits any instance of the target behavior, the teacher returns the item to the student for a brief (20- or 30-second) reinforcement interval. After the interval ends, the item is restricted again and the process is repeated. No verbal attention of any kind is used in this condition. If the student does not demonstrate any target behavior, the teacher would hold the object the entire session. If the student exhibited a high level of target behavior, the student might have the item for most of the session.

ESCAPE CONDITION

This condition is a test of a target behavior's sensitivity to negative reinforcement in the form of a break from work activities. This condition can be done with routine chores and work tasks or with academic demands commonly found in classroom situations. Regardless of whether academic or occupational demands are presented, the procedures remain the same. However, the academic demand condition will be used for explanatory purposes. The teacher is seated next to the child at a worktable or desk. The teacher presents demands to the child to engage in academic material that is difficult or that has previously been associated with target behavior. A regimented prompting sequence is used that commonly involves a verbal, gestural, and physical prompt to ensure compliance with the task demand. Prompts are commonly spaced 5 seconds apart to allow for compliance. This prompting sequence continues until a target behavior is demonstrated, at which point the teacher would remove the work activity and turn away from the student for a brief (20- or 30-second) reinforcement interval. At the end of the interval, the demands resume and the process is repeated. If the student does not demonstrate any target behavior, the teacher would prompt work demands the entire session. If the student exhibited a high level of target behavior, the student might not complete any work during the session.

ALONE CONDITION

Although difficult to utilize in a classroom setting, the alone condition is a test for a target behavior's sensitivity to automatic positive or negative reinforcement. Although some behaviors are under the control of outside social factors as described in the conditions above, others are maintained by the very sensations they produce or alleviate. An example of automatic positive reinforcement would be a child's hitting himself/herself in the head and that blow to the head triggering the release of endogenous endorphins in the brain, and that sensation being enough for the child to continue to produce it through repeated self-injury. An example of automatic negative reinforcement might be a child's scratching his/her skin excessively to alleviate an itch. In both examples, no social variable delivered by the teacher maintained the behavior. Each was maintained by internal stimulation of some kind. The test for this type of reinforcement is the alone condition. The logic of the condition suggests that behavior that occurs as frequently in the absence of all social variables is not reinforced by those variables. If it were, the frequency of the target behavior would be higher in a condition that contains a social variable. A child would be placed in a room by himself/herself or in a setting isolated from all external sources of stimulation. Safety and covert observation factors are adhered to, such that the child cannot cause undue injury to himself/herself. The teacher would videotape or observe through a one-way mirror or window.

CONTROL CONDITION

A control condition is used to provide another condition that contains many of the variables and situation used in the other conditions. Teacher attention, teacher proximity, availability of play items and materials, and other setting factors are presented in the control condition so at least one other condition in addition to the test condition contains these relevant variables. The target behaviors in all other conditions are compared with the level of target behaviors in the control condition. The condition begins with the teacher and student in a play situation in which the teacher delivers attention (praise or neutral statements) at least once every 30 seconds, remains close to the student, and interacts with the students in a typical play manner.

Conditions are presented in a random order, with the stipulation that all conditions in the analysis are used before any are used a second time. Some behavior analysts have used 15-minute conditions (e.g., Iwata et al., 1982) and others have used 10- and even 5-minute conditions (Mueller, Wilczynski, Moore, Fusilier, & Trahant, 2001; Wallace & Iwata, 1999). A short break is usually given between the conditions. Depending on the availability of time for the analysis, multiple presentation of each condition can occur in a single day or across several days. The condition is considered final when the level of behavior in any one condition is consistently above the level of behavior in the other conditions. The degree of separation between level of behavior in different conditions also plays a part in ending an analysis. If the condition containing the most target behaviors is of only a marginally higher level than the other conditions, the analysis might be extended to gain more confidence in the results. If a condition that contains the most target behaviors is the only condition that contains a target behavior and there is a very high level of behavior across conditions, fewer series of conditions are needed to make a confident decision about results. These decisions are made on a case-by-case basis by behavior analysts examining graphical representations of the data collected during the analysis (Mace & Mauk, 1995; Mace, Vollmer, Progar, & Mace, 1998).

The utility of functional analysis is in the identification of reinforcers for problem behavior. This is because those reinforcers can be used in the intervention to decrease the targeted behaviors. For example, if a target behavior is maintained by attention, attention can be used in the intervention. If breaks from work are reinforcing problem behavior, breaks from work can be used in the intervention. This is typically accomplished by manipulating the contingencies under which the reinforcer (attention, breaks from work, tangibles items, etc.) is available.

When a child is demonstrating a target behavior, some reinforcer follows the behavior. In a behavioral intervention, there is a two-step process to change that behavior–consequence relationship. First, the child must learn that the target behavior no longer leads to the reinforcer. If adult attention was reinforcing the throwing of toys, the child must not get attention for throwing toys. Second, the child must get attention for other things. This process (withholding a reinforcer for some behaviors and delivering the reinforcer for some other behaviors) is called differential reinforcement. Behavior analysts do not want to stop children from accessing reinforcers for behaviors as much as they want to change the way in which children get those things. To this end, new communicative response can replace problem behavior, as can incompatible behaviors (deliver attention for sitting in the seat and withhold attention for the child who gets out of their seat), and a variety of other appropriate behaviors can be used to replace problem behavior.

Common criticisms of functional analysis in the classroom mostly center on time and training issues (Nelson, Roberts, Bullis, Albers, & Ohland, 2000; Nelson, Roberts, Mathur, & Rutherford, 1999). That is, some have described functional analysis as too time consuming or too difficult to train others to perform. Related to assessment time, researchers have made many variations to functional analysis procedures that have led to reduced assessment time (e.g., brief functional analyses; Derby et al., 1992; Northup et al., 1991). Conditions have been shortened from 15 to 5 minutes. Fewer conditions are presented overall, and any functional analyses present only those conditions that might contain a reinforcer for a specific target behavior rather than presenting all the conditions. The incorporation of descriptive functional assessment data has helped streamline the analysis process. The time to conduct an analysis ultimately depends on the child's behavior and can at times reach extended periods. However, if a child's behavior is so complex that extended analysis time is needed, it is also likely to be complex enough to persist in the face of ill-conceived intervention based on lack of assessment information. Recent research in training staff to implement complex behavioral protocols has demonstrated that functional analysis methods can be trained to very high levels of integrity in very little time (Iwata et al., 2000; Moore, Edwards, et al., 2002; Mueller et al., in press). The criticism that teachers cannot be trained to analyze very complex behavior is simply not valid. For example, in Moore et al., teachers were asked to implement functional analysis conditions in training sessions with consultants. After receiving brief training using role-play, rehearsal, and performance feedback, all teachers increased their procedural integrity from very low to very high levels and then continued to implement functional analyses with high integrity in their classrooms with referred children.

Very complex behaviors can be increased or decreased by very common social variables. Some of those variables (an-tecedents) occur before problem behavior and can set up situations in which children are likely to demonstrate those behaviors. Antecedents to problem behavior can include aversive demands situations in and out of the classroom, little or no attention from adults and peers, and the restriction of preferred items. Other variables follow problem behavior and make those problem behaviors more likely to occur in the future. Some of those consequent variables include attention, preferred tangible objects, breaks from work, breaks from attention, aversive situation avoidance, and through the sensory stimulation produced by those behaviors. Situations in which children demonstrate severe behaviors very frequently contain many antecedents and many of the common consequences listed above. To isolate and test which of those variables are affecting the problem behavior, functional analysis is used. By creating small test and control situations the common social and sensory variables that occur together can be teased apart and assessed independently. Over time, the conditions containing the target behavior's reinforcers will contain more problem behavior than those that do not. That vital assessment information can then be used to design effective interventions aimed at decreasing those problem behaviors.

See also: Brief Functional Analysis; Functional Assessment of Academic Behavior (FAAB); Functional Assessment Informant Record—Teacher (FAIR-T)

BIBLIOGRAPHY

Berkson, G., & Mason, W. A. (1963). Stereotyped movements of mental defectives: 3. Situational effects. *American Journal of Mental Deficiency, 68,* 409–412.

Berkson, G., & Mason, W. A. (1965). Stereotyped movements of mental defectives: 4. The effects of toys and the character of the act. *American Journal of Mental Deficiency, 70,* 511–524.

Carr, E. G., Newsome, C. D., & Binkoff, J. A. (1976). Stimulus control of self destructive behavior in a psychotic child. *Abnormal Child Psychology, 4,* 139–153.

Derby, K. M., Wacker, D. P., Sasso, G., Steege, M., Northup, J., Cigrand, K., et al. (1992). Brief functional assessment techniques to evaluate aberrant behavior in an outpatient setting: A summary of 79 cases. *Journal of Applied Behavior Analysis, 25,* 713–721.

Hanley, G. P., Iwata, B. A., & McCord, B. E. (2003). Functional analysis of problem behavior: A review. *Journal of Applied Behavior Analysis, 36,* 147–185.

Iwata, B. A., Dorsey, M. F., Slifer, K. J., Bauman, K. E., & Richman, G. S. (1982). Toward a functional analysis of self injury. *Analysis and Intervention in Developmental Disabilities, 2,* 3–20.

Iwata, B. A., Wallace, M. D., Kahng, S., Lindberg, J. S., Roscoe, E. M., Conners, J., et al. (2000). Skill acquisition in the implementation of functional analysis methodology. *Journal of Applied Behavior Analysis, 33,* 181–194.

Lovass, O. I., Freitag, G., Gold, V. J., & Kassorla, I. C. (1965). Experimental studies on childhood schizophrenia: Analysis of self-destructive behavior. *Journal of Experimental Child Psychology, 2,* 67–84.

Lovaas., O. I., & Simmons, J. Q. (1969). Manipulation of self-destruction in three retarded children. *Journal of Applied Behavior Analysis, 2,* 143–157.

Mace, F. C., & Mauk, J. E. (1995). Biobehavioral diagnosis and treatment of self-injury. *Mental Retardation and Developmental Disabilities Research Review, 1,* 104–110.

Mace, F. C., Vollmer, T. R., Progar, P. R., & Mace, A. B. (1998). Assessment and treatment of self-injury. In T. S. Watson & F. M. Gresham (Eds.), *Handbook of child behavior therapy* (pp. 413–430). New York: Plenum.

Moore, J. W., & Edwards, R. P. (2003). An analysis of aversive stimuli in classroom demand contexts. *Journal of Applied Behavior Analysis, 36,* 339–348.

Moore, J. W., Edwards, R. P., Sterling-Turner, H. E., Riley, J., DuBard, M., & McGeorge, A. (2002). Teacher acquisition of functional analysis methodology. *Journal of Applied Behavior Analysis, 35,* 73–77.

Moore, J. W., Edwards, R. P., Wilczynski, S. M., & Olmi, D. J. (2001). Using antecedent manipulations to distinguish between task and social variables associated with problem behavior exhibited by children of typical development. *Behavior Modification, 25,* 287–304.

Moore, J. W., Mueller, M. M., Dubard, M., Roberts, D. S., & Sterling-Turner, H. E. (2002). The influence of therapist attention on self-injury during a tangible condition. *Journal of Applied Behavior Analysis, 35,* 283–286.

Mueller, M. M., Edwards, R. P., & Trahant, D. (in press). Translating multiple assessment techniques into an intervention selection model for classrooms. *Journal of Applied Behavior Analysis.*

Mueller, M. M., Wilczynski, S. M., Moore, J. W., Fusilier, I., & Trahant, D. (2001). Antecedent manipulations in a tangible condition: The effects of stimulus preference on aggression. *Journal of Applied Behavior Analysis, 34,* 237–240.

Nelson, J. R., Roberts, M. L., Bullis, M., Albers, C., & Ohland, B. (2000). Functional behavioral assessment: Looking beyond applied behavior analysis. *Behavioral Interventions, 15,* 25–29.

Nelson, J. R., Roberts, M. L., Mathur, S. R., & Rutherford, R. B. (1999). Has public policy exceeded our knowledge base? A review of the functional behavioral assessment literature. *Behavioral Disorders, 24,* 169–179.

Northup, J., Wacker, D., Sasso, G., Steege, M., Cigrand, K., Cook, J., et al. (1991). A brief functional analysis of aggressive and alternative behavior in an outclinic setting. *Journal of Applied Behavior Analysis, 24,* 509–522.

Wallace, M. D., & Iwata, B. A. (1999). Effects of session duration on functional analysis outcomes. *Journal of Applied Behavior Analysis, 32,* 175–182.

Additional Readings for Nonprofessionals

http://www.aabt.org (The Association for the Advancement of Behavior Therapy)

http://www.abainternational.org (The Association for Behavior Analysis)

Additional Readings for Professionals

Gresham, F. M., & Lambros, K. M. (1998). Behavioral and functional assessments. In T. S. Watson & F. M. Gresham (Eds.), *Handbook of child behavior therapy* (pp. 3–22). New York: Plenum.

Iwata, B. A., Kahng, S., Wallace, M. D., & Lindberg, J. S. (2000). The functional analysis model of behavioral assessment. In J. Austin & J. E. Carr (Eds.), *Handbook of applied behavior analysis.* Reno, NV: Context.

MICHAEL M. MUELLER

Functional Assessment Informant Record—Teacher (FAIR-T)

The FAIR-T (Edwards, 2002) is an instrument developed for use in educational settings to assist in the identification of problem behaviors of children and environmental factors that may influence those problem behaviors. The identification of environmental variables that may be functionally related to behavior is referred to as functional assessment. Although there are several ways to obtain information regarding potential functional relationships, one procedure is to use interviews, checklists, rating scales, and similar instruments. The FAIR-T is an example of this procedure in which a child's teacher acts as the informant in providing information from which functional hypotheses may be developed.

OVERVIEW OF THE FAIR-T

Many functional assessment procedures that involve obtaining information from a third-party informant rely on a lengthy interview. The FAIR-T was designed to be more time efficient by first having the teacher independently complete a checklist and then participate in an interview to expand and clarify ambiguous information. The FAIR-T has four sections: (a) a section requesting basic referral information, (b) a section in which problem behaviors are identified along with their frequency and severity, (c) a section in which events are identified that typically precede the problem behavior (i.e., antecedents), and (d) a section in which events are identified that typically follow the problem behavior (i.e., consequences). Each of these sections is described further below.

Basic Referral Information (pp. 1–2)

After providing the name of the student and the name of the teacher, the teacher identifies the child's school, age, gender, and the date the form is completed. The teacher is then asked to provide some general information about the child's problems and to describe how the referred student differs from other children who were not referred. The next three items provide information about the referred child's academic performance in basic skill areas as compared with other students in the class. Next are two items that solicit information about medical conditions or medications. The teacher is then asked to describe any previous procedures that have been attempted to deal with the student's behavior. The next three items provide information about the child's typical activity schedule and suggest optimal times to conduct direct observations.

Behaviors (p. 3)

This section seeks information that can aid in setting priorities for treatment. The teacher is first asked to provide a specific description of one to three problem behaviors. If more than one behavior is described, the teacher is asked to list them in order of their severity. The next four items require the teacher to rate each identified problem behavior in terms of how manageable and disruptive it is and to report how often each behavior occurs and how long it has been present.

Antecedent Events (p. 4)

This section contains 16 items that explore the relationship between an identified problem behavior and a variety of antecedent events that may be functionally related to the problem behavior. When functional relationships exist between antecedent events and problem behaviors, the antecedent is typically associated with an increased frequency of occurrence of the problem behavior. In many cases, modifying or eliminating certain antecedent events can result in substantial decreases in the occurrence of the problem behavior. For each item, the teacher checks "yes" or "no" as to whether the problem behavior often follows the identified antecedent. If the teacher has identified more than one problem behavior, these 16 items are completed separately for each identified behavior. The teacher is asked if the problem behavior occurs more often during a certain type of task, during easy tasks, during difficult tasks, during certain subject areas, during new material, when the child is asked to stop a behavior, when the child is asked to begin a new activity, during transition periods, when the child's normal routine has been disrupted, when a request from the child has been denied, when specific persons are either present or absent, or following some other behavior. In addition, the teacher is asked if there is anything he/she could do to ensure occurrence of the problem behavior, whether there are any events in the child's home that precede occurrence of the problem behavior in school, and whether the problem behavior is more likely to occur in certain settings such as large or small group activities, bathrooms, recess areas, on the bus, and so on.

Consequent Events (p. 5)

The teacher is first asked to identify by checking "yes" or "no" whether each of a series of consequent events occurs following the problem behavior. As with the Antecedents section, the teacher completes a separate page for each problem behavior being assessed. If events that frequently follow the problem behavior are identified, it is reasonable to hypothesize that these events may be functioning as positive or negative reinforcers for the problem behaviors. Teachers are also asked if

they avoid presenting any particular task to the student because of the occurrence of problem behavior. This question is important because classroom observation cannot identify this type of historical contingency. The teacher is asked whether other problem behaviors frequently follow occurrence of the identified problem. When problem behaviors occur in a sequence, each subsequent behavior can function as a positive reinforcer for the behavior that precedes it, and it is important that this sequence of behaviors be interrupted early. Finally, the teacher is asked whether the child typically receives any positive consequence such as praise when appropriate or desirable behavior is exhibited. This question is asked because one of the best ways of decreasing problem behaviors is to increase appropriate behavior.

THE FOLLOW-UP INTERVIEW

It is not expected that a completed FAIR-T, by itself, will be sufficient to generate hypotheses about the function of problem behavior. Successful use of the FAIR-T requires a follow-up interview by an experienced behavioral specialist. Information from the FAIR-T can, however, help the specialist focus the interview on areas most likely to yield useful information.

Much of the information from the first two sections of the FAIR-T is used for case management rather than for functional assessment purposes. However, if the child is identified as having academic deficiencies in comparison to other children in the classroom, such deficiencies may be contributing to the problem behaviors, and further information needs to be obtained during the follow-up interview. If unsuccessful interventions have been attempted in the past, specific details need to be obtained in order to determine whether similar interventions should be avoided or just need to be modified. Any items checked by the teacher in the sections focusing on antecedent and consequent events should be explored during the follow-up interview. By focusing the follow-up interview on areas most likely to yield productive hypotheses about functional relationships, the FAIR-T can substantially reduce the time needed to conduct an informant assessment. If, for example, none of the task items in the section focusing on antecedent events is checked, the follow-up interview can exclude escape from tasks as an area needing further exploration. Alternatively, if the problem behavior were indicated as occurring more often following certain types of tasks, more information about those tasks would be sought during the follow-up interview. If transition periods are identified as being associated with problem behaviors, whether those transitions involve changing tasks, changing subject areas, changing locations within the classroom, transitioning to a different classroom, and so on will need to be determined. If the presence or absence of certain persons is associated with increased problem behaviors, information about their behavior when they are present needs to be explored. Information obtained from the section dealing with consequent events will normally need clarification before functional hypotheses can be generated. When the teacher indicates that problem behavior is often followed by access to preferred activity, the nature of that activity and how it differs from the activity preceding occurrence of the problem behavior needs to be determined. The specific nature of peer or teacher attention would need to be clarified if the teacher indicates that such attention frequently follows the problem behaviors. If the teacher reports that task termination frequently follows problem behavior or that presentation of certain tasks is avoided, the specific nature of those tasks needs to be determined. When the teacher indicates that he/she provides praise or other positive consequences when desirable behavior occurs, the follow-up interview may need to focus on whether there is evidence that these consequences function as positive reinforcers for the child in question, whether they may have been presented too infrequently or in a delayed manner, or whether some other factor may be interfering with their effectiveness.

THE FAIR-T AND OTHER FUNCTIONAL ASSESSMENT PROCEDURES

Once information has been obtained from the FAIR-T and clarified through the follow-up interview, hypotheses regarding functional relationships between environmental events and problem behavior can be generated. Further clarification of functional hypotheses and/or supportive evidence for such hypotheses can be obtained from direct classroom observations. The final step in a complete functional assessment would be experimental validation of hypotheses through systematic manipulation of the hypothesized functional variables and observation of the effect on the occurrence of problem behavior. Some recent research has suggested that hypotheses derived from the FAIR-T are consistent with information obtained through direct observation and are supported by experimental analysis (Doggett, Edwards, Moore, Tingstrom, & Wilczynski, 2001; Moore, Doggett, Edwards, & Olmi, 1999). A practical and cost-effective approach may be to use the FAIR-T alone to develop functional hypotheses; then develop and evaluate interventions based solely on these hypotheses (Doggett, 2000). Validity of the FAIR-T-based hypotheses would be supported if such interventions were successful. Additional, more extensive functional assessment procedures would only be indicated when such interventions were not successful.

See also: Functional Analysis; Functional Assessment of Academic Behavior (FAAB); Positive Reinforcement

BIBLIOGRAPHY

Doggett, R. A. (2000). *Functional assessment and treatment: Using data from informant assessments to develop functionally-based interventions to reduce problem behavior in general education classrooms.* Unpublished doctoral dissertation, University of Southern Mississippi, Hattiesburg.

Doggett, R. A., Edwards, R. P., Moore, J. W., Tingstrom, D. H., & Wilczynski, S. M. (2001). An approach to functional assessment in general education classroom settings. *School Psychology Review, 30,* 313–328.

Edwards, R. P. (2002). A tutorial for using the Functional Assessment Informant Record for Teachers. *Proven Practice: Prevention and Remediation Solutions for Schools, 4,* 31–33.

Moore, J. W., Doggett, R. A., Edwards, R. P., & Olmi, D. J. (1999). Using functional assessment and teacher-implemented functional analysis outcomes to guide intervention for two students with Attention-Deficit/Hyperactivity Disorder. *Proven Practice: Prevention and Remediation Solutions for Schools, 2,* 3–9.

Skinner, B. F. (1953). *Science and human behavior.* New York: Macmillan.

Additional Readings for Professionals

Doggett, R. A., Mueller, M. M., & Moore, J. W. (2002). Functional Assessment Informant Record for Teachers: Creation, evaluation, and future research. *Proven Practice: Prevention and Remediation Solutions for Schools, 4,* 25–30.

McComas, J. J., & Mace, F. C. (2000). Theory and practice in conducting functional analysis. In E. S. Shapiro & T. R. Kratochwill (Eds.), *Behavioral assessment in schools* (2nd ed., pp. 78–103). New York: Guilford.

RON P. EDWARDS
R. ANTHONY DOGGETT

Functional Assessment of Academic Behavior (FAAB)

Functional Assessment of Academic Behavior (FAAB) (Ysseldyke & Algozzine, 2002) is a data collection and analysis system for identifying aspects of a student's learning environment that can be altered to enhance student academic success. A learning environment represents all the variables and conditions external to the child that may promote or inhibit a student's optimal academic success. Drawing from Bronfenbrenner's systems-ecological framework (1979), which emphasizes the need to examine child development in the context of multiple systems or environments, FAAB provides a structure for collecting data about both the student's home and the school learning environment. It additionally aids in measuring the continuity between these environments—in other words, the degree to which the student's family and school have shared expectations for the student—and in communicating frequently about the student's progress. These data are then used to develop feasible interventions to support the student in mastering important school-related skills and concepts.

Instead of assessing inherent characteristics of the student that affect learning, FAAB emphasizes the need to identify variables within the environment that can be altered to facilitate student learning. It consequently represents a functional assessment of student learning and brings a problem-solving approach to the practice of school psychology. FAAB offers users a guide for examining the interaction of student and environment over time, in an attempt to empirically investigate characteristics that promote student achievement. Focus is placed on measuring the degree to which factors known to increase student academic success (e.g., academic engaged time, daily routine, home–school communication) are present in the student's entire learning environment.

FAAB is intended to guide prereferral and intervention assistance teams in developing proactive intervention strategies for students experiencing learning difficulties. Professionals select data collection tools from a variety of observation and interview forms available in the FAAB manual to obtain information from the teacher, student, and parents. These tools measure student–environment fit according to the 23 components described briefly in Table 1. These 23 characteristics were identified as necessary for optimal student learning based on a comprehensive literature review, and correspond to aspects of student learning in home and school environments, as well as the connection between these environments.

The FAAB manual describes a specific process for conducting an assessment. First, a teacher completes the instructional-needs form, which is a checklist and free-response form that allows teachers to identify instructional strategies they have found to be effective for the student, as well as potential modifications they could make that might foster student learning. At this time, parents also complete a checklist to indicate concerns with their child's school experiences and ways in which they can support their child's learning at home. Following administration of these checklists, the assessor observes the student in the classroom, paying special attention to the teacher's instructional planning, delivery, management, and evaluation strategies that affect student learning. This allows the assessor to carefully examine the degree to which components of effective instruction are present, and whether the instruction matches the needs of the child. After the observation, the student may also be interviewed to ascertain what the student learned and experienced during the observation, as well as to understand his/her overall classroom experiences. Similarly, teacher and parent interview forms are available to collect further information about both the home and school environments.

Following data collection, the assessor integrates and analyzes the data using the instructional environment checklist (both regular or annotated versions are available), which involves rating the degree to which each of the 23 components exists in the student's total learning environments. All ratings are qualitative judgments—judgments by a professional about the extent to which each of the factors is present. The assessor then meets with a team of professionals, including the teacher, parent, administrators, and other support personnel, to plan an instructional intervention for the student. A variety of specific interventions are offered in the manual, corresponding to each of the 23 FAAB components. The team chooses intervention strategies to implement in order to meet the student's instructional needs. This process allows for a direct link between assessment and specific intervention strategies. An intervention documentation record is available to evaluate the effects of interventions, and to help in determining whether modifications in the intervention plan are necessary.

See also: Functional Behavioral Assessment; Mathematics; Reading; Spelling: Academic Interventions; Writing (Written Language)

BIBLIOGRAPHY

Bronfenbrenner, U. (1979). *The ecology of human development.* Cambridge, MA: Harvard University Press.

Additional Readings for Nonprofessionals

Algozzine, B., Ysseldyke, J., & Elliott, J. (1997). *Strategies and tactics for effective instruction* (2nd ed.). Longmont, CO: Sopris West.
Christenson, S. L., & Sheridan, S. L. (2001). *Schools and families: Creating essential connections for learning.* New York: Guilford.
Ysseldyke, J., & Algozzine, B. (2002). *TIPS: Pamphlets for parents.* Longmont, CO: Sopris West.

Additional Reading for Professionals

Ysseldyke, J. E., & Christenson, S. L. (1987). Evaluating students' instructional environments. *Remedial and Special Education, 8*(3), 17–24.

JAMES E. YSSELDYKE
SARA E. BOLT

Functional Behavioral Assessment

The words *function* and *functional* have many uses in the English language. For example, *function* can be used as a noun meaning "to have a purpose" or as a verb meaning "to operate." In addition, the derivative *functional* has been used in several professional disciplines including education, occupational and physical therapy, and psychology. Persons in education often

Table 1. FAAB Support for Learning Components

Component	Definition
Instructional-environment components	
Instructional match	The student's needs are assessed accurately, and instruction is matched appropriately to the results of the instructional diagnosis.
Instructional expectations	There are realistic, yet high, expectations for both the amount and accuracy of work to be completed by the student, and these are communicated clearly to the student.
Classroom environment	The classroom management techniques used are effective for the student; there is a positive, supportive classroom atmosphere; and time is used productively.
Instructional presentation	Instruction is presented in a clear and effective manner; the directions contain sufficient information for the student to understand the kinds of behaviors or skills that are to be demonstrated; and the student's understanding is checked.
Cognitive emphasis	Thinking skills and learning strategies for completing assignments are communicated explicitly to the student.
Motivational strategies	Effective strategies for heightening student interest and effort are used with the student.
Relevant practice	The student is given adequate opportunity to practice with appropriate materials, and a high success rate. Classroom tasks are clearly important for achieving instructional goals.
Informed feedback	The student receives relatively immediate and specific information on his/her performance or behavior; when the student makes mistakes, correction is provided.
Academic engaged time	The student is actively engaged in responding to academic content; the teacher monitors the extent to which the student is actively engaged and redirects the student when the student is unengaged.
Adaptive instruction	The curriculum is modified within reason to accommodate the student's unique and specific instructional needs.
Progress evaluation	There is direct, frequent measurement of the student's progress toward completion of instructional objectives; data on the student's performance and progress are used to plan future instruction.
Student understanding	The student demonstrates an accurate understanding of what is to be done and how it is to be done in the classroom.
Home-support-for-learning components	
Home expectations and attributions	High, realistic expectations about schoolwork are communicated to the child, and the value of effort and working hard in school is emphasized.
Discipline orientation	There is an authoritative, not permissive nor authoritarian, approach to discipline, and the child is monitored and supervised by the parents.
Home-affective environment	The parent–child relationship is characterized by a healthy connectedness; it is generally positive and supportive.
Parent participation	There is an educative home environment, and others participate in the child's schooling and learning, at home and/or at school.
Structure for learning	Organization and daily routines facilitate the completion of schoolwork and support for the child's academic learning.
Home–school-support-for-learning components	
Shared standards and expectations	The level of expected performance held by key adults for the student is congruent across home and school, and reflects a belief that the student can learn.
Consistent structure	The overall routine and monitoring provided by key adults for the student have been discussed and are congruent across home and school.
Cross-setting opportunity to learn	The variety of learning options available to the youth during school hours and outside of school time (i.e., home and community) supports the student's learning.
Mutual support	The guidance provided by, the communication between, and the interest shown by adults to facilitate student progress in school is effective. It is what adults do on an ongoing basis to help the student learn and achieve.
Positive, trusting relationship	The amount of warmth and friendliness, praise and recognition, and the degree to which the adult–youth relationship is positive and respectful. It includes how adults in the home, in the school, and in the community work together to help the student be a learner.
Modeling	Parents and teachers demonstrate desired behaviors, and commitment and value toward learning and working hard in their daily lives, to the student.

use the word *functional* to refer to academic procedures. Many teachers provide instruction to their students in "functional academics" or educational material that allows them to interact more easily in society. Functional academics include learning how to count money, balance a checkbook, measure and weigh varying amounts of distances and volumes, and read common street and highway signs. Occupational and physical therapists often measure the "functional range of motion" performed by their patients. During this procedure, they evaluate how high a person can lift his/her arm, how far out he/she can stretch his/her leg, or how far to the left or right a person can turn his/her head. Finally, psychology has used *function* and its derivatives throughout history with different meanings (Ervin, Ehrhardt, & Poling, 2001). For example, *functionalism* examined how different parts of the mind *functioned* or *worked* to produce conscious thoughts to assist people in making decisions about their environment. Psychodynamic psychologists used *function* to indicate the "underlying meaning" behind a particular behavior. A psychologist practicing from this point of view proposes that a person may cry because he/she is angry or depressed. Finally, behavioral psychologists have used the words *function* and *functional* to refer to the purpose of the performance of a particular action. Another way of looking at it would be to try to identify the motivation for engaging in a specific behavior. It is this last definition that was intended for use in the procedure "functional behavior assessment."

DEFINITION OF FBA AND FUNCTIONS OF BEHAVIOR

Functional behavior assessment (FBA) refers to the use of a variety of methods to determine the reason for a behavior in a particular situation. In addition to evaluating the behavior of concern, FBA uses a collection of procedures to identify the events that precede the behavior and the events that follow the behavior. Relatedly, FBA has also been defined legally through due process hearings and civil court cases (Drasgow & Yell, 2001). In 1998, a hearing officer in Texas defined FBA in the following manner:

> The general purpose of functional behavioral assessment is to provide the IEP team with additional information, analysis, and strategies for addressing undesirable behavior, especially when it is interfering with a child's education. The process involves some variant of identifying the core or "target" behavior; observing the pupil (perhaps in different environments) and collecting data on the target behavior, antecedents and consequences; formulating a hypothesis about the cause(s) of the behavior; developing an intervention(s) in changing the behavior. (Independent School District No. 2310, p. 333)

In addition, FBA has been defined as "a process that searches for an explanation of the purpose behind a problem behavior" (OSEP Questions and Answers, 1999). In short, FBA refers to the process used to answer the question "Why does this person perform this behavior in this situation?"

Events that precede behavior are labeled as *antecedents* and include such events as establishing operations, setting events, and discriminative stimuli. Establishing operations alter a person's motivation to perform a given behavior. For example, people often eat faster and find food more tasty when they are hungry as opposed to when they have a full stomach. Setting events are removed in time and place from the performance of a given

behavior but still affect the performance of the behavior. For example, a child may be less likely to complete a math assignment in class after witnessing an argument between her parents before coming to school in the morning. Discriminative stimuli occur immediately before the performance of behavior. For example, a child may say "No!" to a teacher after being given an instruction to sit down in his seat. The instruction from the teacher is the discriminative stimulus in this example.

The events that follow the performance of behavior are called *consequences*. Although many people in society use the words *punishment, discipline,* and *consequences* synonymously, consequences also refer to those events that motivate a person to perform certain behaviors. In fact, an FBA is designed to identify the consequent events that motivate a person to engage in behavior, most typically problematic behavior. Once identified, these consequent events can be used to encourage the person to engage in more appropriate behaviors called *replacement behaviors*. In a seminal article on self-injury, Carr (1977) proposed three reasons for self-injurious behavior (SIB) that greatly influenced future applications of FBA with other problematic behaviors. Carr suggested that individuals engage in certain behaviors (e.g., SIB) in order to obtain positive reinforcement, negative reinforcement, or self-stimulation, which is a unique form of positive reinforcement. Positive reinforcement refers to those consequent events a person "obtains," such as social attention (e.g., smiles, hugs, praise), material items (e.g., toys, books, money), or edible items (e.g., candy, favorite foods). One example of self-stimulation is the endorphin release, obtained by long-distance runners, often called a runner's high. Negative reinforcement refers to those consequent events a person *avoids* or *escapes* such as social attention (e.g., being bullied on the playground) and instructional or academic demands (e.g., being asked to complete a difficult math worksheet, homework, or to clean up a room). Sometimes a person's behavior serves both functions. For example, a child who disrupts class may be sent out of the room (allowing them to avoid nonpreferred work) and to the counselor's office (allowing them to obtain preferred adult attention) to discuss their inappropriate behavior. In addition, a particular behavior may serve different functions in different contexts. For example, arguing may get a child sent to the hall (allowing them to escape work) at school. However, later that day, arguing may assist the child in obtaining a preferred material activity (e.g., driving the car) after a long debate with his/her parents at home. Finally, the function or purpose of behavior can change over time.

LEGAL ISSUES AND FBA

As mentioned previously, FBAs are often performed to identify the events that motivate or encourage a person to perform problematic behavior. FBA gained popularity beyond being considered a "best practice" in 1997 when the amendments to the Individuals with Disabilities Education Act (IDEA) mandated the use of FBAs to develop positive behavioral supports and interventions for children with identified disabilities who display problematic behavior in the school setting. Gresham, Watson, and Skinner (2001) paraphrased this action by indicating that federal law specifically states

> The team must address through a behavioral intervention plan any need for positive behavioral strategies and supports (614(d)3(B)9i). In response to disciplinary actions by school personnel, the IEP team must, within 10 days, meet to develop a functional behavioral assessment plan to collect information. This information should be used for developing or reviewing and revising an existing behavior intervention plan to address such behaviors (615(k)(1)(B)). In addition, states are required to address the in-service needs of personnel (including professionals and paraprofessionals who provide special education, general education, related services, or early intervention services) as they relate to developing and implementing positive intervention strategies (653(c)(3)(D)(vi)).

In school settings, FBAs are usually conducted in response to problematic behavior that results in some disciplinary action. Previous problematic behaviors have included (a) disruptive behaviors that disrupt the student's learning or the learning of his/her peers, (b) noncompliant or rule-breaking behavior, (c) verbal or physical abuse, (d) destruction of property, and (e) aggression toward others (Drasgow & Yell, 2001). Unfortunately, most school disciplinary practices are reactive and, in many cases, reward the student for engaging in inappropriate behavior. Typical responses by school personnel are presented in a hierarchy called the "discipline ladder" and usually include calling the student to the office to "talk to them" about the problem behavior; calling the parents; sending the student out of the classroom to the hallway; placing them in detention, in-school suspension, or out-of-school suspension; and expulsion from school. Such punitive practices do not teach alternative behaviors and serve to motivate the student to perform the problematic behaviors again in the future. However, IDEA ended the utilization of such practices by mandating the development of a positive behavior support plan that proactively addresses the problematic behavior by requiring school personnel to teach the student new replacement behaviors and to alter the environmental events (e.g., antecedents and consequences) that set off or motivate the student to engage in problematic behavior.

Federal regulations require that an FBA plan be developed within 10 days following the utilization of specific disciplinary actions with students receiving special education services. These instances include (a) suspensions or placements in an alternative setting that exceed 10 cumulative school days or amount to a change in placement, (b) placement in an interim alternative educational setting for 45 calendar days for weapons or drug offenses, or (c) placement in an interim alternative educational setting by a process hearing officer for behavior that is dangerous to self or others (Drasgow & Yell, 2001). Although federal law mandates action after utilization of these three disciplinary procedures, school personnel do not have to wait until the performance of problematic behavior reaches these levels of offense. In fact, Drasgow and Yell encourage school personnel to take action as soon as a pattern of problem behavior is established because doing so would demonstrate evidence that school personnel had the student's best interest at hand and did not want to deny the opportunity for a free appropriate public education (FAPE).

PHASES OF FBA

Although FBA has gained popularity since the reauthorization of IDEA in 1997, there is a lack of consensus concerning exactly what procedures should be used to conduct a comprehensive functional behavioral assessment (Cone, 1997; Ervin, Ehrdardt, & Poling, 2001). In fact, federal law has refused to detail the exact components, allowing local school systems considerable freedom and latitude in establishing their own procedures. Despite this ambiguity, there is some guidance from the professional literature. For example, Gresham, Watson, and Skinner (2001) strongly cautioned that "FBA is not a single test or observation, but rather a multimethod strategy involving observations, interviews, and review of records regarding student behavior, its antecedents, and its consequences. The central goal of an FBA is to identify environmental conditions that are associated with the occurrence and nonoccurrence of problem behaviors" (p. 158). Using this guidance, authors have published manuscripts outlining specific phases that should be conducted within an FBA (e.g., Cone, 1997; Doggett, Edwards, Moore, Tingstrom, & Wilczynski, 2001; Ervin, Radford, Bertsch, Piper, Ehrhardt, & Poling, 2001; Moore, Doggett, Edwards, & Olmi, 1999; Sterling-Turner, Robinson, & Wilczynski, 2001; Watson & Steege, 2003). In a very comprehensive article on FBA procedures, Sterling-Turner et al. (2001) outlined four specific phases for inclusion in the FBA process. Phase I includes the "descriptive phase" and involves collecting data on the problem behavior and environmental events from both indirect and direct sources. Indirect sources of information typically include student record reviews, interviews with important persons, and behavior rating scales. Record reviews should include a review of attendance, classwork and homework grades, performance on schoolwide assessments (e.g., Iowa Tests of Basic Skills), performance on comprehensive assessments (e.g., intelligence tests, achievement tests, adaptive behavior measures, behavior rating scales), goals and objectives on the individualized education plan (IEP), and discipline records.

Several interviews and rating scales have been developed for use with teachers and parents. Examples of structured and semistructured interviews include the *Functional Assessment Interview* (FAI) (O'Neill et al., 1997) and the *Functional Assessment Informant Record for Teachers* (FAIR-T) (Edwards, 2002). A good student interview is the *Student Assisted Functional Assessment Interview* (SAFAI) (Kern, Dunlap, Clarke, & Childs, 1994). Finally, behavioral rating scales include the *Motivation Assessment Scale* (MAS) (Durand & Crimmins, 1988), the *Problem Behavior Questionnaire* (PBQ) (Lewis, Scott, & Sugai, 1994), and the *Functional Analysis Screening Tool* (FAST) (Goh, Iwata, & DeLeon, 1996). These indirect sources of information should assist in (a) developing a concrete and precise definition of the problem behavior, (b) identifying the periods of the day behavior occurs and does not occur, (c) identifying the antecedent events that are associated with the occurrence of problem behavior, (d) identifying the consequent events that motivate the student to perform problem behavior, and (e) identifying successful and unsuccessful intervention attempts that have been used to address the problem behavior in the past (Sterling-Turner, Robinson, & Wilczynski, 2001).

Natural observations of the student's performance of problem behavior in the classroom environment or in other important settings (e.g., hallway, lunchroom, bathroom, playground) address the direct methods included in the descriptive phase. One of the most common types of direct observation procedures included in an FBA is the *A-B-C assessment* (Bijou, Peterson, & Ault, 1968), which records the occurrence of antecedent events, behaviors, and consequent events. Recording of the problem behavior and environmental events as they naturally occur in a specific setting helps the observer develop a better understanding of why the student may engage in such behaviors.

Phase II is called the "interpretive phase" and involves forming hypotheses or "educated guesses" about the reasons behind the performance of problem behavior. For example, after reviewing data from indirect and direct methods, school personnel may develop a summary statement that reads, "When Chris is given a math worksheet involving multiplication problems, he will crumble the paper up and throw it on the floor in order to avoid having to finish the worksheet." Another example is, "When Carla is seated in a reading group with her peers, she will make silly faces in order to obtain social attention from her peers." Such written comments are called summary statements and provide an interpretation of the data that has been gathered to test during the third phase of FBA.

Phase III is called the "verification phase" and involves "testing out" the educated guesses formed during the interpretive phase. Usually, changes are made in the natural environment that are designed to increase the probability that problem behavior and desired behavior will occur. In the example with Chris, the teacher could conduct a condition in which she presents him a multiplication worksheet to see if he throws it on the floor as predicted. A few moments later, she could hand him a preferred assignment (e.g., coloring worksheet) to see whether he chooses to complete it on the basis of enjoyment of the task. If she notices this expected pattern after handing out other multiplication and coloring worksheets, then she has "verified" the hypothesis statement. In the example with Carla, the teacher could have her sit with peers for some assignments and sit alone for other assignments. If Carla makes silly faces only when seated with peers, then the teacher has "verified" the hypothesis statement. A review of the different types of conditions was reported by Sterling-Turner, Robinson, and Wilczynski (2001).

Verification of the summary statements during phase III allows school personnel and parents to develop proactive interventions referred to as positive behavior support (PBS) plans. PBS plans should be designed to change the environmental events that set off (antecedents) and maintain (consequences) the problem behavior and teach the student replacement behaviors that serve the same function as the problematic behaviors. As such, PBS plans are typically composed of a "package" of intervention components as opposed to one single change in the student's educational programming. For example, a student who avoids academic work like Chris does may need to have the academic material placed on his instructional level and be instructed in the use of replacement behaviors for seeking assistance with academic material. In addition, consequent events would need to be designed such that Chris is reinforced for completing his work without displaying problematic behaviors. For Carla, an appropriate intervention may involve seating her with peers who are not likely to attend to problematic behavior, teaching her how to cooperate in group activities, and reinforcing the display of appropriate behavior following the group activity perhaps with free time with preferred peers.

As such, this fourth and final phase is called "treatment implementation and monitoring." Legally, PBS plans should clearly define the problem behaviors and the desired replacement behaviors. Methods for data collection (e.g., observations, self-monitoring forms, etc.) of both behaviors should be identified on the plan and used regularly to review progress. The specific steps of the treatment should also be clearly listed in the PBS plan. All school personnel interacting with the child should be educated on the plan and should be able to perform it with accuracy. All components of the plan must be agreed upon by the parents and should be included on the IEP. Finally, the plan should be reviewed regularly for accuracy of implementation and/or modification. Accuracy of implementation is called *treatment integrity*. Treatment integrity means that the plan is being carried out exactly as agreed upon in the IEP meeting. If review reveals that the plan is not being carried out accurately and consistently, then retraining may need to be undertaken. As mentioned previously, behaviors may change in their function or purpose over time. As such, plans may need to be modified, and additional FBA data may need to be collected in order to properly address the problem behavior. Therefore, FBA is a process that occurs across time. In other words, these steps in an FBA may need to be conducted several times throughout a student's schooling career.

CONCLUSION

In conclusion, Drasgow and Yell (2001) developed a checklist for conducting legally correct and educationally appropriate FBAs that parents and school personnel may find helpful. The authors suggested that (a) an IEP team be convened early after a pattern of problem behavior has been established, (b) school officials ensure that the persons conducting the FBA are qualified, (c) the parents be notified early enough to provide meaningful input into the assessment, (d) the FBA include several indirect measures, direct observations in a variety of settings, experimental manipulations of the environmental events contributing to the performance of problem behavior (if necessary), and summary statements, (e) the FBA be conducted in a timely manner, and (f) the IEP team develop a comprehensive PBS plan based on the information gathered during the FBA process. Engaging in such proactive procedures would positively address the problem behavior of students with disabilities. Failure to conduct legally competent and educationally appropriate FBAs will surely lead to a denial of FAPE for the student and legal sanctions against the school district (Drasgow & Yell, 2001).

See also: Antecedent Analysis; Brief Functional Analysis; Functional Analysis; Functional Assessment Informant Record—Teacher (FAIR-T); Functional Assessment of Academic Behavior (FAAB); Positive Behavioral Supports

BIBLIOGRAPHY

Bijou, S. W., Peterson, R. F., & Ault, M. H. (1968). A method to integrate descriptive and experimental field studies at the level of data and empirical concepts. *Journal of Applied Behavior Analysis, 1*, 175–191.

Carr, E. G. (1977). The motivation of self-injurious behavior: A review of some hypotheses. *Psychological Bulletin, 84*, 800–816.

Cone, J. D. (1997). Issues in functional analysis in behavioral assessment. *Behavior Research Therapy, 35*, 259–277.

Doggett, R. A., Edwards, R. P., Moore, J. W., Tingstrom, D. H., & Wilczynski, S. M. (2001). An approach to functional assessment in the general education classroom. *School Psychology Review, 30*, 239–251.

Drasgow, E., & Yell, M. L. (2001). Functional behavioral assessments: Legal requirements and challenges. *School Psychology Review, 30*, 239–251.

Durand, V. M., & Crimmins, D. B. (1988). Identifying the variables maintaining self-injurious behavior. *Journal of Autism and Developmental Disorders, 18*, 99–117.

Edwards, R. P. (2002). Functional Assessment Informant Record for Teachers. *Proven Practice: Prevention and Remediation Solutions for Schools, 4*, 31–38.

Ervin, R. A., Ehrhardt, K. E., & Poling, A. (2001). Functional assessment: Old wine in new bottles. *School Psychology Review, 30*, 173–179.

Ervin, R. A., Radford, P. M., Bertsch, K., Piper, A. L., Ehrhardt, K. E., & Poling, A. (2001). A descriptive analysis of the empirical literature on school-based functional assessments. *School Psychology Review, 30*, 193–210.

Goh, H. L., Iwata, B. A., & DeLeon, I. G. (1996, May). *The functional analysis screening tool.* Poster presented at the meeting of the Association for Behavior Analysis, San Diego, CA.

Gresham, F. M., Watson, T. S., & Skinner, C. H. (2001). Functional behavioral assessment: Principles, procedures, and future directions. *School Psychology Review, 30*, 156–172.

Independent School District #2310, 29 IDELR 330 (SEA MN 1999).

Individuals With Disabilities Education Act Amendments of 1997, Pub. L. No. 105–17, 20 U.S.C. Chapter 33, §1400 *et seq.*

Kern, L., Dunlap, G., Clarke, S., & Childs, K. E. (1994). Student-assisted functional assessment interview. *Diagnostique, 19*, 29–39.

Lewis, T. J., Scott, T. M., & Sugai, G. (1994). The problem behavior questionnaire: A teacher-based instrument to develop functional hypotheses of problem behavior in general education classrooms. *Diagnostique, 19*, 103–115.

Moore, J. W., Doggett, R. A., Edwards, R. P., & Olmi, D. J. (1999). Using functional assessment and teacher-implemented functional analysis outcomes to guide intervention for two students with Attention-Deficit/Hyperactivity Disorder. *Proven Practice: Prevention and Remediation Solutions for Schools, 2*, 3–9.

O'Neill, R. E., Horner, R. H., Albin, R. W., Sprague, J. R., Storey, K., & Newton, J. S. (1997). *Functional assessment and program development for problem behavior: A practical handbook* (2nd ed.). Pacific Grove, CA: Brooks/Cole.

OSEP Questions and Answers. (1999, March 12). *Federal Register, 64*(48), 12617–12632.

Sterling-Turner, H. E., Robinson, S. L., & Wilczynski, S. M. (2001). Functional assessment of distracting and disruptive behavior in the school setting. *School Psychology Review, 30*, 211–226.

Watson, T. S., & Steege, M. W. (2003). *Conducting school-based functional behavioral assessments: A practitioner's guide.* New York: Guilford.

Additional Readings for Nonprofessionals

www.nasp.org
www.pbis.org

Additional Readings for Professionals

Alberto, P. A., & Troutman, A. C. (2003). *Applied behavior analysis for teachers* (6th ed.). Englewood Cliffs, NJ: Prentice–Hall.

Watson, T. S., & Steege, M. W. (2003). *Conducting school-based functional behavioral assessments: A practitioner's guide.* New York: Guilford.

R. ANTHONY DOGGETT
LAURA M. BAYLOT

Functional Communication Training

Functional Communication Training (FCT) is a procedure designed to increase communication skills *and* to reduce problem behavior (e.g., aggression, self-injury, tantrums, etc.) by teaching individuals appropriate ways to communicate what they need or desire. FCT is based on the premise that all behavior, regardless of its form (e.g., verbal statements, nonverbal behavior, or problem behavior such as aggression), is communicative. Essentially, with FCT, the goal is to teach appropriate communication behavior as a replacement for problem behavior. Numerous studies have documented that teaching functionally equivalent communication skills often results in significant decrease or elimination of problem behaviors (e.g., Durand, 1999; Steege et al., 1990; Wacker et al., 1990).

There are several essential components in the successful use of FCT in the treatment of problem behavior. First, the reason(s) why the behavior is occurring—in other words, the preferred outcome of behavior—must be determined. Although there are a number of "messages" that a behavior may communicate, the preferred outcome will always result in one of three broad categories: (a) gaining something positive (attention, a pleasurable activity, a food item, etc.), (b) avoiding or escaping something unpleasant (e.g., specific tasks, avoiding social interactions, etc.), or (c) sensory consequences (e.g., self-stimulation or arousal reduction). A functional behavior assessment is conducted to determine why problem behavior is occurring.

Second, it is important that the communication response to be taught to replace the problem behavior results in the same desired outcome, or expresses the same communicative message, as was identified for the problem behavior during the functional behavior assessment. In other words, the message of the communication response and that of the problem behavior must correspond. When the appropriate communication response results in the same functional outcomes as the problem behavior (i.e., they are functionally equivalent responses), the individual no longer "needs" to exhibit problem behaviors to get his/her needs met. Over time, this results in the consistent use of the appropriate communicative behavior and a decrease in problem behavior.

Third, the newly acquired communication response needs to be as efficient as, or more than, the problem behavior. For example, if the FCT response requires more effort or is too elaborate, then the individual may simply prefer to display problem behavior as a way of getting his/her needs met. Examples of FCT have included teaching a student whose problem behavior was motivated by social attention from his teachers to ask "Am I doing good work?" as an alternative to disruptive behavior, teaching a child with autism to say "I'm having fun" as a replacement for sensory-maintained screaming behavior, and teaching a student whose problem behavior was motivated by avoidance of academic tasks to request a brief break or to ask for assistance.

Although FCT procedures often involve the teaching of verbal responses, other communication strategies have been found to be very effective with individuals with expressive language impairments. For example, several studies have demonstrated the utility of teaching individuals to communicate functionally equivalent responses through the use of gestures, sign language, pictures, symbols, or mechanical devices (e.g., voice output devices). The selection of the type of communication system is done on the basis of the individual's expressive communication skills. Finally, the effectiveness of FCT is increased when the communication response is incorporated into the individual's overall support program. Although in many cases direct instruction (e.g., discrete trial teaching) may be used initially to teach a communicative response, incidental teaching procedures within naturally occurring environment results in increased generalization and maintenance of communication behavior. Successful FCT is characterized by regular use of functional communication methods instead of other "problem" behaviors during everyday activities.

See also: Discrete Trial Teaching; Functional Analysis; Functional Behavioral Assessment

BIBLIOGRAPHY

Durand, M. (1999). Functional communication training using assistive devices: Recruiting natural communities of reinforcement. *Journal of Applied Behavior Analysis, 32,* 247–267.

Steege, M., Wacker, D., Cigrand, K., Berg, W., Novak, C., Reimers, T., et al. (1990). Use of negative reinforcement in the treatment of self-injurious behavior in children with severe multiple disabilities. *Journal of Applied Behavior Analysis, 23,* 459–467.

Wacker, D., Steege, M., Northrup, J., Sasso, G., Berg, W., Reimers,. T., et al. (1990). A component analysis of functional communication training across three topographies of severe behavior problems. *Journal of Applied Behavior Analysis, 23,* 417–429.

Additional Readings for Nonprofessionals

Durand, M. (1990). *Severe behavior problems: A functional communication training approach.* New York: Guilford.

Reichle, J., & Wacker, D. (Eds.). (1993). *Communication alternative to challenging behavior: Integrating functional assessment and intervention strategies.* Baltimore: Brookes.

Additional Readings for Professionals

Carr, E. G., & Durand, V. M. (1985). Reducing behavior problems though functional communication training. *Journal of Applied Behavior Analysis, 26,* 157–172.

Durand, V. M., & Carr, E. G. (1991). Functional communication training to reduce challenging behavior: Maintenance and application in new settings. *Journal of Applied Behavior Analysis, 24,* 251–264.

Mark W. Steege
Rachel Brown-Chidsey

Gg

Gardner's Theory of Multiple Intelligences

Howard Gardner was the son of German refugees. Born in Scranton, PA, in 1943, he conducted all of his postgraduate work at Harvard University. The theory of multiple intelligences was the result of his involvement in research on cognitive and symbol-using capacities. While involved in this research, he conducted projects involving normal functioning children, gifted children, and adults with brain damage. The theory of multiple intelligences was conceived by Gardner as he tried to synthesize these different lines of work (*Short Biography of Howard Gardner*, 2003).

Gardner did not believe that intelligence could be measured with traditional assessments. He felt that these assessments did not encompass the breadth of human capabilities. Gardner's theory posits that human beings are not in possession of a singular intelligence, but have the potential to, and in most cases do, possess many different forms of intelligence.

Howard Gardner's interest in the development of creativity and artistic abilities led him to explore the multifarious nature of intelligence (Gardner, 1983). Originally, he believed that there were seven intelligences: linguistic, logical/mathematical, bodily kinesthetic, spatial, musical, interpersonal, and intrapersonal. He later added naturalistic intelligence and two tentative intelligences, spiritual and existential (Sattler, 2003). With these additions, the possible total number of intelligences is ten. Gardner did not deny the existence of other intelligences and constantly searched for other viable intelligences to support his theory (Gardner, 1983). Gardner aspired to discover intelligences that met certain psychological and biological spec-

ifications and to compile a comprehensive list of abilities valued by human cultures (Gardner, 1983).

The process an "intelligence candidate" must pass through has two levels (Gardner, 1983). Gardner referred to the initial stage as the "prerequisite of intelligence." To qualify as an intelligence, the candidate must possess a set of problem-solving skills and have the potential for identifying or creating problems. Gardner felt that the ability to identify and create problems is important because this "... lays the groundwork for acquisition of new knowledge." Gardner incorporated the "prerequisite of intelligence" into his theory to ensure that his intelligences would be genuinely important and useful in some specific cultural setting. After an intelligence candidate passed the "prerequisite of intelligence" test, the candidate moves on and must meet the "criteria of intelligence." There are eight criteria that Gardner calls the "eight signs of an intelligence." Gardner points out that simply because an intelligence meets all eight signs or fails to meet all eight signs does not mean that the candidate intelligence will necessarily be rejected or accepted as a viable intelligence. Gardner said of the process, "... the selection (or rejection) of a candidate intelligence is reminiscent more of artistic judgment than of scientific assessment."

The eight signs of an intelligence in Gardner's criteria of intelligence are potential isolation by brain damage; the existence of idiot savants, prodigies, and other exceptional individuals; an identifiable core operation or set of operations; a distinctive developmental history, along with a set of expert "end-state performances"; an evolutionary history and plausibility; support from experimental psychological tasks; support for psychometric findings; and susceptibility to encoding into a symbol system. Potential isolation by brain damage simply means the intelligence is located in a specific part of the brain or, in other words, the intelligence still functions in spite of damage to other parts of the brain. The existence of idiot savants, prodigies, and other exceptional individuals illustrates that intelligence can exist in isolation, as in the case of the idiot savant, or can be strikingly absent as in individuals with autism. This category's function, according to Gardner, is "conformation by negation of certain intelligences." An identifiable core operation or set of operations is "the existence of one or more basic information-processing operations or mechanisms, which can deal with specific kinds of input." For example, an individual's ability to imitate dance movements may be a core operation of bodily kinesthetic intelligence. A distinctive developmental history, along with a definable set of expert "end state" performances, means that to be classified as an intelligence under this category, the evolutionary history and purpose of the candidate intelligence must be traceable and include a mastery level. This includes tracing the evolutionary antecedents of the intelligence, including competencies that are shared with other species; for example, apes exhibit social behaviors similar to those of humans.

Gardner also indicated that it is important to identify periods of rapid growth in human prehistory that may have caused different populations to develop more advanced forms of or deficits in some intelligences. Gardner specified that evidence gained from standardized assessments and empirical research must be considered when contemplating the addition of an intelligence. The intelligence candidate's susceptibility to encoding into a symbol system is the final "sign" or criterion of an intelligence. Two examples of symbol systems are language and mathematics. Through this process, Gardner identified eight intelligences and two possible intelligences. The following paragraphs outline the basic characteristics of Gardner's intelligences.

Linguistic intelligence encompasses activities that relate to words and language (O'Brien & Burnett, 2000). Individuals with linguistic intelligence enjoy activities such as reading and writing, telling stories, and doing crossword puzzles. They demonstrate strength in language arts, speaking, writing, reading, and listening. They are very successful in the traditional classroom.

Logical/mathematical is the second intelligence and involves inductive and deductive reasoning skills. This intelligence includes the ability to work with geometric shapes, recognize patterns, and make connections between pieces of information (O'Brien & Burnett, 2000). Individuals with this intelligence are very successful in the traditional classroom. They enjoy activities such as strategy games and experiments. They are drawn to arithmetic problems and are interested in patterns, categories, and relationships.

Bodily kinesthetic intelligence is related to the knowledge of bodily function and movement. This intelligence includes the ability to express emotion and language through movement. Bodily kinesthetic individuals process knowledge through bodily sensations. Often, individuals with this intelligence are athletic, and good at dancing or crafts. They learn best through

activity: games, movement, hands-on tasks, and building. They are often labeled overactive or diagnosed with ADHD (Sattler, 2003).

Spatial intelligence includes the ability to visualize objects and to develop mental images. Individuals with spatial intelligence think in images and pictures. They are fascinated with mazes, jigsaw puzzles, and drawing. They often daydream. They enjoy charts, graphs, maps, tables, illustrations, art, puzzles, and costumes (Sattler, 2003).

Individuals with *musical intelligence* learn well through songs, patterns, rhythms, instruments, and musical expression. Sensitivity to environmental sounds, human voice, and instruments are hallmarks of this intelligence. Individuals with musical intelligence have the ability to recognize rhythms, beat, and tonal patterns (O'Brien & Burnett, 2000).

People with *interpersonal intelligence* are often leaders and good communicators. They understand the feelings of others and are able to have empathy for the beliefs and feelings of others. They are noticeably people-oriented and outgoing. They learn best when they are allowed to work in groups or with a partner.

Intrapersonal individuals are often labeled shy. They are aware of their own feelings. They are self-motivated and are intuitive about what they learn and how it relates to them. *Intrapersonal intelligence* abilities include knowledge of self, which includes metacognition (thinking about thinking), knowledge of emotional responses, self-reflection, and awareness of metaphysical concepts.

Naturalist intelligence consists of individuals who love the outdoors, animals, and field trips. They like and can easily detect subtle differences in meaning and patterns in nature. Gardner noted that a person with naturalist intelligence "... is able to recognize flora and fauna, to make other consequential distinctions in the natural world, and use this ability productively." Some examples of productively using this ability are hunting, farming, and careers in the field of biological science (Multiple Intelligences, 2003).

The two potential intelligences are *existentialist intelligence* and *spiritual intelligence*. Individuals with existentialist intelligence learn in the context of the "big picture" (Sattler, 2003). Individuals with existentialist intelligence ask questions like "why are we here?" and "what is our role in the world?" Individuals with this intelligence are often seen in the field of philosophy. Individuals with spiritual intelligence are concerned with the cosmic. They also recognize the spiritual state as the ultimate state of being.

For the past 15 years, Gardner has been working with colleagues to design performance-based assessments to evaluate the existence of multiple intelligences. His goal is to use the results of these assessments to create a more personalized curriculum, instruction, and assessment for children so that they can reach their full potential. Gardner feels that our educational system is not prepared to meet the needs of all the intelligences, and that, because of this deficit, gifted and talented children are often diagnosed as ADHD.

See also: *Gf–Gc* Theory of Intelligence; Intelligence Quotient (IQ)

BIBLIOGRAPHY

Gardner, H. (1983). *Frames of mind: The theory of multiple intelligences*. New York: Basic Books. [Paperback, 1985]

Multiple intelligences. (2003). Retrieved January 12, 2003, from http://www.multiintell.com/

O'Brien, P., & Burnett, P. C. (2000). Counseling children using a multiple intelligences framework. *British Journal of Guidance and Counseling, 28*, 353–371.

Sattler, J. M. (2003). *Assessment of children: Cognitive applications* (4th ed.). San Diego: Author.

Short biography of Howard Gardner. (2003). Retrieved January 16, 2003, http://pzweb.harvard.edu/PIs/HG.htm

Additional Reading for Nonprofessionals

Surf Aquarium (2003). Retrieved January, 12, 2003, from http://surfaquarium.com/intelligences.htm

Additional Reading for Professionals

Gardner, H. (1993). *Multiple intelligences: The theory in practice*. New York: Basic Books.

PENNY WARD

Gf–Gc Theory of Intelligence

A BRIEF HISTORICAL PERSPECTIVE

Unlike Spearman who conceptualized intelligence as a single entity, or *g*, Cattell (1941) envisioned it as being composed of two distinct factors—fluid and crystallized. Fluid Intelligence (*Gf*) encompassed inductive and deductive reasoning abilities influenced by both biological and neurological factors and incidental learning through interaction with the environment (Taylor, 1994). Crystallized Intelligence (*Gc*) consisted largely of acquired knowledge and abilities reflecting the influences of acculturation (viz., verbal–conceptual knowledge; Gustafsson, 1992; Taylor, 1994). These two factors formed the basis for a true dichotomous theory of intelligence in contrast to the popular verbal–performance conceptualization used by David Wechsler (1939) that only reflected different ways of measuring general intelligence. Despite research that expanded

Gf–Gc theory from 2 to 10 factors, the "*Gf–Gc*" designation persists and has caused misunderstandings of its multiple, not two-factor, structure (Horn & Noll, 1997; Woodcock, 1993).

EVOLUTION OF *Gf–Gc* THEORY

In the mid-1960s, Horn (1965) expanded Cattell's original *Gf–Gc* model by identifying four additional abilities including visual perception or processing (*Gv*), short-term memory (Short-Term Acquisition and Retrieval [SAR] or *Gsm*), long-term storage and retrieval (Tertiary Storage and Retrieval [TSR] or *Glr*), and speed of processing (*Gs*). By 1968, additional analyses led Horn to add auditory processing ability (*Ga*) to the theoretical model and refine the definitions of *Gv*, *Gs*, and *Glr*. More recently, three factors were added, including one that represents a person's quickness in reacting (reaction time) and making decisions (decision speed; called *Gt* by Horn, 1991, and Correct Decision Speed [CDS] by Carroll, 1993), one that represents a person's quantitative ability or knowledge (*Gq*), and a third that reflects facility with reading and writing (*Grw*) (Horn, 1985, 1988, 1991; Woodcock, 1994). Thus, the current *Gf–Gc* conceptualization, sometimes known as modern *Gf–Gc* theory, is composed of 10 *broad* abilities that themselves were composed of several related but distinct *narrow* abilities. Noteworthy is the fact that these last two abilities (i.e., *Gq* and *Grw*) are often conceived of by practitioners—who routinely conduct psychoeducational assessments—as academic achievements rather than cognitive abilities.

THE CATTELL–HORN–CARROLL (CHC) THEORY OF COGNITIVE ABILITIES

In 1993, John Carroll's meta-analysis of the intelligence literature led him to conclude that modern *Gf–Gc* theory was by far the best conceptualization of the structure of cognitive abilities within the psychometric tradition. On the basis of his research, Carroll formulated his own theory, called the *three-stratum theory* of cognitive abilities. Except for a few notable differences in classification and terminology, Carroll's model of the structure of intelligence closely mirrored the Cattell–Horn model. Carroll's model included a higher order *g* factor that subsumed eight broad cognitive abilities that, in turn, subsumed approximately 70 narrow abilities (Carroll, 1993). The Cattell–Horn model did not include a higher order *g* factor because they viewed *g* as a statistical artifact rather than a real entity.

Despite the differences between the Cattell–Horn and Carroll models, the striking similarities between them allowed for a rather natural integration. McGrew (1997) and Flanagan, McGrew, and Ortiz (2000) presented perhaps the first such integrated framework as a foundation for a new and innovative approach to the measurement and interpretation of abilities known as the *Cross-Battery approach*. Later, during the course of the development of the *Woodcock–Johnson III* (WJ-III) (Woodcock, McGrew, & Mather, 2001), Richard Woodcock, in consultation with John Horn and John Carroll, formally proposed the designation *Cattell–Horn–Carroll theory* (or CHC theory) to describe the integrated model that emanated from the work of McGrew and colleagues. Because the original *Gf–Gc* two-factor theory (Cattell, 1941) evolved into the current CHC multifactor structure through decades of systematic programs of validity research (see McGrew & Flanagan, 1998, and Horn & Noll, 1997, for a summary), it is the most well-supported theory of the structure of cognitive abilities currently available.

CHC THEORY: A TAXONOMY OF COGNITIVE ABILITIES

The impact of CHC theory as the best supported, evolving model of the structure of intelligence lies in its strong network of empirical support. When theoreticians, researchers, and practitioners operate from a well-defined and well-validated set of cognitive constructs, an understanding of intelligence is facilitated, as is communication among disciplines. A brief description of the abilities that comprise CHC theory follows.

Fluid Intelligence (*Gf*)

The mental operations applied to relatively novel tasks that cannot be performed automatically reflect *Gf*. These operations may include forming and recognizing concepts, perceiving relationships among patterns, drawing inferences, comprehending implications, problem solving, extrapolating, and reorganizing or transforming information. Inductive and deductive reasoning are generally considered to be the hallmark narrow-ability indicators of *Gf* but it also includes specific types of reasoning, for example, Quantitative Reasoning (QR).

Crystallized Intelligence (*Gc*)

The breadth and depth of a person's acquired knowledge of a culture and the effective application of this knowledge represent *Gc*. This store of primarily verbal or language-based knowledge represents abilities that have been developed largely through the "investment" of other abilities during educational and general life experiences (Horn & Noll, 1997). A rather unique aspect of *Gc* not seen in the other broad abilities is that it appears to be both a store of acquired knowledge (e.g., lexical knowledge, general information, information about culture) as well as a collection of processing abilities (e.g., oral production and fluency, listening ability).

Quantitative Knowledge (*Gq*)

An individual's store of acquired quantitative declarative and procedural knowledge is known as *Gq*. The store of acquired mathematical knowledge includes the ability to use quantitative information and manipulate numeric symbols. *Gq* abilities are typically measured by achievement tests.

Reading/Writing Ability (*Grw*)

The acquired store of knowledge that includes basic reading and writing skills required for the comprehension of written language and the expression of thought via writing is the essence of *Grw*. It includes both basic abilities (e.g., reading, decoding, spelling) and complex abilities (e.g., comprehending written discourse and writing a story). Although the research underlying the classification of these narrow abilities certainly indicates that they are very closely related abilities (Woodcock, 1994), Flanagan and colleagues (2002) use a more distinct designation, where *Grw-R* refers to those abilities that relate directly to reading and *Grw-W* to those that encompass writing.

Short-Term Memory (*Gsm*)

The ability to apprehend and hold information in immediate awareness and then use it within a few seconds characterizes *Gsm*. It is a limited-capacity system, as most individuals can retain several pieces of information in this system at one time. Examples include the ability to remember a telephone number long enough to dial it, or the ability to retain a sequence of spoken directions long enough to complete the tasks specified in the directions.

Visual Processing (*Gv*)

The ability to generate, perceive, analyze, synthesize, store, retrieve, manipulate, transform, and think with visual patterns and stimuli is called *Gv* (Lohman, 1992). These abilities are measured frequently by tasks that require the perception and manipulation of visual shapes and forms, usually of a figural or geometric nature (e.g., a standard Block Design task). An individual who can mentally reverse and rotate objects effectively, interpret how objects change as they move through space, perceive and manipulate spatial configurations, and maintain spatial orientation would be regarded as having good *Gv* ability.

Auditory Processing (*Ga*)

In the broadest sense, auditory abilities "are cognitive abilities that depend on sound as input and on the functioning of our hearing apparatus" (Stankov, 1994, p. 157) and reflect "the degree to which the individual can cognitively control the perception of auditory stimulus inputs" (Gustafsson & Undheim, 1996, p. 192). Auditory Processing is the ability to perceive, analyze, and synthesize patterns among auditory stimuli, and to discriminate subtle nuances in patterns of sound (e.g., complex musical structure) and speech when presented under distorted conditions. Although *Ga* abilities do not require the comprehension of language (*Gc*) per se, they are important in the development of language skills.

Long-Term Storage and Retrieval (*Glr*)

The ability to store information in and fluently retrieve new or previously acquired information (e.g., concepts, ideas, items, names) from long-term memory represents *Glr*. This ability has been prominent in creativity research, where it has been referred to as idea production, ideational fluency, or associative fluency. It is important not to confuse *Glr* with *Gc*, *Gq*, and *Grw*, which represent to a large extent an individual's stores of acquired knowledge. Specifically, *Gc*, *Gq*, and *Grw* represent *what* is stored in long-term memory, whereas *Glr* is the *efficiency* by which this information is later retrieved.

Processing Speed (*Gs*)

Mental quickness is often mentioned when talking about intelligent behavior. *Gs* is the ability to fluently and automatically perform cognitive tasks, especially when under pressure to maintain focused attention and concentration. "Attentive speediness" encapsulates the essence of *Gs*. *Gs* is measured typically by fixed-interval timed tasks that require little in the way of complex thinking or mental processing (e.g., the Wechsler Symbol Search and Digit Symbol/Coding tests).

Correct Decision Speed/Reaction Time (*Gt*)

In addition to *Gs*, a second broad speed ability is found in the CHC taxonomy. Correct Decision Speed (CDS) and Reaction Time (*Gt*), as proposed by Carroll, subsume narrow abilities that reflect an individual's quickness in reacting (reaction time) and making decisions (decision speed). CDS is typically measured by recording the time an individual requires to provide an answer to problems on a variety of tests (e.g., letter series, classifications, vocabulary; Horn, 1988, 1991). Because CDS appeared to be a much narrower ability than *Gt*, it is subsumed by *Gt* in CHC theory.

In summary, *Gf–Gc* theory has evolved considerably since its initial two-factor conceptualization. To date, it represents perhaps the most sophisticated and empirically defensible theoretical framework of the structure of cognitive abilities within the psychometric tradition. Because *Gf–Gc* theory underlies modern intelligence tests (e.g., WJ-III) and approaches to interpretation (e.g., the Cross-Battery approach) and ongoing *Gf–Gc* research continues to enrich our understanding of cognitive processing and influence the development of new and revised intelligence batteries (e.g., SB:V, WISC-IV), it will continue to be a leading paradigm for scientists and practitioners alike for many decades to come.

See also: Gardner's Theory of Multiple Intelligences; Intelligence Quotient (IQ); Woodcock–Johnson III-Tests of Achievement

BIBLIOGRAPHY

Carroll, J. B. (1993). *Human cognitive abilities: A survey of factor-analytic studies.* Cambridge: Cambridge University Press.

Flanagan, D. P., McGrew, K. S., & Ortiz, S. O. (2000). *The Wechsler intelligence scales and CHC theory: A contemporary approach to interpretation.* Boston: Allyn & Bacon.

Flanagan, D. P., & Ortiz, S. O. (2001). *Essentials of cross-battery assessment.* New York: Wiley.

Flanagan, D. P., Ortiz, S. O., Alfonso, V. C., & Mascolo, J. (2002). *The achievement test desk reference: Comprehensive assessment and learning disability.* Boston: Allyn & Bacon.

Horn, J. L. (1965). *Fluid and crystallized intelligence: A factor analytic and developmental study of the structure among primary mental abilities.* Unpublished doctoral dissertation, University of Illinois, Champaign.

Horn, J. L. (1985). Remodeling old theories of intelligence: *Gf–Gc* theory. In B. B. Wolman (Ed.), *Handbook of intelligence* (pp. 267–300). New York: Wiley.

Horn, J. L. (1988). Thinking about human abilities. In J. R. Nesselroade & R. B. Cattell (Eds.), *Handbook of multivariate psychology* (rev. ed., pp. 645–685). New York: Academic Press.

Horn, J. L. (1991). Measurement of intellectual capabilities: A review of theory. In K. S. McGrew, J. K. Werder, & R. W. Woodcock (Eds.), *Woodcock–Johnson technical manual* (pp. 197–232). Chicago: Riverside.

Horn, J. L. (1994). Theory of fluid and crystallized intelligence. In R. J. Sternberg (Ed.), *Encyclopedia of human intelligence* (pp. 443–451). New York: Macmillan.

Horn, J. L., & Noll, J. (1997). Human cognitive capabilities: *Gf–Gc* theory. In D. P. Flanagan, J. L. Genshaft, & P. L. Harrison (Eds.), *Contemporary intellectual assessment: Theories, tests, and issues* (pp. 53–91). New York: Guilford.

Lohman, D. F. (1994). Spatial ability. In R. J. Sternberg (Ed.), *Encyclopedia of human intelligence* (pp. 1000–1007). New York: Macmillan.

McGrew, K. S. (1997). Analysis of the major intelligence batteries according to a proposed comprehensive *Gf–Gc* framework. In D. P. Flanagan, J. L. Genshaft, & P. L. Harrison (Eds.), *Contemporary intellectual assessment: Theories, tests, and issues* (pp. 151–180). New York: Guilford.

McGrew, K. S., & Flanagan, D. P. (1998). *The intelligence test desk reference (ITDR): Gf–Gc cross-battery assessment.* Boston: Allyn & Bacon.

Stankov, L. (1994). Auditory abilities. In R. J. Sternberg (Ed.), *Encyclopedia of human intelligence* (pp. 157–162). New York: Macmillan.

Taylor, T. R. (1994). A review of three approaches to cognitive assessment, and a proposed integrated approach based on a unifying theoretical framework. *South African Journal of Psychology, 24,* 183–193.

Woodcock, R. W. (1993). An information processing view of *Gf–Gc* theory [WJ-R Monograph]. *Journal of Psychoeducational Assessment,* Special Edition, 80–102.

Woodcock, R. W. (1994). Measures of fluid and crystallized intelligence. In R. J. Sternberg (Ed.), *The encyclopedia of human intelligence* (pp. 452–456). New York: Macmillan.

Woodcock, R. W., McGrew, K. S., & Mather, N. (2001). *Woodcock–Johnson III tests of achievement.* Itasca, IL: Riverside.

Dawn P. Flanagan
Samuel O. Ortiz

Gifted and Talented

The concept of giftedness and exceptional talents is centuries old. However, the idea of intellectual giftedness as a measurable entity arose at the same time that intelligence testing became common in American culture, during the first few decades of the twentieth century. Children who were gifted, according to test results, were sometimes placed in special programs so their talents could be nourished (Delisle, 1992). The notion of a genetic basis of intelligence also rooted itself firmly during these early years, with the active encouragement of bright couples to have babies and the forced sterilization among the dullest members of society (the Eugenics movement). Despite these darker activities, the early years of the gifted and talented (G/T) movement in the United States provided us with a stunning longitudinal study of children identified as gifted—initiated by Terman (Sears, 1979).

The G/T movement in the United States eventually dissociated from the Eugenics movement, coming into its own as a reaction to the 1957 launching of Sputnik by the Soviet Union. Americans were caught off-guard by their own slowness in developing a space program, and by the lack of educational emphasis on advanced math and science skills. Public schools were urged to identify the brightest students and place them in special classes to prepare them to "race for space." The impetus initially given to the G/T movement during this initial competition provided the underpinnings, in terms of government encouragement and support, that continues today.

IDENTIFICATION OF CHILDREN WHO ARE GIFTED AND TALENTED

Currently, the federal definition of G/T includes children deemed capable of high performance in one of several areas, including intelligence, creativity, the arts, leadership, or specific academic areas. The definition also includes terminology indicating that services ordinarily provided by the school are deemed inadequate to meet the child's needs, replicating the model for services provided to children under special education. Identification criteria for children with gifted abilities or special talents can vary widely from state to state, depending upon resources and demographic characteristics.

THEORETICAL MODELS FOR IDENTIFICATION AND INTERVENTION

A number of models have been proposed for identifying and enhancing gifts and talents in children (Davis & Rimm, 1998). Among the earlier models were Bloom and Krathwohl's taxonomy combining educational and affective objectives, and Guilford's Structure of Intellect Model, emphasizing a three-dimensional model based on operations, content, and products. Related to Guilford's model, and offering explicit applications to educational arenas, is Taylor's Multiple Talent Totem Pole Model. Later models for identification and intervention include Betts' Autonomous Learner Model (ALM) and a succession of applied models by Renzulli. Betts' model, designed primarily for implementation in pull-out programs, provides a dimensional outline for classroom activities, ranging from orientation to in-depth study. Renzulli provides some of the best documentation of effectiveness for his models, which have included the Enrichment Triad, Revolving Door Identification, and School-wide Enrichment Model. Renzulli's models share a concern for identification and interventions that can be carried out across regular and special classroom settings and activities, reaching a broader target audience. Other models exist; the reader is referred to Davis and Rimm (1998) for examples.

TYPES OF PROGRAMS

Application of interventions for children who are gifted and/or talented varies widely in type of setting and in goals, with developmental issues frequently kept in mind. At the elementary level, services are frequently provided in pull-out programs, that is, children attend a special class only a few hours a week and attend the regular classroom for the majority of schooltime. Goals in early grade levels usually focus on enrichment or developing higher order thinking skills. Middle schools and high schools are more likely to segregate children in tracks according to ability, often providing accelerated academic instruction and opportunities to earn college credit. Special summer programs are often offered in larger communities or in university settings.

CURRENT ISSUES AND CONTROVERSIES

Proponents and critics of G/T programs raise several concerns regarding identification and intervention. Controversies usually center on the issue of excellence versus equality (Davis

& Rimm, 1998). In practical terms, these controversies include problems in the underidentification and underdevelopment of gifts and talents in children from varied cultures and ethnic backgrounds, in females, in children with disabilities, and in children who show very specific creative talents.

One additional area provides constant debate, and frequent lobbying, on behalf of children who are G/T. Funding sources vary widely from state to state and community to community. In some school districts, funding is tied to federal guidelines, with services provided under special education. In others, state or local funding may or may not be provided, providing an ongoing focus for change from parents, teachers, and proponents of G/T services.

BIBLIOGRAPHY

Davis, G. A., & Rimm, S. B. (1998). *Education of the gifted and talented* (4th ed.). Boston: Allyn & Bacon.

Delisle, J. (1992). *Guiding the social and emotional development of youth.* New York: Longman.

Sears, P. S. (1979). The Terman genetic studies of genius, 1922–1972. In A. H. Passow (Ed.), *The gifted and talented: Their education and development* (Vol. 78, pp. 75–96). Chicago: University of Chicago Press.

Additional Readings for Nonprofessionals

Coleman, L. J., & Cross, T. L. (2001). *Being gifted in school—An introduction to development, guidance, and teaching.* Waco, TX: Prufrock Press.

Gardner, H. (1983). *Frames of mind: The theory of multiple intelligences.* New York: Basic Books.

Additional Readings for Professionals

Boatman, T. A., Davis, K. G., & Benbow, C. P. (1995). Gifted education. In A. Thomas & J. Grimes (Eds.), *Best practices in school psychology III* (pp. 1083–1096). Washington, DC: National Association of School Psychologists.

Heller, K. A., Monks, F. J., Sternberg, R. J., & Subotnik, R. F. (Eds.). (2000). *International handbook of giftedness and talent* (2nd ed.). New York: Elsevier Science.

SHERRY K. BAIN

Goddard, Henry Herbert

Henry Herbert Goddard graduated with his Bachelor of Science degree in 1887 from Haverford College, Pennsylvania, and earned his Master of Arts degree from the same college by 1889. Goddard moved to Worcester, Massachusetts, where he earned his Ph.D. in psychology from Clark University in 1899. In 1906, after several years of teaching at several schools, Goddard moved to New Jersey, where he had accepted a position as the director of research for the Study of Feeble-Mindedness at the Vineland Training Institute.

At the institute, Goddard studied children with developmental delays and children with mental retardation. In order to estimate children's abilities, Goddard used the best current method of assessment—various anthropometric techniques designed by James McKeen Cattell (correlating current academic performance levels with tests of dynamometer pressure, rate of movement, sensation areas, pressure causing pain, least noticeable differences in weight, reaction to sound, time for naming colors, bisection of a 50-cm line, judgment of 10 seconds' time, and number of letters remembered on one hearing) even though it had been shown that almost no correlation existed between any of Cattell's anthropometric tests and current academic performance levels.

Goddard realized the need for an assessment tool to differentiate between normal and feeble-minded children. He also recognized the need for discernment of varying levels of mental ability. Goddard traveled to France to study the work of Binet and Simon on intelligence testing. Goddard supervised the English translation of the 1908 Binet–Simon scales and brought this new method of mental assessment back to the United States. In New Jersey, Goddard normed the English translation of the scales on 400 Vineland Training Institute children and 2,000 New Jersey public school children. Goddard found a significant difference between most of the children from the public schools and the children from Vineland, convincing him of the validity of the instrument. Goddard became a believer in the scales and began promoting the use of his translation by holding classes to instruct teachers on the administration and scoring of the tests. Goddard quickly translated the 1911 release of the Binet–Simon scales, which remained the standard for intelligence testing in the United States until Lewis M. Terman revised the scales as the Stanford–Binet intelligence tests.

Goddard learned the significance of genetics studying under G. Stanley Hall at Clark University and read Gregor Mendel's paper "Experiments on Plant-Hybridization." The basic tenet of the Mendelian principles was that characteristics of plants were inherited from the genes of the parent plants. Goddard recognized that many of the children at Vineland had siblings who were also feeble-minded. Goddard began to examine the relationships between the feeble-minded children at Vineland and began work on his infamous study *The Kallikak family: A study in the heredity of feeble-mindedness.* Goddard tested 22-year-old Deborah Kallikak in 1911 and determined she was a "moron," the term he coined to describe the highest level of feeble-mindedness, which was the most common. Goddard created the name Kallikak, claiming it meant "the nameless one," but has root words of bad and good in Greek. Goddard traced Deborah's ancestry back to Martin Kallikak Sr., an American Revolution soldier from a good family.

Goddard traced the lineage from Martin Sr. and a feeble-minded barmaid to an illegitimate child, Martin Jr., which produced a "bad" side of the family. Martin Sr. married a wealthy and worthy Quaker girl, and produced the "good" side of the family. Goddard claimed that Martin Jr.'s branch of the family had produced 143 feeble-minded people, on the basis of interviews, testing, and examination of occupation and standing in the community. He claimed that of the 495 descendents of the Quaker-wife branch of the family, only 3 were "somewhat mentally degenerate people." Goddard's work was accepted in the psychological and political realm. Many studies replicated his methodology with other families. Goddard served on the Eugenics Section of the American Breeders' Association and the Committee for the Heredity of the Feeble-Minded, both of which recommended sterilization of the feeble-minded. Many states implemented such practices, which stayed in place until the 1960s.

In 1913, Goddard was invited by the U.S. commissioner of immigration to study immigrant screening procedures used at Ellis Island to keep idiots and lunatics out of the country. Goddard convinced Immigration to administer the Binet and the DeSanctis tests to immigrants, through translation when necessary, to refuse admission to the United States. The tests were unfair because they were questions about American products and people, rather than universally understood concepts. Because of Goddard's methods of screening, deportation of immigrants increased from the previous 5 years by 350 percent in 1913 and 570 percent in 1914.

In 1918, Goddard moved to the Ohio State Bureau of Juvenile Research to be the director. In 1922, Goddard began working with intellectually gifted children and special education in the Cleveland public schools to promote "gifted children education." He encouraged what he called "enrichment" rather than rapid promotion. Goddard wrote of the Cleveland program providing classes for the gifted in which they produced plays, made detailed sculptures, and designed complex mathematical games. The program was the most progressive and extensive in the country at the time, with over 600 children participating. Unfortunately, no follow-up studies were ever held, so there are no data on what type of adults these gifted children became.

See also: Binet, Alfred; Hall, G. Stanley

BIBLIOGRAPHY

Hothersall, D. (1984). *History of psychology.* New York: Random House.
Sokal, M. M. (1988). James McKeen Cattell and the failure of anthropometric mental testing, 1890–1901. In L. T. Benjamin, Jr. (Ed.), *A history of psychology: Original sources and contemporary research* (pp. 310–319). New York: McGraw-Hill.

NICHOLAS E. HODA

The Good Behavior Game

When dealing with problem behaviors in the classroom, teachers typically focus on individual students and their unique problem behaviors. However, implementing an intervention that can be applied to the entire classroom can be more economical, both in terms of time and money. Utilizing only one intervention for the class also frees the teacher from having to monitor several individual plans at one time. In addition, group activities can be used as reinforcers, which may be less expensive and less time-consuming than supplying students with individualized reinforcers. Such classroom-based interventions utilize group contingencies to manage behavior. Group contingencies can be categorized into three types: independent, dependent, and interdependent. An independent group contingency allows each group member access to reinforcement on the basis of his/her own performance (e.g., "whoever finishes writing their spelling words can get a game or puzzle from the shelf after I've checked their work"). A dependent group contingency allows members of a group access to reinforcement on the basis of the behavior of a selected member or members of the group, sometimes chosen randomly (e.g., "everyone can get a game or puzzle from the shelf as soon as Derek and Susan put their books away and straighten their desks"). Finally, interdependent group contingencies allow members of a group access to reinforcement on the basis of a group criterion of performance (e.g., "everyone will be able to get a game or puzzle from the shelf this afternoon if there are no more than five rule violations by the class by 2:00 p.m.").

DESCRIPTION

The Good Behavior Game (GBG) is an intervention based on interdependent group contingencies and capitalizes on team competition, group conformity, and peer influence. Because access to reinforcement depends on the performance of the group, group members tend to encourage appropriate behavior and/or discourage inappropriate behavior by their peers in the group or classroom. The GBG is typically designed to decrease disruptive classroom behaviors. To implement the game, the class is divided into teams. Teams' names are posted in the classroom (e.g., on the blackboard) and the teacher announces rules the teams must follow in order to win the game. Rules are based on target behaviors the teacher would like to reduce (e.g., talking without permission). Teams receive a mark against them each time a rule is broken by any member of the team. The team with the fewest marks wins; however, if both teams have fewer marks than a set criterion, both teams can "win." The winning team(s) receives rewards for its good behavior.

In the first investigation that introduced the GBG, Barrish, Saunders, and Wolf (1969) implemented the game with 24 students in a fourth-grade classroom. Observers recorded out-of-seat and talking-out behavior of students in math and reading periods. After obtaining baseline levels of the behaviors, the teacher introduced the game and explained to the students that they would be divided into teams in order to play the game. Students had to stay seated and could talk only when given permission in order to avoid receiving marks against their team on the chalkboard. The team with the fewest number of marks would win the game; or for both teams to win, each had to have fewer than five marks. The winning team(s) received several rewards, including the opportunity to wear victory tags and to have a star placed by the name of each member of the winning team(s) on the winner's chart. In addition, the winning team was allowed to line up first for lunch; or if both teams won, they were allowed to leave early for lunch. Combining a multiple-baseline design across math and reading periods, as well as a withdrawal design in reading, the game reduced out-of-seat and talking-out behavior significantly during math and reading only when it was introduced in those respective periods. The game was popular with the teacher, students, and other school officials.

RESEARCH SUPPORT: APPLICATIONS, SETTINGS, POPULATIONS, AND REINFORCERS

Since the introduction of the GBG, numerous studies have been conducted to replicate the initial results and to investigate the game's effectiveness in other settings with other target behaviors. Researchers have also attempted to analyze the individual components of the intervention to determine the impact of each element. Although there have been some variations in results across studies, effective components of the game appear to include the formation of teams, establishment of criteria for winning, use of feedback to teams, and consequences/reinforcement for winning.

The focus of the GBG is usually the reduction of disruptive classroom behavior. Thus, students must avoid earning points against the team. However, researchers have also found the game successful when rules are stated positively and when the focus is on increasing appropriate behavior rather than decreasing problem behaviors. For example, researchers have demonstrated increases in appropriate social behaviors during volleyball lessons, compliance, and the work output of trainees and students. The GBG has also been successful in increasing or improving some academic behaviors such as assignment and work completion, active participation, attention to task, as well as compositional variables and ratings of creativity in written stories. In one of the more unique adaptations of the GBG, researchers modified the game to target the toothbrushing skills of first and second graders (Swain, Allard, & Holborn, 1982). "The Good Toothbrushing Game" was successful in improving the oral hygiene of participating students.

Although the GBG is usually implemented with students in regular education classrooms, studies have also been conducted in a school library, a rehabilitation setting, self-contained special education classrooms, and a transitional classroom. In addition, studies have included such diverse populations as preschoolers, adult residents in a state hospital, students diagnosed as emotionally disturbed and at risk for behavior disorders, and second-grade students in a Sudanese classroom. The GBG has been shown to be overwhelmingly successful in reducing disruptive behavior across these diverse settings with the various targeted populations.

One advantage of utilizing the GBG is the ability to use group activities or privileges as reinforcers that are commonly available in most classrooms, such as extra free time, extra recess time, leaving for lunch early, playing games in the classroom, and participation in special projects. These types of activities and privileges are often easier to access by the teacher than are more tangible types of reinforcers and require little or no financial investment. Tangible reinforcers, however, such as edibles, victory tags, stars on a winner's chart, and stickers have also been used with success. Two studies have even used letters to parents (Saigh & Umar, 1983) or dorm counselors (Salend, Reynolds, & Coyle, 1989) praising the behavioral improvement of team members. Thus, there is a vast array of potential reinforcers from which the teacher can choose, and although not studied systematically, it is good practice to allow some student input into the generation of potential reinforcers for the winning team(s).

INTERMEDIATE AND LONG-TERM EFFECTS

Many studies have demonstrated the GBG's direct, short-term effectiveness, but only a few have gathered follow-up data to assess its potential intermediate or long-term indirect impact. These researchers have found lower end-of-year teacher ratings of aggression and shyness in first graders who participated in the GBG compared with these students' ratings by the teacher at the beginning of the year (Dolan et al., 1993). In addition, first-grade males from this same group who participated in the GBG throughout first and second grades, and who were initially rated high in aggression, ultimately had lower ratings of aggression by their teachers several years later as well as into middle school (Kellam, Rebok, Ialongo, & Mayer, 1994). Some of these same researchers have also found that a classroom-based intervention that included the GBG with several other strategies may be effective in reducing antecedent behaviors, such as shyness and aggression, that are associated with later drug abuse, affective disorders, and conduct disorders (Ialongo, Poduska, Werthamer,

& Kellam, 2001). The classroom-based intervention was found to be more effective than a family-focused intervention in reducing these antecedent target behaviors. Subsequently, students who had participated in this classroom-based intervention in the first grade exhibited fewer behavior problems and less need for mental health services in the sixth grade compared with their peers who had received the family-focused intervention. Thus, the GBG appears to provide some preventative benefits when used in early elementary school for at-risk students.

CONCLUSIONS

Since 1969, considerable research has shown the GBG to be a versatile, relatively easy-to-implement, and effective interdependent group contingency procedure that can be used to manage a variety of behaviors across diverse age groups of students in classrooms and other academic settings. The game is usually popular with teachers and students, and has been used with diverse populations, from preschoolers to adult residents in a state hospital, as well as with Sudanese children in one cross-cultural investigation (Saigh & Umar, 1983). The GBG has been effective not only in reducing disruptive group/classroom behavior, but also in increasing appropriate social behaviors, some academic behaviors, and even oral hygiene. More recent studies indicate that the GBG may also be effective in preventing the escalation of problem behaviors into more serious disorders.

See also: Group Contingencies; Positive Reinforcement

BIBLIOGRAPHY

Barrish, H. H., Saunders, M., & Wolf, M. M. (1969). Good Behavior Game: Effects of individual contingencies for group consequences on disruptive behavior in a classroom. *Journal of Applied Behavior Analysis, 2,* 119–124.

Dolan, L. J., Kellam, S. G., Brown, C. H., Werthamer-Larsson, L., Rebok, G. W., Mayer, L. S., et al. (1993). The short-term impact of two classroom-based preventive interventions on aggressive and shy behaviors and poor achievement. *Journal of Applied Developmental Psychology, 14,* 317–345.

Ialongo, N., Poduska, J., Werthamer, L., & Kellam, S. (2001). The distal impact of two first-grade preventive interventions on conduct problems and disorder in early adolescence. *Journal of Emotional and Behavioral Disorders, 9,* 146–160.

Kellam, S. G., Rebok, G. W., Ialongo, N., & Mayer, L. S. (1994). The course and malleability of aggressive behavior from early first grade into middle school: Results of a developmental epidemiologically-based preventive trial. *The Journal of Child Psychology and Psychiatry, 35,* 259–281.

Saigh, P. A., & Umar, A. M. (1983). The effects of a good behavior game on the disruptive behavior of Sudanese elementary school students. *Journal of Applied Behavior Analysis, 16,* 339–344.

Salend, S. J., Reynolds, C. J., & Coyle, E. M. (1989). Individualizing the good behavior game across type and frequency of behavior with emotionally disturbed adolescents. *Behavior Modification, 13,* 108–126.

Swain, J. J., Allard, G. B., & Holborn, S. W. (1982). The Good Toothbrushing Game: A school-based dental hygiene program for increasing the toothbrushing effectiveness of children. *Journal of Applied Behavior Analysis, 15,* 171–176.

Additional Reading for Nonprofessionals

Tankersley, M. (1995). A group-oriented contingency management program: A review of research on the good behavior game and implications for teachers. *Preventing School Failure, 40,* 19–24.

Additional Readings for Professionals

Harris, V. W., & Sherman, J. A. (1973). Use and analysis of the "Good Behavior Game" to reduce disruptive classroom behavior. *Journal of Applied Behavior Analysis, 6,* 405–417.

Hayes, L. A. (1976). The use of group contingencies for behavioral control: A review. *Psychological Bulletin, 83,* 628–648.

DANIEL H. TINGSTROM
AIMEE T. MCGEORGE

Goodenough–Harris Drawing Test

The *Goodenough–Harris Drawing Test* (Harris, 1963), or "Draw a Man" test, is a nonverbal test of intelligence requiring the child to draw a person. The test may be administered to children aged 3 to 15; however, norms are more useful for children aged 5 to 12. Although it is recommended that the test be administered individually to preschool children, it may be administered to older children in groups.

ADMINISTRATION

The child is provided with a pencil and a test booklet and is then asked to fill in the information requested on the front of the test booklet, including name, gender, grade, date of test, age, date of birth, and father's occupation. Next, the child is asked to draw a picture of a "whole man, not just his head and shoulders" (Harris, 1963, p. 240). When the drawing is completed, the administrator is to offer praise for the drawing and then to ask the child to draw a picture of a woman. When this drawing is completed, more praise is given. Finally, the child is asked to draw a picture of himself/herself. The child is told to "take care and make this last one the very best of the three" (Harris, 1963, p. 241). Younger children are given short rest periods between the drawings. No time limit is given for the pictures; however, most children finish all three drawings within 15 minutes. The manual cautions administrators against offering any criticisms or suggestions during the test administration. Children who wish to start over during the test are allowed to do so.

USES OF THE TEST

The Goodenough–Harris is designed to measure intellectual maturity, an ability involving "perception (discrimination of likenesses and differences), abstraction (classification of objects), and generalization (assigning newly experienced objects to the correct class)" (Sattler, 1992, p. 311). This is not to be confused with intelligence, despite the manual's claims of a substantial correlation between the two. The most appropriate use of the test is as a screening instrument to select children who may need further assessment. The Goodenough–Harris does have its strengths as a screening measure of cognitive ability. It is easily and quickly administered individually or to groups, and is not culturally biased. The test may be most effective for children in the lower intelligence ranges; however, decisions of diagnosis, placement, and intervention should never be based on the Goodenough–Harris alone.

SCORING

There are two different scoring scales for the Goodenough–Harris: the Point Scale and the Quality Scale. When using the Point Scale, points are given based on the presence of body parts or certain details within the drawings. Each item is scored as either *pass* (1 point) or *fail* (0 points). The raw score for each drawing consists of the total number of points. There are 73 items for the Draw-a-Man test and 71 for the Draw-a-Woman test.

When using the Quality Scale, the child's drawing is compared with 12 model drawings representing a continuum from the lowest level of maturity to the highest. The child's score is thus the number of the drawing that most closely resembles his/her own. The Quality Scale is less precise, yet may be scored much more quickly than the Point Scale.

NORMING AND STANDARDIZATION

For the Point Scale, norms are provided for ages 3 through 15. However, norms are provided only in whole-year intervals, thus no differentiation is made between a child who is 6 years and no months, and one who is 6 years and 11 months. Norms for boys and girls are provided separately. Raw scores from both the Point Scale and Quality Scale may be converted to standard scores in which the mean is 100, with a standard deviation of 15.

The Point Scale was standardized with a sample of nearly 3,000 children selected from four geographic regions of the United States. Although the sample was chosen to be representative of the population at that time, few would argue that it is representative of the population now, nearly 40 years later. The Quality Scale was standardized through the rating (on a 1–12 scale) of 240 drawings by children aged 5 to 15.

RELIABILITY AND VALIDITY

The Goodenough–Harris is reported to be reliable as assessed by test–retest methods and interrater reliability. However, the test is not reported to be a valid predictor of scores on other intelligence measures or measures of academic achievement (Scott, 1981). Thus, using the test to predict either IQ or academic achievement or even as a screening device is inappropriate.

See also: Intelligence Quotient (IQ)

BIBLIOGRAPHY

Harris, D. B. (1963). *Goodenough–Harris Drawing Test manual.* New York: Harcourt Brace Jovanovich.
Sattler, J. M. (1992). *Assessment of children* (3rd ed.). San Diego, CA: Author.
Scott, L. H. (1981). Measuring intelligence with the Goodenough–Harris Drawing Test. *Psychological Bulletin, 89,* 483–505.

Additional Reading for Professionals

Abell, S. C., Horkheimer, R., & Nguyen, S. E. (1998). Intellectual evaluations of adolescents via human figure drawings: An empirical comparison of two methods. *Journal of Clinical Psychology, 54,* 811–815.

ADAM D. WEAVER

Grief

Most children will experience the death of a close or special person prior to graduation from high school. Grief may also occur following other losses (e.g., the death of a pet, parental divorce). Although loss includes a variety of experiences, herein, the emphasis is on the *death* of a close or special person. Children of all ages may experience grief. Practitioners and scholars have highlighted the significance of loss during childhood on subsequent development. Bowlby (1980) emphasizes that "loss of a loved person is one of the most intensely painful experiences any human being can suffer" (p. 7). Available research indicates that youth are vulnerable to psychological, behavioral, and social problems both immediately and following a loss. Thus, it is important that adults are aware of the developmental considerations regarding children's grief.

Grief has been characterized as the emotional and behavioral experiences in response to a loss and is described as the sequence of subjective states that follow loss and accompany mourning (Bowlby, 1980). Mourning and bereavement refer to the larger process of adaptation and coping following a loss, including the grief response and attempts to understand and create meaning from the loss. Support to facilitate healthy bereavement may be offered from caring adults through individual support, group support, family support, and counseling services as appropriate (Lehmann, Jimerson, & Gaasch, 2001; Wolfelt, 2002). An individual's grief will be impacted by a myriad of factors including the individuals' characteristics, context, circumstances of the loss, developmental history, and available supportive adults.

Although it is necessary to appreciate individual differences among bereaved youth, it is also clear that an understanding of death depends on one's developmental level, including cognitive and socioemotional development as well as past experiences (Bertoia & Allan, 1988). Following a loss, a variety of behaviors and feelings often accompany grief in children, including denial, panic, anger, guilt, sadness, anxiety, preoccupation, hyperactivity, short attention span, withdrawal, and repression of feelings. There is an assortment of common emotional, cognitive, physical, and social reactions that youth may experience (see Table 1). Any of these common behaviors and feelings may produce problems later if they persist and if the child does not cope with the loss in a healthy way. There are many variations of healthy mourning and grief responses. Children from different cultural backgrounds have varying beliefs about death, which will influence their grief and coping strategies. The grief experience of a child is also influenced by his/her emerging understanding of death.

DEVELOPMENTAL CONSIDERATIONS IN CHILDREN'S UNDERSTANDING OF DEATH

There are developmental differences in how children of different ages understand and interpret death (Speece & Brent, 1996). Research has yielded four important components of children's understanding of the concept of death: (1) universality, (2) irreversibility, (3) nonfunctionality, and (4) causality. The following provides an overview regarding developmental trends in understanding each of these components, along with important cognitive and socioemotional developmental considerations.

Table 1. Common Grief Reactions in Children and Adolescents

Common *Emotional* Grief Reactions
  Anger
  Sadness/Longing
  Anxiety
  Helplessness
  Shock/Denial
  Depression
  Guilt
  Relief
  Shame
  Mood swings
  Repression of feelings/Apathy
  Hypersensitivity

Common *Cognitive* Grief Reactions
  School difficulties
  Distraction
  Attention span
  Decline in performance
  Spiritual questions
  Memory problems
  Confusion
  Preoccupation with death

Common *Physical* Grief Reactions
  Illness/Somatic complaints
  Sleep disturbance
  Crying and sighing
  Decline in energy
  Eating disturbance
  Hyperactivity
  Susceptibility to health problems
  Gastrointestinal disturbance
  Numbing/Heaviness/Tingling

Common *Social* Grief Reactions
  Changes in personality and family role
  Changes in relationships with peers and adults
  Withdrawal
  Acting out/Increased need for attention
  Aggression/Fighting
  Tantrums/Outbursts
  Regression

Universality refers to the understanding that all living things eventually die. Universality includes three closely related dimensions: all-inclusiveness (e.g., every living thing will die), inevitability (e.g., each living thing will die eventually), and unpredictability (e.g., death may occur at any moment to any living thing). In general, during the first 5 years of life, children do not understand the universality of death. Regarding inclusiveness, younger children are more likely than older children to think that death is avoidable if one is especially clever or lucky. By age 10, children usually begin to understand that death is universal and inevitable.

Irreversibility refers to the understanding that once the physical body dies, it cannot become alive again. Younger children are more likely to view death as reversible or temporary, not fully understanding the irrevocability and finality of death. Young children often believe that death can be reversed spontaneously, through wishful thinking, praying, or magical and medical interventions (Speece & Brent, 1996). By age 10, as children enter the primary grades, most understand the concept of irreversibility (e.g., that death is final).

Nonfunctionality refers to the understanding that once a living thing dies, all of the typical life capabilities of the living thing (e.g., walking, eating, thinking) cease. Research indicates that younger children are more likely than older ones to think that the dead continue to be able to perform various functions. Such functions include both internal (e.g., thinking, knowing) and external (e.g., walking, eating) functions. Although this area has received less attention than others in research, it appears that an understanding of nonfunctionality is often present by age 11.

Causality refers to the abstract and realistic understanding of internal and external causes of death—abstract in the sense that the possible causes are not restricted to a particular individual or event, but are applicable to all living things in general, and realistic in the sense that the specified causes would be generally accepted by most mature adults as valid causes of death. Research indicates that younger children are more likely than older children to provide unrealistic causes of death (e.g., bad behavior, stepping on cracks, eating a specific food) or to list specific concrete causes (e.g., guns, driving fast). Younger children are also more likely to focus on external causes (e.g., violence) than internal causes (e.g., kidney failure, cancer). Understanding of the causality component of the concept of death often continues to develop through early adolescence.

COGNITIVE AND SOCIOEMOTIONAL DEVELOPMENTAL CONSIDERATIONS

A number of studies have demonstrated concordance between children's understanding of death and Piaget's general theory of cognitive development. It is during Piaget's concrete operational stage (ages 7–10), when reduced egocentricity and improved capacity for reasoning are present, that children tend to develop a more adult understanding. As children border Piaget's formal operational stage (ages 11–12), their thinking becomes truly logical, able to handle multiple variables at once and capable of dealing with abstract ideas. Likewise, their understanding of death is often consistent with an adult understanding. It is suggested that the basic understanding of death that develops in early and middle childhood serves as a foundation for the development of a more complex concept during late childhood and adulthood.

As children develop verbal skills they are likely to use words such as *die* and *dead*; however, young children often do not comprehend the meaning of these words. Although children's "understanding" of death will influence their grief reactions, the ability to grieve depends on one's ability to "feel." Thus, any child mature enough to love is mature enough to grieve (Wolfelt, 2002). Thus, even though a young child may not have a fully developed understanding of death, and may lack the terms associated with internal feelings (e.g., sad, anxious, guilty), it is apparent that they will be affected by the loss of a close or special person. Although studies reveal few differences in children's grief reactions among girls and boys, Silverman and Worden (1992) reported that girls were more comfortable expressing their feelings, and hypothesized that this was related to early socialization. Studies in the United States that examine the effects of religion on children's understanding of death concepts have found very few significant differences in children's understanding of death concepts or common grief reactions. Although the available research does not provide specific guidelines to attend to when working with grieving children from diverse backgrounds, it is important that we appreciate the influence of children's developmental history on their grief reactions and understanding of death concepts.

Age by itself explains very little regarding children's grief, as age is a rather general index of a wide range of correlated environmental and biological variables. Most studies report that at around age 10, children understand each of the key components of the death concept (e.g., universality, irreversibility, nonfunctionality, and causality). It should be recognized that as children vary, so does their understanding of death and their grief experiences. Each youth's grief and understanding of death may only be understood through listening to each child share his/her ideas and grief experiences.

See also: Coping; Crisis Intervention; Divorce; Stress

BIBLIOGRAPHY

Bertoia, J., & Allan, J. (1988). School management of the bereaved child. *Elementary School Guidance and Counseling, 23,* 30–38.

Bowlby, J. (1980). *Attachment and loss: Loss, sadness, and depression.* New York: Basic Books.

Lehmann, L., Jimerson, S., & Gaasch, A. (2001). *Grief support group curriculum facilitators handbook.* Philadelphia: Brunner & Routledge.

Silverman, P. R., & Worden, J. W. (1992). Children's reactions in the early months after the death of a parent. *American Journal of Orthopsychiatry, 62,* 93–104.

Speece, C., & Brent, S. (1996). The development of children's understanding of death. In C. Corr & D. Corr (Eds.), *Handbook of childhood death and bereavement* (pp. 29–50). New York: Springer.

Wolfelt, A. (2002). Children's grief. In S. E. Brock, P. J. Lazarus, & S. R. Jimerson (Eds.), *Best practices in school crisis prevention and intervention* (pp. 653–674). Bethesda, MD: National Association of School Psychologists.

Additional Readings for Nonprofessionals

Doka, K., & Davidson, J. (1998). *Living with grief: Who we are, how we grieve.* Philadelphia: Brunner & Mazel.

Wolfelt, A. (1996). *Healing the bereaved child: Grief gardening, growth through grief and other touchstones for caregivers.* Ft. Collins, CO: Companion.

Additional Readings for Professionals

Corr, C. A., & Corr, D. M. (Eds.). (1996). *Handbook of childhood death and bereavement.* New York: Springer.

Lehmann, L., Jimerson, S., & Gaasch, A. (2001). *Mourning child grief support group curriculum: Early childhood edition.* Philadelphia: Brunner & Routledge.

Webb, N. B. (1993). *Helping bereaved children: A handbook for practitioners.* New York: Guilford.

Worden, W. (1996). *Children and grief: When a parent dies.* New York: Guilford.

SHANE R. JIMERSON

Group Contingencies

Contingencies are used daily in educational environments to prevent inappropriate behaviors and encourage and maintain desired behaviors. These contingencies include both reinforcement and punishment and involve individuals and groups. Contingencies specify several components, among them the target behavior(s), criteria(on) for success, and the consequences for meeting or not meeting the criteria(on).

With individual contingencies, each of the components is constructed to meet the needs of a particular student. For example, Joe may receive extra computer time (reinforcing consequence) contingent upon him scoring 80 percent or higher (criterion) on his mathematics assignments (target behavior). The primary advantage of individual contingencies is that specific components can be adjusted for each child. Thus, although 80 percent on mathematics assignments may be an appropriate criterion and target behavior for Joe, who typically scores 60 percent on math assignments, this target behavior and criterion would be inappropriate for Sam, who typically scores 98 percent on mathematics assignments. In addition, although computer time may be a high-quality reinforcer for Joe, it may be inappropriate for Sam, who hates working or playing on computers. By adjusting the target behaviors, consequences, and criteria on the basis of each student's preferences, abilities, and past performance, educators can effectively encourage or discourage behaviors. The primary disadvantage of individual contingencies is that it is extremely difficult for educators to manage different contingencies for each child and target behavior. Thus, educators often use in-

dependent group contingencies (Skinner, Cashwell, & Dunn, 1996).

INDEPENDENT GROUP CONTINGENCIES

With independent group contingencies, the target behaviors, criteria, and consequences are the same for all students in a group (e.g., a class) and each student receives access to consequences on the basis of his/her own performance. These contingencies are used in all schools. For example, if a school or classroom has rules that indicate inappropriate behaviors and punishments for those behaviors, then they are using an independent group punishment system. In addition, if educators give students grades contingent upon their performance on the same test, they are implementing independent group contingencies.

There are many advantages associated with independent group contingencies. First, it is much easier for teachers to manage contingencies where the target behaviors, criteria, and consequences are the same for everyone. In addition, educators, administrators, parents, and children consider them fair. Because of this, such contingencies are often used when high-stakes consequences are involved. For example, independent group contingencies are often used when assigning grades and when delivering serious punishment (e.g., suspending students) for dangerous behaviors (e.g., fighting, bringing weapons to school).

Although independent group reinforcement and punishment procedures are commonly used, there are limitations associated with these procedures. First, because specific consequences have different effects across students, such procedures are not effective for all students. Second, because students have different abilities, skills, and levels of self-control, it is difficult to set a criterion that is appropriate for each target behavior across all students. For example, a criterion of 80 percent on a mathematics assignment may be too high for some students. Thus, these students may not even try to earn the reward. For other students, 80 percent may be too low, thus they could actually receive additional reinforcement for poorer academic performance.

When using independent group contingencies, some students receive consequences and others do not. In most instances, peers are aware as to who received the consequences and who did not. Thus, educators are indirectly providing feedback to peers regarding classmates' performance. This feedback may cause peers to view students who typically earn reinforcement for desired behavior as smart and those who typically receive punishment for inappropriate behavior as bad. When this occurs often enough, those who do not earn reinforcers or who are frequently punished may belittle reinforcers and those who earn access to them (e.g., only geeks like playing on computers).

In addition, some students who are not attempting to earn reinforcers may engage in disruptive behaviors designed to decrease the probability of peers' earning their reinforcement.

Independent group contingencies impose limits on available reinforcers because some students earn them and others do not. For example, some reinforcers (principal kissing a pig, listening to music while completing independent seat-work, going on a field trip) are difficult to deliver to some students but not to others. Therefore, when implementing independent group reinforcement programs, educators often use tangible reinforcers because they can be easily delivered to some students and not to others. This causes additional problems when students who did not earn tangible rewards obtain them (a) by stealing them from peers, (b) by purchasing them, or (c) when a peer shares.

INTERDEPENDENT GROUP CONTINGENCIES

Interdependent group contingencies are less common in schools, but can be extremely effective. With interdependent group contingencies, all or none of the students in a group receive access to the same consequence on the basis of some aspect of the group's behavior. For example, a teacher may agree to come to school dressed like a clown (reinforcement) contingent upon the class averaging 90 percent (group criterion) on their reading test (target behavior).

There are numerous advantages associated with interdependent group contingencies. It is easier to deliver a wide variety of reinforcers to all or none of the students. Because all students have access to reinforcers, they are less likely to belittle the reinforcers or the activities that cause the group to earn them. Students cannot determine peers' performance on the basis of their access to consequences. Thus, these contingencies do not encourage students to perceive one another differently (e.g., children who receive reinforcers are "smart," those who do not are "stupid") on the basis of access to consequences. In addition, because access to consequences is contingent upon each student's own behavior or performance and his/her classmates', students may encourage one another to do well in order to increase the likelihood of the group earning reinforcement. The classwide group celebration when everyone earns the reinforcement also can increase the quality of the reinforcers.

Although there are advantages associated with interdependent group contingencies, there are also disadvantages. First, each student's access to consequences is based on his/her own behavior and his/her classmates' behavior. Thus, with interdependent group punishment, students who did not behave poorly may be punished because of their peers' behavior. Such procedures can occasion emotional reactions from students who may threaten or aggress against classmates who caused them to be punished. Thus, interdependent group *punishment* should not be used. Similar reactions may occur if a particular group of students is judged to have caused the group to fail to earn a reward. Thus, it may be best to use these contingencies with behaviors where each student's performance is not public or known to his/her peers (e.g., academic assignments).

With interdependent group rewards, consequences must be selected with care. For example, consider that a particular consequence is a reinforcer to some students but a punisher to others. For those who find the consequence punishing, they are actually encouraged to sabotage the group's performance so that they can escape and avoid this aversive consequence. One procedure that may address this concern is to have students help develop a pool or group of reinforcers and randomly select the reinforcer from that pool.

Interdependent group reinforcement programs have been used to reduce inappropriate behaviors, enhance academic performance, and reward students on a schoolwide basis (Skinner, Skinner, & Sterling-Turner, 2002). For example, in my community we have recently had a spate of principals kissing pigs or coming to school dressed as clowns because their entire school body met a group goal—selling X amount of coupon-books to raise funds for the school.

Despite the strength of independent group contingencies, such procedures should not be used with punishment because access to consequences is based on peers' behaviors. In addition, although some have proposed giving students group grades, it is not recommended because student grades are high-stakes consequences that also reflect individual achievement. For example, a student who fails to learn should not be given a high grade (e.g., an A on his/her report card). However, we do recommend using such a procedure to *supplement* grades. For example, Popkin and Skinner (2003) offered group reinforcers for academic performance in order to supplement, but not replace, the current grading system and found average increases in performance exceeding two letter grades.

DEPENDENT GROUP CONTINGENCIES

Dependent group contingencies are perhaps the least used contingency in schools. There are good reasons for this. With these contingencies, all students receive access to consequences on the basis of the performance of one particular student. These are the least fair contingencies because, with the exception of the target student, everyone else's fate is controlled by someone else's behavior. Thus, as with interdependent group contingencies, dependent group punishment should be avoided. In addition, grades and other high-stakes consequences should not be given to all students contingent upon the performance of a target student. In addition, such procedures can encourage excessive and inappropriate peer pressure, all directed at the target student.

Despite these limitations, dependent group contingencies can be used in educational settings, but they must be used with care. For example, after each student's performance has been evaluated (e.g., test-graded), educators could randomly select a student and deliver reinforcement to the entire group contingent upon that student earning the reinforcement. It is critical for educators to identify and make public the randomly selected student if, and only if, the student's performance met the criterion. Thus, the entire group may praise and cheer the student who earned them the reward. Because students do not know who the target student is, they cannot apply excessive pressure (e.g., threaten) to that one student. In addition, because they cannot identify whose performance resulted in their failing to meet a group goal, they cannot target a particular student for aggression.

CONCLUSION

Some may question whether or not group contingencies should be used in educational settings. However, in most instances, educators are already using such procedures; they just don't realize it. Successful use of group contingencies requires educators to carefully consider the different types of contingencies available (e.g., reinforcement and punishment, and individual, independent, interdependent, and dependent), and contingencies components (target behaviors, criteria, and consequences). Careful consideration of these factors can allow educators to effectively reduce undesirable behaviors and encourage desirable behaviors using efficient and practical procedures while minimizing predictable negative side effects and maximizing positive side effects associated with such procedures.

See also: Negative Reinforcement; Peer Pressure; Positive Reinforcement; Punishment

BIBLIOGRAPHY

Popkin, J., & Skinner, C. H. (2003). Enhancing academic performance in a classroom serving students with serious emotional disturbance: Interdependent group contingencies with randomly selected components. *School Psychology Review, 32*, 282–295.

Skinner, C. H., Cashwell, C., & Dunn, M. (1996). Independent and interdependent group contingencies: Smoothing the rough waters. *Special Services in the Schools, 12*, 61–78.

Skinner, C. H., Skinner, A. L., & Sterling-Turner, H. E. (2002). Best practices in utilizing group contingencies for intervention and prevention. In A. Thomas & J. Grimes (Eds.), *Best practices in school psychology* (4th ed., pp. 817–830). Washington, DC: National Association of School Psychologists.

Additional Readings for Nonprofessionals

Cashwell, C. S., Skinner, C. H., Dunn, M., & Lewis, J. (1998). Group reward programs: A humanistic approach. *Humanistic Education and Development, 37*, 47–53.

Skinner, C. H., Skinner, C. F., Skinner, A. L., & Cashwell, T. C. (1999). Using interdependent contingencies with groups of students: Why the principal kissed a pig at assembly. *Educational Administration Quarterly, 35*, 806–820.

Additional Readings for Professionals

Kelshaw, K., Sterling-Turner, H. E., Henry, J., & Skinner, C. H. (2000). Randomized interdependent group contingencies: Group reinforcement with a twist. *Psychology in the Schools, 37*, 523–533.

Skinner, C. H., Cashwell, T. H., & Skinner, A. L. (2000). Increasing tootling: The effects of a peer monitored interdependent group contingencies on students' reports of peers' prosocial behaviors. *Psychology in the Schools, 37*, 263–270.

CHRISTOPHER H. SKINNER

Group Counseling

Group Counseling is a dynamic, complex, and extensively utilized treatment approach that involves the use of interpersonal process to assist children and adults with a wide array of issues, ranging from serious psychological pathology (e.g., severe depression) to normal developmental issues (e.g., how to get along with others). Subsequently, the two primary foci are remediation and prevention. When directed at the remediation of psychological problems, the goals of group counseling may include helping children cope with a parental divorce, death of a loved one, sexual abuse, school adjustment, and behavioral disorders. By contrast, the preventive use of group counseling might aim to facilitate healthy development such as social skills development, early exposure to career options, and the proper display of emotions.

Corisini and Rosenberg (1955), in a classic paper, eloquently outlined the mechanisms at work in group counseling. The nine mechanisms Corisini and Rosenberg discuss are considered the faculties that provide the power of a group process in bringing about therapeutic change. They are the following:

- *Acceptance.* This involves the development of respect and empathic understanding between group members and is a foundational characteristic that supports the development of trust within a group. Acceptance works against the feelings of alienation that members often bring to the process.
- *Ventilation.* In a group, members have a venue for expressing feelings and concerns that have remained unspoken previously.
- *Spectator Therapy.* One way to understand oneself is to understand how others deal with their problems. In a group, members gain perspective on themselves and learn by observing others work-through their concerns.

- *Feedback.* Groups are unique in that they provide honest assessments to individuals as to how the other group participants see and experience them. Hearing that someone believes "you are always making excuses for your behavior" can cause the hearer to begin reflecting upon their attitudes and thereby bring about change.

- *Universalization.* The experience of realizing that there are other people who think, feel, and behave similarly to oneself decreases feelings of isolation. Often when children (or adults) are experiencing a particular life difficulty, they falsely believe that they are unique in their problem, leading to a tendency to feel ashamed and lonely. The power of group counseling is that it can provide the unique experience that "I am not alone in my suffering" so that together "we can work to overcome our challenges."

- *Reality Testing.* Groups afford the opportunity for members to practice behaving in a new way within the relative safety of the therapeutic environment. The social relationships within the group provide an ideal setting to see how others are affected when new attitudes, values, actions, or relationship skills are acted out.

- *Altruism.* Most people possess a desire to help others and to see others succeed. Groups can accentuate this desire when members assist one another in making changes. This can be brought about by offering support and encouragement as well as by being the sounding board from which people learn how they are affecting others.

- *Interaction.* Humans are social creatures and are inherently motivated toward social relatedness. Groups allow for intense involvement with others in real and powerful ways, creating feelings of cohesiveness for all involved.

- *Installation of Hope.* The belief that things can and will get better is a powerful predictor of change. Because of their potential to offer support, connection, and acceptance, groups serve to instill and maintain a hopeful attitude among members.

Although the mechanisms outlined above address the processes at work in psychotherapeutic group work, in school settings the use of group counseling is predominately for preventative purposes. Nevertheless, elements of the remedial approach to group psychotherapy will be utilized to assist children without severe disorders in developing healthy self esteem, healthy coping/social skills or to teach decision making or other "life skills." As part of their job requirements, many school counselors are expected to provide developmental guidance to students. Developmental guidance group processes typically involve a structured use of groups wherein psychoeducation (teaching about psychological topics) is combined with psychological interventions (techniques that facilitate psychological change). It

is also likely that mental health personnel in the schools (i.e., school counselors, school psychologists, or social workers) will be called upon to provide group counseling for children who display problematic behaviors such as fighting, aggressiveness with peers, violent outbursts, noncompliance to classroom rules, or evidence of problems at home that are affecting the child's adjustment.

Practically, the economics of scale involved in group work, for example, seeing eight children together for 1 hour rather than one child during the same period of time, is an efficient use of resources. In schools, inpatient care facilities, youth centers, mental health centers, and other treatment localities, group counseling is the preferred method of service delivery because of the fact that multiple individuals can be served by a single mental health professional. Given that it is also a powerful approach it is not surprising that it is so often the treatment of choice.

A word of caution regarding the use of group counseling is warranted. Although rare, it is possible that some individuals are poorly suited to benefit from group counseling or may have a negative experience with groups. The use of confrontation, scapegoating, violation of group members' confidentiality, or pressure to comply with the groups' directives can be quite threatening for some people. Therefore, careful pre-group screening and strong group leadership is of great importance.

See also: Family Counseling; Individual Counseling

Additional Reading for Nonprofessionals

Gladding, S. T. (2003). *Group work: A counseling specialty.* Upper Saddle River, NJ: Merrill Prentice Hall.

Additional Readings for Professionals

Corey, G. (2004). *Theory and practice of group counseling* (6th ed.). Belmont, CA: Brooks/Cole.

Trotzer, J. P. (1999). *The counselor and the group: Integrating theory, training, and practice.* Philadelphia: Accelerated Development.

Yalom, I. (1995). *The theory and practice of group psychotherapy* (4th ed.). New York: Basic Books.

J. Scott Young

Guadalupe Organization, Inc. v. Tempe Elementary School District

Guadalupe v. Tempe was a class action suit filed on behalf of elementary school children of Mexican American and Yaqui Indian descent in the community of Guadalupe, Arizona. Originally filed in 1972, the suit was settled by consent decree, in which both parties negotiated a settlement before going to trial. Similar to other cases alleging misclassification of minority students (*Diana v. State Board of Education*, 1970; *Larry P. v. Riles*, 1970), the plaintiffs claimed that Hispanic and Native American children were overrepresented in special education programs in their district. These children were often classified as mentally retarded and placed in self-contained classes.

ALLEGATIONS OF PLAINTIFFS

The plaintiffs claimed that the overrepresentation of Hispanics and Native Americans in special education was a violation of equal protection and civil rights laws. They alleged that due process rights were violated because referrals and placement decisions were often made without parental notification, consent, or participation. In addition, the plaintiffs claimed that students being diagnosed and placed on the basis of verbal IQ scores was unfair to students with limited English proficiency. Finally, the plaintiffs complained that the district did not adequately fund special education programs or provide special education students with appropriate educational opportunities (Reschly & Bersoff, 1999).

SETTLEMENT

Because *Guadalupe v. Tempe* was settled by consent decree, the case never went to trial; however, the settlement was approved by the court. The agreement focused on two things. First, the school district would take steps to ensure that parents were not denied their due process rights concerning referral and placement decisions. The second part of the agreement

dealt with reforms in assessment methods. As in the *Diana v. State Board of Education* (1970) decision, the consent decree required that children be assessed in their primary language or through the use of nonverbal measures if the child had limited English proficiency. In addition, the agreement required that the district's assessment of referred children include a multifaceted evaluation including a parent interview and an assessment of the child's adaptive behavior. The agreement dealt very little with special education funding or programming changes (Reschly & Bersoff, 1999).

The *Guadalupe* suit and consent decree were important in safeguarding the rights of minorities in public education. Although the consent decree was important in establishing ethical and procedural guidelines for school psychologists, many of these guidelines were later incorporated into the Education of the Handicapped Act (EHA) in 1975 and the Individuals with Disabilities Education Act (IDEA) in 1991.

See also: Adaptive Behavior Assessment; *Diana v. State Board of Education*

BIBLIOGRAPHY

Reschly, D. J., & Bersoff, D. N. (1999). Law and school psychology. In C. R. Reynolds & T. B. Gutkin (Eds.), *The handbook of school psychology* (3rd ed., pp. 1077–1112). New York: Wiley.
Sattler, J. M. (1992). *Assessment of children* (3rd ed.). San Diego, CA: Author.

Additional Reading for Professionals

Reschly, D. J. (1979). Nonbiased assessment. In G. Phye & D. Reschly (Eds.), *School psychology: Perspectives and issues* (pp. 215–253). New York: Academic Press.

ADAM D. WEAVER

Hh

Habits

Simply defined, habits are repetitive, voluntary behaviors that occur across many different situations. Most individuals, at some point in their lives, will engage in a habit. Some of the most common habits include nail biting, thumb/finger sucking, foot tapping/shaking, teeth grinding, and hair twirling/pulling. Habits are generally harmless and go away without treatment. Some habits, however, can cause physical, social, academic/occupational, and psychological discomfort for the individual who exhibits them and/or their caregivers/teachers. For instance, a 5-year-old child who thumb-sucks in public may cause embarrassment for parents and may be teased by peers for thumb-sucking at kindergarten. In this situation, the thumb-sucking does not cause damage to the teeth but results in negative social interactions with others. Physical problems can also occur with bruxism (irregular and premature wear on teeth, malocclusion, damage to the temporomandibular joint, muscle tenderness in the face and neck), nail biting (scarring and infection of the nail bed and/or cuticles, shortening of tooth roots due to excessive pressure), and thumb-sucking after the age of 6 (overbites, malocclusions, and narrowing of the dental arches, deformities of the thumb). Because habits may sometimes result in negative physical, social, or psychological consequences, they should be closely monitored and treated, if necessary.

Historically, repetitive behaviors were referred to as "nervous habits," implying that the individual engaging in them was nervous or that they were indicative of more serious underlying psychopathology. Recent research suggests that children with habits are no more nervous or psychologically distressed than children without habits (Friman, Larzelere, & Finney, 1994). There is some evidence to support the hypothesis that habits may be related to increased anxiety or tension (Glaros & Melamed, 1992; Woods & Miltenberger, 1996). Of the possible explanations for the etiology of habits, perhaps the most parsimonious and likely is that habits are learned behaviors that take shape over time and continue because they either provide some sort of kinesthetic or tactile stimulation to the individual (automatic positive reinforcement) or result in the reduction of stimulation (automatic negative reinforcement). For instance, some children may suck their thumb because placing the thumb in the roof of the mouth feels good (tactile stimulation). Others may suck their thumb when they get into trouble or are upset because doing so reduces the feelings of upset or stress (automatic negative reinforcement). It is conceivable that some habits develop and persist because they become conditioned reinforcers by being paired with another stimulus that is either a conditioned reinforcer (e.g., watching cartoons) or unconditioned reinforcer (e.g., food, sleep). For example, a child might learn that twirling her hair while trying to go to sleep results in her falling asleep faster than if she did not twirl her hair.

TREATMENT

Habit reversal is the most effective treatment for habits. Azrin and Nunn (1973) developed the original 13-component habit-reversal procedure, which has subsequently been shortened to a three-component one. This shortened procedure is referred to as Simplified Habit Reversal and includes (a) awareness training, (b) competing response training, and (c) social support. The purpose of the awareness training component is to teach the child to become more aware of their habit or tic. After the child has become more aware of their habit and the other behaviors associated with it, a competing response is selected that is physically incompatible with the target response (e.g., hands clasped tightly together for thumb-sucking). The child is told to engage in the competing response, and prompted if necessary, for 1 minute contingent upon the occurrence of the habit. The third component is social support training. The purpose of social support training is to provide someone who will prompt and praise the competing response and to positively reinforce the absence of the habit (differential reinforcement).

In some cases, alternative treatments may be necessary. For instance, Watson and Allen (1993) successfully treated thumb-sucking and hair pulling in a 5-year-old by attaching a post to the child's thumb, which interfered with the tactile stimulation provided by thumb-sucking. In addition, they simultaneously implemented a grab bag reward system for positively reinforcing the absence of thumb-sucking and hair pulling. Another very effective treatment for eliminating thumb-sucking, but usually inappropriately used by parents, involves placing an unpleasant-tasting substance on the thumb (e.g., Stopzit, Thumbz, Ambisol). There is a specific protocol for using this procedure, that includes a reinforcement program and both contingent and noncontingent applications, and removal, of the substance (Friman & Leibowitz, 1990). Because many children who engage in habits do so with a preferred object (sometimes called a transitional object and may be a blanket, pillow, stuffed animal, etc.), removing the transitional object may result in cessation of the habit (Watson, Meeks, Dufrene, & Lindsay, 2002). Because of the highly specific nature of the interventions described here, parents should obtain the assistance of a professional before using any of them. It is also extremely important to note that punishment, by itself, is rarely effective for stopping habits and often increases the frequency and intensity of negative interactions between the child and parents/caregivers. For this reason, any type of treatment program for habits should always involve a very strong positive reinforcement component.

See also: Differential Reinforcement; Motor Tics; Negative Reinforcement; Positive Reinforcement; Vocal Tics

BIBLIOGRAPHY

Azrin, N. H., & Nunn, R. G. (1973). Habit reversal: A method of eliminating nervous habits and tics. *Behavior Research and Therapy, 11,* 619–628.

Friman, P. C., Larzelere, R., & Finney, J. W. (1994). Exploring the relationship between thumb-sucking and finger sucking. *Journal of Pediatric Psychology, 19,* 431–441.

Friman, P. C., & Leibowitz, M. J. (1990). An effective and acceptable treatment alternative for chronic thumb and finger sucking. *Journal of Pediatric Psychology, 15,* 57–65.

Glaros, A. G., & Melamed, G. G. (1992). Bruxism in children: Etiology and treatment. *Applied and Preventive Psychology, 1,* 191–199.

Watson, T. S., & Allen, K. D. (1993). Elimination of thumb-sucking as a treatment for severe trichotillomania. *Journal of the American Academy of Child and Adolescent Psychiatry, 32,* 830–834.

Watson, T. S., Meeks, C., Dufrene, B., & Lindsay, C. (2002). Sibling thumb sucking: Effects of treatment for targeted and untargeted siblings. *Behavior Modification, 26,* 412–423.

Woods, D. W., & Miltenberger, R. G. (1996). Are persons with nervous habits nervous? A preliminary examination of habit function in a nonreferred population. *Journal of Applied Behavior Analysis, 29,* 259–261.

Additional Readings for Nonprofessionals

Hadley, N. H. (1984). *Nail biting.* New York: Spectrum. http://www.tigerchild.com/pages/1741.asp

Additional Readings for Professionals

Peterson, A. L., Campose, R. L., & Azrin, N. H. (1994). Behavioral and pharmacological treatments for tic and habit disorders: A review. *Journal of Developmental and Behavioral Pediatrics, 15,* 430–441.

Watson, T. S., & Sterling, H. E. (1998). Habits and tics. In T. S. Watson & F. M. Gresham (Eds.), *Handbook of child behavior therapy* (pp. 431–450). New York: Plenum.

Woods, D. W., & Miltenberger, R. G. (Eds.). (2001). *Tic disorders, trichotillomania, and other repetitive behavior disorders: Behavioral approaches to analysis and treatment.* Boston: Kluwer.

T. STEUART WATSON

Hall, G. Stanley

Credited with receiving the first Ph.D. in Psychology granted in the United States and with founding the American Psychological Association in 1892, G. Stanley Hall is regarded as a pioneer of American psychology. Although his contributions to psychological research and theory are minimal, Hall left his mark on the field by establishing several scholarly journals and through his efforts to gain respect for professional psychology in America.

BEGINNINGS

Granville Stanley Hall was born in Ashfield, Massachusetts, in 1844 to a family that valued education as both parents had taught school for several years. Hall briefly taught school before enrolling in Williams College in 1863. There, he studied philosophy after periods of interest in religion and literature. Following his graduation in 1867, Hall enrolled at Union Theological Seminary in New York City, with plans of becoming a clergyman. After a year of enjoying many of the new experiences and opportunities available in the city, Hall began to lose his zeal for joining the clergy. When financial assistance became available from a local businessman, Hall made his way to Germany to study philosophy and theology. After his money ran out, Hall returned to Union Theological Seminary for his final year in 1871.

ACADEMIA

With no interest in being a clergyman, Hall began trying to secure a position at a college. It was 2 years before he was granted a post at Antioch College in Ohio teaching English literature. After 4 years at Antioch College, Hall was informed that the institution could no longer afford to keep him. Hall then left for Harvard, where he was offered an instructorship in English. While there, he began work on a Ph.D. in philosophy under a young assistant professor, William James. Hall completed his Ph.D. in psychology in 1878, the first conferred in the United States.

Again, Hall had trouble finding an academic position for some time, until he was invited by the president of Harvard to give a series of lectures on education. Partly because of the success of his lectures at Harvard, Hall was invited in 1882 to lecture at Johns Hopkins University. The next year, he established the first psychology laboratory in the United States at Hopkins. In 1884, Hall was appointed Professor of Psychology in the Department of Philosophy at Johns Hopkins. James McKeen Cattell, John Dewey, and Edmund Sanford were among Hall's students at Hopkins.

In 1888, Hall was named president of the newly established Clark University in Worcester, Massachusetts. Hall's plan was to make Clark a center of research and science, emphasizing graduate instruction, and surpass Johns Hopkins. To that purpose, he put together "perhaps the strongest research faculty to ever grace an American university" (Sokal, 1990, p. 114). In addition to President, Hall also served as Professor, and brought with him many bright students from Johns Hopkins. Unfortunately, as the university's benefactor and founder, Jonas Clark, began to reduce his financial support, many of the best professors and students began to leave. Hall's personality and administration style were also frequently blamed for the deterioration of Clark University's prestige in the 1890s and early 1900s (Sokal, 1990).

ESTABLISHING PROFESSIONAL AND SCIENTIFIC PSYCHOLOGY

In 1892, Hall invited 26 of the brightest American psychologists to Clark University to establish the first scientific organization of psychologists. These 26 would become charter members of the American Psychological Association (APA), and Hall was elected the first president. Although he would continue to exert his influence on American psychology, Hall's control of the APA would not last long. Within a few years, the APA was dominated by followers of William James, and Hall no longer even attended meetings (Watson & Evans, 1991).

Hall also left his mark on professional psychology through the establishment of several journals. While a professor at Johns Hopkins University in 1887, Hall founded the *American Journal of Psychology*, the first English-language journal devoted to psychology (Watson & Evans, 1991). Hall dedicated the new journal to promotion of new scientific psychology in place of traditional philosophical psychology and remained editor until 1921. In 1893, while at Clark, Hall founded his second journal, the *Pedagogical Seminary* (now the *Journal of Genetic Psychology*), dedicated to research in child study and educational psychology. The new journal may have been part of an attempt to improve public opinion of Clark University, as the university was experiencing financial difficulty and negative publicity locally. The journal, however, was a success with educators and circulation was unexpectedly large. Finally, in 1917, Hall founded *The Journal of Applied Psychology*, dedicated to research in applied settings.

CHILD STUDY AND EDUCATIONAL PSYCHOLOGY

In 1885, Hall offered the nation's first workshop for kindergarten teachers. In addition, his interest and research in children's thinking led to the popularity and public enthusiasm of the "child study" movement of the late 1800s. Although there were many limitations in much of the early research and many psychologists spoke out against the movement, the child-study movement led directly to the empirical study of children. By the early 1900s, the term *educational psychology* had replaced *child study*. Hall's legacy to the fields of clinical psychology and educational psychology persist today, if not in theory and scholarship, in honor of his vision and tireless efforts to professionalize psychology at least.

See also: American Psychological Association—Division 16

BIBLIOGRAPHY

G. Stanley Hall: Founder of the Journal of Genetic Psychology: Biography. (1991). *Journal of Genetic Psychology, 152,* 397–403.

Sokal, M. M. (1990). G. Stanley Hall and the institutional character of psychology at Clark 1889–1920. *Journal of the History of the Behavioral Sciences, 26,* 114–124.

Watson, R. I., Sr., & Evans, R. B. (1991). *The great psychologists: A history of psychological thought* (5th ed.). New York: HarperCollins.

Additional Reading for Nonprofessionals

Hilgard, E. R. (1996). Perspectives on educational psychology. *Educational Psychology Review, 8,* 419–431.

Additional Readings for Professionals

Nance, R. D. (1970). G. Stanley Hall and John B. Watson as child psychologists. *Journal of the History of the Behavioral Sciences, 6,* 303–316.

White, S. H. (2002). G. Stanley Hall: From philosophy to developmental psychology. In W. E. Pickren (Ed.), *Evolving perspectives on the history of psychology* (pp. 279–302). Washington, DC: American Psychological Association.

ADAM D. WEAVER

Hobson v. Hanson (1967, 1969)

Throughout the mid-twentieth century, aptitude testing was used in public schools to assign students to varying levels of classes. In 1967, Hanson challenged this method of determining education levels in Washington, DC, public schools and turned to the courts to have the equal-protection clause enforced because blacks were not receiving an equal education. Hanson claimed that the lower-level tracks had inferior amenities, lesser teaching, and inadequate programs. Hobson and the school system argued that the tracking system was created in order to advance learning opportunities for black students who did poorly on the aptitude testing. However, the school placed 95 percent of the blacks in the school in the lowest track even though they comprised 90 percent of the district's population. Grades, teachers' recommendations, and various standardized aptitude tests and achievement tests determined the placement of each student, according to the school district.

Judge Wright determined that the group aptitude test scores were the most important factor for educational track placement. Thus, the tests were scrutinized for their capacity to determine the ability levels of students. The court determined that the tests did not determine ability level, but rather showed the differences on achievement in terms of environmental influences. The judge ruled that the tests were biased to the poor and to blacks because these groups had fewer learning opportunities than middle- to upper-class children, so the differences in scores were influenced by this to some degree. He also noted that the tests lacked the ability to determine the relative influence of environment and "innate" ability. Judge Wright also ruled that the tests were "standardized primarily on and are relevant to a white middle-class group of students, they produce inaccurate and misleading test scores when given to lower-class and Negro students." Of the disproportionate assignment to tracking levels, Judge Wright ruled that because it grouped students by race and that lower tracks provided lesser educational opportunities, it was in violation of the equal-protection clause. He also found that the school district tracks were stigmatizing and unbending, and banned the school district from use of the tracking system.

Hobson v. Hanson resulted in a new criterion for tests to be used for placement purposes. Judge Wright established that these tests should be able to measure innate ability. However, tracking systems are not necessarily based on innate ability levels. Nonetheless, it lessened the importance of aptitude testing for placement purposes in education. Still, Judge Wright did not prohibit unequal assignment of students, but he did bring to the forefront the practice of segregation by testing.

See also: Diana v. State Board of Education

BIBLIOGRAPHY

Jacob-Timm, S., & Hartshorne, T. S. (Eds.). (1998). *Ethics and law for school psychologists* (3rd ed.). New York: Wiley.

Reynolds, C. R., & Gutkin, T. B. (Eds.). (1999). *The handbook of school psychology* (3rd ed.). New York: Wiley.

NICHOLAS E. HODA

Homework

Homework has been described as a complex, multifaceted activity that is a common ground where parent, student, and formal school activities intersect (Hoover-Dempsey, Bassler, & Burrow, 1995). Homework, when used as a means to review past work and rehearse current work, is one of many highly effective academic tools fostering long-term academic growth and success in school. Any teacher-developed homework system should include clear instructions, procedures leading to completion, and evaluation of completion accuracy (Belfiore & Hutchinson, 1998).

CLEAR INSTRUCTIONS

Belfiore and Hutchinson (1998) suggest all homework assignments must begin with specific written and/or verbal instructions that are functional and age-appropriate, so that students can independently complete the required assignment(s). Instructions to be included in all homework assignments should include information regarding homework outcome, deadline for completion, and grading. In addition, homework instructions may include (a) assignments of responsibilities if homework requires group participation, (b) information linking outcomes to statewide standards, (c) strategies to use if help is needed, and (d) strategies for self-management. Instructions for homework should also take into consideration the native home language. If the parents' first language is not English, but homework instructions are, the opportunity for parent support and the student's completion of homework may be diminished.

Although homework is most effective when the focus is on fluency of learned materials (i.e., practice), some teachers will assign new materials for homework. Waldron (1996) suggests homework that introduces new materials or new strategies, should be previewed and begun in school before the student leaves for home, allowing the teacher to answer any questions that may arise later. This in-class preparation for homework is especially critical for students who may not have the time, resources, and/or assistance to complete homework at home (Belfiore & Hutchinson, 1998). In general, this recommendation makes sense for all types of homework. Teachers, students, as well as parents need to be "on the same page" to ensure accurate homework completion within the deadlines prescribed.

COMPLETION PROCEDURES

Once instructions are established, delivered, and understood, students must begin the act of homework completion. Homework, like other academic related routines (e.g., note taking, study skills), is best mastered when the steps to homework completion can be operationally defined, task analyzed, and, ultimately, self-managed. One example of a homework routine that has been used in an urban after-school program requires students to answer a sequence of "yes/no" questions: (a) "Is all my homework in the folder?" (b) "Do I have a pencil?" (c) "Begin homework?" (d) "Is all homework complete?" (e) "Did someone check my homework?" and (f) "Is homework back in folder?" When students in the after-school program were first introduced to the homework routine, the teacher walked all students through the skill sequence, as well as initialed all homework routine checklists (step e). Once students began to master the homework routine steps, the teacher randomly checked the routine, while students continued to self-manage. The shift from teacher-delivered to student-directed is critical for effective self-management of any academic routine. Alternatively, the homework routine can be sent home along with the homework, with the parent initially assisting the student in homework and routine completion.

Although several authors (e.g., Hoover-Dempsey et al., 1995) correctly point out that parents play a significant role in forming the attitudes and work habits that underlie success in homework, parental involvement, for whatever reason, is not always present. In efforts to better guarantee homework completion and accuracy when parental/caregiver support is not always a certainty, after-school clubs (like the one described

above) allow all students to complete homework in school. In addition, after-school clubs allow for the assistance of teachers on-site, to answer questions that may arise while completing the assignment.

The last requirement when completing homework is returning the homework to school. In the example above, students in the after-school program returned all completed homework, in the folder, to the teacher in charge before leaving the school. In this instance, the homework never left the school. When assigned homework is to be completed outside of school, options for turning in homework should include time (e.g., before first bell, at 9:30) and location (e.g., homework collection file, teacher desk).

OUTCOME EVALUATION

The third step of any homework activity requires the monitoring of completion and accuracy. To address this component of homework evaluation, O'Melia and Rosenberg (1994) created Cooperative Homework Teams (CHT). Heterogeneous teams of three to four students were organized to evaluate homework completion and accuracy. Following overnight homework assignments, the CHT met and evaluated the assignments the next day. O'Melia and Rosenberg (1994) found that homework completion and homework accuracy increased in those CHT that evaluated, graded, revised, and regraded homework during team time the next day. Belfiore and Hutchinson (1998) state that explicit instruction and homework engagement are necessary and important steps, but without the final step of outcome evaluation, the usefulness of the homework activity is questionable. Including these three steps increases the likelihood that homework will function as the academic tool it was designed to be.

See also: Academic Interventions for Written Language and Grammar

BIBLIOGRAPHY

Belfiore, P. J., & Hutchinson, J. M. (1998). Enhancing academic achievement through related routines: A functional approach. In T. S. Watson & F. M. Gresham (Eds.), *Handbook of child behavior therapy* (pp. 83–97). New York: Plenum.

Hoover-Dempsey, K. V., Bassler, O. C., & Burrow, R. (1995). Parents' reported involvement in students' homework: Strategies and practices. *The Elementary School Journal, 95,* 435–450.

O'Melia, M. C., & Rosenberg, M. S. (1994). Effects of cooperative homework teams on the acquisition of mathematics skills by secondary students with mild disabilities. *Exceptional Children, 60,* 538–548.

Waldron, K. A. (1996). *Introduction to special education: The inclusive classroom.* Boston: Delmar.

Additional Readings for Nonprofessionals

Heron, T. E., & Harris, K. C. (2001). *The educational consultant.* Austin, TX: Pro-Ed.

Mims, A., Harper, C., Armstrong, S. W., & Savage, S. (1991). Effective instruction in homework for students with disabilities. *Teaching Exceptional Children, 24,* 42–44.

Additional Readings for Professionals

Hall, A. M., & Zentall, S. S. (2000). The effects of a learning station on the completion and accuracy of math homework for middle school students. *Journal of Behavioral Education, 10,* 123–138.

Miller, D. L., & Kelley, M. L. (1994). The use of goal setting and contingency contracting for improving children's homework performance. *Journal of Applied Behavior Analysis, 27,* 73–84.

Olympia, D. E., Sheridan, S. M., Jenson, W. R., & Andrews, D. (1994). Using student-managed interventions to increase homework completion and accuracy. *Journal of Applied Behavior Analysis, 27,* 85–99.

PHILLIP J. BELFIORE

Huntington Learning Centers

Huntington Learning Centers are franchised businesses designed to provide assistance to students experiencing academic difficulties. Founded in 1977 by Raymond and Eileen Huntington, the centers are very similar to the more widely recognized Sylvan Learning Centers. Huntington centers provide an on-site diagnosis of the academic problem and offer individualized programs and assistance. Huntington offers programs for math, reading, writing, phonics, study skills, and other related areas.

Although the diagnostic testing will provide information to the Huntington staff about the student's specific area(s) of weakness, all of the programs focus on building basic skills. For example, a basic study skill may be writing down homework assignments and test dates, whereas a basic skill of math could be addition or subtraction. The programs then build on these basic skills so that the student increases his/her performance in the area identified in the diagnostic assessment.

Huntington emphasizes the development of students' self-confidence and motivation as well as improved academic performance. The center staff provides frequent positive reinforcement such as stickers, candy, drinks, and time to work problems with peers. By providing immediate rewards for academic performance, Huntington's goal is to make learning more fun and productive. Huntington's philosophy is that most students are caught in a "failure chain," or a cycle of frustration and failure. Making learning more fun and recognizing student success allows this cycle to weaken.

Many children with academic difficulties have skill deficits, or areas where they do not have a specific skill such as adding or reading at grade level. However, some children also have performance deficits. These are the students who have the ability or skill to do the task, but for whatever reason do not perform the task accurately or even at all. Huntington's programs are designed to resolve both skill and performance deficits.

Regardless of the academic area in which the student receives tutoring, he/she always begins with academic material that he/she is capable of doing. Students progress to more difficult material as performance and self-confidence increase. Huntington reports that 90 percent of students with reading difficulties and 80 percent of students with math difficulties have improved grades in school. This is based on parental report and is not documented by controlled studies from outside sources. Although Huntington also reports that the majority of parents would recommend their services, consumers should be aware that Huntington's services have not been systematically compared to any of the other tutoring services or to other academic interventions.

Huntington Learning Centers are accredited by the Commission on International and Trans-Regional Accreditation, and all of the teachers are certified. Services are available for children aged 5–17. Like most of the other private tutoring companies, Huntington offers test preparation for the American College Test (ACT) and the Scholastic Aptitude Test (SAT). The ACT and SAT are the two most widely used entrance exams for admission to college. Huntington states that most students' scores increase by 200 points after taking their prep course.

Some school districts have contracted with private companies like Huntington to improve student performance. Two elementary schools in Washington, DC, hired Huntington to improve reading scores in eighth-grade students. One school reported that 31 percent of students advanced a full grade level whereas many other students had more modest gains. The report from the second school indicates that the greatest improvements were in vocabulary, followed by reading comprehension (Tress, 1998). It is possible that many other districts have used Huntington's services and failed to report the results. However, consumers should be aware that there are very little data available from outside sources that substantiate Huntington's claims.

Huntington Learning Centers can be contacted via their Web site, www.huntingtonlearning.com or via telephone, 1-800-CAN-LEARN. Other parent and teacher resources are also available on Huntington's Web site, including advice for increasing involvement at home, improving grades, and preparation for college. Fees are not advertised on the Web site and vary significantly by location. Parents are advised to directly contact the Huntington center in their area to obtain current prices.

See also: Academic Interventions for Written Language and Grammar; Kaplan, Incorporated; Sylvan Learning Centers

BIBLIOGRAPHY

Hunting Learning Center. Retrieved September 15, 2002, from http://www.huntingtonlearning.com.
Tress, M. H. (1998). Schools and tutoring companies tailor programs for student success. *Curriculum Administrator, 34,* 38–40.

Additional Readings for Nonprofessionals

Greene, L. J. (2002). *Roadblocks to learning: Understanding the obstacles that sabotage your child's academic success.* New York: Warner Books.

Shore, K. (1998). *Special kids problem solver: Ready to use interventions for helping all students with academic, behavioral, and physical problems.* Englewood Cliffs, NJ: Prentice–Hall.

Additional Readings for Professionals

Eckert, T. L., Ardoin, S. P., Daly, E. J., & Martens, B. K. (2002). Improving oral reading fluency: A brief experimental analysis of combining an antecedent intervention with consequences. *Journal of Applied Behavior Analysis, 35,* 271–282.
Skinner, C. H., & Robinson, S. L. (2002). Interspersing additional easier items to enhance mathematics performance on subtests requiring different task demands. *School Psychology Quarterly, 17,* 191–205.

NANCY FOSTER

Ii

Impulse Control Disorders

Impulsive behavior is both a basic aspect of human behavior and a feature of several psychological disorders found in children and adolescents. Impulsive behavior can describe individuals who act without previous planning or anticipation of the consequences of their behavior, who make decisions that fail to consider alternative courses of action or who are simply acting in a carefree manner. Impulse control disorders in children and adolescents are viewed from two distinct vantage points. First, there are specific psychological disorders found in children and adolescents that are associated with symptoms of impulsivity and lack of control (i.e., Attention-Deficit/Hyperactivity Disorder, Conduct Disorder, Bipolar Disorder), but other symptoms must be present for a diagnosis to be made. Specific impulse control disorders, which may be diagnosed during childhood/adolescence and defined primarily by impulsivity or a loss of control, include Intermittent Explosive Disorder (see entry in this volume), Pyromania, Kleptomania, Pathological Gambling, and Trichotillomania (see entry in this volume). These disorders are as striking in their differences as they are in their similarities. In this group, Pyromania and Kleptomania are disorders most frequently seen in the child/adolescent population.

CHARACTERISTICS

As a general class of problems, impulse control disorders have several common features. There is a *failure to resist* an impulse or drive to initiate an act that is harmful to oneself or to others. There may or may not be *conscious resistance* to performing the behavior and the behavior may or may not

be premeditated. There is often an *increased tension* or *arousal*, which leads up to the impulsive act and the act may be followed by a *sense of relief, gratification,* or *pleasure* upon completion. There may or may not be a sense of guilt or self-regret associated with the impulsive act.

BASE RATES

Less than 5 percent of shoplifting cases are associated with a diagnosis of Kleptomania. The disorder may begin in childhood or adolescence and continue into adulthood, despite multiple convictions for shoplifting. Fire setting is a major problem in children and adolescents. Over 40 percent of arson-related offenses involve individuals under the age of 18 (*DSM-IV-TR*; American Psychiatric Association, 2000). Juvenile fire setting is often associated with Conduct Disorder, Attention-Deficit/Hyperactivity Disorder, or Adjustment Disorder. Although arson is a major source of property damage, studies indicate that the diagnoses of pyromania represent a small fraction of perpetrators, with estimates ranging from 1 to 4 percent. Similarly, although childhood fire setting is quite common, rarely is the diagnosis of pyromania made. This suggests that efforts should be directed toward evaluating fire-setters first for other diagnoses such as conduct disorder, antisocial personality disorder, substance abuse, or other conditions where judgment can be impaired (mental retardation, psychosis, etc.).

CAUSES AND CONTRIBUTORY FACTORS

Both neurobiological factors and psychological origins have been identified. The serotonin system is believed to be more important in the expression of impulsivity, and lowered serotonin levels have been associated with impulsive behavior (Reist, 1997). Serotonin may serve as a behavioral restraint; checking for signals of nonreward, punishment, and uncertainty apart from some pharmacologic manipulations support this model. For example, animals with impaired serotonin levels (due to blockade of serotonin synthesis or lesions of specific nuclei) exhibit behavior described as hyperirritable and hyperexciteable. Social learning models developed by Kolko and Kazdin (1989) suggest that early learning experiences, parental and family influences/stressors/pathology, and individual personal repertoires (behavioral, motivational, and cognitive) may put children at risk for impulse control problems, including fire setting. Most school-age children with fire-setting behavior have histories of school failure and multiple behavior problems (Kolko, 2002; Rasanen, Hirvenoja, Hakko, & Vaisanen, 1995). More recently, impulse control disorders with these features have been identified in terms of an obsessive–compulsive spectrum, which produces the specific behaviors.

KLEPTOMANIA

The diagnostic criteria for Kleptomania include a recurrent failure to resist impulses to steal objects that are not needed for personal use or for their monetary value; an increasing sense of tension immediately before committing the theft; and pleasure, gratification, or relief at the time of committing the theft. The stealing is not typically committed to express anger or vengeance, is not in response to a delusion or a hallucination, and is not better accounted for by Conduct Disorder, Mania, or Antisocial Personality Disorder. The diagnosis of Kleptomania is reserved for individuals who engage in shoplifting of items they neither want nor need. Although the diagnosis is made most frequently in adult women (average age at presentation is about 35 years), the age of onset is much younger (<20 years old). Individuals with this disorder also have high rates of depression and social isolation. Bulimia may also be associated with this disorder.

PYROMANIA

Pyromania is typically diagnosed when there is deliberate and purposeful fire setting on more than one occasion. Typically, the diagnosis occurs more frequently in males with poor social skills and learning problems. Tension or affective arousal occurs before the act and there is fascination with, interest in, curiosity about, or attraction to fire and its situational contexts. To receive the diagnosis of Pyromania, the fire setting is not done for monetary gain, as an expression of sociopolitical ideology, to conceal criminal activity, to express anger or vengeance, to improve one's living circumstances, in response to a delusion

or hallucination, or as a result of impaired judgment. Conduct Disorder, Mania, or Antisocial Personality Disorder are also ruled out.

INTERVENTIONS OR THERAPIES

Effective psychological interventions for impulse control disorders have typically focused on multicomponent strategies using a variety of cognitive and cognitive–behavioral strategies. Social skills training, educative overcorrection, relaxation training/stress management, stimulus control, and response cost procedures coupled with experiential activities (visits to burn units/hospitals, etc.) have been used with considerable success (Koles & Jenson, 1985; Opdyke & Olasov-Rothbaum, 1998). Cognitive–behavioral therapy has been used often in conjunction with medications such as lithium and SSRI antidepressants (e.g., naltrexone or paroxetine). Although success has been successfully demonstrated across the short term (Feeney & Klykylo, 1997; Grant & Kim, 2002), systematic long-term treatment studies are lacking. Impulse control disorders can have a chronic course despite repeated legal and personal consequences.

See also: Antisocial Behavior; Attention-Deficit/Hyperactivity Disorder; Conduct Disorder; Intermittent Explosive Disorder; Trichotillomania

BIBLIOGRAPHY

Feeney, D. J., & Klykylo, W. M. (1997). Treatment for kleptomania. *Journal of the American Academy of Child and Adolescent Psychiatry, 36,* 723–724.

Grant, J. E., & Kim, S. W. (2002). Adolescent kleptomania treated with naltrexone: A case report. *European Child and Adolescent Psychiatry, 11,* 92–95.

Koles, M. R., & Jenson, W. R. (1985). Comprehensive treatment of chronic firesetting in a severely disordered boy. *Journal of Behavior Therapy and Experimental Psychiatry, 16,* 81–85.

Kolko, D. (2002). *Handbook on firesetting in children and youth.* San Diego: Academic Press.

Kolko, D. J., & Kazdin, A. E. (1989). The Children's Firesetting Interview with psychiatrically referred and non-referred children. *Journal of Abnormal Child Psychology, 17,* 609–624.

Opdyke, D., & Olasov-Rothbaum, B. (1998). Cognitive–behavioral treatment of impulse control disorders. In V. Caballo (Ed.), *International handbook of cognitive and behavioral treatments for psychological disorders* (pp. 417–439). Oxford, England: Pergaman

Rasanen, P., Hirvenoja, R., Hakko, H., & Vaisanen, E. (1995). A portrait of the juvenile arsonist. *Forensic Science International, 73,* 41–47.

Reist, C. (1997). Serotonin and impulsivity. *Directions in Psychiatry, 17,* 297–301.

Daniel E. Olympia
William R. Jenson

Inclusion

Inclusion succeeded mainstreaming to further integrate students with and without disabilities into the common educational setting. The practice of mainstreaming students with disabilities into the general/regular education setting developed out of the civil rights movement in the years between 1954 and 1975. The term *mainstreaming* retained its popularity through the end of the 1980s when the terminology and philosophy of mainstreaming was supplanted by *inclusion*.

The differences between mainstreaming and inclusion are in the degree of integration and cooperation between general/regular and special education service delivery systems. One published definition proposed "Inclusion schools embrace the values of diversity and learning communities. Student needs (i.e., academic and/or social) are accomplished through the implementation of combined resources and supports within one setting" (Reddy, 1999, p. 10). The values of inclusion were advocated for by three divergent groups and long-term goals: (a) dismantle and eliminate special education, (b) reduce the costs of special education service delivery, or (c) maximize the normalization of the educational experiences of disabled populations while maintaining the support services of special education within the inclusion setting (Reddy, 1999). The contrast between these goals demonstrates the division within the inclusion debate.

Within a system that promotes inclusion, roles and practices are often modified. The special education teacher is likely to adopt new roles and practices to enable students within the inclusion classroom. The *inclusion classroom* describes a general/regular education setting that adopts practices to serve an integrated population. Within the context of the inclusion classroom, the special education teacher is often described as an *inclusion teacher*. The inclusion teacher adopts new roles and engages in *inclusion practices* that might include (a) coteaching with the general/regular education teacher, (b) preteaching skills, concepts, or vocabulary, (c) supervising peer tutors or integrated study periods, (d) monitoring progress of students, (e) developing individualized study materials, or (f) working within small groups of students with disabilities to structure learning activities. These inclusion practices are broadly described as adapting and modifying instruction and curriculum. The practice of adapting curriculum and instruction retains the substance of instructional objectives of general education, but activities and materials are adapted to facilitate inclusion. For example, in a high school science inclusion class, a reading assignment might be adapted by the inclusion teacher for a student with a reading disability using strategies like preteaching important terms and highlighting the important content in the textbook to emphasize the most important concepts (and

limit student reading). Adaptive practices are most appropriate for students with disabilities who exhibit a general level of functioning that closely approximates their class peers without disabilities. Children whose skills are significantly lower than their peers often require modification of curriculum and individualized instructional objectives. *Modified* activities within a content area diverge in their instructional objectives (unlike adapted activities) but are parallel in the content emphasis of the inclusion class. For example, in a high school science inclusion class, a reading assignment might be modified for a student with a developmental delay (mental retardation, autism) so that the student categorizes pictures into concept groups while other students learn technical vocabulary and read chapters. The distinction between adaptive and modified activities in the inclusion setting is defined by the overlap of instructional objectives. The cooperation and integration of services and activities are indispensable within the inclusion school/classroom.

IDEOLOGY AND RESEARCH

By the mid-1980s, the Regular Education Initiative (REI) had begun to expand the boundaries of what had been described as mainstreaming (Reynolds, Wang, & Walberg, 1987). REI initiated the movement toward inclusion. The goal of REI was to improve general and special education by combining the service delivery systems. The goal was based on the assumptions that (a) students served by both general/regular education and special education are more similar than different, (b) quality instructional practices are similar across populations, (c) quality instruction and placement is not dependent on categorical labels, (d) classrooms can be managed and modified to serve a diverse group of students across settings, and (e) segregated placement is inherently discriminatory (Reynolds et al., 1987). These assumptions were generally accepted among inclusion advocates despite empirical evidence to the contrary. For example, the most comprehensive review (meta-analysis) of the research at that time suggested there was an interaction between disability types and the effects of either self-contained or general/regular education placement (Calberg & Kavale, 1980). For example, students with specific learning disabilities and emotional/behavior problems tended to demonstrate positive effects when placed in pull-out programs and self-contained remedial settings. Students with severe developmental disabilities (autism, mental retardation) tended to demonstrate more positive effects when integrated into the general/regular education setting. Advocacy for a broad policy of inclusion continues despite research-based evidence to the contrary (Kavale, 2000). The most recent reviews of research suggest the actual physical placement might be of less importance than the actual instructional practices (Forness, 2001; Kavale & Forness, 1999). These findings are inconsistent with inclusion because they support an emphasis on *what is done* and not *where it is done*. Although such research does inform the inclusion debate, it does not resolve it. Inclusion is premised by an egalitarian philosophy that emphasizes values that elude research, such as the diversity, acceptance, and community. The research tends to address measurable outcomes such as academic and functional skill development.

SCHOOL-BASED PRACTICES

Deno (1970) presented the Cascade Model for service delivery to define the physical placement options for students with varying degrees of exceptionality (mild to severe). These placement options ranged from the general/regular education classroom to a residential/hospital setting. The Cascade Model was replaced by problem solving models within the context of inclusion. Problem solving models are consistent with inclusion because they are less setting-specific. These models emphasize resource allocation relative to educational objectives and deemphasize that service provision is site-specific settings. For example, the Heartland Problem Solving Model provides a schematic to guide resource allocation and service delivery within an inclusion school (Tilly, 2002). The schematic provides a framework to match problem severity with the appropriate inclusion resources that are necessary to solve the problem. The problem solving model emphasizes neither the physical setting nor the disability status. Instead, the emphasis is placed on student needs relative to the allocation of available resources. Within the problem solving system, educators "create ways that service intensity can be varied in direct proportion to individual student needs within and outside special education boundaries. This situation is desirable from a student learning standpoint and cost efficient from a resource allocation standpoint" (p. 23). Although problem solving models have not been popularized in practice to the same degree as inclusion practices, recent government reports and legislation encourage the practice of problem solving within an inclusion system. For example, recent legislation has focused on early intervention and promotion of academic skills to prevent the academic deficits and disabilities ("No child left behind," 2001). That is, early intervention and prevention of learning problems through the use of problem solving and integrated service delivery has gained emphasis on a national level (President's Commission on Excellence in Special Education, 2002).

Early prevention and intervention is one example of how inclusion practices continue to develop. These practices are consistent with inclusion because they emphasize the integration of service delivery systems (general education, special education, Title 1, Parent Volunteers, Teacher Associates). Within the developing prevention and intervention models, school communities have begun to integrate and distribute resources to solve and prevent problems in the school community.

See also: Mainstreaming

BIBLIOGRAPHY

Calberg, C., & Kavale, K. (1980). The efficacy of special versus regular class placement for exceptional children: A meta-analysis. *The Journal of Special Education, 14,* 295–309.

Deno, S. L. (1970). Special education as developmental capital. *Exceptional Children, 37,* 229–237.

Forness, S. R. (2001). Special education and related services: What have we learned from meta-analysis? *Exceptional Children, 9,* 185–197.

Kavale, K. A. (2000). History, rhetoric, and reality. *Remedial & Special Education, 21*(5), 277–296.

Kavale, K. A., & Forness, S. R. (1999). *Efficacy of special education and related services.* Washington, DC: American Association on Mental Retardation.

No child left behind. (2001). pp. 107–110.

President's Commission on Excellence in Special Education. (2002). *A new era: Revitalizing special education for children and their families* (Report No. ED-02-PO-0791). Washington, DC: Author.

Reddy, L. A. (1999). Inclusion of disabled children and school reform: A historical perspective. In L. R. Reddy (Ed.), *Inclusion practices with special needs students: Theory, research, and application* (pp. 3–24). New York: Hawthorne.

Reynolds, C. R., Wang, M. C., & Walberg, H. J. (1987). The necessary restructuring of special education. *Exceptional Children, 53,* 391–398.

Tilly, W. D. (2002). Best practices in school psychology as a problem-solving enterprise. In A. Thomas & J. Grimes (Eds.), *Best practices in school psychology IV* (pp. 21–36). Bethesda, MD: National Association of School Psychologists.

Additional Readings for Professionals and Nonprofessionals

Kavale, K. A. (2000). History, rhetoric, and reality. *Remedial & Special Education, 21,* 277–296.

Pfeiffer, S. I., & Reddy, L. R. (Eds.). (1999). *Inclusion practices with special needs students: Theory, research, and application.* New York: Hawthorne.

Prasse, D. P. (1995). Best practices in school psychology and the law. In J. Grimes & A. Thomas (Eds.), *Best practices in school psychology III* (pp. 41–50). Bethesda, MD: National Association of School Psychologists.

Sands, D. J., Kozleski, E. B., & French, N. K. (2000). *Inclusive education for the 21st century.* Belmont, CA: Wadsworth.

THEODORE J. CHRIST
ELIZABETH A. LYONS

Individual Counseling

Individual counseling was born out of psychoanalytic theory first developed by Sigmund Freud. Many of the basic tenets of other popular theories either build on the concepts of psychoanalytic theory or are a reaction against this theory. Since the birth of individual counseling, many theories and approaches have been introduced and many more are still emerging. Though there are many theories, there are some basic similarities among them.

Most theories focus on one or more of the following types of change: (1) affective or feeling, (2) cognitive or thinking, and (3) behavior or action. The differences appear in the focus of change and on how much emphasis is given to that particular type of change. Other important aspects shared among theories are support, trust, feedback, therapeutic alliance, insight, modeling, education, challenging, acceptance, and hope, to name just a few (Lambert & Bergin, 1994). Carl Rogers (1961) introduced perhaps three of the most well-known therapist qualities: (1) congruence, genuineness, and realness; (2) unconditional positive regard or acceptance and caring; and (3) empathy or truly understanding the client's world. Although these attributes are born of Rogers's Person-Centered Therapy, many counselors integrate them into their work, regardless of which approach they are using.

Many counselors do not adhere to just one theory or technique, but consider themselves integrative in that they combine concepts and procedures to best help the client. However, research has shown that some therapies are more effective for certain disorders. In particular, behavioral, cognitive, and cognitive–behavioral techniques have been shown to be especially effective in treating fear and anxiety, phobias, depression, and global adjustment. Although research in the area of humanistic approaches has not been as methodical as that of the behavioral, cognitive, and cognitive–behavioral approaches, they are shown to be a factor in building self-esteem.

Although there are over 200 theories of counseling, a few are considered the most influential. Sigmund Freud and psychoanalytic theory and Carl Rogers and person-centered theory have already been mentioned. Other important theorists and theories are Alfred Adler and individual psychology; Viktor Frankl, Rollo May, Martin Buber, James Bugental, and Irvin Yalom and existentialism; Frederick (Fritz) and Laura Perls and Gestalt therapy; Eric Berne and transactional analysis; William Glasser and Robert Wubbolding and reality therapy/choice theory; Ivan Pavlov, B. F. Skinner, J. B. Watson, Joseph Wolpe, Albert Bandura, and Arnold Lazarus and behavioral approaches; Albert Ellis and rational–emotive behavior therapy; Aaron Beck and cognitive therapy; Steve de Shazer and solution-focused brief therapy; and Allen Ivey and developmental counseling and therapy (Capuzzi & Gross, 2003; James & Gilliland, 2003; Parrott, 2003).

Though there are many theories, approaches, and techniques, the goal of individual counseling remains constant—to assist the person in making changes in his/her life that will help alleviate the stress, pain, or discomfort that he/she is experiencing. People seek counseling for many different reasons, but the impetus that brings them is usually that they want something to be different in their lives because they are not where they want to be. Some seek counseling for growth purposes and others to relieve pain. Some clients seek counseling on their own and others are referred by people in their lives who are concerned about them. Others still may be ordered to take part in counseling, for example by the judicial system.

Individual counseling can occur with all ages. Depending on the client's age and the presenting issue, the counselor will adjust techniques and approaches to best help that client. The counselor's role is to assist that person in defining goals, helping him/her formulate a plan to reach those goals, and aiding him/her in carrying out those plans. During this process, it is vital that the counselor and client form a therapeutic connection, which fosters trust and hope.

See also: Family Counseling; Group Counseling; Peer Counseling Programs

BIBLIOGRAPHY

Capuzzi, D., & Gross, D. R. (2003). *Counseling and psychotherapy: Theories and interventions* (3rd ed.). Upper Saddle River, NJ: Merrill/Prentice Hall.

James, R. K., & Gilliland, B. E. (2003). *Theories and strategies in counseling and psychotherapy* (5th ed.). Boston: Pearson Education.

Lambert, M. J., & Bergin, A. E. (1994). The effectiveness of psychotherapy. In A. E. Bergin & S. L. Garfield (Eds.), *Handbook of psychotherapy and behavior change* (4th ed., pp. 143–189). New York: Wiley.

Parrott, L., III. (2003). *Counseling and psychotherapy* (2nd ed.). Pacific Grove, CA: Brooks Cole.

Perry, S., Frances, A. J., & Clarkin, J. F. (1985). *A DSM-III casebook of differential therapeutics.* New York: Brunner/Mazel.

Rogers, C. R. (1961). On becoming a person: A therapist's view of psychotherapy. Boston: Houghton Mifflin.

Additional Readings for Nonprofessionals

Axline, V. M. (1964). *Dibbs: In search of self.* Boston: Houghton Mifflin.

Frankl, V. E. (1994). *Man's search for meaning: An introduction to logotherapy* (4th ed.). Boston: Beacon.

Additional Readings for Professionals

Corey, G. (2001). *Theory and practice of counseling and psychotherapy* (6th ed.). Pacific Grove, CA: Brooks Cole/Wadsworth.

Rogers, C. R. (1961). *On becoming a person: A therapist's view of psychotherapy.* Boston: Houghton Mifflin.

Tammy H. Cashwell

Ingraham v. Wright (1977)

On October 6, 1970, James Ingraham, a 14-year-old eighth grader at Drew Junior High in Dade County, Florida, was asked to leave the stage of the school auditorium by a teacher. Upon slowly leaving the stage, Ingraham, along with other students, were taken to the principal's office to be paddled by the principal, Willie Wright Jr. Ingraham protested the paddling and claimed his innocence. Wright called for the assistant principal, Lemmie Deliford, and the assistant to the principal, Solomon Barnes, to aid him in paddling Ingraham. Ingraham was forced to lie in a prone position, face down across the table, while Barnes held his legs and Deliford held his arms (Lee, 1979). Mr. Wright then inflicted more than 20 strikes to Ingraham's buttocks with a wooden paddle. Ingraham was later taken to a local hospital by his mother, where the doctor diagnosed him with a hematoma causing the area of pain to be tender and large with an abnormal temperature and inflammation. Ingraham was prescribed pain pills, a laxative, sleep pills, ice packs, and was advised to stay home at least a week. On October 9th and 14th, Ingraham returned to the hospital for further treatment and further examinations by another physician. On October 14th, a 6-inch oozing hematoma, swollen, tender, and purplish in color, was observed. Ingraham was advised to rest at home for the next 72 hours.

The case of *James Ingraham v. Wright* was brought before the 1977 Supreme Court. In this case, parents contended that corporal punishment was a violation of a child's basic constitutional rights. The Court agreed to consider whether corporal punishment in the schools constituted "cruel and unusual punishment" as prohibited by the Eighth Amendment to the Constitution, the extent to which paddling is constitutionally permissible, and whether paddling requires due process protection under the 14th Amendment (Jacob-Timm & Hartshorne, 1998). The Court ruled (five to four) that paddling does not require Eighth Amendment protections (Warner, 1999). The Court further ruled that paddling neither violated any substantive rights nor caused any student to suffer any grievous loss. Therefore, the punishments administered to Ingraham and other students at Drew Junior High School did not violate the Cruel and Unusual Punishment Clause of the Eighth Amendment. Specifically, the Court noted that the use of corporal punishment to maintain discipline in the schools does fall under the Cruel and Unusual Punishment Clause because it was historically designed to limit criminal punishments and is not extended to school children (Jacob-Timm & Hartshorne, 1998). More specifically, because of the significant safeguards against abuse provided by the openness of schools and the supervision by the community, the Court stated that "the schoolchild has little need for the protection of the Eighth Amendment"

(Ingraham, 1977, p. 1412). The 14th Amendment protects the right to be free from unjustified intrusions on personal security and states that liberty interests are "implicated" if punishment is unreasonable (Jacob-Timm & Hartshorne, 1998). In this case, Justice Powell, who wrote the majority opinion, ruled that "there can be no deprivation of substantive rights as long as disciplinary corporal punishment is within the limits of common law privilege" (Ingraham, 1977, p. 1415). The Court also held that the due process clause of the 14th Amendment to the United States Constitution does not require notification of charges and an informal hearing prior to infliction of corporal punishment (Lee, 1979). According to the Court, requiring notice and a hearing for every corporal case would "significantly burden the use of corporal punishment as a disciplinary measure" (Warner, 1999). Thus, the Court found that corporal punishment of schoolchildren is not unconstitutional and Ingraham and the students of Drew Junior High, Florida, lost their case (Jacob-Timm & Hartshorne, 1998; Lee, 1979).

See also: Corporal Punishment

BIBLIOGRAPHY

Jacob-Timm, S., & Hartshorne, T. S. (1998). *Ethics and law for school psychologists* (3rd ed.). New York: Wiley.

Lee, V. (1979). *Corporal punishment: A legal analysis of Ingraham v. Wright.* Retrieved September 13, 2002, from http://www.corpun.com

Warner, L. S. (1999). Education and the law: Implications for American Indian/Alaska Native students. In *Next steps: Research and practice to advance Indian education* (chap. 3). (ERIC Document Reproduction Service No. ED 427905)

Additional Readings for Nonprofessionals

Bush Signs Law Protecting Teachers From Lawsuits (2002, January). *School Law News* (30), 5.

Campbell, S. (2002). Spare the rod, spoil the child: Corporal punishment remains popular in America, despite associated risks. *Psychology Today* (35), 5, 6.

Kissel, T. (2000, September). Cruel or unusual punishment: Miami-Dade County has a hands-off policy towards its schoolchildren, but that doesn't mean that corporal punishment has gone away. *Miami New Times.* Retrieved on October 13, 2002, from http://www.miaminewtimes.com/issues/2000-09-07/feature2.html./page1.html

World Corporal Punishment Research. (2003). Factual documentation and resources on corporal punishment around the world. Retrieved October 13, 2002, from http://www.corpun.com

Additional Readings for Professionals

Hyman, I. A., Stefkovich, J. A., & Taich, S. (2002). Paddling and pro-polemics: Refuting nineteenth century pedagogy. *Journal of Law and Education,* 1(31), 74–84.

Lynn, R. (2001). Corporal punishment in American public schools and the rights of the child. *Journal of Law and Education,* 3(30), 554–563.

Thompson, G. E. (2002). Corporal punishment by parents and associated child behaviors and experiences: A meta-analytic and theoretical review. *Psychological Bulletin, 4*(128), 539–580.

ANITRA SHELTON

Intelligence Quotient (IQ)

Intelligence Quotient, or IQ, is a powerful term used in both everyday language and scientific circles to describe a person's mental or cognitive ability. Most typically, the term is used to refer to a person's innate learning ability or the potential one has to learn new information. Those with "high IQs" are said to be fast learners and can acquire new information rapidly whereas those with "low IQs" are said to have difficulty learning. IQ is measured by comparing the performance of an individual on some type of standardized assessment measure with the performance of their same-age peers. As measured by IQ tests, the average score is 100, with a standard deviation of 15 (16 on the Stanford–Binet IV). The standard deviation means that 68 percent of individuals will obtain scores between 85 (the average minus 1 standard deviation) and 115 (the average plus 1 standard deviation).

Scores that fall between 90 and 110 are said to be "average." IQs from 111 to 119 are considered to be "high average" whereas scores that range from 80 to 89 are considered to be "low average." Scores that fall in the 120–129 range are labeled "superior" whereas scores above 130 are regarded as "very superior." In some instances, individuals who score above 130 are labeled as "intellectually gifted," a term that is typically used in education to specify those who are eligible for placement in a program for gifted/talented students. The IQ score required for placement in gifted/talented programs is highly dependent upon the criteria set forth by the particular school district in which a student is enrolled. Scores in the 70–79 range are considered "borderline" scores. Those who score below 70 are usually further assessed to determine if a diagnosis of mental retardation is warranted. Despite the different categorization of IQ scores, one must also consider real differences between scores. That is, although an IQ score of 105 is higher than a score of 99, there are few, if any, real differences in learning ability as reflected by those two scores. Only when there are substantive differences between scores can one make valid inferences about learning. For example, a person with an IQ of 135 is going to learn at a much faster rate than a person with a score of 95, although the IQ score of 95 is an average score.

Although some contend that IQ is largely determined by genetics, there are a number of environmental factors that can affect IQ. Apart from obvious factors such as disease and injury, perhaps the most significant environmental factor is the degree to which young children are exposed to a nurturing and stimulating environment. A nurturing environment is one in which children feel free to explore their surroundings, which provides physical affection, and ensures that all basic needs are met. A stimulating environment is one in which children are exposed to a wide range of experiences and many language-based interactions. Overall, studies suggest that about 30–50 percent of IQ is determined by genetics, whereas the remaining 50–70 percent is determined by environment. IQ is more changeable up to age 8, at which point it becomes stable, barring disease or injury, with little fluctuation in scores.

IQ scores are primarily used in educational settings to assist with diagnosing and classifying children for special education. Although there are serious concerns associated with this practice, there is a long history of doing so and supporters of the practice are quick to point out that IQ scores are moderately good predictors of academic success, with correlations of around .60. Scores on IQ tests between the ages of 3 and 18 have also been found to be good predictors of educational and occupational success as an adult.

Although there are a number of different intelligence theories upon which tests, and therefore IQ scores, are based, the one commonality is that there is a very strong underlying factor (g) that explains intelligence. The theories differ, however, in the emphasis they place on this factor and in the factors that comprise g.

IQ is a term that has been misused and been the subject of controversy and undue emphasis. A high IQ is neither a prerequisite nor a guarantee for success. In fact, most occupations do not require an exceptional IQ for a person to excel in that field. Excellence achieved by those with high IQs probably has more to do with motivation and the drive to achieve than with necessarily having a high IQ.

See also: Adaptive Behavior Assessment; Wechsler Adult Intelligence Scale—Third Edition (WAIS-III); Wechsler Intelligence Scale for Children—Fourth Edition (WISC-IV)

Additional Readings for Nonprofessionals

Gellman, E. (1995). *School testing: What parents and educators need to know.* Westport, CT: Praeger.
http://www.psyonline.nl/en-iq.htm

Additional Readings for Professionals

Block, N. J., & Dworkin, G. (1976). *The IQ controversy.* New York: Random House.
Herrnstein, R. J., & Murray, C. (1994). *The bell curve: Intelligence and class structure in American life.* New York: Free Press.

T. STEUART WATSON

Intermittent Explosive Disorder

The main characteristic of Intermittent Explosive Disorder (IED) is an episode during which a person is unable to resist an aggressive impulse (*Diagnostic and Statistical Manual of Mental Disorders* [4th ed., text rev.] [*DSM-IV-TR*]; American Psychiatric Association, 2000). Another distinctive characteristic is that the aggression expressed during the episode is grossly disproportionate to any provocation or stressor that may have preceded the episode (McElroy, Soutullo, Beckman, Taylor, & Keck, 1998). These episodes cannot be due to medication or substance abuse and must be distinguished from temper tantrums. Even though the behaviors displayed may be tantrum-like (Sheridan & Russman, 1997), the magnitude and intensity of these explosive episodes distinguish them from a more common temper tantrum (Budman, Bruun, Park, Lesser, & Olson, 2000).

The aggressive episodes are discrete, meaning that the onset is abrupt and that the end is clearly distinguishable. According to the *DSM-IV-TR* (American Psychiatric Association, 2000), serious assaults or destruction of property result from these episodes. Hitting another person or making verbal threats are both examples of assaultive acts. Any destruction of property must be a purposeful act. Note that following an explosive outburst, individuals often express remorse or embarrassment over their behaviors.

DIAGNOSIS

Intermittent Explosive Disorder first appeared in the *Diagnostic and Statistical Manual of Mental Disorders* (3rd ed.) (*DSM-III*) (American Psychiatric Association, 1980), replacing the term "explosive personality" used in the previous edition. The *DSM-III* (American Psychiatric Association, 1980) also included a statement regarding the absence of more general signs of aggression or impulsivity between episodes. In the *DSM-IV* (American Psychiatric Association, 1994), not only was this criterion removed, but also it is now believed that "subthreshold" anger can exist between episodes.

IED is classified as an Impulse Control Disorder along with Kleptomania (a recurrent failure to resist impulses to steal unneeded objects), Pyromania (fire setting for pleasure, gratification, or relief of tension), Pathological Gambling, and Trichotillomania (recurrent pulling out of one's hair for pleasure, gratification, or relief of tension that results in noticeable hair loss). Inability to resist impulses and urges to cause harm to self or to others is the common feature among this class of disorders.

Diagnosticians must differentiate IED from Conduct Disorder, Attention-Deficit/Hyperactivity Disorder, substance abuse/use, Antisocial Personality Disorder, Borderline Personality Disorder, psychotic disorders, a Manic Episode, or a general medical condition (e.g., blunt head injuries). It is possible to have a diagnosis of IED and other disorders such as Bipolar Disorder if the IED symptoms appear when there is no active mood disturbance. The differential diagnosis process is a bit complicated but suffice it to say that concurrent diagnoses (e.g., Tourette's Disorder) are possible under several situations.

PRESENTATION

Before the onset of an explosive episode, an increase in tension is often experienced (Budman et al., 2000). Tingling, tremors, tightening of the chest, and head pressure are some of the physical symptoms reported by individuals prior to the episode (*DSM-IV-TR*; American Psychiatric Association, 2000). The stressors that trigger an IED episode are typically minor conflicts with others (McElroy et al., 1998). The impulse that precedes the aggressive act is often irresistible (McElroy et al., 1998). Persons diagnosed with Intermittent Explosive Disorder describe these impulses as the "need to attack or strike out" and as an "adrenaline rush" (McElroy et al., 1998).

During the aggressive acts, an increase in energy and irritability or rage may be readily apparent (*DSM-IV-TR*; American Psychiatric Association, 2000). Some individuals report a temporary loss of awareness (McElroy et al., 1998) whereas others experience racing thoughts during the episode. If successful in resisting the impulse, the person may release the urge in a less destructive way, such as screaming or punching a wall (*DSM-IV-TR*). After the episode has ended, there is a release of tension. A person's emotion following the episode can range from pleasure to remorse. Fatigue and a depressed mood can also follow the episode (*DSM-IV-TR*).

Self-esteem, academic functioning, and interpersonal relationships can all be affected by these episodes. Accounts of childhood from adults with Intermittent Explosive Disorder may show a history of impaired attention, hyperactivity, and extreme temper tantrums. Problematic behaviors such as stealing and fire setting are also frequently noted (McElroy et al., 1998).

PREVALENCE

Some authorities in the mental health arena question whether IED should be an independent disorder (McElroy et al., 1998). Others feel that IED is often seen in combination with other mood disorders, such as depression, but should still be diagnosed as a separate disorder (McElroy et al., 1998). Despite this debate, IED is considered a distinct diagnostic entity in the *DSM-IV-TR* (American Psychiatric Association, 2000). Currently, reliable prevalence data are unavailable. Although some feel that the disorder is underdiagnosed, most conclude IED is rare.

ETIOLOGY

The cause of IED remains unclear but seems best conceptualized as a disturbance in normal biopsychosocial functioning. Indirect evidence comes from neurological exams of individuals with IED that produce "soft" findings (*DSM-IV-TR*; American Psychiatric Association, 2000). A somewhat more specific hypothesis is that there is a malfunction in the "flight versus fight" response that enables individuals to respond to environmental dangers (McElroy et al., 1998). In other words, individuals with IED have misperceptions of their environment, which in turn produces inappropriate responses to psychosocial stressors. Consider that some children may be bumped while getting a drink of water but make no assumption about the intentionality of the person who bumped them. Other children may get bumped but then inaccurately assume that someone bumped them on purpose. This kind of misperception may lead children to interpret otherwise ambiguous stimuli in ways that lead to aggressive responding (e.g., Crick & Dodge, 1996). Finally, mood disorders seem to increase the risk of IED behaviors. There is little conclusive empirical work done to date on identifying causes of irresistible urges to be violent.

TREATMENT

There is no clear treatment of choice for IED in adults or children. Some reports suggest that individuals with IED may respond to treatment with antidepressants. One explanation for this response is that the mood-stabilizing properties of these medications may bolster one's ability to resist urges to be violent. Other treatments focus on reducing risk factors and increasing coping skills. For example, stress inoculation training (SIT) is a preventive treatment approach designed to help individuals develop skills that will enable them to better deal with stressors (Thorpe & Olson, 1997). SIT has proven successful in the treatment of individuals with anger management difficulties. As an individual progresses through SIT, they are led through the phases of a stressful situation such as preparation for the stressor, confrontation of the stressor, coping with the emotions involved, and self-congratulation after successfully handling the stressful experience. As with many treatment strategies, it is recommended that SIT be used in combination with other treatment approaches, such as anger management training. During anger management training, individuals may be asked to compile a list of stressors that provoke anger. Once these stressors are identified, the individual learns to imagine these situations while pairing responses that would compete with the anger, such as relaxation.

In another approach to anger management, Lochman's group (Lochman, Dunn, & Wagner, 1997) categorizes aggression as proactive or reactive. The behavior of proactive aggressive children is displayed to obtain a desired goal or as an intimidation tactic, as seen in "bullying" (Lochman et al., 1997). Reactive aggression, characteristic of an IED episode, functions as a reaction to frustration that lacks self-control. School-based interventions have been designed to help reduce reactive styles of aggression. The Anger Coping Program, which employs a group intervention format, was developed to help reduce aggression in a school setting (Lochman et al., 1997). Group leaders, typically psychologists or counselors, teach children how to take perspective of anger-provoking situations so that they can more accurately perceive the intentions of others. This learning tool would be especially beneficial for children with IED because their perception of environmental stressors is out of sync with the reality of the situation. Children also learn to identify cues of anger such as a racing heart and clenched fists, which are experienced by individuals prior to an IED episode. Finally, by breaking down a problem into simpler components and identifying feelings, choices, and possible outcomes, children are able to improve their problem-solving skills.

Typical strategies for parents to use at home involve a combination of ignoring outbursts and reinforcing desired behaviors. These strategies are easier to implement with younger children than with adolescents. Be forewarned that inconsistent use of behavioral interventions involving ignoring (i.e., an extinction-based strategy) may make things worse! At home, parents of children who exhibit severe behavioral outbursts will likely benefit greatly from involving a behavioral consultant.

See also: Attention-Deficit/Hyperactivity Disorder; Conduct Disorder; Impulse Control Disorders; Oppositional Defiant Disorder; Tantrums; Tourette Syndrome

BIBLIOGRAPHY

American Psychiatric Association. (1980). *Diagnostic and statistical manual of mental disorders* (3rd ed.). Washington, DC: Author.

American Psychiatric Association. (1994). *Diagnostic and statistical manual of mental disorders* (4th ed.). Washington, DC: Author.

American Psychiatric Association. (2000). *Diagnostic and statistical manual of mental disorders* (4th ed., text rev.). Washington, DC: Author.

Budman, C. L., Brunn, R. D., Park, K. S., Lesser, M., & Olson, M. (2000). Explosive outbursts in children with Tourette's disorder. *Journal of the American Academy of Child and Adolescent Psychiatry, 39,* 1270–1276.

Crick, N. R., & Dodge, K. A. (1996). Social information processing mechanisms in reactive and proactive aggression. *Child Development, 67,* 993–1002.

Lochman, J. E., Dunn, S. E., & Wagner, E. E. (1997). Anger. In G. G. Bear, K. M. Minke, & A. Thomas (Eds.), *Children's needs. II: Developmental, problems and alternatives* (pp. 149–160). Bethesda, MD: National Association of School Psychologists.

McElroy, S. L., Soutullo, C. A., Beckman, D. A., Taylor, P., & Keck, P. E. (1998). *DSM-IV* Intermittent Explosive Disorder: A report of 27 cases. *Journal of Clinical Psychiatry, 59,* 203–210.

Sheridan, S. M., & Russman, S. (1997). Temper tantrums. In G. G. Bear, K. M. Minke, & A. Thomas (Eds.), *Children's needs. II: Developmental, problems and alternatives* (pp. 161–169). Bethesda, MD: National Association of School Psychologists.

Thorpe, G. L., & Olson, S. L. (1997). *Behavior therapy: Concepts, procedures, and applications* (2nd ed.). Boston: Allyn & Bacon.

Additional Readings for Nonprofessionals

Phelan, T. W. (1984). *1-2-3: Magic!* Plantation, FL: ADD Warehouse.

Sloane, H. N. (1979). *The good kid book: How to solve the 16 most common behavior problems.* Champaign, IL: Research Press.

Additional Readings for Professionals

Cohen, J. J., & Fish, M. C. (Eds.). (1993). *Handbook of school based interventions: Resolving student problems and promoting healthy educational environments.* San Francisco: Jossey-Bass.

Larson, J., & Lochman, J. E. (2002). *Helping schoolchildren cope with anger: A cognitive–behavioral intervention. The Guilford school practitioner series.* New York: Guilford.

KEVIN J. ARMSTRONG

JESSE HARTLEY

Jj

Jack Bardon Distinguished Service Award

The Division 16 Distinguished Service Award was renamed the Jack Bardon Distinguished Service Award in honor of Jack Bardon, an influential leader in the field of school psychology, who passed away on November 9, 1993. The award is given by the Division of School Psychology of the American Psychological Association to experienced school psychologists who, throughout their careers, have demonstrated exceptional programs of service that merit special recognition. The award is given for accomplishments relating to (a) major leadership in the administration of psychological service in the schools, (b) major contributions in the development and implementation of policy leading to psychologically and socially sound training and practice in school psychology, (c) sustained direction or participation in research that has contributed to more effective practice in school psychology, or (d) the inauguration or development of training programs for new school psychologists or for the systematic nurturance of in-service training for psychologists engaged in the practice of school psychology; or any combination of those. First awarded in 1970, recipients include

1970 Edward French
1971 Frances Mullen
1972 Maria Skodak Crissey
1973 Boyd V. McCandless & David Wechsler (Special Award)
1974 Mary Alice White
1975 T. Ernest Newland
1976 Jack I. Bardon
1977 Virginia Bennett
1978 Beeman Phillips
1979 Rosa A. Hagin
1980 Nadine Lambert
1981 Gilbert O. Trachtman
1982 C. Edward Meyer
1983 Susan Gray
1984 Seymour Sarason
1985 Joseph L. French
1986 John H. Jackson
1987 Calvin L. Dyer
1988 Irwin Hyman
1989 Judith L. Alpert
1990 Thomas Oakland
1991 Thomas K. Fagan
1994 Sylvia Rosenfield & Walter Pryzwansky
1995 Jane C. Conoley
1996 Joel Myers
1997 Stephen DeMers
1998 Jan Hughes & Ronda Talley
1999 James Barclay
2000 Deborah Tharinger
2001 Roy Martin
2002 Jon Sandoval
2003 Mark Shinn

Note: No award was given in 1992 or 1993.

See also: American Psychological Association—Division 16

K. ANGELEQUE AKIN-LITTLE
STEVEN G. LITTLE

Kk

Kaplan, Incorporated

Kaplan, Incorporated is a private business that provides educational services, including test preparation, tutoring, degree and certificate programs, and continuing education. Kaplan has over 180 centers located throughout the world. Forty-two states and the District of Columbia are home to at least one Kaplan center. Kaplan's Web site, www.kaplan.com, contains a location finder for users to find the Kaplan center closest to their zip code.

A subsidiary of the Washington Post Company, Kaplan is recognized as one of the leaders in the test preparation industry. Preparation for the following tests is available through Kaplan: SAT/PSAT, ACT, GRE, GMAT, LSAT, MCAT, DAT, USMLE, NCLEX, TOEFL, and many other state tests. There are several options available for test preparation such as attending classes, receiving individual tutoring, or enrolling in the online version. There is also software available for many of the tests. Some of the tests also have software that can be used on personal data assistants (PDAs). The classroom preparation is available for those students who live close to one of the 1,200 locations that provide Kaplan test prep services (Chambers, 1998). The classes are often offered at high schools and colleges rather than at Kaplan centers. Test prep classes usually occur at least 3 months prior to the actual test. Students receive diagnostic testing to assess their current ability, one-on-one attention from trained teachers, and specific strategies for taking the designated test. The prices range from approximately $600 (ACT prep) to approximately $1,200 (MCAT prep).

The benefits of the online version include 24-hour access to the program, 7 days a week. In addition, some students may not live close to a Kaplan-designated preparation sight. Finally, the online option enables students to prepare when they have less than 3 months before the actual test date. Depending on the test, students may be able to complete the online preparation in as little as 1 month. There are specific online lessons that must be completed; this number varies also with the test. The online version is less expensive than the classroom option. The ACT online is approximately $300 and the SAT is approximately $400.

Private tutoring is the most expensive test preparation option. Students and/or parents should expect to pay significantly more. This option provides the student with one-on-one assistance that is specifically tailored to meet the student's academic and scheduling needs. Prices vary with location, but usually start around $2,000 for most tests.

Finally, Kaplan provides the traditional tutoring similar to other private companies like Sylvan Learning Centers. Named SCORE!, Kaplan tutoring centers are available for students in kindergarten through 10th grade. Kaplan offers two programs: the Advantage Program and the Personal Academic Training. The Advantage Program requires students to attend two 1-hour sessions at a Kaplan center each week. In each program, the student's current ability is determined and a program is designed to meet the child's academic needs. However, in the Advantage Program, the individualized plan is in the form of a computer software program that allows the student to progress through his/her subject or skill area at a computer. Students receive individual assistance through the Personal Academic Training. This program is more similar to traditional learning environments that rely on pencil-and-paper activities. Kaplan centers feature flexible hours and services 7 days a week to accommodate busy schedules. In addition, students enrolled in the Advantage Program may be dropped off at the Kaplan center without an appointment. According to Kaplan, students enrolled in the Personal Tutoring option advance two grade levels within 6 weeks and students in the Advantage Program advance one grade level in 5 weeks. To date, there are no controlled outside studies that validate Kaplan's claims. Consumers must rely on Kaplan's documentation and word-of-mouth to evaluate Kaplan's services.

Kaplan also offers many degree and certificate programs for nontraditional students. Undergraduate programs are available in the following areas: allied health, business, arts and sciences, communications, criminal justice, design/graphic art, education, information technology, paralegal, and vocational training. Certificate programs are available in financial planning, legal nurse consulting, master of laws, and Microsoft network engineer. These programs may be of interest to high school students who are not interested in attending a traditional 2- or 4-year university course.

See also: Academic Interventions for Written Language and Grammar; Huntington Learning Centers; Sylvan Learning Centers

BIBLIOGRAPHY

Chambers, P. (1998, March 9). Testing 1, 2, 3. *Publishers Weekly*, pp. 37–44.

Kaplan, Incorporated. Retrieved September 15, 2002, from http://www.kaplan.com

Additional Readings for Nonprofessionals

Greene, L. J. (2002). *Roadblocks to learning: Understanding the obstacles that sabotage your child's academic success.* New York: Warner Books.

Shore, K. (1998). *Special kids problem solver: Ready to use interventions for helping all students with academic, behavioral, and physical problems.* Englewood Cliffs, NJ: Prentice–Hall.

Additional Readings for Professionals

Dunn, E. K., & Eckert, T. L. (2002). Curriculum-based measurement in reading: A comparison of similar versus challenging material. *School Psychology Quarterly, 17,* 24–46.

Skinner, C. H., & Robinson, S. L. (2002). Interspersing additional easier items to enhance mathematics performance on subtests requiring different task demands. *School Psychology Quarterly, 17,* 191–205.

NANCY FOSTER

Ll

Lau v. Nichols

The landmark case, *Lau v. Nichols*, was a class-action suit filed by non-English-speaking Chinese students alleging that the San Francisco school system failed to adequately provide them with equal educational opportunities. Of the children with limited English proficiency (LEP), approximately 1,000 were provided with supplemental material in English, whereas over 1,800 were taught exclusively in English. The students of Chinese ancestry were expected to obtain a meaningful education based on a curriculum presented in a language in which they were not fluent. In addition, students not meeting proficiency in English were denied high school graduation to ensure that all students in the school district master English before they enter high school. The plaintiffs alleged that the unequal educational opportunities and the disadvantages that the minority children were expected to endure was in violation of the Fourteenth Amendment, which guarantees equal protection under the law.

In 1974, avoiding the Fourteenth Amendment equal protection clause, the U.S. Supreme court decided the case on statutory grounds issued under Title VI of the Civil Rights Act of 1964. Justice Douglas ruled that the San Francisco Unified School District was in violation of Title VI, which prohibits federally funded programs from discriminating on the basis of race, color, or national origin. Douglas wrote:

> there is no equality of treatment merely by providing students with the same facilities, textbooks, teachers, and curriculum; for students who do not understand English are effectively foreclosed from any meaningful education. (*Lau v. Nichols*, 1974)

Douglas argued that requiring students to enter the educational system with needed skills before they can benefit from educational programs defeats the purpose of offering public education. Douglas argued that when children are presented with material in a language with which they are not familiar, they are deprived of receiving useful information. Although the school district provided the LEP child with equal resources, the assets offered are rendered useless without the means to provide interpretation.

The decision in *Lau v. Nichols* has been interpreted to mean that school districts are required to "take affirmative steps" to correct the language deficiency of students with inadequate English proficiency so that they will have the opportunity to participate in a meaningful academic program. The district is also required to provide the same advantages that are offered to other children receiving the same federal funds.

The Court did not issue a federal mandate requiring a bilingual curriculum for the LEP child, but rather left the corrective measures to be taken at the local level. Without providing a particular remedy, the decision required school districts to provide interventions to meet the child's language needs in a timely manner and not simply an "educational dead-end or permanent track." Although the federal government has issued funds for bilingual educational programs to promote the training of bilingual teachers since 1968, many school districts favor teaching English as a second language over bilingual educational programs.

See also: Diana v. State Board of Education

BIBLIOGRAPHY

Lau v. Nichols, 414 U.S. 563 (1974).

Additional Reading for Nonprofessionals

The legal context. (1998, November/December). *Social Education, 62*(7), 428–429.

Additional Reading for Professionals

Office for Civil Rights. (Ed.). (2000). *Programs for English language learners: Resource materials for planning and self-assessments.* Washington, DC: Author.

TONYA SARTOR BUTLER

Learning Disabilities

See: Mathematics; Oral Language; Reading; Written Language Learning Disabilities

---

Leiter International Performance Scale—Revised

The *Leiter International Performance Scale—Revised* (Leiter-R) is an updated version of the original Leiter published in 1929 by Russell Leiter. The current version by Roid and Miller (1997) is based on Carroll's hierarchical theory of intelligence and was designed to nonverbally assess the cognitive development, memory, and attention skills of individuals aged 2 years 0 months to 20 years 11 months. The goal of the test is to provide a global intelligence score that also recognizes the multifaceted nature of cognition (Roid & Miller, 1997). It is intended to be used with individuals who have limited verbal communication skills, including those who have autism, mental retardation, hearing impairment, traumatic brain injury, attention problems, learning disability, and who are second language learners.

TEST CONTENT

The Leiter-R is composed of two primary batteries, the Visualization and Reasoning (VR) and the Attention and Memory (AM). It also has four optional social–emotional rating scales: one each for the parent, teacher, and examiner and a self-report. Each of the two batteries is composed of 10 subtests and the batteries can be used alone or together. The materials for the test include three easel books, response cards, plastic manipulatives, colored picture plates, response grids, response protocols, and a manual. The examiner must supply a stopwatch for many of the subtests.

ADMINISTRATION AND SCORING

Each of the subtests is presented in a "game format" (e.g., Figure Ground is the "find it game") through pantomime and

use of facial expressions. Starting points are dependent on the individual's chronological age and there are teaching items for each subtest to ensure the examinee understands the test questions. Rules are provided for basals, ceilings, and for discontinuation if the examinee cannot complete an item after three nonresponsive minutes. Three types of responses are required: pointing, moving manipulatives, and placing cards in a grid. The Leiter-R generates up to 31 scores, including Brief IQ, Full Scale IQ, composites (all with a mean of 100 and an *SD* of 15), subtest scores (mean = 10, *SD* = 3), percentiles, and optional growth scores.

STATISTICAL PROPERTIES

The VR portion of the Leiter-R was normed on 1,719 typical individuals and was generally representative of the general population in terms of geographic region, socioeconomic status, gender, race, and ethnicity. The AM portion was administered to 763 of the children who were included in the standardization sample. In addition, the test was administered to 692 children who had disabilities.

Reliability and validity are considered strengths with the Leiter-R; test–retest reliability ranged from .75 to .90 for the VR subtests and .65 to .87 for the AM subtests. The reliability of diagnostic decisions was also evaluated and found to be strong. Criterion, content, and construct validity were carefully analyzed and suggest the constructs being measured by the Leiter-R are well supported. For example, the Leiter-R FSIQ correlates at a level of .85 with the WISC-III FSIQ.

INTERPRETATION

The Leiter-R manual provides specific guidelines for the interpretation of results. It recommends that the examiner carefully examine the child's background and use clinical observations to determine whether the child's performance on the day of testing was representative of the child's normal behavior. Interpretation of the scores then proceeds from the Brief or Full Scale IQ (as the best indicator of cognitive ability) to an analysis of the composites (Fluid Reasoning, Fundamental Visualization, and Spatial Visualization), then to an analysis of the subtest scores to identify strengths or weaknesses. Finally, the AM battery can be used along with an investigation of score differences and the rating scales. The level of interpretation depends on the goals of the assessment.

STRENGTHS AND WEAKNESSES

The Leiter-R is considered a multidimensional intelligence test, meaning it measures several factors associated with intelligence (e.g., memory, attention). Because of its nonverbal format, it is useful with a number of populations that cannot be tested with traditional cognitive measures, such as the Wechsler scales. It allows measurement of children as young as 2 years and as old as 20 years 11 months and is considered to be non-biased with respect to culture and language. It is easy to administer, with its picture format and examiner directions printed on the easels. In addition, a comprehensive computer scoring program is available. The statistical properties are considered very good, including excellent standardization, reliability, and validity (Marco, 1999).

Weaknesses for the Leiter-R include the lack of specific nonverbal administration instructions. The standardization sample is somewhat small, with a minimum of 42 individuals at each age range, and the floor is somewhat limited for cognitively impaired 2-year-olds, suggesting much caution in interpretation with young children (Marco, 1999). There is also some variability of subtests across ages so that comparisons cannot always be made as the child becomes older. Despite the limitations, the Leiter-R is a good addition to the nonverbal cognitive assessment tools.

See also: Intelligence Quotient (IQ); Universal Nonverbal Intelligence Test (UNIT)

BIBLIOGRAPHY

Marco, G. L. (1999). Review of the Leiter International Performance Scale—Revised. In L. L. Murphy, J. C. Impara, & B. S. Plake (Eds.), *Tests in print: An index to tests, test reviews, and the literature on specific tests* (Vol. 5, pp. 683–687). Lincoln: University of Nebraska Press.

Roid, G. H., & Miller, L. J. (1997). Leiter International Performance Scale—Revised: Examiner's manual. In G. H. Roid & L. J. Miller (Eds.), *Leiter International Performance Scale—Revised.* Wood Dale, IL: Stoelting Co.

Additional Reading for Nonprofessionals

Gregory, R. J. (1996). *Psychological testing* (2nd ed.). Boston: Allyn & Bacon.

Additional Readings for Professionals

Kamphaus, R. W. (1993). *Clinical assessment of children's intelligence.* Boston: Allyn & Bacon.

McCallum, S., Bracken, B. A., & Wasserman, J. (2001). *Essentials of nonverbal assessment.* New York: Wiley.

DALENE M. McCLOSKEY

Lightner Witmer Award

The Lightner Witmer Award is given by the Division of School Psychology (16) of the American Psychological Association to an individual or individuals in recognition of their early career production of significant scholarly works within school psychology. Simply publishing numerous papers and articles is not considered, by itself, to be sufficient for the award. Instead, the Lightner Witmer Award is given for scholarly activity and contributions that have significantly advanced the profession of school psychology. In addition, award winners are thought to hold exceptional potential and promise to continue to contribute to the research base of the profession for years to come. To be eligible for the award, a person must be within 7 years of receiving their educational specialist or doctoral degree as of September 1 of the year the award is given and must also be a Fellow, Member, Associate, or Student Affiliate of Division 16. A person does not need to have a doctoral degree to be eligible. First awarded in 1973, the following individuals have received the Lightner Witmer Award:

1973 James E. Ysseldyke	1989 Janet Graden &
1974 Ellen C. Bien	Howard Knoff
1976 Judith L. Alpert	1990 Brian Martens &
1977 Thomas R. Kratochwill	Kevin Stark
1978 Emmanual J. Mason	1991 William Erchul
1979 Raymond S. Dean	1992 Sandra Christenson
1980 Cecil R. Reynolds	1993 Susan Sheridan
1981 Terry B. Gutkin &	1994 Gregg Macmann
Frederic J. Medway	1995 Christopher Skinner
1982 Frank M. Gresham	1997 Dawn Flanagan
1983 George W. Hynd	1998 T. Steuart Watson
1984 Stephen Elliott	1999 John Hintze &
1985 Cathy F. Telzrow	Cynthia Riccio
1986 Joe Witt	2000 George H. Noell
1987 Jack Kramer &	2002 Tanya Eckert
Edward Shapiro	2003 Melissa Bray &
1988 Marybeth Gettinger &	Shane Jimerson
Timothy Keith	

Note: No award was given in 1975, 1996, or 2001.

See also: American Psychological Association—Division 16; Witmer, Lightner

K. ANGELEQUE AKIN-LITTLE
STEVEN G. LITTLE

Mm

Mainstreaming

Mainstreaming is generally defined as the early practices used to integrate students with and without disabilities within the general/regular education setting. The practices and philosophical emphases of mainstreaming developed out of the civil rights movement in the 1950s and 1960s. During this time, substantial legal and legislative action was used to promote equitable opportunities in public education for disadvantaged and disabled populations. The term *mainstreaming* was popularized in the 1970s and 1980s to describe integration practices. In the early 1990s, mainstreaming was supplanted by the philosophical and practical shift toward *inclusion.*

The philosophical emphases underlying mainstreaming and inclusion seem to be substantially similar and their distinctions somewhat ambiguous. Both mainstreaming and inclusion practices promoted the integration of students with and without disabilities into a shared learning environment. The level of student integration and the site of remedial services defined the substantive differences between mainstreaming and inclusion practices.

Mainstreaming practices typically preserved the boundaries between general/regular education and special education. Students with disabilities were integrated for the activities that did not require substantial adaptation or modification to the general education instruction and curriculum. The general/regular education personnel served students while they were within the general/regular education setting and the special education personnel served students while they were within the remedial or special education setting. Student placement was considered *mainstream* if they spent more than 20 percent of their school day within the general education setting. In contrast, later inclusion practices did not preserve the boundaries between general/regular and special education. Service systems were integrated to serve the whole child in the general/regular education setting through (sometimes) extensive modification and adaptations in curriculum or instruction within the general/regular education setting. What follows is a brief review of the legal origins of mainstreaming, practical implications, common practices, and the eventual shift toward inclusion.

CASE LAW AND LEGISLATION

The United States Constitution omitted an educational provision, and with this omission the framers relegated the responsibility of education to the states with the language of the Tenth Amendment (1791), "[T]he powers not delegated to the United States by the Constitution, nor prohibited by it to the States, are reserved to the States respectively or to the people." Compulsory education was established within individual states in the years between 1850 and 1950. The educational systems that developed often failed to guarantee equal access and often segregated students by ability, socioeconomic status, or race. These educational systems were challenged in federal courts during the civil rights movement in the years between 1954 and the mid-1980s. It was in the late 1960s through the mid-1980s that mainstreaming arose out of case law and was adopted within federal legislation.

The Fourteenth Amendment (1868) established equal protection under the law and provided an early legal basis for mainstreaming: "No State shall make or enforce any law which shall abridge the privileges or immunities of the citizens . . . nor deny to any person within its jurisdiction the equal protection of the laws." References to the Fourteenth Amendment are found in seminal rulings for separate but equal protection under the law (*Plessy v. Ferguson*, 1869) and later court rulings that integrated educational services for diverse populations (*Brown v. Board of Education*, 1954). These early rulings supported subsequent case law to establish the right of disabled school-age populations to free and appropriate educational services (*Mills v. Board of Education*, 1972) within the least restrictive integrated setting (*Larry P. v. Riles*, 1972; *PARC v. Penn.*, 1972). This case law that supported free educational services within an integrated educational setting for individuals with disabilities was the foundation for mainstreaming. The case law established the rights of students with disabilities to educational opportunities and set the stage for federal legislation.

Section 504 of the Vocational Rehabilitation Act (Vocational and Rehabilitations Act of 1973) codified the standards for nondiscriminatory practices with five mandates for the protection of students' rights within federally supported educational programming. These standards protected students with disabilities by regulating the provision of educational services relative to "(a) location and notification, (b) free appropriate education, (c) educational setting, (d) evaluation and placement, (e) procedural safeguards." In 1975, the Education for All Handicapped Children's Act (Pub. L. 94-142; renamed Individuals with Disabilities Act [IDEA] of 1991) established federal funding to states. This funding was contingent on the school's providing services to handicapped and disabled students. The substance of these provisions included (a) a free and appropriate public education (FAPE), (b) an individualized educational program/plan (IEP), (c) special education services, (d) related services, (e) due process procedures, and (f) services in the least restrictive environment (LRE) (Alexander & Alexander, 1998; Education for all Handicapped Children Act [EHCA] of 1975). In subsequent years, 36 federal court cases were brought to challenge and define the parameters of the right for disabled school-aged children with disabilities to educational opportunities (Martin, 1979). The case law continued to support integrated educational opportunities for students with disabilities. Consistent with mainstreaming, courts continued to reference the ruling of *Brown v. Board of Education*, requiring schools to justify segregated and restrictive placements of students with disabilities.

PRACTICAL IMPLICATIONS OF MAINSTREAMING

Mainstreaming students with disabilities facilitated the early integration of previously segregated student groups. These practices were intended to establish a subset of common learning experiences and equitable educational opportunities to individuals with disabilities. Mainstreaming practices preceded and eventually gave way to the practice of inclusion. Within the context of mainstreaming, students diagnosed with a specific learning disability in mathematics were likely to participate in the general education setting during all but mathematics activities (80 percent of the day in general education). However, students diagnosed with severe developmental disabilities (mental retardation, autism) would be more likely to participate only in nonacademic activities, such as music, art, and physical education (10–20 percent of the day in general education). To meet the mainstreaming requirements, schools had to develop a continuum of services for alternative placement options. This continuum of services was described and defined in the professional literature (Reynolds, 1962). One researcher presented the *Cascade Model* of service delivery (Deno, 1970). The Cascade Model defined six levels of service delivery settings. The least restrictive service delivery setting for students exhibiting mild exceptionality was the general/regular educational classroom. The most restrictive setting to serve students with severe exceptionality was the residential or hospital setting. The intermediate service delivery options included itinerant teacher, resource room, special classes, or a specialized day school. As a result of the mainstreaming emphasis, federal statistics suggest that during the 1984–1985 academic year, 93 percent of school-aged children with disabilities were served within their local general education school building. That statistic evidences substantial improvement of practices from the beginnings of compulsory education up until the 1980s; however, of these students only 25 percent of students spent more than 79 percent of their school day within the general education classroom (U.S. Department of Education, 2001).

As is detailed above, the practice of mainstreaming was promoted first by the courts and then by federal legislation, which was based on issues of civil rights and equal access. The actual or theoretical impact on academic and social growth for differential placements (self-contained or integrated) had a secondary influence. Reviews of the available literature do indeed evidence that the adoption and promotion of mainstreaming practices derived from philosophical orientations, and not research suggesting improved student outcomes within integrated settings (Christopolos & Renz, 1969; Downing, Eichinger, & Williams, 1997; Dunn, 1977; Johnson, 1962; Phillips, 1974). In one recent review of the history of mainstreaming, researchers concluded, "the Dunn article initiated an attitude in special education that eschewed empirical evidence in favor of ideology to produce change . . . but questions remained about what works" (Kavale, 2000, p. 281).

Throughout the 1970s and 1980s, the critical standards and dimensions for what qualified as mainstreaming and LRE continued to develop within the courts and congressional legislation with little deference to empirical research. Instead, the mainstreaming movement was supported primarily by the courts that applied legal standards in place of research outcomes. For example, the *Rockner Standard* (*Rockner v. Walter*, 1983) was often cited in court rulings throughout the 1980s and early 1990s. This standard emphasized the apparent *congressional preference* (legislation) for integrating/mainstreaming student groups. In this context, the courts upheld that alternative placements were appropriate only if *schools demonstrated* substantial benefit to the child within a segregated setting. The legal and philosophical support for mainstreaming shifted toward a more holistic approach to integration toward the late1980s and 1990s. The new approach to integration was termed *inclusion*.

See also: Diana v. Board of Education; Inclusion

BIBLIOGRAPHY

Alexander, K., & Alexander, M. D. (1998). *American public school law* (4th ed.). Belmont, CA. Wadsworth.

Brown v. Board of Education, 347 U.S. 294 (75 S. Ct. 753 [1954]).

Christopolos, F., & Renz, P. (1969). A critical examination of special education programs. *Journal of Special Education, 3,* 371–379.

Deno, S. L. (1970). Special education as developmental capital. *Exceptional Children, 37,* 229–237.

Downing, J. E., Eichinger, J., & Williams, L. J. (1997). Inclusive education for students with severe disabilities: Comparative views of principals and educators at different levels of implementation. *Remedial & Special Education, 18,* 133–142, 165.

Dunn, L. M. (1977). Special education for the mildly retarded—Is much of it justifiable? *Exceptional Children, 35,* 5–22.

Education for All Handicapped Children Act, 20 U.S.C. § 401 (1975).

Johnson, G. O. (1962). Special education for the mentally handicapped—A paradox. *Exceptional Children, 29,* 62–69.

Kavale, K. A. (2000). History, rhetoric, and reality. *Remedial & Special Education, 21*(5), 277–296.

Larry P. v. Riles, 343 F. Supp. 1306 (N.D. Cal. 1972).

Martin, F. (1979). Is it necessary to retest children in special education classes? *Journal of Learning Disabilities, 12,* 35–41.

Mills v. Board of Education, 348 F. Supp. 866 (1972).

Pennsylvania Association for Retarded Children (P.A.R.C.) v. Commonwealth of Pennsylvania, 334 F. Supp. 1257 (D.C.E.E. Pa. 1972).

Phillips, D. (1974). Case history of behavior modification project in a public school. In S. Keller & E. Ribes-Inesta (Eds.), *Behavior modification: Applications to education.* New York: Academic Press.

Plessy v. Ferguson, 163 U.S. 537 (16 S. Ct. 1138 [1869]).

Reynolds, C. R. (1962). A framework for considering some special issues in special education. *Exceptional Children, 28,* 367–370.

Rockner v. Walter, 700 F.2d (6th Cir. 1058 [1983]).

U.S. Department of Education. (2001). *Twenty-third annual report to Congress on the implementation of the Individuals with Disabilities Act.* Washington, DC: Author.

Vocational and Rehabilitations 504 section Act (1973).

Additional Readings for Professionals and Nonprofessionals

Kavale, K. A. (2000). History, rhetoric, and reality. *Remedial & Special Education, 21,* 277–296.

Pfeiffer, S. I., & Reddy, L. R. (Eds.). (1999). *Inclusion practices with special needs students: Theory, research, and application.* New York: Hawthorne.

Prasse, D. P. (1995). Best practices in school psychology and the law. In J. Grimes & A. Thomas (Eds.), *Best practices in school psychology III* (pp. 41–50). Bethesda, MD: National Association of School Psychologists.

Theodore J. Christ
Elizabeth A. Lyons

Mathematics

CURRICULUM-BASED MEASUREMENT

Curriculum-based measurement (CBM) in mathematics is an alternative method of directly monitoring students' performance on basic mathematics skills over time. More specifically, CBM requires students to be provided with daily 1- to 2-minute timed tests called probes. Each probe consists of individual mathematics problems that measure a specific skill (e.g., "two digits plus two digits" addition with carrying). By measuring performance for a specific skill daily, educators can adequately evaluate the effectiveness of instruction and changes in student progress on a day-by-day basis as opposed to more broad measurements of mathematics achievement as measured by end-of-unit tests or annual norm-referenced standardized achievement tests.

Although the purpose of measuring a single domain of mathematics is to ensure that students have mastered a specific skill before moving on to more complex problems that require more complex skills, the purpose of providing a brief time limit is to adequately assess the rate at which students can provide accurate responses. For example, a student who is learning two digits plus two digits addition with carrying may be provided a 2-minute probe that consists of a number of two digits plus two digits with carrying problems. Educators can then measure students' accuracy rates and compare them to some predetermined performance level (e.g., Deno & Mirkin, 1977). If a student's performance is higher than the cutoff score, results would suggest that a student is ready to be presented with a more complex skill. However, if a student does not meet the predetermined cutoff score, results would suggest that a student needs continued instruction and practice of the specific skill.

It is important to note that CBM does not evaluate student performance simply on accuracy alone. Instead, CBM emphasizes the importance of fluency (accuracy and speed together) and measures it by calculating the number of digits that are correct per minute of work on the probe. Research suggests that students who are not only accurate, but also respond quickly (i.e., are fluent) with regard to basic skills, are less likely to exhibit academic problems (Skinner, 1998). Educators measure fluency by calculating the number of digits that are correct per minute of work.

Advantages of CBM of Mathematics Achievement

CBM for mathematics came to be developed primarily as a result of dissatisfaction with more traditional forms of assessment such as norm-referenced standardized achievement tests and criterion reference tests. There are many primary advantages of CBM compared to more traditional methods of mathematics assessment (Elliott & Fuchs, 1997). First, the amount of time required to administer such standardized norm-referenced mathematics tests is considerably larger compared to CBM. Second, unlike norm-referenced and criterion-referenced assessments, 2-minute CBM probes cost very little to develop and administer. Whereas CBM probes can be administered by anyone trained in the use of a stopwatch and simple scoring procedures, other forms of measuring mathematics performance often require the administration to be conducted by a highly trained school psychologist.

Third, CBM offers the advantage of frequent repeated measurement. Whereas traditional forms of assessment generally lend themselves to one or two administrations only because most instruments only have one or two forms, the number of administrations of CBM probes is abundant as new forms can be quickly generated. Fourth, CBM allows for a more sensitive measurement of performance gains. That is, CBM allows educators to measure a specific skill such as two digit plus two digit addition with carrying whereas norm-referenced standardized assessment instruments often only provide an overall mathematics achievement score. Finally, because of CBM's ability to provide sensitive repeated measurement of specific mathematics skills, it can be used as a gauge for measuring the effectiveness of instructional strategies. Because traditional methods of assessment only provide overall mathematics performance and do not allow for frequent measurement, they do not lend themselves to measuring gains in performance over short periods of time nor do they allow for a sensitive evaluation of instructional strategies.

Limitations of CBM of Mathematics Achievement

Although CBM has many advantages in monitoring mathematics performance, it is not without notable limitations. First, there are no universal norms for CBM. That is, CBM does not afford educators good comparisons of student performance on a national level. Because there is no national curriculum, the focus of CBM has been to use local norms to compare students to one another in the same curriculum. Second, there is no consistent standardization. That is, CBM may be presented with students in more than one method, which may result in more than one result. For example, educators may present CBM probes in different formats (e.g., math problems vertically vs. horizontally), for different lengths of time (e.g., 1 vs. 2 minutes) in different settings (e.g., in class vs. in a special room) by different types of people (e.g., teachers vs. school psychologists). All of these variables could affect the outcome of student performance. Finally, although CBM provides a method of understanding a student's problem with respect to a specific type of mathematics task, it does not necessarily specify the most appropriate intervention to remediate the problem. In fact, one of the primary purposes of CBM is to evaluate the effectiveness of interventions.

Despite the limitations, it is apparent that CBM is a viable method for monitoring performance gains and for investigating the effectiveness of instructional strategies. As researchers develop more standardized methods of CBM and incorporate norms to allow for comparison of performance across students, CBM may become an even more effective method for monitoring student progress and making treatment decisions.

BIBLIOGRAPHY

Deno, S. L., & Mirkin, P. K. (1977). *Data-based program modification: A manual.* Reston, VA: Council for Exceptional Children.

Elliott, S. N., & Fuchs, L. S. (1997). The utility of curriculum-based measurement and performance assessment as alternatives to traditional intelligence and achievement tests. *The School Psychology Review, 26,* 224–233.

Skinner, C. H. (1998). Preventing academic skills deficits. In T. S. Watson & F. M. Gresham (Eds.), *Handbook of child behavior therapy* (pp. 61–82). New York: Plenum.

Additional Readings for Nonprofessionals

Fuchs, L. S., Fuchs, D. Hamlett, C. L., & Phillips, N. B. (1994). Classwide curriculum-based measurement: Helping general educators meet the challenge of student diversity. *Exceptional Children, 60,* 518–537.

Wright, J. (2003). Curriculum based measurement: A manual for teachers. Retrieved March 1, 2003, from http://www.jimwrightonline.com/pdfdocs/cbaManual.pdf

Additional Readings for Professionals

Shinn, M. R. (Ed.). (1998). *Advanced applications of curriculum-based measurement.* New York: Guilford.

GARY L. CATES

LEARNING DISABILITIES AND MATH COMPUTATION

Over the last several decades, important advances have been made in understanding the deficits that underlie many learning disabilities. Significant research has been conducted in the area of reading disabilities, and that phenomenon now seems to be better understood. An understanding of disabilities in mathematics appears somewhat more elusive. One difficulty is the complexity of mathematics. Each domain of mathematics (e.g., algebra, geometry, trigonometry) is quite intricate and contains multiple complex subdomains. In addition, children with disabilities in mathematics have unique patterns of strengths and weaknesses; there is no one mathematics disability. In spite of the complexity of the field and the difficulties of research, mathematics education for students with a learning disability cannot be ignored or avoided.

Math difficulties that begin in elementary school often persist through high school and into adult life. These difficulties can impede functioning by otherwise successful adults. Approximately 7 percent of students have significant, persistent difficulties in the areas of mathematics (Fuchs & Fuchs, 2001). For all students diagnosed with a learning disability, more than 50 percent of them have IEP goals in mathematics. Approximately one third of the instructional time in special education resource rooms is spent on mathematics.

According to the National Council of Teachers of Mathematics, four processes should be emphasized: problem solving, reasoning, communicating, and connecting. Although computation is just a small part of mathematics, it is a key skill that underlies all four of these processes. The basic computation skills of students with mathematics disabilities have been studied extensively in the United States, Europe, and Israel (Geary, 1996). These studies have indicated three significant findings: (1) Children with mathematical disabilities often have trouble remembering basic arithmetic facts. They do not remember as many facts as other children and they tend to forget facts more quickly. (2) These children tend to use immature procedures to solve simple computation problems (e.g., counting on their fingers). The children with mathematics disabilities tend to use immature procedures more frequently and for a longer period of time than other children. (3) Children with mathematics disabilities have difficulty solving more complex computation problems. A primary difficulty seems to be sequencing the component steps in solving these more complex problems.

If a child is suspected of having problems with mathematics computation, a number of assessment strategies are available. Formal assessment instruments include standardized survey tests (e.g., Iowa Test of Basic Skills), individually administered tests (e.g., Peabody Individual Achievement Test—Revised) or diagnostic math tests (e.g., KeyMath—Revised).

Informal strategies include informal inventories, error analysis, or curriculum-based assessment. A one-to-one mathematics interview is also an excellent tool for assessing computation skills. A mathematics interview should use manipulatives (e.g., coins, base 10 blocks, geoboards) and a calculator to assess a child's ability to solve computation problems. The examiner should note whether the child talks to himself, exhibits math anxiety, or draws a picture of the problem. This interview will give a clearer picture of a child's strengths and weaknesses in the area of computation.

If a child is found to have difficulties in the area of computation, five key principles should guide remedial and instructional efforts. First, teach the precursors of mathematics learning (e.g., matching and counting). Second, move from the concrete level such as adding two sets of blocks on a table to the semiconcrete level such as adding two sets of tally lines on a page to the abstract level such as adding $3 + 6$. A math concept that progresses through all three stages is more likely to be understood and remembered. Third, give students multiple opportunities for practice and review. These opportunities should be varied and may include such activities as flash cards, computer practice, and games. Fourth, teach generalization skills. Students need to be able to generalize their math learning to new settings and situations. Practices such as teaching skills to a mastery level, having discussions about situations in which to apply new skills, and providing students with a variety of examples and experiences during instruction can all facilitate generalization. Finally, teach mathematics vocabulary. Vocabulary words such as addend, sum, minuend, subtrahend, and difference will help students as they learn basic computation skills.

A foundational skill for computation is the basic math facts. Obviously, students need to know and understand the 100 basic addition, subtraction, multiplication, and division facts before they can solve more complex computation problems. Two programs that have reported success in teaching basic math facts to students with learning disabilities are MATHFACT (Thornton & Toohey, 1982/1985) and Strategic Math Series (Mercer & Miller, 1991/1993). Lerner (2003) also provides an excellent list of activities for teaching basic mathematics computation skills.

Students with a learning disability need to move beyond accuracy with basic computation facts to mastery. Mastery learning implies a level of automaticity where students respond to a math problem without hesitating or having to think about the answer. Some techniques that may improve computation speed are (a) setting a rate goal, (b) charting performance, (c) challenging students to beat their last score, (d) drilling difficult problems with flash cards, and (e) providing rate practice in small intervals.

A final principle in the techniques for improving computational skills in students with learning disabilities is a positive attitude toward math. Many students with a learning disability have a history of math failure. This history can result in negative attitudes toward math. Teachers and parents should address the affective components of math instruction. Students need to be involved in setting challenging, but attainable, goals. The relevance of math skills to daily life should be emphasized. Finally, communicating positive expectations to students is essential.

BIBLIOGRAPHY

Fuchs, L., & Fuchs, D. (2001). Principles for the prevention and intervention of math difficulties. *Learning Disabilities Research & Practice, 6*, 85–95.

Geary, D. C. (1996). Mathematical disabilities: What we know and don't know. *Learning Disabilities* [online]. Retrieved August 19, 2002, from http://www.ldonline.org/ld_indepth/math_skills/geary_math_dis.html

Lerner, J. W. (2003). *Learning disabilities: Theories, diagnosis, and teaching strategies* (9th ed.). Boston: Houghton Mifflin.

Mercer, C. D., & Miller, S. P. (1991/1993). *Strategic math series* (A series of seven manuals: Addition Facts 0–9; Subtraction Facts 0–9; Place Value: Discovering Tens and Ones; Addition Facts 10 to 18; Subtraction Facts 10 to 18; Multiplication Facts 0 to 81; Division Facts 0 to 81). Lawrence, KS: Edge Enterprises.

Thornton, C. A., & Toohey, M. A. (1982/1985). *MATHFACT: An alternative program for children with special needs* (A series of four kits: Basic Addition Facts; Basic Subtraction Facts; Basic Multiplication Facts; Basic Division Facts). Brisbane, Australia: Queensland Division of Special Education.

Additional Readings for Nonprofessionals

Heddens, J. W., & Speer, W. R. (1997). *Today's mathematics. Part II: Activities and instructional ideas* (9th ed.). Upper Saddle River, NJ: Merrill/Prentice Hall.

Thornton, C. A., & Toohey, M. A. (1985). Basic math facts: Guidelines for teaching and learning. *Learning Disabilities Focus, 1*, 44–57.

Additional Readings for Professionals

Carnine, D. (1997). Instructional design in mathematics for students with learning disabilities. *Journal of Learning Disabilities, 30*, 134–141.

Deshler, D., Schumaker, J., Lenz, B., Bulgren, J., Hock, M., Knight, J., et al. (2001). Ensuring content area learning by secondary students with learning disabilities. *Learning Disabilities Research & Practice, 16*, 96–108.

KENT COFFEY

LEARNING DISABILITIES AND MATH REASONING

Mathematics has been described as "a universal language," "a key to opportunity," and "the invisible culture of our age." Humans in our culture use math to develop a grocery budget, calculate the effects of a salary increase, and determine the tax on a video game. Mathematics is central to success in school and ultimately in life. This is equally true for students in general education and those with a learning disability. The Individuals with Disabilities Education Act of 1997 specified two mathematics problem areas for students with a learning disability: mathematics calculation and mathematics reasoning. Math reasoning can be thought of as solving novel problems when the means are not immediately apparent. Difficulties in math reasoning can affect a student's ability to problem solve, to apply appropriate strategies, and to think critically about mathematical concepts.

Children with a learning disability may well have difficulty in math reasoning. For many students with any type of academic learning disability, their math skills progress about 1 year for every 2 years of school attendance. As a result, over 60 percent of students with a learning disability achieve below grade level in mathematics. Approximately 26 percent of students with a learning disability receive instruction for problems in math. These significant math problems often include math reasoning as well as problems in calculation.

In a summary of math difficulties among students with learning disabilities, Montague (1996) noted that deficits in memory, strategies, and processes could impact a student's ability to conceptualize a problem, learn algorithms, and address a problem mathematically. In addition, problems with language and communication may interfere with students' ability to read, write, and discuss ideas about mathematics. These difficulties are at the heart of problems in math reasoning.

Assessment of problems with math reasoning begins with standardized tests or informal measures to gauge general math skills. A wide range of knowledge and skills would be examined at this level (e.g., time, money, basic operations, word problems, and measurement). Assessment of specific math skills may involve standardized diagnostic instruments, but are more typically measured by informal methods. This level of assessment begins to identify deficits and specific instructional objectives. The third level of assessment would examine problem solving and math reasoning. Informal methods such as gathering authentic work samples or administering teacher-constructed tests are most frequently used because they are well suited to evaluate math reasoning skills. Informal tests can examine the students' ability to apply mathematics to real-world situations and solve novel problems. A final step in the assessment process would be to examine the students' attitude toward mathematics. A diagnostic interview can provide useful information about anxiety or other feelings about math.

Mathematics instruction has been significantly influenced by the goals of the National Council of Teachers of Mathematics (NCTM). This group has identified curriculum and evaluation standards for grades K–12. Four themes are consistent across the grade levels: problem solving, reasoning, communicating, and connecting. These standards, however, make no overt or explicit reference to students with a learning disability. This presents a distinct challenge for both parents and teachers. How should math education be structured to meet the unique needs of students with a learning disability while addressing the NCTM standards?

The amount of research on mathematics instruction has increased significantly over the last decade. Some research indicates that poor or poorly designed instruction is one major cause of math difficulties in students with a learning disability. This makes decisions about what should be taught and how it should be taught extremely important. Carnine (1998) recommended five strategies that are especially useful in structuring math education for students with a learning disability: focusing on big ideas, teaching conspicuous strategies, making efficient use of time, communicating strategies in an explicit manner, and providing practice and review to promote retention.

A temptation that exists for both parents and teachers is to focus math instruction on computation alone. This practice ignores higher order skills such as problem solving and math reasoning. Students with a learning disability need to be able to solve real-world problems that they might face in industry or higher education. Problem solving should progress from simpler to more complex and emphasize an authentic context. Students should receive instruction on strategies that will assist in problem representation and problem solution.

When teaching problems in math reasoning, graduated coaching is especially helpful. Graduated coaching allows instruction on complex and multistep reasoning problems that might be too difficult for independent work. Students can use the support provided by appropriate coaching/questioning so as to be successful with math reasoning problems and other higher order math tasks.

BIBLIOGRAPHY

Carnine, D. (1998). Instructional design in mathematics for students with learning disabilities. In D. Rivera (Ed.), *Mathematics education for students with learning disabilities* (pp. 119–138). Austin, TX: Pro-Ed.

Montague, M. (1996). What does the "New View" of school mathematics mean for students with mild disabilities? In M. C. Pugach & C. L. Warger (Eds.), *Curriculum trends, special education, and reform: Refocusing the conversation* (pp. 84–93). New York: Teachers College Press.

Additional Readings for Nonprofessionals

Lovitt, T. C. (1995). *Tactics for teaching* (2nd ed.). Englewood Cliffs, NJ: Prentice–Hall.

National Council for Teachers of Mathematics. (2000). *Principles and standards for school mathematics.* Reston, VA: Author.

Staudacher, C., & Turner, S. (1994). *Practical mathematics for consumers* (2nd ed.). Paramus, NJ: Globe Fearon.

Additional Readings for Professionals

Bley, N. S., & Thornton, C. A. (1995). *Teaching mathematics to students with learning disabilities* (3rd ed.). Austin, TX: Pro-Ed.

Rivera, D. (Ed.). (1998). *Mathematics education for students with learning disabilities.* Austin, TX: Pro-Ed.

Stein, M., Silbert, J., & Carnine, D. (1997). *Designing effective mathematics instruction: A direct instruction approach* (3rd ed.). Upper Saddle River, NJ: Merrill/Prentice Hall.

Kent Coffey

Mattie T. v. Holladay (1979)

Mattie T. v. Holladay was a 1977 class-action lawsuit in the U.S. District Court for the Northern District of Mississippi in which the plaintiffs, 26 children with disabilities and their parents, filed charges against the Mississippi State Department of Education (MSDE) as well as six local school districts (Postlewaite, 1977) for violations under the Education of the Handicapped Act, Part B (EHA-B) and Section 504 of the Rehabilitation Act of 1973, as amended (Friedman, 1978/1979). When the plaintiffs requested, by subpoena, to review certain educational records, excluding all identifiable information, the school districts denied the request. The school districts claimed that under the Family Educational Rights and Privacy Act of 1974 (FERPA), the plaintiffs were required to provide prior notice to the parents of the children before reviewing the records. A federal district court ruled that FERPA did not require the plaintiffs to give prior notice to the parents because the subpoena called for nonidentifiable records. The federal district court ruling removed a significant barrier for legal discovery in education suits (Postlewaite, 1977).

On July 28, 1977, Judge Orma R. Smith ruled that the MSDE had violated plaintiffs' rights under the EHA-B and that two local school districts had violated the plaintiffs' rights under Section 504 of the Rehabilitation Act of 1973, as amended (Friedman, 1978/1979). Specifically, the court ruled that state education officials violated plaintiffs' rights under the EHA-B by failing to guarantee (a) procedural safeguards for children with disabilities and their parents/guardians, such as prior notice of a change in educational placement and the right to an impartial due process hearing to contest evaluation and placement decisions; (b) a plan to locate and identify all children in the state with disabilities requiring special education assistance; (c) the use of nondiscriminatory assessment and evaluation procedures used for classification and placement in special education of children with disabilities; and (d) the education of children with disabilities in general education settings with their nondisabled peers to the greatest extent possible (Friedman, 1978/1989).

This case culminated in a 1979 consent decree between the parties that resulted in several additional requirements and responsibilities of the MSDE. The MSDE was required to (a) employ a team of consultants to examine special education evaluations of children with disabilities, special education programs, as well as individualized education programs (IEPs); (b) submit a personnel assessment report to examine the training needs of personnel as well as a written training program that provided details of possible future training programs; (c) create a system for accountability so that Learning Resource Centers and Regional Screening Teams could make placement recommendations when determining a child's eligibility; and (d) collect and maintain data on the number of black and white children enrolled in what used to be referred to as Educable Mentally Retarded (EMR) special education classes (Kraft, n.d.).

The local school districts were found to have violated the plaintiffs' rights under Section 504 of the Rehabilitation Act of 1973 by failing to ensure the necessary and appropriate educational services (Friedman, 1978/1979). The court ordered the districts to thoroughly evaluate and individually test each plaintiff within 20 days of the order to determine the child's educational needs. Also, within 30 days of completing each child's evaluation, the districts were to provide the child with the appropriate services on the basis of his/her needs (Friedman, 1978/1979).

The ruling established that individuals have federal grounds for action under the EHA-B and that state departments of education are responsible for implementing policies, overseeing local school districts, and requiring compliance with the EHA-B; it also established the rights of students with disabilities to immediate and appropriate educational placement under Section 504 (Friedman, 1978/1979). Finally, this case set guidelines and clearly defined the timelines for identification, referral, evaluation, program development, and placement in special education (Kraft, n.d.). This was the first ruling under the Education of the Handicapped Act of 1974 (Friedman, 1978/1979), which was later amended by The Education for All Handicapped Children Act of 1975 (Pub. L. 94-142). This latter law was further amended and renamed the Individuals with Disabilities Education Act in 1990.

BIBLIOGRAPHY

Friedman, P. R. (1978/1979). Mental retardation and the law: A report on status of current court cases. *Yearbook of Special Education*, 194–215.

Kraft, R. (n.d.). *Non-discrimination in assessments*. Retrieved July 10, 2002, from www.ppmd.org/publications/nondiscrimination_in_assessments.html

Postlewaite, J. (1977). Mattie T. v. Holladay: Denial of Equal Education. *Amicus*, 2(3), 38–44.

DANIEL H. TINGSTROM
DANNELL S. ROBERTS

McCarthy, Dorothea

Dorothea McCarthy was born on March 4, 1906, in Minneapolis, Minnesota. She attended the University of Minnesota, where she obtained B.A. (1925) and Ph.D. (1928) degrees in psychology. McCarthy was one of the first to receive a Ph.D. in child psychology from the Institute of Child Development located at the university. She later married Dr. Robert T. Rock on June 9, 1934, with whom she had a daughter (Duchan, 2001).

Upon receiving her Ph.D., Dr. McCarthy became a National Research Council Fellow in child development until 1929. She then worked for the California Bureau of Juvenile Research as a clinical psychologist for 2 years before accepting the position as director of a nursery school and associate professor at the University of Georgia from 1930 to 1932. She continued her work with children as the director of the Child Guidance Clinic and associate professor at Fordham University. McCarthy also served the American Psychological Association as President of the Division of Developmental Psychology (Division 7) in 1960–1961 (Duchan, 2001).

One of McCarthy's primary research interests was the normal language development of children. She examined various phases and individual differences in the speech and language of children. She also investigated how children differed in language ability when entering school, and gender differences. McCarthy's findings suggested that girls were typically more advanced in language abilities when compared with boys of the same chronological age. She attributed this finding to society's acceptance of girls playing more conversation-based games whereas boys were expected to play more active games and rely less on speech (McCarthy, 1954).

McCarthy's additional research interests included babbling in infancy as a predictor of later intelligence, mother–child relationships and speech problems, environmental factors in the home, and language disabilities. She concluded that language disorders were not a disability that occurred in isolation. Rather, she attributed nonorganic language disorders to the emotional insecurity that a child developed from living in dysfunctional households. McCarthy claimed that the most influential factor in predicting a child's language skills is personality of the parent, along with other environmental variables in the household.

McCarthy theorized that a child raised in a relaxed and safe environment is more likely to excel in learning trials when compared with a child exposed to a threatening and frustrating home environment. When a child is subjected to an unsafe home environment, their tendency is to withdraw from others and become defensive (McCarthy, 1954). Thus, McCarthy believed that educational disabilities in children were due to emotional insecurities and not to mental disabilities.

While training under Dr. Florence L. Goodenough at the Institute of Child Development, McCarthy became convinced that the cognitive abilities of children could be measured during early childhood. Her continued experiences with psychometric tools in settings such as nurseries and child day-care centers brought her attention to how preschool children and learning-disabled children were not being accurately assessed with traditional instruments. She was concerned that, although progress was being made in the development of scales for older children, less effort was being dedicated to the assessment of young children (McCarthy, 1972).

Dr. Anna Speisman Starr, clinical psychologist at Rutgers University, invited McCarthy to participate in her research on the differential diagnosis among persons with mental retardation. Both Starr and McCarthy acknowledged the limitations of the tools used to assess young children with mental retardation. Their concern was that many children were labeled with a disability when assessed with an instrument that was not designed to accurately measure children at young ages. McCarthy's research in this area motivated her desire to develop a measurement that could reliably measure young children. Subsequently, the McCarthy Scales of Children's Abilities (MSCA) was developed in 1972 as a more sensitive instrument to assess the abilities of preschool children.

Dorothea McCarthy was a pioneer in the field of psychology, particularly in the assessment of young children. Her research in the area of language development guided the practice of many speech pathologists in the 1960s. Her contributions in these and other areas led to numerous advances in the understanding of children and their development.

See also: Bayley Scales of Infant Development—2nd Edition; Intelligence Quotient (IQ)

BIBLIOGRAPHY

Duchan, J. (2001) *Dorothea Agnes McCarthy 1906* [online]. Available at http://www.acsu.buffalo.edu/~duchan/historysubpages/dorotheamccarthy.html

McCarthy, D. (1954). Language disorders and parent–child relationships. *Journal of Speech & Hearing Disorders, 19*, 514–523.

McCarthy, D. (1972). *McCarthy Scales of Children's Abilities.* New York: The Psychological Corporation.

Additional Readings for Professionals

McCarthy, D. (1960). Language development. *Monographs of the Society for Research in Child Development, 25*, 5–14.

McCarthy, D. (1959, November). Measurement of cognitive abilities at the preschool and early childhood level. *Proceedings of the Conference on Testing Problems, Educational Testing Service*, pp. 10–25.

TONYA SARTOR BUTLER

Mental Disorders

The American Psychiatric Association publishes periodic updates to its *Diagnostic and Statistical Manual of Mental Disorders* (*DSM*). The most recent edition (*DSM-IV-TR*; American Psychiatric Association, 2000) offers this definition of a mental disorder:

> . . . a clinically significant behavioral or psychological syndrome or pattern that occurs in an individual and that is associated with present distress (e.g., a painful symptom) or disability (i.e., impairment in one or more important areas of functioning) or with a significantly increased risk of suffering death, pain, disability, or an important loss of freedom. In addition, this syndrome or pattern must not be merely an expectable and culturally sanctioned response to a particular event, for example, the death of a loved one. Whatever its original cause, it must currently be considered a manifestation of a behavioral, psychological, or biological dysfunction in the individual. Neither deviant behavior (e.g., political, religious, or sexual) nor conflicts that are primarily between the individual and society are mental disorders unless the deviance or conflict is a symptom of a dysfunction in the individual, as described above. (p. xxxi)

On the basis of this definition, a behavior or pattern associated with a variety of problems in day-to-day living that do not cause distress or impairment would not be included as a mental disorder. For example, it is expected that individuals may show heightened levels of arousal in response to everyday stressors like exams, for students; finding parking, for the urbanite; or returning a library book on time. Demonstrating an expected level of anxiety consistent with local cultural norms would not qualify one to be diagnosed with a mental disorder. In addition, even if someone in mainstream USA were identified as a communist (political), Muslim (religious), or gay/bisexual—in spite of the local culture not supporting behaviors associated with these lifestyles—none of these factors would qualify one for a mental disorder.

The *DSM* is to be used to diagnose serious difficulties with functioning. The *DSM-IV-TR* (American Psychiatric Association, 2000) lists 10 major categories of clinical disorders usually first diagnosed in infancy, childhood, or adolescence. They include Mental Retardation, Learning Disorders, Motor Skills Disorder, Communication Disorders, Pervasive Developmental Disorders, Attention-Deficit and Disruptive Behavior Disorders, Feeding and Eating Disorders of Infancy or Early Childhood, Tic Disorders, Elimination Disorders, and finally, Other Disorders of Infancy, Childhood, or Adolescence. There are too many other categories to list here, but of special relevance to school psychologists and parents may be Substance Abuse, Eating Disorders, Mood Disorders, Anxiety Disorders, Sleep Disorders, and Adjustment Disorders.

Ultimately, one must distinguish between everyday problems of living and a mental disorder on the basis of the level of distress or impairment caused by the behavior pattern in question. If a parent thinks his/her child may meet criteria for a mental disorder, the parent should contact a local mental health provider. It is often the case that a school psychologist or a pediatrician can help make a referral for appropriate evaluation and treatment recommendations. Although it is true that children may outgrow some common problems with simply the passage of time, early treatment may dramatically reduce the amount of negative impact felt by a child.

See also: Anxiety; Attention-Deficit/Hyperactivity Disorder; Depression in Children and Adolescents; *Diagnostic and Statistical Manual of Mental Disorders*; Encopresis; Enuresis; Learning Disabilities; Tics

BIBLIOGRAPHY

American Psychiatric Association. (2000). *Diagnostic and statistical manual of mental disorders* (4th ed., text rev.). Washington, DC: Author.

Additional Reading for Nonprofessionals

http://www.nasponline.org (National Association of School Psychologists)

Additional Reading for Professionals

House, A. E. (2002). *DSM-IV diagnosis in the schools.* New York: Guilford. (Updated 2002)

KEVIN J. ARMSTRONG

Mental Health Consultation

School psychologists typically deliver psychoeducational services to students either (a) directly or (b) indirectly by working with adult staff members such as teachers. Consultation is said to occur when a school psychologist works in a collegial, cooperative relationship with a staff member (termed *consultee*) to improve the learning and adjustment of students (Erchul & Martens, 2002). Mental health consultation, behavioral consultation, and organizational development consultation are considered the three major theoretical/conceptual models of consultation used by school psychologists (Reschly, 1976). Of these, mental health consultation is the oldest, and its creation and aspects of its subsequent development may be traced to community psychiatrist Gerald Caplan (Erchul, 1993a).

ORIGINS

In Israel in 1949, Gerald Caplan and his small clinical staff were charged with the daunting task of attending to the mental health needs of 16,000 adolescent immigrants. Further complicating this work were the adolescents' living in more than 100 residential institutions, transportation within Israel at that time was difficult, and there were about 1,000 initial requests for assistance. Given these obstacles to implementing a standard model of referral/diagnosis/psychotherapy of individual clients, Caplan developed a new approach to service delivery that would use limited professional resources more efficiently (Caplan & Caplan, 1999).

Specifically, instead of meeting with individual clients at a central Jerusalem clinic, Caplan and his staff traveled to the many institutions to meet with the caregivers of the referred adolescents. Supportive, collegial discussions with these caregivers about their clients often resulted in the caregivers' returning to work with a fresh, enhanced perspective that resulted in better management of client problems. By focusing his staff's professional energies on consultative activities that improved the functioning of caregivers, Caplan thought that the mental health of many more clients could be positively affected than was possible through traditional one-on-one therapy. The contemporary practice of mental health consultation emerged from the described approach, which Caplan originally named "counseling the counselors" (Caplan & Caplan, 1999, p. 3).

THE CONSULTANT–CONSULTEE RELATIONSHIP

Mental health consultation (MHC) specifies unique characteristics of the consultant–consultee working relationship. These characteristics distinguish MHC from other professional relationships such as supervision, teaching, and psychotherapy, and include

1. The consultative relationship is essentially triadic, involving a consultant (e.g., psychologist) and one or more consultees (e.g., teachers) and clients (e.g., students). Though considered professionals in their own right, consultees typically lack the training and experience that consultants possess.
2. The desired working relationship in MHC is coordinate and nonhierarchical, and ideally there is no power differential between consultant and consultee.
3. Consultee work-related problems—not personal problems—are the basis for consultative discussion.
4. Because the consultant has no administrative responsibility for or formal authority over the consultee, the

ultimate professional responsibility for the client's welfare remains with the consultee.

5. The consultee's participation in MHC is considered voluntary in that the consultee retains the freedom to accept or reject whatever guidance the consultant may offer.

6. Messages exchanged between consultant and consultee are regarded as confidential, unless the consultant believes someone will be harmed if silence is kept.

7. MHC has a twofold purpose: (a) to help the consultee with a current professional problem and (b) to equip the consultee with added insights and skills that will permit him or her to deal effectively with similar future problems, ideally without the consultant's assistance. This latter aspect builds a strong case for MHC as a method to achieve the primary prevention of mental health and educational problems (Caplan & Caplan, 1999).

THE FOUR TYPES OF MENTAL HEALTH CONSULTATION

Caplan has specified four types of consultation based on two major considerations: (a) whether the content focus of consultation is a client problem versus an administrative problem and (b) whether the primary goal is providing information from the consultant's area of expertise versus improving the consultee's problem-solving capacity.

Client-centered case consultation may be the most familiar type of consultation performed by school psychologists. For example, a teacher who is experiencing difficulty with a student may seek out a school psychologist who then evaluates the student, arrives at a diagnosis, and offers recommendations concerning how the teacher might best work with the student. The primary goal of client-centered case consultation is to develop a plan for dealing with a client's difficulties, with consultee education or skill development seen as secondary.

Consultee-centered case consultation, which emphasizes the difficulties a consultee faces with a particular client, is the type of MHC most closely linked to Caplan. The primary goal of consultee-centered case consultation is to remediate the deficits in the consultee's professional functioning that are contributing to difficulties in handling the present case, with client improvement seen as secondary.

Program-centered administrative consultation resembles client-centered case consultation, except that a program is the focus. Specifically, the consultant considers the problems surrounding the development of a new program or some aspect of organizational functioning.

Consultee-centered administrative consultation is the fourth type of MHC. Its goal is to improve the professional functioning of members of an administrative staff, and is generally based on a more broadly defined consultant role. For example, the consultant may not confine discussion to problems brought to his/her attention by consultees, but instead may be active in identifying and assessing a variety of organizational problems.

SOURCES OF CONSULTEE DIFFICULTY AND THEIR REMEDIATION

Particularly when operating within the consultee-centered types of MHC, it is critical for a consultant to assess the possible sources of consultee difficulty, which are lack of knowledge, lack of skill, lack of self-confidence, and lack of objectivity. Although the first three mentioned are relatively straightforward, lack of objectivity appears more complex. Lack of objectivity occurs when consultees lose their customary professional distance when working with clients and then cannot apply their skills effectively to solve a current work problem (Caplan & Caplan, 1999). Caplan has stated that, when supervisory and administrative mechanisms are functioning well in an organization (and lack of knowledge and lack of skill therefore can be ruled out as explanations), most occurrences of consultee ineffectiveness will be attributable to a lack of objectivity (Erchul, 1993b).

Caplan has delineated five major types of consultee lack of objectivity: direct personal involvement, simple identification, transference, characterological distortion, and theme interference. To restore consultee objectivity, Caplan has proposed several verbally mediated (i.e., theme interference reduction, verbal focus on the client, parable) and nonverbally mediated psychodynamic techniques (i.e., nonverbal focus on the client, nonverbal focus on the consultation relationship; Caplan & Caplan, 1999).

MORE RECENT DEVELOPMENTS

The original conception of the mental health consultant was that of a clinically trained professional whose home base was outside the consultee's work setting. However, as the practice of consultation has grown, consultants have been hired more frequently as regular staff members of organizations. With the emergence of internal consultants have come challenges to some time-honored beliefs regarding consultation. For example, a school psychologist serving as an internal consultant may find it difficult to act nonhierarchically in a school when he/she possesses more knowledge about learning, instruction, and behavior management than some teachers. In addition, organizational factors may force a school psychologist to adopt a direct, hands-on service approach rather than the indirect, advisory approach prescribed by MHC.

Recognition of these and other constraints of the internal consultant's role has led to the development of a different type of interprofessional communication termed *mental health collaboration*. Interestingly, Caplan has asserted that mental health collaboration eventually must replace MHC as the most frequent mode of interprofessional communication used by consultants who are staff members of an organization (Caplan, Caplan, & Erchul, 1994). Time will tell if this transformation will occur within the field of school psychology.

See also: Conjoint Behavioral Consultation; Direct Behavioral Consultation

BIBLIOGRAPHY

Caplan, G., & Caplan, R. B. (1999). *Mental health consultation and collaboration.* Prospect Heights, IL: Waveland.

Caplan, G., Caplan, R. B., & Erchul, W. P. (1994). Caplanian mental health consultation: Historical background and current status. *Consulting Psychology: Practice and Research, 46*(4), 2–12.

Erchul, W. P. (Ed.). (1993a). *Consultation in community, school, and organizational practice: Gerald Caplan's contributions to professional psychology.* Washington, DC: Taylor & Francis.

Erchul, W. P. (1993b). Reflections on mental health consultation: An interview with Gerald Caplan. In W. P. Erchul (Ed.), *Consultation in community, school, and organizational practice: Gerald Caplan's contributions to professional psychology* (pp. 57–72). Washington, DC: Taylor & Francis.

Erchul, W. P., & Martens, B. K. (2002). *School consultation: Conceptual and empirical bases of practice.* New York: Kluwer Academic/Plenum.

Reschly, D. J. (1976). School psychology consultation: "Frenzied, faddish, or fundamental?" *Journal of School Psychology, 14,* 105–113.

Additional Reading for Nonprofessionals

Brown, D., Pryzwansky, W. B., & Schulte, A. C. (2001). *Psychological consultation: Introduction to theory and practice* (5th ed.). Boston: Allyn & Bacon.

Additional Readings for Professionals

Meyers, J., Brent, D., Faherty, E., & Modafferi, C. (1993). Caplan's contributions to the practice of psychology in schools. In W. P. Erchul (Ed.), *Consultation in community, school, and organizational practice: Gerald Caplan's contributions to professional psychology* (pp. 99–122). Washington, DC: Taylor & Francis.

Trickett, E. J., Barone, C., & Watts, R. (2000). Contextual influences in mental health consultation: Toward an ecological perspective on radiating change. In J. Rappaport & E. Seidman (Eds.), *Handbook of community psychology* (pp. 303–330). New York: Kluwer Academic/Plenum.

WILLIAM P. ERCHUL

Merrill, Maud

Maud A. Merrill (James) (1888–1978) began her career in psychology as a graduate student at Stanford in 1919, where she later became a faculty member in the Department of Psychology (Seagoe, 1975). Prior to her education at Stanford, Merrill was a research assistant at the Minnesota School for Feeble-Minded. Much of her research was related to the education of *special class children*, and she published an article detailing a scale to measure reading ability. Using select passages of Century Oldstyle text, Merrill determined the average reading rate for children Grades 1 through 6 (Merrill, 1919). Merrill suggested that to determine a child's reading ability, a test should be given to the child using the passages that correspond to the child's mental age (Merrill, 1919).

When Lewis Terman began his second revision of the Stanford–Binet intelligence scale, he recruited Maud Merrill as his main assistant (Seagoe, 1975). Terman was particularly interested in Merrill's experience with mental institutions and mental disabilities (Seagoe, 1975). Once the second revision was completed, Merrill evaluated its effectiveness, and in 1937 it was published in the book *Measuring Intelligence.* Merrill also assisted in Terman's third revision of the Stanford–Binet published in 1960 after Terman's death.

Participation in the revision of the Stanford–Binet was not Merrill's only contribution to the field of psychology. Merrill assisted Catherine Cox in evaluating the biographies of 300 geniuses, the findings of which were reported in the second volume of *Genetic Studies of Genius.* Cox, accompanied by several assistants including Merrill, searched for people considered to be geniuses and estimated the IQ of each person based on biographical information (Cox, 1926). Merrill also compiled and edited a volume of writings that were published as *Studies in Personality* in honor of Lewis Terman's 65th birthday.

Merrill published *Problems of Child Delinquency* in 1947, in which she discussed the environment, personality, and characteristics of delinquent children. In "Oscillation and progress in clinical psychology," an article published in *Journal of Consulting Psychology* in 1951, Merrill focused on the growth of clinical psychology and the changing roles of the clinician in the 1950s.

See also: Terman, Lewis M.

BIBLIOGRAPHY

Cox, C. M. (1926). *Genetic studies of genius. II. The early mental traits of three hundred geniuses.* Stanford, CA: Stanford University Press.

Merrill, M. A. (1919). A scale for the individual measurement of reading ability. *Journal of Educational Psychology, 10,* 389–400.

Seagoe, M. V. (1975). *Terman and the gifted.* Los Altos, CA: William Kaufmann.

Additional Reading for Nonprofessionals

Fagan, T. K., & Warden, P. G. (1996). *Historical encyclopedia of school psychology.* Westport, CT: Greenwood.

Additional Readings for Professionals

McNemar, Q., & Merrill, M. A. (Eds.). (1942). *Studies in personality: Contributed in honor of Lewis M. Terman.* New York: McGraw-Hill.

Merrill, M. A. (1918). The ability of special class children in the "Three R's". *The pedagogical seminary, 25.*

Merrill, M. A. (1947). *Problems of child delinquency.* Boston: Houghton Mifflin.

Merrill, M. A. (1951). Oscillation and progress in clinical psychology. *Journal of Consulting Psychology, 15,* 281–289.

Terman, L. M., & Merrill, M. A. (1937). *Measuring intelligence.* Boston: Houghton Mifflin.

JENNIFER T. FREELAND
JENNIFER A. RENN

Metropolitan Achievement Readiness Test

The *Metropolitan Achievement Readiness Test* (MRT) is one of the achievement assessment series originally developed in the 1930s for use in the New York City public schools. With a long history of revised editions, this readiness test is intended to evaluate a child's basic and advanced skills in reading and mathematics in prekindergarten through first grade. The sixth edition consists of two levels (Nurss & McGauvran, 1995). Level 1 is intended to assess the skills in prekindergarten children. Level 2 is intended to assess skills in middle kindergarten through beginning first-grade children. This readiness test is the latest in a line of tests with a history of support by test reviewers.

Level 1 of the current version of the MRT consists of five tests: Beginning Reading Skill Area (composed of Visual Discrimination, Beginning Consonants, and Sound–Letter Correspondence); Story Comprehension; and Quantitative Concepts and Reasoning. A Prereading Composite is also offered. At Level 2, the five tests are the same with Beginning Reading Skills composed of three tests with some variability from Level 1 (Beginning Consonants, Sound–Letter Correspondence, and Aural Cloze with Letter). The MRT is individually administered at Level 1, but group administered at Level 2. Types of scores available include percentile ranks, normal curve equivalents, scaled scores, and standard scores (Level 1 only). Administration time is estimated to be 80–90 minutes. A determination of skill level is provided with ratings of proficiency, acquisition, and need instruction on the basis of performance. However, the rating is based on the raw score and it is uncertain how the criteria for these categories were determined.

It is important to note that in his review of the current MRT, Kamphaus (2001) indicated several cautions worthy of consideration. First, the MRT should be used only for screening (some skills are assessed with only one item). Second, the development and other psychometric aspects of the latest MRT have also been questioned or the psychometric information is inadequate. Kamphaus concurs with other test reviewers, indicating that the test has inadequate validity studies to support its use and that it lacks application to current learning theories. Historically, reviewers have expressed a concern for a lack of attention to fairness and bias in testing, and lack of adequate interpretation and application unless local norms are developed and used (Kamphaus, 2001; Ravitch, 1994). For example, a frequent difficulty with readiness tests in general is the child's unfamiliarity with and lack of exposure to the tasks and materials. This leads the evaluator to underestimate the child's ability. Furthermore, although the MRT is individually administered at Level 1, it is group administered at Level 2. Many children may not be prepared to govern their own behavior during test taking and may require individual attention and assistance not provided to those at Level 2 (i.e., middle kindergarten through middle first grade).

In summary, although this test might provide users with information about a child's readiness in areas of reading and mathematics, caution is advised about this instrument. It is likely that other readiness tests with stronger psychometric properties and theoretical foundation will provide more conclusive information for those who are interested in determining a child's basic skills and abilities in mathematics and reading areas.

See also: Metropolitan Achievement Tests

BIBLIOGRAPHY

Kamphaus, R. W. (2001). Review of the Metropolitan Readiness Tests, 6th ed. In B. S. Plake & J. C. Impara (Eds.), *The fourteenth mental measurements yearbook* (pp. 747–749). Lincoln, NE: Buros Institute of Mental Measurements.

Novak, C. (2001). Review of the Metropolitan Readiness Tests, 6th ed. In B. S. Plake & J. C. Impara (Eds.), *The fourteenth mental measurements yearbook* (pp. 749–751). Lincoln, NE: Buros Institute of Mental Measurements.

Nurss, J. R., & McGauvran, M. E. (1995). *Metropolitan Readiness Tests, 6th ed.* San Antonio, TX: Psychological Corporation.

Ravitch, M. M. (1994). Review of the Metropolitan Readiness Tests, 5th ed. In J. C. Impara & L. L. Murphy (Eds.), *Buros desk reference: Psychological assessment in the schools* (pp. 387–390). Lincoln, NE: Buros Institute of Mental Measurements.

Additional Readings for Nonprofessionals

Lyman, H. B. (1997). *Test scores and what they mean.* Boston: Allyn & Bacon.

http://www.early-education.org.uk (The British Association for Early Childhood Education)

http://www.naeyc.org (National Association for the Education of Young Children)

Additional Readings for Professionals

Bracken, B. A. (2000). *The pychoeducational assessment of preschool children* (3rd ed.). Boston: Allyn & Bacon.

Nuttal, E. V., Romero, I., & Kalesnik, J. (1999). *Assessing and screening preschoolers: Psychological and educational dimensions* (2nd ed.). Boston: Allyn & Bacon.

CARLEN HENINGTON

Metropolitan Achievement Tests

The *Metropolitan Achievement Tests* (MAT) were originally developed in the 1930s for use in New York City public schools. With a long history of revised editions, this battery of achievement tests has been considered to be a relatively strong battery (Sattler, 1994). The Eighth Edition (METROPOLITAN8) is the most recent in a long line of achievement tests from Harcourt Educational Measurement (Harcourt, n.d.). This battery of tests assesses student achievement in five academic areas: reading, mathematics, language, science, and social studies. From edition to edition, some variability in tests and curriculum areas can be found; however, with each edition, the test developers have attempted to address the criticisms of the previous edition.

THE METROPOLITAN8

The METROPOLITAN8 is intended to measure foundation skills and critical thinking processes in children, with and without special needs, in grades K through 12 (Harcourt, n.d.). The battery consists of 12 subtests, although not all the subtests are administered to all 13 age groups. Similar to most of the previous editions, the METROPOLITAN8 offers assessments for reading, mathematics, and language, with individual subtests in four other subject areas.

The Total Reading score is composed of the following subtests (corresponding grade level in parentheses): Sounds and Print (K.0–4.5), Reading Vocabulary (1.5–12), Reading Comprehension (1.5–12). The total number of items and the time for administration depend on the child's grade level, ranging from 40 items for 30 minutes at K level to an upper limit of 110 items for a total of 90 minutes in reading at the 3.5–4.5 level. At the younger levels, emergent literacy assessment is available, and open-ended reading is available to assess student comprehension through open-ended questions.

The Total Mathematics score is composed of the following subtests: Mathematics (K to 1.5 and 9 to 12), Mathematics Concepts and Problem Solving (1.5 to 9.5), Mathematics Computation (1.5 to 9.5). The total number of items and the time for administration range from 30 items for 30 minutes at the K level to a high of 78 items for 50 minutes at the 5.5 to 9.5 level.

Language (30 to 48 items), Spelling (30 items), Science (30 to 40 items), and Social Studies (30 to 40 items) are individual subtests with administration times ranging from 25–30 minutes at the lower levels to 40–48 minutes at the upper levels. If all subtests are administered to the lower levels, the battery takes approximately 100 minutes. At the middle and upper levels, the battery requires approximately 5 hours to administer all the subtests appropriate for those grade levels.

The instrument comes with a variety of related materials intended to assist the classroom teacher in making individual educational decisions and in developing curriculum modifications to meet their students' needs. These teacher aids assist the teacher in identifying individual reading levels for each child and include on-level reading lists and materials to track reading progress. Also available is information to assist in the diagnosis of academic difficulties and comparison of reading skills typical for a particular grade level. Process and content scores allow evaluation of skills, strategies and processes, and knowledge in each subject area. The tests provide typical scale scores (e.g., percentiles, grade equivalents, normal curve equivalents). Practice tests are available through grade 8. The publishers indicate that the METROPOLITAN8 can be customized in a variety of ways through their *Select* service (e.g., select specific tests in booklet format, change order of tests, customize answer sheets). Alternative versions of the tests are available, including Braille, large print, and audiotaped versions. The METROPOLITAN8 was normed in 1999–2000. Age groups in the norm sample were grouped in half-year increments (e.g., 1.5 is a first-grade level).

In summary, the METROPOLITAN8 is the latest in a long line of readily recognizable achievement tests available to classroom teachers. It provides assessment in the typical subject areas and utilizes modern technology to provide the user with flexibility to tailor the assessment process to his/her needs.

See also: Curriculum-Based Measurement

BIBLIOGRAPHY

Harcourt. (n.d.). *Metropolitan Achievement Tests* (8th ed.). Retrieved October 18, 2003, from http://www.hemweb.com/trophy/achvtest/mat8info.htm

Sattler, J. M. (1994). Review of Metropolitan Achievement Tests (7th ed.). In J. C. Impara & L. L. Murphy (Eds.), *The Buros desk reference: Psychological assessment in the schools* (pp. 28–35). Lincoln, NE: Buros Institute of Mental Measurements.

Additional Readings for Nonprofessionals

Grissmer, D., Flanagan, A., Williamson, S., & Kawata, J. (2001). *Improving student achievement: What state NAEP tests scores tell us.* Santa Monica, CA: Rand.
Lyman, H. B. (1997). *Test scores and what they mean.* Boston: Allyn & Bacon.

Additional Readings for Professionals

Plake, B. S., Impara, J. C., & Spies, R. A. (Eds.). (in press). *The sixteenth mental measurements yearbook.* Lincoln, NE: Buros Institute of Mental Measurements.
Sattler, J. M. (2001). *Assessment of children: Cognitive applications* (4th ed.). San Diego, CA: Author.

CARLEN HENINGTON

Mills v. Board of Education of the District of Columbia (1972, 1980)

Mills v. Board of Education of the District of Columbia (1972) pertained to supporters of Peter Mills and six other school-age children with disabilities who were denied a publicly supported education from the District of Columbia Public School system. The supporters of these children requested that the school district provide these children free and appropriate public education. Prior to the court case, these children received labels such as *behavior problem, retarded, epileptic, brain-damaged and hyperactive,* and *brain-damaged and retarded* (*Mills v. Board of Education of the District of Columbia,* 1972). On the basis of the evaluation of each of these children, it was determined that they could all benefit from an appropriate education.

At the beginning of the 1971–1972 school year, the legal guardians of Mills and six other children were told by the school district that each of the children would receive some type of education either through the public school or through grants paying for private schools. However, none of these children received the instruction promised to them because of a number of reasons, including suspension, expulsion, or exclusion. The representatives of Mills and the six other children sued on behalf of all school-age children in the school district who were excluded from a public education in the District of Columbia. The plaintiffs requested that all children in the district who had been denied a publicly sponsored education be given a free and appropriate education. During this court case, it was recommended that a comprehensive plan for the assessment, treatment, and education of children with physical or mental difficulties be implemented for individuals ranging from 3 to 21 years of age. This recommendation served as a precursor to Public Law 94-142, the Education for All Handicapped Children Act of 1975 (Prasse, 1995).

At the time of this case, it was revealed that the laws in the District of Columbia stated that all children who live in the District of Columbia were allowed admittance into the public schools at no cost to the child or their family. The Board of Education of the District of Columbia may excuse a child from attending school if it is determined that he/she cannot mentally or physically benefit from school. However, if it is shown that the child can profit from special instruction it is required that the child attend classes.

The judgment ruled in favor of Mills and the other children in the district and included a number of decisions that were eventually included in the Education for All Handicapped Children Act of 1975 (Prasse, 1995). The rulings stated that no child who is eligible for a public education in the District of Columbia be denied a public school education unless there is a reasonable alternative such as special education or grants that would allow attendance to a private school. In addition, the court ruled that the District of Columbia school system must provide a free and appropriate publicly supported education to all children of school age residing in the district regardless "of the degree of the child's mental, physical, or emotional disability or impairment." Furthermore, insufficient funds in the school district could not be a factor for denying education to school-age children. The decree stated that a child will not be suspended from public school for more than 2 days because of disciplinary reasons without being given an appropriate hearing and without providing educational services while the child is suspended. The judge also requested that announcements should be placed in the news media to inform other children to come forward if they had been denied an education from the District of Columbia public school system.

The district was given deadlines by which publicly supported education was to be awarded to those identified in the plaintiff class. This decree also stated that the school district must develop an encompassing plan to address the way in which children would be identified, assessed for eligibility of special services, and placed into such services. It required that this plan include specific information about the curriculum, teacher qualifications, and other services necessary to provide educational programs to identified children (*Mills v. Board of Education of the District of Columbia,* 1972). However, the school system did not comply with the orders by the court, and in 1975, the defendants were held in contempt. In 1980, the plaintiffs sought additional assistance and requested that the order be enforced by the court (Sellers, 1984).

The Mills case served as a model for later cases in which children with disabilities were denied a public education. A similar case was *Pennsylvania Association for Retarded Citizens (PARC) v. Commonwealth of Pennsylvania* (1972). Both cases served as models for Pub. L. 94-142 in 1975. The Mills case was somewhat different from PARC in that the Mills ruling applied not only to children with mental retardation but to children with behavior problems and other physical and mental disabilities. The Mills case was one of the first to address the concern that each child should be provided an equal education. In addition, the Mills and PARC cases were among the first to require that a "child find" be instituted to locate and identify all children with disabilities (Jacob-Timm & Hartshorne, 1998).

BIBLIOGRAPHY

Jacob-Timm, S., & Hartshorne, T. S. (1998). *Ethics and law for school psychologists* (3rd ed.). New York: Wiley.

Mills v. Board of Education of the District of Columbia, 384 F. Supp. 866 (1972). Retrieved August 23, 2002, from the LexisNexis database.

Prasse, D. P. (1995). Best practices in school psychology and the law. In A. Thomas & J. Grimes (Eds.), *Best practices in school psychology III* (pp. 41–50). Washington, DC: National Association of School Psychologists.

Sellers, J. M. (1984). Civil rights papers: Washington lawyers' committee for civil rights under law: Public education legal services project: A private sector initiative in the area of public education. *Howard Law Journal, 27,* 1471. Retrieved September 16, 2002, from the LexisNexis database.

Additional Readings for Nonprofessionals

Fischer, L., & Sorenson, G. P. (1996). *School law for counselors, psychologists, and social workers* (3rd ed.). White Plains, NY: Longman.

Yell, M. L. (1998). *The law and special education.* New Jersey: Merrill.

Additional Readings for Professionals

Fagan, T. K., & Wise, P. S. (1994). *School psychology: Past, present, and future.* White Plains, NY: Longman.

Herr, S. S. (1999). Special education law and children with reading and other disabilities. *Journal of Law and Education, 28,* 337. Retrieved September 16, 2002, from the LexisNexis database.

KAREN I. DITTMER-MCMAHON

Moral Reasoning in Children and Adolescents

Moral reasoning can be defined as a form of practical reasoning directed toward drawing conclusions about what is right or wrong, what should be done in principle, and assigning intentions to behaviors in particular situations (Richards, 2003). The development of moral reasoning in children and adolescents is currently of great social concern owing to the increased incidents of school violence, teenage pregnancy, and teenage suicide. Moreover, providing the needed formation to young people at home and school in order to help them face novel or perplexing moral questions as adults (e.g., euthanasia, abortion, surrogate motherhood, cloning) is of paramount concern to parents and educational professionals.

Although contemporary psychology has provided some guidance to parents and others responsible for the formation of young people, the study of moral reasoning has an extensive philosophical, theological, and political history. Sixth-century Greek philosophers, who did not live by structured religious doctrine, developed foundational principles regarding moral reasoning in Western civilization. Early Greeks accepted that the immortality of the gods justified a divine supremacy over mortal man. In hierarchical fashion, kings represented temporal supremacy and therefore were vested with the authority to dictate standards of morality. Moral reasoning was viewed as nothing more than habits or customs; right and wrong was determined by the will of the gods and/or the monarchy. During that time, no theological or philosophical rationale was assigned to moral issues. It was not until economic conditions resulted in a division among social classes that speculative morality began to emerge. Nonetheless, when systematic moral examination began to develop, the discourse was primarily philosophical rather than theological (Robinson, 1981).

For generations, Homer's *Iliad* and *The Odyssey* provided the standard to guide ancient Greek civilization. Schoolchildren were formed in moral thinking through the memorization of the Homeric epics. Although Homer's gods were instructive, they presented the early Greeks with a great deal of latitude in regard to a model for right conduct. Robinson (1981) maintains that Greek moral behavior was polarized between the Dionysian and the Apollonian philosophies. Dionysus was the god of fertility and represented drunkenness and hedonism. This philosophy promoted living a self-focused life directed by individual passions. In contrast, Apollo represented the life of reason, restraint, order, and justice. Robinson contends that those attempting to understand the human person, from the time of antiquity to the present day, have been faced with the challenge of untangling the web of passion and reason represented in the Dionysian and Apollonian worldviews.

Three primary Greek philosophers set the metric by which all other scholars in the Western world would measure their ideas about moral thought until the beginning of the twentieth century. Socrates (469–399 B.C.), one of the most influential Greek philosophers, is known only through the writings of others. Primarily, Socrates is portrayed through the writing of his student Plato. Although a practical man, Socrates believed that the unexamined life was not worth living. He compared the soul (the animating force within the human person) to the political State. Whereas the State was made up of three classes (merchants, auxiliaries, and counselors), Socrates maintained that the soul was guided by three principles: the rational, the appetitive, and the passionate (Book IV, 441; in Robinson, 1981). Through the dialogues between Socrates and his contemporaries, Socrates reveals that the just individual is one who achieves harmony among these three principles such that "reason controls appetite and, as an auxiliary to reason, passion strengthens the resolve" (Book IV, 443; in Robinson, 1981, p. 61).

Disillusioned with the Greek city-state political structure following the execution of his mentor, Plato (427–347 B.C.) dedicated his life to philosophy and the formation of the Greek citizenry (Oliver, 1999). He believed the world consisted of eternal, objective concepts (forms) by which the value of things and human actions (virtue) could be assessed. Plato concluded that unjust rulers were individuals who were ignorant of the perfection of forms of governance and, thus, lacked the virtue necessary to be in a position of authority. Similar to his mentor Socrates, Plato believed that morality and justice were ultimately a controlled balance of reason, desire, and self gratification.

Although the focal point of morality for Socrates and Plato was justice, Aristotle (384–322 B.C.), a student of Plato, focused on the development of a systematic framework for understanding truth. In addition, Aristotle believed that it was necessary to move beyond the philosophical speculation of his mentor and focus on the reality of the natural world. Aristotle also believed that the natural world followed consistent laws that were revealed through detailed accumulative observations. He utilized a simple method of logical reasoning (syllogism) to analyze complex issues at a particular level in order to identify universal truths level. "The most important contribution of Aristotle . . . is his distinction between theoretical or speculative order and the practical order, the order of contemplation as against the order of action" (Sullivan, 1992, p. 52). Aristotle maintained that wisdom and virtue were the mark of a well-formed person. Attaining happiness required the knowledge of goodness and the virtue to act with wisdom and moderation. The impact Aristotle has had on moral reasoning through philosophy, religion, science, and politics is immeasurable (Soccio, 1998).

Beginning in 334 B.C., Alexander the Great, a devoted student of Aristotle, was responsible for introducing Greek culture, and thus Western philosophy and moral thought, to the people he conquered throughout much of the civilized world (e.g., Persia, Asia Minor, Egypt). By 148 B.C., Rome had conquered Greece and the distinction between the Eastern and Western minds, with their respective histories and philosophies, was becoming apparent. The concept of European culture, central to Christian philosophy, began to develop during the second century as differences between the Roman troops of the western empire—"the Europeans"—and the troops in the eastern sector of the empire—"the Orientals"—became more distinct.

Although moral, philosophical, and theological beliefs of the early Roman Christians shared similarities with pagan Greek views, the Doctors of the Western Church (e.g., St. Ambrose, St. Jerome, St. Augustine) began to designate doctrine specific to the Roman Catholic Church during the fourth century. Much of the Church structure was based on the Roman form of government, and a long succession of European rulers identified Catholicism as the official religion (Oliver, 1999). For nearly 12 centuries, the Roman Catholic Church dominated Western thought and, thus, moral formation.

The Protestant Reformation of the sixteenth century not only resulted in substantive changes in the religious and political structure of Europe (and ultimately all of the Western world), but philosophical development as well. Whereas many practices of the Catholic Church were being brought into question, similarly philosophers were engaging in discourse regarding the human person. This period is significant in that these philosophical debates were being conducted separate from formal religious and political structures.

Philosophy's newfound independence gave rise to revolutionary developments in Western thought and ushered in the Enlightenment. No longer was it necessary for individuals to rely on religious practices to guide moral reasoning. The scientific revolution of the seventeenth and eighteenth centuries promised an objective and systematic means for addressing cultural challenges. Although the conflict between science and religion was troubling to many, scholars nonetheless welcomed the challenge of carefully navigating the intellectual waters between the two.

Without question, modern philosophical thinking began with the French philosopher René Descartes (Soccio, 1998). Although Plato and Aristotle had drawn distinctions between the body and the soul or mind, Descartes' philosophy of human rationality was founded on that distinction (i.e., Cartesian dualism). Descartes' search for unquestionable certainties led him to conclude that reason is superior to sense evidence. Only reason could establish clear and distinct ideas and give meaning to the human experience. Otherwise, Descartes believed that no reliable distinction could be drawn between reality and illusion (Soccio, 1998). Although few present-day philosophers will agree to the rigid Cartesian distinction between body and mind, Descartes established a new philosophical and scientific method of thought that would later be examined and modified by other scholars of the Enlightenment period (e.g., Locke, Hume, and Kant). In addition, the Romantics would counter the Enlightenment and view rationality as a threat to the preservation of human individuality and creativity. Nonetheless, modern psychological theory related to moral development continues to be highly influenced by the philosophies developed during the Enlightenment.

Although Sigmund Freud, Erik Erikson, and Jean Piaget would examine the development of moral reasoning in children and adolescents, longitudinal research initiated in the 1960s by Lawrence Kohlberg (1964, 1976, 1984) most directly addressed the issue and continues to serve as the contemporary authority. Influenced by Piaget's (1932) work, Kohlberg proposed a stage theory of moral reasoning (Wade & Tavris, 2002). His study presented nine hypothetical moral dilemmas to 72 boys from two Chicago suburbs. The boys were equally divided among three age groups (10-, 13-, and 16-year-olds), two social classes (middle and working class), and those high and low in sociometric popularity. Twelve delinquent boys and 12 auxiliary participants were also included at different points in the study. Kohlberg concluded that children advance through 3 two-stage levels of moral development (Wade & Tavris, 2002). At the Preconventional level, children initially obey rules out of fear of punishment. Later, children at the first level obey because they believe it is in their best interests. At the second level, Conventional, the 10- or 11-year-old begins to conform to the conventional adult perspective of morality. Later in the second level, young children begin to understand law and justice. Finally, at the third level of moral development, the Postconventional level, individuals realize that others may have differing values of morality. Kohlberg maintains that few people reach the highest level of Postconventional morality, the stage at which the moral standard is based on a universal understanding of human rights.

Kohlberg's theory of moral development is not without critics, and the results of his study have been challenged. Based primarily on the logic of moral reasoning, Robinson (1981) argues that Kohlberg's work ignores issues such as property rights and the common good of society. Wade and Tavris (2002) identify three limitations of Kohlberg's moral development theory. They maintain that it discounts educational and cultural influences related to moral reasoning. Next, they indicate that the research does not take into consideration the situational aspects of moral reasoning. Finally, Wade and Tavris point out the inconsistency between moral reasoning and behavior as a factor not accounted for in Kohlberg's longitudinal study. The most celebrated critic of the Kohlberg theory, however, is Carol Gilligan (1982). Gilligan's work drew distinctions between the traditional masculine-oriented ethics of justice that has dominated Western thought throughout history and the feminine-oriented ethics of care. Gilligan pointed out that the majority of women in studies subsequent to Kohlberg's original research did not arrive at the advanced levels of moral reasoning. In fact, Soccio (1998) reported "Kohlberg himself thought that, as a rule, women were excluded from the highest stages of moral development. Thus, if Kohlberg's theory is sound, then women are morally inferior to men." Gilligan brought into question the validity of a theory of moral development based on rules and duties while ignoring relationships and intimate concern for one another.

Historical analysis of the development of moral reasoning in Western culture suggests a complex interplay between passion and reason, as well as philosophical, religious, and political structures. Whereas parents once relied on the Church or the *Polis* to direct them in the appropriate formation of their children, they now tend to rely on social sciences. Religious and political approaches addressing the formation and maintenance of society have been replaced by scientific/empirical methods. Regardless of the historic era or the guiding structure of moral development, philosophical truths that endure across time, specific individuals, and social orders serve as the foundational moral compass. St. Thomas wrote, "the study of philosophy is that we may know not what men have taught but what the truth of things is" (see Sullivan, 1992).

Socrates and Plato identified control of self through reason as a means of becoming morally just. Aristotle viewed wisdom and virtue as the fundamental elements of morality. Early Christian doctors of the Church (e.g., St. Augustine, St. Thomas Aquinas) integrated the wisdom of the pagan Greeks with scripture in order to provide extensive social guidance based on charitable acts. Descartes developed scientific methods to guide reason in order to separate passion and reason. Finally, researchers from the twentieth century, such as Kohlberg, identify developmental stages utilizing the scientific method to examine the process by which children and adolescents strike a balance between passion and reason to become morally responsible individuals within a social environment. Therefore, persons interested in the moral formation of young people in the twenty-first century must not expect to find "the answer" in a single psychological study, or a single parenting book, or an individual scholar. Rather, the informed person must examine the consistent moral elements that have served civilizations well throughout history.

See also: Antisocial Behavior; Development

BIBLIOGRAPHY

Gilligan, C. (1982). *In a different voice: Psychological theory and women's development.* Cambridge, MA: Harvard University Press.

Kohlberg, L. (1964). Development of moral character and moral ideology. In M. Hoffman & L. W. Hoffman (Eds.), *Review of child development research.* New York: Russell Sage.

Kohlberg, L. (1976). Moral stages and moralization: The cognitive–developmental approach. In T. Lickona (Ed.), *Moral development and behavior.* New York: Holt, Rinehart & Winston.

Kohlberg, L. (1984). *Essays in moral development. Vol. 2: The psychology of moral development: The nature and validity of moral stages.* San Francisco: Harper & Row.

Piaget, J. (1932). *The moral judgment of the child.* New York: Macmillan.

Richards, M. (2003). *History of philosophy.* New York: Barnes & Noble.

Robinson, D. N. (1981). *An intellectual history of psychology* (rev. ed.). New York: Macmillan.

Soccio, D. J. (1998). *Archetypes of wisdom: An introduction to philosophy.* Belmont, CA: Wadsworth.

Sullivan, D. J. (1992). *An introduction to philosophy: The perennial principles of the Classical Realist Tradition.* Rockford, IL: Tan.

Wade, C., & Tavris, C. (2002). *Invitation to psychology* (2nd ed.). Upper Saddle River, NJ: Prentice-Hall.

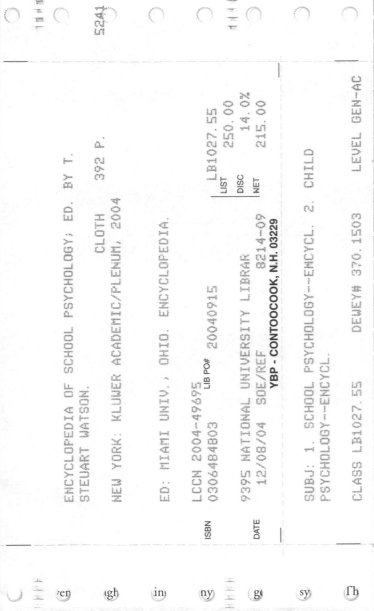

score. No subtest scores are available. The composite score can be converted into a perceptual quotient (overall performance relative to others the same age) with a mean (statistical average) of 100 and a standard deviation (the average variability of scores) of 15 points. Likewise, a perceptual age (the age at which the individual's score reflects an average score) can also be obtained from the composite score. The authors report no statistical information with regard to reliability or validity of the scores, but point out that these data were strong in the original version.

A second version of the test is available that presents the items in a vertical rather than horizontal format to accommodate hemispatial visual neglect (the tendency to not acknowledge stimuli on either the left or right side when a lesion on the opposite side of the brain is present).

See also: Bender Visual Motor Gestalt Test—Second Edition

BIBLIOGRAPHY

Colarusso, R. R., & Hammill, D. D. (1996). *Motor-free visual perception test—revised.* Novata, CA: Academic Therapy Publications.

Additional Reading for Nonprofessionals

Leonard, P., Foxcroft, C., & Kroukamp, T. (1988). Are visual–perceptual and visual–motor skills separate abilities? *Perceptual & Motor Skills, 67,* 423–426.

Additional Readings for Professionals

Bolgna, N. B. (2001). Review of the Motor-Free Visual Perception Test—Revised. In B. S. Plake & J. C. Impara (Eds.), *The fourteenth mental measurements yearbook* (pp. 784–785). Lincoln, NE: Buros Institute of Mental Measurements/University of Nebraska Press.

Volpe-Johnstone, T. (2001). Review of the Motor-Free Visual Perception Test—Revised. In B. S. Plake & J. C. Impara (Eds.), *The fourteenth mental measurements yearbook* (pp. 785–787). Lincoln, NE: Buros Institute of Mental Measurements/University of Nebraska Press.

GARY L. CATES

lationships (being able to mentally manipulate objects in space and see them in relation to other objects), visual discrimination (ability to discriminate among features of objects), figure–ground discrimination (ability to discriminate an object from its background), visual closure (ability to see complete figures when only portions are presented), and visual memory (ability to recall dominate features or sequences of objects). Data from these five areas are aggregated to provide an overall composite

Motor Tics

According to Lees (1985), motor tics are sudden, rapid, repetitive, nonrhythmic motor movements involving discrete muscle groups. Motor tics vary in intensity and form, and can be simple or complex. Simple motor tics involve one or more muscle groups that coordinate to create a single motor movement that is brief and has no apparent purpose. Examples of simple motor tics include mouth stretching and head jerking. Complex motor tics involve several coordinated muscle groups that mimic normal movements, are more complicated, longer in duration, and appear to have some purpose (Lees, 1985). Examples of complex motor tics include twisting and bending the body, making obscene gestures, or rotating the body. Findley (2001) states that children with complex motor tics are also likely to have one or more simple tics.

Motor tics can be a symptom of a tic disorder. According to Findley (2001), tic disorders that may involve motor tics include transient tic disorder, chronic tic disorder, or Tourette Disorder (TD). Transient tic disorder involves one or more motor and/or vocal tics that occur multiple times per day, almost every day, for less than 1 year. Chronic motor tic disorder involves one or more motor tics that occur multiple times per day, almost every day, for a year or longer. TD involves multiple motor tics and at least one vocal tic, which have been present for at least 1 year. Childhood tics lasting 1 year or more typically continue for at least a few more years (Findley, 2001).

ONSET, PREVALENCE, AND COURSE

Shapiro, Brunn, Shapiro, and Sweet (1978) state that tic disorders primarily occur in childhood for a majority of children. Childhood tics are typically more intense between 11 and 14 years of age, but then tend to become less intense during puberty and even milder by adulthood. Motor tics typically begin between 2 and 14 years of age, with the average age of onset being between 6 and 8 years of age. Tic disorders are typically more prevalent in males than females, with rates in males ranging from 6 to 18 percent and 3 to 11 percent in females (Findley, 2001). According to Lees (1985), motor tics can vary in form, and are only limited by the types and number of movements they mimic. Some individuals with tics only exhibit one or two tics and others show larger numbers of tics. The first and most frequent motor tics typically involve the upper part of the face in movements such as eye blinking or grimacing. Tics tend to become less common farther from the head, with toe shaking or curling being the least common motor tics. According to Findley (2001), tics typically occur in clusters and their frequency fluctuates over weeks and months. New tics may develop spontaneously over time and may develop from observing others.

ETIOLOGY

Three areas have been studied as possible contributing factors to tics. These include genetic influences, neurological factors, and environmental factors. According to Findley (2001), research suggests that several genes likely contribute to the development of tic disorders (a polygenic effect). There is

approximately a 15% chance that an individual will develop chronic tics if a family member has a tic disorder. Neurological variables found to contribute to tic disorders involve brain regions responsible for motor control, inhibiting processes, and higher order cognitive processing. Persons with tics are believed to have overactive dopamine systems (Findley, 2001).

Findley (2001) states that various environmental factors may also contribute to the development of tics, such as stress, perinatal difficulties, and autoimmune and infectious processes. These complications can cause a greater vulnerability to more severe tics. Although it is unlikely that tics are acquired and maintained solely through operant processes, it has been demonstrated that providing attention for tics may increase tics significantly (Watson & Sterling, 1998). Other environmental events that have been found to worsen tics include being anxious, angry, self-conscious, being in the presence of others who are critical of tics, and discussing tic symptoms. Silva, Dinohra, Barickman, and Friedhoff (1995) conducted a Tourette Syndrome survey that found 78 percent of subjects had an increase in tics during upsetting or anxious events, and tics in 50 percent of subjects increased when experiencing fatigue or emotional trauma. It was also found that children with more severe tics reacted to a larger number of environmental factors, whereas environmental factors had less of an effect on children with less severe tics.

COMORBIDITY

Findley (2001) asserts that Attention-Deficit/Hyperactivity Disorder (ADHD) and Obsessive–Compulsive Disorder (OCD) are the conditions most commonly comorbid with tic disorders. It is estimated that 50 percent of children with TD also have ADHD, and 30 percent have OCD. However, between 11 and 80 percent of children with TD exhibit obsessive–compulsive behaviors but do not meet the full criteria for OCD. Other anxiety-based disorders such as phobias and depression have also been found to be elevated in people with tic disorders.

ASSESSMENT

Because of the high frequency, variability, and similarity to other more complex movements, motor tics can be difficult to measure and record. According to Carr and Rapp (2001), primary assessments should be conducted by a medical professional to determine if a tic disorder exists. Any medical conditions that may be contributing to the tic disorder can then be identified. If no medical conditions seem to be apparent, other methods should be used to assess the situation. Nonmedical tic assessment methods commonly consist of direct observation, self-monitoring, interviews, and reports from the individual or family members. Carr and Rapp (2001) state that direct observation is typically conducted using video and audio recorders to monitor the frequency of tics. Self-monitoring of tic occurrence has been used but may lead to significant reductions in tic frequency simply because the individual is more aware and cautious of the tics.

Despite the availability of direct observation methods, research has relied primarily on clinician rating scales of tic severity. Such scales typically ask clinicians to rate the frequency, complexity, intensity, interference, and level of impairment produced by the tics.

TREATMENT

Watson, Howell, and Smith (2001) state that the most commonly used treatments for tic disorders are pharmacological treatment and behavior therapy. Severe cases have also been treated with surgical intervention. Pharmacotherapy, the most common of which involves neuroleptics, helps decrease the intensity and frequency of tics by blocking the effects of the neurotransmitter dopamine. The most effective neuroleptics include haloperidol and pimozide, but these medications tend to produce aversive side effects ranging in severity from dry mouth and restlessness to muscle spasms, the most severe effect being seizures. More recent medications used for tic disorders include guanfacine and clonidine. Both of these medications are generally seen as less effective but more tolerable than the neuroleptics.

According to Watson et al. (2001), the most effective and widely used behavioral treatment for motor tics is habit reversal. Habit reversal trains the individual to become more aware of the tics and then to emit a response that competes with the tic. For example, a competing response for a motor tic consisting of a head jerk may involve tensing the neck muscles to block the tic from happening. The competing response is typically used for 1 minute, contingent on the occurrence of the tic or its antecedents. Social support is also a component of habit reversal that is sometimes used to promote the use of the competing response. Social support involves praising and prompting the correct use of the competing response by a child's parent(s) or a significant person in an adult's life. According to Watson et al. (2001), studies suggest up to a 93 percent decrease in tics using habit reversal.

See also: Attention-Deficit/Hyperactivity Disorder; Depression in Children and Adolescents; Habits; Tourette Syndrome; Vocal Tics

BIBLIOGRAPHY

Carr, J. E., & Rapp, J. T. (2001). Assessment of repetitive behavior disorders. In D. W. Woods & R. G. Miltenberger (Eds.), *Tic disorders, trichotillomania, and other repetitive behavior disorders: Behavioral approaches to analysis and treatment* (pp. 9–27). New York: Kluwer Academic.

Findley, D. B. (2001). Characteristics of tic disorders. In D. W. Woods & R. G. Miltenberger (Eds.), *Tic disorders, trichotillomania, and other repetitive behavior disorders: Behavioral approaches to analysis and treatment* (pp. 53–67). New York: Kluwer Academic.

Lees, A. J. (1985). *Tics and related disorders.* New York: Churchill Livingstone.

Shapiro, A. K., Bruun, R. D., Shapiro, E. S., & Sweet, R. D. (1978). *Gilles de la Tourette Syndrome.* New York: Raven.

Silva, R. R., Dinohra, M. M., Barickman, J., & Friedhoff, A. J. (1995). Environmental factors and related fluctuation of symptoms in children and adolescents with Tourette's disorder. *Journal of Child Psychology and Psychiatry, 36,* 305–312.

Watson, T. S., Howell, L. A., & Smith, S. L. (2001). Behavioral interventions for tic disorders. In D. W. Woods & R. G. Miltenberger (Eds.), *Tic disorders, trichotillomania, and other repetitive behavior disorders: Behavioral approaches to analysis and treatment* (pp. 73–91). New York: Kluwer Academic.

Watson, T. S., & Sterling, H. E. (1998). Brief functional analysis and treatment of a vocal tic. *Journal of Applied Behavior Analysis, 31,* 471–474.

Additional Readings for Nonprofessionals

Handler, L. (1998). *Twitch and shout.* New York: Dutton.

Kushner, H. I. (1999). *A cursing brain.* Cambridge, MA: Harvard University Press.

Shimberg, E. F. (1995). *Living with Tourette syndrome.* New York: Fireside.

Additional Readings for Professionals

Leckman, J. F., & Cohen, D. J. (1999). *Tourette's syndrome: Tics, obsessions, compulsions.* New York: Wiley.

Woods, D. W., & Miltenberger, R. G. (Eds.). (2001). *Tic disorders, trichotillomania, and other repetitive behavior disorders: Behavioral approaches to analysis and treatment.* New York: Kluwer Academic.

DOUGLAS W. WOODS
ANDREA M. BEGOTKA

Nn

National Standards for School Psychology Training Programs

National standards for the preparation of school psychologists define the training experiences that should be included in school psychology graduate programs and the competencies that should be acquired by candidates through such training. Such standards, and their application through a program review process, provide the means by which school psychology defines and evaluates quality training and helps to assure that those entering the profession are able to provide a range of effective services that positively affect children, youth, families, and other clients.

Although there are other professional organizations that have standards for training and/or internships (e.g., the American Psychological Association's standards for doctoral programs in psychology, Association of Psychology Postdoctoral and Internship Centers criteria for internships, Council of Directors of School Psychology Programs guidelines for internships in school psychology), the National Association of School Psychologists (NASP) is the only national organization with recognized, comprehensive standards specific to the training of school psychologists. NASP standards are approved by the National Council for Accreditation of Teacher Education (NCATE). NASP is one of 18 affiliated professional specialty organizations whose standards are applied as part of the NCATE accreditation process. NASP also independently reviews and approves programs.

NASP first established guidelines for the graduate preparation of school psychologists in 1972, and has updated and revised its training standards regularly since that time. NASP's most recent *Standards for Training and Field Placement Programs in School Psychology* (NASP, 2000) was approved in 2000. The approval process involved soliciting input from a variety of professional organizations representing psychology, school psychology, and allied professions, as well as opportunities for input from practitioners, trainers, administrators, graduate students, and consumers. NASP standards must undergo two readings and approval by the NASP Delegate Assembly. Standards to be applied as part of the NCATE accreditation process must also be approved by NCATE through its Specialty Area Studies Board.

NASP's training standards define the training, experiences, and professional competencies that must be demonstrated to provide high-quality school psychological services. NASP training standards address five key areas:

- Program Context/Structure
- Domains of School Psychology Training and Practice
- Field Experiences/Internship
- Performance-Based Program Assessment and Accountability
- Program Support/Resources

These areas are described below.

PROGRAM CONTEXT/STRUCTURE

NASP training standards in this area are intended to assure that "school psychology training is delivered within a context of program values and clearly articulated training philosophy, goals, and objectives" and that training includes "a comprehensive, integrated program delivered by qualified faculty, as well as substantial field experiences necessary for the preparation of competent school psychologists whose services positively impact children, youth, families, and other consumers" (NASP, 2000, p. 1). Specific standards require such elements as

- The need for an integrated and sequential program clearly identified as being in school psychology
- A programmatic commitment to understanding and responding to human diversity
- Opportunities for affiliation with colleagues, faculty, and the profession
- Qualified faculty (at least two with specialization in school psychology) who are actively engaged in the profession
- Professional development opportunities for practicing school psychologists

In addition, specialist programs must consist of a minimum of 3 years of full-time graduate study or the equivalent, including at least 60 graduate semester hours and a 1-year, 1200 clock hour supervised internship. Doctoral programs must consist of at least 4 years of full-time study or the equivalent, including at least 90 graduate semester hours and a 1-year, 1500 clock hour supervised internship.

DOMAINS OF SCHOOL PSYCHOLOGY TRAINING AND PRACTICE

The "Domains of School Psychology Training and Practice," which share some traits with other NASP standards and guidelines, define specific competencies to be possessed by entry-level professionals. Such competencies include both foundational knowledge and professional skills needed to deliver effective services that positively affect outcomes in each domain and are based on the extensive analysis provided by Ysseldyke et al. (1997) in *School Psychology: A Blueprint for Training and Practice II*.

The domains are reproduced below exactly as they appear in the NASP training standards (NASP, 2000). Further descriptions of the domains may be found in the appendixes that accompany the standards.

- *Data-based decision making and accountability:* School psychologists have knowledge of varied models and methods of assessment that yield information useful in identifying strengths and needs, in understanding problems, and in measuring progress and accomplishments. School psychologists use such models and methods as part of a systematic process to collect data and other information, translate assessment results into empirically based decisions about service delivery, and evaluate the outcomes of services. Data-based decision making permeates every aspect of professional practice.

- *Consultation and collaboration:* School psychologists have knowledge of behavioral, mental health, collaborative, and/or other consultation models and methods and of their application to particular situations. School psychologists collaborate effectively with others in planning and decision-making processes at the individual, group, and system levels.

- *Effective instruction and development of cognitive/academic skills:* School psychologists have knowledge of human learning processes, techniques to assess these processes, and direct and indirect services applicable to the development of cognitive and academic skills. School psychologists, in collaboration with others, develop appropriate cognitive and academic goals for students with different abilities, disabilities, strengths, and needs; implement interventions to achieve those goals; and evaluate the effectiveness of interventions. Such interventions include, but are not limited to, instructional interventions and consultation.

- *Socialization and development of life skills:* School psychologists have knowledge of human developmental processes, techniques to assess these processes, and direct and indirect services applicable to the development of behavioral, affective, adaptive, and social skills. School psychologists, in collaboration with others, develop appropriate behavioral, affective, adaptive, and social goals for students of varying abilities, disabilities, strengths, and needs; implement interventions to achieve those goals; and evaluate the effectiveness of interventions. Such interventions include, but are not limited to, consultation, behavioral assessment/intervention, and counseling.

- *Student diversity in development and learning:* School psychologists have knowledge of individual differences, abilities, and disabilities and of the potential influence of biological, social, cultural, ethnic, experiential, socioeconomic, gender-related, and linguistic factors in development and learning. School psychologists demonstrate the sensitivity and skills needed to work with individuals of diverse characteristics and to implement strategies selected and/or adapted on the basis of individual characteristics, strengths, and needs.

- *School and systems organization, policy development, and climate:* School psychologists have knowledge of general education, special education, and other educational and related services. They understand schools and other settings as systems. School psychologists work with individuals and groups to facilitate policies and practices that create and maintain safe, supportive, and effective learning environments for children and others.

- *Prevention, crisis intervention, and mental health:* School psychologists have knowledge of human development and psychopathology and of associated biological, cultural, and social influences on human behavior. School psychologists provide or contribute to prevention and intervention programs that promote the mental health and physical well-being of students.

• *Home/school/community collaboration:* School psychologists have knowledge of family systems, including family strengths and influences on student development, learning, and behavior, and of methods to involve families in education and service delivery. School psychologists work effectively with families, educators, and others in the community to promote and provide comprehensive services to children and families.

• *Research and program evaluation:* School psychologists have knowledge of research, statistics, and evaluation methods. School psychologists evaluate research, translate research into practice, and understand research design and statistics in sufficient depth to plan and conduct investigations and program evaluations for improvement of services.

• *School psychology practice and development:* School psychologists have knowledge of the history and foundations of their profession; of various service models and methods; of public policy development applicable to services to children and families; and of ethical, professional, and legal standards. School psychologists practice in ways that are consistent with applicable standards, are involved in their profession, and have the knowledge and skills needed to acquire career-long professional development.

• *Information technology:* School psychologists have knowledge of information sources and technology relevant to their work. School psychologists access, evaluate, and utilize information sources and technology in ways that safeguard or enhance the quality of services (NASP, 2000, pp. 2–3).

FIELD EXPERIENCES/INTERNSHIP

Supervised field experiences and internship are critical to the training of effective school psychologists. NASP standards in this area are intended to assure that "...candidates have the opportunity to apply their knowledge, to develop specific skills needed for effective school psychological service delivery, and to integrate competencies..." (NASP, 2000, p. 3). In addition, one of the core NASP beliefs as reflected in its standards is that those preparing to be school psychologists should have some supervised internship or equivalent experience that occurs in a school setting. Specific standards require such elements as

• Supervised practica and internship that involve the integration and application of the full range of school psychology competencies and domains

• Collaboration between the training program and field sites that includes a written internship plan and both formative and summative evaluation of intern performance

• An internship that is completed on a full-time basis over 1 year or on a half-time

• Basis over 2 years, and that includes at least 600 hours in a school setting

• At least 2 hours of supervision per full-time week by a credentialed school psychologist or, for non-school settings, a psychologist credentialed for that setting

PERFORMANCE-BASED PROGRAM ASSESSMENT AND ACCOUNTABILITY

Standards in this area are intended to assure that training programs systematically assess candidates and various program components, and use the resulting information to "...monitor and improve program quality" (NASP, 2000, p. 4). A key aspect of program accountability is the performance-based assessment of candidates and the services they provide. Specific standards in this area are

• Multiple evaluation procedures including such measures as performance portfolios, field supervisor evaluations, and candidate performance on licensing/certification exams

• Published criteria for the admission and assessment of candidates that include both academic and professional competencies, as well as professional work characteristics needed for effective practice as a school psychologist (including respect for human diversity, communication skills, effective interpersonal skills, ethical responsibility, adaptability, and initiative/dependability)

• A systematic, valid process to ensure that all candidates are able to "...integrate domains of knowledge and apply professional skills in delivering a comprehensive range of services evidenced by measurable positive impact on children, youth, families, and other consumers" (NASP, 2000, p. 4)

In order to assist programs in the development and implementation of performance-based measures, NASP distributes *A Guide for Performance-Based Assessment, Accountability, and Program Development in School Psychology Training Programs* (Waldron, Prus, & Curtis, 2000) as a companion to its standards.

PROGRAM RESOURCES/SUPPORT

NASP standards in this area address the resources needed to support the training program and its faculty and students. Specific elements include

- Faculty resources and support, including maximum teaching load and student-to-faculty ratio needed to ensure sufficient candidate access to faculty instructors, mentors, and supervisors
- Candidate support, including advisement, supervision, and opportunities for funding and other assistance needed to attain their educational objectives
- Adequate physical resources such as office and clinic facilities
- Accommodations for the special needs of candidates and faculty with disabilities
- Adequate library and information technology resources and services

THE NASP PROGRAM REVIEW AND APPROVAL PROCESS

The application of NASP standards occurs through a rigorous, evidence-based review process in which programs must prepare and submit extensive written documentation of compliance with standards. Each review is initially conducted by two or three trained school psychology trainers, administrators, and/or practitioners who may not be from the same state in which the program is located or have any potential "conflict of interest" that might bias their review. Reviewers evaluate the program's compliance with each standard. Most standards in the areas of Program Context/Structure, Field Experiences/Internship, Performance-Based Program Assessment and Accountability, and Program Support/Resources are evaluated from the perspective of both official program or institutional policy and actual practice. Standards related to the "Domains of School Psychology Training and Practice" are evaluated on the basis of evidence of the performance of program candidates/graduates. Programs must document that each domain is *addressed, assessed,* and *attained.*

Individual reviews are then considered by NASP's five-member Program Approval Board, which makes final judgments on program compliance with each standard and determines whether or not programmatic evidence warrants approval. NASP-approved programs located in institutions accredited by NCATE also receive NCATE's "nationally recognized" status. Doctoral programs in school psychology accredited by the American Psychological Association (APA) receive NASP approval through a streamlined process that includes only the documentation of APA accreditation status and program internship requirements consistent with NASP standards.

NASP PROGRAM APPROVAL AND ITS RELATIONSHIP TO SCHOOL PSYCHOLOGY CREDENTIALING

NASP approval has important implications for the graduates of training programs. Graduates of approved programs are automatically eligible for the National Certificate in School Psychology (NCSP), pending documentation of an internship consistent with NASP standards and the attainment of a passing score on the Praxis II Examination in School Psychology administered by the Educational Testing Service (ETS). Graduates of nonapproved programs may be eligible for national certification, but must submit additional documentation of preparation and field experiences consistent with NASP standards, and complete a performance review involving one or more case studies.

Each individual state establishes its own standards for school psychology training and practice. However, many states have chosen to use the NASP standards, or their equivalent, for the approval of training programs and/or for the credentialing of school psychologists for employment in the public schools.

In summary, NASP standards and the corresponding program approval process play important roles both in evaluating the quality of programs, and in helping to assure that graduates of approved programs possess the competencies needed to provide effective school psychological services. Ultimately, the goal of such standards is to positively affect not just the profession and its training programs, but the children, schools, families, and other clients served by school psychologists.

See also: Doctoral Training Programs in School Psychology; Ethical Standards

BIBLIOGRAPHY

National Association of School Psychologists. (2000). *Standards for training and field placement programs in school psychology.* Bethesda, MD: Author.

Waldron, N., Prus, J., & Curtis, M. (2000). *A guide for performance-based assessment, accountability, and program development in school psychology training programs.* Bethesda, MD: National Association of School Psychologists.

Ysseldyke, J., Dawson, P., Lehr, C., Reschly, D., Reynolds, M., & Telzrow, C. (1997). *School psychology: A blueprint for training and practice II.* Bethesda, MD: National Association of School Psychologists.

JOSEPH PRUS
PATTI L. HARRISON

Negative Reinforcement

Negative reinforcement is a key concept associated with B. F. Skinner's model of learning, operant conditioning. In negative reinforcement, a specific behavior is strengthened (i.e., reinforced) by the cessation or avoidance of an aversive stimulus, condition, or event. In other words, a particular behavior results in the elimination of something unpleasant to the organism; therefore, the behavior is more likely to occur again in the future to avoid or escape from the aversive stimulus, event, or condition (i.e., consequence). The consequence that evokes the avoidance or escape behavior is known as the negative reinforcer.

Negative reinforcement is often confused with another operant term, *punishment*. The premise behind *reinforcement* is that the frequency of behaviors increases as a result of specific environmental consequences. The confusion of negative reinforcement and punishment often seems to stem from general connotations associated with the term *negative*, which for many individuals may suggest something untoward. However, in the language of operant conditioning, the term *negative* refers to removing a condition, event, or stimulus from the environment. Therefore, negative reinforcement is said only to occur when an increase in behavior is seen as a result of removing an environmental stimulus. In contrast, punishment results in a decrease in behavior because of the introduction of something aversive or the removal of a preferred stimulus.

A common example of negative reinforcement might be as follows. When 3-year-old Sam sees candy at the checkout line at the grocery store, he begins to beg and cry for the candy. Although Sam's mother does not want him to have candy, she is embarrassed by his temper tantrum in the store, and buys him a candy bar. On subsequent trips to the grocery, Sam's mother quickly gets him a candy bar at the checkout line as soon as he asks for one to avoid Sam's temper tantrum. In this case, the mother's candy buying behavior has been negatively reinforced. She buys a candy bar (behavior) to avoid Sam's temper tantrum (aversive event). Another example of negative reinforcement might be taking medicine for an illness. If taking a certain medicine (behavior) eliminates Joan's headache (aversive experience), Joan may be more likely to use that medication in the future the next time she has a headache (escape). Negative reinforcement may also be seen in students' behavior at school. For example, Marc may learn that breaking his pencils and tearing his papers leads to termination of difficult academic tasks. A child with autism who finds attention aversive may learn that banging his/her head against the wall makes the teacher leave him or her alone.

Although negative reinforcement occurs naturally in the environment to shape behavior, practitioners, teachers, and parents can capitalize on this procedure to modify behavior of clients, students, or their own children. For example, a teacher who determines that a student's disruptive classroom behavior is maintained by escape from aversive academic tasks could use negative reinforcement to increase work completion. The teacher could set an initial criterion for behavior (e.g., completion of two mathematic problems without any disruptive behavior) that, if met, would result in a temporary break from the assignment. As disruptive behaviors decreased, the teacher could increase the amount of work required for escape from the task until the child is working at levels similar to other students in the class. Similarly, some parents complain that their child tantrums to avoid completing simple tasks such as household chores. Parents could teach their child an alternative behavior such as a polite request (e.g., "May I take a break, please?") that would result in a temporary escape from the task. Again, as the child's behavior improved, the amount of time or number of tasks he/she would have to complete before taking a break would be increased slowly over time.

See also: Positive Reinforcement; Punishment

Additional Readings for Nonprofessionals

Harrison, J., & Gunter, P. (1996). Teacher instructional language and negative reinforcement: A conceptual framework for working with students with emotional and behavioral disorders. *Education and Treatment of Children, 19*, 183–197.

Hineline, P. N. (1977). Negative reinforcement and avoidance. In W. K. Honig & J. E. R. Staddon (Eds.), *Handbook of operant behavior* (pp. 364–414). Englewood Cliffs, NJ: Prentice-Hall.

Additional Readings for Professionals

Iwata et al. (1987). Negative reinforcement in applied behavior analysis: An emerging technology. *Journal of Applied Behavior Analysis, 20*, 361–378.

Lalli, J. S., Vollmer, T. R., Progar, P. R., Wright, C., Borrero, J., Daniel, D., Barthold, C. H., Tocco, K., & May, W. (1999). Competition between positive and negative reinforcement in the treatment of escape behavior. *Journal of Applied Behavior Analysis, 32*, 285–296.

HEATHER E. STERLING-TURNER
KIMBERLY D. BELLIPANNI

Note Taking

Note taking has been discussed as one of several academic routines that is pervasive throughout all of schooling (Belfiore & Hutchinson, 1998). Academic routines, of which note taking is included, may be defined as a skill chain (i.e., a task analysis) necessary for academic achievement across multiple curriculum content areas. Belfiore and Hutchinson (1998) suggest that note taking involves information gathering from two generic outlets. First, information for note taking may come from topic-specific, teacher-delivered lectures, presentations, or group discussions. Second, information for note taking may come from a media source (e.g., written materials, electronic/Internet site, software). Note taking is not copying; but rather, information obtained during note taking must be transcribed, reorganized, coded, and reduced into some meaningful outline or template format.

Belfiore and Hutchinson (1998) suggest there is a content and process when developing a routine for note taking. First, the structure of note taking must be addressed (i.e., "how does it look?"). When looking at structure, educators should develop a system for the physical act of taking notes. For example, Pauk (www.usu.edu/arc/ideassheets/cornell.htm, n.d.) suggests a split-page method for taking notes. In this strategy, during the lecture, full notes are written on the larger right column of the note page. Following the lecture, key words, terms, and phrases are written on the smaller left column of the note page. This type of note taking structure also creates a study guide for test preparation. Students can cover the right column, read the key words and phrases in the left column, and recall the context from which those words and phrases were taken. Conversely, students can cover the left column of words and phrases, read the full notes on the right column, and recall the vocabulary when given the context. Other structures for taking notes may include graphic organizers and note outlines. Using these devices during lectures or readings requires students to discriminate main topics, subtopics, and key points given throughout the lecture, discussion, or within media source. Organizers and outline templates are developed to match with the lecture or media source. For example, if the lecture has one main idea, four subtopics within the main topic, and five key points within each subtopic, then the template will reflect space for those numbers. This method of using templates and advanced organizers has been shown to be effective for students requiring academic support. Students identified as needing academic support often have a difficult time taking full notes when presented in a lecture or group discussion format. For these students, the templates provide a visual prompt system allowing students to better discriminate the key elements of the lecture from the nonessential elements that often accompany lectures. The template is accompanied by note takers or an audiotape of the entire lecture. During the lecture, the student completes the template, and following the lecture the student adds additional lecture information from the note taker or audiotape.

Once the structure of taking notes has been established, the process for note taking must be addressed. Spires and Stone (1989) developed a Directed Note-taking Activity (DNA), which includes a structured self-monitoring strategy. In a DNA, self-monitoring may occur prior to taking notes (e.g., "What is the purpose of the assignment/lecture?"), while taking notes (e.g., "Am I discriminating between main topic and subtopics?"), and after taking notes (e.g., "Did I achieve the goal of the lesson?") (Spires & Stone, 1989). Spires and Stone (1989) believe a lack of comprehension following note taking may be the result of students' not having engaged in self-monitoring. The process of self-monitoring (SM) during note taking provides additional cues that result in more effective and efficient product (Belfiore & Hutchinson, 1998). Requiring students to follow a prescribed set of steps maximizes successful note taking. One example of a note-taking routine requiring SM might include such steps as (a) gathering all necessary materials, (b) attending to lecture and completing template, (c) getting full notes (from note taker or audiotape), (d) comparing full notes with template and adding missing pieces, and (e) reviewing.

An alternative SM note-taking routine not requiring the outline template and full note comparison is the Cornell Note-Taking System (www.usu.edu/arc/ideassheets/cornell.htm, n.d.). This procedure, using the split page structure, includes six steps: recording (writing facts and ideas), reducing (reorganizing facts and ideas into key words, phrases, and questions), reciting (stating out loud and in one's own words facts and ideas to be learned), reflecting (self-questioning for application, synthesis, and critique), reviewing (frequently reciting ideas and facts), and recapitulating (summarizing notes on the bottom of the split page).

Regardless of the structure and the process of taking notes, the central priority for any note-taking activity is organization and clarity. As a precursor for academic studying and test taking, note taking sets the stage. Without organized notes that reflect the main theme and the subthemes of a lecture, discussion, or media source, studying and test taking become difficult and highly inefficient propositions.

See also: Academic Interventions for Written Language and Grammar; Study Skills and Test Preparation

BIBLIOGRAPHY

Belfiore, P. J., & Hutchinson, J. M. (1998). Enhancing academic achievement through related routines: A functional approach. In T. S. Watson & F. M. Gresham (Eds.), *Handbook of child behavior therapy* (pp. 83–97). New York: Plenum.

Note-taking: Cornell method. (n.d.). Retrieved September 4, 2002, from www.usu.edu/arc/ideas sheets/cornell.htm

Spires, H. A., & Stone, P. D. (1989). The directed note-taking activity: A self-questioning approach. *Journal of Reading, 33,* 36–39.

Additional Reading for Nonprofessionals

Pauk, W. (2000). *Essential study strategies.* Upper Saddle River, NJ: Prentice-Hall.

Additional Readings for Professionals

Eggen, P. D., & Kauchak, D. P. (2001). *Strategies for teaching: Teaching content and thinking skills.* Boston: Allyn & Bacon.

Laidlaw, E. N., Skok, R. L., & McLaughlin, T. F. (1993). The effects of note-taking and self-questioning on quiz performance. *Science Education, 77,* 75–82.

PHILLIP J. BELFIORE

Nutrition

Nutrition is a science composed of many disciplines studying foods, nutrients, other food components, and health. Nutrients are chemical substances used by the body for growth and good health. They have essentially one of three bodily functions: (1) to provide energy, (2) to provide structural components, and (3) to regulate functions. Our bodies require six categories of nutrients each day (Brown et al., 2002; Mitchell, 2003). Although not one of the six categories of nutrients, fiber is also important for gastrointestinal functioning.

Carbohydrate: Carbohydrate is a very important component of diets throughout the world. It is the least expensive and most abundant source of energy. It includes simple sugars as well as complex carbohydrates. Examples of some food sources are whole grains, cereals, fruits, vegetables, and milk. Function: Provides energy (4 kilocalories per gram).

Protein: Protein is found in products of animal origin and in plants such as legumes, dried beans, nuts, and seeds. Proteins differ in quality. Higher quality proteins contain the nine essential amino acids (the building blocks of protein). Some higher quality protein sources include animal products such as dairy products (milk, cheese, and eggs), meat, fish, and poultry. Plant sources, except for soybeans, are lower quality, but when eaten in certain combinations (such as dried beans and rice) can provide complete protein. Functions: Primarily provides structural components (provides amino acids for building of muscle, bone matrix, and connective tissue), provides energy (4 kilocalories per gram), and regulates body functions

Fat: Fats provide the most energy per gram. Because of their important functions, some dietary fat intake each day is important for health. Some food sources include meats, dairy products, and plant products (nuts, seeds, and avocado). Functions: Primarily provides energy (9 kilocalories per gram) and provides structural components (membrane formation).

Vitamins: Vitamins perform a variety of specific functions in the body. Thirteen vitamins have been discovered. Vitamins have been classified into two types: fat-soluble (vitamins A, D, E, and K) and water-soluble (B-complex and vitamin C). Eating a variety of foods is the best way of meeting the body's vitamin needs. Function: Regulates body functions (normal growth).

Minerals: Humans require 15 minerals. Unlike the other categories of nutrients, minerals carry a charge in solution, which is related to many of the functions of minerals. Like vitamins, eating a variety of foods is the best way to meet the body's needs. Functions: Regulates body functions (sodium and potassium regulate water balance) and provides structural components (calcium and phosphorus provide building materials for bones).

Water: Adults are approximately 60 percent water and cannot survive more than a few days without it. Sources of water include beverages, soups, fruits, and vegetables. Functions: Regulates body function (regulates stable body temperature) and provides structural components (gives structure and form to our bodies).

Scientific research has shown that what we eat affects our health. The Food and Nutrition Board of the National Academy of Sciences has developed the *Dietary Reference Intakes,* which are reference values of these nutrients and which provide estimates of nutrient intakes to be used for planning and assessing diets of healthy individuals and groups (U.S. Department of Agriculture, 2003). However, the U.S. Department of Agriculture developed 10 simple dietary recommendations (grouped into three healthy messages) to help Americans over the age of 2 years make healthy food choices, called the *Dietary Guidelines for Americans* (U.S. Departments of Agriculture and Health and Human Services, 2000). It is the cornerstone of the federal food, nutrition, and policy programs. They are recommendations that help individuals to be productive, enjoy life, and feel good. They specifically help children to experience positive growth and development and to do well in school. Healthful eating early in life can help prevent chronic disease later in life.

Aim for fitness

1. Aim for a healthy weight.
2. Be physically active each day.

Build a healthy base

3. Let the Food Guide Pyramid guide your food choices.
4. Choose a variety of grains daily, especially whole grains.
5. Choose a variety of fruits and vegetables daily.
6. Keep food safe to eat.

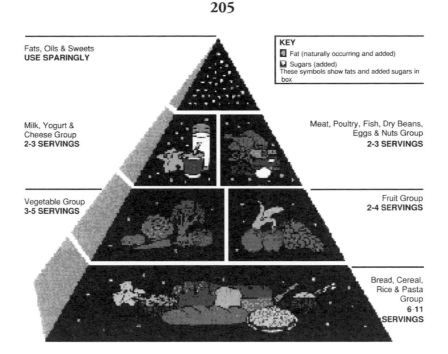

Figure 1. Food guide pyramid.

Choose sensibly

7. Choose a diet that is low in saturated fat and cholesterol and moderate in total fat.
8. Choose beverages and foods to moderate your intake of sugars.
9. Choose and prepare foods with less salt.
10. If you drink alcoholic beverages, do so in moderation.

The Food Guide Pyramid that the *Dietary Guidelines for Americans* mentions was designed to take the scientific knowledge on foods and nutrients and develop a practical tool to help Americans make healthy food choices (U.S. Department of Agriculture, 1992). Foods contain the six categories of necessary nutrients mentioned earlier. In order to get all the nutrients, it is important to eat a variety of foods. The Food Guide Pyramid helps individuals do this. The shape of the pyramid means that individuals should eat more of what is at the bottom of the pyramid compared with the top. The Food Guide Pyramid (Figure 1) is divided into six food categories: (1) bread, cereal, rice, and pasta group (6–11 servings), (2) vegetable group (3–5 servings), (3) fruit group (2–4 servings), (4) milk, yogurt, and cheese group—preferably fat-free or low-fat (2 or 3 servings), (5) meat, poultry, fish, dry beans, eggs, and nuts group—preferably lean or low-fat (2–3 for a total of 5–7 ounces), and (6) fats, oils, and sweets (sparingly). The exact number of servings an individual should consume depends on calorie needs, which generally depends on age and activity level. The United States Department of Agriculture has also developed a pyramid for children aged 2–6 years.

Nutrition is important for good health and productivity. By simply applying the principles of moderation and variety in the foods consumed and following these simple guidelines and recommendations, individuals can learn to live healthy, productive lives.

BIBLIOGRAPHY

Brown, J. E., Isaacs, J. S., Krinke, U. B., Murtaugh, M. A., Stang, J., & Wooldridge, N. H. (2002). *Nutrition through the life cycle.* Belmont, CA: Wadsworth/Thomson Learning.

Mitchell, M. K. (2003). *Nutrition across the lifespan* (2nd ed.). Philadelphia: Saunders.

U.S. Department of Agriculture. (1992). *The food guide pyramid* (Home and Garden Bulletin, No. 252). Washington, DC: U.S. Government Printing Office.

U.S. Departments of Agriculture and Health and Human Services. (2000). *Nutrition and your health: Dietary guidelines for Americans* (5th ed.) (Home and Garden Bulletin, No. 232). Washington, DC: U.S. Government Printing Office.

U.S. Department of Agriculture, National Agricultural Library, Food and Nutrition Information Center (2001). *Dietary reference intakes (DRI) and Recommended Dietary Allowances (RDA).* Retrieved November 14, 2003, from http://www.nal.usda.gov/fnic/etext/000105.html

Additional Readings for Nonprofessionals

U.S. Department of Agriculture (2003). *Center for Nutrition and Policy and Promotion.* Retrieved February 1, 2003, from http://www.usda.gov/cnpp

U.S. Department of Agriculture (2003). *Interactive Healthy Eating Index and Physical Activity Tool.* Retrieved February 1, 2003, from http://www.cnpp.usda.gov/ihei.html

Additional Readings for Professionals

Groff, J. L., & Gropper, S. S. (1999). *Advanced human nutrition and metabolism* (3rd ed.). Belmont, CA: Wadsworth/Thomson Learning.

Worthington-Roberts, B., & Williams, S. R. (2000). *Nutrition throughout the life cycle* (4th ed.). Boston: McGraw-Hill.

ELIZABETH M. YOUNG

Oo

Obesity

Obesity is defined as having excessive body fat. It is estimated that at least 25 percent of children and adolescents in the United Stated are obese, with the number increasing each decade. Childhood obesity represents a serious social problem because of the likelihood of obesity persisting into adulthood and the resulting health, medical, social, and occupational costs associated with being obese.

Although body weight is frequently used to determine if a child is carrying excessive fat, a more accurate method is to calculate the Body Mass Index (BMI), which takes into account the height of the child. BMI is calculated by converting weight in pounds to kilograms and dividing by height (in meters) squared. The criteria for childhood obesity are a BMI above the 95th percentile, body weight above the 95th percentile, and a triceps skin-fold measurement above the 85th percentile. The triceps skin-fold measurement is used to take into account weight that is lean body mass as opposed to fat. The percentile ranges are based on standardized tables based on age and gender.

The prevalence rates for obesity differ according to ethnicity, age, gender, and socioeconomic status. Hispanic and African American children are more likely to be obese than Caucasians. Children of Asian descent are least likely to be obese. There is, generally, an inverse relationship between socioeconomic status and obesity. That is, as economic status increases, the likelihood of obesity decreases. Conversely, as economic status decreases, the likelihood of obesity increases. Rates of obesity are lowest among very poor and very wealthy children. As children age, the rates of obesity increase, perhaps because the activity level of older children is less than that of younger children. Females, particularly Hispanic and African American, have the highest risk for becoming obese.

The reasons behind the rising rates of childhood obesity are numerous. In brief, one must consider both environmental and genetic factors to adequately explain obesity. Environmental factors include such issues as television viewing; physical activity level; number of meals eaten outside the home; parental modeling of eating, dietary, and exercise habits; and parental prompts to eat. In general, increased television viewing is associated with increased obesity because children tend to eat more while watching TV and watching TV is a sedentary activity. Obese children are less likely to engage in physical activity than their nonobese peers are. Parents who eat more healthy and engage in regular exercise are less likely to have children who are obese. Children who eat more meals outside the home tend to be more obese than children who eat fewer meals away from home. Research has indicated that parents of obese children provide more food for their children to eat and offer more prompts to eat and "clean their plate" than parents of nonobese children.

It is estimated that genetics accounts for about 30 to 40 percent of the explanation for why children are obese. For instance, children with one obese parent are more likely to be obese than children for whom neither parent is obese. Children with two obese parents are even more likely to be obese. Having said that, however, it is difficult in these circumstances to separate the effects of genetics from the effects of parents' modeling poor eating and exercise habits and creating an environment in which children are likely to overeat and become obese.

MEDICAL/HEALTH IMPLICATIONS OF OBESITY

If a child's obesity persists through adolescence, their chances of becoming nonobese as an adult are 28 to 1. Obesity carries with it a number of health concerns, among them increased risk of hypertension, cardiovascular disease,

207

hyperlipidemia, orthopedic problems, diabetes, and impaired occupational functioning. These problems not only affect the obese individual but his/her family, friends, employers, and society at large.

PSYCHOLOGICAL IMPLICATIONS OF OBESITY

Obese children suffer an increased risk of a number of psychological and emotional difficulties related to their body size. Obese children are often teased about their weight, which eventually can cause emotional distress, reductions in self-esteem, and increased risk for depression. Children who are obese are viewed by their peers as less intelligent, less attractive, and less competent than nonobese children. In addition, they are often viewed as lazy and mean. These views about obese children often persist and intensify in the adolescent years. As a result, obese children may view themselves in a significantly negative light and develop body image problems and eating disorders. These negative feelings about themselves and their appearance are likely to be carried into adulthood.

TREATMENT

Although there are a number of treatment approaches and alternatives available, only a limited few have empirical data supporting their effectiveness over the long term. For instance, Epstein and colleagues use a family-based approach that employs behavior management, wise food selection, weekly and monthly meetings, and exercise.

The essential behavior management techniques include self-monitoring, stimulus control, eating management, positive reinforcement, and mild negative consequences. Their results indicated that 30 percent of the obese children were no longer obese, even after 10 years. Other programs with impressive results confirm the integral components of weight loss for children: family involvement, structured exercise program, making better food choices, changing eating behavior, behavior management strategies, and long-term treatment. It is safe to say that fad diets (grapefruit diet, severe caloric restriction, etc.) are not going to be effective for reducing childhood obesity rates and actually interfere with the acquisition and development of healthier eating and exercising behaviors.

See also: Eating Disorders; Nutrition; Sports

BIBLIOGRAPHY

Epstein, L. H., Masek, B. J., & Marshall, W. R. (1978). A nutritionally based school program for control of eating in obese children. *Behavior Therapy, 9,* 766–788.

Epstein, L. H., Valoski, A., Wing, R., & McCurley, J. (1994). Ten-year outcomes of behavioral family-based treatment for childhood obesity. *Health Psychology, 13,* 373–383.

Additional Readings for Professionals and Nonprofessionals

Cooper, Z., Fairburn, C. G., & Hawker, D. M. (2003). *Cognitive–behavioral treatment of obesity: A clinician's manual.* New York: Guilford.

Fairburn, C. G., & Brownell, K. D. (Eds.). (2002). *Eating disorders and obesity.* New York: Guilford.

Wadden, T. A., & Stunkard, A. J. (Eds.). (2002). *Handbook of obesity treatment.* New York: Guilford.

T. Steuart Watson
Tonya Sartor Butler

Obsessive–Compulsive Disorder

DIAGNOSIS, PREVALENCE, AND COURSE

Obsessive–Compulsive Disorder (OCD) is classified as a type of anxiety disorder under the revised fourth edition of the *Diagnostic and Statistical Manual of Mental Disorders* (*DSM-IV-TR*). Broadly defined, OCD is the persistent and pervasive presence of obsessions and compulsions that are time consuming (i.e., more than 1 hour a day) and cause impairments in daily functioning (American Psychiatric Association, 2000). Obsessions, the cognitive component of OCD, are recurrent and intrusive thoughts, impulses, or images that interfere with daily activities. Obsessions are viewed by the client as unwanted and that cause significant stress. Compulsions, on the other hand, are repetitive behavior patterns (overt or covert) the individual engages in to prevent or alleviate anxiety associated with obsessions; the client does not view these behaviors as "enjoyable" or "fun." Examples of common compulsive behaviors include washing, cleaning, checking, ordering (e.g., eating foods in a particular order), counting, other repetitive overt and covert behaviors (e.g., repeating words silently), and seeking reassurance from others. Although the diagnostic criteria for adults with OCD require that they recognize the thoughts and behaviors are self-imposed and unreasonable, this criterion does not need to be applied to children given their developmental status. In addition, the diagnostic criteria stipulate that disturbances in behavior cannot be related to direct physiological effects of any substance (e.g., drugs, medication) or a general medical condition; nor can obsessive and compulsive behavior be limited to one thought content or activity such as hair pulling (e.g., Trichotillomania; American Psychiatric Association, 2000).

Because OCD was not extensively studied in child and adolescent populations until the mid-1980s, prevalence rates and demographic variables are tentative and mixed. In the typically developing child population, 1–2.3 percent of children are diagnosed with OCD (American Psychiatric Association, 2000), although other reviews place prevalence rates up to 4 percent (Wewetzer et al., 2001). Discrepancies in rates may be a function of the population sample (clinical vs. community) or the diagnostic criteria applied (*DSM* vs. the *International Statistical Classification of Diseases and Related Health Problems— Tenth Revision [ICD-10]*). A high proportion of adults with OCD retrospectively report that symptoms began in childhood or adolescence (American Psychiatric Association, 2000), with the average age of onset for males being around 6–15 years and for females 20–29 years. Given the age onset data, it is not surprising that sex ratio data suggest higher rates of OCD in boys than in girls, at a 3:2 ratio in clinical samples (Fireman, Koran, Leventhal, & Jacobson, 2001).

DIFFERENTIAL DIAGNOSIS/COMORBID CONDITIONS

Most children display some level of ritualistic behavior at one point or another during the course of normal development. It is not uncommon for children, especially young children, to have preferences for routines such as ordering toys or bedtime rituals. From a diagnostic standpoint, what distinguishes OCD from normal developmental rituals is the degree of anxiety present when rituals are interrupted or prohibited. In addition, ritualistic behaviors associated with OCD are excessive in nature and appear atypical in nature (e.g., laying out clothes in the form of a body, checking lights).

Many of the psychiatric syndromes listed in the *DSM-IV-TR* have thought disorders that include excessive worry, recurrent/intrusive thoughts, and associated anxiety. Therefore, there are a number of differential diagnoses for OCD, the least of which are all other anxiety disorders. Although making these judgments can be difficult, the clinician should focus on the presence of the obsessions and compulsions to assist in diagnosis. That is, classic OCD symptoms are viewed by the affected individual as beyond their control, inappropriate, and not enjoyable. In addition, the ritualistic behaviors must serve to terminate anxiety brought on by the obsessive thoughts. Finally, there must be an impairment in functioning (American Psychiatric Association, 2000). Obsessive–compulsive personality disorder (OCP; see *DSM*, Axis II, personality disorders) should be differentiated from OCD. In OCP, there must be a general pattern of controlling behaviors that is not present in OCD. Children and adolescents should not receive a diagnosis of OCP as the diagnostic criteria stipulate that the onset of OCP occurs in early adulthood (American Psychiatric Association, 2000).

Finally, clinicians should be careful to rule out substance use or medical conditions before giving a diagnosis of OCD. Some neurological disorders may present with OCD-like symptoms, including encephalitis and brain injury.

Comorbidity data suggest that the majority of children with OCD will have at least one other diagnosis. Depression, additional anxiety disorders, developmental disabilities, oppositional defiant disorder, and attention deficit disorder are the most commonly reported concomitant diagnoses (Swedo, Rapoport, Leonard, Lenane, & Cheslow, 1989). Depression and associated anxiety disorders are the two most commonly occurring comorbid disorders; studies suggest these symptoms appear following the onset of OCD symptoms and behaviors (Swedo et al., 1989).

ETIOLOGY

As with most psychiatric disorders, the exact cause of OCD is unclear. However, emerging evidence suggests that OCD is a neurobehavioral disorder caused by irregularities in the circuits involved in connecting the frontal cortex (specifically, the orbitofrontal cortex) and parts of the basal ganglia (Grados & Riddle, 2001). The specific pathways thought to be disrupted are associated with the limbic system, which plays a large role in the regulation of mood and motivation (Grados & Riddle, 2001). The primary neurotransmitter implicated in OCD is serotonin; however, this evidence is based on response to medication. Given the mixed results of symptom response to specific psychotropics, some researchers have suggested that although serotonin may play a role in OCD, it may function to control other neurotransmitters, specifically dopamine, which in turn mediates OCD symptoms (Grados & Riddle, 2001).

Although there appears to be a neurological dysfunction that may predispose certain individuals to OCD, the importance of learning and conditioning in this disorder cannot be overlooked. The combination of classically conditioned anxiety and the negatively reinforcing effects of ritualistic behavior on anxiety serve to maintain both the obsessive and compulsive components of the disorder.

ASSESSMENT

A thorough assessment of children with OCD includes a comprehensive evaluation of the child's development and psychosocial functioning, including the child's medical records and developmental and family history. Interviews should be conducted with the affected child, parents, teachers, and any other significant adults in the child's life. It should be noted again that children may not be aware of the inappropriateness of the obsessions and/or compulsions. If possible, direct observations should be employed to provide further information about the child's obsessive and/or compulsive behavior. There are several scales to assess the presence of OCD symptoms and behaviors. The Children's Yale–Brown Obsessive Compulsive Scale (CY-BOCS) is the most commonly used instrument and is often used as not only a diagnostic tool but as a measure of treatment effects as well. Other scales used for diagnostic purposes include the Leyton Questionnaire, Anxiety Disorders Interview Schedule (ADIS), the Obsessive Compulsive Rating Scale, the NIMH Global Obsessive–Compulsive Rating Scale, the Padua Inventory, and the Structured Clinical Interview for *DSM* Axis I (SCID-I).

TREATMENT

Treatment of OCD in both adults and children may be focused in three areas: (a) pharmacological, (b) behavioral, and (c) cognitive. Adult-focused research has shown that psychotropics tend to have greater effects on the obsessional components of OCD whereas behavior and cognitive–behavioral strategies (CBT) tend to have more substantial effects on compulsive behaviors. To date, no comparative studies (i.e., medication vs. psychotherapy) nor combinative ones (e.g., medication + behavior therapy) have been conducted with child or adolescent populations.

Grados and Riddle (2001) provide a review of psychopharmacological treatment of children and adolescents with OCD and cite specific effects of a number of psychotropics that act on serotonin (tricyclic antidepressants and serotonin-specific reuptake inhibitors), including clomipramine (Anafranil), fluoxetine (Prozac), fluvoxamine (Luvox), sertraline (Zoloft), each of which has been shown to be effective in reducing OCD. It should be noted that these medications carry a significant risk of negative side effects for use in children; in addition, fluoxetine and sertraline are associated with increased motor activity in children, while paroxetine and fluvoxamine tend to be sedative. Paroxetine (Paxil) and citalopram (Celexa), although effective in the treatment of adults with OCD, have yet to be investigated or approved for use in children and adolescents (Grados & Riddle, 2001).

CBT is the gold-standard, first-line treatment for OCD in both adult and pediatric populations. (It should be noted, though, that comparative studies of CBT to other psychotherapies, including behavioral treatments alone, have not been conducted with children and adolescents.) March and Mulle (1998) have constructed a 14-week CBT treatment protocol, supported by research findings, for use in clinical settings. This protocol is readily adaptable to use by psychologists working in the schools as well. Regardless of the treatment protocol used, research has consistently shown the core component of CBT to be the behavioral component Exposure and Response

Prevention Training (ERP). In ERP, the client is exposed to an anxiety-provoking stimulus or thought (obsession) and the attenuating response (compulsion) is then prevented. For example, a child who worries that he/she has left the lights on in another room of the house and therefore the house may catch fire would be asked to leave a room (exposure to the precipitating event for obsessive thought) and then not allowed to go back and check the lights (response prevention). Behaviorally, ERP functions to extinguish the negatively reinforcing effects of the compulsive behavior. Other components of the standard CBT procedure involve cognitive therapy such as altering self-talk or cognitive restructuring. In addition, when working with children and adolescents, family therapy is encouraged so that parents and other caregivers can be trained in the treatment protocols as well as in modifying their own behavior in response to the child's behavior, such as providing positive reinforcement in the form of attention or reassurance for OCD behaviors.

See also: Anxiety; Depression in Children and Adolescents; *Diagnostic and Statistical Manual of Mental Disorders*; Tics; Trichotillomania

BIBLIOGRAPHY

American Psychiatric Association. (2000). *Diagnostic and statistical manual of mental disorders* (4th ed., text rev.). Washington, DC: Author.

Fireman, B., Koran, L. M., Leventhal, J. L., & Jacobson, A. (2001). The prevalence of clinically recognized obsessive–compulsive disorder in a large health maintenance organization. *American Journal of Psychiatry, 158,* 1904–1910.

Grados, M. A., & Riddle, M. A. (2001). Pharmacological treatment of childhood obsessive–compulsive disorder: From theory to practice. *Journal of Clinical Child Psychiatry, 30,* 67–79.

March, J. S., & Mulle, K. M. (1998). *OCD in children and adolescents: A cognitive–behavioral treatment manual.* New York: Guilford.

Rapoport, J. L., & Inoff-Germain, G. (2000). Practitioner review: Treatment of obsessive–compulsive disorder in children and adolescents. *Journal of Child Psychology and Psychiatry, 41*(4), 419–431.

Swedo, S. E., Rapoport, J. L., Leonard, H., Lenane, M. C., & Cheslow, D. L. (1989). Obsessive–compulsive disorder in children and adolescents: Clinical phenomenology of 70 consecutive cases. *Archives of General Psychiatry, 46,* 335–341.

Wewetzer, C., Jans, T., Muller, B., Neudorfl, A., Bucherl, U., Remschmidt, H., et al. (2001). Long-term outcome and prognosis of obsessive–compulsive disorder with onset in childhood or adolescence. *European Child and Adolescent Psychiatry, 10,* 37–46.

Additional Reading for Nonprofessionals

March, J. S., & Mulle, K. M. (1998). *OCD in children and adolescents: A cognitive–behavioral treatment manual.* New York: Guilford.

Additional Readings for Professionals

Grados, M. A., & Riddle, M. A. (2001). Pharmacological treatment of child-hood obsessive–compulsive disorder: From theory to practice. *Journal of Clinical Child Psychiatry, 30,* 67–79.

March, J. S., Franklin, M., Nelson, A., & Foa, E. (2001). Cognitive behavioral therapy for pediatric obsessive compulsive disorder. *Journal of Clinical Child Psychology, 30,* 8–18.

March, J. S., & Mulle, K. M. (1998). *OCD in children and adolescents: A cognitive–behavioral treatment manual.* New York: Guilford.

Rapoport, J. L., & Inoff-Germain, G. (2000). Practitioner review: Treatment of obsessive–compulsive disorder in children and adolescents. *Journal of Child Psychology and Psychiatry, 41*(4), 419–431.

HEATHER E. STERLING-TURNER
G. THOMAS SCHANDING, JR.

Oppositional Defiant Disorder

Oppositional Defiant Disorder (ODD) "consists of an enduring pattern of uncooperative, defiant, and hostile behavior toward authority figures that does not involve major antisocial violations, is not accounted for by the child's developmental stage, and results in significant functional impairment" (Vitiello & Jensen, 1995, p. 2317). ODD is classified as a Disruptive Behavior Disorder along with Attention-Deficit/Hyperactivity Disorder (ADHD), Conduct Disorder (CD), and Disruptive Behavior Disorder—Not Otherwise Specified (NOS). According to Christophersen and Mortweet (2001), there are more office visits to mental health professionals for these disorders than any other childhood disorder, encompassing approximately 55 percent of all office appointments in their clinical practice.

DIAGNOSTIC FEATURES

According to the *Diagnostic and Statistical Manual of Mental Disorders* (4th ed., text rev.) (*DSM-IV-TR*) (American Psychiatric Association, 2000), several important criteria must be met in order for a child to obtain the clinical diagnosis of ODD. The essential feature of ODD is "a recurrent pattern of negativistic, defiant, disobedient, and hostile behavior toward authority figures that persists for at least 6 months" (p. 100). Furthermore, this pattern must be characterized by the frequent occurrence of at least four of the following behaviors: (a) arguing with adults, (b) actively refusing to comply with adult rules and expectations, (c) deliberately engaging in behaviors that annoy others, (d) blaming others for mistakes or misbehavior, (e) being easily annoyed by other individuals, (f) being resentful and angry, (g) or being spiteful or vindictive. These behaviors must occur more frequently than is typically observed in other children of

the same age and gender. In other words, such behaviors cannot simply be the result of the "terrible twos" or traditional "adolescent rebellion." These behaviors must occur within the developmental period, which is before the age of 18 according to the guidelines set forth by the American Psychiatric Association (2000). Furthermore, these behaviors must interfere with important life activities such as occupational, academic, or social functioning. For example, these behaviors must occur often and be severe enough to cause the child to obtain failing grades in school, stop him/her from maintaining a job, or inhibit him/her from forming important social relationships with adults or peers. Finally, these behaviors cannot be better explained by another mental health disorder such as CD, Antisocial Personality Disorder, Psychotic Disorder, or Mood Disorder (e.g., childhood depression).

PREVALENCE AND COURSE

Prevalence rates of 2 to 16 percent have been reported depending on the definition of ODD used, the population of individuals sampled, and the diagnostic methods used. ODD appears to be more prevalent in males than in females before puberty and peaks at about 6 years of age (Christophersen & Mortweet, 2001). However, the behaviors associated with ODD seem to be displayed equally by boys and girls during the adolescent years (American Psychiatric Association, 2000). The frequency and intensity of oppositional behaviors increase with age, and males tend to display more persistent and confrontational behaviors over the years. This increase in behaviors is probably the result of improvement of developmental abilities over time. In other words, children mature in physical and mental abilities as they get older. As such, the high-intensity temper tantrums displayed by a preschooler with a clinical diagnosis of ODD become the argumentative behavior, precocious drug and alcohol use, and low frustration tolerances displayed by an adolescent with ODD. Finally, the behaviors associated with ODD can serve as precursors to the future development of CD in some cases. However, Vitiello and Jensen (1995) optimistically noted that most cases of ODD do not result in a final diagnosis of CD.

COMORBIDITY

ODD can be displayed with other mental health disorders. In diagnostic terms, this dual display of disorders is called "comorbidity." For example, a study by Biederman et al. (1996) found that 65 percent of boys who had ADHD also met criteria for ODD. Vitiello and Jensen (1995) found that 90 percent of children diagnosed with CD also met criteria for ODD. In addition, ODD has also been associated with some learning problems and the internalizing disorders of anxiety and depression. For example, Thomas and Guskin (2001) found that 45 percent of their sample of children with disruptive behaviors also displayed internalizing problems.

FAMILIAL PATTERN

Children diagnosed with ODD seem to come from families in which one or both parents have been diagnosed with a Mood Disorder, ODD, CD, ADHD, Antisocial Personality Disorder, Substance-Related Disorder, or Depressive Disorder. Furthermore, marital problems seem to be associated with the development of ODD in children. Finally, and most important, ODD appears to be the direct result of a disruption in appropriate childcare (e.g., experiencing a succession of different caregivers or punitive, inconsistent, and neglectful parenting practices; American Psychiatric Association, 2000).

ASSESSMENT OF ODD

Comprehensive assessment of a childhood disorder like ODD should be both multimethod and multiinformant. The American Academy of Child and Adolescent Psychiatry (1997) has suggested that information about the performance of behaviors associated with ODD should come from several sources such as interviews, behavioral rating scales, direct observations, standardized testing, record reviews, and physical examination. Furthermore, information should come from several individuals who are knowledgeable about the child, including the parents, teachers, and even the student.

Indirect methods of obtaining information about children and adolescents include interviews, behavioral rating scales, and record reviews. One interview that has been consistently updated and deemed appropriate by empirical research is the *Diagnostic Interview Schedule for Children* (DISC) (Shaffer, Fisher, Lucas, Dulcan, & Schwab-Stone, 2000). Both global and specific behavioral rating scales should be used in the assessment of ODD. Broad or global rating scales that screen for both internalizing and externalizing disorders include the *Child Behavior Checklist* (CBCL) (Achenbach, 1991) and the *Behavior Assessment System for Children* (BASC) (Reynolds & Kamphaus, 1992). Specific rating scales used in the differential diagnosis of ODD can include the *Disruptive Behavior Rating Scale* (Barkley & Murphy, 1998), *Eyberg Child Behavior Inventory* (ECBI) (Eyberg, 1999a), and *Sutter–Eyberg Child Behavior Inventory* (SECBI) (Eyberg, 1999b). Finally, medical and school records should be reviewed to examine the impact that the behaviors associated with ODD have had on the child's developmental and school functioning.

Direct observations typically involve recording the interactions between the child and parents under naturalistic and analogue conditions. Specific conditions have been outlined in empirical literature (Moore, Edwards, Wilczynski, & Olmi, 2001). However, clinicians should generally look at the types of instructions given to the children by the parents, types of disciplinary strategies used by the parents, rates of compliance with parental expectations, and types of problematic behaviors displayed by the child. Because some children with ODD display learning problems, standardized testing may need to be conducted. Such testing should evaluate the child's performance on intelligence tests, achievement tests, and adaptive behavior measures.

TREATMENT

Both pharmacological interventions and behavioral treatment have been proposed for treating the problems associated with ODD. There is currently very limited support for the use of medication in the treatment of children diagnosed with ODD without other comorbid disorders. However, empirical research does support the use of stimulants (e.g., Ritalin, Adderall) and tricyclic antidepressants with children diagnosed with comorbid ADHD and ODD (Christophersen & Mortweet, 2001).

The American Psychiatric Association (2000) noted that a "vicious cycle in which the parent and child bring out the worst in each other" often occurs between caregivers and children diagnosed with ODD. Patterson (1986) referred to this cycle as the "coercive process" in which children learn to avoid displaying problematic behavior in order to escape parental criticism.

Unfortunately, the performance of these defiant and negative behaviors leads to the future use of more aversive strategies by the parents. As such, behavioral parent training has been suggested as the best treatment for families and children with ODD. One example of an empirically based treatment package is *Parent–Child Interaction Therapy* (PCIT) (Hembree-Kigin & McNeil, 1995). PCIT is composed of two components, including Child Directed Interaction (CDI) and Parent Directed Interaction (PDI). In CDI, parents learn how to provide positive social attention (i.e., time-in) to their children while engaging in fun activities and during more naturalistic activities (e.g., working on homework, sitting quietly at a restaurant). In PDI, parents learn how to set up household rules, provide effective instructions to their children, and implement appropriate consequent strategies (i.e., time-out) for the display of disruptive behavior. Treatment is usually conducted by psychologists or other mental health professionals in clinical settings over the course of six to eight sessions with homework assignments designed to promote generalization to other environments (e.g., home, shopping mall, restaurant).

CONCLUSION

ODD involves a pattern of hostile, negativistic, and disruptive behaviors that often leads to impairments in major life activities such as attending school, keeping a job, and developing social relationships. Children with ODD may experience other problems like ADHD and learning problems. As such, the assessment for ODD should be both multimodal and multiinformant in nature. Because ODD is usually a result of living in a household that uses punitive and coercive parenting strategies, treatment should be aimed at teaching the child appropriate behaviors by changing the methods of parenting. Currently, medication is not considered to be appropriate as a first line of treatment for ODD unless the behaviors occur in conjunction with other disorders like ADHD.

See also: Antisocial Behavior; Parenting; Parent Training; Tantrums

BIBLIOGRAPHY

Achenbach, T. M. (1991). *Manual for the Child Behavior Checklist/4–18 and 1991 profile.* Burlington: University of Vermont, Department of Psychiatry.

American Academy of Child and Adolescent Psychiatry. (1997). Practice parameters for the assessment and treatment of children, adolescents, and adults with attention-deficit/hyperactivity disorder. *Journal of the American Academy of Child and Adolescent Psychiatry, 36*(Suppl.), 85S–121S.

American Psychiatric Association. (2000). *Diagnostic and statistical manual of mental disorders* (4th ed., text rev.). Washington, DC: Author.

Barkley, R. A., & Murphy, K. R. (1998). *Attention-deficit hyperactivity disorder* (2nd ed.). New York: Guilford.

Biederman, J., Faraone, S. V., Milberger, S., Jetton, J. G., Chen, L., Mich, E., et al. (1996). Is childhood oppositional defiant disorder a precursor to adolescent conduct disorder? Findings for a four-year follow-up study of children with ADHD. *Journal of the American Academy of Child and Adolescent Psychiatry, 35,* 1193–1204.

Christophersen, E. R., & Mortweet, S. L. (2001). *Treatments that work with children: Empirically supported strategies for managing childhood problems.* Washington, DC: American Psychological Association.

Eyberg, S. M. (1999a). *Eyberg Child Behavior Inventory.* Odessa, FL: Psychological Assessment Resources.

Eyberg, S. M. (1999b). *Sutter–Eyberg Student Behavior Inventory—Revised.* Odessa, FL: Psychological Assessment Resources.

Hembree-Kigin, T. L., & McNeil, C. B. (1995). *Parent–Child Interaction Therapy.* New York: Plenum.

Moore, J. W., Edwards, R. P., Wilczynski, S. M., & Olmi, D. J. (2001). Using antecedent manipulations to distinguish between task and social variables associated with problem behaviors exhibited by children of typical development. *Behavior Modification, 25,* 287–304.

Patterson, G. R. (1986). Performance models for antisocial boys. *American Psychologist, 41,* 432–444.

Reynolds, C. R., & Kamphaus, R. W. (1992). *Behavior Assessment System for Children (BASC).* Circle Pines, MN: AGS Publishing.

Shaffer, D., Fisher, P., Lucas, C. P., Dulcan, M. K., & Schwab-Stone, M. E. (2000). NIMH Diagnostic Interview Schedule for Children Version IV (NIMH DISC-IV): Description, difference from previous versions, and reliability of some common diagnoses. *Journal of the American Academy of Child and Adolescent Psychiatry, 39,* 28–38.

Thomas, J. M., & Guskin, K. A. (2001). Disruptive behavior in young children: What does it mean? *Journal of the American Academy of Child and Adolescent Psychiatry, 40,* 44–51.

Vitiello, B., & Jensen, P. (1995). Disruptive behavior disorders. In H. I. Kaplan & B. J. Sadock (Eds.), *Comprehensive textbook of psychiatry* (6th ed., pp. 2311–2319). Baltimore: Williams & Wilkins.

Additional Readings for Nonprofessionals

Christophersen, E. R. (1998). *Beyond discipline: Parenting that lasts a lifetime* (2nd ed.). Shawnee Mission, KS: Overland Press.

Christophersen, E. R. (1998). *Little people: Guidelines for commonsense child rearing* (4th ed.). Shawnee Mission, KS: Overland Press.

Additional Readings for Professionals

Barkley, R. A. (1997). *Defiant children. A clinician's manual for assessment and parent training* (2nd ed.). New York: Guilford.

McMahon, R. J., & Forehand, R. L. (2003). *Helping the noncompliant child. Family-based treatment for oppositional behavior* (2nd ed.). New York: Guilford.

R. ANTHONY DOGGETT
LAURA M. BAYLOT

Oral Language Learning Disabilities

Oral language is divided into the two categories of speech (expressive language) and listening (receptive language). The development of oral language skills is critical for later learning. For example, oral language skills lay a foundation for learning to read and write. Because oral language skills develop before abilities in reading and writing, they are considered as the *primary* language system. Moreover, by acquiring oral language skills, a child learns about other linguistic aspects such as grammar, vocabulary, and different types of sentences.

Not all children, however, develop language skills as expected. Approximately 8 percent of children do not acquire speech and language at or near the expected age (Tallal, Miller, Jenkins, & Merzenich, 1997). Oral language problems have been closely associated with the reading and writing problems exhibited by children with learning disabilities. One oral language problem that is characteristic of some children with learning disabilities involves deficits in phonological (or phonemic) awareness. Difficulties with phonological awareness are exhibited in problems with focusing on and manipulating phonemes, or the sounds of language. For example, changing a single phoneme or language sound such as *bat/cat* or *pit/put* can alter the meaning of what has been spoken. An informal way in which parents and teachers can assess a child's phonological awareness is to have the child count, by tapping out, the number of sounds he/she hears in a word presented orally. Thus, the following results would be expected for each respective word presented orally to the child: *oh* (one sound), *at* (two sounds), *dad* (three sounds), and *stop* (four sounds). As with all language skills, there is a developmental progression to acquisition. That is, a child 5 years of age would be expected to show better developed phonological awareness skills than a child 3 years of age.

Some children with learning disabilities may have difficulty comprehending what they hear. This comprehension problem may involve a single word, but more than likely will be evidenced with more complex units of speech such as sentences or longer speech units. Oftentimes, children with oral receptive language problems are misidentified as having behavior disorders because of their failure to comply with oral directives such as, "OK, class. Please sit down, get out your math books, and open to page 37." A child with oral receptive language problems may comprehend the first direction ("sit down") or the final direction ("open to page 37"), but may miss out on the entire sequence of directions.

Although problems with phonological awareness and listening comprehension are representative of oral receptive language difficulties, some children with learning disabilities may have difficulty with oral expressive language (speech). A specific oral expressive language problem often exhibited by children with learning disabilities is difficulty with word finding, often called *dysnomia*. This problem is evidenced when children cannot quickly and automatically name objects and are slow to recall the correct words (Lerner, 2003). Sometimes, the child may describe what the object is used for instead of recalling the object's name. A bright 12-year-old child with learning disabilities was observed calling a stapler a "paper putter-togetherer." Informal assessment procedures for dysnomia involve having the child name objects when actually presented with them (e.g., a pen), or when presented with pictures or photographs of them (e.g., an airplane).

Other oral expressive language problems are related to children simply having difficulty in producing speech or in talking. These children can understand speech, have no physiological problems such as muscular paralysis that prevents them from talking, and may do well on nonverbal tasks. Yet, they have a condition known as *expressive aphasia* that makes speaking difficult.

STRATEGIES TO IMPROVE ORAL LANGUAGE SKILLS

The following strategies from Lerner (2003) may help parents and teachers improve the oral language skills of children.

Oral Receptive Language

Clapping Names. Have the children clap out the syllables in their names and the names of their friends. Examples: An-dre-a (three claps), Paul (one clap), Ja-son (two claps).

Rhyming Game. The parent or teacher chooses words that rhyme with *head* or *feet*. The parent or teacher then asks the children a riddle, the answer to which rhymes with either *head* or *feet*. The children respond to the riddle by pointing to the body part (*head* or *feet*) that rhymes with the answer to the riddle. Example: [Parent/Teacher] "When I am tired, I go to____." Each child would then point to his/her *head*, which rhymes with the answer *bed*.

Same/Different. Say pairs of words (e.g., dog–dog, milk–melt, pat–pet, rain–rain) and have the child indicate if the words sound the same or different.

Listening Comprehension. Have children listen to a short story and then indicate which of the three events happened first, second, and third (last) in the plot.

Oral Expressive Language

The following strategies from Lerner (2003) can help teachers and parents develop oral expressive language skills in children.

Naming. Have the children name as many objects as they can in a room, classroom, backyard, and so on. Or, have the children name as many objects as they can in a category of objects. For example, if the category is *colors*, have the children name as many colors as they can.

Missing Words. Have the children supply a word that completes a riddle. For example, "The postman delivers the____."

Plurals. Show the children a single object (e.g., a pencil) and have them tell you what it is. Then show them two of that object (e.g., two pencils) and have them tell you what they are.

Fill In the Blanks. Have the children fill in the blanks given a sentence orally with only a few words provided. For example, *Bob went____ the store and____ a toy truck.*

Oral language skills can be developed using word games and word play. Parents and teachers who engage their children in such activities on a regular basis can help them acquire skills that will help them learn to read and write.

See also: Academic Interventions for Written Language and Grammar; Written Language Learning Disabilities

BIBLIOGRAPHY

Lerner, J. (2003). *Learning disabilities: Theories, diagnosis, and teaching strategies* (9th ed.). Boston: Houghton Mifflin.

Tallal, P., Miller, S., Jenkins, W., & Merzenich, M. (1997). The role of temporal processing in developmental language-based learning disorders: Research and clinical implications. In B. Blachman (Ed.), *Foundations of reading acquisition and dyslexia* (pp. 49–66). Mahwah, NJ: Erlbaum.

Additional Readings for Nonprofessionals

German, D. (2001). *It's on the tip of my tongue.* Chicago: Word Finding Materials.
Scientific Learning. (1995). *FastForWord.* Berkeley, CA: Author.

Additional Reading for Professionals

Adams, A., Foorman, B., Lundberg, I., & Beeler, T. (1998). *Phonemic awareness in young children.* Baltimore: Brookes.
Coyne, M., Kame'enui, E., & Simmons, D. (2001). Prevention and intervention in beginning reading: Two complex systems. *Learning Disabilities Research and Practice, 16,* 62–73.
Torgesen, J. (1997). The prevention and remediation of reading difficulties: Evaluating what we know from research. *Journal of Academic Language Therapy, 1,* 11–47.

G. FRANKLIN ELROD

Otitis Media

Otitis Media (OM) is a broad medical term referring to an inflammation of the middle ear. Structurally, the middle ear is a small air chamber containing three small bony structures: the malleus, incus, and stapes. The function of the middle ear is to conduct sound waves received by the external ear to the structures and nerves in the inner ear. The outer border of the middle ear is the ear drum (tympanic membrane [TM]), a thin membrane that conducts sound wave vibrations from the external ear canal to the bones in the middle ear. Internally, the middle ear is bordered by the Eustachian tube, a short channel that connects the middle ear to the back of the throat. Functionally, the Eustachian tube serves to drain fluid produced in the middle ear as well as keeping the air space in the chamber at an equalized pressure.

There are several types of OM diagnosed by physicians. OM is distinguished from otitis externa (often called "swimmer's ear"), which is an infection or inflammation of the external ear canal. Acute Otitis Media (AOM) refers to the presence of an infection in the middle ear, usually precipitated by an upper respiratory infection. AOM is characterized by pain; fever; a discolored, bulging, immobile TM; presence of purulent fluid (pus); and drainage (otorrhea). Chronic Otitis Media (COM) is defined as a recurrent or persistent infection and/or presence of fluid in the middle ear (chronic otitis media with effusion). Chronic Suppurative Otitis Media is an inflammation

of the middle ear lasting at least 6 weeks, with accompanying drainage through a ruptured TM or surgical intervention (see treatments below). Finally, Otitis Media with Effusion (OME) is diagnosed when there is presence of fluid and air bubbles in the middle ear without signs of infection. In addition to lack of infection, OME is further distinguished from AOM by a thickened, "dull" (bluish or yellow in color as opposed to red [infection] or gray [normal]) TM and accompanying fluid is thick (serous) as opposed to purulent. However, the presence of fluid results in an immobile TM, which occurs with AOM and COM. OME often follows an active ear infection and may last a few days to months (Beers & Berkow, 1999).

There are several associated problems with OM. The pressure and fluid present in OM decrease the mobility of the TM, usually resulting in some minor hearing loss due to impaired conduction of sound waves via the TM. Although the various types of OM typically resolve on their own or with minor medical treatment (see treatments below), the pressure and fluid buildup associated with OM may cause the TM to rupture. Rare but serious complications as a result of OM and spreading infection can also occur, including meningitis, mastoiditis (infection of the mastoid process, a part of the temporal bone located behind the ear), cholesteatoma (a cyst or abscess in the middle ear), tympanosclerosis (permanent thickening and possible calcification of the TM), and/or sensorineuronal hearing loss as a result of damage from infection moving to the inner ear structures (Beers & Berkow, 1999).

OM is the most common pediatric medical diagnosis. Eighty percent of all children will have at least one episode of OM, regardless of subtype, by 2 years of age. By 4 years of age, 80 percent of children will have had at least one diagnosis of OME. Rates of AOM are similar, with 80 percent of children having at least one AOM episode by age 3; 50 percent of children will have had three or more bouts of AOM by the 3rd year of life (Auinger, Lanphear, Kalkwarf, & Mansour, 2003). A recent review of the National Center for Health Statistics data on rates of OM showed that higher rates of OM occurred in higher socioeconomic status (SES) groups, but this finding may be an artifact of sampling procedure and the potential underdiagnosis of low-SES groups as a result of poor access to health care. In fact, the largest increase in OM diagnosis from 1988 to 1994 occurred within the low-SES strata (Auinger et al., 2003). Sex ratios vary slightly depending on the type of OM diagnosis but, generally, OM is slightly more prevalent in males (Auinger et al., 2003).

Prevalence rate data suggest that children are highly susceptible to OM, especially AOM and OME. The primary reason that OM is more frequent in children is that their Eustachian tubes are smaller, shorter, and more horizontally placed (shallower angle to back of throat) than are adult Eustachian tubes. As such, the Eustachian tubes do not drain fluid as efficiently, thus allowing fluid to accumulate in the middle ear, which, in turn, allows bacteria to harbor. The Eustachian tubes and the adenoids (small group of tonsillar tissue made up of lymph tissue located at the end of the Eustachian tube) may also become infected and swollen, constricting fluid drainage even further. Additional reported risk factors for developing OM include propped bottle feeding, group day care, second-hand smoke, allergies, asthma, and access to health care. Auinger et al.'s (2003) review suggests that group child care, allergies, and asthma are the only risk factors confirmed by statistical analysis. Supported risk factors for AOM developing into COM or OM include earlier onset of AOM and being male (Auinger et al., 2003).

Assessment and treatment of OM is done by either a primary care physician or a Ear, Nose, and Throat (ENT) specialist. The American Academy of Pediatrics has published guidelines for the management of OM in children. The standard therapy for OM with infection is a course of antibiotics (Hoberman, Marchant, Kaplan, & Feldman, 2002). However, some members of the medical community have asserted that the overuse and overprescription of antibiotics for minor ear infections has contributed to the increasing rates of antibiotic-resistant bacteria. Data from the Agency for Healthcare Quality and Research (2000) show that approximately 80 percent of AOM cases will resolve on their own in 1–7 days without medical intervention, calling into question antibiotic prescription practices. Immediate antibiotic treatment for OME is not recommended, but a trial may be considered at 6 weeks, if none have been prescribed earlier (American Academy of Pediatrics, 1994). Other medical interventions that may be used include myringotomy, a small surgical incision and suction to remove and allow fluid to drain from the inner ear, or placement of pressure-equalizing (PE) tubes (also called tympanostomy tubes). PE tubes are small, flexible cylinders placed in the TM following a myringotomy to keep the TM open, allowing fluid to drain and thereby improve hearing. PE tubes remain in the ears for approximately 6–9 months. Adenoidectomy (removal of adenoids) and tonsillectomy (removal of tonsils) may also be performed, although there is some controversy about the effectiveness of these procedures in resolving OM. The 1994 American Academy of Pediatrics guidelines for the treatment of OME do not recommend adenoidectomy and tonsillectomy, on the basis of their analysis of data suggesting no evidence for their use. However, studies that are more recent suggest that adenoidectomy, in conjunction with PE tube placement, lowers the risk of subsequent bouts of AOM and the need for multiple PE tube procedures (Coyte, Croxford, McIsaac, Feldman, & Friedberg, 2001).

Aside from concerns of excessive antibiotic use, a concern to both the medical community and education professionals is the impact of diminished hearing on cognitive, language, and social development. Although persistent hearing loss may place a child at higher risk for delays in language acquisition (American Academy of Pediatrics, 1994), research results have been mixed with regard to the bearing of OM on developmental outcomes. Cited reasons for differences across studies include failure to control for variables such as social class and age; use of retrospective parental report of frequency of OM; use of small *N* designs; differences across studies in definitions of the type of OM, hearing status, and assessment instruments. For example, Paradise et al. (2003) compared immediate and delayed tube placement on developmental outcomes. No differences in developmental outcomes were found when comparing the two groups with respect to the timing of tube placement or with controls without a history of middle ear infection. Significant correlations for *duration* of middle ear infection were found for both developmental outcomes (longer duration, lower scores on developmental measures) and parent report measures of stress and child behavior (higher perceived stress and negative view of child behavior with longer duration); however, SES was a better predictor in developmental scores. Micco, Gallagher, Grossman, Yont, and Vernon-Feagans (2001) found evidence that COM can affect language acquisition, depending on the level of hearing loss. Children with hearing loss at a threshold of >20 decibels are at significantly greater risk for diminished language acquisition. Lindsay, Tomazic, Whitman, and Accardo (1999) conducted a prospective analysis over 8 years that focused on middle ear problems and subsequent developmental diagnoses. These authors used a categorical analysis (major ear problems defined as at least one PE tube placement vs. minor ear problems defined as a history of OM) and found that SES was a predictor for *type* of diagnosis at school age. That is, children with major ear problems from low-SES backgrounds were more likely to be diagnosed with articulation disorders, middle-SES children were more likely to be diagnosed with attention-deficit/hyperactivity disorder, and high-SES children were more likely to be diagnosed with language problems. Casby (2001) conducted a meta-analysis of OM developmental impact and found no evidence to support a history of OM negatively affecting developmental status; however, the author was careful to note limitations of the studies and regarded findings as a heuristic for further refined research. Even though data are mixed, it is highly recommended that children with OME lasting at least 3 months be evaluated and monitored for hearing impairments. In addition, a history of OM should be considered when conducting a special education placement evaluation.

See also: Articulation Disorder; Attention-Deficit/Hyperactivity Disorder; Development; Oral Language Learning Disabilities

BIBLIOGRAPHY

Agency for Healthcare Quality and Research. (2000, June). *Management of acute otitis media* (Summary, Evidence Report/Technology Assessment, No. 15). Retrieved November 2, 2003, from http://www.ahrq.gov/clinic/epcsums/otitisum.htm

American Academy of Pediatrics. (1994). Managing otitis media with effusion in young children. *Pediatrics, 94,* 766–773.

Auinger, P., Lanphear, B. P., Kalkwarf, H. J., & Mansour, M. E. (2003). Trends in otitis media among children in the United States. *Pediatrics, 112,* 514–520.

Beers, M. H., & Berkow, R. (Eds.). (1999). *The Merck manual of diagnosis and therapy* (17th ed.). Rahway, NJ: Merck Research Laboratories, Merck & Co.

Casby, M. W. (2001). Otitis media and language development: A meta analysis. *American Journal of Speech–Language Pathology, 10,* 65–81.

Coyte, P. C., Croxford, R., McIsaac, W., Feldman, W., & Friedberg, J. (2001). The role of adjuvant adenoidectomy and tonsillectomy in the outcome of the insertion of tympanostomy tubes. *New Journal of Medicine, 344,* 1188–1195.

Hoberman, A., Marchant, C. D., Kaplan, S., & Feldman, S. (2002). Treatment of acute otitis media consensus recommendations. *Clinical Pediatrics, 41,* 373–390.

Lindsay, R. L., Tomazic, T., Whitman, B. Y., & Accardo, P. J. (1999). Early ear problems and developmental problems at school age. *Clinical Pediatrics, 38,* 123–132.

Micco, A. W., Gallagher, E., Grossman, C. B., Yont, K. M., & Vernon-Feagans, L. (2001). Influence of chronic otitis media on phonological acquisition. *Clinical Linguistics & Phonetics, 15,* 47–51.

Paradise, J. L., Dollaghan, C. A., Campbell, T. F., Feldman, H. M., Bernard, B. S., Colborn, K., et al. (2003). Otitis media and tympanostomy tube insertion during the first three years of life: Developmental outcomes at the age of four years. *Pediatrics, 112,* 265–277.

Additional Reading for Nonprofessionals

Campbell, T. F., Dollaghan, C. A., Rockette, H. E., Paradise, J. L., Feldman, H. M., Shribery, L. D., et al. (2003). Risk factors for speech delay of unknown origin in 3-year-old children. *Child Development, 74,* 346–357.

Additional Reading for Professionals

Campbell, T. F., Dollaghan, C. A., Rockette, H. E., Paradise, J. L., Feldman, H. M., Shribery, L. D., et al. (2003). Risk factors for speech delay of unknown origin in 3-year-old children. *Child Development, 74,* 346–357.

HEATHER E. STERLING-TURNER

Pp

Pain Syndromes: Recurrent

Recurrent pain is characterized by repeated painful episodes experienced across several months that occur in the absence of a well-defined medical cause. The most common types of recurrent pain syndromes involve headaches or abdominal/stomach pain. Those most affected are typically school-aged children and adolescents who are usually healthy and pain free between episodes. Recurrent headaches have been observed in about 2–3 percent of all children under 10, and about 4–15 percent of all adolescents. The typical onset is at around 6–7 years of age, with headaches typically becoming more prevalent with age; adolescent girls typically experience more headaches than do adolescent boys. Recurrent abdominal pain (RAP) occurs in about 10–15 percent of school-aged children. Combined, recurrent pain syndromes can occur in as many as 30 percent of all children, representing a major health problem for school-aged children (McGrath, 1990).

HEADACHES

The two most common types of headaches in children are migraine and tension headaches (Barlow, 1984). Migraines are characterized by pain on one side of the head, usually pulsating in quality, moderate or severe in intensity, aggravated by routine physical activity, and associated with light and noise sensitivity. They typically last anywhere from 4 to 72 hours. In contrast, tension headaches are characterized by pain that is pressing or tightening in quality, mild or moderate in intensity, does not worsen with routine physical activity, and is experienced on both sides of the head and sometimes down the back of the neck. It is not unusual for children to experience a combination of these two types of headaches, with frequent mild, pressing pain, and occasional severe, pulsating pain. Generally, the intensity and the quality are the best indicators of the type of headache.

ABDOMINAL PAIN

Recurrent abdominal pain typically involves at least three episodes of pain over at least 3 months, sufficient to interfere with daily activities and with no known medical cause (Barr, 1983). Onset is rarely before the age of 5 and tends to peak at 9–10 years of age. Although not necessary for diagnosis, there are a number of common symptoms. Pain location is usually around the bellybutton and is generally described as a diffused (i.e., scattered) and aching sensation rather than a sharp and concentrated pain. However, on occasion children are seen with pain symptoms severe enough to result in a trip to the hospital emergency room. Duration of the pain symptoms is usually short (less than 3 hours) and is usually during waking hours. Associated symptoms include nausea and vomiting, flushing, perspiration, and palpitations. Pain is rarely alleviated through medication. Finally, school absence is higher in children with RAP.

MEDICAL AND PSYCHOLOGICAL CONSIDERATIONS

Initial steps in understanding and treating pain syndromes involve ruling out medical causes. This is typically done by a physician and may include a family doctor as well as specialists such as neurologists, allergists, and gastroenterologists. For recurrent headaches, the most common organic causes to rule out include recent infections, increased intracranial pressure from excessive fluid or swelling, solid tumors, diseases such as hypertension, or dental problems such as malocclusions or temporomandibular joint disorder. The diagnosis of RAP is made by elimination of medical problems such as constipation, lactose intolerance, ulcers, abdominal epilepsy, infections (e.g., Crohn's disease), diabetes, and congenital anomalies (e.g., Hirschprung's disease).

Efforts to identify common emotional/behavioral characteristics or psychological diseases of children with recurrent pain syndromes have proven inconclusive. However, it is clear that the longer children endure episodes of pain, the more likely they are to develop other emotional difficulties such as anxiety and depression. Note that these conditions are a result rather than a cause of the recurrent pain episodes.

ORIGINS OF PAIN SYNDROMES

If disease exists, treatment can be relatively efficient and effective in eliminating the child's pain. However, once medical disease has been ruled out, the pain syndrome is understood to be multidimensional in nature and complex. Episodes of pain can be affected by factors both outside and within the individual, many of which can be modified to alter the experience of pain. A variety of models have been offered to account for recurrent pain syndromes, some of which view pain syndromes as "all in the child's head." However, this position has been widely rejected. The most prominent model currently available regarding pain syndromes takes a biobehavioral approach, in which both medical and environmental factors are seen as being important (e.g., Allen & Mathews, 1998).

The biobehavioral model of recurrent pain syndromes views the individual as possessing a nervous system that is highly sensitive and somewhat overresponsive to everyday, typical sources of stress in the environment. Indeed, both headaches and abdominal pain appear to be related to an inherited sensitivity or overreactivity to everyday events. Environmental stress can come from any situation that requires the individual to adjust and adapt. Common situations that can trigger pain episodes include academic demands, emotional distress, fatigue, emotional excitement, exercise, odors, temperature changes, and diet (e.g., nitrates, caffeine, lactose, yeast, MSG, etc.). In this model, the reactivity of the individual is not what is unusual. What is different is that the nervous system reacts sooner and does not recover or calm down as quickly as is typical in others. Over time, this continuing reactivity can result in pain. The model emphasizes that it is not stress that causes the pain syndrome and nor is it the body's reactivity that causes pain, rather it is the combination of the two that can trigger painful episodes. In this model, the physical reactivity is very real and so is the pain that is experienced.

The environment can also have an impact on pain syndromes via learning factors (Rachlin, 1985). The experience of pain is influenced, in part, by how parents model their own experience of pain and coping with pain. Children's experience of pain is also influenced, in part, by how people react to that pain and whether the caregivers encourage or support independence in management of pain. Finally, children's experience of pain is influenced, again in part, by the control they have over pain relief. In general, children who have never observed or experienced independent management of their own pain and who rely primarily on inactivity to achieve pain relief, typically experience more pain symptoms and dysfunction as a result of their pain. In sum, the consequences of pain are closely related to the level of disability created by pain in children and adolescents.

TREATMENT

Treatment for pain syndromes typically focuses on four different approaches. These might be used in isolation or, more commonly, in a multimodal approach that incorporates one or more of the approaches in some combination. These approaches involve medical management, identifying and controlling significant pain triggers, teaching self-regulation skills for managing physical sensitivity, and using parents to support and encourage independent management of pain symptoms.

Medical Management

Medical management of RAP is rarely used. Over-the-counter remedies have not been shown to be effective. Sedative medications or those that directly impact the intestines have also not been found to be effective and in some cases can be associated with aggravated symptoms. High-fiber diets are prescribed by some physicians and have been found to have some benefits.

Common drug treatments for headaches fall into two categories: drugs taken to reduce pain and drugs taken to prevent onset of pain (Singer, 1994). Because most simple over-the-counter medications have few side effects, they are the first line of treatment for children with recurrent headaches. Preventive medications do have a higher likelihood of side effects such as nausea, sedateness, fatigue, and lightheadedness, but there are no studies indicating the extent to which these might affect daily functioning and/or school performance in children. In part, this is due to the fact that most medications administered in the treatment of childhood headaches have been demonstrated as effective with adults only. Reviews of drug treatment of childhood headache show that medications do not reliably control pain in children. Subsequently, drug treatment of headache activity is highly individualized, and the effectiveness and possible side effects should be closely monitored by the child's physician. The general consensus is that the use of daily medications is neither necessary nor desirable for children and that behavioral pain management is a viable alternative to drug therapy.

Controlling Triggers

The longer children experience recurrent headaches, the larger the number of triggers that are likely to be present. In cases in which clear pain triggers are identified, attempts to eliminate or control these triggers may prove valuable. Eliminating obvious sources of significant academic, emotional, dietary, or physical stress makes sense; however, often the most significant source of stress is the pain syndrome itself. In addition, environmental triggers do not reliably account for a significant number of headaches or stomachaches. Finally, eliminating triggers often involves significant changes in lifestyle for the child and the family (i.e., changing diet), making it a relatively challenging intervention. As a result, although this can be an important treatment for some children, it is rarely a sufficient treatment by itself.

Learning Self-Regulation

Learning to control the physical sensitivity and overreactivity associated with pain syndromes is regarded as one of the most effective treatments available and is the most researched area of treatment regarding pain syndromes in children. Self-regulation training for children typically involves either biofeedback training or progressive muscle relaxation or some combination of the two, and these treatments have been found to be quite effective (Hermann, Blanchard, & Flor, 1997). There are other self-regulation strategies that can be used with children, such as visual imagery, controlled breathing, and hypnosis; however, none of these strategies have the research support of biofeedback and relaxation.

In biofeedback, *bio* refers to body and *feedback* refers to information. Biofeedback, then, is simply a means of giving children information about what their body is doing so that they can learn to control the reactivity. Computerized devices provide children with information about moment-to-moment changes in physical reactivity (e.g., body temperature, muscle tension, breathing rate), helping children learn to reduce and stabilize reactivity. Frequent use of biofeedback may reduce reactivity and thereby prevent the onset of painful episodes. Treatment can involve 8–12 clinic-based sessions over 6–10 weeks. However, home-based programs are more efficient and accessible to more children. A typical treatment might involve four clinic visits across 8 weeks, with most learning occurring during daily home practice. Indeed, there is a strong relation between amount of home practice and improvement in pain.

Relaxation programs teach children to control reactivity by tensing and relaxing different muscle groups in sequence. The cycles of tensing and relaxing provide their own feedback and help teach children to identify escalating levels of reactivity

and to bring it under control. Children are typically asked to practice regularly at home and often listen to tapes that talk them through the muscle relaxation exercises.

Encouraging Independence

Treatment may also involve teaching children to independently manage their pain. Parents may be asked to change how they and others respond to pain symptoms. Parents may be given specific guidelines on how to create an environment in which children independently use the self-regulation skills they have been taught. Although it is natural for children to wait for a parent to alleviate the pain for them, parents are typically asked to do less for their child in terms of directing pain management efforts and are asked to do more in terms of encouraging adaptive, active coping. Recommendations may direct parents to pay less attention to pain behaviors, pay more attention to adaptive coping, and insist upon continuation of normal activities, chores, and responsibilities. Parents who follow these types of guidelines have been found to have children who control pain better (Allen & Shriver, 1998).

PROGNOSIS

Clinical evidence does suggest that some children recover from pain syndromes without treatment, but there are no clear indicators of who may become pain free and who will continue to suffer. It is clear, however, that treatment outcome is dependent upon a number of factors. Headache frequency prior to treatment is a strong predictor of treatment outcome. Extremely low or extremely high headache frequency prior to treatment is associated with poorer treatment outcome. Outcome is also strongly associated with treatment adherence, where daily practice and use of self-regulation skills produce better outcomes than less frequent use. In addition, children experience better outcomes when parents encourage independent management of the pain syndromes. Overall, when implemented as prescribed, treatment can be expected to produce reductions in pain, improvements in adaptive behavior, increases in school attendance, reductions in medication usage, and fewer activities missed.

LIMITATIONS

Although multimodal treatment of pain syndromes in children has proven effective, there continue to be important directions for research and study. Recurrent pain is a complex phenomenon affected by complex biological and environmental interactions that are different for children than for adults. Children present unique challenges and warrant research that targets them specifically. Scientists currently are exploring not only which treatments are effective, but for which children. It is clear there are individual differences in responses to behavioral and medical treatments, but there is also uncertainty in predicting how an individual will respond. Scientists are also exploring strategies for managing pain syndromes in primary care and school settings, where children are frequently seen. In addition, scientists are exploring how to provide parents with clear guidance in selecting from treatment options. Comparisons of behavioral and drug treatments are in progress as are studies regarding the role of alternative therapies with children, such as physical therapy and chiropractic adjustments. In the near future, children and their families will be able to make more informed decisions about which medical and behavioral treatments are best suited to their needs, where these treatments should be delivered, and how they are likely to respond.

See also: Anxiety; Coping; Depression in Children and Adolescents

BIBLIOGRAPHY

Allen, K. D., Elliott, A. E., & Arndorfer, R. (2002). Behavioral pain management for pediatric headache in primary care. *Children's Health Care, 31*(3), 175–189.

Allen, K. D., & Mathews, J. R. (1998). Management of recurrent pain in children. In T. S. Watson & F. M. Gresham (Eds.), *Handbook of child behavior therapy: Ecological considerations in assessment, treatment, and evaluation* (pp. 263–285). New York: Plenum.

Allen, K. D., & Shriver, M. D. (1998). Role of parent-mediated pain behavior management strategies in biofeedback treatment of childhood migraine headaches. *Behavior Therapy, 29*, 477–490.

Barlow, C. F. (1984). *Headaches and migraine in childhood.* Philadelphia: Lippincott.

Barr, R. G. (1983). Recurrent abdominal pain. In M. D. Levine, W. B. Carey, A. C. Crocker, & R. T. Gross (Eds.), *Developmental behavioral pediatrics* (pp. 521–528). Philadelphia: Saunders.

Hermann, C., Blanchard, E., & Flor, H. (1997). Biofeedback treatment for pediatric migraine: Prediction of treatment outcome. *Journal of Consulting and Clinical Psychology, 65*, 611–616.

Levine, M. D., & Rappaport, L. A. (1984). Recurrent abdominal pain in school children: The loneliness of the long distance physician. *Pediatric Clinics of North America, 31*, 969–991.

McGrath, P. A. (1990). *Pain in children: Nature, assessment and treatment.* New York: Guilford.

Rachlin, H. (1985). Pain and behavior. *The Behavioral and Brain Sciences, 8*(1), 43–83.

Singer, H. S. (1994). Migraine headaches in children. *Pediatrics in Review, 15*, 94–101.

Zeltzer, L. K., Barr, R. G., McGrath, P. A., & Schechter, N. L. (1992). Pediatric pain: Interacting behavioral and physical factors. *Pediatrics, 90*(5), 816–821.

Additional Readings for Nonprofessionals

Headache—Hope through research. (2001). National Institute for Neurological Disorders and Stroke. Retrieved May 11, 2002, from http://www.ninds.nih.gov/health_and_medical/pubs/headache_htr.htm

Informational resources for headache sufferers. (2002). National Headache Foundation. Retrieved October 7, 2002, from http://www.headaches.org/consumer/educationmoduleindex.html

Additional Readings for Professionals

Friedrich, W. N., & Jaworski, T. M. (1995). Pediatric abdominal disorders: Inflammatory bowel disease, ruminating/vomiting, and recurrent abdominal pain. In M. C. Roberts (Ed.), *Handbook of pediatric psychology* (2nd ed., pp. 479–497). New York: Guilford.

McGrath, P. A., & Hillier, L. M. (Eds.). (2001). *The child with headache: Diagnosis & treatment.* Seattle: International Association for the Study of Pain Press.

Keith D. Allen

Parent Training

Parent training refers to the targeted teaching of parenting skills to parents with the intent of changing child behavior. Parent training differs from parent education approaches in that there is an expectation in parent training for parents to acquire skills and demonstrate changes in their behavior so that positive changes in child behavior may occur. Parent education refers more broadly to providing parents with parenting information to improve child outcomes, but not necessarily targeting actual parent behavior change. Parent training may take place as part of a parenting group or in individual sessions. Parent training is most often conducted by professionals in health services fields such as psychologists, counselors, social workers, and other health providers (e.g., mental health nurses). Parent training may take place in outpatient clinical settings (e.g., psychologist's office), hospital settings, churches, or schools (e.g., school psychologists or school counselors).

Casual perusal of any local bookstore will reveal a vast array of parenting books, guidelines, and parent training packages. Some of the more common parent training packages include Parent Effectiveness Training (PET) and Systematic Training for Effective Parenting (STEP). Because of the passive nature in which parenting skills are presented in packages and books (e.g., primarily reading and/or watching video) there is little expectation for actual parent behavior change. In fact, the majority of parenting packages and books available, although based in theory or on research, are best described as parent education materials, not parent training materials. Parent training requires an active approach that includes actual modeling by a parent trainer, guided practice for the parent, in vivo practice for the parent, and corrective and reinforcing feedback on parental skill acquisition. These teaching techniques are commonly used in parent training to teach specific parenting skills. The skills that are taught are based on empirical research demonstrating what parental behaviors most probably affect child behavior.

Although there are many theories regarding parenting and parental effects on child behavior, parent training procedures based on a behavioral model of parent–child interaction have typically garnered the most empirical support for actual parent and child behavior change. Many of the behavioral parent training models are based on a two-stage model of parent training that includes differential reinforcement and time-out. Differential reinforcement refers to providing reinforcement (often social attention such as verbal praise and positive physical touch) immediately following the child behavior that is desired, such as following directions, playing independently, or talking respectfully. Time-out is a punishment or discipline procedure that refers to removing a child's access to reinforcement (removing social attention and access to toys and other preferred items or activities) immediately following undesired behavior such as not following directions, tantrums, or talking disrespectfully. Time-out often involves having a child sit in a chair for a short (15 seconds to 4 or 5 minutes), previously specified amount of time, with release from the chair dependent upon the child being quiet. There are wide variations in how differential reinforcement and time-out may be effectively applied given the child behaviors of concern, parent characteristics and skills, and ecological variables (e.g., number of children in family, size of living space, access to reinforcing activities/items, etc.). Along with other considerations, such as communication and negotiation strategies and development of clear rules, parent training often involves variable implementation of these two procedures tailored to the child and family's unique situation.

THREE EXAMPLES OF PARENT TRAINING APPROACHES

An early model of parent training based on research examining parent–child interaction was developed by Forehand and McMahon in the 1970s and published in their book on parent training in 1981 (Forehand & McMahon, 1981). This model includes a Child's Game component in which parents are taught how to provide differential reinforcement for compliant or other desired child behavior. Parents are then taught how to provide effective commands to increase the probability of child compliance. Finally, parents are taught effective implementation of time-out procedures as a response to noncompliant behavior or other undesired behavior. This model of parent training is commonly used today.

A similar, but more structured, approach to parent training is a model called Parent–Child Interaction Therapy (PCIT) developed by Sheila Eyberg and Cheryl McNeil (Hembree-Kigin & McNeil, 1995). There appears to be more emphasis

in this approach on improving positive parent–child interactions prior to implementing discipline or time-out procedures. This approach explicitly teaches parents specific child-directed interaction skills during the first phase, called Child Directed Interaction. During the second phase, termed Parent Directed Interaction, parents are taught how to provide effective commands and implement time-out for negative child behavior. PCIT is very similar to the parent training model proposed by Forehand and McMahon, but is different in that there are more explicit criteria required for parents to meet in each phase of the parent training process.

A third model of parent training commonly used was developed by Carolyn Webster-Stratton. This model of parent training is similar to that of Forehand and McMahon's and PCIT in that this program also incorporates effective implementation of differential reinforcement and time-out. The parent training model developed by Webster-Stratton differs, however, in that the parent training is delivered in parent training groups, whereas the other two approaches are individualized. As such, the training approach used by Webster-Stratton also uses videos in addition to the parent training to assist with delivering information and to help model parenting skills (Webster-Stratton & Hancock, 1998).

The characteristic common to all three of these popular approaches to parent training is that they incorporate direct teaching techniques and an explicit focus on changing parent behavior to effect child behavior. Although noncompliance (i.e., not following directions) is a common problem addressed in parent training, there are many child problems that can be addressed through parent training. Types of child problems that have been addressed in parent training include oppositional behavior, conduct disorder and juvenile delinquency, behaviors associated with attention-deficit/hyperactivity disorder, feeding problems, pain management, phobias, behavior problems associated with developmental disabilities, medical compliance and chronic illness, weight management, and many others.

PARENT TRAINING AND SCHOOL PSYCHOLOGY

Parent training is an educational service that is mandated by the Individuals with Disabilities Education Act (1997). Parent training is included as a related service for families with children receiving special education services because it is recognized that positive parent–child interaction and positive parental support of child development and education are necessary to effective education, particularly for children who need extra help at school. Professionals in the schools most likely to provide parent training services will be school psychologists or school counselors. School psychologists can provide parents with education about their child's disability as well as specific training in how to more effectively manage child behavior or solve other child-related problems.

See also: Differential Reinforcement; Parenting; Time-Out

BIBLIOGRAPHY

Forehand, R. L., & McMahon, R. J. (1981). *Helping the noncompliant child: A clinician's guide to parent training.* New York: Guilford.

Hembree-Kigin, T. L., & Bodiford McNeil, C. (1995). *Parent–Child Interaction Therapy.* New York: Plenum.

Webster-Stratton, C., & Hancock, L. (1998). Parent training: Content, methods, and processes. In E. Schaefer (Ed.), *Parent training* (pp. 98–152). New York: Wiley.

Additional Readings for Nonprofessionals

Forehand, R., & Long, N. (1996). *Parenting the strong-willed child.* Lincolnwood, IL: Contemporary Books.

Patterson, G., & Forgatch, M. (1987). *Parents and adolescents living together.* Eugene, OR: Castilia.

Additional Readings for Professionals

Forehand, R. L., & McMahon, R. J. (1981). *Helping the noncompliant child: A clinician's guide to parent training.* New York: Guilford.

Hembree-Kigin, T. L., & Bodiford-McNeil, C. (1995). *Parent–Child Interaction Therapy.* New York: Plenum.

Schaefer, E. (1998). *Parent training.* New York: Wiley.

MARK D. SHRIVER

Parental Pressure

Parental pressure is a concept that is widely used but rarely well defined. The term refers to the effects that parental behaviors have on children's functioning. For example, someone may say that the high school quarterback on the football team is "pressured" by his parents to perform well during games so that he can obtain an athletic scholarship to college. This pressure may refer to any or all of a wide variety of parent behaviors including cheering their son at games, talking with their son frequently about football and college scholarships, expressing displeasure at poor performance during games or practice, expressing worry about paying for college without a scholarship, providing actual reward or punishment dependent upon performance during a game, and deemphasizing academic achievement as the son's road to college. None of the preceding examples is inherently good or bad, but each may serve to provide pressure on child behavior. It may well be that the parents are not con-

sciously aware of how their behavior, talk, and/or expectations affect their child's behavior or their child's perceptions of what he thinks his parents value most. The example above is but a small sample of what parental pressure may refer to. Essentially, parental pressure refers to how parents influence their children's behavior, whether it is intentional or not. The term *pressure* has a somewhat negative connotation, which may lead some to conclude that it is an undesired effect of parental behavior on child performance. However, parental pressure may also be positive and lead to desired effects on child performance.

BRIEF SUMMARY OF RESEARCH ON PARENTAL PRESSURE

Researchers in psychology and education have attempted to study the effects of parental pressure on child, adolescent, and adult child behavior, expectations, and perceptions for at least 50 years. A large focus of the research has been on how parental pressure may affect children's academic performance. Other areas of child behavior that have been examined in relation to parental pressure include classroom behavior, early reading performance, medical career choices, athletic performance, eyewitness reporting, and eating disorders. Much of the research is based on surveys of children's/adolescents' perceptions of parental expectations. Some of the research also examines parents' reports of their expectations and values. More recently, there has been an emphasis in the research literature examining cross-cultural differences within American subcultures (e.g., Asian American, African American, European American) in parental pressure and academic performance based on surveys of college students.

In general, a summary of the research literature suggests that parental pressure that is exemplified by coercive or punishment-oriented parent behaviors tends to have negative effects on children's and adolescents' performance in school and in other endeavors. In contrast, parental pressure that is exemplified by support, high but realistic expectations/goals, and positive reinforcement tends to have positive effects on children's and adolescents' performance.

PARENTAL PRESSURE AND SCHOOL PSYCHOLOGY

How parents talk about school, monitor and encourage academic achievement, set expectations or goals for academic performance, and establish positive and/or negative consequences for school performance may all affect a child's academic performance and behavior in the classroom. For children who may experience difficulties at school, a school psychologist may work with the parents to assess parental pressure for school behavior and academic achievement. The school psychologist can work with the parents to establish positive parental behaviors to support positive child behaviors at school and promote academic achievement in the classroom. The school psychologist may work with parents by educating them regarding appropriate expectations and goals for their child, setting up strategies to monitor homework completion, and training parents to establish positive reinforcement programs to encourage appropriate classroom behavior and academic achievement.

See also: Parenting; Parent Training

Additional Reading for Professionals and Nonprofessionals

Grolnick, W. S. (2003). *The psychology of parental control: How well-meaning parenting backfires.* Mahwah, NJ: Erlbaum.

MARK D. SHRIVER

Parenting

Parenting refers to an extremely wide range of behaviors or events that essentially encompass the socialization of children by the adults with whom they live. Parenting is most often conducted by the biological mother and/or father of a child, but may also refer to the care and/or guidance provided by extended family members (e.g., grandparents, aunts, and uncles), adoptive parents, or foster parents and other types of legal guardians (i.e., residential care). Parenting not only refers to the care and guidance provided by humans, but also to the care and guidance provided by other species toward their young to ensure survival. Parenting is a difficult term to specifically define given the wide range of behaviors the term encompasses. This difficulty with definition, however, has not stopped people from exploring the effects of parents on children. Historical evidence suggests that the importance and effects of parenting have been discussed throughout recorded history.

Given the lack of a clear definition on parenting and the wide range of behaviors the term encompasses, research on parenting tends to focus on specific characteristics of the parent, the child, or the interaction between them when examining the effects of parenting. Likewise, there is not yet a widely accepted comprehensive theory regarding parenting, although there are various theoretical approaches to the topic. Below, a very brief history of the topic of parenting is presented. A select few of the more common current theories regarding parenting are presented. Next, some of the more common lines of research on parenting are discussed. Finally, the relationship between the topics of parenting and school psychology is reviewed.

BRIEF HISTORY OF PARENTING

Tomb paintings and stories from ancient Egypt (ca. 2000–1800 B.C.E.) suggest that the Egyptians valued children. Children are depicted in play. They are depicted with their mothers and fathers. Children's toys have been found in tomb excavations, and the Egyptians kept records of all births (French, 1995). In Babylonia, the Huammurabi law code (ca. 1750 B.C.E.) contained many laws pertaining to how parents were to care for children (French, 1995). In Greece, during the fourth century B.C.E., Plato and Aristotle wrote about the proper care of children by parents, and it is in writings from Greece that we find the first evidence of systematic observation and theorizing about parenting (French, 1995).

More recently, John Locke wrote *Some Thoughts Concerning Child Rearing* (1693/1978), which was a popular manual concerning raising children in Western Europe and America in the early 1700s (Holden, 1997). Likewise, Rousseau discussed his views of appropriate child care in his book *Emile* (1762/1956). *The Care and Feeding of Children* by Luther Emmett Holt, a physician, was published in 1894 and was the most popular book on child care for almost 50 years (Holden, 1997). Benjamin Spock, also a physician, is probably the most recognized name in parenting advice in the latter half of the twentieth century with the sixth edition of his famous child care book published in 1992 titled *Dr. Spock's Baby and Child Care*. For most of history, writing and advice on parenting has been dominated by philosophers, physicians, and religious leaders (Holden, 1997). In the twentieth century, psychology began to develop as a discipline independent of philosophical inquiry, and psychologists began exploring parenting more systematically.

PARENTING THEORIES

In psychology, as well as in other disciplines such as philosophy, religion, and medicine, there are many worldviews or theories regarding why people and/or animals behave the way they do. These theories have implications for how a person studies or describes parenting effects on children. One of the first systematic theories of child development that included hypotheses regarding parenting effects was that of psychoanalytic theory developed by Sigmund Freud in the early twentieth century. Although his work generated interest in the area of child development and parenting, research has not been supportive of most of his contentions.

Behaviorism, a philosophy of science proposed by B. F. Skinner, was especially popular in the early twentieth century and continues to provide important avenues for the study of parenting and child care as well as effective parenting interventions to improve child care. Theoretical approaches that have developed from the behavioral tradition have included Social Learning theory and Ecological theory.

In developmental approaches to parenting, stages and sequences of maturation common across children are studied. In addition, children take an active role in the socialization process through cognitive processes (e.g., assimilation of cognitive schema, internalization of rules) that develop naturally during maturation. Parents are viewed as facilitators of children's developmental maturation processes through the parents' influence on a child's environment.

It can probably be asserted that most theoretical orientations recognize that genetics plays a role in child development, behavior, and parenting. Behavioral genetics is a research approach to studying parenting based on studies of the influence of parents' genes on behavior. This approach to research has become more prevalent with the advent of the Human Genome Project.

RESEARCH IN PARENTING

Mammals, particularly primates, are often used to study parenting. The use of animals allows for more frequent and intensive observation of parenting behaviors than would be possible with humans. In addition, biological influences on parenting behaviors can be more readily studied with animals. Primates, such as chimpanzees, are particularly useful for studying parenting given their close genetic similarities with humans. Observations of animal behavior in the laboratory as well as in more natural settings allow for examination of differences in parenting behaviors among species, based on environmental factors, learning principles, and biology. Specific biological variables that have been studied include hormonal influences on mothers' parental behaviors postnatal, during infancy, and later childhood. Hypotheses can be generated from the study of animals regarding the learning principles and biological principles that may affect human parenting.

Parenting research in humans has explored the effect of biological variables on parenting, ecological variables on parenting, specific parental characteristics (genetics and behavioral), and specific variables affecting the parent–child relationship/interaction. Much of the research on the psychobiology of parenting has focused on mothers, particularly in relation to their interaction with infants. Changes in physiology associated with pregnancy have been examined and attempts have been made to correlate physiological changes with maternal behavior. Likewise, maternal physiological responses to infant cues (smell, vocalizations, sight, touch) have been examined in terms of endocrine profiles as well as heart rate and galvanized skin response. These physiological responses to infant characteristics and behavior are examined to determine if there are correlations with maternal behavior.

Ecological variables that have been examined for their effects on parenting behavior include cross-cultural differences, socioeconomic variables (e.g., low income vs. high income), racial and ethnic differences, marital status, as well as family structure (e.g., number of siblings, extended family as child caretaker). The interaction between ecological variables and psychobiological variables will affect parental behavior and parent–child interactions.

Research on parenting has often led to the differentiation of particular parent characteristics that are assumed to have differential effect on child behavior. Common parental traits or classifications that have been proposed include authoritarian, authoritative, and permissive. These classifications of parental characteristics differ along a continuum, according to the degree of warmth and control exhibited by parents toward their children. The authoritarian parent is one who attempts a high degree of control over a child but exhibits little warmth toward the child. The authoritative parent has more balanced degrees of control over a child and warmth, whereas the permissive parent exhibits little attempt to control the child and high degree of warmth or acceptance.

Another research area in parenting examines the effects of the interaction between parents and their children. Specific parental behaviors such as monitoring, commands, and contingent social attention are examined for effects on child compliance. Likewise, more attention is being paid also to the degree to which child behaviors and characteristics influence parental behavior. For example, parenting a child with a physical disability requires a different degree of parental behavior (i.e., monitoring, physical care). Likewise, children who are more oppositional to parental control will affect subsequent efforts by their parents in attempting to control them. It is the research on parent–child interaction that has led to effective treatment approaches for child disorders, such as Attention-Deficit/Hyperactivity Disorder and Oppositional Defiant Disorder as well as other behavioral pediatric disorders such as sleep problems, eating, and toileting.

PARENTING AND SCHOOL PSYCHOLOGY

Many variables affect parenting behavior (e.g., genetic, biological, ecological, proximal environmental events, parental learning history, child behavior/characteristics). Parenting will have an effect on child behavior and outcomes. Research on child academic performance has suggested that parenting behaviors can enhance or inhibit academic performance. Children who come from homes that have stable, two-parent families, with frequent monitoring of the children, balanced and effective discipline approaches, high yet appropriate expectations for academic performance, as well as an environment supportive of academic performance (books available, structured study time, positive remarks about education) tend to do better in school than children without these parental supports. For this reason, school psychologists are encouraged to include parents in problem-solving activities when children are having difficulty at school. This form of collaborative teamwork between schools and parents is believed to improve a child's success in schools.

See also: Attention-Deficit/Hyperactivity Disorder; Oppositional Defiant Disorder; Parent Training; Sleep Disorders

BIBLIOGRAPHY

French, V. (1995). History of parenting. In M. H. Bornstein (Ed.), *Handbook of parenting: Vol. 2. Biology and ecology of parenting* (pp. 263–284). Mahwah, NJ: Erlbaum.

Holden, G. W. (1997). *Parents and the dynamics of child rearing.* Boulder, CO: Westview.

Additional Reading for Nonprofessionals

Bornstein, M. H. (Ed.). (1995). *Handbook of parenting* (Vols. 1–4). Mahwah, NJ: Erlbaum.

Additional Readings for Professionals

Borkowski, J. G., Landesman Ramey, S., & Bristol-Power, M. (2002). *Parenting and the child's world: Influences on academic, intellectual, and social–emotional development.* Mahwah, NJ: Erlbaum.

Bornstein, M. H. (Ed.). (1995). *Handbook of parenting* (Vols. 1–4). Mahwah, NJ: Erlbaum.

Holden, G. W. (1997). *Parents and the dynamics of child rearing.* Boulder, CO: Westview.

MARK D. SHRIVER

Pavlov, Ivan

MOTIVES, EMOTIONS, AND MEDICINE

Pavlov always considered his research to be physiology—he wanted to understand the workings of the brain. But his findings are important to all of us for several reasons. For one, Pavlov's work shows how fears and phobias are created, and many current treatments for phobia are based on his findings.

More generally, Pavlov showed how environments, like those in schools, can produce feelings of well-being and comfort *or* feelings of stress and anxiety. A second major application lies in drug effects—Pavlov's findings tell us why placebo effects occur and how learning affects our response to all medicines.

Ivan Petrovich Pavlov was born the son of a priest in Ryazan, Russia, in 1849 and began his higher education at a theological seminary. He then attended Petersburg University and finally the Imperial Medical Surgical Academy, where he earned a medical degree in 1883. His research on the physiology of digestion won him a Nobel Prize in 1904 and an international reputation that prepared an enthusiastic reception for his psychological work.

Hence, he was well known when his *Conditioned Reflexes* appeared in translation in 1927. Although Americans had heard news of the conditioned reflex and some had made use of it in theoretical writings, few grasped its real significance. Even today, it is rare when Pavlov is understood by American psychologists. He was not the "Pavlov" who is encountered in many psychology textbooks.

THE BODY AS LIVING MACHINE

The thinkers of the past several centuries had passed on the legacy of Descartes, a legacy that lives on in our commonsense views of the mind. According to this view, which is really the only one that we are taught, we each have (or we are) a mind trapped in the physical structure of a body. We are "ghosts in machines." We tend to regard the body as a marvelous machine that is constantly carrying out all kinds of complicated functions, but it is still a machine. Like Descartes, we effectively treat the body as dead and inert, no different from a robot; clay that is not really "us," but a structure that is animated by a supernatural ghostly "mind," made of different stuff.

Pavlov's views, and those of his colleagues, were quite different. For them, the body is also a machine and it is also marvelous, but it is a *living* machine and therein lies the difference. A body composed of living parts does not require a separate ghost/mind to guide it. There is mind, of course, but it is the product of the workings of the living body —it is not a separate entity.

Given a mechanical (living) body and its functioning (the mind), how do we understand its workings? Pavlov believed that this was the business of physiology and that the psyche was best studied through investigation of the physiological activity of the brain. Pavlov's work showed how the adjustments we make as the conditions of the world change around us can be understood as the workings of an integrative mechanism, controlled largely by the cerebral cortex. The significance of Pavlov's work was seen differently by early American psychologists.

PAVLOV'S INSIGHT

Pavlov had the insight to see the significance of a common and trivial occurrence. As recounted in countless textbooks, popular articles, and cartoons, Pavlov noticed that his dogs salivated when things that had previously accompanied food were present. Such salivation represented a learned reflex, which Pavlov first called a "psychic reflex," and it was just that bare fact that was of such interest to the Americans. At birth, or after a period of maturation, we have a set of reflexes that do not depend upon the conditions of our individual experience—they are "unconditional." In textbook parlance, a conditioned stimulus (CS) signaling an unconditioned stimulus (UCS) produces a conditioned response (CR) that is similar to the unconditioned response (UCR). So a UCS such as food in the mouth produces a UCR including chewing, salivation, swallowing, secretion of digestive enzymes, and other reactions. The sight of food, acting as a CS, produces those reactions also, but in a weaker form known as the CR. Salivation is the easiest part of the CR to measure.

Instead of the sight of food, the sound of a bell, of bubbling water, or hearing the word "food" can become a signal, or conditioned stimulus. Thus, new cues can call out old reflexes. Can we then account for all of our behavior and experience as the accumulation of conditioned reflexes? If we decide that we can, we part company with Pavlov. Nevertheless, that finding is still important. Imagine—whenever a strong stimulus (it need not be food) is reliably signaled by a weaker stimulus, the weaker stimulus comes to produce the reaction of the strong stimulus. Consider two examples.

• Jimmy's parents use mealtime to criticize him, hoping to make him a better person. Their harangues upset his stomach and make him feel anxious. Soon the cues associated with mealtime (dining room, parents, even food) produce anxiety and upset stomach. The weaker context cues produce the effect that the powerful stimulus (parents' criticisms) produces. This is classical conditioning just as surely as is the dog's salivation to a bell. This may create a problem that haunts Jimmy for years. You can imagine that the same thing can happen at school, if Jimmy were regularly taunted by bullies or embarrassed by a scolding teacher. All the stimuli associated with school would become anxiety-producing.

• When you were a child and were sick, a parent gave you medicine that made you feel better. You also received medicine from a doctor or nurse and later you took prescriptions to the drugstore. The medicines acted as a UCS and your improvement in health was the UCR. Now you may feel better when you take a sugar pill, as long as a doctor, nurse, or similar figure tells you it will help. The next time you buy an over-the-counter remedy, such as an antacid, look at the insert that describes the results of clinical trials. You may see that the drug was reported

effective in 80% of tested cases, whereas the placebo (sugar pill) cases were effective only 55% of the time. That 55% is the CR that accounts for a large part of the effectiveness of *all* drugs.

THE MIND OF THE GLANDS—THE WHOLE BODY IS ALIVE

In 1896, S. G. Vul'fson was assigned by Pavlov to work out the mechanisms controlling salivation, and it was Vul'fson who discovered the unusual "mind" of those glands. Vul'fson found that the salivary glands reacted differently to different foods and to nonfood substances even when visually presented—when he "teased" the dogs. We have no direct control over the salivary glands, yet they react to things that we see and smell—they alone, among glands, have a "mind" in some sense! Another researcher, I. T. Tolochinov, discovered extinction of the CR and pointed out that CRs have been observed in the "knee reflex" and the eyeblink reflex—in both cases these were "reflexes at a distance." Pavlov called them *conditional reflexes*.

In any event, the CR itself was not an end and Pavlov never believed that it might serve as a unit of analysis. Yet, early American psychologists did propose such a possibility. From their point of view, one's personality is simply compounds and sequences of reactions to conditioned stimuli (CSs). This includes private experience, because the CR to food, or to other UCSs, includes the thought of food and the pleasures of eating. American researchers and theorists adopted the vocabulary used by Pavlov and concentrated on the specific conditions that produce Pavlovian conditioning, later called classical conditioning, or simply conditioning.

INHIBITION IN THE BRAIN: MORE INTERESTING THAN YOU THINK

Inhibitory action in the nervous system was a controversial issue during the nineteenth century. Pavlov believed that his data showed that excitation and inhibition are brain processes aroused by UCSs and that these processes become attached to CSs. So a reliable signal for food or for electric shock is very excitatory and might be called a strong CS+, noting that the "+" means that it is a strong signal, not that it signals something "good." A reliable signal for no food or shock would become strongly inhibitory and might be called a strong CS−, realizing that the "−" means that it signals "no UCS." An excitatory CS produces a strong reaction (CR) and an inhibitory CS produces an *opponent* reaction—not *no* reaction, but one opposite to what one might expect. Look at what happened to Konorski's dog!

KONORSKI'S DOG WON'T EAT AND CHRIS FREEZES UP IN CLASS

Pavlov's evidences for inhibition are complex and difficult to describe, so we will consider only three interesting and easily described cases. The first was described by Jerzy Konorski (1948), a Pavlovian who ran a physiological institute in Warsaw. Imagine a hungry dog that is occasionally fed a small bit of food and this always occurs just after a green light flashes. At other times, a tone is sounded briefly and no food is ever delivered. When neither tone nor light is on, nothing happens and during this period and during periods when the tone is on, the dog appears to be waiting for the light. Soon the light becomes a CS+ and the tone becomes a CS−. What of the no-tone/no-light periods?

Is that interval also a CS−? There is no response from the dog, just as is the case during the tone, which explicitly signals "no food." The problem with the notion of inhibition is that it is not obvious whether lack of response means that inhibition is present or simply that excitation is absent. Moreover, inhibition means an actual *suppression* of responding that would otherwise occur.

When offered food during the light, the dog eats and it eats when food is offered during the no-stimulus interval. But, when offered food just after the tone, the dog refuses—it turns away and if food is forced on it, it spits it out. This indicated to Konorski that the tone elicited an "antieating" response, because it has become a reliable predictor of "no food" and thus inhibitory.

Imagine a comparable situation in a classroom, where Chris is never called on to answer a question. An unexpected question from the teacher does not simply produce "no response," it produces a "freezing up," so that Chris cannot even *speak*. Contrast this with the child who is always called on or who is occasionally called on—freezing up does not happen to her. The parallel with Konorski's dog is clear.

THE PARADOX OF INHIBITION

A second phenomenon associated with inhibition has been called the "paradox of inhibition." In delayed conditioning, a CS is presented and remains on during a delay period and a UCS is then presented. For example, Kimmel (1966) presented human subjects tones that remained on for a few seconds until painful electric shock (the UCS) was delivered. One component of the response to such a UCS is perspiration, which can be measured as a change in skin conductance, the galvanic skin response (GSR). As trials continued, typically to a dozen or more, the GSR diminished and in some cases even decreased to levels below baseline. That is, the subjects appeared to be more relaxed than they were before the experiment began. How can that be?

Pavlov believed that stimuli present when no UCS ever occurs become inhibitory—the CR is suppressed. In delayed conditioning, the delay interval itself never features a UCS and it therefore becomes inhibitory, as does the CS present during its duration. In fact, that is the case during early trials with food or shock or other UCSs and the CR occurs throughout the interval. Over a few trials, the CR diminishes in the early part of the interval so that a pattern of increased responding through the interval appears.

Given that, it makes sense that if the interval is sufficiently brief, responding may be suppressed through the whole interval and even during the UCS itself, even when the UCS is painful shock. Kimmel found that when the shock was presented alone, a strong UCR occurred and the subjects reported pain. They even reported that it was painful when their GSR had diminished. Interestingly, they also reported "organism-wide tranquility!"

Kimmel's findings are only one instance of this effect that was reported originally by Pavlov (1927, Lecture 3). Humans show the effect when a noxious puff of air is the UCS and the CR "eyeblink" comes to be inhibited. Dogs show it when they refuse to eat when the interval between CS/UCS trials is reduced from 10 minutes to 90 seconds. If a different CS+ is presented, they "ate avidly," as they did when no CS was present. In all of these cases, the CS specifically inhibited the CR and the UCR. A salient example of this effect occurs in drug addiction, where it appears as tolerance, so that more and more of a drug is required to produce the same effect.

REAL EXPERIMENTAL NEUROSIS

A third inhibitory phenomenon played a large part in Soviet psychiatry and was interpreted as the result of conflict between excitation and inhibition. Experimental neurosis may be produced by presenting an impossible discrimination problem, the original involving a circle and an ellipse. Dogs were presented a circle (CS+) with food and an ellipse (CS−) without food and their salivation to the CS+ and CS− was recorded. They quickly learned to salivate only during the CS+. Gradually, the stimuli were made more similar, as the ellipse was made more nearly circular, until the subject could no longer distinguish between the two shapes. When the forms could no longer be discriminated, the dog became agitated, it barked, salivated, bit at its harness, and generally went berserk. To prevent injury, the dog is removed and placed in a kennel, where it may remain "insane" for months or years.

A similar effect occurs in pigeons discriminating colors and in children learning successively subtle concepts. When a simple series of problems has been learned, with each problem slightly more difficult than the last, few or no errors occur if the difficulty of the problems increases gradually enough. But, if too large a step is taken and the subject cannot deal with the current problem, its behavior becomes irregular and something amazing happens. When we revert to the earlier and easier problems, we find that our subject *can no longer solve them* (Terrace, 1963)! Therein lies the danger in programmed learning that presents material in carefully crafted order of increasing difficulty, so that errors are seldom made. What happens when the child cannot deal with the latest level of difficulty? If too large a step is taken, will earlier learning be erased?

CLASSICAL CONDITIONING IN MEDICINE

Of the myriad applications of conditioning to medicine, none is more famous than that of Ader and Cohen (1982) finding that the body's immune system can be conditioned. Diseases like AIDS, MS, allergies, and a host of others occur because of a lack of immune response or an overly strong response. Systemic lupus erythematosus, commonly called "lupus," occurs when the immune system reacts too strongly, so that healthy tissues are destroyed and death results. Ader and Cohen were using the drug cyclophosphamide to induce nausea in rats, when they noticed their subjects succumbing to a variety of infections—the drug was depressing the immune systems! They then applied the drug to mice bred to contract lupus and found that it extended their lives. This benefit was due to suppression of the immune response, which they subsequently showed could be conditioned.

In brief, one group of mice (C100) received weekly pairings of a saccharine taste and an injection of the drug. A second group (C50) received the same treatment, except that on half the occasions the drug was replaced by saline solution. The third group (NC50) was treated as was the C50 group, except that the saccharine taste and injections occurred on different days. A final group received only saccharine and saline, unpaired. Their genes ensured that all mice would die, but the longevity of the C50 group showed that the immune system suppression had become a CR. Both the C50 and the NC50 mice had the same amount of drug, saccharine, and saline. But the taste/drug pairing for the C50 group meant that conditioning could occur. On average, the C50 group members outlived the NC50 mice by almost a month and a half—an increase of about 25 percent.

Ader and Cohen suggested that conditioning accounts for the placebo effects that have been reported for thousands of years. We are accustomed to CS (medicine/doctor)– feeling better, so that the "health response" becomes a CR. Turkkan (1989) surveyed many cases of placebo that fit this mold, as well as some nocebo (harmful) effects that have been reported.

PAVLOVIAN CONDITIONING, BEHAVIOR THERAPY, AND PANIC

The only major form of psychotherapy that almost always *works* is the treatment of phobias through counterconditioning and systematic desensitization, a method credited to Wolpe (1958). Of course, Watson and Jones used the method decades earlier (Watson, 1929) and, in fact, Wolpe points out that Erofeeva, a woman researcher in Pavlov's laboratory in 1912, actually first demonstrated the method. She showed that electric shock applied to a dog's body surface could become a signal for food and so produce salivation rather than flinching.

Another application of Pavlovian conditioning to psychotherapy demonstrated the *establishing* of a powerful fear reaction—in fact, a panic reaction. Campbell, Sanderson, and Laverty (1964) used a tone CS and the UCS was an injection of succinylcholine, which produces an immediate respiratory paralysis! The human subjects believed that they were "suffocating and dying," a panic state if ever there was one. A single pairing was enough to produce powerful conditioned responses and thus an artificial panic attack had been produced.

SEMANTIC CONDITIONING

Semantic conditioning is a way of using classical conditioning to assess the similarity of meaning in words and symbols and in gauging what Razran (1961) called "meaning load."

This procedure involves establishing a CR to a word, sentence, or numerical expression as a CS+ and (usually) presenting a second CS, which is made inhibitory by presenting no UCS with it.

The UCSs include food, a cold disk on the skin, and electric shock. A 13-year-old boy, Yuri, was conditioned to salivate to sentences and numbers. For example, after the Russian words for "good" and "bad" were established as CS+ and CS−, respectively, a number of test sentences were presented with no UCS. The CRs to the original CSs generalized to other stimuli similar in meaning—semantics—for the subject. So, classical conditioning even influences the effects that words have on us, a powerful determinant of our moods, emotions, and the tone of our lives.

PAVLOV'S RUSSIAN RIVALS

Pavlov's method was to correlate gross behavioral functions with gross brain functions, unlike the traditional and rival neurophysiologists, who were concerned with nervous and synaptic conduction. Pavlov did not keep abreast of this literature and was out of touch by 1920. There was a lot of competition between the Pavlov School and the physiologists for research support.

Until the 1920s, dominant positions in academic physiology were held by the neurophysiologists—the so-called Sechenov School. They were displaced in the 1920s by the Pavlov School. Inhibition was a key bone of contention. Pavlov's approach became dominant in Soviet science from the 1920s until at least the early 1960s. For Pavlov and his school, the whole body is important in constituting the psyche. It took Western psychology most of the twentieth century to appreciate this.

See also: Skinner, B. F.; Watson, John B.

BIBLIOGRAPHY

Ader, R., & Cohen, H. (1982). Behaviorally conditioned immunosuppression and murine systemic lupus erythematosus. *Science, 215,* 1534–1536.

Campbell, D., Sanderson, R., & Laverty, S. G. (1964). Characteristics of conditioned response in human subjects during extinction trials following a single traumatic conditioning trial. *Journal of Abnormal and Social Psychology, 66,* 627–639.

Kimmel, H. D. (1966). Inhibition of the conditioned response in classical conditioning. *Psychological Review, 73,* 232–240.

Konorski, J. (1948). *Conditioned reflexes and neuron organization.* Cambridge: Cambridge University Press.

Pavlov, I. P. (1927). *Conditioned Reflexes.* New York: Oxford University Press.

Razran, G. (1961). The observable unconscious and the inferable conscious in current Soviet psychology: Interoceptive conditioning, semantic conditioning, and the orienting reflex. *Psychological Review, 68,* 81–147.

Terrace, H. S. (1963). Errorless transfer of a discrimination across two continua. *Journal of the Experimental Analysis of Behavior, 6,* 223–232.

Turkkan, J. S. (1989). Classical conditioning: The new hegemony. *Behavioral and Brain Sciences, 12,* 121–179.

Watson, J. B. (1929). *Behaviorism* (3rd ed.). New York: Norton.

Wolpe, J. (1958). *Psychotherapy by reciprocal inhibition.* Stanford, CA: Stanford University Press.

Additional Reading for Nonprofessionals

Malone, J. C. (1991). *Theories of learning: A historical approach.* Belmont, CA: Wadsworth.

Additional Readings for Professionals

Gray, J. A. (1979). *Ivan Pavlov.* New York: Penguin.

Pavlov, I. P. (1955). *Selected works.* Moscow: Foreign Languages Publishing House.

Rescorla, R. A. (1988). Pavlovian conditioning: It's not what you think it is. *American Psychologist, 43,* 151–160.

JOHN C. MALONE
JUSTIN HALL
MARIA E. A. ARMENTO

Peer Counseling Programs

Students helping their peers succeed academically is not a new concept in schools. Tutoring programs with students knowledgeable in a subject area have been successful in helping less-able peers achieve. As peer tutoring programs expanded, the value of peers in assisting their classmates outside of the academic arena was recognized. Students are often the first to know about the problems their peers are experiencing and peers may be more likely to approach a classmate than an adult. School-aged youth helping one another is a compelling concept in which they assist in a number of capacities, including referral sources, information providers, hosts of new student orientation, and facilitators of groups (Robinson, Morrow, Kigin, & Lindeman, 1991).

Although the term *peer counselor* is often used to describe the special relationship between classmates assisting one another outside of academic concerns, the terms *peer facilitator* or *peer helper* are more accurate. Students are not trained to be counselors. Rather these students are taught skills to assist their peers with problems and concerns. For the purposes of this article, this individual will be termed as a *peer facilitator*. Schools have implemented several types of basic peer programs with students in various roles, including teacher or counselor assistant, tutor, mentor, and leader of small groups.

TEACHER/COUNSELOR ASSISTANT

Peers assist teachers by grading papers, teaching a difficult concept, or serving as a teacher's aide. Students who have difficulty discussing personal or academic issues with an adult can seek out a peer facilitator who has been trained in communication, listening, referral resources, and limits of confidentiality.

PEER TUTORS

Literature abounds with successful results when students assist others with academic difficulties. Peers can be approximately the same age, or older students can be selected to work with younger students. One peer tutoring program developed in a Midwest high school improved grades, reduced stress, and enhanced socialization skills (Corn & Moore, 1992). Although these programs often benefit the student being tutored as well as the tutor, what is often missing from these programs is a systematic approach to teaching tutors skills outside of instructional help. For instance, auxiliary skills that assist in academic performance include note taking, time management, following directions, etc., and can be taught to the tutors, who in turn can teach these skills to their tutee.

MENTORS

Many school-aged youth feel isolated and lonely and do not have the skills to form peer relationships. Countless students need a special person who will show interest in them and listen to their concerns. At times, an older, popular peer facilitator will be paired with a younger student who has difficulties. For example, one school paired popular, high school athletes with younger, struggling students just to "hang out" for an hour, 1 day a week (Studer & Siehl, 1994). In other cases, peer facilitators provide an orientation to new students and meet with these students on a regular basis, visit hospitalized students, or assist as a "secret buddy" or a playground friend.

LEADER OF GROUPS

More students can participate in small groups when peers are trained as leaders. A peer facilitator program implemented in a middle school, trained eighth-grade students to work in small groups with sixth-grade students identified with behavioral problems (Corn & Moore, 1992). Peers focused on topics of self esteem, attitude, discipline, attendance, and academic achievement. Following this "peer-vention," behavior improved among the students receiving help. In another school, owing to a student suicide, peers were trained in empathy skills, active listening, and suicide risk assessment and were encouraged to seek out isolated, lonely peers to develop a relationship with them. This strategy indicated the importance of additional training for peer facilitators (Stuart, Waalen, & Haelstromm, 2001).

Program success depends on careful selection of peer facilitators, which is conducted in several ways (Myrick, 1994). In one Midwest high school, teachers and counselors recommended students who exemplified the desired traits of empathy, concern, and confidentiality. In another school, middle school students were asked to list the name of one classmate with whom they would feel most comfortable discussing a problem. Because the identified students represented various subcultures in the school, a wider population of students was motivated to seek assistance (Studer & Siehl, 1994).

Regardless of the type of peer group that is formed, training and supervision are vital. Although some programs stress academics and others focus on developmental concerns (Tobias & Myrick, 1999), the group purpose dictates the type of training students receive. Typically, peers learn about the characteristics of a helping relationship, communication and listening skills, and vital issues in which the assistance of a professional is necessary. Other types of training include personal growth activities, acceptance of diversity, self-assessment, micro-counseling skills, crisis management, and boundary setting (Robinson et al., 1991). The length of training depends upon the purpose of the peer program and the age of the peers. Students in the secondary school may meet 1 hour, 2 days a week, with additional training throughout the year. Training may occur over lunch, or in a course with credit. In elementary schools, the training consists of fewer hours, but varies according to the purpose of the peer project (Myrick, 1994).

Successful peer facilitation programs require systematic organization with clearly defined goals. These programs have enhanced the personal growth and perceptions of the school climate, not only for the students who were assisted, but also for peer facilitators (Robinson, Morrow, Kigin, & Lindeman, 1991). Furthermore, a foundation for career patterns may be established. For example, in one follow-up study, peer facilitators were still involved in an informal helping relationship 5 years following the program training (Robinson et al., 1991). For peer facilitators, the training may assist the individuals in personal problem solving, developing leadership skills, and communicating more effectively. For the students assisted, relationships are built and academic, career, and personal/social growth are often enhanced.

Peer programs cannot exist without financial and administrative support. School personnel, most commonly school counselors, are effective in coordinating the program and training the peers because of their knowledge of the school milieu and the students. Additional crucial factors include an evaluation component, as well as supervision and support for peer helpers themselves, because these individuals are under the same pressures as the peers they assist (Studer & Siehl, 1994; Tobias & Myrick, 1999). Furthermore, in this age of educational reform, evaluative data may provide critical evidence that peer programs are supportive resources that embrace and support the educational mission of the school by reaching out to more students.

Various types of peer programs are found in today's schools. Peer assistants, tutors, mentors, and group leaders assist their classmates in a variety of ways; and when these programs are systematically organized, success is evident. However, the effectiveness of these programs is contingent upon peer selection, administrative support and funding, evaluative strategies, and an enthusiastic program coordinator.

See also: Crisis Intervention; Peer Mediation; Peer Pressure

BIBLIOGRAPHY

Studer, J. R., & Siehl, P. M. (Summer, 1994). Working together—peers, school, parents, and community. *Kappa Delta Phi Record*, pp. 180–183.

Tobias, A. K., & Myrick, R. D. (1999). A peer facilitator-led intervention with middle school problem-behavior students. *Professional School Counseling, 3*, 27–33.

Suggested Readings for Nonprofessionals

Potter, G. B., Gibbs, J. C., & Goldstein, A. P. (2001). *The EQUIP implementa-tion guide: Teaching youth to think and act responsibly through a peer-helping approach.* Champaign, IL: Research Press.

Tindall, J. A. (1989). *Peer power: Book 2 Applying peer helper skills.* Muncie, IN: Accelerated Development.

Tindall, J. A., & Gray, H. D. (1985). *Peer power: Becoming an effective peer helper. Book 1, Introductory Program.* Muncie, IN: Accelerated Development.

Suggested Readings for Professionals

Corn, K. L., & Moore, D. D. (1992). Reaching for the S.T.A.R.S—students teaching and reaching students: A two-faceted peer facilitating program at Greenfield-central high school. *The School Counselor, 40,* 68–72.

Robinson, S. E., Morow, S., Kigin, T., & Lindeman, J. M. (1991). Peer counselors in a high school setting: Evaluation of training and impact on students. *The School Counselor, 39,* 35–40.

Stuart, C., Waalen, J. K., & Haelstromm, E. (2001). Many helping hearts: An evaluation of peer gatekeeper training in suicide risk assessment. *Death Studies, 27,* 321–333.

JEANNINE R. STUDER

Peer Mediation

Conflict is a normal part of our society. Superheroes fighting battles and assaulting the enemy are common on Saturday morning TV. People in physical combat in the media become America's idols as they emerge victorious. In addition, violence is widespread in video games because a "high scorer" is selected on the basis of the number of "kills." With the pervasiveness of aggression in all aspects of our world, the lines between reality and fantasy are often blurred. Yet, conflict does not just take place outside the doors of the school building. The rising pace of violence has propelled many school districts to take steps in reducing violence among school-aged youth. These methods range from purchasing and monitoring metal detectors and hiring campus police, to teaching students positive methods of handling disagreements, including implementing conflict mediation programs. These programs are based on the premise that cooperation is based on reasoning leading to increased empathy and problem solving. Some of the conflict resolution methods include classroom curriculum, peaceable classroom, peaceable school, and mediation programs (Crawford & Bodine, 1996).

- *Classroom curriculum* strategies are taught in a separate course or during classroom time set aside for instruction in conflict resolution.
- *Peaceable classroom* techniques integrate conflict management strategies into the core curriculum. In addition,

teachers learn classroom management techniques that assist in creating a caring, nurturing environment.
- *Peaceable school* methodologies build upon the peaceable classroom concepts by expanding the strategies outside the classroom and into the entire school system. All individuals within the school system model these concepts.
- *Mediation programs* teach identified youth or adults mediation skills to assist disputing youth reach a resolution. Peer mediation programs that encompass problem-solving skills, communication, listening skills, creative thinking, and personal responsibility have been successful.

A successful peer mediation program involves identifying and training a diverse group of students from various social, academic, and cultural backgrounds to serve as peer mediators. Peer mediators are trained in active listening skills, understanding nonverbal behaviors, restating facts, clarification through open-ended questions, and issues surrounding confidentiality (Humphries, 1999; Schrumpf, Crawford, & Usadel, 1991). Intensive training occurs at the beginning of the program during the academic year, with at least one classroom period per week set aside for additional training sessions (Bickmore, 2002).

The mediation begins when disputants trying to settle a problem voluntarily approach a peer mediator. In the elementary grades, mediators generally work in teams of two in the lunchroom, classroom, or playground. In the upper-level grades, mediation is generally more formal, with a designated place (usually an empty office or classroom) and time scheduled in advance. Peer mediation involves specific steps in which disputants are helped to solve their own problems. The steps outlined by Schrumpf et al. (1991) include opening the session, gathering information, focusing on common interests, evaluating options, and writing the contract.

STEP 1: OPENING THE SESSION

The mediator welcomes the disputants and leaves time to make introductions. The purpose of mediation, consequences for not settling the conflict, and the rules of the mediation are all explained at this time. Ground rules usually include (a) no interrupting, (b) no name-calling or bodily contact, (c) telling the truth, and (d) agreeing to solve the problem.

STEP 2: GATHER INFORMATION

Each disputant is given an opportunity to tell his/her side of the story without interruptions. After the first disputant has spoken, the mediator summarizes the information and then asks the second disputant to tell his/her side of the story without interruption. The mediator again summarizes the shared information. Each disputant has an opportunity to provide additional information, which is summarized by the mediator, until both individuals understand the conflict.

STEP 3: FOCUS ON COMMON INTERESTS

This vital step assists disputants to take a different perspective of the problem by finding common interests or points of view. By finding a common ground disputants can formulate a mutual goal that assists in creating a solution to the problem.

STEP 4: BRAINSTORM OPTIONS

The mediator asks the disputants to creatively think of ideas that would solve the dispute. As ideas are generated, other solutions are proposed. Options can even be created by weaving suggestions together. Brainstorming involves the following rules: (a) being creative, (b) not judging ideas, and (c) thinking of as many alternatives as possible.

STEP 5: EVALUATE OPTIONS AND CHOOSE A SOLUTION

The disputants are asked to review the list of options, evaluate each one, and agree on a solution that is satisfactory to each of them. The mediator discusses the chosen option and an agreement is reached.

STEP 6: WRITING THE CONTRACT

The mediator prepares a written contract that outlines the agreement. This document is written in the words of the disputants and includes only the solutions to which both disputants agreed. All parties sign the contract and a copy is given to each of the mediation members. Before leaving the session, all individuals shake hands and the mediator thanks the disputants for their participation.

There are numerous advantages to peer mediation programs: (a) peer mediators have better attitudes toward school, with improved academic performance; (b) parents report improvements in attitudes and grades; and (c) school principals claim a decrease in discipline referrals (Carruthers, Sweeney, Kmitta, & Harris, 1996) and an improvement in school climate (Bickmore, 2002). Yet, there are also potential disadvantages in peer mediation programs: (a) students can be dissatisfied for not being provided with the appropriate training or the opportunity to apply their mediation skills; (b) the enormous amount of time it takes to design, implement, and evaluate a program requires financial support and time; and (c) ongoing practice with realistic scenarios is necessary to reinforce training (Humphries, 1999; Thorsen-Spano, 1996).

Conflict resolution programs are successful when included in the early grades and reinforced throughout the entire school curriculum. Peer mediators selected from a cross section of the school population are provided with training and skills throughout the school year. When peer mediation programs are provided with the financial support and time for implementation, positive results are carried over into relationships outside of the school halls.

See also: Conflict Resolution; Crisis Intervention; Peer Pressure

BIBLIOGRAPHY

Bickmore, K. (2002). Peer mediation training and program implementation in elementary schools: Research results. *Conflict Resolution Quarterly, 20,* 137–160.

Humphries, T. L. (1999). Improving peer mediation programs: Student experiences and suggestions. *Professional School Counseling, 3,* 13–19.

Additional Readings for Nonprofessionals

Crawford, D. K., & Bodine, R. J. (1996). *Conflict resolution education: A guide to implementing programs in schools, youth-serving organizations, and community and juvenile justice settings* (Report No. UDO31548). Washington, DC: Education Research Information Clearinghouse. (ERIC Document ED 404426).

Schrumpf, F., Crawford, D., & Usadel, H. C. (1991). *Peer mediation: Conflict resolution in schools.* Champaign, IL: Research Press.

Additional Readings for Professionals

Carruthers, W. L., Sweeney, B., Kmitta, D., & Harris, G. (1996). Conflict resolution: An examination of the research literature and a model for program evaluation. *The School Counselor, 44,* 5–18.

Thorsen-Spano, L. (1996). A school conflict resolution program: Relationships among teacher attitude, program implementation, and job satisfaction. *The School Counselor, 44,* 19–27.

JEANNINE R. STUDER

Peer Mentoring

Mentoring comes from a Greek word meaning "enduring," and is defined as a trusted relationship between a youth and an adult. Peer mentoring is a deliberate, conscious, voluntary relationship between two people of equal standing (i.e., mentor and peer) in an organization whereby the mentor supports his/her peer.

TYPES

The two types of mentoring are natural mentoring and planned mentoring. Natural mentoring occurs through friendship, collegiality, teaching, coaching, and counseling. Natural mentoring relationships occur without planning and typically do not have a preestablished timeline. In contrast, planned mentoring occurs through structured programs in which mentors and participants are selected and matched through formal processes. Planned peer mentoring is supported by the organization and acknowledged by supervisors. Usually, an established time frame is predetermined.

RELATIONSHIP

Peer mentors provide peers with a supportive, safe, confidential environment to explore and discuss their questions, concerns, anxiety, and discouragement. In this peer environment, fear of judgment, reprisal, demotion, or termination is nonexistent. Through continued involvement, a peer mentor offers support, guidance, and assistance as his/her peer goes through a difficult period, faces new challenges, or works to correct earlier problems. Most often, a peer mentor is a more experienced compatriot who establishes trust and acts as a role model, guide, and/or cheerleader.

UNIQUELY QUALIFIED

Peer mentors bring knowledge based on personal experience to the relationship. A peer mentor is uniquely qualified to help his/her peer succeed. Peer mentors know firsthand the challenges his/her peer faces and can offer valuable strategies to meet those challenges with confidence and success. Peer mentors "know the ropes" because they have previously traveled a similar path. They offer a supportive environment reflecting empathy, camaraderie, and encouragement. Mutual respect is inherent in a peer mentor relationship. Peer mentors encourage right behavior and prevent or correct harmful actions. Peer mentors offer honest advice, provide an inside view on what really goes on, advocate by protecting his/her peer from mistreatment, promote the peer's positive traits and aptitudes, and groom the peer for future responsibilities.

PURPOSES

Mentoring exists in different venues: universities and colleges, schools and communities, religious institutions, professional industry, business workplace, government institutions, court-mandated programs, recreational programs, and athletic organizations. Education peer mentoring relationships focus on helping mentored peers improve academic achievement, schedule classes, and/or traverse cumbersome bureaucracy. Specific examples include assisting with adjustment to college, writing, study skills, résumé development, and locating student services. Vocational peer relationships exist to help peers develop the necessary skills to enter or continue on a career path. Work-related examples may include orientation to a new office environment, honing Internet search skills, practicing interview techniques, or understanding and choosing a benefit package. Personal development mentoring supports peers during phases of personal or social stress and provides guidance for problem solving and decision making. Examples may include stress management, time management, or creating a written plan of action and a decision tree.

Examples of peer mentor relationships include a high school youth encouraged to tutor an elementary school student who has a learning disability. A female manager shares her strategy with other working women to break the "glass ceiling." A medical student or nurse nurtures an incoming peer medical or nursing student. A businessman takes a new staff member "under his wing." A single, working parent provides finance and time management wisdom to other single, working parents. An experienced faculty member advises a junior colleague on work expectations. A successful business owner offers fledgling entrepreneurs ideas on how to get started.

BENEFITS

Empirical research findings are limited and focus on traditional mentoring relationships (i.e., adult–child). However, a few studies and program evaluations do support positive claims. A survey was sent to the parents of children and volunteers involved with the Big Brothers, Big Sisters programs. They discovered that a majority of respondents reported an increase in child self-esteem, that Little Brothers and Little Sisters experienced increased exposure to cultural and educational services, youth peer relationships were better, a more positive relationship with teachers, an increase in school grades, and improved family relationships (Big Brothers, Big Sisters, 2001). In an evaluation of a Baltimore-based mentoring project (i.e., Project RAISE), McPartland and Nettles (1991) discovered that mentoring relationships had positive effects on grades in English and school attendance, but this did not enhance promotion rates or increase achievement test scores. A strongly implemented one-on-one mentoring relationship was the key to positive outcomes. In a different study, participants in different mentoring programs were found to have higher levels of college enrollment and higher educational aspirations than those without mentors (Cave & Quint, 1990). Dennison (2000) found that older students mentoring younger peers resulted in increases in self-esteem, enhanced attitude toward school, and increased on-task behavior.

In summary, peer mentoring is a unique and supportive relationship between mentor and peer. Natural (unstructured) and planned (structured) peer mentoring models exist. Peer mentors are uniquely qualified owing to their own personal and like experiences to empathize and guide peers. Mentors create an environment built on trust that is safe and where shared information is held in confidence. Peer mentoring exists in a variety of settings and for purposes such as educational, vocational, and personal goal achievement. A number of exemplary peer mentoring model programs were provided. Benefits cited include boost in child self-esteem, exposure to cultural diversity, increase in school attendance, and improved relationships.

See also: Peer Counseling Programs; Peer Mediation

BIBLIOGRAPHY

Big Brothers, Big Sisters of Finney County. (2001). *Corporate mentoring program.* Retrieved December 8, 2003, from http://www.gardencity.net/bbbs/corporatementor.html

Cave, G., & Quint, J. (1990). *Career beginnings impact evaluation: Findings from a program for disadvantaged high school students.* New York: Manpower Demonstration Research Corporation. (ERIC Number ED 325598).

Dennison, S. (2000). A win–win peer mentoring and tutoring program: A collaborative model. *Journal of Primary Prevention, 20,* 161–174.

McPartland, J. M., & Nettles, S. M. (1991). Using community adults as advocates or mentors for at-risk middle school students: A two-year evaluation of Project RAISE. *American Journal of Education, 99,* 568–586.

Additional Readings for Nonprofessionals

Bordenkircher, T. G. (1991). *A directory of youth mentoring programs and materials.* Pittsburgh, PA: The Plus Project on Mentoring.

Diambra, J. F. (2003). Peer advising: A bargain for students, faculty and program. *The Link, Quarterly Newsletter for the National Organization for Human Service Education, 24*(2), 5–7.

Newman, M. (1990). *Beginning a mentoring program.* Pittsburgh, PA: PLUS (Project Literacy U.S.).

Additional Readings for Professionals

Dearden, J. (1998). Cross-age peer mentoring in action: The process and outcomes. *Educational Psychology in Practice, 13,* 250–257.

Pyatt, G. (2002). Cross-school mentoring: Training and implementing a peer mentoring strategy. *Mentoring & Tutoring: Partnership in Learning, 10,* 171–177.

Web-Based Resources

Peer Resources. (n.d.). Retrieved December 8, 2003, from http://www.peer.ca/peer.html

The Mentor Center, The International Center about Information about New Teacher Mentoring and Induction. (n.d.). Retrieved December 8, 2003, from http://www.teachermentors.com/MCenter%20Site/MCategoryList.html

JOEL F. DIAMBRA

Peer Pressure

Peer pressure has been defined as pressure to think or behave according to peer-determined expectations (Clasen & Brown, 1985). Not all researchers have operationalized the term in the same manner. For example, some researchers have simply studied relationships between friends' behavior, whereas others have included a measure of the degree of pressure individuals feel to think or behave in a certain manner. The latter is considered to be a more accurate reflection of peer pressure, as studies examining only relationships between friends' behavior often do not take into account the effects of selection (tendency to choose friends with similar beliefs and interests).

A construct frequently confused with peer pressure is peer conformity. Although related, peer pressure (an attitude or perception) differs from peer conformity (a behavioral disposition). Peer conformity indicates an individual's willingness to comply with peer pressure. Consequently, peer pressure and peer conformity are often studied together because they are highly correlated and both are predictive of future behavior. A third variable related to peer pressure and conformity is the desire to be popular or to identify with an elite crowd. This factor has been found to explain some peer behavior, but it has not proven to be a good predictor of future behavior.

PERCEIVED PEER PRESSURES

Clasen and Brown (1985) identified five areas of behaviors wherein adolescents reported experiencing peer pressure: involvement with peers (spending free time with friends), school involvement (academic and extracurricular), family involvement, conformity to peer norms (clothes, music), and misconduct (drugs, sexual intercourse, delinquent behavior). Pressure for peer involvement was considered greater than pressure for school or family involvement. Perceived pressure for misconduct was much lower than all other behaviors but increased over time until grade 9.

DEVELOPMENTAL TRENDS IN CONFORMITY

Conformity to peer pressure tends to follow an inverted U-shaped age pattern, with peer conformity increasing through childhood, peaking between the sixth and ninth grade, and then declining. This pattern has been replicated in numerous studies but to varying degrees. The degree of conformity to peer pressure varies on the basis of type of behavior involved—antisocial, neutral, or prosocial. Children and adolescents are more likely to conform to pressure from peers to engage in neutral activities (e.g., sports, entertainment, and restaurants) and prosocial behaviors (e.g., participating in charitable activities or helping a new student) than antisocial behaviors. However, although less common, developmental changes over time are more pronounced for antisocial behaviors than other behaviors, with a sharp increasing trend starting in the third grade and peaking in the ninth grade. Conformity to peer pressure to engage in neutral behaviors also has been found to peak during the ninth grade but, relative to antisocial behaviors, changed very little over time. Conformity to peer pressure to engage in prosocial behaviors has been found to peak during the sixth grade. Conformity to peer pressures tends to increase with age, whereas conformity to parental pressure tends to decrease with age. Adolescents report valuing parental approval more than peer approval but when forced to make a choice, adolescents are more likely to be influenced by peers.

EFFECT OF FRIENDS ON RISK BEHAVIORS

Peer pressure has been linked to achievement, substance abuse, sexual behavior, risk-taking behavior, and delinquency. Despite a tendency to associate the term *peer pressure* with negative outcomes, peers have been found to play an important role in both harmful and beneficial activities. In a longitudinal study, Maxwell (2002) examined peer influence (i.e., having a friend who engages in the behavior) on five risk behaviors: cigarette smoking, alcohol consumption, marijuana use, chewing tobacco use, and sexual intercourse. Adolescents with a friend engaging in any of the five behaviors were twice as likely to engage in the behavior a second time. Peer influence was especially strong for nonusers to begin smoking marijuana and tobacco. However, influence was found in both directions—pressure to begin and pressure to refrain or quit—for alcohol and chewing tobacco use, indicating that peers provide positive influences as well.

Peer crowd affiliation has been associated with varying degrees of peer pressure across three areas of behavior: misconduct, school involvement, and family involvement. Adolescents identified as members of the druggie-tough crowds reported more pressure to engage in misconduct than jock-populars and loners, whereas jock-populars reported more pressure for school and family involvement and more pressure to not engage in misconduct (except drinking) than the other groups.

RISK AND PROTECTIVE FACTORS

The study of sex differences in susceptibility to negative peer pressure has produced mixed results that may be the result of differences in the measures used. Measures using explicit examples of peer pressure resulted in higher susceptibility among males, whereas more subtle examples of peer pressure resulted in higher susceptibility among females. When different types of behaviors are examined, boys and girls tend to be equally susceptible to peer pressure in most areas, with the exception of antisocial behaviors. Girls have been found to show less conformity than boys on antisocial behaviors (Brown et al., 1986).

Family factors such as parenting style, monitoring, and family composition have all been associated with peer influence susceptibility. Authoritative parenting styles consisting of clear rules and consequences combined with an emphasis on developing autonomy have been associated with fewer deviant behaviors among adolescents. Parental monitoring, which includes adolescents' spending time with parents, is a strong predictor of decreased susceptibility to negative peer pressures and less misconduct. When family composition is examined, boys from intact, two-parent families have been found to be less susceptible to negative peer influences than boys from single-parent families and stepfamilies.

See also: Peer Relations; Social Skills Building for Adolescents

BIBLIOGRAPHY

Brown, B., Clasen, D., & Eicher, S. (1986). Perceptions of peer pressure, peer conformity dispositions, and self-reported behavior among adolescents. *Developmental Psychology, 22*, 521–530.

Clasen, D., & Brown, B. (1985). The multidimensionality of peer pressure in adolescence. *Journal of Youth and Adolescence, 14*, 451–468.

Maxwell, K. (2002). Friends: The role of peer influence across adolescent risk behaviors. *Journal of Youth and Adolescence, 31*, 267–277.

Additional Readings for Adolescents

Cherniss, H., & Sluke, S. J. (2001). *The complete idiot's guide to surviving peer pressure for teens.* New York: Alpha Books.

Scott, S. (1997). *How to say no and keep your friends: Peer pressure reversal for teens and preteens.* Amherst, MA: Human Resource Development Press.

Additional Readings for Nonprofessionals

Feller, R. (2001). *Everything you need to know about peer pressure.* New York: Rosen.

http://inside.bard.edu/academic/specialproj/darling/adolesce.htm

http://parentingteens.about.com

Additional Readings for Professionals

Harris, J. (1995). Where is the child's environment? A group socialization theory of development. *Psychological Review, 102,* 458–489.
http://www.focusas.com/PeerInfluence.html

SHERI L. ROBINSON
GABRIELLE ROBERTS

Peer Relations

Children receive social information and support from relationships with parents, teachers, and other adults; however, positive relationships with peers provide a unique source of information that is associated with the development of strong interpersonal skills, self-confidence, autonomy, expressions of empathy, improved academic performance, and overall psychological well-being. As children develop, peers play an increasingly important social role. More time is spent with friends during middle childhood and adolescence than any other time in the life span—with adolescents spending nearly one third of their waking hours with peers.

Peer relations have been studied extensively, and for two primary reasons. First, it provides information regarding the skills and behaviors needed to promote positive peer relations, as well as those behaviors and/or lack of skills associated with poor peer relations. Second, children with poor peer relationships are at increased risk for both short- and long-term negative outcomes, indicating a need for prevention and intervention.

PEER ACCEPTANCE

Early peer relation research focused primarily on peer acceptance or social status (i.e., the degree to which one is liked or disliked by peers). Social status is determined by asking children to rate peers on the basis of how much they would or would not like to play with each of them. Another method often used in conjunction with peer ratings is peer nomination. Children are asked to nominate three peers with whom they would like to spend time and three peers with whom they would not like to spend time. Five classifications of social status have emerged from this method: popular, average, rejected, neglected, and controversial (see Coie, Dodge, & Copotelli, 1982). Most emphasis has been placed on the rejected group, those children actively disliked by their peers, and the neglected status, and those children ignored but not actively disliked by their peers, as these classifications were thought to result in the poorest outcomes.

OUTCOMES

Children who are rejected by their peers are at the greatest risk for negative social and psychological outcomes. Rejected children report higher levels of depression, loneliness, and social anxiety than average or popular children. In addition, they are more likely to be victimized or bullied and to have more difficulty adjusting to school transitions than are other children. In a review of the literature on the relationship between peer relations and future adjustment, Parker and Asher (1987) found that children who were rejected by their peers were more likely than nonrejected peers to drop out of school, engage in criminal activity, and have mental health disorders in adulthood. Low peer status tends to be persistent over time and settings. Once children establish a reputation (negative or positive) among peers, this reputation tends to influence how peers respond to future behaviors. Even if behaviors improve, the negative reputation often self-perpetuates.

Unlike rejected children, there is little evidence to support the notion that neglected children are at risk for future adjustment problems. Neglected-status children are described as shy by their peers and are more withdrawn than their peers. However, no negative long-term effects have been found related to these behaviors. Although neglected-status children may exhibit more problem behaviors than popular children, they are not distinguishable from their average peers. Academically, neglected children have been found to earn higher grades in school, have higher levels of motivation, be better liked by teachers, and engage in higher levels of prosocial and cooperative behavior in the classroom compared with average-status peers (Wentzel & Asher, 1995). It is hypothesized that neglected-status children may be ignored by peers because of conformity to adult expectations and less conformity to peer conventions. Unlike rejected children, neglected children report little interest in changing their behaviors to become more socially accepted, and their status is less stable over time and often changes in different settings.

BARRIERS TO DEVELOPING POSITIVE PEER RELATIONSHIPS

Aggression has been found to be the primary correlate of peer status at all ages. Aggressive and disruptive behaviors have been positively associated consistently with poor peer relations and rejected peer status; however, the type and nature of behaviors associated with peer rejection vary with age. Physical aggression and name-calling are typical of younger peer-rejected children. With age, the types of behavior associated with rejection become more differentiated, with disruptiveness and increasingly subtle and covert forms of aggression (e.g., verbal) becoming the primary behavioral markers of peer rejection. Other behaviors negatively associated with positive peer relations include bossiness, rigidity, dishonesty, and impulsivity.

Other children are ignored, or actively withdraw from peers, limiting opportunities to gain acceptance and develop friendships. These children are likely to obtain a neglected status from peers. Withdrawal becomes increasingly related to low peer status with age, as children begin to recognize in themselves and others that the behavior is atypical. Dissimilarity of any sort, such as physical unattractiveness, disabilities, race, or being a newcomer, increases the likelihood of peer rejection or neglect.

Engaging in some of the behaviors associated with peer rejection does not ultimately lead to rejection. For example, responding aggressively to provoked physical aggression is positively associated with popularity. The effects of negative behaviors can be offset by positive behaviors as seen by children in the controversial social status category. These children are actively liked by some peers and actively disliked by others. They are viewed as cooperative, funny, sociable, and leaders, and also as aggressive and disruptive.

CHARACTERISTICS OF POSITIVE PEER RELATIONS

Specific individual skills have been associated with positive peer relations. Children with good social skills such as assertiveness, knowing how to enter a peer group, and managing conflict tend to be well liked by peers and have quality friendships. Well-liked children are adept at accurately reading and responding to others' emotions, displaying empathy, and self-control as opposed to children with low peer status who are more likely to misinterpret others' behaviors and emotions and react negatively. Indirect influences such as positive parent–child relationships, marked by a supportive, warm parenting style and low levels of conflict (i.e., authoritative style), have been associated with the development of intimacy, conflict resolution skills, and successful relationships with peers and romantic partners.

FRIENDSHIP

More recently, researchers have begun to distinguish between peer acceptance and friendship. Friendships are characterized by reciprocity or social giving and taking between equals, vary in quality, and change developmentally. Friendships marked by intimacy and social support are related to positive attitudes toward school and overall psychological well-being, whereas friendships marked by instability and conflict are related to loneliness, less engagement in school, poorer at-

titudes toward school, and disruptiveness (Hartup & Stevens, 1999). The qualities of friendship children report as important change with age. Preschoolers tend to select friends on the basis of proximity—neighbors or preschool. School-aged children spend more time together and generally become friends on the basis of shared activities and interests. By middle school, children base friendships on more abstract qualities such as loyalty, trust, and self-disclosure and have more rules about group membership (e.g., cliques). When examining the relationships between peer status and friendship, Parker and Asher (1993) found that (a) not all well-accepted children have close friends, (b) many low-status children do have friends, and (c) having a best friend was related to less loneliness regardless of social status. These results support the view that although related, friendships provide unique contributions in the overall social functioning of children.

See also: Peer Pressure; Social Skills Building for Adolescents

BIBLIOGRAPHY

Coie, J., Dodge, K., & Copotelli, H. (1982). Dimensions and types of social status: A cross-age perspective. *Developmental Psychology, 18*, 557–571.

Hartup, W., & Stevens, N. (1999). Friendships and adaptation across the life span. *Current Directions in Psychological Science, 8*, 76–79.

Parker, J., & Asher, S. (1987). Peer relations and later personal adjustment: Are low-accepted children at risk? *Psychological Bulletin, 102*, 357–389.

Parker, J., & Asher, S. (1993). Friendship and friendship quality in middle childhood: Links with peer group acceptance and feelings of loneliness and social dissatisfaction. *Developmental Psychology, 29*, 611–621.

Wentzel, K., & Asher, S. (1995). The academic lives of neglected, rejected, popular, and controversial children. *Child Development, 66*, 754–763.

Additional Reading for Nonprofessionals

http://aboutourkids.org

Additional Readings for Professionals

Bukowski, W., Newcomb, A., & Hartup, W. (Eds.). (1996). *The company they keep: Friendship in childhood and adolescence.* New York: Cambridge University Press.

Ladd, G. (1999). Peer relationships and social competence during early and middle childhood. *Annual Review of Psychology, 50*, 333–359.

http://www.childtrends.org/r_resbrief.asp
http://www.focusas.com/PeerInfluence.html
http://www.smhp.psych.ucla.edu/qf/peersupport.htm

SHERI L. ROBINSON
STEPHANIE PAULOS

Personality Theory: Operant

The term *personality* can be traced back to the Latin term *persona*. A persona was a large mask that an actor wore to symbolize the type of character being played. In a sense, a persona was a symbol of what type of person the actor was. The *Morris Dictionary of Word and Phrase Origins* (1998) states that the term *personality* is used to "sum up the characteristics and attributes that make an individual distinct from his fellow man" (p. 450). A second definition taken from an advanced personality textbook describes personality as "the system of enduring inner characteristics of individuals that contributes to consistency in their behavior" (Delgata, Winstead, & Jones, 1999, p. 4). As reflected by these definitions and especially the latter one, personality is usually thought of as something (e.g., mechanism, agency, force, etc.) within a person that is a fundamental source of their behavior.

The universally implicit and usually explicit assumption that personality is an inner determinant of behavior is a relatively recent development. Just a few centuries ago, the term *personality* was used more as a description of how people behaved than as an answer to questions about why they behaved that way. So, for example, smiling, friendly, active people were described as happy but their cheer was not thought to be due to a "happy personality." This kind of transition in meaning, from external description to inner determinant or, more generally, from adjectives and verbs to nouns, has been common in the history of psychology. For example, the term *anxiety* was originally *anguisse* from the Old French and then *anguish* in Middle English. *Anguisse* referred to choking sensations in the throat and it was helpful in describing feelings pertaining to aversive events. *Anguish* was more generally descriptive. But anxiety has become an explanatory noun (e.g., her anxiety caused her hands to shake; see Friman, Hayes, & Wilson, 1998). Something very similar has happened with the term *personality*.

As psychologically descriptive terms such as *personality* or *anxiety* are established there appears to be an almost evolutionary semantic process that occurs that gradually but inexorably moves them from descriptors and labels to nouns and explanations or from *as if* (e.g., it is as if one had something inside that makes them happy; it is as if one were choking) to *as is* or just *is* status. Said slightly differently, the descriptor becomes a thing and the thing is gradually believed to exist. As indicated above, the assumption (belief) that personalities exist inside people is almost universal. If someone asks why a person is always so active and smiles so much, the answer that it is because he/she has a happy personality is widely acceptable as an answer for most laypersons and many psychologists. Yet the circularity of personality as an explanation is evident in only a cursory examination of the typical use of the term. The term *happy personality*

serves very well as a descriptor for behavior that includes smiling, being active, and so forth. Expanding its service to include an explanation of that behavior, however, is like saying happy people behave that way because that is how happy people behave. Needed are facts about the source of the happy behavior. A caution about the use of explanatory nouns in discussions of psychological activities was provided by Woodworth (1921) many years ago:

> Instead of "memory" we should say "remembering;" instead of "thought" we should say "thinking;" instead of "sensation" we should say "seeing, hearing", etc. But, like other branches, psychology is prone to transform its verbs into nouns; but there are no such things, there are only the activities that we started with, seeing, remembering, and so on. Intelligence, consciousness, the unconscious are by rights not nouns or even adjectives or verbs; they are adverbs. The real facts are that the individual acts intelligently—more or less so—acts consciously or unconsciously, as he may also act skillfully, persistently, excitedly. It is a safe rule, then, on encountering the menacing psychological noun, to strip off its linguistic mask, and see what manner of activity lies behind it. (pp. 5–6)

If the linguistic mask of the term *personality* is stripped away, as Woodworth suggests, what remains is a word that is useful for describing, but not explaining, the general way a person behaves. The linguistic process of turning descriptors into nouns or, more generally, regarding something that is immaterial (e.g., semantic, abstract) as something material is called reification. Reification increases linguistic efficiency but often obscures other information such as the identification of causal variables. In order to account for the causes of behavior it is necessary to look beyond the descriptors such as personality type and toward variables that can account for the operations that are traditionally attributed to personality.

CAN AN OPERANT ACCOUNT OF PERSONALITY BE CONDUCTED?

Operant psychology is widely believed to be unable to supply a satisfactory account of human behavior because it does not address uniquely human capacities such as thinking and feeling. But this is a gross and unfair misconception. Operant psychologists are well aware of the importance of thinking and feeling but address them as human activities (i.e., in their verb or adjectival form) and not as things (i.e., in their noun form). With insidiously oblique mischaracterizations, critics of operant psychology have successfully made it seem as if its adherents do not believe in the existence of human activities that are not directly observable. In actual fact, however, operant psychologists merely prefer to refer to those activities as activities and not as things and require high standards of proof to establish veracity. B. F. Skinner (1974), considered the founder of operant psychology, clearly stated that its critics had grossly mischaracterized it as an approach to human behavior. In fact, operant psychology is often called *radical behaviorism*, and the term *radical* is used because the idea that behaviorism could account for all human behavior, including private human events such as thoughts and feelings, was such a radical notion. Operant psychologists, however, attribute the cause of human behavior to environmental–behavior interactions and not to internalized, reified, hypothetical constructs such as personality. Furthermore, the private world of an individual is thought of as a part of the environment that influences behavior. Thus, a term such as *personality*, which in its descriptive form includes private as well as public events, is not outside the scope of operant psychology.

It is correct that the term *personality* is not behavioral in origin and is not one that is commonly employed (in a technical sense) by behavioral researchers. But rejecting a term or failing to pursue the phenomenon to which it refers because the term is nonbehavioral in origin is not consistent with a behavioral analysis (Friman et al., 1998; Hayes, 1984). A behavioral analysis can be conducted of any psychological term and behavioral analyses of the construct of personality, albeit often incomplete or inaccurate, are included in most personality textbooks.

OPERANT DEFINITIONS OF PERSONALITY

As indicated above, operant psychologists avoid using terms such as *personality* in their reified, explanatory form. Nonetheless it is difficult to communicate without the use of nouns for operant as well as mainstream psychologists. When operant psychologists discuss personality, however, they do so by focusing on consistent trends in behavior and the conditions that set the occasion for behavior. For example, Lunden (1969) defined personality as "the organization of unique behavior equipment an individual has acquired under the special conditions of his development" (p. 7). As another more current example, Staats (1996) defined personality as a concept that referred to groupings of basic behavior repertoires. By basic behavior repertoire he meant a conceptual grouping of responses or response potentials, acquired through operant processes, that describes a "very large 'system' of stimuli that will elicit an emotional response, and will also serve as reinforcing and directive stimuli" (Staats, 1996, p. 111). These definitions, and especially the latter one, reflect the reluctance by operant psychologists to reify the term *personality*, internalize it, and imbue it with causal significance and preference for using it to describe behavior and the conditions that occasion it. Enhancing the utility of this kind of usage is a set of operant principles that account for the acquisition of and maintenance of human behavior but that do not involve reified hypothetical constructs.

OPERANT ACCOUNT OF PERSONALITY

The behavior of newborn children is reflexive and environmental consequences play a very small role. But as the neonate's reflexive movements make contact with consequences (e.g., thumb to mouth followed by soothing sensations), behavior becomes nonreflexive, more "deliberate" movements are made, and these come under the direct and indirect influences of the consequences. Some consequences strengthen behavior and these are called *reinforcement*, and some weaken behavior and these are called *punishment* (an unfortunate choice of terms but the field appears stuck with it). There are two types of reinforcement: positive, which involves consequences (pleasant, preferred) that are presented by the environment (e.g., praise), and negative, which involves consequences (unpleasant, nonpreferred) that are avoided or escaped (e.g., turning off the alarm). There are two parallel types of punishment: positive, which involves consequences (unpleasant, nonpreferred) that are presented by the environment (e.g., scolding), and negative, which involves consequences (pleasant, preferred) that are lost or withdrawn (e.g., point fine). Over the course of a person's early life, these processes develop basic behavioral repertoires and, as indicated above, these make up a person's personality. Please note that this is a very incomplete account (e.g., there are also Pavlovian processes that come into play), but necessarily so for this brief entry.

The stimuli that compose consequences gain their reinforcing and punishing functions through one of two processes: naturally or by being conditioned. Unconditioned or natural reinforcers are presumed to have been established through the contingencies of survival (i.e., evolution). They involve commodities such as food and water that are life-sustaining. No conditioning is necessary for these commodities to obtain their reinforcing effects. An example involves serving a child dinner only after he/she has washed his/her hands. Food for hungry children requires no conditioning to work as a reinforcer. Yet, there are stimuli that gain their function through pairings with unconditioned reinforcers. For example, attention or praise from a parent gains its function through pairings with unconditioned reinforcers such as food. As a result praise will function as a reinforcer for most individuals.

There are multiple variables that influence the potency of reinforcement (and punishment) and a major one involves the schedule of its delivery. There are two general schedules of reinforcement: continuous and intermittent. A continuous schedule involves a reinforcer after every target response and an intermittent schedule involves a reinforcer after a select number of responses. These two schedules have different impacts on the speed at which behavior comes under their control and how long the behavior persists after the reinforcers have been discontinued. A continuous schedule will quickly gain control of a behavior but the behavior will not persist for long if the reinforcer is terminated. An intermittent schedule takes longer to bring a behavior under its control, but the behavior will persist for a longer period of time in the absence of reinforcement.

Another variable that influences the potency of reinforcers (and punishers) is the establishing operation, an environmental event that alters the effectiveness of reinforcers and the frequency of behaviors that are affected by reinforcers. Food deprivation is a common example of an establishing operation. Food will function as a more potent reinforcer if the person has not eaten in a long time. The effects of establishing operations are always fluctuating for humans and can be the cause of variability in one's behavior.

Knowing a little about reinforcement and punishment, and variables that affect their potency sheds some light on the operant view of "personality." Because of the influence of environmental consequences, their scheduled delivery, and the operations that affect the influence, some behaviors occur more frequently and consistently and others less so. There are still other sources of influence, however. For example, specific classes of behavior occur in the presence of particular stimuli and others do not. Stimuli that are present when a person's behavior is reinforced (or punished) and that subsequently set the occasion for that behavior are called *discriminative stimuli*. For example, the child from the earlier example will most likely learn to wash his hands when dinner is being prepared or when he is called to dinner, but not when he is going out to play. The presentation of a stimulus (called to dinner), the response (washing his hands), and the reinforcer (dinner) are what make up a three-term contingency, the core unit in an analysis of behavior.

There are times when an individual will be presented with a novel stimulus and respond in ways that suggest learning with respect to that stimulus has already occurred (even though it has not). This can occur for a number of reasons, but the most typical involves generalization. Generalization is a process where responses occur in the presence of stimuli that are similar in form to established discriminative stimuli but that have not been directly trained (or learned). Generalization can account for the learned basis of a large amount of behavior that at first glance appears to have developed in the absence of learning. For example, the child trained to wash his hands before dinner at home may begin to wash his hands before lunch at school without any training or inducement to do so. Lunch at school is sufficiently similar in form to dinner at home in that it generates responses that have been trained at home (i.e., causes the boy to generalize his learned responses). Over time, however, another process, discrimination, also occurs. If washing hands at school is never reinforced, the boy will learn to discriminate where washing needs to take place (where it is reinforced) and may stop washing at school.

COMPLEX HUMAN BEHAVIOR

All of what has been described so far has been studied using both humans and nonhuman animals (e.g., rats and pigeons). Some relatively recent advances in operant psychology account for more complex forms of human behavior, behavior that distinguishes humans from nonhumans as a species. The overarching class of this behavior is referred to as verbal behavior by operant psychologists and its analysis expands the scope of operant psychology in ways that allow it to address all the activities traditionally associated with the construct of personality.

For example, humans have the ability to predict future results of behavior, to respond to self- or externally generated rules, or more generally, to respond relationally (Friman et al., 1998; Hayes, Barnes-Holmes, & Roche, 2001). Relational responding involves responding to one stimulus in terms of another. This means that humans have the ability to respond not only to the formal properties of stimuli but also to the relations between them. Thus, direct training is not always needed to create discriminative stimuli. For example, a person who directly learned to fear and thus avoid being in small enclosed spaces (e.g., claustrophobia due to an early experience of being trapped in the trunk of a car) may also avoid committed relationships or highly structured jobs because the person begins to feel "trapped" in them. Small enclosed spaces have no formal similarity to committed relationships or structured jobs. But because of the human ability to respond "as if" one condition is similar to another (i.e., to respond relationally) the trapped feeling directly learned in one situation can be experienced in another formally different situation (it is as if one were just like the other). The research and conceptual support underlying responding relationally is large, complex, and notoriously difficult to communicate clearly. This brief note is no substitute for major position papers (e.g., see Hayes et al., 2001).

In addition, humans have the ability to generate rules that maintain behavior across situations and over time. For example, the child from the earlier examples who was reinforced for washing his hands at home and then started washing them at school may have generated a rule like "I need to wash my hands before any meal." This rule will cause the child to wash without the need for reinforcement and even in the face of aversive consequences.

CONCLUSIONS

The term *personality*, as generally used, is an example of a reified construct that was historically used only to describe behavior and that is now also used to explain it. The operant view of personality is more consistent with historical usage. That is, to operant psychologists, *personality* does not refer to something that exists within a person; it refers to consistent patterns of behavior and the conditions that occasion them. The operant view of personality is also radical, in the sense that its analytical tools can address all of the psychological activities conventionally associated with the term, including patterns of thought and feeling.

See also: Personality Theory: Social Learning

BIBLIOGRAPHY

Delgata, V. J., Winstead, B. A., & Jones, W. H. (1999). *Personality* (2nd ed.). Chicago: Nelson Hall.

Friman, P. C., Hayes, S. C., & Wilson, K. (1998). Why behavior analysts should study emotion: The example of anxiety. *Journal of Applied Behavior Analysis, 31*, 137–156.

Hayes, S. C. (1984). Making sense of spirituality. *Behaviorism, 12*, 99–110.

Hayes, S. C., Barnes-Holmes, D., & Roche, B. (2001). *Relational frame theory: A post-Skinnerian account of human language and cognition.* New York: Kluwer Academic.

Lunden, R. W. (1969). *Personality: A behavioral analysis.* Toronto: Collier-MacMillan.

Morris, W., & Morris, M. (1988). *Morris dictionary of word and phrase origins.* New York: Harper & Row.

Skinner, B. F. (1974). *About behaviorism.* New York: Knopf.

Statts, A. W. (1996). *Behavior and personality: Psychological behaviorism.* New York: Springer.

Woodworth, R. S. (1921). *Psychology* (rev. ed.). New York: Henry Holt.

MICHAEL TWOHIG
PATRICK C. FRIMAN

Personality Theory: Social Learning

Psychologists often disagree in their definitions of *personality*, but the term is widely used to describe the individual's characteristic method of seeing and thinking about himself/herself and his/her environment. Personality is typically thought of as something that the individual brings to his/her environment and as something that strongly influences the individual's thoughts, feelings, and behaviors across a wide range of situations. Social learning theories of personality emerged in the 1930s as research psychologists who studied the learning process—such as Clark Hull at Yale University—began to apply learning theory to test and explain elements of Sigmund Freud's theory of psychoanalysis. Although there is no single unified social learning theory of personality, social learning theorists tend to believe that personality develops from an individual's thoughts, motivations, and, most important, what a person learns through experiences with his/her social environment. Social learning theorists combine aspects of behaviorism, imitation, psychological defense mech-

anisms, and cognitive attributes to explain how the learning occurs.

SOCIAL ENVIRONMENT

People do not exist in a vacuum; people are social beings. Social learning theorists stress the importance of the individual's social environment. A social environment includes everything and everyone in an individual's immediate surroundings. As people interact with their social environments, people learn from, and get changed by, their experiences. A person's personality changes and adapts as the behavior of the person is reinforced or punished by his/her social environment. It is not only that people are influenced by their social environments, people also have an impact on their environments, because the social environment is affected by and responds to the person's behavior. Social learning theorists believe that persons usually seek those particular environments that are especially likely to satisfy the person's wants, needs, and desires. The relationship between an individual and his/her social environment is interactive and reciprocal.

INFLUENTIAL SOCIAL LEARNING THEORIES

There are three predominant social theories that focus on the relationship between the behaviors and interactions of an individual with his/her environment. These were developed by John Dollard and Neal Miller (1947), Julian Rotter (1954), Albert Bandura (1977), and Walter Mischel (1999).

DOLLARD AND MILLER'S SOCIAL LEARNING THEORY

John Dollard and Neal Miller's (1947) theory is a drive-reduction theory built upon Clark Hull's idea of drives, and applies behavioristic tenets of learning to Freudian psychoanalytic theory. Prior to Dollard and Miller's work, Freudian theory was resistant to experimental study because many of Freud's concepts were abstract and difficult to measure. Dollard and Miller attempted to translate psychoanalysis into the more traditionally scientific language of learning theory so that many of Freud's beliefs could be objectively and experimentally tested.

Dollard and Miller believed learning requires four components: "[I]n order to learn one must want something, notice something, do something, and get something. Stated more exactly, these factors are drive, cue, response, and reward" (Miller & Dollard, 1947, p. 2). Thus, for Dollard and Miller, an individual wants or needs something (drive). He/she perceives the want or need (cue). He/she does something about the want or need (response). He/she gets something (reward).

Drives

Human beings have wants and needs. The wants and needs are considered drives. Drives activate behavior. When people take action, often the purpose of the action is to satisfy a drive. Drives are divided into two types: primary and secondary. Primary drives are biological in origin and based on individual survival and perpetuation of the species. Primary drives are inborn and all people have the same primary drives during a normal life span, although individual primary drives may vary depending on sexual maturation and age. Secondary drives include all other wants an individual may have. Secondary drives are learned and develop as an individual matures.

Habit Hierarchy

In any given situation, there is a wide range of behaviors that a person might exhibit. Any possible behavior is termed *habit* (Hull, 1934; Miller & Dollard, 1947). On the basis of a person's previous experiences, or learning history, certain behaviors are more likely to occur than others because the individual has learned, through experience, that certain behaviors are more likely to lead to reinforcement (drive reduction). Each individual has a habit hierarchy. The habit hierarchy is based on the likelihood of possible behaviors (habit) occurring. Behaviors that are more likely to occur are ranked higher than those less likely to occur. In order for learning to occur, a habit must change locations in the hierarchy. The drive is then satisfied by the behavior (habit). Because the habit was successful, the individual is more likely to repeat the habit when the drive occurs in the future.

Frustration–Aggression Hypothesis

On the basis of their reading of Freud, Dollard and Miller studied what they called the Frustration–Aggression Hypothesis—the idea that aggression is caused only by frustration and that frustration always causes aggression. Fear and frustration arise when a person who experiences a drive is blocked from satisfying the drive. Aggression is most likely to occur when a primary drive is frustrated or, in other words, left unsatisfied. Fear and aggression may also stem from secondary drive frustrations. Aggression is thought to be a natural reaction to frustration. In this theory fear can lead to frustration or escape behaviors, such as apathy, depression, or withdrawal.

In the absence of escape, frustration compounds, until the person exhibits aggression. Although aggression does not satisfy the blocked drive, the aggressive act can cause rearrangement of the individual's habit hierarchy. The aggressive act moves to the top of the habit hierarchy and the habits related to the unsatisfied drive are moved down the hierarchy.

Approach–Avoidance Conflicts

Approach–avoidance theory explains why some goals (drives) are met and others are not. As one approaches a goal, a conflict can arise between fear and desire. For example, a young adult in a driver's education course may want to drive, but be scared to get behind an automobile's steering wheel. If the fear becomes too great, the habits associated with avoiding driving move to the top of the student's habit hierarchy, and getting behind the wheel moves down the hierarchy. If the student refuses, he/she still has the desire to operate an automobile. The closer the goal is to being obtained, the more likely a person is to attain the goal or avoid the goal. If the fear becomes too great, then escape occurs in order to alleviate the drive of fear, and the original goal is not met.

Psychological Defense Mechanisms

Dollard and Miller used the behavioral notion of negative reinforcement to address the Freudian concept of defense mechanisms. Negative reinforcement is used to describe the situation in which a particular behavior is made more likely to occur due to the removal of an unpleasant or aversive stimulus. In the case of psychological defense mechanisms, an individual's misinterpretation of his/her true motives or of external reality is reinforced by a reduction in the person's experience of anxiety. If a person begins to become aware of undesirable or unacceptable wishes, for example, the person is expected to experience anxiety. Through becoming unaware of the unacceptable and anxiety-arousing wishes, perhaps by introducing competing and distracting thoughts, the person's anxiety disappears. As a result of this process, the person learns to repress, or keep from conscious awareness, unacceptable desires and wishes, and to instead spend his/her time thinking thoughts that are not unpleasant.

JULIAN ROTTER'S SOCIAL LEARNING THEORY

Julian Rotter (1954) theorized three required constructs for social learning to occur: behavior potential, expectancy, and reinforcement value. A parsimonious explanation of Julian Rotter's social learning theory is offered by Funder, "what you are likely to do depends on whether you think you can get something and how badly you want it, under the circumstance." (2001, p. 438).

Behavior potential. Behavior potential (BP) is the chance that "any behavior will occur in any given situation or situations" (Rotter, 1954, p. 105). Behaviors with the highest BP are those most likely to occur and those with the lowest BP are those least likely to occur. Behavior potential is synonymous to Miller and Dollard's habit hierarchy.

Expectancies and locus of control. Expectancy is an individual's belief about how likely performing a behavior will result in obtaining what he/she wants. Why does one open a jar of pickles? Because one wants a pickle and *expects* a pickle to be inside the jar. One usually doesn't open a jar of pickles in hopes of finding peanut butter. Expectancies are learned from the social environment.

Different people have different expectancies, of course, but it is possible to draw a general distinction between people based upon their characteristic expectancies. Rotter's notion of *Locus of Control* refers to the extent to which people tend to view events as under their personal control versus the control of external forces. Persons with an internal locus of control believe that they are in control of their own destinies. An internal locus of control suggests that the person typically expects that his/her behavior has an impact and that action leads to reinforcement. Persons with an external locus of control are more likely to view themselves as passive recipients of luck, fate, or the actions of others.

Reinforcement value. Reinforcement value (RV) is what the reward is worth to the individual. It is subjective to the individual. Faced with two possibilities, an individual will do the one which he/she wants more. For Rotter, needs and reinforcement values can be combined to increase or decrease their values.

In a practical context, the BP could be taking a driver's education course. Why did the driver's education student take the course? Because he/she *expected* to learn how to drive. If the student places a high enough *value* (RV) on driving, then the student will complete the course. A student who may have previously chosen not to take a driver's education course, because he/she lived a block from school and walked everyday, may want to take a photography class at a community college located in a neighboring town. Thus, driving has become more valuable. Not only can the student drive to school, but he/she can also take the photography course.

ALBERT BANDURA AND WALTER MISCHEL'S COGNITIVE SOCIAL LEARNING THEORY

Albert Bandura (1977) and Walter Mischel's (1999) major contributions to social learning theory are the concepts of observational learning, self-efficacy, and reciprocal determinism. Bandura and Mischel moved theory from the realm of social learning to cognitive theories of personality by including *personal cognitive variables* (an individual's thoughts). Bandura's initial social learning theory was a true social learning theory. It

rapidly evolved to include cognitive aspects, and because of an emphasis on *personal cognitive variables* in subsequent theoretical revisions, the end product can be categorized as cognitive psychology.

Modeling

Observational learning—a process called *modeling*—is learning a behavior by watching someone else perform the behavior. If the person being watched (the model) is rewarded, the behavior is more likely to be copied (modeled). Playground jungle gyms offer a possible example of modeling. When first exposed to a jungle gym, some children may look at it and deduce its purpose. Other children may not know what it is or even if it should be touched. However, should an ambivalent child see other children playing and having a good time on a jungle gym, the child does not have to be told the jungle gym's purpose.

Self-Efficacy

Self-efficacy refers to an individual's belief that he/she can successfully master a situation and produce a positive outcome. In other words, one can do something, because one believes that one can do it. Although Rotter's explanation is "what one thinks one can get," self-efficacy is "what one thinks one can accomplish." Self-efficacy is how the little train that could not get up the hill, did.

Reciprocal Determinism

Reciprocal determinism is Bandura and Mischel's term for the triangular relationship between thoughts, behavior, and environment. No single aspect works independently from the others. Using a broad definition of *environment* (immediate surroundings), reciprocal determinism can be observed in a physician's crowded waiting room.

An individual walks into a waiting room (behavior). Everyone in the waiting room looks toward the door as the would-be patient enters. He/she has altered the environment by making it more crowded and because of the other people (part of his/her social environment) looking in his/her direction. Realizing the waiting room is crowded (thought), the would-be patient decides to leave and return later in the day. This final behavior and thought alters the environment again by making it less crowded.

CONTEMPORARY VIEW

There is no single social learning theory of personality. Instead there are several social learning theorists who have made contributions to our understanding of personality. In less than four decades, the social learning perspective served as a bridge between psychology's attempts to reconcile the behaviorist and psychodynamic schools of thought and today's current focus on social cognitive and cognitive–behavioral theories and treatment. During this same period of time, psychological science has moved from searching for a single reason or cause for a given psychological phenomenon to accepting that many factors work together to cause a psychological phenomenon. Biological variables, such as genetic factors, have also received growing attention in recent years. Nevertheless, social learning theory remains in contemporary thought, primarily because it is empirically driven and provides insights as to how environmental factors contribute to learning and behavior.

SOCIAL LEARNING THEORY AND BIOLOGICAL CONSIDERATIONS

A personality does not exist in a social environment without a biological aspect. Recent research concerning neuropsychological factors and behavioral genetics provide a challenge to the early social learning theorist's assumption that behavior is primarily determined by environment. Perhaps this challenge is best answered by remembering that the biological being brings his/her thoughts into an environment. The person is capable of changing aspects of an environment, either purposefully or accidentally. The environment and thoughts play roles in an individual's actions.

It can be argued that all people are the same, yet different. From a biological perspective, all human bodies are substantially similar. All people have circulatory systems, nervous systems, respiratory systems, and other physiological systems. Geneticists indicate that human beings are composed of two types of genes: structural and regulatory. Structural genes provide the blueprints for the formation of bodily structures (heart, lungs, brain, and so on). There are no structural differences between individual people, races, or ethnic groups. No evidence suggests that the biological components that underlie personality differ from person to person.

Regulatory genes act as switches, which turn processes on and off. The visible physical differences between two people can be caused by regulatory genes. A regulatory gene allows the amount of dark skin pigment into a person's skin. Therefore, some people are fair-skinned and others have darker complexions. Environmental influences can also cause physical differences. Every year, people flock to beaches in search of a tan. They knowingly seek out an environment that will change their physical appearance (darker skin). An individual not seeking a tan can unknowingly get one, while being outside on a cloudy day.

Personality can operate in the same manner. An individual can take assertiveness training, in order to become more assertive. The same nonassertive individual could take a job in sales and by observing his/her cohort's behavior, become more assertive by modeling his/her cohort's behavior.

Social learning theories maintain that the personality differences between people are learned through interactions with their social environments. A person plays an active role in selecting many of the environments in which the person finds herself/himself. Needs and wants are why an individual with freedom of choice seeks out environments. Some needs are biologically based on individual survival and species perpetuation. The biologically based needs to eat, drink, and breathe are assumed to be essentially identical across all people. Other needs and wants are learned. The summed total of characteristics and enduring traits considered personality are learned through interactions with physical environments and other people while an individual is developing.

PERSONALITY AND CHANGE

Can personality change? Because social learning theorists believe that personality is learned, their obvious answer is yes. However, psychological change is not as simple as changing a flat tire. Barring biologically based changes, an abrupt change of personality may occur for two reasons: it either *has* to occur, or a person *wants it* to occur. Change has to occur when it is necessary for the person to accommodate significant, and often unexpected, major life events occurring in the social environment.

Change also occurs when one desires it to occur. Ambition to change a personality trait is often unrealized, because the effort expended and the time needed to change a long-standing characteristic require a persistent commitment. The individual can revert to a previous behavior, either through spontaneous recovery of the extinct behavior, or through rationalization (Freud, 1949; Pavlov, 1927; Williams, 1959). No matter how maladaptive a trait, it has thus far got an individual through his/her life. To some degree the undesirable trait works for that person. Even with the desire, motivation, and commitment, change is difficult without an appropriate model to follow. If one has never seen an appropriate model to learn from, then he/she has to develop alternatives from scratch. Personality is not set for life, but it is strongly rooted.

Because personality is believed to be learned and forms over time, an unwilled gradual change is more likely to occur. One would expect that if an assembly line factory worker was around the same people at work for several years, then a mutual socialization would occur and each individual would be changed by the other individuals in that group. However, the amount of change would be limited by the amount of individual differences in the group. Individuals, who choose the same occupations, may start out with much in common.

See also: Personality Theory: Operant

BIBLIOGRAPHY

Bandura, A. (1977). *Social learning theory.* Englewood Cliffs, NJ: Prentice-Hall.

Freud, S. (1949). *An outline of psychoanalysis.* New York: Norton.

Funder, D. C. (2001). *The personality puzzle* (2nd ed.). New York: Norton.

Hull, C. L. (1934). The concept of habit–family hierarchy and maze learning. *Psychological Review, 41,* Part I, 33–52; Part II, 134–152.

Miller, N. E., & Dollard, J. (1947). *Social learning and imitation.* New Haven, CT: Yale University Press.

Mischel, W. (1999). Personality coherence and dispositions in a cognitive–affective personality (CAPS) approach. In D. Cervone & Y. Shoda (Eds.), *The coherence of personality: Social–cognitive bases of consistency, variability, and organization* (pp. 37–60). New York: Guilford.

Pavlov, I. P. (1927). *Conditioned reflexes* (G. V. Anrep, Ed. and Trans.). London: Oxford University Press.

Rotter, J. B. (1954). *Social learning and clinical psychology.* Englewood Cliffs, NJ: Prentice-Hall.

Williams, C. D. (1959). The elimination of tantrum behavior by extinction procedures. *Journal of Abnormal and Social Psychology, 59,* 269.

Additional Readings for Professionals

Bandura, A., & Starr, D. (1986). *Social foundations of thought and action: A social cognitive theory.* Englewood Cliffs, NJ: Prentice-Hall.

Bandura, A., & Walters, R. H. (1963) *Social learning and personality development.* New York, Holt, Rinehart & Winston.

Dollard, J., & Miller, N. E. (1950). *Personality and psychotherapy: An analysis in terms of learning, thinking and culture.* New York: McGraw-Hill.

CHARLES L. SPIRRISON
MARK THOMAS

Physical/Motor Development

The study of physical development involves an examination of several factors of human growth. Researchers look at the variations in height and weight and at the growth of the brain—the increasing number and complexity of the cells that govern activity of the body. An accumulation and refinement of motor skills accompanies the growth of the body and brain. These changes occur in sequences that may vary based on biological factors and experiences.

As the body develops from birth to adulthood, the proportion of the head to the rest of the body decreases significantly, from about one quarter of total body height to about one eighth. This pattern of development (beginning at the head) is called cephalocaudal. The trunk of the body is also more developed than the extremities in early childhood following the rule of proximodistal development. The larger muscle groups of the legs and arms develop before the smaller muscles of the hands and feet (Hughes, 2002).

At birth, the average child weighs approximately 7½ pounds and is about 20 inches in length. Several factors such as the age and health of the mother, prenatal exposure to toxins, and genetics can influence the infant's birth weight and height. The infant can be expected to double in weight in 6 months and triple birth weight by age 1. The typical child will gain approximately 1 inch in height each month until age 1 and reach half the adult height by the second birthday.

The years that follow show a slowing of the growth rate, in which greater variation becomes evident. On average, physical growth for both sexes remains fairly constant, but individual children are likely to experience growth spurts. Boys will tend to be taller and heavier than girls, but this difference reverses between the ages of 10 and 13 years when girls experience a dramatic increase in height. For boys, this increase occurs later, between 13 and 15 years, and eventually results in boys surpassing girls during their adolescent growth spurt (Liebert, Wicks-Nelson, & Kall, 1986).

Differences in nutrition and health cause variation in physical growth. Rates of growth that are adversely affected by acute episodes of poor health generally are followed by a spurt that returns the child to the normal level of growth and make up for what was lost (Fischer & Lazerson, 1984). Undernourishment that results in stunted development usually occurs from lack of fats, protein, and iron. Infants who experience insufficient calorie intake suffer from a wasting of tissue known as marasmus. Kwashiorkor, a condition that results in swollen belly, hair loss, and listlessness, arises from a lack of protein (even with sufficient caloric intake; Hughes, 2002). Iron and fat intake are tied to healthy development of the brain.

The first parts of the brain to develop are those of the inner brain, which are most essential toward survival. The outer brain, the cerebral cortex, which serves as a type of command center for the brain, continues development into later parts of childhood. The most significant period of brain development occurs before the age of two, when the brain cells, known as neurons, experience a rapid increase in number. This increase, called transient exuberance, is accompanied by refinement of the structure of the brain through processes of neural trimming (where unused cells disintegrate) and interconnections between neurons. The structure of the neuron consists of the cell body, dendrites (extending from the cell body), and the axon, which is surrounded by a fatty myelin sheath. The myelin sheath serves in the same fashion as insulation on wiring, increasing the rate of transmission of impulses. Information in the brain is transmitted from the axon of one neuron to the dendrites of neighboring neurons across a gap known as the synapse.

During these first 3 years of life, attention to healthy development of the brain is most critical. Because unused neurons will disintegrate, early stimulation is necessary to prevent loss of certain capabilities, especially those related to emotional response. Although this period of development may be sensitive in this regard, it is also a time when recovery from brain trauma is at its most advantageous. The rapid growth of neurons means that the infant brain has a measure of plasticity in regaining lost functions. Such recovery would not be expected from similar trauma in the adult brain, since neurons do not regenerate in adults.

At birth, the infant's neuromuscular functions are restricted to reflexes related to survival: rooting (turning toward a touch on the cheek with a sucking motion), grasping (closing the fingers around an object in the palm of the hand), the Moro reflex (arching the back and throwing the arms out to the side in response to startle), and the Babinski reflex (fanning out the toes when the bottom of the foot is stroked). The newborn also exhibits a stepping reflex when held upright on a surface. These reflexes fade as muscles come under the infant's control.

The infant is first able to control the larger muscles to develop gross motor skills. The infant at birth may be able to move the head from side to side and, by the end of the 1st month, should be able to raise the head and at the 2nd or 3rd month to use the arms to push up and assist in tracking objects or looking around (Hughes, 2002). The next significant gross motor skill, that of rolling over, occurs between the 4th and 5th months, and sitting up unassisted between the 7th and 8th months (Fischer & Lazerson, 1984).

By the end of the 6th month, the infant may be able to move to the next set of motor skills, the locomotor skills, by pushing up on all fours. Before the child is able to walk, there are several milestones to be reached, and the attainment of these milestones can vary. Babies may drag themselves forward before supporting weight with the legs (age 3 to 6 months). Between 4 and 8 months, the infant should sit without support. The child develops the ability to stand with support from 5 to 10 months and to pull to standing at 6 months. The strength and balance required to walk with support develop between 7 and 12 months, to stand alone at 10 months, and to walk alone between 11 and 14 months. At 3 years, the child should be able to run, hop, and jump, and there is evidence that these and other skills emerge naturally as the child has opportunities (Hughes, 2002; Liebert et al., 1986).

Although infants may reach for objects at 3 months, they may only be able to swipe at them. The ulnar grasp—closing the fingers to the palm—may not be controlled well enough to hold an object until 5 or 6 months of age (Fischer & Lazerson, 1984). The pincer grasp—putting together the thumb and the forefinger—develops at around 12 months (Hughes, 2002). These fine motor movements are essential in developing later cognitive skills as the child learns to manipulate objects, to explore the environment, to draw, and to write. Research indicates that moderate stimulation (as opposed to deprived or greatly enriched environments) is optimal for normal motor development (Fischer & Lazerson, 1984).

Physical development and development of motor skills can vary widely among individuals. Significant delays, however, can indicate more pervasive developmental difficulties. In addition to evaluating growth patterns in children, professionals have a range of diagnostic tools that test the child's gross and fine motor skills. Some warning signs suggesting a need for evaluation include unresponsiveness to voices or faces (especially eye contact), relative weakness on one side of the body, noticeably late development of milestones for motor development, extreme sensitivity to physical stimuli, or disinterest in age-appropriate social interactions (Hughes, 2002).

See also: Cognitive Development

BIBLIOGRAPHY

Fischer, K. W., & Lazerson, A. (1984). *Human development.* New York: Freeman.

Hughes, L. (2002). *Paving pathways: Child and adolescent development.* Belmont, CA: Wadsworth/Thomson Learning.

Liebert, R. M., Wicks-Nelson, R., & Kall, R. F. (1986). *Developmental psychology* (4th ed.). Englewood Cliffs, NJ: Prentice-Hall.

Additional Readings for Nonprofessionals

Bly, L. (1994). *Motor skills acquisition in the first year: An illustrated guide to normal development.* Orlando, FL: Academic Press.

http://www.education.pitt.edu/publications/parentingguides/MotorDevelopment.pdf

Additional Reading for Professionals

Connolly, K. J., & Prechtl, H. F. R. (1981). *Maturation and development: Biological and psychological perspectives.* Philadelphia: Lippincott.

MARK S. COTTER

Piers–Harris Children's Self-Concept Scale (The Way I Feel About Myself)

The *Piers–Harris Children's Self Concept Scale—2* (PHCSCS-2) (Piers, Harris, & Herzberg, 2002) is a widely used measure of psychological health for children and adolescents between the ages of 7 and 18. Like the original scale, which was published in 1969 and revised in 1984, the PHCSCS-2 is used to identify problems with self-concept and the potential need for further psychological intervention. Used in both schools and clinics, the PHCSCS-2 is often administered for routine classroom screening and clinic evaluation (Jeske, 1985). Results of the Piers–Harris help identify specific internal conflicts, methods of coping, and appropriate intervention techniques. A distinguishing characteristic of the PHCSCS-2 is that assessment results are based on the individual child's own perceptions rather than parent or teacher observations.

CHARACTERISTICS OF THE PIERS–HARRIS

The PHCSCS-2 was standardized on a nationally representative sample of nearly 1,400 students, who were recruited from school districts throughout the United States (*The Piers–Harris Children's Self-Concept Scale—2*, 2002). The use of a nationally representative sample provides a vast improvement over the original version of the scale, which was normed on children from a relatively small town in Pennsylvania. Because the PHCSCS-2 is intended for children and adolescents between the ages of 7 and 18, test items were written at a third-grade reading level in an effort to accommodate a wide range of developmental abilities. The format of the items also addresses developmental capabilities. Each item is constructed as a simple descriptive statement requiring a *yes* or *no* response. Respondents are asked to evaluate each statement as it applies to him or her.

In this second revision of the Piers–Harris, the scale has been reduced from 80 to 60 items. However, the revision is psychometrically compatible with the original version because no new items were created and no items were reassigned to different subscales (*The Piers–Harris Children's Self-Concept Scale—2*, 2002).

PHCSCS-2 SCORES

The PHCSCS-2 results in a Total Score that reflects overall self-concept, plus subscale scores (i.e., Behavioral Adjustment, Freedom from Anxiety, Happiness and Satisfaction, Intellectual and School Status, Physical Appearance and Attributes, and Popularity) that identify specific areas related to self-concept. Two validity scales identify inconsistent responding and a tendency to answer without regard to item content. Because the revised scales remain psychometrically equivalent to the original scales, results from the PHCSCS-2 can be compared, for research or clinical purposes, to those obtained using the original test.

All PHCSCS-2 scores can be converted to standard scores (e.g., percentile rank, stanine, or *T*-score; Epstein, 1985). However, some caution should be observed when interpreting the subscales of the PHCSCS. Although many researchers have applied the PHCSCS to a variety of ethnic and racial groups, age groups, and students with mental retardation, some researchers have questions about the actual number of subscales and the stability of those scales. Thus, although a great deal of research exists related to the PHCSCS, more research needs to be conducted to validate scores on the subscales.

Like many standardized assessment instruments, the PHCSCS is now available with computerized scoring and interpretation services. Consumers using the PHCSCS can also submit scores on disk, by fax, or through prepaid mail-in answer sheets. The computerized options result in a detailed interpretive report (i.e., group report, individual report, or school report) that includes a validity section. Because the PHCSCS is used in a variety of settings, reports are carefully constructed to avoid misinterpretation.

Authors of the PHCSCS have added to the strength of the scale through the construction and continued revision of a comprehensive test manual. The manual contains standard information related to scale construction, administration procedures, scoring guidelines, and interpretation protocols. The authors provide additional benefit to test administrators by including an extensive review of the empirical research related to the PHCSCS. The authors add further credibility to the PHCSCS through clear and detailed discussion about limitations and appropriate use (Epstein, 1985).

In summary, the PHCSCS-2 continues to be a highly useful tool for assessing children's self-concept. Extensive research on the scale supports its use for clinical, school, and research purposes. Although some questions have been raised related to subscale stability, the general consensus is that the PHCSCS is psychometrically sound. Improvements in the standardization sample, straightforward discussion of limitations, and a detailed administration manual have helped the authors of the PHCSCS-2 to maintain the usefulness of the scale since its inception in 1969.

See also: Coping

BIBLIOGRAPHY

Epstein, J. H. (1985). Test review of the Piers–Harris Children's Self-Concept Scale. In J. V. Mitchell, Jr. (Ed.), *The ninth mental measurements yearbook* [Electronic version]. Retrieved October 7, 2002, from the Buros Institute's *Test Reviews Online* Web site: http://www.unl.edu/buros

Jeske, P. J. (1985). Test review of the Piers–Harris Children's Self-Concept Scale. In J. V. Mitchell, Jr. (Ed.), *The ninth mental measurements yearbook* [Electronic version]. Retrieved October 7, 2002, from the Buros Institute's *Test Reviews Online* Web site: http://www.unl.edu/buros

Piers, E. V., Harris, D. B., & Herzberg, D. S. (2002). The Piers–Harris Children's Self Concept Scale—2. Los Angeles: Western Psychological Services.

The Piers–Harris Children's Self-Concept Scale—2. (2002). Western Psychological Services. Retrieved October 7, 2002, from http://www.wpspublish.com/wpsf06s20.htm

CARL SHEPERIS
W. JEFF HINTON
CHRIS HORTON

Play Therapy

Play therapy is defined as "the systematic use of a theoretical model to establish an interpersonal process wherein trained play therapists use the therapeutic powers of play to help clients prevent or resolve psychosocial difficulties and achieve optimal growth and development" (Association for Play Therapy, 2002). More simply, play therapy is a therapeutic process with children in which toys are used to help children "play out" their concerns much like adults "talk out" their concerns in the therapeutic relationship (Axline, 1969). The play therapist creates a comfortable environment for the child in an effort to decrease initial worries the child may have and to facilitate communication. Play is considered the natural mode of expression used by children (Axline, 1969). A room filled with toys is the hallmark of a playroom, and therefore the play therapy room as well. This obvious resemblance between both settings connects the comfort of play with the newness of therapy. The selected toys should represent the child's natural environment of home, school, and other situations to which the child might be exposed (i.e., hospital, church, and day care). The types of toys include cars, trucks, soldiers, wild animals, domestic animals, houses, hospitals, churches, dolls, tools, kitchen utensils, sporting goods, and other items that the child might enjoy during the session.

RATIONALE

The rationale behind play therapy is that children experience emotions and events that are beyond their ability to express verbally. Researchers observing children at play have discovered that children reenact traumatic events, engage in role rehearsal, and express wish fulfillment in their play activities, when given a safe environment for free play (O'Connor, 1991).

TYPICAL SESSION

During the session, the child plays with toys while the therapist is observing his/her play. The role of the therapist is to verbally interact with the child during play, when appropriate, by discussing the items he/she chooses to play with as well as the nature of the interaction. The nature of the interaction can be qualified by describing the individual's play as rough, gentle, quick, or slow, or by identifying likes and dislikes. For example, the therapist might say to the child, "I see you are playing with the tools. You are picking up the hammer. I like how you are working." If the child then threw down the hammer and began playing with the animals, a response from the therapist might be, "You decided not to play with the hammer any more. You are now playing with the cars." This example of a possible interaction demonstrates the full attention the therapist provides to the child. This attention illustrates to the child that he/she is the focus of the session, allowing the child to feel safe making choices and encouraging the child to explore without fear of critique or failure. The play therapy room becomes a place of acceptance, a place with no boundaries on self-expression.

COMMON USES

Children with physical, emotional, and cognitive disabilities have been found to positively respond to play therapy. The literature has included specific cases of play therapy being successful with abused children, children with autism, children of divorce, and those with defiance, aggression, attachment disorders, chronic and serious illnesses, depression, hyperactivity, enuresis and encopresis, fears, anxiety, grief, learning disabilities, speech and language difficulties, self-esteem, and trauma (cf. Schaefer & O'Connor, 1983).

PLAY THERAPIST QUALIFICATIONS

The Association for Play Therapy (APT) is a national organization that provides a register of play therapists meeting academic and training criteria. A Registered Play Therapist must have a license or certificate in a mental health field, have provided 500 hours of play therapy and been supervised for 50 clock hours by a registered play therapist. In order to maintain the registration, the play therapist must receive 12 clock hours of continuing education each year. APT publishes a directory of its membership, registered play therapists, and registered play therapist supervisors each year.

CONCLUSION

Play therapy is an intervention derived from the notion that play is the language of children. It is a process designed to assist children with expressing their concerns and fears by communicating via a comfortable medium. Children encounter difficulties in life just as adolescents and adults do. Language acquisition and development is mature in the latter. Children have yet to acquire the necessary skills needed to relay their inner thoughts and emotions. Therefore, placing a child in a setting allowing them to "play out" his/her feelings creates a safe place that individual counseling provides for adults.

See also: Individual Counseling

BIBLIOGRAPHY

Association for Play Therapy, Inc. (2002). *Definition of play therapy.* Retrieved September 10, 2002, from http://www.a4pt.org

Axline, A. (1969). *Play therapy: The inner dynamics of childhood.* Boston: Houghton Mifflin.

Barlow, K., Landreth, G., Landreth, G., Homeyer, L., Bratton, S., & Kale, A. (1995). *The world of play therapy literature* (2nd ed.) Denton, TX: The Center for Play Therapy.

Landreth, G., Homeyer, L., Glover, G., & Sweeney, D. (1998). *Play therapy interventions with children's problems.* Northvale, NJ: Jason Aronson.

O'Connor, K. (1991). *The play therapy primer: An intergration of theories and techniques.* New York: Wiley.

Schaefer, C., & O'Connor, K. (Eds.). (1983). *Handbook of play therapy.* New York: Wiley.

Additional Readings for Nonprofessionals

Axline, V. (1971). *Dibs: In search of self.* New York: Ballantine Books.

Nemiroff, M., & Annunziata, J. (1990). *A child's first book about play therapy.* Washington, DC: American Psychological Association.

Ramirez, L., & Salcines, M. (2000). *Maggie's visit to the play room.* Houston, TX: Double Press.

Additional Readings for Professionals

Ginott, H. (1959). The theory and practice of therapeutic intervention in child treatment. *Journal of Counseling Psychology, 23,* 160–166.

Klein, M. (1975). Symposium on child-analysis. In *Love, guilt, and reparation & other works 1921–1945.* New York: Delecorte Seymour Lawrence.

Landreth, G. (1991). *Play therapy: The art of the relationship.* Bristol, PA: Accelerated Development.

Ray, D., Bratton, S., Rhine, T., & Jones, L. (2001). The effectiveness of play therapy: Responding to the critics. *International Journal of Play Therapy, 10*(1), 85–108.

LAURA M. BAYLOT
KARLA CARMICHAEL

Positive Behavioral Supports

Positive behavior support (PBS) is defined by the Association for Positive Behavior Supports as "an approach to intervention derived from social, behavioral, educational, and biomedical science to achieve reduction in problem behavior and improved quality of life." As such, the focus of PBS is on increasing appropriate behavior and decreasing inappropriate behavior through positive-reinforcement-based strategies. Positive behavior support is applicable across contexts and with diverse populations (The Association for Positive Behavioral Supports [APBS], n.d.). PBS can be used with individuals, families, classrooms, schools, community agencies, and even with large-scale regional and state initiatives. Recent research on the PBS approach suggests that the approach is both effective in addressing its goals and acceptable to those using it (Carr, Horner, et al., 1999; Carr, Levin, et al., 1999).

PBS often focuses on the change at the systems level and takes advantage of multiple intervention components following functional behavior assessment. Unlike approaches that focus on simply decreasing problem behavior, prevention and skill acquisition are hallmarks of the PBS approach. This multifaceted approach allows PBS to target problem behavior reduction and skill acquisition using antecedent and consequence-based strategies.

The critical features of PBS include comprehensive lifestyle change, a life-span perspective, ecological validity, stakeholder participation, and social validity (APBS, n.d.). Lifestyle change relates to increasing skills to facilitate further learning and appropriate behavior acquisition rather than on simply reducing problem behavior. Instead of simply decreasing a problem behavior, the PBS approach would be to increase a skill base to address future learning to plan for similar situations that may arise. The life-span perspective of PBS takes into consideration a person's age, his/her community, his/her family, his/her current skill repertoire, and a person's preferences, and builds choices into intervention. The life-span perspective of PBS encourages including the planning of choice making into intervention so that an individual can control relevant personal decisions to the maximum extent possible.

Ecological validity refers to the extent to which an assessment or treatment is similar to the environment from which a referral is made. The PBS approach strives to ensure a high level of ecological validity by incorporating known stimuli into assessment and treatment planning. If possible, an assessment and treatment would take place in the area from which a referral was made, rather than in a clinical setting or treatment facility. Both assessment and treatment would include the use of relevant caregivers from the referral environment. If an assessment were made in a classroom, the ecologically valid approach of PBS would encourage the assessment and treatment to include the teacher in the classroom to the greatest extent possible. This stakeholder participation is another key aspect of the approach. By incorporating familiar people, family, teachers, friends, and peers into assessment and treatment, the environment will more closely resemble the environment from which the problem behavior occurred (Reuf, Turnbull, Turnbull, & Poston, 1999).

PBS step	Individual child	Schoolwide PBS
Problem Identification	Referral from teacher, family, or community agency	Referral from school
Data Collection (Assessment)	Interview, records review, observation, functional assessment, functional analysis	Interview administration, review of office referral and suspension data, observation in classrooms and common areas
Summary Statements	Hypotheses regarding the function of the problem	Hypotheses regarding which areas are most problematic, which behaviors are most common, review of current procedures for dealing with school discipline
Plan Development	Functionally based program using positive reinforcement to decrease problem behavior and increase appropriate skills	Initiate schoolwide rules, train behavioral expectations, use a schoolwide incentive program to motivate students to demonstrate appropriate behavior
Data Collection (Monitoring)	Collect data to monitor levels of problem and appropriate behaviors	Collect data to monitor changes in office referrals, suspensions, appropriate classroom behavior, and appropriate behaviors that correspond to the behavioral expectations of the schoolwide rules

Through years of research in education, applied behavior analysis, school psychology, and biomedicine, several different treatment approaches could be utilized for any given problem. With the PBS approach, social validity is at the forefront of the decision-making process. Through using empirically validated, socially acceptable treatment and teaching procedures, PBS addresses problems of social importance with nonaversive reinforcement-based systems. Because of the focus on systems, the PBS model has been successfully used and evaluated in many different school settings. Recent research demonstrates effectiveness to address many different issues in a wide variety of school settings (Luiselli, Putnam, & Handler, 2001; Luiselli, Putnam, & Sunderland, 2002; Putnam, Luiselli, Handler, & Jefferson, 2003).

Regardless of setting, PBS uses a data-based problem-solving model composed of Problem Identification, Data Collection (Assessment), Summary Statements, Plan Development, and Data Collection (Monitoring). This problem-solving sequence can look slightly different given the focus on either individual- or systems-level change. To highlight this, the table above represents a brief example of what each step could entail for an individual and a schoolwide PBS system.

In both examples above, the same problem-solving steps were used to identify, assess, form a treatment for, implement, and monitor the success of a system designed specifically for the type of situation used with PBS. PBS is an approach to treatment that uses a variety of methods to ensure best practice, whether the target of intervention is an individual, a classroom, a school, or a larger system such as a school district or regional network of community health care organizations.

See also: Antecedent Analysis; Functional Analysis

BIBLIOGRAPHY

Association for Positive Behavior Supports. (n.d.). http://cfs.fmhi.usf.edu/dares/apbs/

Carr, E. G., Horner, R. H., Turnbull, A. P., Marquis, J. G., Magito McLaughlin, D., McAtee, M. L., et al. (1999). *Positive behavior support for people with developmental disabilities: A research synthesis* (American Association on Mental Retardation Monograph Series). Washington, DC: American Association on Mental Retardation.

Carr, E. G., Levin, L., McConnachie, G., Carlson, J. I., Kemp, D. C., Smith, C. E., et al. (1999). Comprehensive multisituational intervention for problem behavior in the community: Long-term maintenance and social validation. *Journal of Positive Behavior Interventions, 1,* 5–25.

Luiselli, J. K., Putnam, R. F., & Handler, M. W. (2001). Improving discipline practices in public middle schools: Description of a whole-school and district-wide model of behavior analysis consultation. *The Behavior Analyst Today, 2,* 18–27.

Luiselli, J. K., Putnam, R. F., & Sunderland, M. (2002). Longitudinal evaluation of a behavior support intervention in a public middle school. *Journal of Positive Behavior Interventions, 4,* 182–188.

Putnam, R. F., Luiselli, J. K., Handler, M. W., & Jefferson, G. L. (2003). Evaluating student disciplinary practices in a public school through behavioral assessment of office referrals. *Behavior Modification, 27,* 505–523.

Reuf, M. B., Turnbull, A. P., Turnbull, H. R., & Poston, D. (1999). Perspectives of five stakeholder groups: Challenging behavior of individuals with mental retardation and autism. *Journal of Positive Behavior Interventions, 1,* 43–58.

Additional Reading for Nonprofessionals

Office of Special Education Programs Technical Assistance Center on Positive Behavioral Interventions and Supports. http://www.pbis.org/

Additional Reading for Professionals

Sugai, G., Horner, R. H., Dunlap, G., Hieneman, M., Lewis, T. J., Nelson, C. M., et al. (1999). Applying positive behavioral support and functional behavioral assessment in schools. Association for Positive Behavior Supports. Washington, D.C. Retrieved October 21, 2003, from http://www.pbis.org/files/TAG1.doc.

MICHAEL M. MUELLER

Positive Reinforcement

Positive reinforcement occurs when access to a consequence (reinforcement) is delivered contingent upon a behavior meeting a criterion, and this process increases the probability of the student engaging in this behavior in similar situations. Positive reinforcement has been used to increase desired behaviors, maintain desired behaviors, decrease undesirable behaviors, shape new behaviors, and encourage creative behaviors. In fact, positive reinforcement may be the most common procedure used to enhance student learning and manage behaviors.

Positive reinforcement components include (i) target student(s), (ii) target behavior(s), (iii) criteria that must be met to receive access to reinforcers, and (iv) the reinforcer. Each of these variables can influence the type of positive reinforcement program used and the success of the program.

Target Student(s)

Positive reinforcement programs can be developed for individual students or for groups of students. When targeting groups, educators often use group-oriented contingencies. For example, when an educator offers reinforcement to any student who scores 90 percent or better on an exam, the educator is using an independent group reinforcement program to attempt to influence the behavior of the entire class. Parents and educators also implement individual contingency programs to address specific target behaviors of specific students. For example, a teacher may write a behavioral contract where Johnny receives reinforcement (e.g., 10 minutes of computer time) when he completes all of his mathematics homework with a minimum of 85 percent correct.

Target Behavior(s)

Positive reinforcement can be used to target both desirable and undesirable behaviors. When targeting desirable behaviors, educators reinforce the occurrence of those behaviors when they meet or exceed a criterion. For example, an educator concerned with a student not following direction could provide reinforcement when he/she follows directions 90 percent of the time. Offering reinforcement for behaviors students cannot perform (i.e., when they have a skill deficit) will not be effective and may only frustrate students. Therefore, a critical factor when targeting increases in desired behaviors is that students must be able to perform those behaviors.

Differential reinforcement of incompatible behaviors (DRI) or differential reinforcement of lower rate behaviors (DRL) can be used to reduce behaviors. Using DRI, educators reinforce behaviors that are incompatible with the behavior they want to decrease. For example, educators who want to decrease calling out could reinforce hand raising and responding only when called upon to respond. Again, it is critical that the target student be able to perform these incompatible behaviors. Using DRL, educators would reinforce lower rates of calling

out. For example, a student could be given access to computers provided he called out less than eight times during the school day.

Criteria

One of the more difficult tasks when using positive reinforcement is to develop an appropriate criterion for earning access to reinforcement. Baseline data can be used to guide criterion development. Specifically, the criterion would be set higher than baseline when attempting to increase a behavior and lower than baseline when attempting to decrease a target behavior. However, this can still leave a wide range of possible criteria. For example, suppose Johnny is not doing any of his in-class mathematics work. A criterion could be established where he receives reinforcement contingent upon completing 10 percent of his work or 100 percent of his work.

One solution to setting criteria is to use shaping. With this procedure, the criterion begins with a small change in behavior (e.g., 30 percent of the work complete) and then the criterion is gradually increased (e.g., 50 percent and then 70 percent) as the student's behavior improves (Skinner, Skinner, & Armstrong, 2000). Shaping procedures are often used because they allow the student to experience some success, especially when the program is initially implemented.

Another solution is to develop a pool of criteria and randomly select a criterion to earn reinforcement after the behavior(s) have been performed. For example, students could be told that each student whose performance on an exam exceeds a randomly selected criterion would receive ice cream. The teacher could write different criteria on slips of paper (e.g., 50, 60, 70, 80, and 90 percent) and, after the exam is graded, randomly choose a criterion. With this procedure, students whose behaviors rarely meet criteria for earning reinforcement are less likely to give up because they may be able to meet a lower criterion. In addition, students who tend to do well will do their best so that they can meet any criteria that may be randomly selected (Popkin & Skinner, 2003).

Another solution is to offer differential reinforcement for differential performance. With this procedure, students would earn more or higher quality reinforcement for stronger performance. However, any improvement in performance would earn some level of reinforcement. For example, those who score 70 percent on an exam could earn X, but those who score 80 percent would earn $X + Y$ and those who score 90 percent would earn $X + Y + Z$.

Reinforcement

One critical aspect of any positive reinforcement program is the reinforcer itself. Reinforcers can be tangible (e.g., candy, stickers), symbolic (grades), social (praise), exchangeable (tokens or money), and the opportunity to perform activities (e.g., work on the computer). Although each type of reinforcement can be effective, reinforcement quality varies across students. Thus, for Johnny, computer time may be a powerful reinforcer, whereas for another student, Jane, the opportunity to use the computer may not be a reinforcer. When working with groups of students, using token economies allows each student to earn access to preferred reinforcers. Using this procedure, students earn tokens that can be exchanged for a variety of reinforcers (e.g., five tokens can be used to earn computer time or to purchase a pencil). Money serves the same purpose in that individuals can choose to exchange money for preferred reinforcers (e.g., seeing a show, obtaining a tennis racquet). Using randomly selected or unknown reinforcers also can be used to increase students' motivation. For example, students could close their eyes and pick a reinforcer from a "goody bag." As long as the pool of reinforcers contains some reinforcers that are high-quality reinforcers for each student, such procedures can be highly effective (Skinner, Skinner, & Sterling-Turner, 2002). Finally, allowing students to choose reinforcers is a simple procedure for identifying high-quality reinforcers.

In addition to reinforcer quality, reinforcement rate and immediacy are important variables to consider. With respect to reinforcer rate, high-rate reinforcement (reinforcement delivered frequently) is likely to be more effective than low-rate reinforcement. Also, reinforcement that is delivered immediately after target behaviors are performed will have a greater influence on student behavior. Peers and computers often can be used to deliver high rates of immediate reinforcement (e.g., feedback) to students. In addition, educators and parents can often deliver social praise quickly and efficiently.

REINFORCEMENT IS RELATIVE

If students can perform target behaviors, the success of reinforcement is based on relative, as opposed to absolute, levels of reinforcement (Neef, Shade, & Miller, 1994). If students are to choose to engage in desired behaviors, it is critical that reinforcement for desired behavior exceeds reinforcement for other incompatible behaviors. Therefore, reinforcement programs are more likely to be effective when reinforcement for competing behaviors (e.g., walking around the room) is weaker (lower quality, more delayed, lower rate) than reinforcement for desired behaviors (e.g., doing mathematics assignment). This is especially true when desired behaviors take more effort. If all else is held constant (e.g., reinforcement rate, immediacy, and quality), students are more likely to choose to engage in behaviors that require less effort. Therefore, it is important that reinforcement for high-effort behaviors be strong (e.g., high rate, immediate, high quality).

UNINTENTIONAL REINFORCEMENT

If children repeatedly engage in undesirable behaviors, those behaviors are likely being reinforced. However, it may be difficult to determine what is reinforcing those specific behaviors. For example, a child may misbehave, get yelled at, and get sent to the principal's office. In this situation, the reinforcement could be (a) getting yelled at, (b) being allowed to leave the classroom, (c) being able to avoid doing assigned classwork, (d) talking with the principal's secretary, (e) being yelled at by the principal, and so on. Regardless, research on choice behavior suggests that something is reinforcing this behavior. Recently, functional behavioral assessment (FBA) procedures have been developed that assist people by identifying what is a reinforcing behavior (Skinner & Ervin, 2003; Watson & Steege, 2003). This information can then be used to develop effective reinforcement programs designed to reduce undesirable behavior and increase desired behaviors. For example, if FBA data suggest that teacher attention is reinforcing disruptive behaviors, teachers could reduce the rate of reinforcement for these behaviors and increase attention delivered for desirable behaviors.

FADING REINFORCEMENT

Once behaviors become established, it is important that they be maintained. To assist with maintenance, reinforcement rate or quality can be gradually decreased, or the interval between the behavior and reinforcement delivery can be gradually increased. Another procedure for fading reinforcement is to enhance the amount of effort required to earn the reinforcement by altering target behavior or criteria (Popkin & Skinner, 2003). Finally, these fading procedures can be combined. For example, a parent who initially provides extra TV time to his/her child for making good scores on daily academic assignments could eventually provide a delayed, but higher quality, reinforcer (e.g., a slumber party) for strong report card grades.

CONCLUSION

When students engage in desired behaviors or show improvement in academic performance, adults should, and often do, reinforce this behavior. This reinforcement is often unplanned and social (e.g., praise). This incidental reinforcement is often enough to produce meaningful changes in student behavior. However, in other instances, specific reinforcement programs may need to be developed to alter student behaviors. When constructing such programs, careful consideration of components of reinforcement programs (e.g., target behaviors, criteria) and an understanding of the relative strength of reinforcement for desirable behaviors versus competing behaviors should lead to the development of more successful procedures designed to prevent and remedy learning and behavior problems.

See also: Differential Reinforcement; Functional Behavioral Assessment; Group Contingencies; Negative Reinforcement

BIBLIOGRAPHY

Neef, N. A., Shade, D., & Miller, M. S. (1994). Assessing the influential dimensions of reinforcers on choice in students with serious emotional disturbance. *Journal of Applied Behavior Analysis, 27,* 575–583.

Popkin, J., & Skinner, C. H. (2003). Enhancing academic performance in a classroom serving students with serious emotional disturbance: Interdependent group contingencies with randomly selected components. *School Psychology Review, 32,* 282–295.

Skinner, C. H., & Ervin, R. (2003). Functional behavioral assessment of nonverbal behavior. In S. McCallum (Ed.), *Handbook of nonverbal assessment* (pp. 253–276). New York: Kluwer Academic/Plenum.

Skinner, C. H., Skinner, A. L., & Armstrong, K. (2000). Shaping leisure reading persistence in a client with chronic schizophrenia. *Psychiatric Rehabilitation Journal, 24,* 52–57.

Skinner, C. H., Skinner, A. L., & Sterling-Turner, H. E. (2002). Best practices in utilizing group contingencies for intervention and prevention. In A. Thomas & J. Grimes (Eds.), *Best practices in school psychology* (4th ed., pp. 817–830). Washington, DC: National Association of School Psychologists.

Watson, T. S., & Steege, M. W. (2003). *Conducting school-based functional behavioral assessments: A practitioner's guide.* New York: Guilford.

Additional Readings for Nonprofessionals

Skinner, C. H. (in press). Academic egagement. In A. Canter (Ed.), *Helping children at home and school. Part II: Handouts from your school psychologist.* Washington, DC: National Association of School Psychologists.

Skinner, C. H., Waterson, H. J., Bryant, D. R., Bryant, R. J., Collins, P. M., Hill, C. J., et al. (2002). Team problem solving based on research, functional behavioral assessment data, teacher acceptability, and Jim Carey's interview. *Proven Practice: Prevention & Remediation Solutions for Schools, 4,* 56–64.

Additional Readings for Professionals

Billington, E. J., & Ditommaso, N. M. (2003). Demonstrations and applications of the matching law in education. *Journal of Behavioral Education, 12,* 91–104.

Skinner, C. H., Wallace, M. A., & Neddenriep, C. E. (2002). Academic remediation: Educational application of research on assignment preference and choice. *Child and Family Behavior Therapy, 24,* 51–65.

CHRISTOPHER H. SKINNER

Posttraumatic Stress Disorder

Posttraumatic Stress Disorder (PTSD) is a psychiatric disorder that follows exposure to a traumatic incident. Examples of trau- matic incidents include sexual assault, physical attack, hostage taking, kidnapping, severe automobile accident, natural disaster (flood, fire, earthquake), and man-made disaster (war, shelling, terrorist attack). A child or an adult may contract the disorder without being personally threatened or injured in any way. It is sufficient to be present and to witness the pain, suffering, or death of others, whether strangers or loved ones. Most people become upset when exposed to a traumatic incident, especially if they experience intense fear, helplessness, and horror, during the incident or shortly thereafter; they do not reexperience the original incident months, and even years, later. The people who do relive the traumatic event are diagnosed as suffering from PTSD, a disturbance in one's adjustment and lifestyle that persists months, if not years, following the traumatic event. PTSD may occur at any age. It usually begins within 3 months following the traumatic event, but in rare cases may occur years later (American Psychiatric Association, 1994).

CHARACTERISTIC SYMPTOMS OF POSTTRAUMATIC STRESS DISORDER

The traumatic incident may be reexperienced in various ways. Sufferers may have recurrent and intrusive recollections of the event, or have recurrent distressing dreams about it. They may act or feel as if the event were about to recur or were in fact recurring before their eyes. Some people who suffer from this disorder develop maladaptive coping strategies in an attempt to avoid thoughts, conversations, people, or situations that might arouse recollections of the traumatic incident. They withdraw from their customary work and recreational activities, become detached or estranged from family and friends, and become emotionally numb or frozen. Some become hypervigilant, and are continually on guard for fear of recurrence of the terrifying event or the intrusive recollection of the event. As a consequence, they are unable to relax, to sleep normally, or to concentrate on important tasks at hand. Some sufferers experience distress without being able to pinpoint what is bothering them. Others are unable to meet their daily commitments as well as before. Adult workers do less well on the job and get fired, homemakers neglect care of their children and fall behind in their housework. School-age children fall behind in their homework. Preschool children may lose previously acquired bowel (encopresis) or bladder (enuresis) control.

TREATMENT OF INITIAL ACUTE STRESS REACTIONS

It is important to distinguish between the immediate stress reactions of children and adults to a traumatic incident and the chronic posttraumatic stress symptoms described above.

Most people experience nervous agitation, depression, apathy, or other distressing or disorganized feelings and behaviors immediately following exposure to a traumatic event. Return to familiar surroundings, rest, reassurance, and brief therapeutic interventions are usually sufficient for most people to resume their normal routines.

Family members, friends, and trained volunteers as well as mental health workers perform many helpful activities on behalf of distressed people. They provide them with relevant information about the nature of their condition, much like the information that a physician imparts to a child who has broken her leg or an adolescent who has contracted diabetes. Distressed people should be told that (a) the current distress is "normal" and is a direct consequence of the traumatic experience, (b) the distress typically decreases in the weeks ahead as one resumes routine activities, (c) brief forms of psychotherapy, counseling, or what is called debriefing are helpful if the symptoms persists, and (d) prescribed medication to help one relax and to get a good night's sleep is available.

Distressed people benefit from social and emotional support, the reassuring presence of loved ones, friends, teachers, and ministers of their faith, and the encouragement they provide to resume ordinary routines. Two key elements of social support are presence and persistence. Social support is not a one-time exercise, but a persistent effort that extends over time. Verbal support and verbal encouragement are helpful, but the physical presence and side-by-side engagement of the other in beneficial activities are far more therapeutic.

TREATMENT OF RECALCITRANT SYMPTOMS

Some distressed people are unable to regain emotional composure or to resume their normal activities, and as the weeks and months pass, it becomes clear that they require intensive, comprehensive professional treatment if they are to recover. The treatment is tailored to the personal characteristics of the individual or group (age, maturity), the nature of the traumatic incident (duration of the traumatic incident, the extent of injury, damage, or loss of life), and the severity of the symptoms.

PTSD AND SCHOOL PSYCHOLOGY

PTSD is not a respecter of age and may adversely affect teachers as well as children. The traumatic incident that generates the disorder may take place on school premises, in the community at large, or in the personal and private life of the teacher or the schoolchild. We live at a time (a) when deranged adults or schoolchildren have opened fire on children and teachers on school premises and killed or maimed victims and terrorized those who witnessed these terrifying events; (b) when children come to school to learn that a teacher or a classmate was killed

in a drive-by shooting; (c) when a school bus is involved in a highway collision and there is injury and loss of life; (d) when a hurricane ravages a community and destroys the familiar landscape of the children; (e) when a child returns to school after witnessing an accident or a confrontation that injured or killed his parent or sibling; and finally (f) when a teacher or administrator returns to work following a personal tragedy of the order cited above (Milgram, Toubiana, Klingman, Raviv, & Goldstein, 1988).

Many school systems have developed intervention programs for when community crises arise and recruit the efforts of trained professionals to deal with these crises. These programs are designed to prevent the development of stress-related symptoms in many children, to reduce the severity of symptoms that do develop in some children, and to prevent these acute symptoms from becoming chronic and crystallizing into full-blown PTSD in still others. These programs emphasize resumption of normal school activities with a generous, flexible allotment of time for group participation in memorial services, expression of sadness and anger in word and in drawings, organization of self-help groups of children, and self-help groups of parents (Toubiana, Milgram, Strich, & Edelstein, 1988). Individuals who develop chronic debilitating symptoms are appropriate candidates for individual or group psychotherapy. The precise nature of the psychotherapy will depend on the nature of the traumatic event and the prior history, strengths, and resources of the patient. So-called psychodynamic or psychoanalytic therapies attempt to uncover crippling unconscious motivations and experiences. Learning-based therapies attempt to assist patients in freeing themselves of stress-related incapacitating coping behaviors and acquiring constructive coping behaviors. Cognition-based learning therapies emphasize the way people interpret their experiences to their personal detriment and how they may learn to interpret the past and anticipate the future differently in the course of behaving differently in their daily lives. Existential therapies emphasize the personal search for meaning in life, the meaning of why bad things happen to good people, and the meaning of life after the loss of innocence or cherished beliefs that are no longer tenable (Milgram, 1986).

CLOSING THOUGHTS FOR VICTIMS/ SURVIVORS OF TRAUMATIC EVENTS

People exposed to a traumatic event typically ask two questions. The first question is "Will I be the same again? Will I be able to resume my life as I lived it before?" The reassuring answer "Yes" is usually false. The appropriate answer is "No." People who were exposed to traumatic experiences will be different precisely because of these experiences and the particular ways in which they elected to cope with these experiences over time.

The second question is "Why did this happen to me and what am I supposed to do about it?" The appropriate answer, in most cases, is "You bear no direct responsibility for what happened to you, but you are responsible for what you do about it. You may call upon the help of God or society in coping with misfortune. You are fortunate to live in a society that offers social and professional services. You may be personally fortunate to have the guiding hand or reassurance of those who love you. In the final analysis, you are responsible for making something positive out of a negative experience. If you succeed in doing so, the quality of your life will not be diminished by the misfortune that befell you; it may even be enhanced."

See also: Anxiety; Coping; Crisis Intervention; Encopresis; Enuresis; Stress; Traumatic Incidents

BIBLIOGRAPHY

American Psychiatric Association. (1994). *Diagnostic and statistical manual of mental disorders* (4th ed.). Washington DC: Author.

Milgram, N. A. (1986). Attributional analysis of war-related stress: Modes of coping and helping. In N. A. Milgram (Ed.), *Stress and coping in time of war: Generalizations from the Israeli experience* (pp. 9–25). New York: Brunner/Mazel.

Milgram, N. A., Toubiana, Y. H., Klingman, A., Raviv, A., & Goldstein, I. (1988). Situational exposure and personal loss in children's acute and chronic stress reactions to a school bus disaster. *Journal of Traumatic Stress, 1,* 339–351.

Toubiana, Y. H., Milgram, N. A., Strich, Y., & Edelstein, A. (1988). Crisis intervention in a school community disaster: Principles and practices. *Journal of Community Psychology, 16,* 228–240.

Additional Reading for Nonprofessionals

Bard, M., & Sangrey, D. (1986). *The crime victim's book* (2nd ed.). New York: Brunner/Mazel.

Additional Readings for Professionals

Meichenbaum, D. (1994). *A clinical handbook/practical therapist manual: For assessing and treating adults with Post Traumatic Stress Disorder (PTSD).* Waterloo, Ontario: Institute Press.

Solomon, Z. (1993). *Combat stress reaction: The enduring toll of war.* New York: Plenum.

Yule, W. (Ed.). (1999). *Post Traumatic Stress Disorder: Concepts and therapy.* New York: Wiley.

NOACH MILGRAM

Procrastination

Academic procrastination is defined as persistent delay in the start and/or completion of educationally related tasks: home-work assignments for the next class meeting, written reports or term papers, and preparing for and being present at scheduled written or oral exams. Academic procrastination can take the form of doing these assignments at the last possible minute or completing these assignments late, if at all (Milgram & Toubiana, 1999).

Academic procrastination generally has three elements:

a. *Insufficient time allotted:* Students set a time for doing the assignment or the preparation, but as it draws near, find reasons for postponing it; they set a new date and fail to meet that date; or they underestimate the amount of time it will take and schedule doing it just before the deadline and run out of time.

b. *Substandard performance:* Procrastinating students get poorer grades than they might have received had they given the assignments the time and effort that were necessary for them to earn a reasonable grade.

c. *Emotional distress about the work process and the work product:* Procrastinating students are likely to experience emotional distress for two reasons. First, they are not proud of their *work process,* the way they go about doing their assignments; they find it difficult to schedule assignments promptly and efficiently and find it even more difficult to do the assignments according to schedule. Second, they are not proud of their *work product,* the grades they receive on their various assignments. Distress and the concomitant desire to change work habits are essential ingredients in any intervention program to reduce academic procrastination. There are students who have no interest in their studies, invest little time and effort in their studies, experience little or no distress about their work habits or their grades, and are not motivated to change their behavior; instead they wish to change their venue. By the definition suggested here and accepted by many educators, these latter students are not academic procrastinators.

Research on the reasons offered by students for procrastinating on academic assignments identified two major reasons that were significantly associated with actual procrastination: fear of failure and finding the academic assignment aversive. One may ask why students who are afraid they will not do well on academic assignments behave in such a way as to guarantee that they will not do well. Doing schoolwork at the last minute if at all guarantees failure or, at the very least, substandard performance. There are, however, several psychological benefits to putting off doing unpleasant assignments.

There is a short-term benefit in putting the unpleasant assignment out of mind, enjoying other more pleasurable activities, and eventually exposing oneself for a very brief period to the aversive assignment. There is also a long-term benefit in attributing poor grades or academic failure to faulty work habits or to poor time management, failings that are both socially acceptable and ameliorable, rather than to lack of ability, a failing that is socially denigrating and regarded as irreversible. Students who work long and hard and still fail to pass an exam experience far greater distress explaining to themselves or to others why they failed. Students elect to attribute their failure to poor time management, lack of interest in the assignment, or lack of motivation to persevere in doing the task. These excuses enable students to maintain self-esteem and "save face" when they discuss their poor school grades with their peers. Therefore, academic procrastination may be seen as a coping strategy.

CHARACTERISTICS OF ACADEMIC PROCRASTINATORS

When compared with nonprocrastinating peers, procrastinators appear to lack the discipline to persist and perform effectively in frustrating situations. Their parents—in most studies, the mother is cited—are poor models for prompt, disciplined behavior, are less involved in their children's schoolwork, and do not attach great importance to formal education (Milgram, Mey-Tal, & Levinson, 1998). Some students have difficulty in making decisions related to their schoolwork. They lack confidence in their own judgment and vacillate on trivial as well as important matters. In comparison with their more decisive peers, they tend to be anxious, depressed, and lacking in self-esteem (Milgram & Tenne, 2000). There is, however, no "typical profile" of the academic procrastinator and no single prescribed treatment program for all academic procrastinators.

CHARACTERISTICS OF ACADEMIC ASSIGNMENTS THAT ELICIT PROCRASTINATION

Students may find one assignment aversive and another challenging. Some students may procrastinate on preparing for examinations because they are anxious about being in situations that appear to be controlled by others (the teachers who choose the questions) and not procrastinate in preparing written papers because they have access to the information and have ample time to handle the assignment on their terms. Other students have different anxieties and consequently different promptness–procrastination profiles. Generally students procrastinate more on assignments they perceive as unpleasant, boring, or difficult than on assignments that are pleasant, challenging, or easy (Milgram, Srolof, & Rosenbaum, 1988).

ACADEMIC PROCRASTINATION: A STUDENT–ASSIGNMENT INTERACTION

Self-report measures of academic procrastination are not comparable across students differing widely in aspiration or across institutions of higher learning. Students in colleges with high admission standards report higher procrastination rates than students in colleges with lenient or no selection standards. This finding is attributed to the subjective character of self-report measures and to the susceptibility of the student to the demands of the academic setting in which he/she studies. Two students may have 1 month to submit a written book report; one may decide that 2 weeks is ample time to do the assignment and begin working on the 3rd week; another may decide that putting off the start by 1 week is dragging one's feet and begin immediately. The major criterion by which we confirm that students are, indeed, procrastinating on their academic assignments is the absence of any of the following:

(a) Self-report by students about the manner in which they do their assignments or the promptness with which they complete them and pass them in. Many superior students rate themselves high in procrastination because they set extremely high standards for their work process and work product.

(b) Objective notation by teachers or the students themselves as to when the assignments are completed and when they passed it. Students may be comfortable with turning in their work at the last minute or requesting deadline extensions.

(c) Observed discrepancy between the student's academic grades and estimates (from the teacher or the student) of the student's potential for achieving higher grades. Students may be content with lower standards because they do not consider grades important because they have other preferred or pressing priorities to which they devote their time and energy.

We conclude that self-report about schoolwork habits, objective notation about when assignments are completed, and underachievement that may be attributed to academic procrastination are necessary, but not sufficient, conditions for identifying academic procrastination. Many students meet any or all of the above criteria and do not fall into the academic procrastinator category. The decisive criterion is the presence of some degree of emotional distress about work process and work product. Academic procrastinators acknowledge freely that they are dissatisfied with how they go about doing their work and with the grades they receive for their work. Students who do not express dissatisfaction are simply showing the customary behavior of anyone who (a) has no interest in doing something and (b) will not suffer any personally adverse consequences if he does not do it or does it poorly.

A convenient rubric for understanding academic procrastination is the AAA model of coping (Appraisal–Anxiety–Avoidance). Students appraise a given academic assignment and if, as a consequence of their appraisal, they experience anxiety, they will avoid dealing with it by putting it off as much as possible. Students will then resort to excuses, legitimate and fraudulent, to justify granting them extensions to complete their assignments. In principle, students reject making excuses, but in fact, when they find themselves in the actual anxiety-provoking situation, they feel differently and behave differently.

See also: Anxiety; Coping

BIBLIOGRAPHY

Ferrari, J. R., Johnson, J. L., & McCown, W. G. (Eds.). (1995). *Procrastination and task avoidance: Theory, research, and treatment.* New York: Plenum.

Milgram, N. A., Mey-Tal, G., & Levinson, Y. (1998). Procrastination, generalized or specific, in college students and their parents. *Personality and Individual Differences, 25,* 297–316.

Milgram, N. A., Srolof, B., & Rosenbaum, M. (1988). The procrastination of everyday life. *Journal of Research in Personality, 22,* 197–212.

Milgram, N. N., & Tenne, R. (2000). Personality correlates of decisional and task procrastination. *European Journal of Personality, 14,* 141–156.

Milgram, N. A., & Toubiana, Y. (1999). Academic anxiety, academic procrastination and parent involvement in students and their parents. *British Journal of Educational Psychology, 69,* 345–362.

Additional Readings for Nonprofessionals

Bliss, E. C. (1983). *Doing it now: A twelve-step program for curing procrastination and achieving your goals.* New York: Charles Scribner.

Burka, J. B., & Yuen, L. M. (1983). *Procrastination: Why you do it and what to do about it.* Reading, PA: Addison-Wesley.

Knaus, W. J. (1979). *Do it now: How to stop procrastinating.* Englewood Cliffs, NJ: Prentice-Hall.

Additional Readings for Professionals

Ellis, A., & Knaus, W. J. (1977). *Overcoming procrastination.* New York: Institute for Rational Living.

Ferrari, J. R., & Pychyl, T. A. (Eds.). (2000). Procrastination: Current issues and new directions [Special issue]. *Journal of Social Behavior and Personality, 15.*

NOACH MILGRAM

Punishment

Punishment is one of the most misunderstood and controversial terms found in this encyclopedia. Within school settings, punishment procedures have included social disapproval (e.g., verbal reprimands, frowns, the "hairy eyebrow"), aversive procedures (e.g, spanking, raps on the knuckles with a ruler, water mist), forfeiture of earned tokens, recess, and privileges, and the required performance of effortful behavior (e.g., writing sentences 100 times, copying spelling words 50 times after each error on a spelling test). In short, punishment procedures are ingrained within our social framework, schools, communities, and homes. The term *punishment* typically evokes a wide range of opinions and emotional reactions. Most people equate punishment with a negative experience. What, then, is meant by punishment? Moreover, what are the caveats to consider when using punishment? Should punishment procedures be used at all with students in school settings?

In everyday life, punishment is typically viewed as the implementation of a procedure that is aversive, noxious, or painful. Punishment is typically defined in terms of a specific consequence such as spanking, electric shock, verbal reprimands, prison terms, traffic tickets, and time-out, among others.

Within the field of applied behavior analysis, principles such as reinforcement and punishment are defined in terms of their *effect* on future behavior. When an event that follows a behavior results in an increase in the frequency, duration, or intensity of the behavior, the consequence is referred to as reinforcement. Conversely, when the event that follows a given behavior results in a decrease in the frequency, duration, or intensity of the behavior, the consequence is called punishment. A stimulus or event that is reinforcing to one individual may indeed be punishing to another person. For example, although we typically think that giving compliments to others about their dress or appearance is a reinforcing statement, for individuals who are painfully shy, such statements may be highly aversive. In short, to determine whether a stimulus/event is a punisher or a reinforcer, one needs to examine the effect it has on subsequent behavior.

Technically, the term *punishment* refers solely to procedures that reduce the probability or likelihood of a response in the future (Kazdin, 2001). Within the field of applied behavior analysis, there are hundreds of published studies demonstrating the effectiveness of punishment procedures in reducing/suppressing undesirable behaviors. There are two general forms of punishment on the basis of whether aversive events are presented, positive events are withdrawn, or effortful behavior is required after the inappropriate behavior has occurred. In each of these broad areas of punishment, the procedure implemented resulted in a decrease/suppression of the inappropriate behavior.

PUNISHMENT TYPE I

This is perhaps the most familiar form of punishment. This involves the presentation of an aversive or unpleasant event after

---

Punishment Type I: Contingent *presentation* of an aversive stimulus or event that results in a *future decrease* or weakening of behavior rate, duration, or intensity. Examples: spanking, electric shock, verbal reprimands, overcorrection, social disapproval

Punishment Type II: Contingent *withdrawal* of a preferred stimulus or event that results in a *future decrease* or weakening of behavior rate, duration, or intensity. Examples: time-out from reinforcement, response cost

Punishment Type III: Contingent participation in an effortful activity which results in a *future decrease* or weakening of behavior rate, duration, or intensity. Examples: overcorrection, positive practice

---

a behavior has occurred and that results in the future suppression of that behavior. There are two types of aversive events: (a) primary aversive stimuli and (b) secondary, or conditioned, aversive stimuli. Primary aversive stimuli are inherently uncomfortable or painful physical events such as electric shock, spanking, loud noises, bright lights, and so on. When these stimuli follow a specific behavior, the behavior is typically suppressed. Secondary aversive stimuli are acquired through their association with primary aversive stimuli and include such examples as the word "No!," frowns, gestures, and so on. Secondary aversive stimuli are not inherently uncomfortable, but because of their paired association with primary aversive events they gain aversive properties. For example, a young child does not consider frowns from her mother and the word "No" to be inherently aversive. However, if the mother shouts the word "No!" (a loud noise that is aversive) and pairs this with frowning when the child displays inappropriate behaviors (e.g., reaching into a campfire), the word "No" and the frown will, in the future, serve to suppress future behaviors.

Although one may naturally think of primary aversive stimuli to be more extreme than secondary aversive stimuli, that is not always the case. Consider the case of a first-grade student who had a "crush" on his classroom teacher. One day at school he was talking with a classmate during morning story time and the classroom teacher, upon noticing his "disruptive behavior," stopped reading, looked directly at the student, cocked her head to the side, lowered her eyebrow, frowned, and said sternly, "Daniel!" Daniel was crushed emotionally. What we might think of as a mild form of social disapproval can often have devastating effects.

PUNISHMENT TYPE II

In Punishment Type II, the undesirable behavior is followed by the *removal of a preferred event*, resulting in the subsequent decrease in the frequency, duration, or intensity of the response. When one intends to use Punishment Type II behaviors, it is critical that the *reinforcer* that the person loses as a result of undesirable behavior is indeed reinforcing.

The two major forms of Punishment Type II are time-out from reinforcement and response cost.

Time-Out from Reinforcement

Within school settings, this is one of the most frequently used procedures to address problem behaviors. Although the technical term is *time-out from reinforcement*, this procedure is commonly referred to simply as *time-out*. Time-out from reinforcement typically involves removing a student from a reinforcing situation to a neutral or less reinforcing setting following the occurrence of problem behavior. The duration of time-out from reinforcement may range from as little as 30 seconds to as much as 5 minutes. There are two basic forms of time-out from reinforcement: (a) Exclusion Time-Out from Reinforcement and (b) Seclusion Time-Out from Reinforcement.

Exclusion Time-Out from Reinforcement

This involves excluding the student from the immediate reinforcing situation, but not removing the student from the immediate classroom setting. For example, during a small group cooperative learning activity within a social studies class, Lisa displayed disruptive behaviors (e.g., acting out a scene from a recent comedy movie) that clearly were motivated by social attention (e.g., laughs, comments) from classmates. The classroom teacher directed Lisa to leave the immediate situation (i.e., the small group activity), return to her desk within the classroom, and remain seated at her desk for a period of 3 minutes. This resulted in Lisa experiencing a loss of social reinforcement and served to reduce the future occurrences of disruptive behavior.

Seclusion Time-Out from Reinforcement

This involves excluding the student from the immediate reinforcing situation, and removing the student from the immediate classroom setting. For example, during the same small group cooperative learning activity, Lisa's good friend Julie displayed disruptive behaviors (e.g., pretending to pick her nose) that resulted in social attention from classmates. Because Julie's desk was adjacent to the group of students, the teacher directed Julie to leave the classroom and to stand in the hallway for 3 minutes. This resulted in Julie experiencing a loss of social reinforcement and served to reduce subsequent occurrences of disruptive behavior. In more extreme cases, seclusion time-out from reinforcement has included the removal of an individual from classroom settings and placement within specifically designed areas (e.g., "time-out" rooms, isolation areas, principal's office, etc.).

Although most forms of time-out from reinforcement involve implementation of the consequence immediately after the occurrence of the undesirable behavior, there are situations in which delayed implementation of the procedure is effective. With delayed time-out from reinforcement, the *time-out* procedure is implemented minutes or even hours after the occurrence of the problem behavior. For example, David displayed disruptive behaviors during arithmetic class. Ms. Ellie's classroom rules specified that each occurrence of disruptive behavior would result in 3 minutes of time-out during the next scheduled recess. In David's case, this meant that his infraction of classroom rules would result in staying in class for the first 3 minutes of morning recess. This was an effective form of time-out from reinforcement, because the loss of reinforcement (i.e., recess), although delayed, was punishing to David.

Cardinal Rule in Using "Time-Out": Time-out from reinforcement is effective to the degree that the time in environment is reinforcing.

Response Cost

Response cost involves the forfeiture of reinforcement contingent on the occurrence of problem behaviors. Although time-out from reinforcement typically involves the removal of the person from the reinforcing activities, response cost involves the forfeiture of tangible items (e.g., money, tokens, smiley faces, etc.). Typically, response cost consists of some type of fine. Examples of response cost include fines for traffic violations, fees for late filing of income tax returns, charges for bounced checks, and charges for overdue library books, among others (Kazdin, 2001). Response cost is a form of punishment because the loss of reinforcement serves to reduce the probability of the future occurrence of a given behavior. For example, Mary Ann, a 10th-grade student in a special education classroom in which a token economy was used as part of a classwide behavior management system, was required to forfeit 50 previously earned tokens because she displayed swearing behavior. This resulted in a subsequent decrease in swearing behavior.

PUNISHMENT TYPE III

Punishment Type III involves requiring a student to engage in effortful activities as a consequence of problem behavior. The most common form of Punishment Type III is overcorrection. Overcorrection is composed of two components: (a) restitution and (b) positive practice; these components may be used singularly or in combination. Restitution involves correcting the immediate environment contingent on the occurrence of problem behavior. Restitution may involve requiring the student to restore the environment to its original state or to make it better than it was before (hence, the term *overcorrection*). For example, a student who was throwing food in the school cafeteria may be required to restore the immediate environment to its original state by cleaning up the thrown food (restitution) or to improve the state of the cafeteria by not only cleaning up the thrown food, but by mopping the cafeteria and cleaning tables (overcorrection). Both procedures require effortful behavior on the part of the student and, therefore, reduce the likelihood of the behavior occurring in the future.

Positive practice is a procedure in which following the occurrence of problem behavior the student is directed to practice the appropriate behavior over and over and over. For example, a student who slammed a door would be required to open and close the door appropriately 25 times. In this example, the student was required to engage in the appropriate form of the behavior (i.e., practice of the "positive" behavior of closing the door correctly) as a consequence of problem behavior. This serves not only to punish the problem behavior, but to establish the appropriate behavior within the student's repertoire.

POTENTIAL PROBLEMS WITH USING PUNISHMENT

Although effective in reducing problem behaviors, punishment is not without drawbacks. There are several potential *side effects* of punishment that one needs to consider before implementing interventions that involve the use of punishment. For example, punishment may result in social withdrawal, counterpunishment/counteraggression, and emotional side effects and inhibit behaviors other than those actually being punished. Moreover, a major concern with the use of punishment is that although it reduces problem behavior, it does not teach correct behavior.

As noted by Kazdin (2001), punishment is a procedure that should be used cautiously for many reasons, ranging from broad ethical and social issues to more concrete concerns such as possible undesirable side effects. As a general rule other procedures should be used before resorting to punishment-based interventions (Kazdin, 2001).

See also: Time-Out

BIBLIOGRAPHY

Donnellan, A. M., LaVigna, G. W., Negri-Shoultz, N. & Fassbender, L. L. (1988). *Progress without punishment.* New York: Teachers College Press.
Kazdin, A. (2001). *Behavior modification in applied settings.* Belmont, CA: Wadsworth/Thomson Learning.

Additional Reading for Nonprofessionals

Miltenberger, R. G. (2001). *Behavior modification: Principles and procedures.* Belmont, CA: Wadsworth/Thomson Learning.

Additional Readings for Professionals

Sugai, G. M., & Tindal, G. A. (1993). *Effective school consultation: An interactive approach.* Pacific Grove, CA: Brooks-Cole.
Thomas, A., & Grimes, J. (Eds.). (2002). *Best practices in school psychology—IV.* Bethesda, MD: National Association of School Psychologists.

RACHEL BROWN-CHIDSEY
MARK W. STEEGE

Rr

Reactive Attachment Disorder

Reactive Attachment Disorder (RAD), the most severe form of disrupted attachment between child and primary caregiver, is characterized by a marked disturbance in the development of positive social relationships and is assumed to be associated with severe pathological care. The development of RAD is spawned by a deprivation of basic emotional and/or physical needs and/or repeated changes in caregivers (e.g., multiple foster care placements, failed adoptions, or institutionalization). John Bowlby (1988), a pioneer in attachment theory, believed that disturbances in early attachment have lasting effects on human functioning.

ATTACHMENT PROCESS

Attachment to a caregiver is an instinctual process that begins at birth and continues through early childhood as basic needs are met (e.g., food, clothing, diaper changes, shelter, love, comfort, protection, and stimulation). Infants attempt to get their needs met through proximity-seeking behaviors such as whining, crying, screaming, and clinging. Consistent caregiver attention to and fulfillment of infant needs creates a safe and predictable environment, which is a crucial element in the formation of secure attachment. Thus, bonding between caregiver and child also is a critical process.

Bonding and attachment are terms that are often used interchangeably; however, they are not synonymous. Bonding refers to the feelings a caregiver has toward a child, while attachment refers to the feelings a child has toward a caregiver. In Reactive Attachment Disorder, both bonding and attachment are impaired (Hanson & Spratt, 2000).

DEVELOPMENT OF RAD

RAD can be differentiated by either an Inhibited or a Disinhibited subtype (American Psychiatric Association, 2000). Children who are diagnosed with the Inhibited type are characterized by excessive hypervigilance or ambivalence. These children present themselves as shy and withdrawn and fail to imitate and respond socially in a developmentally appropriate manner. The Disinhibited subtype of RAD is warranted if a child fails to discriminate social interactions and exhibits a lack of selectivity in attachments. Disinhibited children will attempt to attach themselves to any attachment figure and often display a pattern of diffuse attachments. Thus, developmentally appropriate stranger anxiety is not present, which may lead to dangerous situations, inappropriate interactions, and further victimization of the child.

In both Inhibited and Disinhibited subtypes, there is an assumption that disturbed behavior is the result of pathogenic care. It should be noted, however, that pathogenic care does not always result in RAD. Some children who have a history of abuse or neglect as well as exposure to multiple caregivers may be able to establish and maintain healthy, secure attachments with significant others across multiple environments. The presence of a support network can mitigate the effects of exposure to traumatic events.

RAD is a syndrome characterized by a set of maladaptive behaviors. Many of these behaviors are similar to other disorders of infancy and early childhood. Thus, it is important to differentiate RAD from other diagnoses. Diagnoses commonly confused with RAD include Mental Retardation, Autistic Disorder, Attention-Deficit/Hyperactivity Disorder, Oppositional Defiant Disorder, Conduct Disorder, and Parent–Child Relational Problems (*Diagnostic and Statistical Manual of Mental Disorders* [4th ed., text rev.] [*DSM-IV-TR*]; American Psychiatric Association, 2000). The effects of RAD also impact academic functioning. Children with RAD often experience academic difficulties, which may be associated with attention problems or hyperarousal as a result of posttraumatic stress. Finally, a child with RAD may also be prone to conduct problems and antisocial behavior. It is important to remember that behaviors manifested by a child diagnosed with RAD are assumed to be a product of grossly pathogenic care.

Although it is necessary to differentiate RAD from other disorders, the possibility of comorbid conditions exists. Children diagnosed with RAD also have experienced concurrent Post-Traumatic Stress Disorder (PTSD), Traumatic-Induced Psychotic Disorder (TIPD), Childhood-Onset Bipolar Disorder (COBD), and Major Depression.

ASSESSMENT AND TREATMENT

Prior to any treatment intervention, a comprehensive assessment using standardized assessment protocols and direct behavioral observation should be conducted. Thorough assessment aids in the formulation of realistic and measurable goals. It is essential that treatment be systemic and include the parent/caregiver. Behavioral parent training aids in the establishment of a consistent environment and may foster greater bonding and attachment experiences (Sheperis, Renfro-Michel, & Doggett, in press). A critical step for parents through this training is the establishment of realistic boundaries within an empathic and nurturing context. Problem behaviors may be reduced through teaching alternative skills, modeling appropriate interactions, reinforcing positive behaviors, establishing concrete rules and clear instructions, and using appropriate discipline.

Treatment of RAD is a complex process including, but not limited to, (a) education about RAD; (b) coordination of appropriate resources and wraparound services; (c) the establishment of support networks, including crisis intervention services; and (d) family counseling.

See also: Attention-Deficit/Hyperactivity Disorder; Autism; Conduct Disorder; Oppositional Defiant Disorder

BIBLIOGRAPHY

American Psychiatric Association. (2000). *Diagnostic and statistical manual of mental disorders* (4th ed., text rev.). Washington, DC: Author.

Bowlby, J. (1988). *A secure base: Clinical applications of attachment theory.* London: Routledge.

Hanson, R. F., & Spratt, E. G. (2000). Reactive attachment disorder: What we know about the disorder and implications for treatment. *Child Maltreatment, 5,* 137–145.

Sheperis, C. J., Renfro-Michel, E., & Doggett, R. A. (in press). In-home treatment of reactive attachment disorder in a therapeutic foster care system: A case example. *The Journal of Mental Health Counseling.*

Additional Reading for Nonprofessionals

Levy, T. M., & Orlans, M. (1998). *Attachment, trauma, and healing: Understanding and treating attachment disorder in children and families.* Washington, DC: Child Welfare League of America.

Additional Readings for Professionals

Ainsworth, M. D., Blehar, M. C., Waters, E., & Wall, S. (1978). *Patterns of attachment.* Hillsdale, NJ: Erlbaum.

Bowlby, J. (1969). *Attachment and loss: Attachment* (Vol. 1). New York: Basic Books.

Sheperis, C. J., Dogget, R. A., Hoda, N. E., Blanchard, T., Renfro-Michel, E., Holdiness, S., et al. (2003). The development of an assessment protocol for reactive attachment disorder. *The Journal of Mental Health Counseling, 25,* 291–310.

Sheperis, C. J., Dogget, R. A., & Renfro-Michel, E. (2003). Disrupted attachment patterns and youth at risk: Understanding and treating disruptive behavior. In D. Rea & R. Stallworth-Clark (Eds.), *Fostering our youth's well-being: Healing the social disease of violence* (pp. 189–199). New York: McGraw–Hill.

CARL SHEPERIS
SACKY HOLDINESS
R. ANTHONY DOGGETT

Reading

ACADEMIC INTERVENTIONS FOR READING COMPREHENSION

Reading is the most frequently targeted academic subject for remediation in the school system (Shapiro, 1996). Interventions that focus on reading often focus on increasing the functional reading skill of comprehension. Increasing reading comprehension makes sense because when most people read, they are reading to gather information or to understand what they are reading. Reading comprehension is an important element of other academic subjects such as science or history. When determining what intervention should be used to increase reading comprehension, educators must first determine if the student is currently reading at an instructional level in her curriculum. It may be the case that students are not reading at their instructional level, which may then interfere with acquiring information to answer comprehension questions. Increasing comprehension skill may be better accomplished if students are reading at a level that is appropriate for their skills (Shapiro, 1996).

Once instructional level has been determined, there are several techniques discussed in the reading literature that have been empirically validated for increasing reading comprehension. These techniques are usually divided into two areas: prereading and postreading (Shapiro, 1996). With prereading interventions, elements of the story are made more salient so that the reader is actively searching (i.e., reading) for certain information while he/she is engaged in the reading passage. Postreading interventions consist of activities that are utilized after the student has read the assigned story or passage.

Prereading Interventions

Prereading interventions consist of providing the participant with facts to examine or questions to answer prior to the actual reading of the passage. One example of a prereading technique that may be utilized to increase reading comprehension is called story mapping (Idol-Maestas & Croll, 1987). When implementing story mapping, the reader (student) is instructed to examine and organize the story while he/she is reading. The reader reads an assigned story or reading passage and is instructed to attend to important elements or items described in the particular passage such as main characters, main ideas, factual information, central themes, and settings. Story mapping could be employed by educators in the classroom quite easily. Before students are required to read an assigned passage, the teacher could administer a worksheet that instructs the students to find certain elements of the passage while they are reading. For example, students may be asked to identify the main character of the story. In this manner, reading comprehension is increased because students are reading to search for relevant information in order to answer comprehension questions. Thus, this gives students opportunities to focus on main points of the story or reading passage to be able to answer comprehension questions.

Another technique that may be used to increase reading comprehension, based on this same premise of story mapping, consists of having the students determine for themselves elements or questions about the story (e.g., setting, main ideas) to focus on while they are reading. This method for increasing reading comprehension is known as self-instruction. During self-instruction, students may be required to reread the story or reading passage several times to find answers to certain comprehension questions. Essentially, they are practicing reading comprehension skills by rereading the assignment to answer questions. Practicing provides students with more opportunities to respond while also increasing total engaged time spent reading. Practicing reading in the self-instruction technique and in the procedure known as rereading may aid in increasing reading comprehension.

Previewing has been demonstrated to be effective in increasing accuracy of comprehension, particularly when combined with other reading interventions (Sindelar & Stoddard, 1991). Previewing may be done by the teacher or another student in the classroom. The person who is previewing reads the story aloud to the student while the student silently follows along. Previewing may also be conducted using a tape of someone reading the passage while the student follows along. Students are then typically asked to reread the story either silently to themselves or back to the previewer. The student is then given the opportunity to answer comprehension questions.

Previewing is often constructed so that classroom peers first preview a story passage and then listen as the student reads the passage back to them. The previewer may correct any errors that the student makes while he/she is reading. Students may then be tested for reading comprehension. In this type of intervention, the techniques of listening previewing and repeated readings are used in conjunction with each other. The student has additional opportunities to practice reading, which may aid in the understanding of the reading material.

It has also been suggested that increasing reading fluency may increase reading comprehension. The literature on reading reports a high correlation between reading fluency and reading comprehension (Jenkins & Jewell, 1993). Students who are fluent in reading are able to acquire information at a faster rate, which may result in less effort exerted for reading and reading comprehension (Skinner, 1998). In addition, if a student is able to read quickly he/she may be able to devote more cognitive resources to comprehending the material (LaBerg & Samuels, 1974).

There have also been many cognitive interventions described in the literature that have been used to increase reading comprehension. These strategies generally consist of having students acquire information from the reading using methods that require them to think or question different elements in their reading assignment, such as predicting story elements (Shapiro, 1996).

Postreading Interventions

There have been several interventions described in the literature regarding postreading techniques. These techniques are implemented to increase reading comprehension once the assigned reading has already been completed.

One postreading technique used to increase reading comprehension is contingent reinforcement (Sulzer-Azaraoff & Mayer, 1986). Accurate responses to comprehension questions can be reinforced in the classroom with tangible rewards (such as school supplies), free time (2-minute "break"), or special errands for the teacher, to name a few. One technique to set up a contingent reinforcement program in the classroom is to have students work at meeting a goal such as exceeding a previous reading comprehension accuracy score. Thus, educators would have to assign students a reading passage, let the students know their previous goal, and ask them to try to reach or exceed their previous goal. Students could then choose a reward based on obtaining or exceeding their accuracy goal.

Not only can the contingent reinforcement technique be used with an individual student exhibiting problems with reading comprehension, but the same technique may also be used in a classwide intervention to increase reading comprehension. Educators may provide a group goal (or group contingency) that the whole class (or varying numbers of the class) must obtain in order to earn a group reward. Educators or practitioners could put different goals, different percentages of the class, and different reinforcers on slips of paper and then place the slips of paper into different containers. The educator may then randomly select the goal the class must meet or exceed on their reading comprehension questions in order to earn the randomly drawn rewards. The percentage or number of students that must obtain this goal may also be randomly selected from slips of paper that are placed in a container.

Increasing reading comprehension may also be demonstrated using corrective feedback provided by either educators or peers in the classroom. The student is asked to read a passage aloud to the educator or peer, who follows along while the student is reading. If the student makes a mistake in the passage, the person chosen to provide feedback will correct the student's mistake while he/she is reading. The educator or peer may also use corrective feedback if the student is stumbling or spending too much time trying to pronounce a word. The student may then be asked to repeat the correct word back to the educator and/or provide the correct word in its phrase. The student may be instructed to repeat the word or the words in its phrase a few times (e.g., three times) back to the educator or peer.

As some of the different techniques described above suggest, peer tutoring has also been used successfully in increasing reading comprehension (Fuchs, Fuchs, Mathes, & Simmons, 1997). Peer tutoring may provide constructive performance feedback for those students exhibiting reading comprehension deficits. Using a peer tutor may also alleviate the burden on teachers to provide individual instruction to all students exhibiting deficits in reading comprehension. Some interventions described above may be modified so that a peer tutor may take the place of the educator or teacher providing assistance. In reading comprehension interventions, such as repeated readings, a student may read aloud to a peer tutor while the peer tutor follows along and provides corrective feedback. A peer tutor may also preview reading passages with the student and engage the student in dialogue regarding central themes such as main events, story endings, or characterization.

To increase students' reading comprehension many of these interventions have been used either separately or together.

The educator must determine what intervention or combination of interventions would be most beneficial to the individual student.

See also: Dyslexia

BIBLIOGRAPHY

Fuchs, D., Fuchs, L. S., Mathes, P. H., & Simmons, D. C. (1997). Peer-assisted strategies: Making classrooms more responsive to diversity. *American Educational Research Journal, 34*, 174–206.

Idol-Maestas, L., & Croll, V. J. (1987). The effects of training in story mapping procedures on the reading comprehension of poor readers. *Learning Disability Quarterly, 10*, 214–229.

Jenkins, J. R., & Jewell, M. (1993). Examining the validity of two measures for formative teaching: Reading aloud and maze. *Exceptional Children, 59*, 421–432.

LaBerg, D., & Samuels, S. J. (1974). Toward a theory of automatic information processing in reading. *Cognitive Psychology, 6*, 293–323.

Shapiro, E. S. (1996). *Academic skills problems: Direct assessment and intervention* (2nd ed.). New York: Guilford.

Sindelar, P. T., & Stoddard, K. (1991). Teaching reading to mildly disabled students in regular classes. In G. Stoner, M. R. Shinn, & H. M. Walker (Eds.), *Intervention for achievement and behavior problems* (pp. 357–378). Washington, DC: National Association of School Psychologists.

Skinner, C. H. (1998). Preventing academic skill deficits. In T. S. Watson & F. M. Gresham (Eds.), *Handbook of child behavior therapy* (pp. 61–82). New York: Plenum.

Sulzer-Azaroff, B., & Mayer, G. R. (1986). *Achieving educational excellence using behavioral strategies.* New York: Holt, Rinehart, & Winston.

Additional Readings for Nonprofessionals

Dawson, P. (1998). Reading to read: An intervention strategy combining CBM and repeated readings. In A. S. Canter & S. A. Carroll (Eds.), *Helping children at home and school: Handouts from your school psychologist* (pp. 203–204). Washington, DC: National Association of School Psychologists.

Vaughn, S., Bos, C. S., & Schumm, J. S. (2000). *Teaching exceptional diverse, and at-risk students in the general education classroom.* Boston: Allyn & Bacon.

www.indstate.edu/soe/blumberg

Additional Readings for Professionals

Baker, S., Gersten, R., & Grossen, B. (2002). Interventions for students with reading comprehension problems. In M. R. Shinn, H. M. Walker, & G. Stoner (Eds.), *Interventions for academic and behavior problems. II: Preventive and remedial approaches.* Washington, DC: National Association of School Psychologists.

Shapiro, E. S. (1996). *Academic skills problems: Direct assessment and intervention* (2nd ed.). New York: Guilford.

JENNIFER T. FREELAND
JENNIFER A. RENN

CURRICULUM-BASED MEASUREMENT OF READING SKILLS

Curriculum-based measurement (CBM) is a set of standardized and specific measurement procedures that can be used to quantify student performance in the basic academic skill areas of reading, spelling, mathematics computation, and written expression. As a variant of curriculum-based assessment (CBA), CBM uses the general education curriculum as the basis for test development and is designed primarily as a measurement and evaluation system that school psychologists and teachers can routinely use to monitor individual student progress and instructional effectiveness.

CBM differs from other forms of CBA in a number of important ways (Fuchs & Deno, 1991). First, the focus of CBM is on broad long-term goal objectives, rather than short-term objectives. With CBM, practitioners specify what they hope students will achieve by year's end. These long-term objectives structure the assessment process throughout the school year, as the same performance objective is continually assessed. Focusing on the broad goals of the curriculum, rather than a series of short-term objectives, allows CBM to attend to the assessment of more general integrated outcomes as they occur in context. The result of such measurement focuses the attention of the assessment on the broader desired outcome of instruction. This is in contrast to more mastery- or criterion-referenced approaches, whereby the assessment material changes, with each new short-term objective requiring the curriculum to be decomposed and compartmentalized for assessment. Second, because it focuses on broad aspects of the curriculum, CBM allows for the assessment of retention and generalization of learning. Using a domain sampling approach to test development, CBM draws on a broad domain of skills representing the current instructional focus, as well as those representing past and future instructional targets. As a result, CBM produces performance indicators that assess current learning in addition to the retention and generalization of previously mastered material. A third distinguishing feature of CBM is that it specifies the measurement and evaluation procedures to be used, including methods for generating test stimuli, administering and scoring tests, and summarizing and making inference from the data collected. This again is in contrast to other forms of CBA where the administration and scoring, as well as test development procedures, are not standardized and left up to the will of the examiner. Using standardized administration and scoring procedures allows for comparison of scores across students, as well as the comparison of scores within students across time.

The process of assessing reading using CBM contains three primary design features: (a) constructing the measurement materials or reading probes as they are often referred to, (b) administering and scoring the reading probes, and (c) organizing the data and decision making. The collective use of these design features can be used for both survey level assessments and monitoring progress over time. Survey level assessment involves the summative assessment of a student's reading skills up and down the reading curriculum with the goal of determining what level of material the student has mastered, what level is instructional, and what level appears frustrational. Once these levels are determined, progress monitoring then involves the formative assessment of a student's reading skill over time with reading materials of relatively consistent difficulty.

To develop measurement materials for use in the survey level assessment of reading, three equivalent reading passages are constructed at each grade level (generally grades 1 through 6). Each reading passage should be of approximately 150–200 words in length (although early grades can be shorter) and should be selected from narrative text only. Expository text or text such as poetry, plays, or songs should not be used for assessment. Although some prefer to simply randomly select text from all possible reading materials in a given year, recent research suggests that the text should probably be purposively sampled and controlled for readability and/or difficulty (Hintze & Shapiro, 1997; Hintze, Shapiro, & Lutz, 1994). This is because the difficulty of text varies considerably within a given grade level and there is no assurance that text selected from a third-grade-level reader will be of third-grade-level reading difficulty. Determining the readability of reading passages can be accomplished with the use of current computer technology as most word processing programs have some form of readability calculation capabilities. In addition to word processors, a number of stand-alone software packages are available that perform the calculations. In developing assessment materials, it is suggested that reading passages with readabilities within the middle half of the year being assessed be selected. For example, passages at the third-grade level with readabilities of 3.3 to 3.7 would be most suitable for assessment. To facilitate assessment, two copies of each passage should be made—one for the student to read from and the other for the examiner to follow along with that has a running word count along the side to aid in scoring.

In administering the CBM reading assessment, the practitioner should begin with the three probes developed for the grade level in which the student is currently placed. The student is asked to read each reading passage aloud while the examiner follows along noting errors (e.g., omissions, substitutions, additions, hesitations, etc.). At the end of 1 minute, the student is asked to stop reading and the examiner quickly scores the reading passage for the number of words read correctly per minute. The second and third reading passages within the grade level are then administered in exactly the same fashion. Once all three reading passages are administered and scored, the median number of words read correctly across the three passages is noted. Using placement standards, the examiner then determines whether the student's reading skills at that grade level are at a mastery, instructional, or frustrational level. The survey level assessment then proceeds with the examiner moving up and/or down grade levels until the three placement standards are determined (i.e., mastery, instructional, frustrational). The results of the survey level assessment should provide an indication of the level in reading where instruction would be most profitable. Generally, this is the level at which the student read at an instructional pace.

In addition to summatively assessing a student's reading skills up and down the curriculum at one point in time, CBM can also be used to formatively monitor the progress of reading development over time. As previously noted, CBM progress monitoring uses reading passages that are selected from long-term goal level material (e.g., the material the student is expected to be able to read comfortably in 1 year's time). Results of the survey level assessment are often helpful in determining goal level material. For example, if a fourth-grade student was found to be instructional at the second-grade level, using fourth-grade material to monitor his/her progress would likely result in little growth because of the fact that the material was too difficult (i.e., frustrational level). Likewise, monitoring the student's growth in second-grade material may be too easy and result in a ceiling effect, again being insensitive to growth over time as a result of instruction. In this case, the material used for instruction would most likely be of third-grade-level difficulty. Although this material might be above the student's assessed instructional level, it represents the material most likely to be sensitive to growth over time.

Developing CBM reading assessment materials follows the same process as that used during survey level assessment, with the exception that rather than developing 3 passages per grade level, upwards of 20 to 30 passages are developed at each grade level. In administering the reading probes, CBM progress monitoring involves only a 1-minute sample at each progress monitoring session (i.e., only one reading probe is administered rather than three). Doing so allows the examiner to assess the reading progress of a student twice a week for 10 to 15 weeks. In addition to collecting data, an extremely important aspect of progress monitoring is graphing the data in a time series fashion. Without a graphic display of the data, decisions about a student's progress are difficult. For most purposes, a simple equal-interval graph is used, with calendar day noted on the horizontal axis, and oral reading rate scaled along the vertical axis. With progress monitoring, decisions regarding performance are indexed to the amount of growth observed over time (i.e., formative assessment), rather than to some benchmark standard as is done in survey level assessment (i.e., summative assessment). Growth over time is usually indexed using ordinary least-squares regression, although easier techniques can also be used (e.g., split-middle techniques). Regardless of the method used, the primary goal of CBM progress

monitoring in reading is to make instructionally relevant decisions regarding the growth of a student's reading skills over time.

BIBLIOGRAPHY

Fuchs, L. S., & Deno, S. L. (1991). Paradigmatic distinctions between instructionally relevant measurement models. *Exceptional Children, 57,* 488–500.

Hintze, J. M., & Shapiro, E. S. (1997). Curriculum-based measurement and literature-based reading: Is curriculum-based measurement meeting the needs of changing reading curricula? *Journal of School Psychology, 35,* 351–375.

Hintze, J. M., Shapiro, E. S., & Lutz, J. G. (1994). The effects of curriculum on the sensitivity of curriculum-based measurement in reading. *The Journal of Special Education, 28,* 188–202.

Additional Readings for Nonprofessionals

Shapiro, E. S. (1996). *Academic skills problems: Direct assessment and intervention* (2nd ed.). New York: Guilford.

Shinn, M. R. (Ed.). (1989). *Curriculum-based measurement: Assessing special children.* New York: Guilford.

Additional Reading for Professionals

Shinn, M. R. (Ed.). (1998). *Advanced applications of curriculum-based measurement.* New York: Guilford.

JOHN M. HINTZE

READING RECOGNITION IN STUDENTS WITH LEARNING DISABILITIES

The act of reading requires students to be able to make sense of a group of symbols on a page and then interpret the meaning of those symbols. These symbols are actually sequences of letters that first must be translated into sounds and then into words. To translate letters into sounds, a student must have a conscious awareness of the sound structure of words and the ability to manipulate sounds into words. This ability is referred to as phonological awareness, which is a prerequisite to a student's ability to comprehend what he/she has read. When a student has phonological awareness, he/she is likely to be a successful reader. Students who cannot manipulate sounds into words are said to have difficulty with fluency (they stumble with words on a page or skip words altogether). Without fluency, it is extremely difficult for students to draw meaning from, or comprehend, what they are reading. When the problem is significant, the student may be identified as learning disabled in reading recognition.

Assessment of Reading Skills

Reading assessments are done to determine a student's current reading ability. Specific strengths and weaknesses, which are helpful when determining instructional objectives, are identified. To ensure that assessments are valid, multiple assessment procedures, including standardized tests, observations, and informal inventories, should be used (Mercer & Mercer, 1993). Each of these types of assessment procedures is then used to develop the student's reading profile.

Standardized Achievement and Reading Survey Tests

Standardized achievement tests, such as the Terra Nova, do one of two things: they compare a student's reading ability to a large group of similar students or they describe the student's performance, rather than compare it in an effort to determine what specific instructional objectives the student has mastered. They are typically used to provide an overall measure of reading achievement. Reading survey tests, such as the Woodcock Reading Mastery Tests, are typically utilized as basic screening measures and can help determine which students are experiencing problems in reading and need further testing (Mercer & Mercer, 1993).

Diagnostic Tests

Unlike achievement and reading survey tests, diagnostic tests allow the teacher to find out how the student attempts to read by pinpointing the student's strengths and weaknesses in the various subskills of reading (Carnine, Silbert, & Kameenui, 1997). Examples of diagnostic tests include profiling reading strengths and weaknesses, identifying students' errors in reading performance, and determining students' prerequisite knowledge and skill deficits.

Criterion-Referenced Tests

While norm-referenced tests compare performance among students, criterion-referenced reading tests (e.g., The Brigance Diagnostic Inventory of Basic Skills, The Classroom Learning Screening Manual, and The Multilevel Academic Skills Inventory) describe student performance according to fixed criteria. For example, the teacher is able to determine, through criterion-referenced testing, whether the student has mastered recognition of the prefix un as in undress or untied.

Informal Reading Assessment

Examining a student's daily work or giving teacher-made tests is known as informal assessment. The teacher can utilize the measures to determine student strengths and weaknesses and to chart progress. Specific types of informal assessment include graded word lists, informal reading inventories, and curriculum-based measurement.

Strategies for Teaching Reading Recognition

The most significant part of selecting appropriate instructional approaches for students with learning disabilities in reading recognition is to understand the student's reading profile. This profile is determined through a battery of assessments (discussed above) that determines the students' needs, their strengths and weaknesses, and what skills require more work. Once it has been determined that the student needs work with reading mechanics, the teacher will develop instructional objectives utilizing one of the code-emphasis developmental reading methods. Some of the more popular approaches are described below.

Phonics Approach

Through the phonics approach, the student learns to associate speech sounds with letter sounds. This is known as grapheme–phoneme associations. The student is taught consonants and blends, and learns to sound out words by blending the two. Many researchers suggest that children need to know phonics or letter–sound correspondence to learn to read text successfully (Mercer & Mercer, 1993). One advantage of the phonics approach for learning disabled students is that it is considered a bottoms-up approach, meaning that students learn a strategy during the beginning of reading instruction and continue to build on that strategy. Instruction is efficient because it allows the teacher to present the maximum number of skills in the minimum amount of time (Carnine et al., 1997).

Linguistic Method

Words are taught in word families with words that have similar spelling patterns. Word-by-word recognition is encouraged. Students are taught that reading is talk written down. The linguistic approach has been found to be effective with older students who have had difficulty with the phonics approach. Another advantage of the approach is that it quickly facilitates the development of a sight word vocabulary. One disadvantage is that students may continue to have difficulty analyzing unfamiliar words.

Multisensory Approach

This approach is often utilized with the phonics and the linguistic methods. It is based on the belief that students learn best when information is presented in several modalities. The multisensory approach utilizes tracing, hearing, writing, and seeing, which are integrated into instruction. This approach is often referred to as the VAKT, or the visual–auditory–kinesthetic–tactile method. Advantages of this approach are that it is effective for a wide variety of learning styles and that it is developmentally appropriate for very young readers. One disadvantage would be the need for a myriad of teaching tools needed for instruction.

Detecting a Learning Disability in Reading

Most students with learning disabilities are identified in second or third grade, because that is the time when independent reading is generally required in school. By the time a student is referred for assessment, there are often significant problems with coding, sequencing, categorizing, organizing, or memorizing (Rodis, Garrod, & Boscardin, 2001). One of the tenets of remediating learning problems is that the earlier the intervention, the more likely the success of the intervention. Parents should be sure to take advantage of preschool screening and should listen to their children read in an effort to be aware of their child's ability to recognize weekly word assignments. If problems are suspected, parents should meet with their child's teacher to discuss their child's progress and to refer their child for initial screening when problems begin to occur.

BIBLIOGRAPHY

Carnine, D. W., Silbert, J., & Kameenui, E. J. (1997). *Direct instruction reading.* Upper Saddle River, NJ: Prentice–Hall.

Mercer, C. D., & Mercer, A. R. (1993). *Teaching students with learning problems.* New York: Merrill.

Rodis, P., Garrod, A., & Boscardin, M. L. (2001). *Learning disabilities and life stories.* Boston: Allyn & Bacon.

Additional Reading for Nonprofessionals

Hardman, M. L., Drew, C. J., & Egan, M. W. (1999). *Human exceptionality: Society, school, and family.* Boston: Allyn & Bacon.

Additional Reading for Professionals

Bigge, J. L., & Stump, C. S. (1999). *Curriculum, assessment, and instruction for students with disabilities.* Belmont, CA: Wadsworth.

SANDY D. DEVLIN

Relational Aggression

It has been well established that aggression predicts peer rejection, negative social adjustment, and long-term adjustment in children. Recently, considerable focus has been placed on distinguishing forms of aggression with two distinct types exhibited by children, Overt Aggression and Relational Aggression. Overt Aggression is defined as physical manifestation of aggression (e.g., hitting, kicking, physical gestures of threats). Relational Aggression is defined as manifestation of aggression in a manner that harms another's interpersonal relationships (e.g., social exclusion, spreading rumors, disrupting friendships). Relational Aggression is sometimes referred to as social aggression, covert aggression, and indirect aggression, although the constructs and definitions of these terms vary slightly from researcher to researcher. Contrary to previous research that indicated that boys are more aggressive than girls, when definitions and descriptors of both types of aggression are used, girls are identified by peers as aggressive as often as boys (Henington, Hughes, Cavell, & Thompson, 1998).

Given the implications of Relational Aggression, researchers have for the past decade, conducted studies to further our understanding of this important correlate of children's current and future adjustment. It appears that both girls and boys engage in Relational Aggression, but the research is inconsistent as to whether there are gender differences in its manifestation and effects. Generally, girls are found to use Relational Aggression slightly more and to find it slightly more distressing than do boys. Most studies indicate that the gender differences increase across children's age with greater differences as children mature. Often these differences are the result of the type of measurement conducted (French, Jansen, & Pidada, 2002).

Research shows that children who exhibit Relational Aggression experience a wide range of distress (e.g., internalizing problems, externalizing problems, social-psychological adjustment difficulties), are more likely to be rejected by their peers, and are at risk for future maladjustment (Crick, Grotpeter, & Bigbee, 2002). In addition, Crick and colleagues' findings are similar for boys and girls, and that relative to Overt Aggression, Relational Aggression has a unique impact on children's adjustment. This relationship is true for the perpetrators of, as well as for those who are the victims of, Relational Aggression (Prinstein, Boergers, & Vernberg, 2001).

Although much of the literature suggests similarities between Relational Aggression and Overt Aggression across gender, there are differences. For example, Prinstein et al. (2001) state that Relational Aggression is associated with diagnostic descriptors of Oppositional Defiant Disorder and Conduct Disorder for girls but not for boys. Henington et al. (1998) found that high levels of Overt Aggression rarely occur in elementary-school-age girls without similarly high levels of Relational Aggression. This relationship was not found for boys. Crick et al. (2002) reported that instances of aggression that are interpersonal (e.g., Relational Aggression) are reported as more distressing by girls than by boys.

Modeling, tutoring, and peer pressure have all been found to be related, potentially as a causal factor, to aggression. Crick et al. (2002) explain aggression from a social information processing perspective in that children perceive cues from the actions of others in their environment; these cues then guide the child's behavior. Furthermore, Crick indicates that for girls, Relational Aggression may be more distressing than for boys. Another perspective may be to view the consequences of Relational Aggression for the aggressor. When children engage in Relational Aggression, they are modeling a specific type of aggression. When this aggression leads to desired outcomes (e.g., another child expresses distress, the child stops an annoying behavior), that form of aggression is more likely to occur in the future. Therefore, the aggression increases and is used in the future. From a discrimination perspective, if girls express greater distress from Relational Aggression than do boys, then a child (regardless of gender) may be more likely to use Relational Aggression with a girl than with a boy in the future.

Much remains to further our understanding of Relational Aggression and its impact on both those who engage in this type of aggression and those who are victims of Relational Aggression. For example, little is known about the specific changes in the manifestation and impact of Relational Aggression on children long term. In addition, there has been little research conducted to determine effective interventions for Relational Aggression.

See also: Conduct Disorder; Oppositional Defiant Disorder; Peer Relations

BIBLIOGRAPHY

Crick, N. R., Grotpeter, J. K., & Bigbee, M. A. (2002). Relationally and physically aggressive children's intent attributions and feelings of distress for relational and instrumental peer provocations. *Child Development, 73*, 1134–1142.

French, D. C., Jansen, E. A., & Pidada, S. (2002). United States and Indonesian children's and adolescents' reports of relational aggression by disliked peers. *Child Development, 73*, 1143–1150.

Henington, C., Hughes, J. N., Cavell, T. A., & Thompson, B. (1998). The role of relational aggression in identifying aggressive boys and girls. *Journal of School Psychology, 36*, 457–477.

O'Donnell, A. S. (2002). Implementation and evaluation of a treatment program for relational aggression and victimization with preadolescent girls. *Dissertation Abstracts International, 63*(6B), 2996.

Prinstein, M. J., Boergers, J., & Vernberg, E. M. (2001). Overt and relational aggression in adolescents: Social-psychological adjustment of aggressors and victims. *Journal of Clinical Child Psychology, 4*, 479–491.

Additional Reading for Nonprofessionals

Taylor, J. (2002). *The girls' guide to friends: Straight talk for teens on making close pals, creating lasting ties, and being an all-around great friend.* New York: Crown.

Additional Readings for Professionals

Crick, N. R., & Grotpeter, J. K. (1995). Relational aggression, gender, and social-psychological adjustment. *Child Development, 66*, 710–722.

Crick, N. R., Werner, N. E., & Casas, J. F. (1999). Childhood aggression and gender: A new look at an old problem. In D. Bernstein (Ed.), *Gender and motivation* (pp. 75–141). Lincoln: University of Nebraska Press.

Nelson, D. A., & Crick, N. R. (2002). Parental psychological control: Implications for childhood physical and relational aggression. In B. K. Barber (Ed.), *Intrusive parenting: How psychological control affects children and adolescents* (pp. 161–189). Washington, DC: American Psychological Association.

CARLEN HENINGTON

Retention

Grade retention refers to the practice of requiring a student who has been in a given grade level for a full school year to remain at that same grade level in the subsequent school year. Grade retention is also referred to as *nonpromotion, flunking, being retained,* and *being held back.* The practice of grade retention has become increasingly popular amid the current sociopolitical zeitgeist emphasizing educational standards and accountability. Grade retention has increased over the past 25 years, with recent estimates indicating that 7 to 9 percent of children in the United States are retained annually. This results in over 2.4 million children retained each year. National data indicate that 30–50 percent of students will be retained at least once by the ninth grade. However, the use of grade retention to address academic achievement and behavior problems is controversial, as evidence from research throughout the past century fails to support the practice of student retention as an effective intervention (Jimerson, 2001). Research provides essential information regarding (a) characteristics of retained students, (b) the effectiveness of grade retention, (c) long-term outcomes associated with grade retention, and (d) students' perspectives regarding grade retention.

CHARACTERISTICS OF RETAINED STUDENTS

Retained students generally have lower achievement relative to the average student in a classroom; however, there are typically grade-level peers who are equally low achieving but promoted. Clearly, it is important to consider other characteristics of retained students, as evidence indicates that low achievement alone is not a distinguishing characteristic among retained and promoted students. Research indicates that compared with equally low achieving and promoted peers, retained students do not have lower IQ scores. However, children who are retained are more likely to have mothers with lower IQ scores than a matched group of promoted children. Parents' involvement in school and their attitude toward their child's education also play a significant role in determining whether a student will be retained. Research also indicates that behavior problems are characteristic among retained students. Those students who are retained are often seen as being significantly less confident, less self-assured, less engaging, and more "immature" than their similarly low achieving peers. Teachers have also reported that the retained students were less popular and less socially competent than their peers. Finally, research has also delineated gender and ethnic characteristics of retained students, indicating that boys are twice as likely to repeat a grade as girls and that retention rates are higher for minority students (see Jimerson, Carlson, Rotert, Egeland, & Sroufe, 1997, for further discussion of characteristics of retained students). Thus, available research indicates that retained students are a diverse group of children with an assortment of challenges that influence low achievement and poor classroom adjustment.

EXAMINING THE EFFECTIVENESS OF GRADE RETENTION

Three meta-analyses provide a summary of studies of grade retention published between 1925 and 1999 (Holmes, 1989; Holmes & Matthews, 1984; Jimerson, 2001). Meta-analysis is a statistical procedure based on the concept of *effect size* (ES). Calculation of effect sizes allows researchers to systematically pool results across studies. Analyses resulting in a negative effect size suggest that an intervention (grade retention in this case) had a negative or harmful effect relative to the comparison groups of promoted students. In examining the effectiveness of grade retention, it is important to consider both academic achievement and social adjustment.

Effects on Academic Achievement

The convergence of research fails to demonstrate academic advantages for retained students relative to comparison groups of low-achieving promoted peers. For instance, the Holmes (1989) meta-analysis indicates that 54 studies yielded negative achievement effects for retained students. Of 9 studies that reported positive short-term achievement effects (during the repeated grade the following year), the benefits were shown to diminish over time and disappear in later grades (Holmes, 1989). The overall effect sizes for academic achievement outcomes in the Holmes and Matthews (1984) and Holmes (1989) meta-analyses were −.44 and −.19, respectively. The most recent meta-analysis examining 20 studies published between 1990 and 1999 (Jimerson, 2001) indicated that only 5 percent of the 169 analyses of academic achievement outcomes resulted in significant statistical differences favoring the retained students, whereas 47 percent resulted in significant statistical differences favoring the comparison groups of low-achieving peers. Of the analyses that did favor the retained students, two thirds of them reflected differences during the repeated year (e.g., second year in kindergarten). Moreover, these initial gains were not maintained over time. Analyses examining the effects of retention on language arts, reading, and math yielded moderate to strong negative effects (ES = −.36, −.54, −.49, respectively). These findings indicate that across published studies, the group of low-

achieving but promoted students outperformed the retained students in language arts, reading, and math. The overall average effect size across academic achievement outcomes was −.39 (Jimerson, 2001). In sum, the results of the meta-analyses of nearly 700 analyses of achievement, from over 80 studies during the past 75 years, fail to support the use of grade retention as an early intervention to enhance academic achievement.

Effects on Social and Behavioral Adjustment

Fewer studies have addressed the social and behavioral adjustment outcomes of retained students. The results of these studies indicate that grade retention fails to improve problem behaviors and can have harmful effects on socioemotional and behavioral adjustment as well. Holmes (1989) examined over 40 studies, including 234 analyses of socioemotional outcomes, and concluded that on average, the retained students displayed poorer social adjustment, more negative attitudes toward school, less frequent attendance, and more problem behaviors in comparison with groups of matched controls. Jimerson (2001) examined 16 studies that yielded 148 analyses of socioemotional adjustment outcomes of retained students relative to a matched comparison group of students and reported that 8 analyses resulted in statistical significance favoring the retained students and 13 analyses were statistically significant favoring the comparison group. The majority of analyses (86 percent) examining socioemotional outcomes indicated no significant differences between those students who were retained and low-achieving but promoted students. The overall average effect size across studies published between 1990 and 1999 was −.22. Furthermore, related research indicated that retained students may be teased or have difficulties with their peers. Overall, results of the meta-analyses of over 300 analyses of socioemotional and behavioral adjustment (from over 50 studies during the past 75 years) fail to support the use of grade retention as an early intervention to enhance socioemotional and behavioral adjustment.

LONG-TERM OUTCOMES ASSOCIATED WITH GRADE RETENTION

There is a considerable amount of literature examining high school dropout that identifies grade retention as an early predictor variable. In fact, grade retention has been identified as the single most powerful predictor of dropping out, even when controlling for other characteristics. A recent review of 17 studies examining factors associated with dropping out of high school prior to graduation suggests that grade retention is one of the most robust predictors of school dropout (Jimerson, Anderson, & Whipple, 2002). All studies of school dropout that included grade retention found that grade retention was associated with subsequent school withdrawal. Several of these studies included statistical analyses controlling for many individual and family level variables commonly associated with dropping out (e.g., socioemotional adjustment, SES, ethnicity, achievement, gender, parental level of education, and parental involvement). Research indicates that retained students are between 2 and 11 times more likely to drop out during high school than non-retained students and that grade retention increases the risk of dropping out by between 20 and 50 percent. The available research indicates that early failure (grade retention) is highly associated with the ultimate school failure (dropping out).

In addition to increasing the likelihood of dropping out of high school, grade retention is associated with other long-term negative outcomes. Although there are few studies examining the long-term effects of grade retention, one prospective longitudinal study followed children for 21 years (Jimerson, 1999). This study provides evidence that retained students have a greater probability of poorer educational and employment outcomes during late adolescence. Specifically, retained students had lower levels of academic adjustment at the end of 11th grade, were more likely to drop out of high school by age 19, and were less likely to receive a diploma by age 20. They were also less likely to be enrolled in a postsecondary education program, received lower education/employment status ratings, were paid less per hour, and received poorer employment competence ratings at age 20 in comparison to a group of low-achieving students. Results from other longitudinal samples yield similar findings, suggesting poorer long-term outcomes for retained students relative to a comparison group of low-achieving but promoted students.

STUDENTS' PERSPECTIVES REGARDING GRADE RETENTION

It is also valuable to consider children's perspectives regarding grade retention. In a study published in 1987, children (first-, third-, and sixth-grade students) were asked to rate 20 stressful life events that included such occurrences as losing a parent, going to the dentist, and getting a bad report card. The results indicated that sixth-grade students reported only the loss of a parent and going blind as more stressful than grade retention. This study was replicated in 2001 and it was found that sixth-grade students rated grade retention as the single most stressful life event, higher than both the loss of a parent and going blind (Anderson, Jimerson, & Whipple, 2002). A developmental trend was noted in both studies, with the reported stress of grade retention increasing from the first to the third, and then to the sixth grade. Thus, research indicates that children perceive grade retention as extremely stressful.

SUMMARY

Cumulative evidence emerging from research during the past century that examines the effectiveness of grade retention consistently indicates the potential for negative outcomes. Considering this cumulative research evidence, it is important to consider evidence-based alternatives to promote the social and cognitive competence of children at risk of academic failure.

See also: Academic Interventions for Written Language and Grammar

BIBLIOGRAPHY

Anderson, G. E., Jimerson, S. R., & Whipple, A. D. (2002). *Students' ratings of stressful experiences at home and school: Loss of a parent and grade retention as superlative stressors.* Manuscript in preparation, University of California, Santa Barbara.

Holmes, C. T. (1989). Grade-level retention effects: A meta-analysis of research studies. In L. A. Shepard & M. L. Smith (Eds.), *Flunking grades: Research and policies on retention* (pp. 16–33). London: Falmer.

Holmes, C. T., & Matthews, K. M. (1984). The effects of nonpromotion on elementary and junior high school pupils: A meta-analysis. *Reviews of Educational Research, 54,* 225–236.

Jimerson, S. R. (1999). On the failure of failure: Examining the association between early grade retention and education and employment outcomes during late adolescence. *Journal of School Psychology, 37,* 243–272.

Jimerson, S. R. (2001). Meta-analysis of grade retention research: Implications for practice in the 21st century. *School Psychology Review, 30,* 420–437.

Jimerson, S. R., Anderson, G. E., & Whipple, A. D. (2002). Winning the battle and losing the war: Examining the relation between grade retention and dropping out of high school. *Psychology in the Schools, 39,* 441–457.

Jimerson, S. R., Carlson, E., Rotert, M., Egeland, B., & Sroufe, L. A. (1997). A prospective, longitudinal study of the correlates and consequences of early grade retention. *Journal of School Psychology, 35,* 3–25.

Additional Readings for Nonprofessionals

Alexander, K., Entwisle, D., & Dauber, S. (1994). *On the success of failure: A reassessment of the effects of retention in the primary grades.* New York: Cambridge University Press.

Shepard, L. S., & Smith, M. L. (1989). *Flunking grades: Research and policies on retention.* London: Falmer.

Additional Readings for Professionals

Ferguson, P., Jimerson, S., & Dalton, M. (2001). Sorting out successful failures: Exploratory analyses of factors associated with academic and behavioral outcomes of retained students. *Psychology in the Schools, 38,* 327–342.

Jimerson, S. R., Ferguson, P., Whipple, A. D., Anderson, G. E., & Dalton, M. J. (2002). Exploring the association between grade retention and dropout: A longitudinal study examining socio-emotional, behavioral, and achievement characteristics of retained students. *The California School Psychologist, 7,* 51–62.

Jimerson, S. R., & Kaufman, A. M. (in press). Reading, writing, and retention: A primer on grade retention research. *The Reading Teacher.*

Pianta, R. C., Tietbohl, P. J., & Bennett, E. M. (1997). Differences in social adjustment and classroom behavior between children retained in kindergarten and groups of age and grade matched peers. *Early Education and Development, 8,* 137–152.

SHANE R. JIMERSON

Rorschach Technique

The theory of personality underlying the Rorschach is that particular characteristics and patterns, whether maladaptive or adaptive, persist within the individual. The Rorschach technique attempts to identify some of these unconscious patterns by measuring deeper personality patterns and providing a psychological view of the *whole person*. Assessment instruments, such as the Rorschach, seek to uncover these hidden patterns and are referred to as projective personality assessment instruments. The Rorschach accomplishes this by exposing the person to pictures of vague inkblots. The inkblot does not form any picture; the image is determined by the person and his/her projections onto the inkblot (Rose, Kaser-Boyd, & Maloney, 2001).

The history of inkblot assessment has been quite controversial and lengthy. The earliest recorded discussion on the use of inkblots occurred in Germany in 1857 in a paper written by Justinus Kerner. Then in 1895, Alfred Binet observed that inkblots could be useful in examining childhood imagination. After Binet's observation, several other investigators in the United States and Europe also began to study inkblots. These included Dearborn (1897), Kirkpatrick (1900), Whipple (1910), and Parsons (1917). In 1917, Szymon Hens, a Polish psychiatrist, developed an inkblot test for his doctoral dissertation. This dissertation then prompted Hermann Rorschach to pursue his previous interest in the inkblot technique.

The Rorschach consists of 10 inkblots that were selected by Hermann Rorschach, the original creator of the Rorschach assessment instrument. Each inkblot is almost symmetrical and is centered on a piece of cardboard that is $6\,3/4'' \times 9\,1/2''$. Five of the cards are black-and-white prints, while the rest are in color. Two of the colored cards are only red-and-black. Each inkblot is unique in design, shading, texture, and color (Rose, Kaser-Boyd, & Maloney, 2001).

The Rorschach is administered individually in two phases. During the first phase, the psychologist records the responses verbatim. This phase typically lasts 10–15 minutes. During the second phase, the psychologist then asks the person to expand on the earlier response. This phase lasts approximately 20–30 minutes. The explanation of the response is then scored.

The Rorschach utilizes several scoring categories: (1) location, where on the print the response was seen; (2) determinants, the features of the inkblot that lead to the response; (3) form level, how well the response fits the inkblot; (4) content, the descriptions of the inkblot by the student; and (5) popularity of the response, the likelihood of others responding the same way (Levitt & Truumaa, 1972; Rose, Kaser-Boyd, & Maloney, 2001).

After the responses are recorded verbatim, the sequence of responses is charted and then scored. The frequency of the responses are recorded according to the total number of whole responses, movement responses, pure color responses, and special scores. Then the ratios, percentages, and derivations are calculated from these frequencies. These numbers are then used to reflect various psychological factors. This scoring procedure can take as long as 2 hours, depending on the complexity of the responses (Levitt & Truumaa, 1972; Rose, Kaser-Boyd, & Maloney, 2001).

The primary argument against the Rorschach technique is that its validity has not been clearly demonstrated owing to its nature as a projective test. Perhaps the most serious limitation is that the scoring of the Rorschach can be very subjective and may reveal as much about the test administrator as the person taking the test. Although a couple of studies have found that the Rorschach is conceptually valid when it is administered appropriately (Rose, Kaser-Boyd, & Maloney, 2001; Weiner, 1996), this does not mean that the instrument can be used in a meaningful manner for either diagnosis or treatment planning.

BIBLIOGRAPHY

Levitt, E. E., & Truumaa, A. (1972). *The Rorschach technique with children and adolescents: Application and norms.* New York: Grune & Stratton.

Rose, T., Kaser-Boyd, N., & Maloney, M. P. (2001). *Essentials of Rorschach assessment.* New York: Wiley.

Weiner, I. B. (1996). Some observations on the validity of the Rorschach inkblot method. *Psychological Assessment, 8,* 206–213.

Additional Readings for Professionals

Exner, J. E. (2000). *Rorschach workbook for the comprehensive system* (5th ed.). New York: Rorschach Workshop.

Exner, J. E., & Weiner, I. B. (1996). *The Rorschach: A comprehensive system* (3rd ed.). New York: Wiley.

Weiner, I. B. (1998). *Principles of Rorschach interpretation.* Mahwah, NJ: Erlbaum.

KIMBERLY R. HALL

Ss

School Refusal

School refusal behavior generally refers to a child-motivated refusal to attend school and/or difficulties remaining in classes for an entire day. The problem is thus a form of school absenteeism that focuses on child-based problems (i.e., not parent-based school withdrawal or family-based emergencies). Specifically, school refusal behavior refers to school-age youth who are completely or partially absent from school, who show severe morning behavior problems (e.g., tantrums, clinging, running away) to try to miss school, and/or who have great distress as they attend school during the day. The latter is often marked as well by somatic complaints and constant pleas for future nonattendance (Kearney & Silverman, 1996).

School refusal behavior may be differentiated from other terms commonly used to describe youth who are absent from school. School refusal, for example, often refers to anxiety-based school refusal behavior and does not cover all youth who miss school illicitly. School phobia refers to the minority of youth who miss school because of a specific fear, which may be one aspect of school refusal. In addition, some children display separation anxiety from parents or other caregivers that precludes school attendance. Finally, truancy refers to absence from school without parental knowledge, a condition often linked to juvenile delinquency or conduct disorder. The term school refusal behavior is meant to encompass all of these terms and all youth who refuse school for illegitimate reasons.

PREVALENCE AND CHARACTERISTICS

School refusal behavior is thought to affect about 5–28 percent of youth at one time during their developmental period (Kearney, 2001). The problem affects boys and girls fairly equally and does not seem closely tied to race or socioeconomic status, although school dropout rates do tend to be higher in minority-status and low-income families (see Absenteeism in this volume). School refusal behavior is marked by many different internalizing and externalizing behavior problems. Common internalizing behavior problems include anxiety, worry, depression, social withdrawal, fear, fatigue, and somatic complaints (especially stomachaches, headaches, nausea, vomiting, diarrhea, and shaking). Common externalizing behavior problems include tantrums, noncompliance, defiance, verbal and physical aggression, running away from school or home, clinging, crying, and refusal to move.

Kearney and Albano (in press) assessed 143 youth with primary school refusal behavior using structured diagnostic interviews. Youth were assessed at university-based specialized clinics for children and adolescents with school refusal behavior. On the basis of combined child and parent reports, separation anxiety disorder was the most common diagnosis in the sample (22.4 percent). Almost one third of the sample (32.9 percent) met criteria for no mental disorder however, meaning that many children with school attendance problems display such behaviors independent of more serious disorders. The remaining sample largely met criteria for generalized anxiety disorder (10.5 percent), oppositional defiant disorder (8.4 percent), major depression (4.9 percent), specific phobia (4.2 percent), social anxiety disorder (3.5 percent), conduct disorder (2.8 percent), attention-deficit/hyperactivity disorder (1.4 percent), panic disorder (1.4 percent), enuresis (0.7 percent), and post-traumatic stress disorder (0.7 percent). Of those youth who did receive a primary diagnosis, 45.8 percent received a second diagnosis, 17.7 percent received a third diagnosis, 6.3 percent received a fourth diagnosis, and 3.1 percent received a fifth diagnosis. The study reaffirmed the heterogeneity of youth with school refusal behavior.

274

Youth with school refusal behavior are also at risk for many short- and long-term consequences. In the short term, school refusal behavior can lead to significant child distress, family conflict, economic problems, declining grades, social alienation, legal difficulties, and friction with school officials. In the long term, school refusal behavior could lead to school dropout, restricted economic opportunities, and occupational and marital problems in adulthood. Long-term outcome studies of youth with school refusal behavior generally indicate that about one third will continue to have serious adjustment problems in adulthood, and another one third will continue to experience some adjustment problems. Overall, the shorter the duration of a child's school refusal behavior, the better his/her prognosis.

School refusal behavior may be triggered by any type of event, including family crises or transitions. Indeed, many cases of school refusal behavior are precipitated by moves to larger school districts or a child's move to a new school building. Regarding the latter, therefore, many children refuse to attend school when entering kindergarten, first grade, middle school, or high school for the first time. Other triggers to school refusal behavior reported in the literature include a school-related frightening event, threats to well-being at school, and changes in teachers or classes. In addition, many students report no clear precipitating event to school refusal behavior and are often as baffled about the situation as their parents and teachers.

CLASSIFICATION

Given the extensive heterogeneity of youth with school refusal behavior, it is perhaps not surprising that classification strategies for this population have also been quite varied. One traditional approach to classification has been to divide the population into those that are more anxiety-based and those that are more delinquent in their behavior. Thus, the dichotomy of school refusal/school phobia/separation anxiety versus truancy has often been espoused. Another traditional classification approach has been to divide the population into acute and chronic types, differentiating youth who refuse school for less than one calendar year and youth who refuse school for longer periods of time, a significant indicator of poor prognosis.

One problem with classifying youth with school refusal behavior according to forms of behavior is that great overlaps occur. For example, many children are anxious about school and subsequently skip classes without knowledge of their parents. Similarly, many youth are both depressed and display aspects of conduct disorder. To address this dilemma, Kearney and colleagues designed a functional model of school refusal behavior based on the primary reasons why children refuse to attend school. Specifically, youth are theorized to refuse school for one or more of the following reasons: (1) to avoid school-related stimuli that provoke a general sense of negative affectivity, (2) to escape aversive social and/or evaluative situations, (3) to pursue attention from significant others, and/or (4) to pursue tangible reinforcement outside of school. The first two functional conditions refer to youth who refuse school for negative reinforcement, or to avoid something noxious at school. The latter two functional conditions refer to youth who refuse school for positive reinforcement, or to obtain something more enticing outside of school. Of course, some youth refuse school for a combination of these reasons as well.

ASSESSMENT AND TREATMENT

Youth with school refusal behavior typically require a comprehensive assessment procedure to identify all the primary forms and functions of their behavior. This procedure often encompasses structured diagnostic interviews, questionnaires regarding internalizing and externalizing behavior problems, behavioral observations of the child and family in the morning and during the school day, and daily ratings of behavior (especially levels of anxiety, depression, and noncompliance). Information from school officials is crucial as well, including a child's past and present school attendance, social interactions, and academic performance and makeup work. In addition, information should be gathered about procedures and obstacles for reintegration into school, rules about absenteeism and related conduct, alternative educational programs, conflict between parents and school officials, and other information relevant to a particular case. Assessment regarding youth with school refusal behavior should involve as many people as possible, including the child, parents, school officials, pediatricians, dating partners, peers, and siblings.

Treatment for youth with school refusal behavior may be prescriptive, with a focus on tailoring treatment to the specific needs of a child and his/her family. This can be done in various ways, with the goal to gradually reintegrate a child into school and maintain full-time attendance without distress. Within a functional model, youth receive prescriptive treatment based on the primary reason they refuse school. For youth who refuse school to avoid stimuli that provoke negative affectivity or to escape aversive social/evaluative situations, child-based treatment focuses on psychoeducation, somatic control exercises to reduce physical symptoms of anxiety (e.g., tension-release relaxation training for shakiness), cognitive therapy to modify irrational thoughts, and gradual reexposure to school. For youth who refuse school for attention, parent-based treatment focuses on establishing daily routines and contingency management. For youth who refuse school for tangible reinforcement outside of school, family-based treatment focuses on contingency contracting to increase incentives for school attendance. Data indicate that a prescriptive treatment approach for this population is highly effective (Kearney & Silverman, 1999).

See also: Absenteeism; Anxiety

BIBLIOGRAPHY

Kearney, C. A. (2001). *School refusal behavior in youth: A functional approach to assessment and treatment*. Washington, DC: American Psychological Association.

Kearney, C. A., & Albano, A. M. (2000). *When children refuse school: A cognitive–behavioral therapy approach—Therapist guide*. San Antonio, TX: The Psychological Corporation.

Kearney, C. A., & Albano, A. M. (in press). The functional profiles of school refusal behavior: Diagnostic aspects. *Behavior Modification.*

Kearney, C. A., & Silverman, W. K. (1996). The evolution and reconciliation of taxonomic strategies for school refusal behavior. *Clinical Psychology: Science and Practice, 3*, 339–354.

Kearney, C. A., & Silverman, W. K. (1999). Functionally-based prescriptive and nonprescriptive treatment for children and adolescents with school refusal behavior. *Behavior Therapy, 30*, 673–695.

Additional Readings for Nonprofessionals

Kearney, C. A. (2003). *Casebook in child behavior disorders*. Belmont, CA: Wadsworth.

Kearney, C. A., & Albano, A. M. (2000). *When children refuse school: A cognitive–behavioral therapy approach—Parent workbook*. San Antonio, TX: The Psychological Corporation.

Additional Readings for Professionals

Chiland, C., & Young, J. G. (1990). *Why children reject school: Views from seven countries*. New Haven, CT: Yale University Press.

Kearney, C. A. (2002). Identifying the function of school refusal behavior: A revision of the School Refusal Assessment Scale. *Journal of Psychopathology and Behavioral Assessment, 24*, 235–245.

Kearney, C. A. (in press). Bridging the gap among professionals who address youth with school absenteeism: Overview and suggestions for consensus. *Professional Psychology: Research and Practice.*

CHRISTOPHER A. KEARNEY

School Threats: Legal Aspects

The Fifth Circuit Court of Appeals noted that the "epidemic of violence in American public schools is a relatively new phenomenon, but one that has already generated considerable caselaw" (*Johnson v. Dallas Indep. Sch. Dist.*, 1994, p. 199). In addressing school violence cases, courts have considered the legal duty of school personnel to exercise reasonable care to protect students from foreseeable harm (Hermann & Remley, 2000). Courts have found that students' acts of violence were foreseeable if students threatened to do harm. Accordingly, school personnel have responded to their legal obligation to ensure student safety by implementing policies such as *zero tolerance* for threatening behaviors. Though the constitutionality of some of these policies has been challenged, courts are supporting the efforts of school personnel as they work to prevent school violence.

Students disciplined for making threats of violence in school settings have alleged violations of their First Amendment right to freedom of expression. These student plaintiffs often cite the precedent-setting *Tinker* case in which the U.S. Supreme Court stated that students do not "shed their constitutional rights to freedom of speech or expression at the schoolhouse gate" (*Tinker v. Des Moines Indep. Community Sch. Dist.*, 1969, p. 506). However, courts consistently note that threats of physical violence are not protected under the U.S. Constitution (*Lovell v. Poway Unified Sch. Dist.*, 1994). Moreover, threats that present a "clear and present danger" have never been afforded First Amendment protection (Hermann & Remley, 2000, p. 433). Thus, in reaching decisions regarding alleged constitutional violations in the discipline of students who threatened to commit violent acts, courts have considered whether these threatening behaviors were indicative of serious threats to do harm.

Some courts have found that for a student's threat to be punishable, the threat must meet an objective "true threat" test (*Lovell v. Poway Unified Sch. Dist.*, 1994, p. 372). A true threat is a threat that a reasonable person would find to be a serious and unambiguous expression of intent to do harm considering the language of the threat, and the context in which the threat was made (Hermann & Remley, 2000). However, considering recent, highly publicized incidents of school violence, courts are more supportive of school personnel in their decisions to take all student threats seriously.

The case of *D. G. v. Independent School District No. 11, Tulsa County Oklahoma* (2000) illustrates the judiciary's current interpretation of the true-threat doctrine. In this case, the court upheld the suspension of an 11th-grade student who had written a poem about killing a teacher. Though the student convinced school personnel that she had written the poem to express her dissatisfaction with the teacher's actions and she never intended to do harm, the school had a zero tolerance policy for student threats. Accordingly, even though neither the teacher nor the school administrators believed that the threat was a true threat, the student was still suspended. The court held that the student's suspension was appropriate, while the threat was being investigated. However, the court added that once a psychologist determined that the threat was not a true threat, the school would be violating the student's constitutional rights if they did not allow her to return to school.

Similarly, a federal appeals court upheld the removal from school of a student who had written a poem that depicted a school shooting in which 28 people died and the shooter killed himself (*Lavine v. Blaine Sch. Dist.*, 2001). The student had told the school counselor that he had thought about committing suicide; the school counselor knew that the student was having serious problems at home; and the student's discipline record included an incident involving a fight. Considering these facts, the principal expelled the student. A psychiatrist evaluated the student and determined that the student was not a threat to others and that the student could safely return to school. Though the student was allowed to return to school, the student's father sued school personnel asserting that his son's removal from school had violated his son's constitutional rights. The court responded by expressing that recent school shootings have "put our nation on edge and have focused the attention of what school officials, law enforcement and others can do or could have done to prevent these kinds of tragedies" (*Lavine v. Blaine Sch. Dist.*, p. 987). The court also emphasized that "the school had a duty to prevent any potential violence on campus" (p. 989). Accordingly, the court held that school personnel acted reasonably by removing the student from school until a psychiatrist determined that the student was not a danger to himself or others.

Courts have also found that school personnel acted appropriately in removing students who threatened harm and when the students had also exhibited prior violent conduct. For example, a federal appeals court upheld a 15-year-old student's suspension for threatening to shoot her school counselor because she was dissatisfied with her schedule (*Lovell v. Poway Unified Sch. Dist.*, 1994). The student defended her actions by stating that she had merely used a figure of speech. The counselor reported that the student did not act in a physically threatening manner, yet the counselor reported that she did feel threatened by the student because the counselor had observed the student's volatile nature and lack of impulse control on other occasions. The court was further persuaded by the frequency of reported school violence incidence and expressed that "in light of the violence prevalent in schools today, school officials are justified in taking very seriously student threats against faculty or other students" (*Lovell v. Poway Unified Sch. Dist.*, p. 372).

Recently, a Pennsylvania district court held that a school acted responsibly in expelling a 15-year-old student who wrote a note stating "There's a Bomb in this School bang bang!!" (*Brian A. v. Stroudsburg Area Sch. Dist.*, 2001, p. 505). In reaching their decision, the court considered the fact that the student was on probation for blowing up a shed on the property of another school. The court found that the student's previous delinquent acts provided evidence of the seriousness of the student's threat.

It is noteworthy that although courts have supported the temporary removal from school of students who make threats, to date courts have been reluctant to find school officials

accountable for school violence. In August, 2000, a court dismissed the lawsuit filed against school personnel in the West Paducah, Kentucky, school shooting (Glaberson, 2000). In spite of evidence that the assailant showed other students his guns when he brought them to school and wrote homicidal and suicidal thoughts in school papers, the court held that only the perpetrator was responsible for the shooting. Similarly, in November 2001, a court dismissed the lawsuits against school officials brought by the families of victims in the Columbine school shooting (Kass, 2001). According to the pleadings in the case, the families had alleged that school officials were negligent in failing to recognize the warning signs from the student assailants. These warning signs included a videotape made for a video production class in which Harris and Klebold enacted a scenario in which they shot other students (McPhee, 2000). Furthermore, in school writing assignments, Harris and Klebold expressed their anger, intent to kill, and that they possessed firearms. The judge held that these warning signs were not enough to predict the impending violence. The victims' families plan to appeal the court's decision to dismiss the case (Kass, 2001).

Although courts are reluctant to hold school personnel liable for injuries sustained as a result of school violence, school personnel are still legally obligated to exercise reasonable care to protect students from foreseeable harm. If a student threatens to harm others, school personnel can be held responsible for injuries related to the student's acts of violence (Hermann & Remley, 2000). Thus, educators need to take appropriate precautions. According to recent school violence jurisprudence, these precautions include taking every threat of school violence seriously.

See also: Crisis Intervention; School Violence Prevention; Threat Assessment

BIBLIOGRAPHY

Brian A. v. Stroudsburg Area Sch. Dist., 141 F. Supp. 2d 502 (M.D. Pa. 2001).

D. G. v. Indep. Sch. Dist. No. 11 of Tulsa County Okla., 2000 U.S. Dist. LEXIS 12197 (N.D. Okla. 2000).

Glaberson, W. (2000, August 4). Judges dismiss civil suits in school killings. *The Times-Picayune*, p. A4.

Hermann, M. A., & Remley, T. P., Jr. (2000). Guns, violence, and schools: The results of school violence—litigation against educators and students shedding more constitutional rights at the school house gate. *Loyola Law Review, 46*, 389–439.

Johnson v. Dallas Indep. Sch. Dist., 38 F.3d 198 (5th Cir. 1994).

Kass, J. (2001, November 29). Columbine seeks closure—out of court. *The Christian Science Monitor*, p. 2.

Lavine v. Blaine Sch. Dist., 257 F.3d 981 (9th Cir. 2001).

Lovell v. Poway Unified Sch. Dist., 90 F.3d 367 (9th Cir. 1996).

McPhee, M. (2000, October 3). Lawsuits criticize teachers DeAngelis, others cited in new papers. *The Denver Post*, p. A06.

Tinker v. Des Moines Indep. Community Sch. Dist., 393 U.S. 503 (1969).

Additional Readings for Professionals

Hermann, M. A. (2002). An ethical and legal perspective on the role of school counselors in preventing violence in schools. *Professional School Counseling, 6*, 46–55.

Hermann, M. A., & Remley, T. P., Jr. (2000). Guns, violence, and schools: The results of school violence—litigation against educators and students shedding more constitutional rights at the school house gate. *Loyola Law Review, 46*, 389–439.

MARY A. HERMANN

School Violence Prevention

School violence is an alarming issue involving a range of negative behaviors that threaten the physical, psychological, and emotional well-being of all individuals on school campuses (National Association of School Psychologists, 2002). It includes low-level aggression such as teasing, harassment, and taunting; and high-level aggression such as physical intimidation and assaults. In its most extreme and visible form, school violence has involved school shootings (Furlong, Kingery, & Bates, 2001). Regardless of the form school violence takes, many questions arise: How much school violence is occurring? Why are students exhibiting such harmful behaviors? What are schools and communities doing to prevent this violence? This entry provides an overview of the prevalence of school violence and related prevention programs. School violence prevention efforts are discussed as being essential to creating safe and supportive school learning environments.

DEFINITION OF TERMS

Studies of school violence have variously used terms such as aggression, conflict, delinquency, conduct disorders, criminal behavior, antisocial behavior, and violence to describe this class of problem behaviors. Aggression is defined as behavior that is intended to harm or injure another. The harm may be physical, social, emotional, or material. There is reactive aggression/impulsive, which is in response to frustrating experiences, and proactive aggression, which is planned to obtain a utilitarian outcome. Another type is relational aggression, which involves harming social relationships through exclusion, such as gossip or spreading rumors. School violence includes all of these types of aggression when they occur on a school campus. Importantly, all types of aggression disrupt a school campus, but they may require different types of responses.

School violence occurs along a continuum of behavior and within a developmental framework. For example, aggressive behavior in younger children typically involves hitting, teasing, kicking, or name-calling. Older youths' behavior may become more serious, even criminal, and is characterized by bullying or physical fighting. More specific examples of aggressive behavior are assaults against other students and staff, sexual harassment, gang activity, and weapon possession. Criminal behaviors may include theft, property offenses, and vandalism. In addition, aggressive behaviors and their motivations differ between males and females; however, even though most serious school violence offenses are committed by males, female violence is increasing (Lamberg, 2002).

SCOPE AND PREVALENCE OF SCHOOL VIOLENCE

The public's perception of school violence is derived primarily from the intensive media attention given to school shootings such as those that occurred in Springfield, Oregon and Columbine, Colorado. This media attention reinforces a link between school violence and school shootings (Rose & Gallup, 2001). However, the level of risk for serious harm in school settings is low when compared with other social settings (the odds of a student dying at school was about 1 in 2 million during 1998–1999; Anderson et al., 2001). In addition, in general, violent crimes for youth aged 10–17 have decreased dramatically in the late 1990s. Despite the relative rarity of extreme forms of school violence, other forms of low-level violence, such as bullying (Nansel et al., 2001), are much more common, and consequently school violence continues to be a major concern for both the public and the educators (Rose & Gallup, 2001).

The incidence of school violence is assessed through state and national studies that draw upon sources such as crime reports, school disciplinary reports, and, most commonly, student self-report surveys. The two most widely used student surveys in the United States are the Center for Disease Control and Prevention's *Youth Risk Behavior Surveillance Survey* (YRBS) and the University of Michigan's *Monitoring the Future Survey* (MTF) (Bates, Furlong, Saxton, & Pavelski, 2002). These surveys explore risky behaviors, including violence- and injury-related incidents on school campuses nationwide among students in grades 9–12. On the basis of these student self-reports, the prevalence of key aggression-related incidents on school campuses is as follows:

1. Bullying, which is recurring physical and nonphysical intimidation of a student by a more powerful student, can have highly negative developmental effects on both the bully and the victim. It is the most common form of school violence and occurs regularly in almost all schools across the United States. In a national study, Nansel et al. (2001) found that bullying involves nearly

30 percent of middle and high school students—13 percent as bullies, 11 percent as victims, and 6 percent as both bully and victim. It occurs most often among males and students in grades 6–8.

2. Physical fights on school property in the past 12 months declined from 16.2 to 14.2 percent (12.3 percent decrease) between 1993 and 1999 (Brenner et al., 1999).

3. The possession of any weapon on school property dropped from 11.8 to 6.9 percent (a 41.3 percent reduction) between 1993 and 1999 (Brenner et al., 1999).

4. Finally, even with increased awareness of school shooting tragedies, school-associated violent deaths between 1992–93 (55 deaths; first-year data available) and 1999–00 (12 deaths; Anderson et al., 2001) declined by 78.2 percent.

These are very promising trends and reflect the concerted efforts of many school districts to increase school safety. However, a U.S. national education goal is to completely eliminate violence on school campuses, and therefore, efforts to reduce its occurrence continue (National Education Goals Panel, 1999).

RISK FACTORS FOR AGGRESSION/VIOLENCE AND PREVENTION STRATEGIES

In developing school safety programs, a first step toward preventing school violence is to identify and understand the individual and social factors that place children and youths at risk for violent victimization and perpetration (Dwyer, Osher, & Warger, 1998). These influences include *individual* (e.g., history of aggression, beliefs supportive of violence, and impulsivity); *family* (e.g., poor caregiver monitoring, poor attachment to caregivers, and exposure to family violence); *peer/school* (e.g., associating with aggressive students, peer rejection, and low school engagement); and *neighborhood* factors (e.g., poverty, availability of weapons, and transiency). In addition, the U.S. Secret Service and the U.S. Department of Education (2002) carefully examined 37 school shooting incidents carried out by students on school campuses in the United States between 1974 and 2000. It was found that school shooters did not have common psychological profiles or common life risk experiences. Nearly half of these students received As or Bs in the classes and about two out of three had no or few discipline problems. What this federal study found, however, was that many school shooters had been bullied at school and nearly all of them had experienced a difficult loss, with many of them being suicidal. Although coming from various backgrounds and having various prior experiences, these youths seem to have planned these attacks as a way to cope with the loss they had experienced.

The link between bullying as the most prevalent form of school violence and school shootings provides further motivation for schools to implement prevention programs that seek to support students in need and to provide them with alternatives to violence.

PREVENTION AND INTERVENTION PROGRAMS

In the late 1990s, one initial response to concerns about school violence was to take a *get-tough* approach and to implement *zero tolerance* discipline strategies. Any occurrence of school weapons possession, drug use, or aggressive threats was immediate grounds for suspension from school. As evidence has been collected, however, it was shown that such strict, inflexible disciplinary responses alone do not reduce the threat of school violence and may create a negative school climate (Skiba & Noam, 2002). In an attempt to balance concerns about school security and to help promote positive, caring school climates (Furlong, Paige, & Osher, 2003), school violence prevention strategies increasingly have taken a school–community perspective. They have also attempted to address the needs of *all* students, not just those who have violated school rules or appear to pose a threat.

Successful school violence intervention and prevention efforts consider school and individual needs as well as the multiple contexts within which violence occurs (Dwyer & Osher, 2000). Some of the school violence prevention programs with evidence supporting their effectiveness and which are being used by many school districts include (see Furlong, Pavelski, & Saxton, 2002) the following:

Families and Schools Together is a comprehensive, multilevel primary and early intervention program for students grades 1–5 who are at risk for developing aggressive behavior. The school-based program teaches students effective conflict resolution/interpersonal problem-solving skills, emotional competence, such as empathy and communication, and prosocial skill developments. Teachers, counselors, psychologists, and other mental health professionals provide additional services through consultation and education. The home-based program provides parent education through modeling and training of appropriate interpersonal skills for students and their families.

The *Second Step Program* (Committee for Children, 2003) is another comprehensive program that provides a schoolwide curriculum for assisting elementary and middle school students in developing skills related to empathy, impulse control, social problem-solving, assertiveness, and anger management. The Second Step Program has been found to decrease school aggressive behaviors while increasing prosocial behaviors.

Life Skills Training concerns substance abuse and violence prevention. Middle or junior high students are taught about self-esteem, self-confidence, dealing with social anxieties, and consequences of substance use. Life Skills Training has successfully decreased risk-taking behaviors, such as tobacco, alcohol, and drug use, while increasing knowledge and awareness of substance use.

The *Bullying Prevention Program* by Dan Olweus is a schoolwide program that is designed to prevent bullying (aggressive behaviors within an interpersonal relationship) in elementary, middle, and high school students. Bullying behaviors and students are assessed and scheduled for conferences with parents and school personnel (teachers, counselors, and mental health professionals). The Bullying Prevention Program has been found to reduce bullying and antisocial behaviors (e.g., vandalism, fighting, theft, and truancy), with improvements in positive social relationships and attitudes.

Striving Together to Achieve Rewarding Tomorrows (CASASTART) was developed by the National Center on Addiction and Substance Abuse at Columbia University and provides intensive services for youths involved in drugs and violence at school and in the community. As a neighborhood-based, school-centered program it coordinates law enforcement, schools, and social services agencies to provide targeted students with tutoring, mentoring, family services, after-school activities, counseling, community policing, juvenile justice intervention, and other incentives. Participating students are assigned case managers to coordinate services, make referrals, and develop case plans. Results show that CASASTART participants become less involved with delinquent peers, have lower levels of violent offenses, exhibit higher levels of positive peer interactions, and are less likely to use drugs.

CREATING SAFE AND CARING SCHOOLS

The National Association of School Psychologists (NASP, 2002) provides recommendations to incorporate strategies and appropriate interventions for schools in the effort to reduce school violence; these include

1. Creating a school–community safety partnership that provides a systematic planning process to understand school safety problems and opportunities.
2. Establishing a comprehensive school crisis response plan to provide support for victims through counseling and recovery programs.
3. Enhancing classroom climate, school climate, and promoting positive school discipline and support to end school violence.
4. Using nonstigmatizing school violence prevention programs as positive methods of school discipline such as solution-focused approaches that include the application of behavior management principles and strategies. Assessments should not identify or profile students as being high risk for committing acts of school violence

because of high false identification rates (most students with behavior difficulties do not commit serious acts of violence).
5. Promoting antiviolence initiatives that include prevention programs for all students by teaching peacemaking, peer mediation, and conflict resolution.
6. Intervening with students who experience significant school behavioral adjustment problems by teaching social skills and self-control.

An example of school–community partnership that uses these program principles to increase school safety was implemented in Cicero, Illinois (Telleen, Maher, & Pesce, 2003). This comprehensive school violence prevention program included community, district, campus, and targeted individual student components. It involved local law enforcement, after-school programs, social skills training, outreach to families in need, gang prevention strategies, and crisis preparation. Such a combined, cross-agency coordinated approach has become the standard model in school violence prevention.

FUTURE DIRECTIONS

In *Safeguarding Our Children: An Action Guide*, Dwyer and Osher (2000) suggest that school safety plans should be based on a three-level approach that includes a schoolwide foundation, early intervention for some students, and intensive interventions for severe cases. It recommends that schools build a school team with trained faculty that contribute a diverse range of expertise, skills, and experience with the shared purpose of creating a safe school. A school team effectively pools resources, meets regularly, creates measurable goals and objectives, and incorporates community organizations into a safety plan. The Action Guide also recommends that two teams be created: one that addresses school performance and one that focuses on individual students. Finally, effective school violence prevention should also include a combination of assessment, consultation, intervention, and program evaluation. On the basis of the model proposed in the Action Guide, the U.S. federal government has funded more than 100 school–community collaborative projects that are implementing comprehensive school violence prevention models (see Furlong, Paige, & Osher, 2003). These projects provide models of how schools can work with communities to prevent and reduce school violence.

School violence prevention involves understanding the multiple influences that develop and maintain violent behavior and recognizing that research-based, multicomponent, multilevel approaches maintained over the long term stand the best chances for success. If the necessary steps are taken, school violence may not only decrease, but the quality of life for all students will improve.

See also: Bullying; Crisis Intervention; School Violence: Legal Aspects; Threat Assessment

BIBLIOGRAPHY

Anderson, M., Kaufman, J., Simon, T. R., Barrios, L., Paulozzi, L., Ryan, G., et al., & the School-Associated Violent Deaths Study Group (2001). School-associated violent deaths in the United States, 1994–1999. *Journal of the American Medical Association, 286*, 2695–2702.

Bates, M., Furlong, M. J., Saxton, J., & Pavelski, R. (2002). Research needs for school crisis prevention program. In P. Lazarus, S. Brock, & S. Jimerson (Eds.), *Best practices in crisis intervention* (pp. 755–770). Washington, DC: National Association of School Psychologists.

Brenner, N. D., Simon, T. R., Krug, E. G., & Lowry, R. (1999). Recent trends in violence related behaviors among high school students in the United States. *Journal of the American Medical Association, 282*, 440–446.

Committee for Children. (2003). *Second step* (3rd ed). Seattle, WA: Author.

Dwyer, K., & Osher, D. (2000). *Safeguarding our children: An action guide.* Washington, DC: U.S. Departments of Education and Justice, American Institutes of Research.

Dwyer, K., Osher, D., & Warger, C. (1998). *Early warning timely response: A guide to safe schools.* Washington, DC: U.S. Department of Education.

Furlong, M. J., Kingery, P. M., & Bates, M. P. (2001). Introduction to the special issue on the appraisal and prediction of school violence. *Psychology in the Schools, 38*, 89–91.

Furlong, M. J., Paige, L. Z., & Osher, D. (2003). The Safe Schools/Healthy Students (SS/HS) initiative: Lessons learned from implementing comprehensive youth development programs. *Psychology in the Schools. 40* 447–457.

Furlong, M. J., Pavelski, R., & Saxton, J. (2002). The prevention of school violence. In S. Brock, P. Lazarus, & S. Jimerson (Eds.), *Best practices in crisis intervention* (pp. 131–149). Bethesda, MD: National Association of School Psychologists.

Lamberg, L. (2002). Younger children, more girls commit acts of violence: Some get help, others receive only punishment. *Journal of the American Medical Association, 288*, 566–568.

Nansel, T. R., Overpeck, M., Pilla, R. S., Ruan, W. J., Simons-Morton, B., & Scheidt, P. (2001). Bullying behaviors among US youth: Prevalence and association with psychosocial adjustment. *Journal of the American Medical Association, 285*, 2904–2910.

National Association of School Psychologists. (2002). Position statement on school violence. Retrieved August 21, 2002, from www.nasponline.org/publications/cq306skiba.html

National Education Goals Panel. (1999). America 2000 goals [Online]. Washington, DC: Author. Retrieved August 24, 2003, from www.negp.gov/webpg210.html

Rose, L. C., & Gallup, A. M. (2001). The 34th Annual Phi Delta Kappa/Gallup poll of the public's attitudes toward the public schools. *Phi Delta Kappan, 84*, 41–56.

Skiba, R. J., & Noam, G. G. (Eds.). (2002). Zero Tolerance: Can suspension and expulsion keep school safe? *New Directions for Youth Development.* San Francisco: Jossey-Bass/Pfeiffer.

Telleen, T., Maher, S., & Pesce, R. C. (2003). Building community connections for youth to reduce violence. *Psychology in the Schools. 40*, 549–564.

U.S. Secret Service & U.S. Department of Education. (2002). *The final report and findings of the safe school initiative: Implications for the prevention of school attacks in the United States.* Washington, DC: Authors.

Additional Readings for Nonprofessionals

Noll, K., & Carter, J. (2002). *Taking the bully by the horns.* Reading, PA: Author. Retrieved September 5, 2002, from http://hometown.aol.com/kthynoll/howorder.htm

Peter, V. J. (2000). *Parents and kids talking about school violence: A Boys Town How-To Book.* Boys Town, NE: Boys Town Press. Retrieved January 18, 2001, from http://www.boystown.org

MICHAEL J. FURLONG
OANH TRAN
ALICIA SOLIZ

Seizure Disorders

DESCRIPTION, CATEGORIES, AND ASSOCIATED CONDITIONS

A seizure is "a sudden discharge of electrical activity in the brain that results in alterations of sensation, behavior, or consciousness" (Ho-Turner & Bennett, 1999, p. 502). The term *epilepsy* is used to refer to a pattern of recurrent, unprovoked seizures (Sachs & Barrett, 1995; Warzak, Mayfield, & McAllister, 1998), whereas *seizure disorder* is a broader term used to refer to all types of seizures, regardless of origin, type, or pattern of occurrence. Seizures range widely from momentary attentional lapses to lengthy convulsions, depending on the area of the brain affected by the seizure and the manner in which the electrical discharge progresses (Franks, 2003). Furthermore, seizures may be precipitated by an acute disturbance, such as a fever, low blood sugar, or trauma. Seizures also may be unpredictable, occurring in the absence of any identifiable environmental precipitant (Franks, 2003; Warzak et al., 1998).

Seizures can be classified by type or by syndrome. There are two main types of seizure: (1) generalized, which starts in both hemispheres of the brain and affects both sides of the body, and (2) partial (or focal), which starts in one area of the brain and often only affects one sensory or motor system (Franks, 2003; Sachs & Barrett, 1995; Warzak et al., 1998). Generalized seizures are associated with impairment in consciousness and include absence seizures (formerly known as *petit mal* seizures, characterized by blank, staring episodes), atonic seizures (characterized by sudden loss of muscle tone), myoclonic seizures (characterized by a myoclonic jerk, or sudden brief contraction of a single muscle group), and generalized tonic–clonic seizures (formerly known as *grand mal* seizures, characterized by loss of consciousness, stiffening of the body [tonic contraction], falling to the ground, and repetitive jerking movements [clonic movements]). Partial seizures can be further delineated as either simple (in which consciousness is not impaired) or complex (in which consciousness is impaired).

Seizure syndromes are characterized by similar seizure type(s) and related symptoms. Among the most common are febrile seizures, Lennox–Gastaut Syndrome, infantile spasms (West Syndrome), Laudau–Kleffner Syndrome, and pseudo-seizures (for further information, see Ho-Turner & Bennett, 1999; Sachs & Barrett, 1995; Warzak et al., 1998).

PREVALENCE, COURSE, AND PROGNOSIS

Seizure disorders are considered the most common neurological disorder of childhood (Franks, 2003; Sachs & Barrett, 1995). Isolated seizures are an especially common occurrence during infancy and early childhood (Ho-Turner & Bennett, 1999) with about 5 percent of children experiencing a seizure at some point, often in response to an acute event, such as a high fever (Franks, 2003). Only about 0.5 to 1 percent of school-age children go on to experience recurrent seizures, which is consistent with prevalence rates for the general population (Cowan, Bodensteiner, Leviton, & Doherty, 1989; Franks, 2003). Seizures are more common in young children 1 to 4 years of age, and in males, with black children having higher rates of generalized seizures (Cowan et al., 1989). Finally, there is a higher prevalence of seizure disorders among children with autism and mental retardation. Up to 25 percent of children with autism (American Psychiatric Association, 2000) and anywhere from 5 to 50 percent of children with mental retardation also have a seizure disorder, with increasing risk as intellectual functioning level declines (Bird, 1997).

Many factors affect the prognosis for children with seizure disorders. In general, onset during adolescence, difficulty establishing control of seizures, a known etiology, and association with mental retardation are associated with poorer prognosis in terms of long-term seizure control (Franks, 2003). However, younger age at onset, a known etiology, longer duration of the disorder, more frequent seizures, and difficulty controlling seizures (and use of more than one antiepileptic medication) are all associated with greater cognitive impairments (Ho-Turner & Bennett, 1999; Sachs & Barrett, 1995).

ASSOCIATED IMPAIRMENTS

Children with seizure disorders often experience a decline in intellectual functioning, and an increase in learning difficulties, behavioral problems, and social problems. It is difficult to differentiate impairment that is directly related to damage caused by the disease process and impairment caused by medications used to control seizures. Regardless of cause, studies have demonstrated mean IQs as much as 10 points below expected values in children with seizure disorders (Sachs & Barrett, 1995). Accordingly, these children often experience learning difficulties that result in academic deficits. Studies also suggest that about 20 percent of children with seizure disorders experience significant behavioral problems in the classroom, including aggression, hyperactivity, oppositionality, and attention-seeking behaviors (Sachs & Barrett, 1995). Finally, children with seizure disorders frequently experience negative social consequences as a result of stigmatization by peers, resulting in social isolation and skills deficits that are compounded by medical restrictions on age-appropriate activities such as sports (Sachs & Barrett, 1995).

ETIOLOGY

Researchers have identified three main factors that impact seizure threshold and, thus, the onset of a seizure disorder (Ho-Turner & Bennett, 1999): (1) genetic factors/family history, (2) onset during infancy and toddlerhood, and (3) environmental stressors. First, evidence in support of a genetic component is based on both animal studies and twin studies. Second, infancy and toddlerhood are reported to be a particularly vulnerable time period for onset of seizure disorders, as at this age children naturally have a lower seizure threshold relative to newborns or adults. Finally, several environmental stressors such as spiking fever, ionic concentrations/metabolic factors, and fatigue have been implicated as contributing to onset of seizure disorders.

Recent evidence also suggests these factors interact in a cumulative manner to determine seizure risk. Therefore, individuals with a strong family history are more likely to have a seizure in the face of an environmental stressor (e.g., high fever; Ho-Turner & Bennett, 1999). However, these factors may have a greater or lesser influence on certain types of seizure disorders. For instance, there is strong evidence for a genetic component in the development of febrile seizures, absence seizures (childhood or juvenile), generalized tonic–clonic seizures, complex partial seizures, and Rasmussen Syndrome (Ho-Turner & Bennett, 1999).

ASSESSMENT

Assessment of seizures requires specialized medical testing by a neurologist. Usually, a neurologist will conduct a physical examination, a neurological examination, and order various tests such as an electroencephalogram (EEG) to detect abnormal electrical signals within the brain. Other tests, such as a computed tomography (CT) scan or magnetic resonance imaging (MRI), may also be used to rule out other organic causes for seizure activity, such as a brain tumor or structural abnormalities. The neurologist will also diagnose the type of seizure and make recommendations for managing and/or preventing future seizures.

TREATMENTS AND EFFECTS ON CLASSROOM BEHAVIOR

The standard of care in the treatment of seizure disorders is antiepileptic (or anticonvulsant) drugs (AEDs) (Sachs & Barrett, 1995; Warzak et al., 1998), although, in some instances, surgery may be necessary for management of uncontrolled seizures (Franks, 2003). Commonly used AEDs include carbamazepine (Tegretol), valproic acid (Depakote, Depakene), phenytoin (Dilantin), ethosuximide, and phenobarbital, although benzodiazepines are used frequently as an adjunct treatment (Handler & DuPaul, 1999; Sachs & Barrett, 1995; Warzak et al., 1998). The medication(s) selected depends on the type of seizure the child experiences and difficulties encountered in attaining adequate seizure control.

Although antiepileptic medications are quite effective in controlling seizures, they also are associated with a wide range of adverse side effects that have important implications for classroom performance. Each medication has a different side effect profile. The main side effects include a variety of cognitive impairments, learning difficulties, behavioral problems, and drowsiness (Handler & DuPaul, 1999). Among the associated cognitive impairments are intellectual decline, cognitive slowing, and problems with attention, memory, and processing speed (Handler & DuPaul, 1999). These deficits, taken in combination with disruptive behavior and drowsiness, set the stage for academic problems. Benzodiazepines are also associated with undesirable side effects, including drowsiness, unsteady gait, dependency, and onset of seizures following sudden withdrawal (Sachs & Barrett, 1995).

Typically, side effects such as sedation quickly remit after the medication is discontinued, although little is known about the potential long-term effects on cognitive functioning with prolonged use. However, the use of phenobarbital, a barbiturate once widely used for seizure control, has been limited in recent years because in addition to side effects such as sedation, overactivity, depression, and deficits in attention and memory, several studies have demonstrated lasting declines in cognitive ability from prolonged use (Handler & DuPaul, 1999; Sachs & Barrett, 1995).

SPECIAL CONSIDERATIONS FOR SCHOOL SETTINGS

There are several issues related to childhood seizure disorders that are particularly salient to the school setting. First, teachers and school personnel should be knowledgeable about the wide range of seizure disorders that occur in childhood, as teacher report may be critical in the identification and proper medical management of seizure disorders (Sachs & Barrett,

1995). Although many teachers are likely to have some basic knowledge regarding generalized tonic–clonic seizures, they may have little knowledge of absence seizures, which are more common in children and may be difficult to distinguish from ADHD-Predominantly Inattentive Type, given similarity of symptoms including staring episodes and difficulties focusing. Also, given higher prevalence of seizure disorders in children with autism and mental retardation, it is particularly important for special education teachers to be knowledgeable about management of seizures in the school setting.

Second, it is important that teachers and other school personnel know how to manage seizure activity. Sources agree that if a student in class experiences a tonic–clonic seizure, the teacher should clear away furniture, help the child down on the floor, place something soft such as a folded jacket under his/her head, and position the head to one side. This will help keep his/her airway clear of saliva and/or vomit. No objects should be placed in the child's mouth. When the child awakens, he/she may be confused or sleepy and should be observed by an adult until alert. If seizure activity lasts longer than 5 to 10 minutes, the child should be treated by a physician before returning to class (Warzak et al., 1998). (These are general recommendations and should be viewed as secondary to the specific advice given by a student's medical provider.)

Finally, although many children with seizure disorders have no significant intellectual impairments, both the seizures themselves and the medications used to prevent seizures place these children at risk for learning and behavioral problems. School personnel should be trained to monitor for academic difficulties and behavioral problems, in addition to typical medication side effects (Sachs & Barrett, 1995). Teachers also should provide appropriate individualized educational plans for children, as indicated, based on cognitive, academic, or behavioral concerns that may arise (Dreisbach, Ballard, Russo, & Schain, 1982). Furthermore, given risk of social stigmatization by peers, teachers and school nurses are advised to provide classmates with basic education about seizures to minimize fears and teasing on the part of peers (for further information see Epilepsy Foundation, n.d.).

See also: Attention-Deficit/Hyperactivity Disorder

BIBLIOGRAPHY

American Psychiatric Association. (2000). *Diagnostic and statistical manual of mental disorders* (4th ed., text rev.). Washington, DC: Author.

Bird, J. (1997). Epilepsy and learning disabilities. In O. Russell (Ed.), *Seminars in the psychiatry of learning disabilities* (pp. 223–244). London: Gaskell.

Cowan, L. D., Bodensteiner, J. B., Leviton, A., & Doherty, L. (1989). Prevalence of epilepsies in children and adolescents. *Epilepsia, 30*, 94–106.

Dreisbach, M., Ballard, M., Russo, D. C., & Schain, R. J. (1982). Educational intervention for children with epilepsy: A challenge for collaborative service delivery. *The Journal of Special Education, 16*, 111–121.

Franks, R. P. (2003). Psychiatric issues of childhood seizure disorders. *Child and Adolescent Clinics of North America, 12*, 551–565.

Handler, M. W., & DuPaul, G. J. (1999). Pharmacological issues and iatrogenic effects on learning. In R. T. Brown (Ed.), *Cognitive aspects of chronic illness in children* (pp. 355–385). New York: Guilford.

Ho-Turner, M., & Bennett, T. L. (1999). Seizure disorders. In S. Goldstein & C. Reynolds (Eds.), *Handbook of neurodevelopmental and genetic disorders in children* (pp. 499–524). New York: Guilford.

Sachs, H., & Barrett, R. P. (1995). Seizure disorders: A review for school psychologists. *School Psychology Review, 24*, 131–145.

Warzak, W. J., Mayfield, J., & McAllister, J. (1998). Central nervous system dysfunction: Brain injury, postconcussive syndrome, and seizure disorder. In T. S. Watson & F. M. Gresham (Eds.), *Handbook of child behavior therapy* (pp. 287–309). New York: Plenum.

Additional Reading for Professionals and Nonprofessionals

Epilepsy Foundation. (n.d.). *General information about K through 12.* Retrieved November 3, 2003, from http://www.epilepsyfoundation.org/answerplace/Social/education/k12/

SARA E. SYTSMA-JORDAN

Selective Mutism

Since 1877, when the first reported case of selective mutism appeared, there has been considerable attention directed toward this uncommon but debilitating condition (Drewes & Akin-Little, 2002). Although varied descriptions and terminology have been employed, the term *elective mutism* has been most commonly used until the advent of the fourth edition of the American Psychiatric Association's (1994) *Diagnostic and Statistical Manual of Mental Disorders*. Since then, the term *elective* has been replaced with *selective* to emphasize that the child exercises control in the selection of settings where, or individuals to whom, he/she speaks. The occurrence of selective mutism is rare, occurring in less than 1 percent of the general population. Onset is usually around the time the child begins attending school.

The specific diagnostic criteria for selective mutism include a consistent failure to speak in specific social situations. Furthermore, the failure to speak must be evident for over 1 month, and not because of lack of knowledge of spoken language, or a communication disorder (*DSM-IV*; American Psychiatric Association, 1994). There can be, and usually are, several associated features including excessive shyness, social isolation and withdrawal, negativism, tantrumming, anxiety, enuresis, vomiting, and controlling or oppositional behavior,

particularly in the home setting (*DSM-IV*; American Psychiatric Association, 1994).

CAUSES

There is considerable ambiguity regarding the cause of selective mutism. Although it has been commonly assumed that the child was exposed to a severe trauma, such as physical or sexual abuse, there is little or no support for such a claim. Others, including Black and Uhde (1992), claim that selective mutism is related to anxiety disorders, especially social phobia and avoidant disorder. However, Kehle, Madaus, Baratta, and Bray (1998) have argued that perhaps the etiology of selective mutism is the result of classical conditioning and is later maintained and strengthened by negative reinforcement. Perhaps this is why children with selective mutism are so highly resistant to intervention (Kehle et al., 1998). For instance, when questions requiring a verbal response are directed to the child, and the child refuses to respond, the requests are often withdrawn and thereby function to strengthen the child's willingness not to talk. In addition, it is not unusual for these children to be socially reinforced by adults and peers for their nonverbal communication. Consequently, the longer the duration of selective mutism, the more resistant it is to intervention (Kehle et al., 1998). Despite these reasonable hypotheses regarding the origin of selective mutism, others have stated that the origin is simply unknown (Stone, Kratochwill, Sladezcek, & Serlin, 2002).

TREATMENT

The most common treatment approaches have been categorized as psychodynamic, family systems, behavior therapy, biological, and a combined behavioral–biological approach. Stone et al. (2002) summarized psychodynamic therapy as involving communication, play, or art in order to identify some assumed underlying cause. Supposedly, when this conflict or cause is uncovered the cure will take place and the child will begin appropriately conversing. Some common psychodynamically based reasons for children having selective mutism are that he/she may be regressing to a preverbal stage of development, or is displaying hostility directed primarily toward the mother. There are no convincing studies to justify this theoretical orientation in the treatment of selective mutism; furthermore, it may even function to create intrafamilial conflict (Kehle et al., 1998).

Interventions that focus on treating the entire family as a unit are based on the assumption that the family members' interactions cause the child's selective mutism. Teachers feel most comfortable with this treatment model in that the origin of the problem is assumed to be within the family, and therefore justifies treating the child outside of the school within the family context (Kehle et al., 1998). Stone et al. (2002) stated that there does appear to be evidence to suggest some degree of heritability, and therefore related family characteristics such as temperament and anxiety should be assessed. Nevertheless, treatment with family therapy is not supported by the research literature (Kehle et al., 1998).

Behavior therapy treatments (e.g., systematic desensitization, successive approximations, positive reinforcement, extinction, stimulus fading, spacing effect, modeling, and self-modeling) are based on learning theory and assume that selective mutism is a learned phenomenon and therefore the child can with carefully designed behaviorally based interventions, effectively be taught to speak appropriately. Generally, behaviorally oriented treatments have been shown to be effective in the remediation of selective mutism.

The biological approach assumes that there is a physiological disorder, or a temperament-based predisposition, that can be attenuated by medication. The work of Black and Uhde (1994) has demonstrated the effectiveness of certain drugs, such as fluoxetine (Prozac), as a treatment.

Finally, in consideration of the successes of both the behavioral and biological approaches, Kehle, Bray, and Theodore (2000) and Kehle et al. (1998) have combined the two into a single behavioral–biological approach to successfully treat children with selective mutism. For example, they used a multicomponent treatment encompassing self-modeling augmented with unknown reinforcement (mystery motivators), self-reinforcement, stimulus fading, and fluoxetine. A detailed definition of the different treatment components is included in Kehle et al. (1998). In brief, (a) self-modeling involves edited videotapes depicting the target behavior (i.e., the child engaged in appropriate verbal behavior in classroom settings); (b) mystery motivator was an unknown positive reinforcer awarded to the student contingent upon appropriate behavior (i.e., the student talking aloud in the classroom with students and teacher present); (c) self-reinforcement is the process of allowing the student to access reinforcers when a desired behavior is performed (i.e., the student can choose from a menu of reinforcers when he/she is viewing the edited videotape that shows them talking; Mace, Belfiore, & Shea, 1989); (d) stimulus fading is defined as the lessening of the discriminative stimulus (i.e., the gradual inclusion of peers, with whom the child with selective mutism has never spoken, into settings that have high probability for speech); (e) the spacing effect is defined as the students' exposure to several spaced viewings of their edited videotapes, rather than single or daily viewing of all their videotapes; and finally, (f) fluoxetine, a serotonin reuptake inhibitor, is an antidepressant. Although these combined intervention studies were based on single cases, they met certain conditions that allowed valid inferences to be drawn about the effects of a combined behavioral–biological-based intervention. Most convincing of these conditions is that all of the children evidenced a rapid,

dramatic, and complete remission of their selective mutism. This provided a strong basis for attributing the effects of treatment to the combined treatment.

In summary, and in concert with Drewes and Akin-Little (2002) and Stone et al. (2002), there is considerable ambiguity regarding the etiology of selective mutism. Nonetheless, the developmental progression of the disorder is relatively clear, with the average age of onset being around 5 years. Finally, the most promising treatments appear to incorporate both behavioral and pharmacological interventions.

See also: Anxiety; Enuresis; Extinction; Negative Reinforcement; Oppositional Defiant Disorder; Positive Reinforcement

BIBLIOGRAPHY

American Psychiatric Association. (1994). *Diagnostic and statistical manual of mental disorders* (4th ed.). Washington, DC: Author.

Black, B., & Uhde, T. W. (1992). Elective mutism as a variant of social phobia. *Journal of the American Academy of Child and Adolescent Psychiatry, 31,* 1090–1094.

Black, B., & Uhde, T. W. (1994). Treatment of elective mutism with fluoxetine: A double-blind, placebo-controlled study. *Journal of the American Academy of Child and Adolescent Psychiatry, 33,* 1000–1006.

Drewes, K. M., & Akin-Little, A. (2002). Children with selective mutism: Seen but not heard. *The School Psychologist, 56,* 37 ff.

Kehle, T. J., Bray, M. A., & Theodore, L. A. (2000, August). *Further support for the use of self-modeling as a treatment for selective mutism.* Paper presented at the annual meeting of the American Psychological Association, Washington, DC.

Kehle, T. J., Madaus, M. M. R., Baratta, V. S., & Bray, M. A. (1998). Augmented self-modeling as a treatment for children with selective mutism. *Journal of School Psychology, 36,* 377–399.

Mace, F. C., Belfiore, P. J., & Shea, M. C. (1989). Operant theory and research on self-regulation. In B. J. Zimmerman & D. H. Schunk (Eds.), *Self-regulated learning and academic achievement: Theory, research, and practice.* New York: Springer-Verlag.

Stone, B. P., Kratochwill, T. R., Sladezcek, I., & Serlin, R. C. (2002). Treatment of selective mutism: A best-evidence synthesis. *School Psychology Quarterly, 17,* 168–190.

Additional Readings for Nonprofessionals

Giddan, J. J., Ross, G. J., Sechler, L. L., & Becker, B. R. (1997). Selective mutism in elementary school: Multidisciplinary interventions. *Language, Speech, and Hearing Services, 28,* 127–133.

Johnson, A., & Wintgens, (2001). *Selective mutism resource manual.* Oxfordshire, UK: Speechmark.

Additional Readings for Professionals

Hadley, N. H. (1994). *Elective mutism: A handbook for educators, counselors, and health-care professionals.* Dordrecht: Kluwer Academic.

Kratochwill, T. R. (1981). *Selective mutism: Implications for research and treatment.* Hillsdale, NJ: Erlbaum.

THOMAS J. KEHLE
MELISSA A. BRAY

Self-Control

Throughout our lives, we are faced with choices between immediate gratification and longer term rewards. Often, these choices must be made at the expense of the alternative. In other words, if a person engages in a behavior that brings about immediate gratification, that person often, by doing so, forgoes the opportunity for a larger longer term reward. There are many examples from our everyday lives that illustrate these types of choices (e.g., exercise, money management, problem behaviors exhibited by children in the classroom), which will be discussed below. However, in behavioral terminology, when a smaller immediate and a larger more distant reward are offered, choosing the immediate gratification is referred to as *impulsivity* and choosing a larger long-term reward is referred to as *self-control* (Logue, 1995; Schweitzer & Sulzer-Azaroff, 1988).

When people make decisions about how they eat, they often make decisions related to self-control. A person may choose to limit the amount of food eaten that is high in fat and cholesterol to lower the chances of heart disease later in life, lose weight, and look better. Because she avoids short-term access to highly preferred food, she is said to exhibit self-control by engaging in a behavior where the delayed benefit may be years away. Because these high-fat foods are highly preferred by some people, it is often very difficult to exhibit self-control, and impulsive choices are frequently demonstrated. The larger delayed reward in this case might take the form of a lowered chance of heart disease later in life, eventual weight loss, and overall better health. Similar examples of self-control and food are seen when eating out, buying groceries, and in unhealthy snacking between meals.

Another example that illustrates the choice between self-control and impulsivity involves money management. People must make decisions about their money every day. These decisions often involve a choice between spending money in order to attain immediate indulgence in the form of tangible items and saving or investing the money for long-term financial security. Investing money entails a longer delay to reward. However, by putting money away in a savings account, a person can build toward larger, delayed benefits such as the purchase of a car or a house, putting children through college, more financially comfortable retirements, and so on. That same person could also choose to simply spend the money on small items that he/she may not need. Spending money on small immediate reinforcers can be thought of as impulsive buying, and people often exhibit this behavior even though they may not have the financial means to do so. When a person saves or invests money for some future consideration, the person is said to be exhibiting self-control.

A final example of self-control in everyday life involves the problematic behavior of schoolchildren. Inappropriate behaviors that occur in the classroom happen for a wide variety of reasons. A student may exhibit inappropriate behavior in order to obtain attention from other students or from a teacher. Or, they may behave inappropriately to escape a nonpreferred task. In the case where the problematic behavior is maintained by peer attention, the child can be thought of as making a decision between immediate gratification and a larger delayed reward. The immediate gratification in this case is the attention received from the child's peers in the classroom. The larger delayed benefit that is lost may take the form of a tangible reward for proper behavior attained at the end of class, the school day, or at home. In the case where the problematic behavior is maintained by escape, the immediate gratification (i.e., the impulsive choice) may take the form of getting out of doing some task that is difficult for the student. When students choose to engage in inappropriate behavior in order to get out of doing an academic task, however, they lose out on the longer term benefit of improvement in academic skills that are not only necessary for further skill acquisition but are imperative later in life.

A great deal of research has investigated the variables that contribute to individuals' engagement in self-control and impulsivity. Of particular interest to many school psychologists are procedures that teach self-control to students who have exhibited impulsive choice making in the past. One procedure that has been examined and demonstrated to be effective in bringing about self-control with impulsive children involves decreasing wait times associated with the larger delayed rewards. For example, Schweitzer and Sultzer-Azaroff (1988) examined this procedure with young children by making both large and small rewards available immediately. Once the children showed consistent preferences for the choice that obtained the large reward, a delay was added to that choice and slowly increased over time. These children, who had initially behaved impulsively, now engaged in self-control following this slow increase of the delay to the large reward.

Another procedure that has been demonstrated effective in bringing about self-control involves the use of distracting activities during the delays to the larger rewards. Dixon and Cummings (2001) used procedures that involved activities during delays to larger rewards with young children who had been diagnosed with autism. The children, after consistently exhibiting impulsive choices, were presented with choices between immediate gratification and larger, delayed rewards in which they were required to engage in alternative, distracting activities while they waited. After the children were repeatedly exposed to the choices that involved the distracting activities while they waited, they consistently showed a preference for self-control choices. Another procedure for increasing self-control has been to combine distracting activities with slow increases in wait times (Dixon et al., 1998). Another procedure has modified the sizes of rewards associated with choices relative to different wait times (Neef, Bicard, & Endo, 2001). Each has been successful in increasing self-control in children.

Procedures that signal the length of wait times have also been examined. Vollmer, Borrero, Lalli, and Daniel (1999) examined the use of signals while treating impulsive aggressive behavior exhibited by children with developmental disabilities. The investigators showed that when offered a choice in which aggressive behavior accessed small amounts of food immediately and appropriate communication allowed the children to access larger amounts of food following delays, the children showed preferences for the small immediate choice. The investigators then examined using signals during the wait times that indicated how long the children had to wait for the larger amounts of food. The use of signals, combined with the slow increase of the wait time, resulted in the children's consistently exhibiting self-control and cessation in behaving aggressively.

Many school psychologists and behavior analysts continue to investigate ways to help children learn to improve their self-control and choice making associated with demonstrating self-control. Learning to tolerate delays in obtaining rewards and gratification is beneficial for children as they develop because many of the most satisfying rewards associated with academics, jobs, and social relationships are delayed and not immediate. The ability to make responsible, delayed gratification choices will play an important role in shaping the lives of children as they mature into young adulthood.

BIBLIOGRAPHY

Dixon, M. R., & Cummings, A. (2001). Self-control in children with autism: Response allocation during delays to reinforcement. *Journal of Applied Behavior Analysis, 34*, 491–495.

Dixon, M. R., Hayes, L. J., Binder, L. M., Manthey, S., Sigman, C., & Zdanowski, D. M. (1998). Using a self-control training procedure to increase appropriate behavior. *Journal of Applied Behavior Analysis, 31*, 203–210.

Logue, A. W. (1995). *Self-control: Waiting until tomorrow for what you want today.* Englewood Cliffs, NJ: Prentice–Hall.

Neef, N. A., Bicard, D. F., & Endo, S. (2001). Assessment of impulsivity and the development of self-control with students with attention deficit hyperactivity disorder. *Journal of Applied Behavior Analysis, 34*, 397–408.

Schweitzer, J. B., & Sulzer-Azaroff, B. (1988). Self-control: Teaching tolerance for delay in impulsive children. *Journal of Experimental Analysis of Behavior, 50*, 173–186.

Vollmer, T. R., Borrero, J. C., Lalli, J. S., & Daniel, D. (1999). Evaluating self-control and impulsivity in children with severe behavior disorders. *Journal of Applied Behavior Analysis, 32*, 451–466.

TERRY S. FALCOMATA
MICHAEL M. MUELLER

Self-Injurious Behavior

Self-injurious behavior (SIB) is assumed to be a voluntary behavior toward oneself that when emitted once or repeatedly causes tissue or sensory damage. Although such acts as attempted suicide and body art (e.g., tattooing and piercing) could be labeled as SIB, school psychologists and other mental health professionals typically define SIB more narrowly by including specific forms of behavior. The common forms of self-injurious behavior may include such acts as banging one's head, knees, or other body parts against hard objects and hitting, kicking, biting, slapping, and scratching oneself.

An estimate of the prevalence rate of SIB among the general public is unavailable primarily because most research on SIB has been conducted in institutions, community programs, hospitals, and schools for persons with mental retardation (Rojahn & Esbensen, 2002). Despite the heavy concentration of research in these settings, the estimated prevalence rate of SIB among individuals with developmental disabilities and mental retardation varies from 5 to 16 percent (Schroeder, Rojahn, & Oldenquist, 1991) with no significant difference in prevalence between males and females (Borthwick, Meyers, & Eyman, 1981).

The relationship of SIB with mental retardation is an important consideration for clinicians as the prevalence of SIB increases with the level of intellectual impairment. A review of numerous studies on the prevalence rate of SIB among individuals with mental retardation suggests that about 5 percent of individuals with mild mental retardation engage in SIB whereas 27–35 percent of individuals with profound mental retardation engage in such behaviors (Rojahn & Esbensen, 2002).

In addition to being associated with mental retardation, SIB has also been shown to have strong associations with specific disorders such as Lesch–Nyhan Syndrome (Anderson & Ernst, 1994), Rett Syndrome (Sansom, Krishanan, Corbett, & Kerr, 1993), Cornelia de Lange Syndrome (Bryson, Sakati, Nyhan, & Fish, 1971), Prader–Willi Syndrome (Symons, Butler, Sanders, Feurer, & Thompson, 1999), and Tourette Syndrome (Trimble, 1989). Research has demonstrated that specific topographies (i.e., forms of SIB) are more prevalent among specific syndromes. For example, nearly 100 percent of individuals affected by Lesch–Nyhan Syndrome engage in some form of self-biting. Likewise, individuals with Cornelia de Lange Syndrome engage in self-hitting, and finger biting (Berney, Ireland, & Burn, 1999), whereas individuals with Prader–Willi Syndrome often engage in skin picking.

CAUSES OF SELF-INJURIOUS BEHAVIOR

Because a variety of syndromes have been demonstrated to have somewhat predictable patterns of SIB, neurobiological models have been emphasized as a framework for understanding SIB. Specifically, research has suggested an association between SIB and levels of neurotransmitters such as dopamine and serotonin. However, it is unclear as to whether the association is due to some natural brain reaction to SIB or if neurotransmitter levels are precursors to SIB.

Although SIB has been demonstrated to be related to neurobiological factors, researchers and clinicians alike realize that SIB is also associated with conditions that do not necessarily have neurobiological causes. First, SIB has been associated with health conditions such as otitis media (inner ear infections), gastroesophageal reflux disease (severe heartburn), sleep deprivation, and menstrual cycles (Thompson & Caruso, 2002). Second, individuals without mental retardation, specific syndromes, or health problems also engage in SIB. For example, some typically developing and otherwise physically healthy children and adolescents may engage in forms of SIB such as knife cutting or self-burning of the skin. Finally, considerable research with animals and humans has suggested that severe social deprivation in the early years of life may contribute to increased incidence of aberrant behavior, including SIB.

ASSESSMENT AND TREATMENT OF SELF-INJURIOUS BEHAVIOR

One treatment for SIB is psychotropic medication. Although stimulants, neuroleptics, anticonvulsants, sedatives, antidepressants, and other drugs have all been used in the treatment of SIB, research on the effects of such medications is mixed. Moreover, psychotropic medications typically result in negative side effects, and the use of such medication to control the behavior of individuals with mental retardation has been deemphasized.

Because the use of psychotropic medications generally does not cure SIB, and current medical technologies do not provide cures for specific syndromes associated with SIB, clinicians have focused on assessing the environmental conditions that trigger and maintain SIB. Clinicians conduct functional assessments and functional analyses to determine which of four specific behavioral functions (i.e., access to tangible items, attention, escape demands, or self-stimulation) the SIB may serve (Iwata, Dorsey, Slifer, Bauman, & Richman, 1982/1994). In addition to assessing consequences and behavioral function, clinicians often assess setting events (specific events in the environment such as loud noises or bright lights) and establishing operations (specific events within the person such as pain or hunger) that

may evoke SIB. By understanding both the antecedents and consequences of SIB, clinicians develop treatments that focus on changing the environment such that the inappropriate SIB is less likely to be evoked or persist over time.

One effective environmental treatment for SIB is extinction, whereby the functional reinforcer (i.e., the consequence that is provided that results in the SIB persisting over time) is withheld. For example, a functional analysis may indicate that a person engages in SIB to gain attention in a classroom setting. In this case, extinction simply requires a teacher to ignore all SIB. Although extinction can be effective, in applied settings the procedure has limited success owing to the difficulty in withholding attention from severe behavior by others (e.g., other students).

As an alternative to extinction, clinicians sometimes prefer differential reinforcement. Differential reinforcement is a procedure that requires extinction of the SIB and, in addition, reinforcement of some other alternate response that is often incompatible with the SIB. In the case of the individual who engages in SIB for attention in a classroom, the clinician may train care providers how to ignore all SIB and how to provide attention on regular intervals for other behavior that does not include SIB (e.g., working on assignments or raising one's hand to gain attention).

An elaborate example of implementing differential reinforcement for the treatment of SIB is functional communication training (FCT). Often used with individuals with mental retardation and/or limited communication, FCT is a method of communication whereby appropriate methods of communication are reinforced and inappropriate SIB ignored. Clinicians, in conjunction with care providers, may train the individual to request attention (or other reinforcers) using a picture exchange system. For example, upon turning in a card that says "play with me" or has a picture of toys on it, the individual is provided with attention and play time. Over time, a general decrease in the rate of SIB is observed, accompanied by an increase in the more appropriate mode of communication.

Another method for treating SIB is punishment. Punishment procedures are used to decrease inappropriate functional behavior by providing an undesirable consequence. For example, research on SIB has demonstrated that when mild punishment is provided such as being guided through a brief period of exercise or chores rather than being provided the functional reinforcer (e.g., attention), rates of SIB decrease.

Although such punishment procedures have been demonstrated to be effective in decreasing SIB, they sometimes are deemed inappropriate due to age, disability, or difficulty to implement. When such punishment procedures are inappropriate, individuals may be provided with brief time-outs through physical restraint. Physical restraint is a less desirable punishment procedure for SIB, which may include padded clothing, helmets, arm restraints, wrist or ankle weights, and various physical holds by a caregiver. These physical restraint procedures are often used in severe cases when the focus of the moment is to safeguard the individual from harming himself/herself.

Several federal and state mandates have led to increased awareness of SIB and the populations most affected. Moreover, such mandates have led to better management of SIB. Current research on SIB is focusing on understanding the relationship between genes, the brain, the environment, and SIB. By understanding these variables and the ways in which they interact, mental health providers will be able to provide better services to individuals with SIB.

See also: Autism; Differential Reinforcement; Extinction; Functional Analysis; Functional Assessment; Negative Reinforcement; Positive Reinforcement; Punishment; Self-Mutilation; Stereotypy

BIBLIOGRAPHY

Anderson, L. T., & Ernst, M. (1994). Self-injury in Lesch–Nyhan disease. *Journal of Autism and Developmental Disorders, 24,* 67–81.

Berney, T. P., Ireland, M., & Burn, J. (1999). Behavioral phenotype of Cornelia de Lange syndrome. *Archives of Disease in Childhood, 81,* 333–336.

Borthwick, S. A., Meyers, C. E., & Eyman, R. K. (1981). Comparative adaptive and maladaptive behavior of mentally retarded clients of five residential settings in three Western states. In R. H. Bruininks, C. E. Meyers, B. B. Sigford, & K. C. Lakin (Eds.), *Deinstitutionalization and community adjustment of mentally retarded people* (Monograph No. 4, pp. 351–359). Washington, DC: American Association on Mental Deficiency.

Bryson, Y., Sakati, N., Nyhan, W., & Fish, C. (1971). Self-mutilative behavior in the Cornelia de Lange Syndrome. *American Journal of Mental Deficiency, 76,* 319–324.

Iwata, B. A., Dorsey, M. F., Slifer, K. J., Bauman, K. E., & Richman, G. S. (1994). Toward a functional analysis of self-injury. *Journal of Applied Behavior Analysis, 27,* 197–209. (Reprinted from *Analysis and Intervention in Developmental Disabilities, 2,* 3–20, 1982)

Rojahn, J., & Esbensen, A. J. (2002). Epidemiology of self-injurious behavior in mental retardation: A review. In S. R. Schroeder, M. L. Oster-Granite, & T. Thompson (Eds.), *Self-injurious behavior. Gene–brain–behavior relationships* (pp. 41-77). Washington, DC: American Psychological Association.

Sansom, D., Krishanan, V. H., Corbett, J., & Kerr, A. (1993). Emotional and behavioral aspects of Rett syndrome. *Developmental Medicine & Child Neurology, 35,* 340–345.

Schroeder, S. R., Rojahn, J., & Oldenquist, A. (1991). Treatment of destructive behaviors among people with mental retardation and developmental disabilities: Overview of the problem. In *Treatment of destructive behaviors in persons with developmental disabilities* (NIH Publication No. 91-2410, pp. 173–230). Washington, DC: U.S. Department of Health and Human Services.

Symons, F. J., Butler, M. G., Sanders, M. D., Feurer, I. D., & Thompson, T. (1999). Self-injurious behavior and Prader–Willie syndrome: Behavioral forms and body locations. *American Journal on Mental Retardation, 104,* 260–269.

Thompson, T., & Caruso, M. (2002). Self-injury: Knowing what we're looking for. In S. R. Schroeder, M. L. Oster-Granite, & T. Thompson (Eds.), *Self-injurious behavior: Gene–brain–behavior relationships* (pp. 3–21). Washington, DC: American Psychological Association.

Trimble, M. (1989). Psychopathology and movement disorders: A new perspective on the Gilles de la Tourette's syndrome. *Journal of Neurology, Neurosurgery, and Psychiatry, 17,* 90–95.

Additional Reading for Nonprofessionals

Schroeder, S. R., Oster-Granite, M. L., & Thompson, T. (Eds.). (2002). *Self-injurious behavior: Gene–brain–behavior relationships.* Washington, DC: American Psychological Association.

Additional Readings for Professionals

Mace, F. C., Vollmer, T. R., Progar, P. R., & Mace, A. B. (1998). Assessment and treatment of self-injury. In T. S. Watson & F. M. Gresham (Eds.), *Handbook of child behavior therapy* (pp. 413–430). New York: Plenum.

Schroeder, S. R., Oster-Granite, M. L., & Thompson, T. (Eds.). (2002). *Self-injurious behavior: Gene–brain–behavior relationships.* Washington, DC: American Psychological Association.

GARY L. CATES

Self-Management

Self-management is a general term that incorporates a variety of procedures designed to alter behaviors. With these interventions, people are taught and encouraged to engage in a variety of behaviors, including self-observing and recording their behaviors, setting goals, scheduling activities, and self-evaluating their behaviors. Self-managed interventions can be as, if not more, effective than teacher- or parent-managed interventions (Fantuzzo, Polite, Cook, & Quinn, 1988). In addition, these procedures may encourage children to take responsibility for their own behavior while reducing demands on teachers and parents.

TARGET BEHAVIORS

One of the most interesting characteristics of self-management procedures is that the same procedures can have the opposite, but desired, effect. When children are taught to observe, record, and evaluate their own *inappropriate* behaviors (e.g., leaving their seat without permission), these behaviors tend to decrease. However, when they are taught to observe, record, and evaluate appropriate behaviors (e.g., complete their homework), these behaviors tend to increase. Another advantage of self-management procedures is that they can be used to target behaviors that cannot be directly observed by others. Thus, self-management procedures may be used in programs designed to alter emotional responses (i.e., reduce anxiety) and cognitive behaviors (e.g., dysfunctional thinking).

SELF-MONITORING

Self-monitoring, a basic form of self-management, requires students to observe and record their own behaviors. The change in target behavior brought about by these behaviors is called *reactivity*. In addition to bringing about changes in target behaviors, self-monitoring may cause students to self-evaluate their behaviors, set goals for observed behaviors, and "self-reinforce" when they meet these goals.

Once target behaviors are selected, children must be taught to observe the presence or absence of target behaviors. This requires clear definitions of target behaviors, and conditions when they should be observed and recorded. Next, students are taught to record the presence or absence of these behaviors under identified conditions. Although several researchers have found that merely instructing students how to observe and record their own behavior can bring about desired changes in behavior, studies suggest that when students accurately, frequently, and immediately self-record, the effects on behavior may be stronger (Shapiro, 1984).

To increase the accuracy of self-monitoring, an independent observer (e.g., teacher, parent, or classmate) also can record the child's behavior. When a child knows that someone else may check the accuracy of their recordings, they are more likely to record accurately, thus increasing the probability of the self-management program being effective.

When targeting low-rate, discrete behaviors, students can record their behaviors immediately after they occur. However, when targeting more continuous behaviors (e.g., staying in seat), recording may have to be cued. For example, a teacher could use a timer with a bell (often used for cooking) to cue all students in the class to record if they are "on task" and the teacher could reset the bell. With such programs, it may be best to start with frequent recording (short intervals between bell rings) and then gradually increase the intervals (Glynn & Thomas, 1974).

SELF-EVALUATION

In some instances, recording behaviors may require students to first evaluate the behavior to determine if it meets the criterion for recording. For example, after an academic response (spelling a word), the student may need to check their work to determine if their response was accurate before they can record the presence of an *accurate* response. In these situations, it is critical to provide efficient procedures that allow students to immediately self-evaluate their responses as such procedures will prevent students from repeating incorrect responding (Skinner & Smith, 1992).

TALKING TO ONE'S SELF: SELF-INSTRUCTION AND SELF-CONTROL

In addition to being taught to self-observe and record their own behaviors, students have been taught to provide instructional cues designed to enhance their responding. For example, a student could be taught to make self-statements when faced with mathematics problems. Thus, a student doing mathematics work may first be taught to say to himself, "What type of problem is this?" The student may then be taught to respond, "It is a division problem, I know that from the symbol." After learning such procedures, it is important for students to practice them by making the self-statement out loud in the presence of an adult who can reinforce correct responding and provide immediate corrective feedback when the student fails to make desired self-statements. After some practice, students can then begin making these self-statements both silently and independently (Meichenbaum, 1977).

INCREASING THE EFFECTIVENESS OF SELF-MANAGEMENT PROCEDURES

In order to increase the probability of students' performing self-management procedures, instructions should be clear, few behaviors should be targeted, and obvious reminders or cues should be available or delivered to remind children to engage in self-management behaviors. Students should practice these self-management behaviors across settings and tasks in order to enhance generalization and maintenance. Even after instruction and practice, educators and parents should monitor students' self-management behaviors and deliver labeled praise (e.g., "very good job checking your work") and other rewards when they perform those behaviors independently. Prompts and/or immediate corrective feedback should be delivered when children fail to engage in self-management behaviors.

Many have suggested that even without specific instruction, observing and recording one's own behavior causes people to set goals related to their own behavior, self-evaluate the observed behavior, and reinforce themselves when they meet these goals. Some believe that it is this self-reinforcement that causes the change in the target behavior. However, one cannot reinforce one's own behavior (Catania, 1975). Thus, parents and educators who instruct and encourage children to engage in self-management procedures should do all they can to encourage both the self-management behaviors (i.e., observing and recording behaviors) and also the change in target behaviors.

Initially, self-management programs may bring about desired target behavior change. However, additional reinforcement is often necessary if these behavior changes are to be maintained over time and across environments. In some instances, this additional reinforcement will not require parents or teachers to change typical routines because changes in target behaviors will bring the student into contact with reinforcers. However, in other instances, the initial change in behavior may not bring the child into contact with reinforcers. For example, consider Frank and Claire. Frank is failing history (40 percent average) and Claire is making a C (75 percent average). Self-management programs designed to enhance study skills are provided and both improve their performance 20 percent. Frank now makes 60 percent and Claire 95 percent. It is likely that Claire's improved performance will bring her into contact with reinforcers (e.g., praise from parents and teachers, increased privileges at school and home). Although Frank improved his performance markedly (50 percent improvement), his performance is still too poor to allow him access to these reinforcers. In this case, it is a folly to hope that teaching Frank to talk to himself, praising his own behavior changes (e.g., "You did very well Frank"), is enough to maintain the changes in his study habits. Instead, adults (e.g., parents, teachers) should monitor and reinforce this significant change in target behavior and use shaping procedures to support Frank's progress.

Sometimes, busy educators and parents may not have the time and resources required to monitor small improvements in target behaviors. One solution is to teach students to self-evaluate their improvements and to then solicit reinforcement when target behaviors improve. Such procedures teach students effective self-management behaviors (e.g., observing and evaluating their own behaviors), while also increasing the probability that desired changes in behavior will be reinforced.

SUMMARY

Although the term *self-management* suggests that educators and parents have little role planning and implementing self-management programs, this is far from the truth. Self-management programs need to be carefully designed and students need to be taught to implement self-management procedures accurately and consistently. After students have acquired and mastered these self-management skills, parents and teachers need to encourage and reinforce students for using these skills and also provide supplemental reinforcement when initial changes in behavior are not sufficient enough to allow students access to typical reinforcement at home or in school.

See also: Behavioral Observation: Self-Constructed

BIBLIOGRAPHY

Catania, A. C. (1975). The myth of self-reinforcement. *Behaviorism, 3*, 199–206.
Fantuzzo, J. W., Polite, K., Cook, D. M., & Quinn, G. (1988). An evaluation of the effectiveness of teacher- vs. student-management classroom interventions. *Psychology in the Schools, 25*, 154–163.
Glynn, E. J., & Thomas, J. D. (1974). Effects of cueing on self-control of classroom behavior. *Journal of Applied Behavior Analysis, 7*, 229–306.
Meichenbaum, D. (1977). *Cognitive–behavior modification.* New York: Plenum.
Shapiro, E. S. (1984). Self-monitoring procedures. In T. H. Ollendick & M. Hersen (Eds.), *Child behavioral assessment: Principles and procedures* (pp. 148–165). New York: Pergamon.
Skinner, C. H., & Smith, E. S. (1992). Issues surrounding the use of self-managed interventions for increasing academic performance. *School Psychology Review, 21*, 202–210.

Additional Reading for Nonprofessionals

Brigham, T. A. (1989). *Self-management for adolescent: Managing everyday problems.* New York: Guilford.

Additional Reading for Professionals

Shapiro, E. S., & Cole C. (1994). *Behavior change in the classroom: Self-management interventions.* New York: Guilford.

CHRISTOPHER H. SKINNER

Self-Mutilation

Self-mutilation (SM) refers to the intentional self-destruction or alteration of body tissue without deliberate suicidal intent (Favazza, 1998). Although often mistaken by professionals and nonprofessionals alike as a suicidal gesture, most individuals who engage in SM, particularly in its most common form, appear to do so as a morbid form of coping and self-help. The behavior often appears to serve the function of providing rapid but temporary relief from stress and tension, providing a sense of security or control, and/or decreasing troublesome thoughts or feelings (Favazza, 1998). Although many individuals who engage in repetitive SM frequently are at high risk for suicidal behavior (Favazza, 1998), the bulk of research findings to date suggests that SM and suicide attempts are distinct and have different etiologies (Ross & Heath, 2002). Self-mutilation is frequently associated with adolescence, as it is typically first exhibited by individuals during this developmental period.

Referred to by a variety of descriptors, including deliberate self-harm, self-injurious behavior, self-wounding, parasuicide, and more colloquially as "cutting," SM must be placed in a cultural context in order to be adequately understood. For example, there are many culturally sanctioned rituals and practices in which individuals mutilate their own body parts or willingly allow others to mutilate them (Favazza, 1999). Several cultures engage in body modification rituals that may serve a variety of functions, including societal control and the maintenance of cultural norms, symbolic rites of passage, and/or the promotion of healing and spirituality (Favazza, 1999). In contemporary Western culture, behaviors such as tattooing and body piercing are commonplace, particularly among adolescents and young adults, but because these practices are culturally sanctioned and not typically indicative of psychopathology they would not be considered forms of SM according to the functional definition described above.

Self-mutilation has a long history (the first recorded account of an incident of SM was in 450 B.C.), although it was not until the 20th century that the first text addressing SM was published and only in recent decades has the phenomenon received attention from professionals and the general public (Favazza, 1998). Current demographic data regarding individuals who engage in SM are sparse, as little empirical research has been generated examining this condition (Ross & Heath, 2002). Much of the research on SM conducted to date has limited generalizability to nonpsychiatric populations, and many studies have had inconsistent definitions of the condition, often combining individuals who engaged in SM with individuals who attempted suicide (Ross & Heath, 2002). As a result, little is known about the demographics of SM in the United States, particularly among children and adolescents, although some conclusions may be tentatively drawn.

Current research indicates, for example, that (a) SM appears to begin most typically in early adolescence, although it can begin earlier, and may persist for years or even decades unless effectively treated; (b) its prevalence may be underestimated and increasing within the adolescent population; (c) it appears to be more prevalent in girls than in boys; (d) self-cutting appears to be the most common form of SM; and (e); it may sometimes, though not always, be precipitated by one or more incidents of sexual or physical abuse (Favazza, 1999; Ross & Heath, 2002). Although some have suggested that ongoing dissociation is a feature of SM and that dissociative experiences correlate highly with childhood trauma such as sexual abuse, research to date has not found a clear and consistent link between these conditions (Favazza, 1998). Recent research does suggest, however, that adolescents who engage in SM may experience more depression and anxiety and greater socioemotional difficulties than adolescents who do not self-mutilate (Ross & Heath, 2002), and that they may experience a number of other disorders or problems including eating disorders, personality disorders, poor impulse control, and substance abuse (Favazza, 1999). In addition, possible predisposing factors to SM may include particular biological conditions, chaotic family relationships, excessive guilt or self-blame, low self-esteem, and dissatisfaction with body shape, image, and/or sexual organs (Favazza, 1999).

Although self-mutilation is not classified as a specific disorder in the *Diagnostic and Statistical Manual of Mental Disorders* (4th ed., text rev.) (American Psychiatric Association, 2000), others have made various attempts at classification and diagnosis. A classification system that has recently received wide acceptance because of its comprehensiveness and clinical utility was developed by Favazza (1998). In this classification system, SM is divided into three observable categories based on the degree of tissue destruction and the rate and pattern of the self-mutilating behavior. These categories include major SM, stereotypic SM, and superficial/moderate SM. This last category has three subtypes: compulsive, episodic, and repetitive.

Major SM refers to infrequent acts such as self-initiated eye removal, castration, and/or limb amputation. Such behaviors are extremely rare in children and adolescents and appear most commonly as associated features of psychotic states, such as schizophrenia. Stereotypic SM refers to acts such as head banging and hitting, and is typically associated with children and adolescents with autism or other developmental disabilities. Current research suggests that psychiatric medication is the most effective treatment for major SM, and that behavioral interventions are most effective for treating stereotypic SM (Favazza, 1998). The third and final type of SM, superficial/moderate SM, refers to acts such as hair pulling and skin picking, which comprise the compulsive type, and to skin cutting and burning, needle sticking, and interference with wound healing, which comprise the episodic and repetitive types. Superficial/moderate SM is the most common form of self-mutilation, with estimates that 1 in every 100 persons engages in it (Favazza, 1998), and is the type of SM most commonly referred to in the popular media. As such, a primary focus of the remainder of this entry will be on superficial/moderate SM and its assessment and treatment. Individuals interested in a more complete description of the assessment and treatment of major and stereotypic SM are encouraged to review other sources (e.g., Favazza, 1999; Iwata, Dorsey, Slifer, Bauman, & Richman, 1994).

Because children and adolescents who engage in superficial/moderate SM are often secretive and reluctant to refer themselves to professionals for treatment, identification and assessment of these individuals can be difficult. Moreover, the lack of standardized assessment instruments for SM, such as rating scales and structured diagnostic interviews, is problematic. If a child or adolescent is suspected of engaging in superficial/moderate SM, however, a comprehensive assessment should include both direct observations and individual interviews with the child/adolescent, caregivers, and other adults who frequently observe the child/adolescent (e.g., school personnel). Behavioral observations should include checking for cuts or burn marks, and the presence of unusually heavy or unseasonable clothing designed to mask scars (Miller, DeZolt, & Trimarchi, 2001). When interviewing a child or adolescent suspected of engaging in SM, the interviewer should directly ask the child/adolescent if she/he is engaging in the behavior. If the child/adolescent is engaging in SM, a suicide risk assessment should immediately be conducted as well. The following conditions also should be assessed, as they may have implications for treatment: (a) degree of anger and its expression; (b) degree of student self-esteem and self-concept; (c) history of abuse, particularly sexual abuse; (d) possible cognitive distortions; and (e) family tolerance for expression of feelings (Favazza, 1999).

In addition, one should enquire about and analyze the events that precipitate acts of SM, including asking about and noting where acts occur and what the goals, benefits, and consequences of the act are for the child/adolescent engaging in SM (Miller et al., 2001). Gathering information about antecedent conditions, behaviors, and consequences of the behavior in order to determine the reason or function of the SM for a given child or adolescent can be potentially useful for linking assessment to effective intervention. For example, the function of SM for one adolescent might be escape (e.g., mounting anxiety and unbearable tension are released), whereas for another it might be attention (e.g., a girl who cuts herself and shows it to her boyfriend to show how deeply he has hurt her). Identical behaviors (e.g., skin cutting) may serve different functions and therefore suggest different interventions to meet individual needs.

To date, there are little outcome data on effective treatments for children and adolescents who engage in superficial/moderate SM. For some individuals, behavioral and cognitive techniques, such as thought stopping, relaxation techniques, behavioral strategies to prevent or delay SM (e.g., removing all sharp objects so the individual cannot engage in skin cutting), and cognitive therapy designed to modify erroneous and distorted thought patterns may be useful (Hawton, 1990). A form of cognitive–behavioral therapy known as dialectical behavior therapy, which is based on the view that those who engage in SM exhibit faulty problem-solving behaviors, low distress tolerance, and inadequate coping skills, has shown some promise for the treatment of SM (Favazza, 1999). Cognitive–behavioral procedures also may need to be combined with some form of pharmacotherapy, such as selective serotonin reuptake inhibitors (SSRIs), which may be effective for dampening the impulsivity of those who engage in SM although these pharmacotherapies do not target SM directly (Favazza, 1999). Treatment of those who engage in SM, particularly repetitive superficial/moderate SM, can be a difficult task. It requires intervention agents who are compassionate and flexible, and who demonstrate sensitivity to individual needs and a commitment to a multidisciplinary approach to treatment.

See also: Anxiety; Body Art; Body Image; Coping; Depression in Children and Adolescents; Functional Analysis; Functional Behavioral Assessment; Impulse Control Disorders; Self-Injurious Behavior

BIBLIOGRAPHY

American Psychiatric Association. (2000). *Diagnostic and statistical manual of mental disorders* (4th ed., text rev.). Washington, DC: Author.

Favazza, A. (1998). The coming of age of self-mutilation. *The Journal of Nervous and Mental Disease, 186*, 259–268.

Favazza, A. (1999). Self-mutilation. In D. G. Jacobs (Ed.), *The Harvard medical school guide to suicide assessment and intervention* (pp. 125–145). San Francisco: Jossey-Bass.

Hawton, K. (1990). Self-cutting: Can it be prevented? In K. Hawton & P. J. Cowen (Eds.), *Dilemmas and difficulties in the management of psychiatric patients* (pp. 91–103). Oxford: Oxford University Press.

Iwata, B., Dorsey, M., Slifer, K., Bauman, K., & Richman, G. (1994). Toward a functional analysis of self-injury. *Journal of Applied Behavior Analysis, 27*, 197–209. (Reprinted from *Analysis and Intervention in Developmental Disabilities, 2*, 3–20, 1982).

Miller, D. N., DeZolt, D. M., & Trimarchi, C. L. (2001). *"Cutters": Working with students who engage in deliberate self-harm.* Poster session presented at the annual convention of the National Association of School Psychologists, Washington, DC.

Ross, S., & Heath, N. (2002). A study of the frequency of self-mutilation in a community sample of adolescents. *Journal of Youth and Adolescence, 31*, 67–77.

Additional Readings for Nonprofessionals

Kettlewell, C. (1999). *Skin game.* New York: St. Martin's Griffin.

Strong, M. (1998). *A bright red scream: Self-mutilation and the language of pain.* New York: Penguin.

Additional Readings for Professionals

Favazza, A. (1996). *Bodies under siege: Self-mutilation and body modification in culture and psychiatry* (2nd ed.). Baltimore: Johns Hopkins University Press.

Walsh, B. W., & Rosen, P. M. (1988). *Self-mutilation: Theory, research, and treatment.* New York: Guilford.

DAVID N. MILLER
DENISE M. DeZOLT

Senior Scientist Award

The Senior Scientist Award is given by the Division of School Psychology (16) of the American Psychological Association annually to a senior scholar in recognition of an outstanding program of research throughout his/her career that has had an impact on school psychology. This award is not given simply for the amount of writing an individual has produced, but rather for a significant and sustained program of research. The program of scholarly work should be of exceptional quality in its contribution to the scientific knowledge base of school psychology training and/or practice. The primary purpose of the award is to recognize the sustained contributions of experienced members of the school psychology community to sound theoretical and research activity over the course of one's career. To be eligible for the award, a person: (a) must be either at least 50 years of age or 20 years postdoctoral by December 31 in the year nominated for the award, and (b) must also be a Fellow, Member, or Associate of Division 16 of the American Psychological Association. First awarded in 1993, award recipients include the following:

1993 Richard Woodcock
1994 Barry J. Zimmerman
1995 Tom Kratochwill
1996 Arnold Goldstein
1997 Alan Kaufman
1998 Jerome Sattler
1999 Terry Gutkin & Cecil Reynolds
2000 Thomas Oakland
2001 Jack Naglieri
2002 George Hynd
2003 Frank Gresham

See also: American Psychological Association—Division 16

K. ANGELEQUE AKIN-LITTLE
STEVEN G. LITTLE

Sexual Development

INFANCY AND CHILDHOOD

Although many people think of sexual development as a process that begins in adolescence, it actually starts at birth and continues through the life span. There is evidence that penile erections and vaginal lubrication and swelling occur in the womb. Baby boys may have erections immediately after birth while baby girls can experience vaginal lubrication and clitoral erections as early as the first 24 hours of life. New parents are often not aware of these changes, perhaps because there are so many other exciting things going on at the time. However, many parents are dismayed and embarrassed that their infant boy loves to "play with himself"! In fact, both infant boys and infant girls may discover that unintended genital stimulation during diaper changes or bath time is pleasurable. Caretakers may soon observe that babies have learned to stimulate their own genitals. This usually occurs earliest in boys, around 6–7 months of age, while girls follow at around 10–11 months of age. (All age ranges provided here are averages, taking into consideration that some children fall outside of the range.) Once infants learn to self-stimulate, they may even become annoyed when interrupted. Around 15–16 months of age, males typically begin to exhibit more obvious masturbation by directly touching and rubbing the penis. In contrast, a little girl at this age is likely to engage in more subtle forms of masturbation like rocking, sitting on her heel, or rubbing on objects (Miracle, Miracle, & Baumeister, 2003).

It is important to realize that infant and childhood self-stimulation of the genitals is not goal-directed toward orgasm. Rather, it is more of a self-comforting, "feel good" activity. Caretakers must be aware of the nature of the behavior in order to respond appropriately. The best advice for caretakers is to treat masturbation like any other normal, private behavior: by telling the child that this is a behavior that they should do in private. Many adults feel uncomfortable when children express their sexuality. However, it is actually very normal behavior and does not represent deviant sexuality.

Friedrich, Fisher, Broughton, Houston, and Shafran (1998) conducted a study on "normal" childhood sexual behaviors in order to determine if some of the troublesome behaviors that parents observe are, in fact, deviant. The researchers found that the majority of parents of children aged 2–5 reported that their child touches his/her "privates" at home and looks at others undress. Around age 3, many children kiss other children. The most important milestone for the 4- to 5-year-olds is that they discover one another's bodies. This may lead to playing games such as "doctor" or "show me." Often, children play these games with children of the same sex. Sex educators advise parents to use this milestone as an opportunity to discuss their child's curiosity. There is no evidence to suggest that this behavior predicts later sexual adjustment or later problems. Because children learn through parental reaction, it is advisable to remain calm and communicate acceptance to the child.

When children reach the age of 5, parents typically report a decline in observable, overt sexual behavior. The majority continue to report that their child touches his/her genitals at home. Children this age remain interested in discovering the body and may watch others undress or look at pictures of naked people. Beginning around the age of 10, as children approach adolescence, they show an increased interest in the opposite sex. They continue to socialize primarily with their same sex, but may group-date. During group dates, they often play games like spin-the-bottle or other games that allow for kissing (Friedrich et al., 1998).

ADOLESCENCE

During adolescence (roughly starting at age 12), children experience a great many physical, emotional, and behavioral changes. For girls, increased estrogen levels lead to growth of underarm and pubic hair as well as fatty tissue in the hips and buttocks. Girls may notice breast tissue growth as soon as 8 or 9, and breasts usually enlarge around age 10. They may wrongly perceive their new rounder hips and budding breasts as weight gain, rather than as a necessary and normal part of the physical changes they are going through. As a result, many young girls become dissatisfied with their bodies and may begin dieting in order to eliminate these unwanted pounds. For many girls, this marks the beginning of an eating disorder.

Also, girls grow taller at a faster rate than boys of the same age, often leaving them feeling awkward. The uterus, cervix, and vaginal walls enlarge and mature, allowing for their first menstrual period. At this point they are now able to become pregnant. Most girls begin menstruating at 12–13 years, but, of course, some girls will start their periods either much earlier or much later. One of the best ways to predict when a girl will start her period is to look to either her mother or an older sister as she will start roughly at the same age. Earlier menstruation is associated with earlier dating and earlier first intercourse (McCammon, Knox, & Schacht, 1993).

Physical changes for boys include the growth of pubic, facial, and body hair as a result of increased testosterone levels. Underarm hair typically appears first and is followed by facial hair, usually as "fuzz" on the upper lip. Only half of the 17-year-old boys in the United States shave, because beard development occurs 2–3 years after mustache hair. Beard and chest hair growth continue to develop through the early twenties. Adolescent boys also experience a deepened voice due to changes in the larynx and vocal chords. There are also several changes in the genitals. The penis and testicles get bigger, and the scrotal sac enlarges and begins to hang from the body. Most boys begin to masturbate to orgasm around age 12. It is usually a year after puberty before ejaculation occurs (usually age 13–14). Nocturnal emissions, or "wet dreams," usually occur about 1 year after first ejaculation and do not necessarily indicate the boy is dreaming about sex. Adolescent boys often experience more frequent, spontaneous erections. Most boys masturbate 2–3 times each week. There is no link between masturbation and sexual activity or sexual adjustment or maladjustment.

Adolescent boys get heavier and taller and their chest and shoulders widen. Boys usually stop growing taller around age 18. Boys are more likely to report more positive feelings about their weight gain, viewing their bodies as muscular, whereas girls often perceive it as "fat." Although many boys are embarrassed to talk about it, estimates indicate that 50 percent of them also experience enlargement of the breast tissue. The good news is that when this occurs, it usually disappears in a year or so.

Boys who physically mature before their peers are rated as more popular, good-natured, and relaxed. The data are mixed for girls. Some studies indicate that early-maturing girls are rated as more confident and popular whereas other studies say they are rated as less popular and self conscious. These findings highlight the importance of communicating with teens about their changing bodies and how to deal with these changes.

Hormonal changes also lead to emotional changes for the adolescent. During puberty, he/she is developing the physical appearance of an adult, and society often endorses sexy and grown-up behavior. Other people in the teen's environment may encourage the adolescent to "just wait to grow up." Such mixed messages may lead to confusion for adolescents as they attempt to sort out how to act.

By age 15, almost all teens have kissed someone of the opposite sex, and girls usually kiss earlier than boys. By 16, most teens have had their first date. The younger the age of dating, the more likely the adolescent is to "go steady" and to have sex. Other factors associated with earlier sex are drug use, having friends who have sex, and having parents with few rules or who do not enforce rules. The best predictor of sexual activity for a girl is whether her best friend of the same sex is having sex. For boys, the best predictor is level of testosterone. Factors associated with teens postponing sex are having higher educational goals, experiencing academic success, and feeling that they can talk to parents. Boys typically have sex for the first time at younger ages than girls.

A common way that teens satisfy curiosity and sexual desire without the risks of sex is by "petting" or "making out." Teens today are also more likely to engage in oral sex, with girls more likely to perform oral sex for males than the other way around. Teenagers who abstain from sex provide the following reasons: family values, threat of getting caught, unwanted pregnancy, and disease risk. Teenagers who have sex cite the following reasons: curiosity, peer pressure, and pressure from one's partner.

Although half of all high school students are sexually active, they do not have sex frequently. Satisfaction with the relationship is the best predictor of frequent sex, and more consistent contraception use. For most teens, contraception use is rare, inconsistent, and involves using ineffective methods. Other factors associated with contraception use include the following: peers use birth control, the female initiating use of birth control, and having sex with a partner who focuses on the long-term consequences of sex. Younger teens are less likely to use birth control because they lack both the information about it and the resources to obtain it. Those with poor academic performance and poor family relationships are also less likely to use contraception.

Teens are more likely to postpone having sex until they are older and they are more likely to use effective methods of birth control when parents have serious, frequent discussions with the teen about sex. In addition to imparting factual information, these conversations allow parents to communicate their attitudes and values about sex to their teen. Teen pregnancy in the United States has declined, but remains one of the highest in the world. Less than 10 percent of high school students receive comprehensive sex education before graduation. The majority report getting their information from peers (yet another reason for parents/guardians to communicate with teens!). Research does not show that sexual experimentation increases when sex education is provided. Although many parents have mixed feelings about schools providing sex education, it is important for both parents and children to be aware of the typical patterns of sexual development.

See also: Sexual Minority Youth

BIBLIOGRAPHY

Friedrich, M. N., Fisher, J., Broughton, D., Houston, M., & Shafran, C. R. (1998). Normative sexual behavior in children: A contemporary sample. *Pediatrics, 101*, E9.

McCammon, S., Knox, D., & Schacht, C. (1993). *Choices in sexuality*. New York: West Publishing.

Miracle, T. S., Miracle, A. W., & Baumeister, R. F. (2003). *Human sexuality: Meeting your basic needs*. Englewood Cliffs, NJ: Prentice–Hall.

Additional Readings for Nonprofessionals

Bell, R. (1998). *Changing bodies, changing lives: A book for teens on sex and relationships* (3rd ed.). New York: Times.

Westheimer, R. (1998). *Dr. Ruth talks to kids*. New York: Aladdin.

Additional Readings for Professionals

Jaccard, J., Dittus, P. J., & Gordon, V. V. (2000). Parent–teen communication about premarital sex: Factors associated with the extent of communication. *Journal of Adolescent Research, 15*, 187–208.

Santelli, J. S., Lindberg, J. D., Abma, J., McNeely, C. S., & Resnick, M. (2000). Adolescent sexual behavior: Estimates and trends from four nationally representative surveys. *Family Planning Perspective, 32*, 156–165, 194.

NANCY G. McCARLEY
NANCY FOSTER

Sexual Minority Youth

Sexual minority youth is a term used to describe a wide variety of young people who are lesbian, gay, bisexual, and transgendered (LGBT). Questioning youth, those who are questioning their sexual orientation or gender identity, are also represented. "Coming out" is a term used to describe recognizing one's status as a sexual minority and acknowledging it to self and others. As society recognizes the rights of sexual minorities and there

is more positive support for them, people are coming out at younger ages. The typical age for coming out used to be during the college years, with males coming out at younger ages than females. Today many more youth are finding the safety and support to acknowledge their feelings and identities during the high school years.

For all children, adolescence is a time of great growth, development of self-awareness, and finding a place in the world. It is a challenge for all young people, with trials and rewards. Sexual minority youth have the additional challenge of developing a sense of self and their place in a world that stigmatizes them for who they love and how they view themselves. With support, their journey can be as rewarding as that of the typical heterosexual teenager.

In order to guide and support sexual minority youth, it is vital for the adults in their lives to have a clear understanding of sexual orientation issues, environmental challenges, and correlates of risk and resiliency. Sexual minority youth, by virtue of their stigmatized existence in society, are more at risk than most adolescents for a range of problems including violent attack, homelessness, depression, sexually transmitted diseases, suicide, and drug and alcohol abuse (Tharinger & Wells, 2000). Sexual minority youth are 2 to 3 times more likely than other teens to attempt suicide and sexual minority youth comprise up to 30 percent of completed suicides. Some studies have found that as many as 30–40 percent of sexual minorities report attempting suicide at some point in their lives. About 25 percent of sexual minority youth are forced to leave their homes, and up to 30 percent of homeless teens may be sexual minorities (Ritter & Terndrup, 2002). A large-scale national survey of sexual minority adolescents revealed that 84.6 percent reported hearing antigay remarks in schools often or frequently, with 23.6 percent reporting hearing remarks from faculty or staff at least some of the time. In addition, 83 percent reported experiencing verbal harassment, 41.9 percent were physically harassed (being shoved, pushed, etc.), and 21.1 percent were physically assaulted by being punched, kicked, or injured with a weapon (Gay, Lesbian and Straight Education Network [GLSEN], 2001). Sexual minority youth are also at higher risk than other teens for experiencing violence in their homes. The harassment and violence is not limited to students who have come out; targets are also adolescents who are *perceived* to be sexual minority by virtue of appearance, nontraditional gender role, or rumor.

In schools, it is vital that all children be protected from harassment and violence. The ethical codes of all major psychological and educational professional organizations make a clear commitment to diversity and the rights of all students. Court decisions have affirmed the responsibility of teachers, principals, and other school officials to protect sexual minority students. In 1996, in the first ruling of its kind, the U.S. Court of Appeals found that the public school system failed to protect a former high school student in Wisconsin from abuse because of perceived sexual orientation and awarded him $900,000 (Buckel, 1996). More recently, the American Civil Liberties Union (ACLU) filed a lawsuit on behalf of a student who was harassed in the Visalia California Unified School District, and a settlement was reached in August 2002, with the district agreeing to train staff and students as part of sweeping reforms to address antigay harassment. In a case filed by the ACLU and The National Center for Lesbian Rights on behalf of five high school students, the Federal Court of Appeals for the Western states issued a decision in April 2003 that holds school officials liable for failing to protect students from antigay harassment (ACLU, 2002, 2003).

A number of programs have been developed by school systems to increase awareness and decrease discrimination, harassment, and violence against sexual minority adolescents. Henning-Stout, James, & Macintosh (2000) reviewed programs and found that successful programs have a number of general commonalities. Successful programs respond directly to the concerns of the community by dealing with harassment issues and level of awareness, are preventative in their focus, increase the safety for all youth, and counter heterosexism. Successful programs are designed through a collaborative effort to tailor programs to the needs of all students, parents, faculty, and staff within the cultural context. GLSEN (Gay, Lesbian and Straight Education Network) also has programs available for implementation for individuals and schools. Their website (www.glsen.org) is an excellent resource for individuals to educate themselves and to learn how one person can have a positive impact on the lives of sexual minority youth.

Heterosexual educators are often hesitant to support sexual minority youth for fear that others will perceive them to be gay. Furthermore, sexual minority educators risk losing their jobs because there are no laws in place in most states to protect them. Gay–straight alliance groups are an excellent way to develop support for sexual minority youth while offering some protection to all.

It is often difficult for school psychologists and other school officials to deal with issues around sexuality in schools because of conservative political environments. In addition, many hold personal views about the appropriateness or inappropriateness of the topic in school settings. Despite ethical and legal mandates, each person makes decisions based on individual values in conjunction with professional standards. For those struggling with issues about supporting sexual minority youth, several things need to be kept in mind. First, all children deserve a harassment and violence-free education. You can support antiharassment efforts without endorsing beliefs of any particular group. Second, about 10 percent of the adult population identifies as gay, lesbian, or bisexual despite living in a harassing, stigmatizing world where most felt isolated during adolescence. Allowing the stigma to continue does not change people; it makes the world a dangerous place for them to live. Third, protecting and supporting sexual minority youth is not about endorsing sexual activity, it is about accepting and advocating for an individual's right to attraction, dating, and love; even when the advocate is having difficulty comprehending those feelings.

See also: Sexual Orientation

BIBLIOGRAPHY

American Civil Liberties Union. (2002, August 13). Lesbian & gay rights: Youth & schools. In groundbreaking federal lawsuit settlement, school agrees to strongest anti-gay harassment program in nation. Retrieved May 10, 2003, from http://www.aclu.org/LesbianGayRights/LesbianGayRights.cfm?ID=10674&c=106&Type=s

American Civil Liberties Union. (2003, April 8). Lesbian & gay rights: Youth & schools. Federal Appeals Court says schools must protect gay students from harassment. Retrieved May 10, 2003, from http://www.aclu.org/LesbianGayRights/LesbianGayRights.cfm?ID=12310&c=106

Gay, Lesbian and Straight Education Network. (2001). GLSEN's national school climate survey [Online]. Retrieved May 10, 2003, from http://www.glsen.org/binarydata/GLSEN_ARTICLES/pdf_file/1307.pdf

Henning-Stout, M., James, S., & Macintosh, S. (2000). Reducing harassment of lesbian, gay, bisexual, transgender, and questioning youth in schools. *School Psychology Review, 29,* 180–191.

Ritter, K. Y., & Terndrup, A. I. (2002). *Handbook of affirmative psychotherapy with lesbians and gay men.* New York: Guilford.

Tharinger, D., & Wells, G. (2000). An attachment perspective on the developmental challenges of gay and lesbian adolescents: The need for continuity of caregiving from family and schools. *School Psychology Review, 29,* 158–173.

Additional Readings for Nonprofessionals

Heron, A. (1994). *Two teenagers in 20: Writings by gay and lesbian youth.* Los Angeles: Alyson.

Parents & Friends of Lesbians & Gays; PFLAG; 1101 14th Street NW, Suite 12030; Washington, DC 20005. Available from http://www.pflag.org

Pollack, R., & Schwartz, C. (1995). *The journey out: A guide for and about lesbian, gay, and bisexual teens.* New York: Puffin/Penguin.

Additional Readings for Professionals

Annotated Bibliography for the Mini-Series on Lesbian, Gay, Bisexual, Transgender, and Questioning Youth: Their Interests and Concerns as Learners in Schools. Retrieved May 10, 2003, from http://www.nasponline.org/advocacy/SPRbiblio.html

Henning-Stout, M., & James, S. (Guest Eds.). (2000). Lesbian, gay, bisexual, transgender and questioning youth: Their interests and concerns as learners in schools [Miniseries]. *School Psychology Review, 29.*

Just the facts about sexual orientation and youth. A primer for principals, educators and school personnel. (1999). Retrieved May 10, 2003, from http://www.glsen.org/templates/resources/record.html?section=114&record=424

Savin-Williams, R. C. (2001). *Mom, dad, I'm gay: How families negotiate coming out.* Washington, DC: American Psychological Association.

AMY M. REES

Sexual Orientation

Sexual orientation is a term used to describe an enduring emotional, romantic, sexual, or affectional attraction to another. Attraction may be toward the same sex (homosexual, gay, lesbian), the opposite sex (heterosexual, straight), or both sexes (bisexual). Sexual orientation is considered an aspect of a person's identity that is not consciously chosen, and there is significant evidence for a biological basis (Bailey, 1995). Although once considered a disorder, in 1973 the American Psychiatric Association removed homosexuality from the list of mental disorders. Physicians, psychologists, and other mental health professionals agree that sexual orientation in and of itself is not related to mental disorders. However, societal stigma and heterosexism (behaviors and attitudes that prize heterosexuality and denigrate homosexuality) can have a negative impact on mental health. So-called "reparative therapies" and "transformational ministries" that claim to change sexual orientation from gay, lesbian, or bisexual to heterosexual have not been found to be effective and also have negative impacts on mental health (Gay, Lesbian and Straight Education Network [GLSEN], 1999).

Although sexual orientation is often viewed as categorical, it is better described on a continuum from exclusively same-sex attraction to exclusively opposite-sex attraction, with varying degrees of both-sex attraction in between. Simple categories do not accurately represent the complexity of human experiences. Many people have had thoughts, feelings, and fantasies about, or behaviors with, the opposite sex, the same sex, or both sexes that do not develop into an enduring attraction. Sexual orientation is dynamic rather than static; people at any age may develop a self-awareness of their sexual orientation.

The term *sexual identity* is used to describe an individual's adoption of a label of heterosexual, gay, lesbian, or bisexual. Sexual orientation is used to refer to the feelings of attraction, while sexual identity is based on the individual's self and social identification. For instance, a person may have an attraction to both sexes (orientation) but choose to identify as gay (identity). General acceptance of terminology changes over time. Currently, *homosexual,* when used to describe a person, is considered to have negative connotations and is generally not appropriate. The term *heterosexual* is considered acceptable. Some object to the use of *straight,* because it implies that nonheterosexuals are *crooked. Sexual minority* is a term that is growing in acceptance in professional language. *Gay, lesbian, bisexual,* and, in some areas, *queer* are terms that are typically used by people for self-identification. In general, it is most considerate of others to accept the label that others have chosen for themselves.

Sexual orientation and sexual identity are different from gender identity. Gender identity, or gender expression, is the person's sense and expression of being male or female. It is a stereotype that masculine women are lesbians and feminine men are gay. Sexual minorities and heterosexuals both exhibit a range of masculine and feminine behaviors that cannot be reliably used to guess sexual orientation.

It is estimated that 6–10 percent of the population is gay or lesbian (Patterson, 1995). However, these numbers do not reflect the diversity of human experience because there are a large number of people who change their self-identification over the course of their lives. In addition, people with a bisexual orientation may identify as heterosexual, bisexual, gay, or lesbian at varying points in their lives. Our ability to develop accurate data about sexual orientation is hindered by the stigma attached in society to being anything other than heterosexual. Most studies are based on self-identification. It is likely that societal pressures affect people's willingness to disclose same-sex attraction. In addition, the societal expectation of heterosexuality (heterosexual assumption) combined with stigma may reduce self-awareness and increase discomfort and denial for same-sex attraction. Although sexual orientation is considered to be an aspect not chosen or subject to voluntary change, social pressures affect self-awareness and identity labels chosen.

Because the majority of people are heterosexual, and our society is organized around that assumption, development of awareness of same-sex attraction and identity as gay, lesbian, or bisexual is a process. A number of models have been developed to describe this process. For a full review, see Ritter and Terndrup (2002). In general, people go through phases of awareness and acknowledgment of feelings to self and possible confusion, exploration of feelings and attraction, finding peers and community, and acceptance and self-identification. The process varies from individual to individual and is greatly affected by availability of positive support in the environment.

Sexual orientation is just one aspect of a person's overall identity. People of all sexual orientations lead rich, rewarding lives. Young people in their teens are capable of recognizing their sexual orientation. Often, young people who are experiencing same-sex attraction are faced with a naive question of "How do you know if you've never done it?" by peers and sometimes well-meaning adults. However, most would never think to apply the same question to a young person who is experiencing socially accepted opposite-sex attraction. Sexual orientation is not dependent on behavior, but is rather a manifestation of feelings.

There are many myths about lesbian, gay, and bisexual people (LGB). LGB people are no more likely to be sexual predators than heterosexuals, because 99 percent of perpetrators of child sexual abuse are *hetero*sexual. "Recruiting" is a myth, but may have developed as a result of misinterpreting the actions of people newly exploring their identity and seeking support from others. People in same-sex relationships may be no more likely to split up than heterosexual couples, with many same-sex relationships lasting throughout the couple's adult life. Bisexuals have monogamous relationships and are no more likely than others to have multiple sexual partners. Children of LGB parents have no more mental health difficulties than other children do. In addition, children growing up in a household with gay or lesbian parents are no more likely to identify as LGB themselves than are children in heterosexual households. LGB individuals exist in all cultures and ethnicities (Bailey, 1995).

See also: Sexual Minority Youth

BIBLIOGRAPHY

Bailey, J. M. (1995). Biological perspectives on sexual orientation. In A. R. D'Augelli & C. J. Patterson (Eds.), *Lesbian, gay and bisexual identities across the lifespan: Psychological perspectives* (pp.). New York: Oxford University Press.

Gay, Lesbian and Straight Education Network. (1999). Just the facts about sexual orientation and youth. A primer for principals, educators and school personnel. Retrieved August 20, 2003, from http://www.glsen.org/templates/resources/record.html?section=114&record=424

Patterson, C. J. (1995). Sexual orientation and human development. *Developmental Psychology, 31*, 3–11.

Ritter, K. Y., & Terndrup, A. I. (2002). *Handbook of affirmative psychotherapy with lesbians and gay men.* New York: Guilford.

Additional Readings for Nonprofessionals

Heron, A. (1994). *Two teenagers in 20: Writings by gay and lesbian youth.* Los Angeles: Alyson.

Parents & Friends of Lesbians & Gays; PFLAG; 1101 14th Street NW, Suite 12030; Washington, DC 20005. Available from http://www.pflag.org

Pollack, R., & Schwartz, C. (1995). *The journey out: A guide for and about lesbian, gay, and bisexual teens.* New York: Puffin/Penguin

Additional Readings for Professionals

Henning-Stout, M., & James, S. (Guest Eds.). (2000). Lesbian, gay, bisexual, transgender and questioning youth: Their interests and concerns as learners in schools [Miniseries]. *School Psychology Review, 29.*

Savin-Williams, R. C. (2001). *Mom, dad, I'm gay: How families negotiate coming out.* Washington, DC: American Psychological Association.

AMY M. REES

Shy Children

Shyness refers to a tendency to be reserved or inhibited in social situations. Childhood shyness is quite common and exists on a continuous dimension, from children who are a little bit nervous to children who are severely anxious in social situations. Children who are at the low end of the continuum may only feel shy in certain situations, such as upon meeting new people or having to perform in front of a large group. These appear to be common feelings, with studies showing that up to 50 percent of young children feel shy in certain social settings (Beidel & Turner, 1998). As such, shy feelings are often transitory and are commonly thought of as part of a normal developmental process. In fact, many children will outgrow their shyness and typically do not require intervention efforts.

On the other hand, children at the higher end of the continuum may become so nervous in everyday social situations, such as at school or at camp, that they may want to avoid these places in order to avoid feeling anxious. Feared and/or avoided situations also may include playing sports or extracurricular activities, attending birthday parties, eating in public, and speaking to unfamiliar people in general. In extreme cases of shyness, children sometimes will not speak to other children or adults and may ask a parent or friend to speak for them. Often, a specific fear of doing or saying something that will be embarrassing prevents shy children from enjoying activities with their peers. Over time, extended avoidance of these types of social situations may result in some degree of social skill deficits (Stemberger et al., 1995). In social settings, blushing, shaking or trembling, tearfulness, and sweating are commonly observed. However, signs of extreme shyness may also be subtle. In fact, because shy children are frequently considered "good" students who do their work and do not bother other children, teachers often do not recognize that these children may be greatly distressed. In addition to their anxiety, other uncomfortable feelings either prior to or during social events are common, such as stomachaches, nausea, or headaches. For children experiencing such intense distress and avoidance, a diagnosis of social anxiety disorder may be warranted. Social anxiety disorder, also called social phobia, is a severe form of shyness and affects approximately 5 percent of children (Davidson et al., 1993). Most studies indicate that social anxiety disorder is evenly distributed among boys and girls, although some studies have found slightly higher rates among girls. Although the average age of onset is midadolescence, young children also may be given the diagnosis. Currently, studies indicate that for children who are socially anxious prior to age 11, recovery in the absence of intervention is unlikely (Davidson et al., 1993). For older socially anxious children/adolescents, feelings of loneliness and depression are not uncommon. In clinical studies, children/adolescents who are both socially anxious and depressed have a poorer prognosis for recovery than those who are socially anxious but not depressed.

Although the precise cause of shyness is not known, most researchers believe that both biological and environmental factors play a significant role. For example, while some children may be temperamentally predisposed to feel shy in social situations, other children, who do not possess the same temperamental predisposition, may display similar shy behavior in social settings. For this latter group of children, a prior significant negative (e.g., embarrassing) social experience is commonly thought to be the cause of such feelings of shyness. Furthermore, temperamental shyness together with early negative social experiences may create a specific risk for the development of social anxiety disorder (Stemberger et al., 1995). In addition, compared to nonshy children, children who are shy are more likely to have a parent who is socially anxious. Indeed, twin studies show that shyness is a strongly heritable trait. However, while a genetic link may be present, family environment has also been shown to play an important role in the development of shyness. Excessive restrictions placed on socialization activities, overprotective parenting, overemphasis on the opinions of others, and modeling of socially avoidant behaviors have been associated with extreme shyness in children. However, early signs of shyness (e.g., prior to age 5) suggest that a biological predisposition is more likely to be present.

The effects of childhood social anxiety over the long term have been found to include a delay in or lack of occupational advancement, a delay in or avoidance of marriage and starting a family, avoidance of leadership roles, and, in some cases, reliance on family members or the public for financial support (Beidel & Turner, 1998). As such, early intervention efforts are often recommended in extreme cases of childhood shyness. Several methods of treatment are available, including cognitive–behavioral therapy (CBT), social skills and assertiveness training (SST), and pharmacological treatments. Recent studies have shown CBT and social skills training to be highly effective in treating socially anxious children (Beidel, Turner, & Morris, 2000). CBT most often involves teaching children techniques to cope with their anxiety while gradually exposing them to feared situations, whereas SST focuses on helping children develop skills such as recognizing social cues and asserting themselves in social settings. Evidence for the effectiveness of pharmacological treatments is somewhat more limited, but promising nonetheless. In general, drugs that prevent the reabsorption of the neurotransmitter serotonin (SSRIs) have been shown to be effective when compared to pill placebo.

See also: Anxiety; Depression in Children and Adolescents

BIBLIOGRAPHY

Beidel, D. C., & Turner, S. M. (1998). *Shy children, phobic adults: The nature and treatment of social phobia.* Washington, DC: American Psychological Association.

Beidel, D. C., Turner, S. M., & Morris, T. L. (2000). Behavioral treatment of childhood social phobia. *Journal of Consulting and Clinical Psychology, 68,* 1072–1080.

Davidson, J. R., Hughes, D. L., George, L. K., & Blazer, G. (1993). The epidemiology of social phobia: Findings from the Duke Epidemiological Catchment Area Study. *Psychological Medicine, 23,* 709–718.

Stemberger, R. T., Turner, S. M., Beidel, D. C., & Calhoun K. S. (1995). Social phobia: An analysis of possible developmental factors. *Journal of Abnormal Psychology, 104,* 526–531.

Additional Reading for Nonprofessionals

Zimbardo, P. G., & Radl, S. L. (1999). *The shy child: Overcoming and preventing shyness from infancy to adulthood* (2nd ed.). New York: McGraw–Hill.

Additional Reading for Professionals

Beidel, D. C., & Turner, S. M. (1998). *Shy children, phobic adults: The nature and treatment of social phobia.* Washington, DC: American Psychological Association.

CANDICE A. ALFANO
DEBORAH C. BEIDEL

Sibling Rivalry

Sibling rivalry may be defined as the contentious feelings that occur between siblings or children in a family. There are many accounts in real life, as well as in movies and plays, of brothers and sisters who have engaged in emotional or physical combat with each other in the form of hitting, pushing, teasing, arguing, name-calling, and similar aversive behaviors. The biblical account of Cain and Abel is an example of sibling rivalry that can get out of control and become sibling abuse, a subject to be discussed later.

Sibling rivalry naturally occurs only in families where there is more than one child. A well-known psychologist is said to have defined the birth of a second child as the "dethroning" of the first child. This comment helps us understand why sibling rivalry occurs and how parents might intervene. Siblings do not choose each other. They simply arrive on the scene when another child is added to the family. The birth of another sibling means that the prior sibling or siblings will have to share with this new addition to the family. Initially, this may be experienced by the original sibling(s) as having to share the attention of mother and father with a newborn infant who requires a lot of their time. As the new sibling grows, it means sharing perhaps a room, toys, and other personal possessions. The sharing that is required of children often is at the root of the hitting, pushing, name-calling, and similar behaviors that constitute sibling rivalry. Children engaging in sibling rivalry often act as if there won't be enough to go around—enough attention, enough parental time, and enough of parents' meeting the many needs that children have.

An important clue for parents in preventing or coping with sibling rivalry is to make sure that each child feels important in his/her own right, or to put it in other words, that there is "enough" for each child. Adele Faber and Elaine Mazlish (1986), in their book *Siblings Without Rivalry*, state: "To be loved equally... is somehow to be loved less. To be loved uniquely—for one's own special self—is to be loved as much as we need to be loved" (p. 89). Parents must determine how they can respond to the uniqueness of each child. It may mean that a mother and her young daughter attend a movie together or go on a shopping trip without other siblings present. A father may go to a ballgame with his son without anyone else present. Children differ in their emotional needs and parents must be sensitive to these differences.

Unfortunately, sibling rivalry can get out of control in a family. When this happens, sibling rivalry becomes sibling abuse. A national study of violence in families found that siblings are the most violent persons in American families (Straus, Gelles, & Steinmetz, 1980). Thus, parents must be aware so that sibling rivalry does not get out of hand. Parents can ask themselves the following three questions in order to determine if sibling rivalry is crossing the fine line into sibling abuse:

1. How long and how frequently has the name-calling, fighting, and so on occurred between the siblings? It is impossible to state a definite period of time when this kind of behavior goes over the line into abuse; however, certainly when parents say they do not want to be around their children because they are constantly fighting, it is obvious the behavior has been going on too long. Another question is the following:
2. Is one child repeatedly a victim of another? A victim is someone who needs help. The child who is the victim in combative sibling behaviors needs for the parent to step in and stop the behavior. In these two questions, parents are looking for a *pattern* of behavior that is occurring.
3. What purpose does the behavior serve the perpetrator? Is this the way one sibling is able to control another sibling? Does the behavior put the perpetrator in a position of power over other siblings?

When parents become concerned about sibling rivalry that is repeatedly occurring in the family, they need to intervene. For example, if a parent sees a child hitting a sibling, the parent should call the child on it and say, "That's not how we treat each other," then give the perpetrator logical consequences for engaging in the behavior, such as no television for a night.

Parents will also find it helpful to intervene in sibling rivalry by calling a family conference. A good time for such a conference is at the dinner table before family members leave the table to do homework or other tasks. The acronym SAFE provides a guide for initiating and conducting a family conference. *S* stands for "stop the action." If two siblings are fighting, a parent needs to stop the behavior perhaps by separating them such as having each go to their rooms. *A* stands for "assessing" in a family conference the facts and feelings regarding what happens when siblings become involved in destructive behavior toward one another. Both the perpetrator and the victim need to relate to what occurs and how they are feeling when they get into a fracas with each other. *F* stands for "find out what works." This means the family members must engage in problem solving based on the facts and feelings that came up earlier. Often setting some simple rules, posted on a refrigerator or cupboard door, cuts down on arguments between siblings. Following are two examples of such rules:

1. No one borrows anything from another person's room without first getting permission to do so.
2. No one enters a closed door, such as a bathroom or bedroom door, without knocking and receiving permission to enter.

Posting a chart with chores siblings must do, such as taking out the trash or emptying the dishwasher and identifying a consequence for the failure to do the task on the designated day, helps to reduce arguments siblings get into over who is supposed to do what, when, and what happens if the chore is not done.

All siblings get into squabbles with each other. The parental response of ignoring the behavior will not make it go away. Also, each child needs to feel from the parents that his/her needs are important—that there is "enough" to go around for every member of the family.

See also: Parenting

BIBLIOGRAPHY

Faber, A., & Mazlish, E. (1987). *Siblings without rivalry: How to help your children live together so you can live too.* New York: Avon.

Straus, M., Gelles, R., & Steinmetz, S. (1980). *Behind closed doors: Violence in the American family.* Garden City, NY: Anchor.

Additional Readings for Nonprofessionals

Faber, A., & Mazlish, E. (1980). *How to talk so kids will listen & listen so kids will talk.* New York: Avon.

Faber, A., & Mazlish, E. (1987). *Siblings without rivalry: How to help your children live together so you can live too.* New York: Avon.

Wiehe, V. (2001). *What parents need to know about sibling abuse.* Springville, UT: Bonneville.

Additional Readings for Professionals

Connelly, E. (2000). *Sibling rivalry: Relational problems involving brothers and sisters.* Philadelphia: Chelsea House.

Wiehe, V. (1997). *Sibling abuse: Hidden physical, emotional, and sexual trauma.* Thousand Oaks, CA: Sage.

VERNON WIEHE

Skinner, B. F.

B. F. Skinner was born in Allegheny, Pennsylvania in 1904 and died in Cambridge, Massachusetts in 1990. He was the best-known promoter of the behavioral approach to psychology, and because of his research, writing, and personal influence, behavioral methods are widely in use in education, treatment of psychopathology, business, advertising, and elsewhere.

Skinner's specific brand of behaviorism, radical behaviorism, differs from other behaviorisms and from the popular perception of behaviorism. Essentially, radical behaviorism is atheoretical and promotes the search for relationships between behavior, including private behavior (e.g., thinking, feeling, imagining), and conditions of life, including conditions that shaped our species. Skinner specifically insisted that private experience, popularly known as "mental life," be included.

Skinner's legacy appears in two main forms, corresponding to the two main journals that report behavioral research. Researchers involved in Experimental Analysis of Behavior (EAB) study the basic processes governing animal and human behavior. Their work appears in the *Journal of the Experimental Analysis of Behavior*. A far larger group deals with Applied Behavior Analysis (ABA), and their research appears in the *Journal of Applied Behavior Analysis*.

BASICS OF SKINNER'S THEORY

Skinner's best work was probably the strategy proposed in the 1930s for the discovery of order in behavior. This was a novel solution to the problem of determining order in any phenomenon and it applies as well to physics and physiology as to psychology. It constitutes an alternative to the molecular/molar "unit of behavior" distinction represented in the views of others.

Skinner's operant conditioning theory and its applications presented in popular books and in the press have made him familiar to the general public. But, the public conception is a very limited one, not surprisingly, and the popular "Skinner" seems to be a composite of newspaper items that describe aspects of behaviorists such as Pavlov and Watson. After noting that Skinner was the most honored and cited contemporary psychologist, yet the most maligned and misunderstood, Hineline (1988) laid much of the blame on Skinner himself. Referring to "problems that have lain for decades at Skinner's door," he suggested that Skinner's approach is "countercultural," and thus invites criticism. Further, Skinner almost never responded to critics and often aimed his writings at popular audiences, inviting

caricature and distortion. We will set the record straight—what *did* Skinner do?

Skinner proposed the intensive study of the behavior of simple organisms, like the rat and the pigeon. If we can discover the principles that govern their behavior, we will find that they apply to behavior in general, including human behavior and experience. In the 1950s, there was a great deal of research on reinforcement schedules and the findings quickly found application in education and treatment of psychopathology, not to mention commercial animal training. But Skinner's point remained unclear to many.

Skinner's message was that an analysis of contingencies, or the relations among stimuli, behavior, and patterns of consequences, is the proper strategy for psychology. An experimental analysis of behavior would account for observable behavior and for experience and mental activity. It will explain attention, remembering, perception, learning, dispositions, traits, and any other activity we might consider. Most important, it means that to change your child's behavior, including performance in school, the key is to arrange conditions (environment, context) to promote the changes you want. By the end of the twentieth century, great progress was made and many held Skinner personally responsible for advances in programmed instruction and behavior therapy. Although that is an exaggeration, his influence in these areas is undeniable.

WHY THEORIES ARE UNNECESSARY

In 1950, Skinner argued against theories, not only in psychology, but in science in general. The puzzlement generated at the time continued for decades and many readers were never able to understand that what Skinner was doing was simply arguing against a specific definition of *theory*, which was cast in terms of intervening variables, the mainstay of all psychological theories.

When someone behaves rudely toward you, you may seek the cause for this by asking someone who knows the offender better than you do. You are told that he/she is a nasty person or a bully, and that accounts for the rudeness toward you. For practical purposes, that might be all that you want to know: that the person often acts this way and that you might do well to avoid him/her in the future. But, you learned only that the *names* you already assigned to the behavior, rudeness and aggressiveness, are appropriate names for that person's behavior much of the time. That is only naming, not explaining, that behavior. When we resort to such naming and say that someone is "aggressive," "industrious," "persistent," "intelligent," "willful," and that he/she has a "great memory," we only name behaviors and when we think we are explaining, we actually have only unfinished causal sequences, not explanations. That is the main ingredient in virtually all psychological theories.

When we refer to intervening variables like habits, drives, and even "learning," we commit the same error. Real explanations lie in the history of the individual and the species. Aggressive behavior may become strong because of the way one was raised, a history of failure, frequent disappointments, chronic pain, or thousands of other reasons. We often don't care what the relevant history is, but Skinner wanted us to know that naming it *aggressiveness* is no explanation. He felt that our knowledge of the conditions that produced the behavior is the only explanation necessary.

But that is not all there is to it—when we look to the past we seek causes for current activities, but those activities require proper description. This is the problem of the "unit of behavior."

THE BEHAVIORAL UNIT

Skinner outlined his strategy for the discovery of order in behavior (summarized in 1938). He showed that the unit of behavior need not be molecular, and it need not be molar. Skinner's rejection of the traditional molecular and molar alternatives and his proposal of a different kind of molar unit has often been misunderstood. In fact, half a century after they were written, Skinner himself seemed to misunderstand them! Skinner tended to emphasize molecular interpretations, despite his earlier arguments against them. His inconsistency concerns his followers and provides fuel for his critics.

Earlier theorists had restricted the analysis of all behavior to the discovery of stimuli that elicit specific responses. But what about spontaneous behavior, which is, by definition, not elicited? A child throws a tantrum for no reasons that we can detect. We find that such behavior is often influenced by the consequences it produces; we can influence the rate of occurrence of such behavior by manipulating such consequences. Skinner called this kind of behavior *operant behavior*.

What we must do is observe instances of our chosen behavior and refine our definition, beginning with the extreme generic case. Our unit, therefore, is not determined in advance. We seek out eliciting stimuli or consequences that influence the behavior in question and then narrow our definition of that behavior until we discover the class of behaviors that vary together in an orderly way. We quickly find that all the behaviors that we label as *aggression* do not act as a unit: different types of aggression are produced and maintained by different things, whether it be frustration due to repeated failure, attention from teachers, or other factors. The *law of effect* specifies that many behaviors are sensitive to the consequences they produce and so can be changed by altering consequences they produce.

THE LAW OF EFFECT

The *theoretical law of effect* attempts to explain why reinforcers work as they do. Is it really important that we know? Skinner long argued that it is not important and that efforts to explain the action of all reinforcers are misdirected. For him, the law of effect is an empirical fact; we find that many events under many conditions act to increase the frequencies of many operants and that is enough.

Until the 1950s, psychologists were very unsuccessful in accounting for behaviors that occur over any appreciable span of time. Ferster and Skinner (1957) were the first to show that the scheduling of reinforcers could produce extremely reliable patterns of behavior that could be maintained as long as was desired, often extending over a considerable fraction of the life of an experimental subject such as the rat. The rule by which reinforcers are delivered is called a *schedule of reinforcement*. The law of effect can be extended by this knowledge in the form of the *matching law*, which holds that relative response rates match relative reinforcement frequencies. This extremely important modification means that behavior is always a matter of *choice* and that one behavior may be altered by changing the consequences of another (see Malone, 1991).

TREATMENT OF HUMAN PSYCHOTICS

Many patients in mental hospitals spend decades as so-called hopeless cases, unresponsive to psychotherapy or to drugs. Such patients often refuse to eat, to dress themselves, and to practice the most basic personal hygiene. Ayllon and Haughton (1962) proposed to apply Skinner's principles to treat a population of such patients diagnosed as chronic schizophrenics. But how may that be done? What could act as a reinforcer to alter the behavior of patients who appear to want nothing and whose files show them to be "out of reality contact," "subject to psychotic intrusions," and suffering from faulty "ego identification" (Ayllon & Haughton, 1962)? In a situation such as this, the therapist considers the reinforcement contingencies that currently maintain the patients' behavior and those that might alter the behavior.

Bear in mind that these patients had been diagnosed as hopeless, had been hospitalized for many years, and initially were incapable of even the most rudimentary self-care. Yet, the alteration of consequences for their behavior transformed them. Ayllon and his colleagues arranged contingencies so that food was available only at specific times and access to TV and other valued activities depended on specific behaviors. Thus, the patients had to go to the dining hall or they didn't eat. They had to accomplish specific behavioral goals, such as dressing themselves, for access to TV. It was simple and smacked of animal training, but it worked. All of this shows us that we must look at behavior over time and if we want to change behavior, we have to consider the consequences produced by *current* unwanted behavior and change them. As long as the bully on the playground gets what he/she wants, the bully will remain a bully.

PRIVATE EXPERIENCE

Skinner was opposed to what he called "methodological behaviorism." This is the view that there is a distinction between public and private events and that psychology (to remain scientific) can deal only with public events. Skinner noted that this is the position that accepts the arid philosophy of truth by agreement; something is real if at least two observers agree. Methodological behaviorism leaves the mind to the philosophers.

Skinner called his own view "radical behaviorism," which does not distinguish between public and private events. Skinner certainly did not deny the existence of private experience, nor did he feel that its study is beyond us. What he did deny is the mind–body dualism of the mentalists and the methodological behaviorists. Thinking is something that we do, just as walking is something that we do. Our names for feelings are words that refer to real stimuli just as words refer to objects we see. To feel pain is a reaction to pain-producing stimulation, just as recognizing a friend is a reaction to other stimulation. It is important, however, to realize that feelings do not make us act. When we touch a hot stove it hurts and it makes us pull the hand away. However, withdrawing the hand is a spinal reflex response that would occur whether we felt pain or not. We do not withdraw because it hurts (Skinner, 1974).

MENTAL AS MOLAR: ARISTOTLE WAS RIGHT

William Baum wrote a book in 1994 that was a frank attempt to present Skinner's ideas more clearly and to eliminate some of the misunderstandings that still prevail. He improved greatly on Skinner by showing immediately how the great difference between radical and methodological behaviorism has practical significance when considering things that have proven difficult to deal with, for example, intelligence, love, and pain.

Aristotle defined things like "love," "virtue," "bravery," and "springtime" as patterns of activities extending over time. There is no instantaneous "pang" of love that characterizes life in any meaningful way and the concept of virtue can mean only a pattern of virtuous acts. Just as spring occurs over time, not with the sighting of a single swallow, love, virtue, and happiness are apprehensible only over time—perhaps a lifetime.

B. F. Skinner never saw how closely Aristotle's interpretation was to that of behavior analysis, but Howard Rachlin surely did. Rachlin's *Behavior and Mind* (1994) shows convincingly that Aristotle was more a radical behaviorist than was Skinner himself. As Rachlin sees it, such "patterns of behavior over time" actually define what we treat as mental. Consider how this applies to pain.

RACHLIN'S PAIN—MOLAR THINKING

In 1985, Howard Rachlin proposed that pain is not a private event, as had been assumed for millennia. Instead, he argued that pain is an overt behavior, with nothing whatever subjective about it. Preposterous as this seems, pain is an odd phenomenon when we consider it closely. Pain is not simply related to the amount and extent of damage to our body. In an article entitled "The perception of pain," Ronald Melzack (1961) wrote that pain is not "a function of the amount of bodily damage alone . . . ." It also depends on our personal history, our expectations, and other factors.

Melzack (1961) and Rachlin (1985) both cite the report of Henry Beecher (1959), an anesthesiologist serving in the army during the Second World War. Beecher noted the wounds suffered by wartime casualties and the proportion of those with a given severity of wound who asked for morphine anesthetic. Only about a third (35%) of them requested anesthesia, whereas 65% refused it, claiming that the pain did not warrant it. These men were not anesthetize because of shock, because they objected to the pain caused by an inept attempt to find a blood vessel to give an injection. When Beecher returned to private life as a physician in Massachusetts, he found that civilian patients with the *same* degree of wounds suffered by the soldiers requested morphine 80% of the time. Why did four fifths of the civilians need anesthesia, whereas only one third of the soldiers did? Beecher felt that this and other evidence made it clear that pain is not directly related to degree of physical injury. For the civilians, their injury was often a "bolt from the blue," a catastrophe occurring against a backdrop of relative comfort and security. It was different for the soldiers, whose injury brought an escape from a battlefield, where death is a constant threat. "Pain" then becomes relative, not an unmistakably private event.

ENDINGS

In describing Rachlin's (1994) molar behaviorism, Baum (1994) was careful to distinguish it from Skinner's view. Though the concept of *mental* or *mind* as "patterns of activity extended in time" derives directly from Skinner's vision, he himself never adopted it, though Skinner did describe his main contribution as the demonstration of the importance of "rate of response," which implies consideration of behavior extended over time.

Rachlin (1994) dispensed with the public/private distinction, whereas Skinner retained it, while denying that there was any real difference between overt and covert stimuli and behavior. Note that the analysis was left at the level of discrete stimuli and responses. Along with the equating of inner and outer, Skinner proposed that all aspects of what is called mind are best construed as activity—behavior—and that behaviors such as seeing and thinking need not imply movement in space. Most important, seeing, thinking, and the rest are modifiable and so may be altered by altering contingencies. The molar behaviorism of Rachlin goes far beyond this view, just as Skinner's view goes far beyond the limited views of most of psychology.

For purposes of understanding your child's behavior remember these simple things:

- Everything that concerns you about your child can best be viewed as *behavior* and behavior can be changed by altering its consequences. Arrange clear and specific consequences for behaviors.
- Do not rely on exhortations, such as "work hard," "do the right thing," and such homilies. Be specific and require 2 hours of studying each night.

Above all, remember that Skinner showed us that children, rats, and pigeons always do as they "should." That is, they do what the context requires. If we want to change what they do, we must change the environment by rearranging the schedules of reinforcements and punishments for specific behaviors.

See also: Pavlov, Ivan; Personality Theory: Operant; Watson, John B.

BIBLIOGRAPHY

Allyon, T., & Haughton, E. (1962). Control of the behavior of schizophrenic patients by food. *Journal of the Experimental Analysis of Behavior, 5*, 343–352.

Baum, W. M. (1994). *Understanding behaviorism: Science, behavior, and culture.* New York: HarperCollins.

Beecher, H. K. (1959). *Measurement of subjective responses. Quantitative effects of drugs.* New York: Oxford University Press.

Ferster, C. B., & Skinner, B. F. (1957). *Schedules of reinforcement.* New York: Appleton-Century-Crofts.

Hineline, P. N. (1988). Getting Skinner straight. In A. C. Catania & S. Harnad (Eds.), *The selection of behavior: The operant behaviorism of B. F. Skinner: Comments and consequences.* New York: Cambridge University Press.

Melzack, R. (1961). The perception of pain. *Scientific American, 204*, 41–48.

Rachlin, H. (1985). Pain and behavior. *Behavioral and Brain Sciences, 8*, 43–83.

Rachlin, H. (1994). *Behavior and mind.* New York: Oxford University Press.

Skinner, B. F. (1938). *The behavior of organisms.* New York: Appleton-Century-Crofts.

Skinner, B. F. (1950). Are theories of learning really necessary? *Psychological Review, 57*, 193–216.

Skinner, B. F. (1974). *About behaviorism.* New York: Knopf.

Additional Readings for Nonprofessionals

Byork, D. (1993). *B. F. Skinner: A life.* New York: Basic Books.

Skinner, B. F. (1948/1976). *Walden II.* New York: Macmillan.

Additional Readings for Professionals

Malone, J. C. (1991). *Theories of learning: A historical approach.* Belmont, CA: Wadsworth.

Skinner, B. F. (1984). Canonical papers of B. F. Skinner. *Behavioral and Brain Sciences, 4* (Whole No. 4).

Verplanck, W. S. (1954). Burrhus F. Skinner. In Estes et al. (Eds.), *Modern learning theory.* New York: Appleton-Century-Crofts.

JOHN C. MALONE
NIGEL O. LAY

Sleep Disorders

Sleep disorders have been reported to occur in 24–47 percent of children (Blampied & France, 1993). The most common sleep disorders include bedtime refusal, sleep onset delay, parasomnias (e.g., disorders of arousal, sleepwalking, night terrors), sleep apnea (i.e., airway obstruction leading to restless inefficient sleep), and sleep disturbances associated with pharmacological treatment (e.g., stimulant therapy for ADHD). Blampied and France (1993) indicated that typical sleep patterns could be best described as an interaction between biological and environmental factors. Biologically, human behavior is largely affected by several cyclic patterns, one of which is the circadian cycle of waking and sleep. Environmentally, sleep is controlled by a number of variables. These variables may include appropriate environmental cues, appropriate bedtime routines, competing consequences for sleep of alternative behaviors (e.g., being allowed to watch television instead of going to bed), and sleep as an establishing operation in that too much or too little sleep can affect overall sleep patterns.

PARASOMNIAS

Normal sleep consists of cycles through light sleep (Stage I) to deep sleep (Stage II) with arousal through Stages III and IV to rapid eye movement (REM) dream sleep, several times a night. Typical sleep cycles are 90 minutes long, with brief awakenings or arousals from Stage IV. Young children sleep very deeply. Arousal from this deep sleep is sometimes incomplete and disturbed. When the child cannot return to a normal state of sleep, they are considered to have a parasomnia. These events span the gamut from the nightmares of REM sleep to night terrors, sleepwalking, and confusion arousal from Stage IV sleep.

Nightmares typically occur in the last third of sleep when REM sleep is most common. The child typically remembers the frightening dream content that may reflect daytime events and stressors. They start as early as 18 months and occur for

10 to 50 percent of children. Nightmares may be treated with brief comforting by the parents in the child's bedroom: Prevention includes positive stories at bedtime and repeated imagining of pleasant thoughts. When recurrent nightmares impair the child's daytime activity, intervention with counseling and the use of tricyclic antidepressants to interrupt the sleep cycle may be warranted.

Night terrors occur in 3 to 5 percent of young children. They typically commence later in life than nightmares and are usually seen after 60 to 90 minutes of sleep. The child displays physiological signs of fear with pupil dilation, sweating, and increased heart rate. The child is not responsive, may lash out at those trying to comfort them, and does not remember the event in the morning. Occurrence tends to happen in clusters, with spontaneous remissions. Treatment initially consists of regular family schedules with adequate sleep. Awakening the child after 1 hour of sleep or 30 minutes before expected events will often interrupt the cycle. If terrors persist, the use of low-dose tricyclic antidepressants is usually effective.

Similar to night terrors, sleepwalking occurs early in the sleep cycle. Children will be difficult to arouse, appear uncoordinated, and tend to wander in inappropriate locations. Children will not remember the event, which may be triggered by life stresses, excessive tiredness, and interruptions of daily schedules. Although routine early awakenings timed to precede expected walking episodes and use of pharmacological agents are usually effective, the child needs to be safeguarded from accidental injury during clusters of sleepwalking episodes.

OBSTRUCTIVE SLEEP APNEA

Obstructive sleep apnea is seen in up to 3 percent of preschool and school-aged children and is caused by airway restriction. The child thrashes around, sleeping fitfully as they search for a position that opens the upper airway. The neat bedcovers of early evening are disheveled as a result of the constant movement. Snoring is commonly observed in up to 70 percent of these children. Parents complain of "legendary" snoring in all sleep positions. One commonly observes the child mouthbreathing and chewing with the mouth open. Parents will use terms such as breath holding, gasping, and choking to describe their child's breathing pattern. Mornings are often trying family experiences as the tired child is coaxed out of bed and into the normal morning routine.

For the school-aged child with sleep disturbance due to upper airway obstruction, physicians and educators are beginning to recognize that inefficient sleep increases risk for educational problems. The student is excessively sleepy at school, easily aroused to opposition, and demonstrates a poor attention span, often leading to overt physical hyperactivity. School-aged child diagnosis and treatment may be difficult, as the source of the exhaustion may not be apparent. The behaviors may be subtle even as they jeopardize the school experience. The child may easily be labeled as oppositional defiant or hyperactive. Pharmaceutical treatment may be initiated for ADHD while diagnostic criteria are being sought for this sleep disorder.

The gold standard for diagnosis is a sleep study. Availability and expense have often relegated this measure to difficult or confusing cases. A sensitive history and physical examination by the pediatrician or otolaryngologist often leads to the correct diagnosis and treatment. Although many rare congenital disorders and occult physical malformation may cause the problem, the most common cause is hypertrophy of the adenoids and/or tonsils. Medical treatment with antihistamine–decongestants or nasal steroids may be effective but surgical treatment with adenotonsillectomy (i.e., removal of adenoids and tonsils) is often required.

Relief from offending symptoms is often permanent. The snoring, restless sleep, and mouth breathing rapidly resolve and are long lasting. Problem behaviors associated with inefficient restless sleep may lead to a premature diagnosis of ADHD, Oppositional Defiant Disorder, or Persistent Developmental Delay. When treatment for upper airway obstruction has been successful, some problem behaviors decrease, permitting withdrawal of behavioral and medical treatment for those problems. Thus, a school-age child with *unexplained* behavioral traits that suggest psychiatric problems, and who also has snoring and restless sleep, deserves a detailed examination of sleep problems before a psychiatric diagnosis is considered and treatment initiated.

SLEEP PROBLEMS ASSOCIATED WITH ATTENTION-DEFICIT/HYPERACTIVITY DISORDER

The diagnosis and pharmacological treatment of Attention-Deficit/Hyperactivity Disorder has increased dramatically in the past 20 years. The incidence has remained consistent at 4 to 8 percent of the population over this period, with increasing sensitivity to diagnosis in young women. Up to 10 or 15 percent of children in some regions may be on pharmacological therapy for ADHD. Although the tendency for stimulant therapy to cause sleep disturbance is well known, it is less well appreciated that sleep disturbance can be a fundamental manifestation of the disorder requiring treatment.

Over 300 double-blind studies have shown the effectiveness of stimulants for the treatment of ADHD. Ten percent of those treated will report problems of insomnia directly related to stimulant therapy. Long-acting preparations of methylphenidate (Concerta, Ritalin LA, Metadate CD) and mixed amphetamine salts (Adderall XR) now account for over 50 percent of prescriptions, and the incidence of sleep problems has risen with these new more convenient preparations. Physicians and therapists often have to adjust dose and timing of these medications to permit effective sleep. Pharmacological aids may be employed if insomnia unresponsive to dose and timing adjustment jeopardizes the observed real positive effect of stimulant therapy.

Many parents report the inability of their child to settle down to sleep when ADHD remains untreated. Older children describe a constant pressure of scattered thought processes, which prevent attention to and concentration on the task at hand—going to sleep. Paradoxically, the use of stimulant medication, including doses just prior to bedtime, will often resolve this inherent sleep problem of ADHD.

The use of diphenhydramine (Benadryl), a common over-the-counter antihistamine and sleep aid, may help with earlier onset of sleep but drowsiness and cognitive deficits may last well into the morning, possibly compromising school performance. A naturally occurring hormone, melatonin, sold as a vitamin or nutritional supplement has proven useful to many practitioners. The Food and Drug Administration (FDA) does not regulate it and variation of concentration and purity between manufacturers and product lines makes dosing a trial-and-error process.

Prescription drugs used in concert with the stimulants help induce sleep in the child with insomnia that is either an inherent property of ADHD or a result of stimulant therapy. Clonidine (Catapres), an antihypertensive, is used commonly before bedtime to reduce motor activity and is quite effective in permitting sleep. Mirtazapine (Remeron), a quadricyclic antidepressant, is also used with great effectiveness. Although neither medication appears to induce tolerance to their effects, practitioners are cautioned that use of these medications for sleep induction in children is an "off label" indication not approved by the FDA. Benzodiazepines (Valium, Ativan, Restoril, etc.) are generally not used because of rapid development of tolerance and abuse potential.

BEDTIME REFUSAL AND POOR SLEEP ONSET DELAY

The refusal of a child to appropriately go to bed and consequently fall asleep can be best described as a chain of events. First, effective bedtime routines begin with a period of quiet, which acts as a setting event for the child to sleep when entering the bed. Specifically, a child will comply more often with the prompt "go to bed" when it is preceded by a period of inactivity versus a period of play. Second, once in bed, effective cues must be present that control falling asleep. For example, a specific

blanket, the closure of a book after reading to the child, turning off the overhead light, or turning on a night-light can serve as cues. Third, a minimal number of sleep-competing activities should be present. Specifically, if the child is allowed to play with a favorite toy or watch a video until sleep onset, significant delays will most likely occur. And fourth, a significant amount of time between recent sleep and bedtime must occur for sleep deprivation to make falling asleep more likely. Using these procedures in isolation or in combination has resulted in a number of effective behavioral interventions.

Antecedent Intervention

Treatments that utilize stimulus control or cues typically have two components: (a) a specific cue or set of cues that control sleep onset and (b) removal of reinforcement for behaviors that compete with sleep (i.e., extinction). Specific cues that have been successful have included positive bedtime routines, providing specific bed-related cues, removal of parental attention, and providing objects and activities that facilitate falling asleep. Essential to the success of these treatments is the use of salient cues that are available for the child should a night awakening occur. Specifically, upon awakening, the cue needs to set the occasion for the child to fall back to sleep. Thus, setting up bedtime routines that include cues that are not available throughout the night (i.e., parent controlled) are countertherapeutic.

Consequence Intervention

Treatments that utilize consequences as a primary treatment for bedtime refusal and poor sleep onset delay focus on establishing contingencies of reinforcement that increase sleep-compatible behaviors. These treatments also include procedures that decrease the occurrence of behaviors that are incompatible with sleep. Specifically, either punishment or extinction contingencies are used to reduce incompatible behaviors. Thus, prior to the implementation of treatment, the contingencies of reinforcement that maintain incompatible behavior must be identified. Once the maintaining contingencies are identified, treatments are prescribed in the same fashion as any other problem behavior. First, a list of sleep-compatible behaviors is developed and subsequently reinforced. Second, the hypothesized reinforcer for incompatible behavior is removed (i.e., an extinction contingency). Unfortunately, the use of an extinction contingency often results in an escalation of problem behavior. This increase in problem behavior is often unacceptable to parents, which, in turn, can lead to poor treatment integrity. Given this potential outcome, it is essential that parents fully understand the negative side effects that can occur when consequence-based treatments are employed. Specifically, when problem behaviors no longer result in desired outcomes (i.e., crying no longer results in getting out of bed) temporarily the problem behavior persists.

Faded Bedtime with Response Cost

To date, the faded bedtime with response cost procedures described by Piazza and Fisher (1991) may provide the most effective tool for treating bedtime refusal and delayed sleep onset without the use of medication. The procedure includes four components. First, a baseline for sleep onset is established by measuring asleep and awake periods within 30-minute intervals throughout the day and night. Once established, a bedtime is determined that should result in rapid sleep onset. Specifically, this initial bedtime is determined by calculating the average sleep onset time during baseline and adding 30 minutes. Next, if the child fails to display sleep behavior within 15 minutes of being introduced to the bed, the individual is removed from the bed for 1 hour (i.e., response cost). This sequence of events is continued until sleep onset is obtained within 15 minutes. Lastly, bedtime is faded back by 30-minute intervals each night until a desired sleep onset time is obtained. The primary drawback to using this routine is that it is labor-intensive.

See also: Attention-Deficit/Hyperactivity Disorder; Oppositional Defiant Disorder

BIBLIOGRAPHY

Blampied, N. M., & France, K. G. (1993). A behavioral model of infant sleep disturbance. *Journal of Applied Behavior Analysis, 26,* 477–492.

Piazza, C. C., & Fisher, W. (1991). A faded bedtime with response cost protocol for treatment of multiple sleep problems in children. *Journal of Applied Behavior Analysis, 24,* 129–140.

Additional Reading for Nonprofessionals

Golbin, A. Z. (1995). *The world of children's sleep: Parents guide to understanding children and their sleep problems.* Salt Lake City: Michaelis Medical Publishing.

Additional Readings for Professionals

Ashbaugh, R., & Peck, S. M. (1998). Treatment of sleep problems in a toddler: A replication of the faded bedtime with response cost protocol. *Journal of Applied Behavior Analysis, 31,* 127–129.

Pearl, P. L. (2002). Childhood sleep disorders: Diagnostic and therapeutic approaches. *Current Neurology and Neuroscience Reports, 2*(2), 150–157.

K. Mark Derby
Stephen Luber
Kimberly P. Weber
Anjali Barretto

Social–Emotional Development

The study of social and emotional development encompasses personality theory, theories of attachment, emotional regulation and expression, moral development, and concepts of the self. Unlike other disciplines that may emphasize an accumulation of attributes or skills, these areas most often view qualitative changes within the individual. The more prominent theorists in social–emotional development have seen growth in terms of stages, or in invariant periods of crisis.

Sigmund Freud (1923) established some of the earliest theories of social–emotional development with his psychosexual theory. In this theory, sexual feelings refer not to sexual acts per se but to activities that produce bodily pleasure—the term for this sexual energy is *libido*, and the area in which it finds its expression is the *erogenous zone*. A child who becomes excessively frustrated or excessively gratified may become fixated at this stage and may regress to the source of bodily pleasure as an adult. The personality develops from the conflicts of the three agencies of the mind—the id (the biological, pleasure-seeking part of the personality), the ego (the reasoning or reality-based agency), and the superego (made up of the conscience and the ego ideal). At each stage of the child's life, the resolution of the struggle within these three agencies will determine the traits of adulthood (Crain, 2000; Hughes, 2002).

The first of the childhood erogenous zones is the mouth, and Freud called the first 2 years of life—when the infant finds gratification through oral sensations—the *oral stage*. In the early part of the stage, the infant has little recognition of another as a separate person. The infant's focus on the self was the basis for what Freud termed *narcissism*. In the later oral stage, the infant develops the urge to bite, and the infant is aware (at a subconscious level) that the infant is driving the mother away.

The second stage, at 2 and 3 years of age, is the anal stage, when the child is focused on the sensation of bowel movements. At this stage, the child experiences the effects of toilet training—the parent seeks to have the child renounce the pleasurable feelings and gain control over instinctual urges. The child may develop either an anal-expulsive (excessively messy) or anal-compulsive trait (excessively orderly) trait when under stress.

Between the ages of 3 and 6 years, the child enters the phallic stage, when the child is focused on the penis. Experiences in this stage differ, of course, for boys and girls. The boy develops, what Freud termed, the *Oedipal complex*, where the boy seeks the love of his mother and feels rivalry with the father. At this stage the child develops defense mechanisms against prohibited feelings. The boy represses his sexual feelings and may identify with the father. Freud reasoned that the girl in the phallic stage experiences *penis envy*. She blames the mother for her lack of a penis and focuses her romantic urges on her father. The girl may repress her feelings of inferiority by becoming more aggressive and assertive.

From age 6 to 11 years, the child enters the *latency stage*. This is a time when the child has resolved issues of earlier stages and can now keep urges and fantasies to a subconscious level. These issues do emerge again though when the child reaches the next stage, the *genital stage*. When the child reaches puberty, the individual is now capable of carrying out feelings and must resolve issues of rivalry and dependence by breaking free of the parents.

Freud's daughter, Anna Freud (1958), developed more of the theories about adolescent crises than her father. Anna Freud described the more complex and varied defense mechanisms: taking flight, contempt, asceticism (denial of pleasure), and intellectualism. Though the validity of Freud's theories is continually questioned by scientists, his work has provided the foundation for other theorists and the therapeutic community (Crain, 2000).

Erik Erikson (1968) developed a theory of stages of development that are similar to Sigmund and Anna Freud's. Like Freud, Erikson believed that the effects of an incomplete resolution of a crisis are retained throughout life. The age frames are similar to Freudian stages, but the crisis in each stage deals with the more social world. Thus, Erikson departed from the notion of the erogenous zones and focused on more general *crises* to be resolved at each age (Fischer & Lazerson, 1984).

The first crisis to be faced by the infant is *trust versus mistrust*. The infant at this stage comes to know—from his caretakers' actions—if the world is a trustworthy place. The next crisis, between the ages of 1 and 3 years, is *autonomy versus shame and doubt*. The child in this stage begins the process of becoming an independent person, made to feel competent or ashamed. The crisis of *initiative versus guilt* occurs from 3 to 6 years of age. Children now begin to develop new abilities, and they strive to use them. As the child pushes new limits, parents may overreact and create feelings of guilt.

Where Freud saw the child in a stage of latency (age 6 to 11 years), Erikson found crisis—*industry versus inferiority*. The child is now emerging more into the wider social world and developing useful skills. The success or failure of the child will result in the relative feelings of competence. The child entering adolescence faces a crisis of *identity versus role confusion*. Adolescents seek ways to determine who they are and begin to concern themselves with their futures. Erikson also proposed crises that extended into later years. These stages he described as *intimacy versus isolation* (young adulthood), *generativity versus stagnation* (adulthood), and *ego integrity versus despair* (old age).

John Bowlby (1988) and Mary Ainsworth and her colleagues (1978) examined the impact of parent–child inter-action from the perspective of *attachment*. Bowlby proposed four phases of attachment: indiscriminate responsiveness to humans (birth to 3 months), focusing on familiar people (3 to 6 months), intense attachment and active proximity-seeking (6 months to 3 years), and partnership behavior (3 years and beyond). Ainsworth described four patterns of attachment: secure, insecure–avoidant, resistant, and disorganized/disoriented attachment. The types of attachments formed in early childhood can be associated with IQ, confidence, conflict resolution, and problem behaviors in later childhood.

Lawrence Kohlberg (1966) and Carol Gilligan (1982) examined the ways in which children develop moral principles. Kohlberg proposed six stages of moral development in a hierarchy he described as Preconventional, Conventional, and Postconventional or Principled. The first two stages (Preconventional) are typified by a reasoning of self-interest. The source of the values guiding a decision lies outside the individual. In Stage 1, the child views obedience to the dictates of authority as a reason for an action, and in Stage 2, the child sees the consequences for self as the reason—avoid punishment and seek an action that will bring a favorable return (Crain, 2000; Fischer & Lazerson, 1984). In conventional morality, reasoning is based on social constructs. In Stage 3, the individual seeks social approval, and in Stage 4, the individual does what is best for social order (Fischer & Lazerson, 1984). Postconventional morals exemplify an internalization and abstraction used in reasoning. Stage 5 is described as an adherence to a social contract and individual rights (Crain, 2000). The highest level of moral development, according to Kohlberg, occurred in Stage 6, where the individual holds to universal principles.

Kohlberg's research showed that individuals did not skip stages and usually did not regress to lower stages. Kohlberg conducted his research on boys, a point at which Carol Gilligan found fault. Gilligan pointed out that Kohlberg's findings focused on rules of formal justice, whereas her findings demonstrate women's emphasis on interpersonal relationships and the ethics of care (Crain, 2000).

The different theories presented here provide a foundation for establishing parenting techniques, therapeutic interventions, and conventions of social justice. Freudian theories are the basis for diagnosis and treatment of emotional disorders in adults and children, and Erikson's contributions, especially those on identity, have been found useful in educational settings (Crain, 2000; Hughes, 2002). The most important contribution of the theorists and research in this area may be the awareness that the life-world of the child is qualitatively different from that of the adult.

See also: Development; Moral Reasoning in Children and Adolescents

BIBLIOGRAPHY

Ainsworth, M. D. S., Blehar, M. C., Waters, E., & Wall, S. (1978). *Patterns of attachment: A psychological study of the Strange Situation.* Hillsdale, NJ: Erlbaum.

Bowlby, J. (1988). *A secure base.* New York: Basic Books.

Crain, W. (2000). *Theories of development: Concepts and applications* (4th ed.). Upper Saddle River, NJ: Prentice–Hall.

Erikson, E. (1968). *Identity, youth, and crisis.* New York: Norton.

Fischer, K. W., & Lazerson, A. (1984). *Human development.* New York: Freeman.

Freud, A. (1936). *The ego and the mechanism of defense.* New York: International Universities Press.

Freud, S. (1923). *The ego and the id* (J. Riviere, Trans.). New York: Norton.

Gilligan, C. (1982). *In a different voice.* Cambridge, MA: Harvard University Press.

Hughes, L. (2002). *Paving pathways: Child and adolescent development.* Belmont, CA: Wadsworth/Thomson Learning.

Kohlberg, L. (1966). Cognitive stages and preschool education. *Human Development, 9,* 5–17.

Additional Reading for Nonprofessionals

http://library.adoption.com/Human-Growth-and-Development/Stages-of-Social-Emotional-Development-In-Children-and-Teenagers/article/3215/1.html

Additional Reading for Professionals

Thompson, R. A. (1998). Early sociopersonality development. In W. Damon (Ed.), *The handbook of child psychology* (5th ed.). New York: Wiley.

MARK S. COTTER

Social Skills Building for Adolescents

Social skills building refers to the teaching of prosocial behaviors that are necessary for adolescents to successfully function in a variety of social contexts (Walker, Todis, Holmes, & Golden, 1988). For example, starting a conversation, requesting help from others, and apologizing represent social skills commonly employed by adolescents. Social skills develop early in childhood and are influenced by numerous factors, including personal characteristics of the child (e.g., physical appearance, language abilities), environmental conditions (e.g., family interactions), and contextual variables (e.g., cultural norms; McFadyen-Ketchum & Dodge, 1998). The development of age-appropriate social skills allows adolescents to establish social relationships, acquire peer acceptance, develop friendships, and adjust to changing social environments (Walker et al., 1988). However, adolescents experiencing social skills deficits

are at greater risk for a variety of negative outcomes, including interpersonal, educational, and psychological difficulties (McFadyen-Ketchum & Dodge, 1998). As a result, adolescent social skills building has been identified as an important undertaking for school professionals (McFadyen-Ketchum & Dodge, 1998).

Although adolescent social skills building can occur informally in the home, school, and community, most skills-building approaches focus on formal instruction that can be concurrently applied to groups of adolescents (i.e., universal program) or individualized to the unique needs of the adolescent (i.e., selected intervention; Gresham, 2002). In general, formal social skills building focuses on four primary objectives: (a) promoting the acquisition of social skills, (b) enhancing the performance of social skills, (c) reducing or removing problem behaviors that interfere with the performance of social skills, and (d) facilitating generalization and maintenance of social skills (Gresham, 2002). Because of the nature of adolescent social skills problems, skills-building approaches will be more likely to focus on the advanced objectives and less likely to focus on basic skill acquisition.

Many behavioral intervention techniques have been employed to train global social skills or alter specific behaviors that impede social competence (McFadyen-Ketchum & Dodge, 1998). To promote adolescents' acquisition of social skills, modeling, coaching, and rehearsal may be required (Goldstein & McGinnis, 1997; Gresham, 2002; Walker, Todis, Holmes, & Golden, 1988). Strategies to enhance adolescents' skill performance may include manipulating environmental antecedents (e.g., peer initiation), as well as manipulating environmental consequences (e.g., verbal praise, contingency contracting; Goldstein & McGinnis, 1997; Gresham, 2002; Walker et al., 1988). The removal of problem behaviors that may interfere with appropriate social skills may involve differential reinforcement, overcorrection, time-out, or systematic desensitization (Goldstein & McGinnis, 1997; Gresham, 2002; Walker et al., 1988). Generalization strategies should be employed throughout social skills building to ensure that adolescents continue to apply newly developed skills with different persons in different settings and situations (DuPaul & Eckert, 1994; Goldstein & McGinnis, 1997; Gresham, 2002; Walker et al., 1988). These strategies are typically embedded within the social skills building technique and may involve using different materials or settings (i.e., training diversely), teaching different responses or relevant behaviors (i.e., exploiting functional contingencies), and incorporating relevant social and physical stimuli (i.e., incorporating functional mediators; DuPaul & Eckert, 1994; Gresham, 2002). The selection of these techniques will vary depending on the social skills addressed and the competencies of the adolescent.

In recent years, a number of formal adolescent social skills building programs have been developed that target global social skills (DuPaul & Eckert, 1994). These adolescent social skills building programs can be implemented with large groups of adolescents under similar conditions. For example, the *Skillstreaming* (Goldstein & McGinnis, 1997) or the ACCEPTS (Walker et al., 1988) curricula are structured to teach a variety of global adolescent social skills that are related to successful social functioning. In the *Skillstreaming* curriculum, adolescent social skills are divided into six skill clusters of increasing difficulty, which include (a) beginning social skills (e.g., listening, giving a compliment), (b) advanced social skills (e.g., giving instructions, convincing others), (c) skills for dealing with feelings (e.g., expressing your feelings, dealing with fear), (d) skill alternatives to aggression (e.g., sharing something, using self-control), (e) skills for dealing with stress (e.g., answering a complaint, dealing with group pressure), and (f) planning skills (e.g., setting a goal, arranging problems by importance; Goldstein & McGinnis, 1997). A number of general teaching considerations have been identified that may promote adolescent social skills building, including limiting the number of social skill instructors (i.e., two per group) and adolescents (i.e., six to eight per group), addressing instructor–student cultural compatibility (i.e., similar cultural experiences), conducting two sessions per week, and selecting adolescent groups that match real-life peers (Goldstein & McGinnis, 1997).

More intensive adolescent social skills building approaches have been developed for adolescents exhibiting more serious social competency problems, such as aggression, or psychological disorders, such as Conduct Disorder and Attention-Deficit/Hyperactivity Disorder. The *Prepare Curriculum* (Goldstein, 1999), which represents an extension of the *Skillstreaming* curriculum (Goldstein & McGinnis, 1997), teaches adolescents interpersonal problem-solving skills related to problematic social events. This curriculum was developed for school professionals involved in the teaching of prosocial competencies to seriously aggressive and withdrawn children. Comprehensive training is provided in this social skills building program, including anger control, moral reasoning, problem solving, empathy, situational perception, cooperation, stress management, recruiting social supports, and understanding and using groups. Throughout this individualized social skills building approach, prescriptive sessions are conducted. For example, sessions addressing empathy training would include readiness training (e.g., empathy preparation skills), perceptual training (e.g., programmed self-instruction), affective reverberation training (e.g., meditation, focusing), cognitive analysis training (e.g., exposure plus guided practice), and communication training.

Recent attention has also been focused on the assessment and training of social–cognitive skills that may be related to the performance of socially competent behaviors. It has been suggested that examining whether deficits exist in adolescents' social–cognitive processing abilities may be useful in social skills building (McFadyen-Ketchum & Dodge, 1998). Six social–cognitive skills related to adolescent social skills building have been identified: (a) ongoing observation and encoding of peer behaviors, (b) accurate interpretation of peer behaviors, (c) evaluating and identifying appropriate responses, (d) constructing appropriate responses, (e) selecting appropriate responses, and (f) engagement of responses (McFadyen-Ketchum & Dodge, 1998). Teaching adolescents to engage in these social–cognitive skills may improve their ability to consistently engage in appropriate social behavior across situations.

To date, most of the research examining the effectiveness of adolescent social skills building approaches has been conducted with preadolescent handicapped boys exhibiting serious social skills problems (McFadyen-Ketchum & Dodge, 1998). Adolescent social skills building approaches targeting specific prosocial behaviors have been found to be effective in changing selected behaviors for short periods of time (Goldstein, 1999; Goldstein & McGinnis, 1997; McFadyen-Ketchum & Dodge, 1998; Walker et al., 1983). Unfortunately, these types of adolescent social skills building approaches have not resulted in maintenance and generalization of treatment effects (DuPaul & Eckert, 1994; McFadyen-Ketchum & Dodge, 1998). Adolescent social skills building approaches targeting global or social–cognitive skills training have resulted in modest changes in prosocial behavior (McFadyen-Ketchum & Dodge, 1998). These types of approaches have demonstrated maintenance and generalization of treatment effects (Goldstein, 1999; Goldstein & McGinnis, 1997; McFadyen-Ketchum & Dodge, 1998). However, minimal evidence supports the extent to which these approaches lead to socially valid improvements as assessed by others (McFadyen-Ketchum & Dodge, 1998). Clearly, additional research is warranted that examines the extent to which adolescent social skills building approaches improve prosocial behaviors and patterns across settings, person, and time and that these changes lead to socially valid improvements as assessed by others (Gresham, 2002; McFadyen-Ketchum & Dodge, 1998).

See also: Adaptive Behavior Assessment; Shy Children; Social Skills Building for Elementary Children

BIBLIOGRAPHY

DuPaul, G. J., & Eckert, T. L. (1994). The effects of social skills curricula: Now you see them, now you don't. *School Psychology Quarterly, 9*, 113–132.

Goldstein, A. P. (1999). *The Prepare Curriculum: Teaching prosocial competencies* (2nd ed.). Champaign, IL: Research Press.

Goldstein, A. P., & McGinnis, E. (1997). *Skillstreaming the adolescent: New strategies and perspectives for teaching prosocial skills* (2nd ed.). Champaign, IL: Research Press.

Gresham, F. M. (2002). Best practices in social skills training. In A. Thomas & J. Grimes (Eds.), *Best practices in school psychology—IV* (4th ed., pp. 1029–1039). Bethesda, MD: National Association of School Psychologists.

McFadyen-Ketchum, S. A., & Dodge, K. A. (1998). Problems in social relationships. In E. J. Mash & R. A. Barkley (Eds.), *Treatment of childhood disorders* (2nd ed., pp. 338–368). New York: Guilford.

Walker, H. M., Todis, B., Holmes, D., & Golden, H. (1988). *The Walker social skills curriculum: The ACCESS program.* Austin, TX: Pro-Ed.

Additional Reading for Nonprofessionals

Christophersen, E. R., & Mortweet, S. L. (2002). *Parenting that works: Building skills that last a lifetime.* Washington, DC: American Psychological Association.

Additional Reading for Professionals

Goldstein, A. P., & McGinnis, E. (1988). *The Skillstreaming video: How to teach students prosocial skills* [Videotape]. Champaign, IL: Research Press.

Tanya L. Eckert
Arnold P. Goldstein
Melissa L. Rosenblatt
Blair D. Rosenthal

Social Skills Building for Elementary Children

Smiling, complimenting, and helping others represent social skills commonly employed by children. Teaching children prosocial behaviors that are necessary for successful functioning in a variety of social contexts is referred to as social skills building (Walker et al., 1983). These skills develop early in childhood and are influenced by numerous factors. For example, personal characteristics such as physical attractiveness, athletic ability, and academic skills are related to children's social skills development (Walker et al., 1983). Additional environmental (e.g., family factors) and contextual variables (e.g., cultural expectations) can also be related to children's social competence and peer acceptance (McFadyen-Ketchum & Dodge, 1998). Children who develop age-appropriate prosocial behaviors have the prerequisite skills necessary to establish social relationships, acquire peer acceptance, develop friendships, and adjust to changing social environments (Walker et al., 1983). Children experiencing social skills deficits are at greater risk for a variety of negative outcomes, including interpersonal, educational, and psychological difficulties (McFadyen-Ketchum & Dodge, 1998; Patterson, Reid, & Dishion, 1992; Webster-Stratton, 1993). Teaching children with social skills deficits has been identified as an important objective for school professionals (McFadyen-Ketchum & Dodge, 1998; Webster-Stratton, 1993).

Although the typical development of childhood social skills occurs incidentally in the home, school, and community, most formal social skills building is applied to groups of children (i.e., universal training programs) or individualized to meet the unique needs of the child (i.e., selected intervention programs; Gresham, 2002). Social skills building approaches for children focus on four primary objectives: (a) promoting the acquisition of social skills, (b) enhancing the performance of social skills, (c) reducing or removing problem behaviors that interfere with the performance of social skills, and (d) facilitating generalization and maintenance of social skills (Gresham, 2002). For many children experiencing social skills problems, skills building approaches target the acquisition of critical social skills related to prosocial behavior in school and related social situations (McFadyen-Ketchum & Dodge, 1998).

Most social skills building approaches for children either teach global social skills or alter specific behaviors that impede social competence (McFadyen-Ketchum & Dodge, 1998). Initially, modeling, coaching, and rehearsing basic social skills are used to promote children's acquisition of social skills (Gresham, 2002; McGinnis & Goldstein, 1997). In addition, changing or manipulating factors in a child's environment can enhance children's social skills (Gresham, 2002; McGinnis & Goldstein, 1997). In some cases, it may also be necessary to reduce problem behaviors (e.g., temper tantrums, aggression) that interfere with the development of social skills (Gresham, 2002; McGinnis & Goldstein, 1997). Finally, social skills building should employ generalization strategies to ensure that children continue to apply social skills in different settings and situations (DuPaul & Eckert, 1994; Gresham, 2002; McGinnis & Goldstein, 1997). For example, social skills building that uses different materials or settings (i.e., training diversely), teaches multiple responses (i.e., exploit functional contingencies), and incorporates related social or physical stimuli (i.e., incorporate functional mediators) enhances the likelihood that children will use these skills in social settings.

Recently, social skills building approaches have focused on the training of social–cognitive skills that may be related to the development of social competence. It has been suggested that children's social skills problems may develop as a result of social–cognitive processing difficulties and specific training in these skills may improve the performance of socially competent behaviors (McFadyen-Ketchum & Dodge, 1998). The six social–cognitive skills identified include (a) ongoing observation and encoding of peer behaviors, (b) accurate interpretation of peer behaviors, (c) evaluating and identifying appropriate responses, (d) constructing appropriate responses, (e) selecting appropriate responses, and (f) engagement of responses (McFadyen-Ketchum & Dodge, 1998). Providing children with specific training in these social–cognitive skills may improve their ability to consistently engage in age-appropriate social skills in a variety of situations.

In recent years, a number of formal social skills building programs for children have been developed that target global social skills (DuPaul & Eckert, 1994). These social skills building programs can be implemented with groups of children using similar procedures (Gresham, 2002). For example, the *Skillstreaming* curriculum (McGinnis & Goldstein, 1997) is structured to teach a variety of global social skills and social–cognitive skills that are related to children's successful social functioning. These skills are divided into six skill clusters of increasing difficulty, which include (a) beginning social skills (e.g., using nice talk, asking a favor), (b) school-related skills (e.g., following directions, trying when it is hard), (c) friendship-making skills (e.g., joining in, playing a game), (d) dealing with feelings (e.g., feeling left out, deciding how someone feels), (e) alternatives to aggression (e.g., dealing with feeling mad, deciding if it is fair), and (f) dealing with stress (e.g., dealing with mistakes, wanting to be first; McGinnis & Goldstein, 1997). Social skills building may be enhanced if sessions are conducted twice a week for 15 to 20 minutes and the number of social skill instructors and children is small (i.e., two instructors, 6 to 8 children; McGinnis & Goldstein, 1997). Other important considerations include assessing the cultural compatibility of children and instructors and identifying child groups that match real-life peers (McGinnis & Goldstein, 1997).

Another formal social skills building program for children that targets global social skills related to school functioning is the *ACCEPTS* (Walker et al., 1983) curriculum. Initially developed for children with handicapping conditions, this program could be adapted for use with nonhandicapped children exhibiting social skills difficulties. In the *ACCEPTS* curriculum, a number of procedures been developed for social skills building, and include (a) determining the child's social skills deficits, (b) general instructional procedures for teaching social skills, (c) scripts for teaching social skills to children, (d) videotaped illustrations of social skills, (e) role-play activities for practicing social skills, and (f) social skill activities that vary depending on the teaching format. Five social skill components are taught, and include (a) classroom skills (e.g., listening to your teacher, doing your best work), (b) basic interaction skills (e.g., eye contact, using the right voice), (c) getting along skills (e.g., sharing), (d) making friends (e.g., good grooming), and (e) coping skills (e.g., when someone says No). It is strongly recommended that moderate pretraining in the curriculum be provided (Walker et al., 1983).

One social skills building program that adopts a family–child–school-based approach to training was developed by Webster-Stratton (1993). This program was specifically developed for young children with behavior problems and combines parent management training, specific training in strategies to improve children's social skills, and home–school collaboration instruction. Many of the strategies used in this approach to social skills building are based on extensive work completed by Patterson and colleagues (1992). However, this group approach includes videotape vignettes that illustrate successful and unsuccessful parent–child interactions as well as specific parent education on issues related to adult well-being (e.g., coping, anger management, problem-solving strategies; Webster-Stratton, 1993).

To date, most of the research examining the effectiveness of social skills building approaches for children has been conducted with handicapped boys exhibiting serious social skills problems (McFadyen-Ketchum & Dodge, 1998). These studies suggest that social skills building approaches that target specific prosocial behaviors have been found to be effective for short periods of time (McFadyen-Ketchum & Dodge, 1998; Walker et al., 1983). For example, children are able to learn specific social skills that allow them to adapt to their social environment and increase the number of contacts with peers (McFadyen-Ketchum & Dodge, 1998; Walker et al., 1983). However, these types of social skills building approaches have not resulted in changes of global measures of social competence (e.g., peer acceptance), nor have they resulted in maintenance and generalization of treatment effects (DuPaul & Eckert, 1994; McFadyen-Ketchum & Dodge, 1998). Research examining the effectiveness of social–cognitive social skills building programs has suggested modest changes in children's prosocial behavior as well as maintenance and generalization of treatment effects (McFadyen-Ketchum & Dodge, 1998; McGinnis & Goldstein, 1997). Minimal evidence has been established regarding the extent to which social–cognitive skills building programs lead to socially valid improvements as assessed by others (McFadyen-Ketchum & Dodge, 1998). Research examining the effects of family–child–school-based approaches has demonstrated significant changes in children's prosocial behaviors (McFadyen-Ketchum & Dodge, 1998; Webster-Stratton, 1993). The preliminary evidence regarding the maintenance, generalization, and social validity of these effects has been positive (Webster-Stratton, 1993).

See also: Shy Children; Social Skills Building for Adolescents

BIBLIOGRAPHY

DuPaul, G. J., & Eckert, T. L. (1994). The effects of social skills curricula: Now you see them, now you don't. *School Psychology Quarterly, 9*, 113–132.

Gresham, F. M. (2002). Best practices in social skills training. In A. Thomas & J. Grimes (Eds.), *Best practices in school psychology—IV* (4th ed., pp. 1029–1039). Bethesda, MD: National Association of School Psychologists.

McFadyen-Ketchum, S. A., & Dodge, K. A. (1998). Problems in social relationships. In E. J. Mash & R. A. Barkley (Eds.), *Treatment of childhood disorders* (2nd ed., pp. 338–368). New York: Guilford.

McGinnis, E., & Goldstein, A. P. (1997). *Skillstreaming the elementary school child: New strategies and perspectives for teaching prosocial skills.* Champaign, IL: Research Press.

Patterson, G. R., Reid, J. B., & Dishion, T. J. (1992). *Antisocial boys.* Eugene, OR: Castilia.

Walker, H. M., McConnell, S. R., Holmes, D., Todis, B., Walker, J., & Golden, H. (1983). *The Walker social skills curriculum: The ACCEPTS program.* Austin, TX: Pro-Ed.

Webster-Stratton, C. (1993). Strategies for helping school-aged children with Oppositional Defiant Disorder and Conduct Disorders: The importance of home–school partnerships. *School Psychology Review, 22,* 437–457.

Additional Readings for Nonprofessionals

Christophersen, E. R., & Mortweet, S. L. (2002). *Parenting that works: Building skills that last a lifetime.* Washington, DC: American Psychological Association.

Webster-Stratton, C., & Herbert, M. (1994). *Troubled families—Problem children.* New York: Wiley.

Additional Readings for Professionals

Goldstein, A. P., & McGinnis, E. (1988). *The Skillstreaming video: How to teach students prosocial skills* [Videotape]. Champaign, IL: Research Press.

Webster-Stratton, C. (1987). *Parents and children: A 10 program videotape parent training series with manuals* [Videotape]. Eugene, OR: Castilia.

Tanya L. Eckert
Arnold P. Goldstein
Melissa L. Rosenblatt
Blair D. Rosenthal

Social Stories

The social story intervention, first described in the early 1990s, was designed to teach children with autism to communicate more effectively and to enhance their social behavior. A social story is an individualized short story that adheres to a specific format, including an objective description of a social situation, activity, or skill in terms of relevant social cues and expected responses (Gray, 1998; Gray & Garand, 1993). They are designed to fit each child's specific target situation and are written from the perspective of the child with an autistic spectrum disorder. They have been used to describe a change in routine (e.g., field trips, fire drills, substitute teachers), teach academics (e.g., counting the number of children in line) and self-care skills, personalize social skills, and reduce fears, aggression, and obsessive behaviors (Gray, 2000; Gray & Garand, 1993). The objective of each social story is to provide the child with an appropriate response to a given situation.

The original social story format suggested using a combination of sentence types: descriptive, perspective, and directive sentences (Gray & Garand, 1993). Descriptive sentences describe a target situation by defining where and when it takes place, who is involved, what they are doing, and why they are doing it. They may also describe the physical properties of the room in which the situation occurs or the scenery if outdoors. Descriptive sentences must be included in every social story and are the only required sentence type (Gray, 2000); for example, "At recess many boys and girls sit under the tree."

Perspective sentences describe the perspective of the other individuals in the situation: "My teacher will be happy if I raise my hand before I talk." Directive sentences direct the child as to the response he/she is expected to provide in that situation. They typically begin with "I will try" to allow for a less rigid interpretation of the story: "I will try to be quiet when I'm in the library."

Recently the variety of sentence types has been expanded to include affirmative, partial, control, and cooperative sentences (Gray, 2000). Affirmative sentences generally direct the child to subscribe to a rule: "Only one boy at a time may jump from the diving board." Partial sentences can help demonstrate comprehension by asking the child to fill in the missing word from the story: "When I am talking to someone, I will try to _____ at their face." Control sentences help the child develop an appropriate strategy for remembering information in the story or for explaining metaphors. "When someone says I changed my mind, I can think of an idea becoming better like a caterpillar, changing into a butterfly" (pp. 13–15). Cooperative sentences describe how others can help the student learn a new skill. "My teacher can help me put on my coat."

Although the length of each social story may vary, the most successful social stories reportedly adhere to a "social story ratio" of sentence types. This ratio suggests that for every 0 to 1 directive sentence (including partial or control sentences), 2 to 5 descriptive, perspective, or affirmative sentences should be used because too much direction may confuse the child (Gray, 1998; Gray & Garand, 1993).

Gray and Garand (1993) suggested that social story construction should adhere to the following guidelines: (1) positively state behaviors (e.g., "I will try to speak in a quiet voice" rather than "I will not scream"), (2) write at a comprehension level that is at or slightly below the child's level, (3) write from the child's perspective using a first-person format as if he/she were writing the story, (4) ensure the story answers questions such as who is involved, what is happening, where will the activity take place, when it will occur, and why must the child behave in that manner, (5) keep it short for children who do not yet read, (6) incorporate the child's interests when possible, (7) use words such as *sometimes* and *usually* to ensure a literal interpretation, (8) consider using a question for the title (e.g., "Why I Should Speak Quietly"), and (9) if using illustrations, consider line drawings because of their limited detail.

When first implementing the social story, Gray (1998) recommended having an adult sit slightly behind the child, with the story placed in front of the child so he/she is not distracted by another person's presence. During the first presentation, the adult should read the story to the child and ask questions to check comprehension. Thereafter, the child may read the story to the adult, or for nonreaders, the adult may continue to read the story to the child before the target situation occurs. Eventually the social story can be faded by increasing the number of days between review. Below is a sample social story:

> There are lots of people in the library. Some people are sitting. Some people are reading quietly. Some people are talking. The people who are talking are using quiet voices. I will also try to use a _____ voice when I am talking in the library.

Note: The books by Gray (1994, 2000) are the best sources on this topic for both parents and professionals.

See also: Autism; Social Skills Building for Adolescents; Social Skills Building for Elementary Children

BIBLIOGRAPHY

Gray, C. (1994). *The original social story book.* Arlington, TX: Future Horizons.
Gray, C. (1998). Social stories 101. *The Morning News, 10*(1), 2–6. Michigan: Jenison Public Schools.
Gray, C. (2000). *The new social story book.* Arlington, TX: Future Horizons.
Gray, C., & Garand, J. D. (1993). Social stories: Improving responses of students with autism with accurate social information. *Focus on Autistic Behavior, 8*, 1–10.

DOROTHY SCATTONE

Special Education Identification and Placement

In general, acknowledging that a child may need special education services is the responsibility of a concerned parent, teacher, family member, or school official. An adult who works closely with a particular child may witness his/her difficulty with reading assignments, writing drills, mathematical concepts, behavior, speaking, mobility, and/or general health. Some educators who observe a child struggling with certain subjects or adjusting to the school setting may choose to intervene on their own, as do some parents. However, when these informal interventions fail to yield results or significant improvements, more formal procedures should be exercised for dealing with a child's academic, behavioral, and/or medical issues. These formal procedures are the first steps in identifying the need for special education.

There are many different ways for determining which individuals require education beyond a regular-education curriculum. Moreover, special education services, resources, definitions, testing procedures, and identification procedures are constantly evolving owing to the ever-changing American educational landscape. Also, new legislation, judicial decisions, classification parameters, and instructional techniques affect how students are identified and placed in special education programs. Finally, identifying what children and adolescents qualify for special education services differs from state to state, and often between school districts within one state (Kidder-Ashley, Deni, & Anderton, 2000). Despite the fluid nature of the identification process, the most important constant is that each child suspected of needing special education receives a psychoeducational battery to determine the services for which he/she qualifies. However, crucial information must be gathered by teachers and family members before a child is referred for psychoeducational testing and prior to a child's placement in an appropriate special education program.

Educational planning teams, student assistance teams, and student study teams are but a few of the terms used to describe a group of adults responsible for deciding which children are ready and eligible for psychoeducational testing and which are not (MacMillan, Gresham, Bocian, & Siperstein, 1997). In essence, convening these teams is the first official component in identifying an individual's special education needs. Most states use some sort of educational team approach composed of regular education teachers, special education teachers, support personnel, specialists (speech–language pathologist, school counselors, behavioral specialists), and school psychologists. Parents of the children in question are often invited to attend. These teams meet at the request of a teacher or parent and are charged with developing special interventions, to be implemented in the regular education setting and based on the information provided by a regular-education teacher, which may positively affect a child's academic achievement or behavior. Once the team has elected the special interventions, a student's teacher(s) enacts the academic and/or behavioral intervention(s) and monitors the child's progress. After a set period of time has elapsed, the team is reconvened to determine the effectiveness of the interventions. If it is determined that the child's academic and behavioral needs were adequately addressed by the interventions, then the interventions are left in place and the teacher is encouraged to continue monitoring the child's progress. If, however, the intervention(s) did not yield significant, measurable improvements, then the child may be referred to a school psychologist for psychoeducational testing as a means to pinpoint what academic, behavioral, learning processing, and/or adaptive issues the child may be experiencing.

PSYCHOEDUCATIONAL TESTING

The Individuals with Disabilities Education Act (IDEA), which was reauthorized in 1997 and is a direct successor of

Public Law 94-142 (approved by Congress in 1975), is the federal law used to enforce the provision of special education services in U.S. schools and school districts (Whorton, Siders, Fowler, & Naylor, 2000). This law mandates that school districts must have clear procedures for determining which children and adolescents within their district qualify for special education programs, including children who are not enrolled in public schools or are of preschool age. Because of IDEA, school districts must also publish the procedures they use in identifying what children are eligible for psychoeducational testing and special education placement.

Prior to a child being identified as eligible for special education, they must be tested by a certified professional within the school district, whether that professional works directly for the school district or is contracted to work with the school district (such as a counseling psychologist in private practice; Kidder-Ashley et al., 2000). Students may not be tested by a school psychologist until the parent of the child in question has granted consent for their child to be tested. Furthermore, a parent has the right to disagree with the student assistance team's recommendation for testing. The vast majority of U.S. school districts depend on the decision of student study teams, educational planning teams, student assistance teams, and so on to refer children for psychological testing.

The psychological tests, or psychoeducational batteries, administered to children who are referred for testing vary depending on the presenting problem of a child (MacMillan et al., 1997). For example, if a student assistance team is of the opinion that a child has difficulty with math or writing, then the school psychologist may administer separate tests to measure intelligence, academic achievement, and learning process. Moreover, if a child is suspected of having some type of mental handicap (also known as mental disability or mental retardation), then the school psychologist may administer an adaptive behavior test in addition to intelligence, achievement, and learning processing tests. Furthermore, if a child is being referred for testing regarding abnormal or severe behavior, the school psychologist may administer a behavior/emotional checklist, a personality measure, or a projective test wherein the child is directed to draw pictures, which are then analyzed by the school psychologist, in addition to previously noted measures. In short, school psychologists, with their extensive level of expertise and knowledge in a variety of measures, determine what tests to use and when to use them, depending on the referred student. The results of a child's psychoeducational battery determine if a child is eligible for placement in special education or not. In addition, psychological testing results provide insight and information as to how best to assist a particular child, and in the development of his/her educational plan (MacMillan et al., 1997).

PLACING INDIVIDUALS IN SPECIAL EDUCATION

The federal government recognizes and funds 12 different types of special education classifications, as outlined by IDEA (Whorton et al., 2000). The 12 classifications are as follows: autism, deaf–blind, hearing impaired, mental retardation, visual impairments, traumatic brain injuries, speech and/or language impairments, specific learning disabilities, serious emotional disturbance, other health impairments, orthopedic impairments, and multiple disabilities. Some of these classifications, such as deaf–blind, other health impairments, and orthopedic impairment, require little, if any, psychological tests conducted by a school psychologist. However, becoming eligible for the majority of these classifications depends on how a child performs on a set of psychoeducational tests.

The federal government allows each state some flexibility in setting the requirements for determining if a child is eligible for services in a specific category. In addition, most states recognize the special education classification of *developmentally delayed* for those children under the age of 5, and some states also fund gifted and talented programs under the direction of district-level special education departments (Whorton et al., 2000). In short, although the federal government mandates and administers funding for special education programs, state and individual school districts are responsible for establishing testing criteria as well as placing children in specified special education programs.

Once a school psychologist has completed the psychoeducational testing of a particular child, a case conference is convened at the child's school or within the school district to decide what special education placement, if any, is best suited for the child. The meeting that occurs after the completion of the psychoeducational battery is usually referred to as the initial case conference (MacMillan et al., 1997). The conference is attended by a school psychologist, a regular education teacher, a special education teacher, a school counselor, and the parent of the child in question. Although the meeting may be considered a placement meeting, placement in a special education program does not occur until the school psychologist has shared the psychoeducational findings with the conference participants, and until the various options are presented to the parent of the child in question.

Although MacMillan and Forness (1998) reported some controversy with using intelligence tests (IQ tests) to measure a child's ability, intelligence tests are widely used and highly regarded by most school psychologists. IQ tests are considered to be the cornerstone for most psychoeducational batteries and are extremely important when it comes to special education placement (MacMillan et al., 1997). However, since individual states set their own guidelines and parameters for how a child qualifies for special education services, it is up to the school psychologist and school officials to review psychoeducational results and how the results are interpreted within each state and school district.

Regardless of the services for which a child qualifies, the members of an initial case conference must ensure that a child is provided with a free appropriate public education (FAPE) prior to placement, by developing an individual educational plan (IEP) related to their specified special education placement (MacMillan et al., 1997). Individual education plans are written on the basis of the results of a child's psychoeducational testing and vary depending on the program for which a child qualifies (Whorton et al., 2000). Although educators are responsible for coordinating and implementing special education interventions in line with a child's needs, the parents and related school personnel must agree to a child's IEP before it is put into action. Finally, all participants in the initial case conference must decide on the least restrictive environment (LRE) in which the IEP is to be carried out. That is, a child who qualifies for special education placement should not be stigmatized or completely isolated from his/her peers because of his/her special education placement, and, therefore, the school must guarantee that the child in question spends as much time as possible with his/her peers (McMillan et al., 1997).

CONCLUSION

Identifying and placing children and adolescents in special education is a complicated, intricate endeavor, whereby many individuals, regulations, assessments, and variables interact. For this reason, a team approach is most advantageous in identifying which children should participate in psychoeducational testing in order to determine their eligibility and placement in special education programs. Despite the many controversies related to the use of psychoeducational tests for determining special education placements, such as testing bias against ethnically and racially diverse children (MacMillan & Forness, 1998), overrepresentation of certain children in behavioral and emotional programs based on their home environment (Frey, 2002), and large numbers of children of low socioeconomic status in learning disabled programs (Blair & Scott, 2002), school psychologists and the tests they administer are the most common methods of identifying and placing children in special education programs. Once testing results have been presented to all interested parties, parents and educators are encouraged to find out and solidify their role in order to meet the educational needs of children and adolescents who qualify for placement in special education programs.

See also: Academic Interventions for Written Language and Grammar; Autism; Learning Disabilities

BIBLIOGRAPHY

Blair, C., & Scott, K. (2002). Proportion of LD placements associated with low socioeconomic status: Evidence for a gradient? *The Journal of Special Education, 36*, 14–22.

Frey, A. (2002). Predictors of placement recommendations for children with behavioral or emotional disorders. *Behavioral Disorders, 27*, 126–137.

Kidder-Ashley, P., Deni, J., & Anderton, J. (2000). Learning disabilities eligibility in the 1990s: An analysis of state practices. *Education, 121*, 65–72.

MacMillan, D., & Forness, S. (1998). The role of IQ in special education placement decisions: Primary and determinative or peripheral and inconsequential? *Remedial and Special Education, 19*, 239–258.

MacMillan, D., Gresham, F., Bocian, K., & Siperstein, G. (1997). The role of assessment in qualifying students as eligible for special education: What is and what's supposed to be. *Focus on Exceptional Children, 30*, 1–18.

Whorton, J., Siders, J., Fowler, R., & Naylor, D. (2000). A two decade review of the number of students with disabilities receiving federal monies and the types of educational placements used. *Education, 121*, 287–297.

Additional Reading for Nonprofessionals

deBettencourt, L. U. (2002). Understanding the differences between IDEA and Section 504. *Teaching Exceptional Children, 34*, 16–23.

Additional Reading for Professionals

Warner, T., Dede, W., Garvan, C., & Conway, T. (2002). One size does not fit all in specific learning disability assessment across ethnic groups. *Journal of Learning Disabilities, 35*, 500–508.

JOSÉ A. VILLALDA
SHELLY F. SHEPERIS

Spelling: Academic Interventions

Spelling is a very important skill and has been linked to academic competence. Because the English language has irregularities, learning to spell can be quite difficult (Hallahan, Kauffman, & Lloyd, 1999). Spelling requires that a person either write or say the correct sequence of letters that form the word to be spelled. To write words, a student must convert phonemes (sounds) into graphemes (letters). Reading and spelling are similar, but in spelling we hear sounds and write letters whereas in reading we see letters and say sounds (Hallahan et al., 1999). Much of what we know about spelling comes from the literature dealing with spelling errors. Most of this work tells us that students make most of their mistakes in the middle of words by altering a single phoneme (Graham, 1999). As students move through the grades they employ a wide variety of rules such as "*i* before *e* except after *c*" when attempting to spell words.

Most of the students who have difficulty in spelling are also children with learning disabilities in reading and written language. These students spell few words correctly like other children and youth, write words that are close to those produced by young children who display problems in morphology, generate words that have some of the phonetic features of correct words, do not make errors by reversing letters, and fail to employ diacritical markings to sound out words correctly. Spelling is assessed from both standardized (e.g., Wide Range Achievement Test—Revised) as well as informal means, such as graded wordlists or employing the list of the most commonly misspelled words.

Spelling words can be scored by counting words, letters, and two-letter sequences as correct. Although not the most exact manner to score spelling, teachers tend to employ the number of words correct as their measure (Hallahan et al., 1999). Of all the academic skills, spelling is probably the most common type of skill where teachers monitor the progress of their students.

There is a great deal of debate regarding how best to teach spelling to students, especially since there is much ambiguity in the way letters sound and how they are written. These methods of instruction have ranged from use of invented spelling, where children "make up or invent" how the word should be spelled, to more structured commercial approaches to spelling instruction, such as *Spelling Mastery* (Dixon, Engelmann, Meirer, Steely, & Wells, 1998). Finally, an important aspect of spelling instruction involves the selection of words that are to be spelled. Hallahan et al. (1999) suggested that lists of words that students learn should include the following categories: regular words; high-frequency, less-regular words; words that require context to determine which spelling, such as *forth* and *fourth* and "demon" words that are the most frequently misspelled words in English, such as *the*.

BEST PRACTICES IN SPELLING

Many best practices in spelling instruction have empirical support for their use in the general and special education settings. These practices range from the use of such commercially available programs as *Morphographic Spelling* (Dixon et al., 1998), computer programs to teach spelling (i.e., Compu Spell), to student self-managed practice procedures such as copy, cover, and compare (McLaughlin & Skinner, 1996).

Curriculum-Based Interventions

Unfortunately, only a few curriculum interventions in language arts to assist students in spelling have been evaluated. Two exceptions, *Spelling Mastery* (Dixon et al., 1998) and *Morphographic Spelling, The Auditory In Depth Program* (Lindamood & Lindamood, 1978), have empirical support for their use. Both of these programs are skill-based and develop skills in phonics. The *Spelling Mastery* program is based on the principles of Direct Instruction and it correlates well with their *reading* series, *Reading Mastery*. The *Auditory In Depth Program* has also been adapted for use with personal computers found in the classroom.

Technology-Based Interventions

The outcomes of such interventions in the teaching of spelling have been comparable to outcomes when compared with traditional paper-and-pencil procedures such as copy, cover, and compare, or add-a-word. In addition, the cost of computers as well as the software can place this intervention strategy out of reach in most classrooms. Combining spelling instruction with such devices as the Language Master or placing tests on audiocassettes so they can be dictated whenever a student is ready to take the exam has been shown to be helpful for children with mild disabilities. Teachers have reported that after the initial setup has been factored into the curriculum, such devices can be beneficial in providing students individualized instruction and allowing them to progress rapidly through spelling texts.

Use of Consequences

There have been several studies that have shown that employing such consequences as free time, allowances, and teacher attention and praise can be useful in teaching children to spell.

Time Delay

Time delay involves having the teacher or tutor pause for approximately 3 seconds after asking the student to spell a word. If the student spells the word correctly during the pause, he/she earns a reward. If the student does not respond correctly, the teacher/tutor gives the answer and the reward is withheld. Gradually the teacher/tutor increases the delay. This has been effective even when students practice their spelling on a computer.

ACTIVE STUDENT RESPONDING PROCEDURES

Much of the literature dealing with effective spelling instruction has employed additional opportunities for students to practice their spelling. Many of these practices are easy for teachers to employ in their respective classrooms and are highly evaluated by parents and students.

Daily Practice with Smaller Lists of Words

Several research teams have found that breaking the size of the spelling unit down into a small number of words and employing daily practice sessions can be helpful to students in general as well as special education at the elementary school level.

Tutoring by Peers, Other Students, or Parents

There is a wealth of data that tutoring by adults and/or peers can improve the spelling achievement of students on end-of-the-week as well as standardized tests. Various manuals are available for teachers to set up such programs in their classrooms. Using parents in the home can provide additional practice over and above that employed in the classroom. Lists of words that have been used have ranged from the most commonly misspelled words to weekly wordlists from the spelling curricula in the classroom. A unique set of procedures employing student tutors and testers and same-day retakes of exams have been shown to increase the number of lessons completed by students in a self-contained special education classroom (McLaughlin, 1991).

Copy, Cover, and Compare

These procedures developed by C. H. Skinner and his colleagues and Williams and his coworkers at Gonzaga University have been able to increase the spelling performance of children across a wide variety of disability designations and grade levels (Skinner, McLaughlin, & Logan, 1997). Copy, cover, and compare is a self-managed self-drill and practice procedure. Copy, cover, and compare involves just a few straightforward steps. First, the student looks at the correct spelling of a word. Next, the student covers the word and writes or orally spells the word. The student then uncovers the word and evaluates his/her answer by comparing it to the original word. If the student determines that his/her last response was accurate, the student moves to the next word and repeats the procedure. If the child finds that his/her spelling of the word had an error, they implement some type of error correction procedure (e.g., repeat the copy, cover, and compare procedure or write the word and its correct spelling three times in rapid succession, etc.) before going on to the next word. Another aspect of copy, cover, and compare includes a procedure in which a small number of words are learned and when a word is mastered 3 days in a row, that word is removed and another word is added (flowlists). That word will reappear on the list in five school days and if the students spells the word correctly, it is permanently removed from the list. The retention of spelling words using these procedures has been impressive. Finally, these procedures have been shown to be just as effective as computer-based programs such as CompuSpell,

whose limitations are the number of computers in a classroom and the cost of the software.

Interspersal Procedures

This procedure requires that you employ spelling lists that contain known as well as new or unknown words. Outcomes with such procedures have been very positive in spelling and in other academic areas.

Academic Positive Practice

This procedure requires the student to write over their errors. Error drill or academic positive practice has been effective in increasing the spelling performance of children in both general and special education classroom settings.

CONCLUSIONS

The teaching of spelling is very difficult but does have an impressive database for teachers and care providers to employ. Most of the interventions are cost effective (e.g., copy, cover, and compare, peer tutoring strategies, consequences), rely on additional practice (copy, cover, and compare, classwide peer tutoring, CompuSpell, academic positive practice, providing daily practice with short wordlists, personalized systems of instruction [PSIs] in spelling, etc.), use known and unknown words in lists (interspersal, academic positive practice, CompuSpell, copy, cover, and compare), and teach spelling each day (*Morphographic Spelling* or copy, cover, and compare).

See also: Reading; Writing (Written Language)

BIBLIOGRAPHY

Dixon, R., Engelmann, S., Meirer, M., Steely, D., & Wells, C. (1998). *Spelling mastery*. Chicago: Scientific Research Associates.

Graham, S. (1999). Handwriting and spelling instruction for students with learning disabilities: A review. *Learning Disability Quarterly, 22,* 78–98.

Graham, S. (2000). Should the natural learning approach replace spelling instruction? *Journal of Educational Psychology, 92,* 235–247.

Hallahan, D. P., Kauffman, J. M., & Lloyd, J. W. (1999). *Introduction to learning disabilities* (2nd ed.). Boston: Allyn & Bacon.

Hubbert, E. R., Weber, K. P., & McLaughlin, T. F. (2000). A comparison of copy, cover, and compare, and a traditional spelling intervention for an adolescent with a conduct disorder. *Child & Family Behavior Therapy, 22*(3), 55–68.

Lindamood, C. H., & Lindamood, P. C. (1978). *The A. D. D. program: Auditory discrimination program.* Hingham, MA: Teaching Resources.

McAuley, S. M., & McLaughlin, T. F. (1992). Comparison of add-a-word and CompuSpell programs with low achieving students. *Journal of Educational Research, 85,* 362–369.

McLaughlin, T. F. (1991). Use of personalized system of instruction with and without a same-day retake contingency on spelling performance of behaviorally disordered children. *Behavioral Disorders, 16*, 127–132.

McLaughlin, T. F., & Skinner, C. H. (1996). Improving academic performance through self-management: Cover, copy, and compare. *Intervention in School and Clinic, 32*, 113–118.

Skinner, C. H., McLaughlin, T. F., & Logan, P. (1997). Cover, copy, and compare: A self-managed academic intervention across skills, students, and settings. *Journal of Behavioral Education, 7*, 295–306.

Additional Readings for Nonprofessionals

Haring, N. G., Lovitt, T. C., Eaton, M. E., & Hansen, C. L. (1978). *The fourth r: Research in the classroom.* Columbus, OH: Merrill.

McLaughlin, T. F., & Skinner, C. H. (1996). Improving academic performance through self-management: Cover, copy, and compare. *Intervention in School and Clinic, 32*, 113–118.

Additional Readings for Professionals

Graham, S. (1999). Handwriting and spelling instruction for students with learning disabilities: A review. *Learning Disability Quarterly, 22*, 78–98.

Hull, M. A. (1981). *Phonics for the teacher of reading: Programmed for self-instruction* (3rd ed.). Columbus, OH: Merrill.

Skinner, C. H., McLaughlin, T. F., & Logan, P. (1997). Cover, copy, and compare: A self-managed academic intervention across skills, students, and settings. *Journal of Behavioral Education, 7*, 295–306.

T. F. McLaughlin
Kimberly P. Weber
Anjali Barretto

Sports

Sports are considered any games pursued for diversion. Sports have existed since the beginning of humanity. Most sports in this country including track and field, all of the variations of football, and the stick and bat games (e.g., baseball, field hockey, and softball) can be traced to England. Even sports that originated outside of England (e.g., basketball, gymnastics, and golf) use English methods of organization for their sports (Crosset, Bromage, & Hums, 1998).

Sport programs organized by adults for children began to flourish at the start of the twentieth century. One of the first organizers of these activities was the Young Men's Christian Association (YMCA). The programs sought to promote values such as cooperation, discipline, and character development. By the 1940s, most youth programs resembled their pro sport counterparts in terms of organization and administration. All of these programs were specifically designed for boys (Berryman, 1996). Programs for women and girls did not develop until after the passage of Title IX of the Educational Amendments Act, which required those schools receiving any government funding provide equal opportunities for participating in sporting activities for males and females.

It is estimated that between 20 and 30 million children are involved in interscholastic sports. There are a number of sport opportunities that parents and children might pursue. Sports, especially youth sports, should be a vehicle for promoting a life-long commitment to an active lifestyle and mass participation in these activities. However, fewer adults than ever are active and physically fit.

What do parents want from their child's sport program? According to Murphy (1999), there are seven basic motivators for parents to involve their children in sport programs. Sport programs can help parents bond with their children. Going to games, providing transportation, helping with fundraising, and providing coaching make parents feel good about spending quality time with their children. Organized sports give parents the satisfaction of knowing their child is located somewhere safe and wholesome. A child's successful sports experience can often add excitement and meaning to an adult's life. Some research indicates that children involved in sports have been found to feel more physically fit and happy, have higher levels of self-confidence, and perform better in school. Participation in sports may enhance self-control, which is important in the development and maturation process. If a child receives good technical advice and develops good practice habits, his/her skill level will rise in that particular sport. Many parents concerned about their children's social development will encourage involvement in sports to help them meet and interact with other children.

Murphy (1999) also warns parents of the pitfalls of parental overinvolvement. Parents or guardians can sometimes become "overidentified" with their child's sports performance. Parents' feelings of euphoria when a child succeeds or disappointment when he/she fails are often overemphasized. Parents can have unrealistic expectations about their children's professional or athletic scholarship potential. They sometimes compare their child's performance to other children on the team and make judgments about their children's effort or the fairness of decisions by coaches (e.g., playing-time decisions). These feelings are quickly identified by children and may be added to the pressure to perform to please their parents.

Smith, Smith, and Smoll (1983) provide reasons children give for sports participation. The activity must be considered "fun." The sport must allow the child to be active and involved. The physical and mental challenge that they are facing should be equal to the skills that they possess. A challenge too difficult may lead to anxiety. A challenge too easy may lead to boredom. If you see your child standing around or sitting on the bench most of the time, he/she will most likely become disinterested. The desire to be skilled and to improve also drives sport participants. The physical ability to move fast and jump high are thrills at any age. When children do not improve (not challenged or skills too difficult), they are likely to lose interest in the activity.

Sports activities are also a good setting for children to develop lasting friendships with their peers. Teamwork and cooperation can be positive influences in shaping adolescent behavior. Social recognition such as school letters and trophies can be reinforcers for sports participation. Although competition can be a driving force, too much or too little competition can reduce participant interest. Finally, children play sports to gain recognition from their parents and coaches. Many participants refer to their former coaches as *father* or *mother* figures.

Sports can be a healthy diversion for both parents and children. It can enhance the development of social and physical skills. It is important for adults to understand children's motivations for sports participation as well as the drawbacks of parental overinvolvement.

See also: Nutrition; Title IX

BIBLIOGRAPHY

Berryman, J. W. (1996). The rise of boys' sports in the United States, 1900 to 1970. In F. I. Smoll & R. E. Smith (Eds.), *Children and youth in sport: a biopsychosocial perspective* (pp. 1–15). New York: Brown & Benchmark.

Crosset, T. W., Bromage, S., & Hums, M. A. (1998). History of sport management. In L. P. Masteralexis, C. A. Barr, & M. A. Hums (Eds.), *Principles and practice of sport management* (pp. 1–2). New York: Aspen.

Murphy, S. (1999). *The cheers and the tears.* New York: Jossey-Bass.

Smith, N. J., Smith, R. E., & Smoll, F. L. (1983). *Kid sports: A survival guide for parents.* New York: Addison-Wesley.

Additional Reading for Nonprofessionals

Smith, R. E., Smith, N. J., & Smoll, F. L. (1990). *Parents' complete guide to youth sports.* Reston, VA. American Alliance for Health, Physical Education, Recreation and Dance.

Additional Readings for Professionals

Cross, N., & Lyle, J. (1999). *The coaching process: Principles and practice for sport.* Guildford: Klug. Lynn. Butterman-Heinemann.

Martens, R. (1997). *Successful coaching.* Champaign, IL. Human Kinetics.

EMILE CATIGNANI

State School Psychology Associations

A current listing of state associations with links to their websites, if available, may be found online at http://www.nasponline.org/information/links_state_orgs.html

Stereotypy

The term *stereotypy* is typically used to describe repetitive behavior that is invariant and appears to serve no social function. Some common examples include body rocking, hand flapping in front of the eyes, head weaving, and hand mouthing, among others. Although the literature suggests that some forms of stereotypy (e.g., body rocking) are more common than others, there have been dozens if not hundreds of response forms called stereotypy. With some exceptions, stereotypy is usually only deemed problematic when exhibited by individuals diagnosed with developmental disabilities (DD) and autism. Among individuals with developmental disorders, stereotypy tends to occur long after the behavior stops in typically developing children. Thus, stereotypic-like behavior does occur with typically developing children, but it usually stops at an early phase of development. Because stereotypy often persists in individuals with developmental disorders, the behavior tends to disrupt learning and positive social interactions. For example, it is difficult to teach or even talk to a person when he/she is rocking back and forth at a high rate. There is sometimes social stigma attached to the behavior, such as when other children stare at or tease an individual who engages in stereotypy.

In general, researchers tend to agree that repetitive behavior should be categorized as "stereotypy" using the following criteria: (a) the behavior is voluntary (as opposed to a reflex), (b) the behavior lacks variability (i.e., the behavior looks the same every time it occurs), (c) the behavior persists over time (e.g., for at least several months), (d) the behavior is relatively immutable when faced with environmental changes, and (e) the behavior is out of synchrony with the individual's expected age-related development (Berkson, 1983).

PREVALENCE

Although several studies have attempted to identify the prevalence of various forms of stereotypy, the results are difficult to interpret because of the use of indirect measures (e.g., parental report), the inclusion of typically developing children, and the focus on behaviors that are more commonly referred to as habits (e.g., thumb sucking). For example, Troster (1994) surveyed caregivers at residential-care facilities for developmentally typical children. The results of the survey indicated that the most prevalent forms of "stereotypy" for children aged 10 months to 3 years were thumb sucking (72 percent), hair twisting/manipulation (22 percent), and body rocking (22 percent). For children aged 3 to 5 years, thumb sucking remained the most common stereotypy (26 percent), whereas the most prevalent repetitive behavior in children 6 to 11 years old was nail biting/chewing (17 percent). Although the results of Troster's study are interesting, it could be argued that thumb sucking is an age-typical "habit" that does not disrupt learning and carries little social stigma. In addition, the use of survey methodology rather than direct observation probably influenced the accuracy of the prevalence estimates.

To date, a study by Berkson, Tupa, and Sherman (2001) represents one of the most comprehensive investigations of the early development of stereotypy in children with DD. Berkson et al. (2001) conducted observations of 39 children with DD who were 40 months of age or younger to screen for the presence or absence of various repetitive behaviors (e.g., body rocking, head banging, self-scratching). Of particular interest, Berkson et al. found that 33 of the 39 children (nearly 85 percent) engaged in body rocking while positioned in one or more body postures (i.e., supine, four-point, seated, or standing). Although this study did not provide evidence that each child would have continued to engage in stereotypy as he/she develops, it did show that these behaviors may be directly observed and identified as aberrant at a very young age. Rojahn (1986) also reported that a high percentage of noninstitutionalized individuals with DD engaged in stereotypy, especially if they also engaged in self-injurious behavior. However, specific summary statistics are difficult to glean from Rojahn's data because he included some response forms that most other researchers do not call stereotypy (e.g., self-restraint).

CAUSES

There is some agreement that many stereotyped behaviors (e.g., hand gazing, body rocking) that are exhibited by individuals with DD share commonalities with developmentally normal behavior (e.g., Schwartz, Gallagher, & Berkson, 1986). Thus, at one level, developmental models of stereotypy are appropriate. However, the causes underlying stereotypy are not addressed directly by developmental models. Developmental models describe when behavioral phenomena typically occur, but do not emphasize how or why behavioral phenomena occur.

Behavioral models hypothesize that repetitive behavior produces "feedback" or "self-stimulation," implicating the role of reinforcement (e.g., Lovaas, Newsom, & Hickman, 1987). Reinforcement is when stimulation that behavior produces makes the behavior more likely to occur in the future. The notion is that stereotypy produces a form of stimulation that keeps the behavior going—similar to how one might strum a guitar to hear the music or read a book to learn a story. There is a lot of evidence supporting the reinforcement hypothesis, and this evidence takes three forms: (a) individuals will engage in stereotypy even when they are alone, which shows that the behavior somehow maintains itself, independent of the social environment; (b) individuals will engage in other behavior (like

schoolwork) in order to earn access to stereotypy if stereotypy is restricted, showing that there must be something pleasing about the behavior; and (c) individuals will stop engaging in stereotypy if the sensation (stimulation) from the stereotypy is somehow cut off or blocked (similar to how one might stop strumming the guitar if the guitar strings made no sound).

Primarily on the basis of research conducted with nonhumans (e.g., rodents, primates), neurobiological researchers contend that stereotypy is the product of biochemical imbalances or deficiencies. In contrast to behavioral models, neurobiological models emphasize neurobiological mechanisms, rather than reinforcement, as the originating and maintaining source(s) of stereotypy. Various animal models have been developed using impoverished rearing conditions, injections of neurotransmitters, and the application of stress-inducing events (e.g., restricting the movement of the animal). Also, outcomes of treatment studies with humans using pharmacological agents provide some support for neurobiological mechanisms (Sprague & Newell, 1996).

Central to the study of stereotypy in nonhumans is the arrangement of environmental conditions early in the animal's development, which presumably affect the animal's brain development and, hence, subsequent behavior. Various studies have shown changes in levels of stereotypy as a function of deprivation from stimulation during early development. Likewise, studies have shown that altered levels of dopamine, serotonin, corticosterone, or a combination of these neurochemicals can exert a direct influence on the exhibition of repetitive behavior (Sprague & Newell, 1996). Given the limited data on the effects of pharmacological agents in reducing stereotypy in humans however, it is unclear as to what extent animal models accurately describe the processes that govern human behavior.

It should be emphasized that developmental, behavioral, and neurobiological models regarding the occurrence of stereotypy should not be viewed as mutually exclusive. For example, perhaps a particular level of environmental stimulation is required to establish proper neurochemical activity and brain development during critical developmental stages or phases. If proper brain development does not occur, it is possible that deficits of a particular neurotransmitter may establish stereotypic behavior as more reinforcing than it would have been otherwise. It is also possible that the particular movement occurs originally as a function of a neurochemical abnormality, but persists as a result of reinforcement. A relatively unexplored area of research is the combined neurobiological and behavioral assessment and treatment of stereotypy.

BEHAVIORAL INTERVENTIONS

Several behavioral interventions, such as environmental enrichment (EE) and differential reinforcement (DR), have been used to treat stereotypy in individuals with DD. EE is a viable treatment because it involves the placement of alternative sources of stimulation (e.g., music, television, toys) into the individual's environment. The idea is that other forms of stimulation will compete with, and thereby reduce, stereotypy. Several studies support this notion, although it is clear that not all stereotypy is so easily treated. Differential reinforcement involves providing preferred stimulation contingent upon (as a consequence for) a more desirable behavior. For example, turning on a radio may be reinforced with access to juice. The idea is that if the person learns alternative ways to obtain stimulation, he/she may engage in less stereotypy. The use of a socially mediated reinforcer (such as juice delivered by another person) may be gradually eliminated when the individual has learned to obtain stimulation through alternative behavior (an acceptable form of automatically reinforced behavior).

We recently conducted a study to examine the effects of behavioral interventions for children who exhibited three or more forms of stereotypy (Rapp, Vollmer, & Dozier, 2001). This multiphase investigation yielded several potentially interesting outcomes. First, in terms of the amount of time each participant engaged in specific forms of stereotypy, we found that nearly every participant showed orderly and consistent preferences for specific stereotyped behaviors. That is, the proportion of time spent engaging in a given behavior remained similar across observations and each individual spent the most time engaged in one particular form of stereotypy. Second, treatment of the most preferred form of stereotypy resulted in an increase in a formerly less preferred stereotypy for nearly every participant. That is, as one form of stereotypy decreased, other forms of stereotypy increased. Third, for half of the participants, a reduction in the most preferred stereotypy was correlated with a reduction in another highly preferred, yet untreated, stereotypy. That is, as one form of stereotypy decreased, other forms of stereotypy decreased along with it. These findings may be important because treating one form of stereotypy has indirect effects on other forms of stereotypy.

SUMMARY

Stereotypy is a term used to describe highly repetitive behavior displayed primarily by individuals with DD and autism. Although prevalence statistics vary and are in some ways confounded, it is clear that stereotypy occurs in a high proportion of individuals with developmental disorders. There is no known single cause of stereotypy, but it appears that reinforcement and neurochemical abnormalities play a role. It is also known that response forms that are similar to stereotypy occur in typically developing children. Behavioral interventions show promise for decreasing the frequency of stereotypy, but little work has been done in combining behavioral and neurobiological assessment and treatment models. Overall, the most promising behavioral approach to date is to teach alternative skills that may replace stereotypy, via environmental enrichment or differential reinforcement. Finally, researchers and practitioners should be aware that changing the frequency of one form of stereotypy is likely to influence the frequency of other forms of stereotypy (sometimes in an undesired direction).

See also: Autism; Differential Reinforcement; Positive Reinforcement; Self-Injurious Behavior

BIBLIOGRAPHY

Berkson, G. (1983). Repetitive stereotyped behaviors. *American Journal of Mental Deficiency, 88*, 239–246.

Berkson, G., Tupa, M., & Sherman, L. (2001). Early development of stereotyped and self-injurious behaviors. I. Incidence. *American Journal on Mental Retardation, 106*, 539–547.

Lovaas, O. I., Newsom, C., & Hickman, C. (1987). Self-stimulatory behavior and perceptual reinforcement. *Journal of Applied Behavior Analysis, 20*, 45–68.

Rapp, J. T., Vollmer, T. R., & Dozier, C. L. (2001, May). Assessment of stereotypy in children with Autism using response restriction. In B. Iwata (Chair), *Applications of response deprivation and response restriction methodology*. Symposium presented at the Annual Meeting of the Association for Behavior Analysis, New Orleans, LA.

Rojahn, J. (1986). Self-injurious and stereotypic behavior of noninstitutionalized mentally retarded people: Prevalence and classification. *American Journal of Mental Deficiency, 91*, 268–276.

Schwartz, S. S., Gallagher, R. J., & Berkson, G. (1986). Normal repetitive and abnormal stereotyped behavior of nonretarded infants and young mentally retarded children. *American Journal of Mental Deficiency, 90*, 625–630.

Sprague, R. L., & Newell, K. M. (Eds.). (1996). *Stereotyped behavior: Brain–behavior relationships*. Washington, DC: American Psychological Association.

Troster H. (1994). Prevalence and functions of stereotyped behaviors in nonhandicapped children in residential care. *Journal of Abnormal Child Psychology, 22*, 79–97.

Additional Reading for Nonprofessionals

Berkson, G., & Tupa, M. (2000). Early development of stereotyped and self-injurious behaviors. *Journal of Early Intervention, 23*, 1–19.

Additional Readings for Professionals

Hanley, G. P., Iwata, B. A., Thompson, R. H., & Lindberg, J. S. (2000). A component analysis of "stereotypy" for alternative behavior. *Journal of Applied Behavior Analysis, 33*, 285–296.

Powell, S. B., Newman, H. A., Pendergast, J. F., & Lewis, M. (1999). A rodent model of spontaneous stereotypy: Initial characterization of developmental, environmental, and neurobiological factors. *Physiology and Behavior, 66*, 355–363.

Ringdahl, J. E., Vollmer, T. R., Marcus, B. A., & Roane, H. S. (1997). An analogue evaluation of environmental enrichment: The role of stimulus preference. *Journal of Applied Behavior Analysis, 30*, 203–216.

Vollmer, T. R. (1994). The concept of automatic reinforcement: Implications for behavioral research in developmental disabilities. *Research in Developmental Disabilities, 15*, 187–207.

TIMOTHY R. VOLLMER
JOHN T. RAPP

Stress

Stress means different things to different people. Stress is frequently defined as a cause of physical and mental illness ("He suffers from stress," "Her problems are due to stress") and just as frequently is defined as an end result ("She is all stressed out"). This lack of clarity makes it necessary to adopt an unusual format in presenting this topic. A starting point in understanding stress is to compare the difference between two distinct, but complementary, orientations to the etiology or cause of psychiatric disorders, the historically prior psychiatric orientation and the more recent stress-related orientation (Milgram, 1998).

ANXIETY AND THE HISTORICAL PSYCHIATRIC ORIENTATION

The traditional psychiatric orientation states that some people become extremely anxious and respond "abnormally" to routine life events that ordinarily elicit normal or constructive responses in most people. Most children are able to deal effectively with the developmental tasks of separation from parents and entering peer group relations, and later are able to cope with the physiological and psychological changes associated with adolescent maturation. Some children and adolescents are unable to traverse these milestones. They lack the repertoire of social, emotional, and cognitive skills necessary for adaptation to normal milestones and the accompanying tribulations, become extremely anxious, and develop maladaptive behaviors to deal with their anxiety rather than adaptive behaviors to deal with life challenges.

These deficiencies are due to (a) pathological genetic vulnerability (e.g., hereditary transmission of heightened vulnerability to psychiatric disorders that existed in parents or grandparents), (b) an early painful life experience (e.g., death of a sibling, sudden separation from parents, parent divorce in childhood), (c) recurrent adverse experiences during childhood (e.g., psychological rejection or deprivation, disruptive home environment), or more likely (d) a combination of two or more of the above. This approach highlights anxiety, both conscious and unconscious, as the driving force in the development of psychopathology. It focuses on the difficulties that vulnerable children and adults encounter in coping with ordinary milestones and occasional tribulations and attributes these difficulties to inherent or acquired vulnerabilities.

THE STRESS AND COPING ORIENTATION

The stress-related orientation, by contrast, deals with normal people who come to our attention because they are responding abnormally to abnormal life events. It focuses on intense, stressful life events regarded as detrimental by any observer (e.g., traumatic physical or sexual assault, witnessing violent acts, being present in the vicinity of Ground Zero on 9/11). Most people exposed to these stressful life events exhibit adverse stress reactions and recover under favorable postexposure circumstances.

Some suffer the persisting effects of the initial exposure long after the upsetting experience has ended and develop severe stress reactions or posttraumatic stress disorder. Their inability to recover following exposure to stressful life events may be due to the following:

(a) The unique and idiosyncratic character of any given stressful event for each participant in the event. Consider the different immediate experience of the resident in upper Manhattan upon learning of what happened in lower Manhattan, the bystander in lower Manhattan who witnessed the collapse of the Twin Towers and then fled north from the scene of destruction, and the fireman who removed the charred bodies of fellow workers from the conflagration. No two people are ever witness to the same stressful event.

(b) The unique and idiosyncratic character of the implications of any given stimulus event for each person affected by it. Consider the short- and long-term consequences of 9/11 for the resident in upper Manhattan who subsequently learns that his wife had been shopping in the area of the tragedy and was killed; the bystander who reaches safety, but whose livelihood is threatened by the immediate economic changes that affect the entire area; and the fireman who receives public approbation for his heroic efforts, but cannot tolerate certain food odors because they conjure up the horrific images of charred human flesh, and who has chronic sleep disturbance due to recurrent nightmares. The consequences of a stressful event are never the same for any two people affected by the event.

(c) Personal vulnerabilities and deficiencies that predated the stressful event. It may be noted that the factors considered responsible for the subsequent psychological disturbance are remarkably similar in the two orientations. They both deal with features of the person and features of the life events to which the person has responded. The first emphasizes preexisting vulnerabilities and the features of stressful life events long past in childhood or adolescence. The second emphasizes the features and implications of the recent stressful life event that precipitated the psychological disturbance. The two orientations are not mutually exclusive, some disorders fall in an overlap category, and people with preexisting psychiatric disorders may also become exposed to highly stressful life circumstances.

CONCEPTUALIZATION OF STRESS

One way of defining stress is in terms of stimulus events that lead to changes in the organism. A life event is stressful to the extent that it requires the individual to change or adapt in coping with the frustrations, conflicts, and/or pressures brought about by the event. Investigators of the epidemiology of psychiatric and medical disorders assess the stressfulness (or demand for change and adjustment) inherent in different life events by obtaining normative ratings of social readjustment by judges across a broad range of stressful life events. In this manner investigators add up the stressfulness ratings of those life events that occurred in a person's life and obtain a measure of overall stressfulness (Dohrenwend & Dohrenwend, 1974). These measures are then correlated with physical and mental health and yield important knowledge on the deleterious effects of stress on health for large populations in society.

This approach is faulty when it is applied to the diagnosis and treatment of a given individual because: (1) it assumes that all stressful events have adverse health consequences, when, in fact, only undesirable events are potentially detrimental, and (2) because it assumes a uniform ordinal scaling of stressful life events for all people, it ignores the idiosyncratic features of the stressful event to which each person is exposed, and it ignores the different implications of the stressful event for each individual.

STRESS AS AN IMBALANCE BETWEEN STIMULUS DEMAND AND RESPONSE SUPPLY

Lazarus (1991) defines stress in terms of a person–environment interaction in which events place demands upon the individual that are not immediately or easily met by his/her response repertoire. Some demands are perceived as a challenge and are welcomed by the individual and may be regarded as instances of what may be called positive or health-promoting stressful interactions (e.g., learning how to drive a car, tackling a new and difficult assignment, climbing a mountain). Other demands are unexpected and threaten to overwhelm the individual (e.g., imminent bankruptcy, serious illness or incapacity, death of a loved one). The response to exposure to a given event is a series of cognitive appraisals: "Does this event apply to me or to others? Is the hurricane heading my way or will it bypass my town?" If the answer to this primary cognitive appraisal is positive, a secondary cognitive appraisal follows: "Is my home insured? Can I get out in time? Or should I retire to my hurricane-proof lower basement?" The answers that one gives to these appraisals determine one's emotional reactions (e.g., self-recrimination that the house is not properly insured against hurricane damage, fear of injury or loss of life) and one's planning and behavior in the hours and days ahead. As events unfold, appraisals change, emotions change, and people adapt their behavior to changing requirements of the new situation. For Lazarus, the continuing appraisal of threat and damage and of the resources that are available to cope with threat and damage determine one's emotions and resulting adaptive behavior. People may make faulty appraisals of the event, either exaggerating or minimizing the imminent threat or damage; in a similar manner people may also make faulty appraisals of the resources that can be called upon to deal with these events and their consequences. Faulty appraisals lead to ineffective or inappropriate coping behaviors.

Hobfoll (1989) added a new dimension to the person–environment interaction by emphasizing the notion of conservation of resources. People strive to obtain, retain, and protect those possessions or resources that they value. Stress represents an interaction in which valued resources are threatened or lost or an anticipated increase in certain resources following the investment of other resources does not occur. Resources may be material objects (e.g., loved ones, health, wealth, personal possessions), immaterial conditions (e.g., living with happily married parents, enjoying the friendship and respect of age peers), personal characteristics (e.g., self-esteem, personal values, moral integrity), and energies (e.g., having the time to do what one has to do and what one wants to do, possessing the knowledge and information necessary to pursue one's goals). People invest resources in any one category in order to protect or conserve threatened resources or to restore damaged resources.

The professional terminology utilized in the stress and coping orientation refers to stressors (aspects of the stimulus situation perceived as threatening and taxing one's adaptive capacities), stressor-mediating variables (aspects of the stimulus situation, the person, and their interaction that affect the stressor–stress reaction relationship), acute stress reactions (transient, adaptive, and maladaptive emotions and behaviors), and chronic stress disorders (crystallized clinical syndromes that follow from maladaptive efforts to rectify this imbalance and that may undergo spontaneous remission, respond to treatment, or become chronic).

In summary, constructive and potentially destructive stressful interactions are endemic in modern life. Individuals, groups, and society as a whole are called upon to utilize effectively their resources to prevent damage from taking place, to minimize damage when it does occur, and to rehabilitate those who have suffered damage.

See also: Anxiety; Coping; Posttraumatic Stress Disorder; Traumatic Incidents

BIBLIOGRAPHY

Dohrenwend, B. S., & Dohrenwend, B. P. (Eds.). (1974). *Stressful life events: Their nature and effects.* New York: Wiley.

Hobfoll, S. E. (1989). The conservation of resources: A new attempt at conceptualizing stress. *American Psychologist, 44*, 513–524.

Lazarus, R. S. (1991). *Emotion & adaptation.* New York: Oxford University Press.

Milgram, N. A. (1998). Children under stress. In T. H. Ollendick & M. Hersen (Eds.), *Handbook of child psychopathology* (3rd ed., pp. 505–533). New York: Plenum.

Additional Readings for Nonprofessionals

Davis, M., Eshelman, E. R., & McKay, M. (1991). *The relaxation & stress reduction workbook* (3rd ed.). Oakland, CA: New Harbinger.

Schaffer, M. (1982). *Life after stress.* New York: Plenum.

Additional Readings for Professionals

Breznitz, S. (Ed.). (1983). *The denial of stress.* New York: International Universities Press.

Garmezy, N., & Rutter, M. (Eds.). (1983). *Stress, coping, and development in children.* New York: McGraw-Hill.

Lystad, M. (Ed.). (1988). *Mental health response to mass emergencies: Theory and practice.* New York: Brunner/Mazel.

NOACH MILGRAM

Study Skills and Test Preparation

Study skill strategies are the link between note taking (i.e., teacher-presented educational materials and methods organized by students) and test taking (i.e., student-presented educational materials and methods assessed by teachers). Mastering effective study skills is only beneficial if that which is being studied corresponds to that which is being tested. Ultimately, effective study skills are only effective if the resulting exam, presentation, or project is sufficiently mastered when assessed.

Often, study skill strategies are not considered as an educational priority until after poor test performance is demonstrated. A generic educational sequence may be represented by the following: (a) materials to be mastered are presented by a teacher, or located by a student within a media source, (b) presented or located materials are transcribed and organized by students (taking notes), (c) organized materials are studied by students, (d) teacher-presented materials are organized for assessment, and (e) assessment is completed by students and evaluated by teacher. The first three (a, b, and c) are components of the test

preparation environment, whereas the last two (d and e) are components of the test environment.

Lawrence (2002) suggests a disconnect may exist between the test environment and the test preparation environment, resulting in poor academic performance. This disconnect is apparent in one of two ways. First, the methods for completing a test may not match the way in which materials were presented by the teacher. For example, if the testing methodology requires students to apply and critically evaluate material but the classroom lecture presents to students names, date, and vocabulary, then the *method* presented in class does not match test requirements, resulting in poor test performance. Second, the materials for completing a test may not match the organized notes taken by the student. For example, if the testing materials require the student to list key conflicts and subconflicts from a novel but the student only takes notes on conflicts in general, then the *materials* do not match test requirements, resulting in poor test performance.

This second example is related more to an organizational disconnect between teacher-presented lecture and student-organized notes. Student study skills may be effective (i.e., material that was studied was mastered), but the materials studied were incorrect. This problem with studying can be resolved by teacher-developed note-taking templates or advanced organizers (Belfiore & Hutchinson, 1998). In this case, study skills are enhanced because the note-taking template ensures that the content and structure of the materials presented are in line with the test expectation. For example, if there are three key conflicts and two subconflicts in a novel, then the template guide will provide a visual cue, allowing for the exact number on the note-taking template. Students take notes with the template, study the template content and format, and are tested on materials in that format. Using the template is an effective study skill strategy because the materials presented in class match the materials (a) studied and (b) required for testing.

The first example above is related more to a strategic disconnect between student study strategies and test requirements. After exploring the demands between test requirements and study strategies, and noting poor test performance, Lawrence (2002) developed a 10-week unit using Question–Answer Relationships (QARs) (Raphael, 1982) to integrate study skills and test-taking skills. A key element of the Lawrence (2002) program was a system to differentiate study question types. If students could study notes and text using the same strategy that the test would require, test performance would increase. Students were taught to discriminate question type by following a red–yellow–green light cue. Green-light questions require students to go right to a single location in the text or notes to find the answer (i.e., literal comprehension). Yellow-light questions required students to slow down, think, and search several locations in the text or notes for the answer. Red-light questions required students to stop and think about what the question is asking. Answers for red-light questions cannot be found only in the text or notes, but additional application or synthesis is needed. Student test performance improves by helping students discriminate test question type and study strategy related to the test question type (Lawrence, 2002). The study strategy, in this case, improves test performance because the methods required for answering test questions were practiced using the same method when taking and studying notes.

Note-taking, test-preparation (i.e., study skill strategies), and test-taking strategies coexist, with the success criteria being test performance or project presentation outcome. Accuracy in notes taken requires a match between that which was teacher-presented and that which was student-transcribed, and organized into a note format. Once accurate materials are available for studying, the questioning strategy of the test or project should be incorporated into the study skills. When students have accurate notes (i.e., materials) and knowledge of the testing environment (i.e., method), student academic performance is enhanced.

See also: Academic Interventions for Written Language and Grammar; Note Taking

BIBLIOGRAPHY

Belfiore, P. J., & Hutchinson, J. M. (1998). Enhancing academic achievement through related routines: A functional approach. In T. S. Watson & F. M. Gresham (Eds.), *Handbook of child behavior therapy* (pp. 83–97). New York: Plenum.

Lawrence, K. M. (2002). Red light, green light 1–2–3: Tasks to prepare for standardized tests. *The Reading Teacher, 55,* 525–528.

Raphael, T. E. (1982). Question-answering strategies for children. *The Reading Teacher, 36,* 186–190.

Additional Reading for Nonprofessionals

Clemmons, J., & Laase, L. (1995, July/August). Build the study skills your students need most. *Instructor,* 87–90.

Additional Reading for Professionals

Scruggs, T. E., & Mastropieri, M. A. (1986). Improving the test-taking skills of behaviorally disordered and learning disabled children. *Exceptional Children, 53,* 63–68.

PHILLIP J. BELFIORE

Stuttering

Stuttering is a speech disorder in which the normal fluency or timing of speech is disrupted. According to the diagnostic criteria for stuttering in the *DSM-IV* (American Psychiatric Association, 1994), these speech disruptions can include repetitions of word sounds, syllables, or whole words, prolongations of word sounds, and blocking or pausing between words or within a word when attempting to speak (pauses may be filled with sounds such as "uh" or silent). Other types of speech patterns that may constitute stuttering include speaking with observable physical tension, substituting words to avoid commonly stuttered words, and interjections. It is not uncommon for stutterers to exhibit tension or struggle behaviors such as head movements, facial grimacing, eye blinks, body movements, or other tic-like behaviors while attempting to speak. In such cases, it may appear that the child is struggling through the stuttered words in an attempt to speak fluently. Stuttering is diagnosed when one or more of these disfluencies occurs frequently and interferes with the individual's ability to communicate or disrupts academic or occupational achievement (American Psychiatric Association, 1994).

It is estimated that stuttering occurs in close to 1 percent of the general population (Bloodstein, 1995) and approximately 5 percent of preschool children (Leung & Robson, 1990). Stuttering typically starts in children between the ages of 2 and 7 years and has a peak onset at 5 years of age. According to the *DSM-IV,* 98 percent of the time the onset of stuttering occurs before the age of 10 years. Stuttering is more common in boys than girls, by a ratio of 3:1. Fortunately, stuttering will spontaneously remit without any treatment in a large percentage of children who stutter. However, because not all stuttering ceases without treatment, Miltenberger and Woods (1998) suggest that a child's stuttering should be treated if it has not stopped within 6 to 12 months after onset.

Although the causes of stuttering are not entirely clear, it is thought that genetic factors may underlie the disorder and that neurological factors, such as problems with interhemispheric lateralization, play a role in stuttering (Miltenberger & Woods, 1998). Furthermore, anxiety is reported to be associated with exacerbation of stuttering (American Psychiatric Association, 1994). Regardless of the underlying factors that give rise to stuttering, it is clear that the physiology of stuttering involves disruption of airflow during speech production. This disruption may involve irregular breathing, prolonged exhalation, and cessation of breathing during speech (Woods, Twohig, Fuqua, & Hanley, 2000). Because of the relationship between disruption of airflow and stuttering, one of the most successful approaches to treatment is Regulated Breathing, a procedure in which the child is taught to regulate airflow while speaking in an attempt to produce fluent speech and inhibit stuttering.

OVERVIEW OF REGULATED BREATHING

Azrin and Nunn developed and evaluated Regulated Breathing as a treatment for stuttering in 1974. Regulated Breathing is a behavioral treatment package that includes the following components: awareness training, relaxation training, competing response training, motivation training, and generalization training. Azrin and Nunn implemented the Regulated Breathing treatment in a 1- to 2-hour treatment session with 14 stutterers aged 4 to 67 years and produced large decreases in stuttering for all participants. Subsequent to this study, a number of researchers have evaluated Regulated Breathing and variations of the procedure with child and adult stutterers and have found the treatment to be largely successful in decreasing stuttering to low levels (see Woods et al., 2000, for a review). A more detailed description of the Regulated Breathing treatment is provided below.

REGULATED BREATHING: TREATMENT DESCRIPTION

The goal of regulated breathing is to help the child become more aware of each instance of stuttering and interrupt it or prevent its occurrence with the use of a competing response that involves regulating airflow during speech. The child learns the techniques in session and carries out the techniques throughout the day with the help of a significant other who provides social support. What follows is a description of each of the treatment components.

Awareness Training

Four techniques are used to help the child become aware of each instance of stuttering. In *response description*, the child describes the particular speech patterns involved in his/her stuttering. In *response detection*, the child practices identifying each instance of stuttering, with praise and feedback from the therapist, while speaking in session. In *situation awareness training*, the child identifies commonly stuttered words or situations associated with stuttering. In the *early warning* procedure, the child identifies the physical sensations (e.g., muscle tension) or behaviors (e.g., body movements) that precede each instance of stuttering. By the end of the awareness training procedure, the child should be in a position to identify each instance of stuttering as soon as it occurs or is about to occur.

Relaxation Training

Because stuttering is often associated with tension or anxiety, the therapist teaches the child to relax by assuming relaxed postures and breathing diaphragmatically (slow, rhythmic deep breathing). The child practices in session and is then taught to use the procedures to produce relaxation when experiencing tension or anxiety.

Competing Response Training

In this phase of treatment the child is taught to breathe diaphragmatically (as learned during relaxation training) and to begin speaking after a slight exhalation of air. The point is to increase a type of response (speaking on an exhale) that is incompatible with the interrupted airflow typically associated with stuttering. To help the child learn and practice this breathing and speaking pattern in the treatment session, the therapist may place the child's fingers in front of the child's mouth to let him/her feel the warmth of his/her breath when starting to exhale. The child is instructed to start speaking once the child feels his/her breath. Initially the child is instructed to speak for shorter durations and, as the child begins speaking fluently, the durations of speech are lengthened. If stuttering should occur, the child is taught to stop speaking immediately, exhale slightly, and begin speaking again on the exhale. This prevents the struggle that is often associated with stuttering and replaces it with the proper breathing and speaking pattern. After successfully practicing this technique in session, the child is instructed to use the technique outside of the treatment session when speaking.

Motivation Training

Three techniques are used in an attempt to increase compliance with the treatment. First, in the *inconvenience review*, the therapist and the child (and the child's parents) review all of the inconveniences or problems associated with stuttering. Second, the therapist teaches a parent to provide *social support*. In the social support procedure, the parent is instructed to praise the child for talking fluently and for correctly using the competing response. The parent also reminds the child to use the competing response when the parent observes an instance of stuttering. Finally, in the *public display* procedure the therapist instructs the child to practice using the competing response to speak fluently in situations where stuttering was most likely to occur prior to treatment.

Generalization Training

In order to increase the likelihood that the child will use the procedures in stuttering-prone situations outside of the treatment sessions, the therapist implements *symbolic rehearsal*. In this procedure, the child is instructed to imagine using the techniques and successfully inhibiting stuttering in difficult situations outside of the session.

SUMMARY OF OUTCOME RESEARCH

Researchers have shown that Regulated Breathing and simplified versions of the procedure are effective in the treatment of stuttering exhibited by children and adults (Woods et al., 2000). Furthermore, Regulated Breathing is more efficient than other successful treatments for stuttering. Regulated Breathing is often implemented in a few treatment sessions and has been shown to produce lasting and clinically significant decreases in stuttering in children. With Regulated Breathing, decreases in stuttering are obtained without the corresponding decreases in speech rate that often characterize some other treatments for stuttering. In fact, Regulated Breathing most often is associated with increases in speech rate for the recipients of the treatment. Finally, Regulated Breathing has received high ratings of treatment acceptability, showing that treatment recipients like the procedure.

See also: Anxiety; *Diagnostic and Statistical Manual of Mental Disorders*; Treatment Acceptability

BIBLIOGRAPHY

American Psychiatric Association. (1994). *Diagnostic and statistical manual of mental disorders* (4th ed.). Washington, DC: Author.

Azrin, N. H., & Nunn, R. G. (1974). A rapid method of eliminating stuttering by a regulated breathing approach. *Behaviour Research and Therapy, 12,* 279–286.

Bloodstein, O. (1995). *A handbook on stuttering.* San Diego, CA: Singular Publishing.

Leung, A., & Robson, W. L. (1990). Stuttering. *Clinical Pediatrics, 29,* 489–502.

Miltenberger, R. G., & Woods, D. W. (1998). Speech disfluencies. In T. S. Watson & F. M. Gresham (Eds.), *Handbook of child behavior therapy* (pp. 127–142). New York: Plenum.

Woods, D. W., Twohig, M. P., Fuqua, R. W., & Hanley, J. M. (2000). Treatment for stuttering with regulated breathing: Strengths, limitations, and future directions. *Behavior Therapy, 31,* 547–558.

Additional Readings for Nonprofessionals and Professionals

http://www.nsastutter.org/ (National Stuttering Foundation)
http://www.stuttering.com/ (National Center for Stuttering)
http://www.stutterisa.org/ (International Stuttering Association)
http://www.stuttersfa.org/ (Stuttering Foundation of America)

RAYMOND G. MILTENBERGER

Sylvan Learning Centers

Sylvan Learning Centers are individually owned businesses that specialize in tutoring students experiencing academic difficulties. Sylvan Centers are designed to assist students in grades kindergarten through 12. Established in 1979, Sylvan has over 900 centers in the United States, Canada, Hong Kong, and Guam and is accredited by the Commission on Internet and Trans-Regional Accreditation. Most students who contact Sylvan receive reading, writing, or math tutoring. However, the centers also offer study skills assistance and preparation for college entrance exams.

The three major components of the tutoring system that Sylvan refers to as "The Sylvan Advantage" are (1) skills assessment, (2) "Mastery Learning," and (3) personalized instruction. The skills assessment is a battery of tests that assess a student's ability across academic areas. The information is then used to develop a comprehensive analysis of each student's academic performance. According to Sylvan, students often have "skill gaps," or areas of learning that serve as a foundation for later skills. Sylvan's services are designed to complete these skill gaps so that the student can complete more advanced academic tasks.

The center uses the information obtained in the skills assessment to develop a program tailored to a student's individual needs. For example, a student with difficulty completing algebra problems would receive a different program than a student with a reading comprehension problem. In addition, independent work is emphasized. Students learn to check their work as they progress with a certified teacher close by to provide assistance and feedback as needed.

Starting with the original skill gap that was identified in the initial assessment, students must master each skill before advancing to the next, higher skill. The student must demonstrate the skill accurately—three to five times—before progressing. This is what Sylvan refers to as Mastery Learning.

The entire process is designed to reward students with praise and tokens for academic performance in order to allow them to experience the rewards associated with academic success. Sylvan uses a token system wherein students earn tokens contingent on academic progress. These tokens can be traded in at the on-site store to receive specific items like games, puzzles, or candy. Teachers also provide frequent verbal praise during every tutoring session. One of Sylvan's goals is for students to learn to take pride in their success and develop confidence in their ability.

Parents or guardians of students can also expect to attend conferences with Sylvan staff to discuss student progress. Academic achievement is continually assessed to ensure that students maintain their knowledge throughout the tutoring process. Most centers offer a guarantee that students will advance by a minimum of one grade level by the first progress assessment. The first skill check typically occurs after 36 hours of tutoring. Failure to progress by one grade level typically results in the student receiving an additional 12 hours of tutoring free. According to Sylvan's Web site, 80 percent of students improve one grade level within 36 hours of tutoring.

Sylvan Learning Centers also provide online tutoring for students in third through ninth grades. The online version is very similar to the person-to-person tutoring and includes skills assessment, individualized programs, and emphasis on mastery learning. All of the consultations between parents and teachers are conducted via phone and the student receives tutoring through the computer from a certified Sylvan teacher. Following the initial telephone contact with the parent, the student completes the skills assessment on the computer. The results are provided to the parent over the telephone and the student receives the equipment he/she will need to complete the online tutoring. Sylvan will ship the student a digital pen, a digital writing pad, and a headset. The headset allows the student to talk directly to his Sylvan tutor as the tutoring occurs. By connecting to the student's computer, the student can provide written communication to the teacher with the digital pen and paper. This allows students to write answers to questions or problems as they typically do in school and avoid having to type responses. Online tutoring sessions are designed to last 1 hour and occur two to four times weekly. The cost for online tutoring is similar to the traditional center-based tutoring. There are additional fees for use of the headset and digital equipment. Fees range from $250 to $450 per month, depending on the location of the Sylvan center as well as the services provided.

Although Sylvan claims that most students advance one grade level in their skill deficit area, there are no controlled studies from outside sources that have investigated Sylvan's effectiveness. Thus, consumers must rely on anecdotal reports from others and Sylvan's own publications to evaluate their claims of effectiveness. In the past, some school districts have contracted with tutoring businesses and may be able to provide data indicating any changes in academic progress (Tress, 1998).

Sylvan learning centers may be contacted through their Web site www.sylvanlearningcenter.com or at 1-888-EDUCATE. The Web site contains additional information on the services and process.

See also: Academic Interventions for Written Language and Grammar; Huntington Learning Centers; Kaplan, Incorporated

BIBLIOGRAPHY

Sylvan Learning Center. Retrieved September 15, 2002, from http://www.sylvanlearningcenter.com

Tress, M. H. (1998). Private tutoring companies and public school districts. *Curriculum Administrator, 34,* 1–4.

Additional Readings for Nonprofessionals

Greene, L. J. (2002). *Roadblocks to learning: Understanding the obstacles that sabotage your child's academic success.* New York: Warner.

Shore, K. (1998). *Special kids problem solver: Ready to use interventions for helping all students with academic, behavioral, and physical problems.* Englewood Cliffs NJ: Prentice–Hall.

Additional Readings for Professionals

Glaeser, B. J., & Pierson, M. R. (2002). An instructional model for improving reading comprehension for students with and without learning disabilities during content instruction. *Proven Practice, 4,* 11–17.

Skinner, C. H., & Robinson, S. L. (2002). Interspersing additional easier items to enhance mathematics performance on subtests requiring different task demands. *School Psychology Quarterly, 17,* 191–205.

NANCY FOSTER

Tt

Tantrums

Tantrums, or temper tantrums, represent a major childhood behavioral concern. Typically a collection of several behaviors that may involve self-injury or aggression toward others, tantrums may include, but not be limited to, throwing oneself to the floor, kicking, pounding fists, crying, screaming, flailing, head banging, or a combination thereof (Goldstein, 1999).

Typically lasting between 1 and 4 minutes, tantrums may be triggered by factors such as frustration, fatigue, hunger, illness, or changes in routine. Often, tantrums are preceded by a period of whining, irritability, and/or defiance. The event often begins with a confrontation of some sort (e.g., a request or instruction to complete a task by a teacher/caregiver and a refusal to comply by the child or a refusal of a child's request). As the tantrum begins to subside, the child may begin to cry or sob. In most cases, the child eventually regains composure and attempts to reestablish contact with the caregiver.

Among young children, those between the ages of 1 and 2 are most likely to exhibit tantrumming behavior. However, only about half of children in this age group exhibit frequent or chronic tantrums. The topography of tantrums seen in this age group may include crying, biting, hitting, kicking, screaming, screeching, arching the back, throwing themselves on the floor, pounding or flailing arms, breath holding, head banging, and throwing objects.

Tantrums may also occur in older children. For instance, preschoolers aged 3–4 may engage in any of the above behaviors during a tantrum, as well as stomping, yelling, whining, criticizing others, shaking fists, and slamming doors. In addition to the tantrumming behaviors seen in younger children, students 4 and above may also exhibit swearing, self-criticism, striking out at others, deliberately breaking objects, and threatening others (Goldstein, 1999).

Tantrums are also commonly seen in children with developmental disabilities, and may include many of the same behaviors described above. However, children with developmental disabilities, especially those in the moderate to severe/profound range, may be more likely to exhibit self-injurious behavior, such as head banging, biting oneself, and slapping oneself, during a tantrumming episode.

TREATMENT OF TANTRUMMING BEHAVIOR

In preschool age children, tantrums are rarely a sign of serious behavioral or emotional concern. However, when a child begins to frequently use tantrumming as a problem-solving tool, serious concern may be warranted (Goldstein, 1999). Such tantrums may interfere with a child's quality of life in several ways. For example, child–parent interactions may become stressed if the child's behavior is aversive, or punishing, to the parents. In addition, parents may become hesitant to take children to public places, such as stores or restaurants, for fear that the child will engage in embarrassing tantrumming behavior. Furthermore, tantrums in the school setting or other learning situations may result in substantial loss of time engaged in academic activities, and may also alienate a child from his/her peers. Finally, as noted previously, tantrums may be associated with more severe behaviors such as aggression or self-injury (Vollmer & Northup, 1996).

Traditional interventions for tantrums have included extinction (e.g., ignoring) and punishment (e.g., time-out). However, these treatments may be associated with negative side effects. For example, extinction may result in a temporary increase in the frequency or intensity of the tantrum. Furthermore, punishment procedures may provoke emotional behavior and reduce positive interactions between the parent and child (Vollmer & Northup, 1996). Because of the potential negative side effects of these traditional treatments for tantrumming, other interventions should be considered initially. For example, a differential reinforcement procedure (e.g., differential reinforcement of other behavior [DRO]) may be a useful technique for treating tantrumming behavior.

As noted previously, tantrums may be triggered by any of several possible factors. In fact, several studies have indicated that tantrums may serve distinctive functions for individual children. Thus, an important consideration in the treatment of this behavior is the function that the tantrum serves for the individual. It may be useful, then, to utilize functional analysis procedures to identify contingencies that maintain tantrums and increase the probability that an effective intervention will be implemented (Vollmer & Northup, 1996).

See also: Differential Reinforcement; Extinction; Functional Behavioral Assessment; Punishment; Self-Injurious Behavior; Time-Out

BIBLIOGRAPHY

Goldstein, A. (1999). *Low-level aggression.* Champaign, IL: Research Press.
Vollmer, T. R., & Northup, J. (1996). Functional analysis of severe tantrums displayed by children with language delays. *Behavior Modification, 20,* 97–116.

Additional Reading for Professionals and Nonprofessionals

Forehand, R., & Long, N. (2002). *Parenting the strong-willed child* (2nd ed.). Chicago: Contemporary Books.

D. Joe Olmi
Melissa D. Scoggins

Tarasoff v. Board of Regents of California

Remley and Herlihy (2001) noted that when the interests of society outweigh an individual's right to privacy, privacy can no longer be guaranteed. In the context of providing mental health services, courts have held that the interests of society outweigh a client's right to privacy when a client threatens to harm others. Accordingly, many state legislatures and courts have imposed a duty on mental health professionals to engage in reasonable efforts to prevent clients from harming others.

The seminal case addressing the obligation of mental health professionals to prevent clients from harming others is

Tarasoff v. Regents of University of California (1976). In this case, Poddar, a graduate student at the University of California at Berkeley, told the psychologist he was seeing at the university counseling center that he intended to kill his girlfriend when she returned home from a trip to Brazil. Though Poddar did not mention the girlfriend's name, the girlfriend was readily identifiable as Tatiana Tarasoff. The psychologist considered the threat to be serious, so he initiated proceedings to have Poddar committed for psychiatric evaluation and contacted the campus police. The campus police questioned Poddar, but released him on the basis of their determination that the student was not dangerous. Poddar did not receive a psychiatric evaluation because the psychologist's supervisor at the university counseling center ordered that no such action take place. When Poddar's girlfriend returned from her trip, Poddar killed her.

The Supreme Court of California held that when "a therapist determines, or pursuant to the standards of his profession should determine, that his patient presents a serious danger of violence to another, he incurs an obligation to use reasonable care to protect the victim against such danger" (*Tarasoff v. Regents of University of California*, 1976, p. 340). The court found that this duty could include warning the intended victim. Though Tarasoff was out of the country at the time the threat was made, the court stated that the psychologist could have notified Tarasoff's family members of Poddar's violent intentions so that the family members could have notified her. The court found Tarasoff's subsequent murder at the hands of Poddar might have been prevented by such notification.

In spite of its holding, the *Tarasoff* court did acknowledge the importance of open and confidential psychotherapeutic dialogue (*Tarasoff v. Regents of University of California*, 1976). The court further noted that a therapist should not routinely reveal these confidential communications because such disclosures could seriously disrupt the patient's relationship with the therapist. When such disclosures are necessary, the court suggested that they be made discreetly in order to preserve the privacy of the patient.

The *Tarasoff* holding is based on California law and is only persuasive authority for courts in other jurisdictions. Yet, the court's findings have been utilized as a foundation for establishing mental health professionals' duty to warn potential victims when clients express violent intentions. Other courts have adopted, extended, limited, and rejected the *Tarasoff* holding. The case is such a well-known precedent that the duty to warn is often referred to as the "*Tarasoff* duty."

Some courts have limited the duty to warn to clearly identifiable potential victims (i.e., *Swan v. Wedgwood Family Services*, 1998). Courts have also extended the duty to warn to include foreseeable victims (i.e., *Hedlund v. Super. Ct. of Orange County*, 1983). Courts have differed when ruling on the duty to warn potential victims who knew of the danger. Some courts have found that there is no duty to warn when the victim already knew of the danger (i.e., *Boulanger v. Pol*, 1995), whereas others have extended the duty to protect victims who already knew of the potential danger (i.e., *Hutchinson v. Patel*, 1994). The court in *Peck v. Counseling Services of Addison County* (1985) even extended the duty to warn to clients' threats to property.

The Supreme Court of Ohio found that since the *Tarasoff* decision, a majority of courts have "concluded that the relationship between the psychotherapist and the outpatient constitutes a special relationship which imposes upon the psychotherapist an affirmative duty to protect against or control the patient's violent propensities" (*Estates of Morgan v. Fairfield Family Counseling Center*, 1997). However, the court continued by stating that psychotherapists are not expected to render perfect predictions of future violence, they are simply expected to use their best professional judgment to make informed assessments of the clients' propensity for violence and to take reasonable precautions to prevent harm from occurring.

Not all state courts have embraced the *Tarasoff* doctrine. In 1999, the members of the Texas Supreme Court unanimously rejected the *Tarasoff* duty (*Thapar v. Zezulka*, 1999). Basing its decision on the Texas statute governing mental health professionals' legal duty to protect clients' confidentiality, the court found that it was unwise to impose a duty to warn on mental health practitioners.

Several state legislatures have codified the *Tarasoff* duty (Remley & Herlihy, 2001). These statutes were often designed to protect mental health professionals from civil liability for breaching confidentiality when a client poses a danger to others. The statutes usually limit the duty owed by mental health professionals and specifically describe the action required by the mental health professional.

Counselors may also have a duty to warn potential victims of nonviolent acts that can result in harm. For example, the duty to warn may be implicated when a counselor believes that an HIV-positive client is planning to have unprotected sex or share needles with a reasonably identifiable person (Ahia & Martin, 1993). Glosoff, Herlihy, and Spence (2000) found that only Utah has a state statute that extends counselors' duty to warn to clients' possible transmission of communicable diseases. Whether other states will find that mental health professionals have a duty to warn in this situation has not been decided.

The multiple interpretations of the *Tarasoff* duty and the lack of statutory and case law addressing this duty as it relates to school personnel add complexity to the application of the *Tarasoff* duty in school settings. The basic standard of care for school personnel is clear; courts have uniformly held that school personnel have a duty to protect students from foreseeable harm (Hermann & Remley, 2000). Preventing students from harming other students seems to be implicit in this duty. Whether warning students of other students' threats of violence against them is included in this duty has yet to be determined.

BIBLIOGRAPHY

Ahia, C. E., & Martin, D. (1993). *The danger-to-self-or-other exception to confidentiality.* Alexandria, VA: American Counseling Association.

Boulanger v. Pol, 900 P.2d 823 (Kan. 1995).

Estates of Morgan v. Fairfield Family Counseling Center, 673 N.E.2d 1311 (Ohio 1997).

Glosoff, H. L., Herlihy, B., & Spence, E. B. (2000). Privileged communication in the counselor–client relationship. *Journal of Counseling & Development, 78,* 454–462.

Hedlund v. Super. Ct. of Orange County, 669 P.2d 41 (Cal. 1983).

Hutchinson v. Patel, 637 So.2d 415 (La. 1994).

Peck v. Counseling Services of Addison County, 499 A.2d 422 (Vt. 1985).

Remley, T. P., Jr., & Herlihy, B. (2001). *Ethical, legal, and professional issues in counseling.* Upper Saddle River, NJ: Prentice–Hall.

Swan v. Wedgwood Family Services, 583 N.W.2d 719 (Mich. App. 1998).

Tarasoff v. Regents of University of California, 551 P.2d 334 (Cal. 1976).

Thapar v. Zezulka, 994 S.W.2d 635 (Tex. 1999).

Additional Readings for Professionals and Nonprofessionals

Isaacs, M. L. (1997). The duty to warn and protect: Tarasoff and the elementary school counselor. *Elementary School Guidance and Counseling, 31,* 326–342.

Isaacs, M. L., & Stone, C. (1999). School counselors and confidentiality: Factors affecting professional choices. *Professional School Counseling, 2,* 258–266.

Pietrofesa, J. J., Pietrofesa, C. F., & Pietrofesa, J. D. (1990). The mental health counselor and the "duty to warn." *Journal of Mental Health Counseling, 12,* 129–137.

Waldo, S. L., & Malley, P. (1992). Tarasoff and its progeny: Implications for the school counselor. *The School Counselor, 40,* 46–54.

MARY A. HERMANN

Television Violence and Aggressive Behavior in Children

Modern concerns about the effects of viewing violence on television are nothing new. In fact, it was not long after televisions were introduced into American homes that researchers began examining the effects of viewing TV violence on child behavior. Today, a large body of research shows TV violence is a significant environmental influence on children's development of aggression. Indeed, this finding is one of the most rigorously tested and consistent results in the field of child development.

The best studies in this area show that the effects of TV violence account for about 10 percent of the variability in all child aggression. Coie and Dodge (1998) illustrate the meaning of this statistical finding by pointing out that 10 percent is approximately equal to the effect of cigarette smoking on cancer.

Given this significant finding, it is no surprise that concerns about TV violence have maintained across generations.

Although the significance of the findings described above should not be underestimated, it is important to note that much of the research in this area is correlational in nature. That is, researchers have found that children who view TV violence are also rated or observed to be more aggressive; however, no direct causal link between the two has been documented (i.e., this type of research cannot show that children who watch violent TV subsequently become more aggressive). Scientists approach this kind of research with some skepticism because these data could point to a variety of conclusions other than TV violence causing aggressive behavior. Nevertheless, the large volume of research in this area lends considerable support for the notion that viewing TV violence contributes to aggressive behavior.

In addition, a limited number of controlled laboratory research lends further credence to this conclusion. In laboratory settings, researchers are able to control the kind/amount of violence to which the child has exposure as well as the frequency/intensity of pre- and postviewing aggressive responding. The most well-known example of this kind of research was conducted by Bandura and his colleagues in which children who played in a room with a "Bobo" doll before and after watching violence on TV were more aggressive toward the doll afterwards (Bandura, Ross, & Ross, 1963). Such work better demonstrates the causal link between TV viewing and aggression; however, the extent to which laboratory work can be generalized to real-world settings is still in question.

In their review, Coie and Dodge (1998) discuss a number of ways in which viewing TV violence might have an effect on child aggression. First, viewing violent actors who benefit from their actions may provide the child with ideas about strategies that may be effective for them in the future. Second, watching TV violence repeatedly may "desensitize" children to the negative emotions it may initially provoke. In fact, laboratory studies show children have decreased physiological responses to aggression over repeated viewing. Finally, watching programs with violent content may alter children's understanding of reality. Research has shown that those who frequently watch TV violence believe real-world violence is more common and the world is less safe, justifying the use of their own real-world aggression. All of these are plausible mechanisms, but no one pathway has more research than another does.

The teacher, parent, or practitioner can prevent or decrease the apparent negative effects of TV violence on children in two ways. First, research findings suggest that children who are initially aggressive are more likely to choose violent TV programming. Indeed, Coie and Dodge (1998) describe the relationship between TV violence viewing and aggression as reciprocal in nature. Thus, the prevention and early intervention

of aggression in very young children, regardless of TV viewing preferences, seems an important starting point.

Second, a number of studies have documented beneficial effects of "inoculating" viewers to the influences of TV. In one example (Huesmann, Eron, Klein, Brice, & Fischer, 1983), experimenters taught third graders to understand that TV violence was not real, the use of special effects and that in real life people do not use such tactics to solve problems. In addition, the children were asked to create a film showing other children "who had been fooled by TV" what they had learned. Results showed the children who received the intervention were better educated about TV violence and received lower peer-nominated aggression scores than a similar group receiving no treatment.

In summary, the things that children see on TV obviously have an influence on their behavior. The extent of the influence may be unknown and is confounded by other events in the environment. TV is a powerful medium that has the potential to exert both positive and negative influence on the viewer. It is the parent's responsibility to ensure that their children are not harmfully affected by the images they see on TV.

BIBLIOGRAPHY

Bandura, A., Ross, D., & Ross, S. A. (1963). Imitation of film-mediated aggressive models. *Journal of Abnormal and Social Psychology, 66*, 3–11.

Coie, J. D., & Dodge, K. A. (1998). Aggression and antisocial behavior. In W. Damon & N. Eisenberg (Eds.), *Handbook of child psychology. Vol. 3: Social, emotional, and personality development* (5th ed., pp. 779–862). New York: Wiley.

Huesmann, L. R., Eron, L. D., Klein, R., Brice, P., & Fischer, P. (1983). Mitigating the imitation of aggressive behaviors by children's attitudes about media violence. *Journal of Personality and Social Psychology, 44*, 899–910.

JODI POLAHA

Terman, Lewis M.

When Lewis Terman first worked on the Stanford–Binet intelligence test revision in 1916, he probably had no idea that it would ultimately affect the world of psychometrics (the study of psychological measures using quantitative tests) as much as it did. In fact, one might never expect Terman to achieve much of anything when considering his family circumstances. Terman stated in his autobiography that if one did a statistical study of his ancestors, one would assume he would grow up a farmer and that his education would have ended after high school. Terman was the 12th of 14 children and had a strange curiosity regarding the personality traits of others. He remarked that he and his siblings often mimicked and made fun of those with any differences from the rest of the population (Terman, 1961). Although this type of behavior may be common in children, Terman eventually made this passion for individual differences a theme in his many research interests.

Terman earned his baccalaureate degrees in the areas of science, classics, and pedagogy at Normal College, Indiana. In 1905, he received his Ph.D. in psychology from Clark University and immediately afterwards became a school principal in Los Angeles from 1906 to 1910. In 1910, he obtained a position as an assistant professor at Stanford University in the education department and remained there for the rest of his career. Terman eventually moved up in rank to head of the Department of Psychology at Stanford until his retirement in 1942 (Minton, 1999).

Perhaps Terman's greatest achievement was in the area of intelligence testing. His first major research project focused on developing an American version of the intelligence scale developed by French scientist Alfred Binet in 1905. In 1916, Terman and his graduate students conducted an extensive revision of the scale that became known as the Stanford–Binet Intelligence Scale and published the results in the influential book *The Measurement of Intelligence* (Terman, 1916). The revision introduced the term *Intelligence Quotient*, or *IQ*, and became one of the most widely used tests of intelligence. An additional revision was made in 1937 with Maud A. Merrill (Minton, 1999). Terman's devotion to intelligence testing provided a concrete method for determining differences among individuals on the basis of intellect and also introduced the idea of a continuum of intelligence that can fall between the severely retarded and the superior (Maloney, 1987). The work conducted on the Stanford–Binet would prove to be the foundation upon which group testing research would be conducted.

In 1917, Terman, along with a group of other psychologists, played a key role in developing intelligence tests for the army during World War I that could be administered to large numbers of individuals at one time. The tests, known as the Army Alpha and Army Beta, would later be adapted to be introduced to school populations and eventually lead to the development of the National Intelligence Tests for Grades 3 to 8 in 1920 (Minton, 1999). Other group-administered tests would follow, including The Terman Group Tests of Mental Ability and The Stanford Achievement Tests (Terman, 1961). Throughout the 1920s, Terman promoted the use of standardized tests in schools in order to classify students in groups of the same ability (homogeneous groups) and thus "track" students according to such abilities throughout their academic career (Minton, 1999).

One homogeneous group to which Terman dedicated a large part of research was the gifted. Terman began work with gifted children in 1922 when he sampled approximately 1,500 elementary and high school students in California with IQ scores of 135 and above in order to identify characteristics of gifted children and follow their progression through their years of development. In 1924, he published the results of his initial investigation in *Genetic Studies of Genius*, concluding that gifted children were well-rounded and had skills that could later be harnessed for leadership positions. For many years through the 1980s, the group was assessed by Terman and others, with whom he had made arrangements to conduct assessments even after his death. Overall, the study demonstrated that the gifted sample achieved above-average career success and held high degrees of personal satisfaction (Minton, 1999).

Although Terman later conducted research on gender identity assessment and psychological factors associated with marital happiness (Minton, 1999), it is his work in intelligence testing and among the gifted population that would have such a profound impact on the field of psychology. The Stanford–Binet proved to be the impetus for the testing movement in America and is the psychometric basis for most measures of intellectual and academic functioning even today (Freeland & Watson, 2001).

See also: Binet, Alfred; Gifted and Talented

BIBLIOGRAPHY

Freeland, J., & Watson, T. S. (2001, April). *The ancestry of concurrent validity of commonly administered tests by school psychologists: The Stanford–Binet is the great grandfather of them all.* Poster presented at the 33rd annual meeting of the National Association of School Psychologists, Washington, DC.

Maloney, M. P. (1987). Mental retardation. In R. J. Corsini (Ed.), *Encyclopedia of psychology* (Vol. 2, 2nd ed., pp. 397–399). New York: Wiley.

Minton, H. L. (1999). Lewis Madison Terman. In J. A. Garranty & M. C. Carnes (Eds.), *American national biography* (Vol. 21, pp. 455–456). New York: Oxford University Press.

Terman, L. M. (1961). Lewis M. Terman: Trails to psychology. In C. Murchison (Ed.), *A history of psychology in autobiography* (Vol. 2, pp. 297–331). New York: Russell & Russell.

Additional Readings for Nonprofessionals

Minton, H. L. (1988). *Lewis M. Terman: Pioneer in psychological testing.* New York: New York University Press.

Seagoe, M. V. (1975). *Terman and the gifted.* Los Altos, CA: William Kaufmann.

Additional Readings for Professionals

Chapman, P. D. (1988). *School as sorters: Lewis M. Terman, applied psychology, and the intelligence testing movement, 1890–1930.* New York: New York University Press.

Hilgard, E. R. (1957). Lewis Madison Terman. *American Journal of Psychology, 70,* 472–479.

CANDICE BARR

Test of Written Language—3rd Edition

The Test of Written Language—3rd Edition (TOWL-3) (Hammill & Larsen, 1996) is a norm-referenced instrument used to assess the written language of children aged 7 to 17. The primary purpose of a norm-referenced instrument is to compare an individual's performance to a particular norm group. Except for one small portion of the TOWL-3, the test is not timed. The TOWL-3 has two equivalent forms (A and B) that are interchangeable and may be administered as pre and post measures. The TOWL-3 requires approximately 90 minutes to administer and may be given individually to one student or to a group of students. The TOWL-3 was designed to (a) identify students with written language difficulties, (b) determine students' strengths and weaknesses, (c) document students' progress, and (d) conduct research in written language (Hammill & Larsen, 1996).

The third edition of the TOWL examines three basic components of written language performance, including conventional, linguistic, and cognitive language (Hammill & Larsen, 1996). These components refer to the ability to (a) appropriately apply the rules of punctuation, spelling, and capitalization; (b) appropriately use grammar and meaning; and (c) express ideas in a coherent manner. Contrived and spontaneous formats are two ways in which these components are evaluated in the TOWL-3. Tests that use a contrived format measure small, isolated components of written language (e.g., spelling, punctuation, and capitalization). The spontaneous format measures written language within a meaningful writing task. Using this format, students are provided a picture and are instructed to write a story about the picture. The student stories are scored for a variety of writing skills, including spelling, punctuation, capitalization, format, plot, sentence structure, and readability. In addition, handwriting can be reviewed and informally scored.

SUBTESTS

A total of eight subtests comprise the TOWL-3. The contrived format is utilized in the subtests of Spelling, Style, Vocabulary, Sentence Combining, and Logical Sentences. In the Vocabulary subtest, the student writes a sentence using a word given by the examiner. The Spelling and Style subtests ask the student to write dictated sentences, which are reviewed for punctuation, capitalization, and spelling errors. In the Logical Sentences subtest, the student must make an illogical sentence into one that makes sense, whereas the Sentence Combining

subtest requires the student to make one longer sentence out of two or three smaller sentences.

The spontaneous format, which requires a student to write a story about a picture, is utilized in the final three subtests (i.e., Contextual Conventions, Contextual Language, and Story Construction). These three subtests are evaluated for spelling, punctuation, vocabulary quality, sentence construction, grammar, and compositional aspects (e.g., interest to reader).

SCORES

The eight subtests are combined to create three different composite quotients: Overall Writing, Contrived Writing, and Spontaneous Writing. The Overall Writing composite score describes a student's performance in written language using both contrived and spontaneous formats and includes all eight subtests. Scores on the TOWL-3 are reported as Scaled scores for the individual subtests and Standard scores on the composite quotients. Scaled scores have an average of 10 with the Average range falling between 7 and 13. Standard scores have an average of 100 with the Average range falling between 85 and 115. For both subtests and quotients, 84 percent of all students will score within the Average range.

NORM GROUP

In 1995, the TOWL-3 was standardized in 25 states with 2,217 participants, which comprised the normative group (Hammill & Larsen, 1996). Based on the 1995 U.S. Census data, this sample was generally representative of the nation regarding gender, residence, race, ethnicity, geographic area, family income, educational attainment of parents, and disabling condition. It appears that the normative group was adequate for the appropriate standardization of the TOWL-3.

RELIABILITY AND VALIDITY

Results of a test should be dependable. Dependability means that test scores are reliable (i.e., reproducible and stable) and valid (i.e., meaningful). A variety of research studies have been conducted to determine the dependability of the TOWL-3 (Hammill & Larsen, 1996). Overall, the TOWL-3 is dependable and the composite quotients may be used to make individual decisions about individual students. However, the TOWL-3's ability to identify students with special needs is somewhat unclear (Salvia & Ysseldyke, 1998). More validity studies in this area would be useful (Sattler, 2001).

As with many norm-referenced tests, the TOWL-3 is only moderately helpful in designing interventions to improve writing ability. According to the authors, "the TOWL-3 does not yield the detailed kind of information that is essential for designing instructional programs for individual students" (Hammill & Larsen, 1996, p. 43) and the authors recommend that teachers review a student's permanent products to identify writing areas for remediation. Although suggestions for remediation of writing skills are provided, these recommendations are vague at best.

See also: Academic Interventions for Written Language and Grammar; Writing (Written Language)

BIBLIOGRAPHY

Hammill, D. D., & Larsen, S. C. (1996). *Test of Written Language—3rd Edition: Examiner's manual.* Austin, TX: Pro-Ed.

Salvia, J., & Ysseldyke, J. E. (1998). *Assessment* (7th ed.). Boston: Houghton Mifflin.

Sattler, J. M. (2001). *Assessment of children: Cognitive applications* (4th ed.). La Mesa, CA: Author.

MERILEE MCCURDY

SAMUEL Y. SONG

Thorndike, Robert L.

The Thorndike family has been carrying on a tradition in the field of psychometrics, the study of measuring psychological factors, across many generations. R.L. Thorndike is the son of Edward L. Thorndike, a famous psychometrician, and the father of Robert M. Thorndike, who is also a leader in the field. R.L. Thorndike once described his family as a sandwich, with the two slices of bread being his father and his son, while he deemed himself the ham in the middle (Thorndike, 1990).

While at Columbia University, Thorndike researched distinct learning abilities in rats and earned his Ph.D. in 1935. Thorndike remained at Columbia throughout his career, becoming head of the Department of Psychological Foundations in 1957 and eventually retiring and leaving the college in 1980. Throughout his tenure, his dedication to the design and analysis of achievement tests would have a large impact on how the field of psychology views the measure of intelligence (Cronbach, 1992).

With the onset of World War II, many psychologists were recruited to participate in the evaluation of existing procedures and to develop new assessments to predict the future achievement of pilots, bombardiers, and navigators in training programs and on-the-job performance. Then-Major R.L. Thorndike and others noted many errors that made existing tests unstable and thus proceeded to guide the design and interpretation of reliability studies. The report was featured in the influential journal *Personnel Selection* in 1949 (Cronbach, 1992).

The project also identified distinct ability patterns that predicted future success of men enlisted in the Air Force and ensued with Thorndike's follow-up study with E.P. Hagen (Ten Thousand Careers, 1963). The results demonstrated that individual test performance was correlated with (related to) occupational level later in life.

Thorndike applied his work on ability testing to other settings when he developed a group mental test to be used in schools. The original work was done in 1954 in collaboration with Irving Lorge and evolved into the Cognitive Ability Test (CAT), after later revisions with Hagen in 1986. The Cognitive Ability Test provided a profile or spread of four scores rather than a single score, unlike the predominant IQ test at the time, the Stanford–Binet. Thorndike's son, Robert, believed the test to be a "major milestone" in the testing movement (p. 412, 1990). Despite the purported advantage of separating the various aspects of intelligence into different components, the CAT never reliably differentiated between the four components, and led Thorndike to conclude that a general cognitive ability measure is more accurate for predicting functioning than are the individual aspects of intelligence (Cronbach, 1992). This idea of a general intelligence, known as the *g* factor of intelligence, would go on to influence many aspects of the testing movement throughout the history of psychometrics.

Thorndike went on to conduct comparative research of achievement testing in other countries that have influenced education in the United States. His involvement in intelligence testing in applied settings and using test scores to predict future success later influenced test reliability measures and the field of vocational assessment/guidance.

See also: Binet, Alfred; Terman, Lewis M.

BIBLIOGRAPHY

Cronbach, L. J. (1992). Robert Thorndike (1910–1990): Obituary. *American Psychologist, 47,* 1237.

Thorndike, R. L. (1990). Origins of intelligence and its measurement. *Journal of Psychoeducational Assessment, 8,* 223–230.

Thorndike, R. L. (1990). Would the real factors of the Stanford–Binet fourth edition please come forward? *Journal of Psychoeducational Assessment, 8,* 412–435.

Additional Readings for Nonprofessionals

Michell, J. (1999). *Measurement in psychology: Critical history of a methodological concept.* New York: Cambridge University Press.

Sheehy, N., Chapman, A. J., & Conroy, W. A. (1997). *Biographical dictionary of psychology*. New York: Routledge Reference.

Additional Readings for Professionals

Barnette, W. L. (1976). *Readings in psychological tests and measurements* (3rd ed.). Baltimore: Williams & Wilkins.

Thorndike, R. L., & Hagen, E. P. (1991). *Measurement and evaluation in psychology and education* (5th ed.). New York: Wiley.

CANDICE BARR

Threat Assessment in the Schools

During the 1997–1998 school year, there were 60 reported school-related deaths (48 homicides, 12 suicides) in the United States alone. From 1994 to 1998, a total of 668,000 teachers were victims of nonfatal violent crimes (e.g., assault, rape, or robbery). During the 1999–2000 school year, there were 13 school-related deaths, a sharp decrease from previous years. The percentage of high school students in 1999 reportedly threatened or injured with a weapon has remained at a constant 7 to 8 percent, with 15 percent of high school students reportedly being victims of physical aggression.

It remains that there are instances of aggressive behavior directed at others perpetrated by students in our schools who might be deemed dangerous, who display behaviors that may forewarn school officials of such occurrences. No one would disagree that these students need to be identified through systematic means in an effort to predict/prevent future occurrences. Conversely, there are those students who engage in behaviors perceived to be threatening, who are, in fact, not dangerous or at risk for engaging in aggressive behaviors toward others. One would also argue that these students should be addressed differently than those perceived to be dangerous. A proactive assessment procedure could prevent violence toward others, as well as prevent students who are not at significant risk for engaging in violent behavior from being suspended, expelled, or alternatively placed.

THE NEED FOR THREAT ASSESSMENT

According to the United States Secret Service (O'Toole, 2000), threat assessments in the schools are vitally important for three reasons. First and foremost, the assessment will increase the likelihood that the school environment is safe and that the students and their parents will perceive themselves as safe in schools. Second, the Secret Service (O'Toole, 2000) specifically states that assessment is needed to replace the "zero tolerance"

policies in schools that call for the immediate expulsion of the student in the event that a threat is made. Third is to comply with *Tarasoff v. Regents of the University of California* (1976), which spoke of the obligation to inform potential victims of a threat made toward them. Although *Tarasoff* is not a federal law, most states have adopted it in some form (Borum & Reddy, 2001).

PURPOSE OF THREAT ASSESSMENTS

According to Borum et al. (1999), the purpose of a threat assessment "is to determine the nature and degree of risk a given individual may pose to an identified or identifiable target" (p. 324). It should be noted that the assessment is not to determine whether or not a threat was made, but rather if the person who made the threat *poses* a threat (Fein, Vossekuil, & Holden, 1995). Borum and his colleagues (1999) distinguish this approach from profiling techniques in that there is a discernable target.

Older methods of assessment have focused on the potential for violent behavior as if it was part of a person's disposition (Borum et al., 1999). If this were true, then identifying the dispositions that were highly correlated with violent acts would facilitate proactive measures to stop these events from occurring, hence the beginning of the movement for behavioral profiling. Behavioral profiling did not prove to be a lucrative endeavor.

Although no one would argue that threat assessment could be a very important function for school psychologists, research has failed to suggest a set of characteristics that would perfectly correlate with violent behaviors. The current views are that it is the interaction of environmental events that places a person at increased risk of committing a violent act. Thus, the thrust of threat assessment models is to collect data regarding the potential environmental variables that are currently interacting in a person's life, which could influence him/her to consider violent activities.

U.S. SECRET SERVICE THREAT ASSESSMENT PROTOCOL

The United States Secret Service (O'Toole, 2000) suggested a model for assessing the level of risk associated with individuals in schools. This model diverges from the previously used profiling methods and forces an assessment of numerous variables that interact to influence the level of risk associated with an individual. The model was based on the procedures used by the Secret Service to assess the level of risk associated with those who threaten to injure or assassinate public officials. A general overview of the model and its specific uses in the schools is presented.

The Secret Service defines a threat as "an expression of intent to do harm or to act out violently against someone or something. A threat can be spoken, written or symbolic" (O'Toole, 2000, p. 6). In other words, threatening statements can be made in a variety of ways and can indicate a variety of targets. Regardless of the medium used or if the target is a person or a building, all threats must be taken seriously.

In general, the Secret Service indicated three critical factors that should be assessed during a threat assessment: the existence of specific plausible details about plans or preparations for violent acts, the emotional content of the threat, and the precipitating stressors that may have triggered the threat. The degree to which these factors exist for the person will lead to a decision as to what level of threat (i.e., low, medium, or high) the person poses to his/her intended target. A low-level threat is a threat that is associated with minimal risks for violent acts. Specifically, a low-level threat is characterized by vague or nonexistent plans and suggests that the person is unlikely to follow through. A moderate-level threat is one that seems possible, yet is unlikely. The content of the threat suggests that the person has given some thought to the details and planning, but has not taken steps to fully plan the event. Finally, a high-level threat is a threat that is serious and indicates an imminent risk to the safety of the intended victim(s).

As a specific model, the Secret Service proposed a "Four Pronged Assessment Approach" aimed at systematically assessing the individual, the individual's social context, the individual's family, and school factors associated with the individual in order to make competent decisions about the level of threat posed by an individual. As a goal, the assessor is not assessing the details of the threat. Instead, the assessor must assess if the perpetrator has the "intention, the ability, or the means to act on the threat" (O'Toole, 2000, p. 10).

In regard to specific guidelines for schools, the Secret Service (O'Toole, 2000) suggests that the assessment process be carried out through the use of a properly trained multidisciplinary team of professionals with one coordinator. The team can consist of any number of professionals, including but not limited to law enforcement, district administrators, mental health personnel, and other school staff or outside consultants. Regarding the coordinator, no specific suggestions are given except that the individual should be sufficiently trained to oversee the assessment process.

THREAT ASSESSMENT TEAM (TAT) MODEL

The proposed TAT model is based on the general model of threat assessment suggested by the United States Secret Service (O'Toole, 2000), but with additional details relevant to the school environment. The model is currently utilized by personnel in schools served by the University of Southern Mississippi School Psychology Service Center. It is proposed here that a school psychologist should act as the threat assessment team coordinator owing to the extensive training and experience school psychologists receive in consultation, assessment, and crisis intervention.

The TAT is an organized group of school personnel (teachers and administrators) and outside personnel who assemble immediately upon notice of a threat. The TAT must *always* work *immediately* after any threat has been reported so as to efficiently assess the potential for violent behavior and to intervene if necessary. In addition, the TAT is also charged with planning and monitoring the implementation of detailed interventions and/or disciplinary recommendations in follow-up to the assessment.

Table 1 depicts the suggested team members and their respective responsibilities. All team members should be trained in their respective duties. Specifically, the team requires two *leaders*—the TAT Coordinator (i.e., school psychology

Table 1. Suggested TAT Members and Their Respective Responsibilities

TAT Coordinator	Works closely with the school's principal, leading the team through an efficient assessment process
	Is responsible for the majority of the assessment procedure including interviews with children, teachers, and parents/guardians as well as administration and scoring of rating scales and psychological testing
	Compiles the final report
Principal or Principal's Designee	Chairs the TAT
	Receives reports of all threats
	Is responsible for removing the perpetrator from the school population, for obtaining background information, and for contacting all outside persons, including parents, other TAT members, community services, etc.
Other TAT Members	May include guidance counselor, SAT Chair, perpetrator's teacher, school police officer, and/or community consultants
	Called in order to reach conclusions about the seriousness of the threat and what future actions will be implemented
	Future actions that will be discussed include additional assessment and/or placement, disciplinary action, school intervention, or assistance with community services
	May be responsible for monitoring the behavior of the child in the future as well as monitor the progress of any interventions

consultant) and the school's principal or designee. The TAT Coordinator does exactly as the title suggests: coordinates the activities of the team, is responsible for the collection of data, and completes the final assessment report. The report should include descriptions of the threat, a synthesis of all data collected, and suggested responses such as disciplinary actions, therapeutic intervention, or referral to outside agencies. The TAT Coordinator may complete the majority of the data collection alone or he/she may delegate to other qualified members of the team.

The principal of the school serves as the actual "chair" of the team. The participation of the school's principal in this role is strongly suggested owing to his/her administrative responsibility and authority. The effective implementation of the team's activities depends on the immediate response of all involved parties, including administrators, parents, teachers, and students. It is also the principal's responsibility to review and coordinate implementation of recommendations that may be suggested as part of the assessment process. In the absence of a principal on site at the time of a threat, the principal may designate someone to act on his/her behalf. It is suggested, however, that the designated person be an administrator who is also trained in the activities and responsibilities of the team. The TAT Coordinator should be informed of the principal's absence and the designee.

Additional TAT members could include district level administration, law enforcement, guidance counselors, teachers, Student Assistance Team (SAT) representatives, and/or other agency personnel. In general, the team members may assist in data collection, may provide the team with data of their own (e.g., reports of previous contact with the student), and/or may participate in the review of assessment data determining the level of risk associated with the threat. In addition, other members may be responsible for monitoring the implementation of the intervention, the progress of the child, and notifying appropriate parties if further intervention or a change in intervention is necessary. Specific team members may vary depending on the nature of the threat.

TAT PROCEDURE

When a threat is reported to an administrator (i.e., principal or assistant principal), the TAT Coordinator is immediately notified. Cell phones dedicated to emergency use only can be an important tool in the notification process in the event of a reported threat. The implementation steps of the threat assessment process follow.

Step 1: Initial Data Collection

The purposes of this initial step are to ensure the safety of the school building immediately following the report of a

threat and to gather preliminary data regarding the threat and the perpetrator. The procedure begins with a report of a threat. As noted earlier, a threat is defined as any written, gestural, or spoken expression of intent to destroy school or community property that could potentially result in harm to self or others or to cause pain and/or injury to self or others. All threats must be immediately reported to the building principal. When the principal receives the report of the threat, he/she immediately activates the TAT, contacts the TAT Coordinator, and removes the perpetrator from his/her class to a room designated by the principal or principal's designee. As in a case of threatened suicide, the student should remain under constant adult supervision until the Coordinator arrives to begin the assessment. Once the assessment begins, the principal or principal's designee notifies the perpetrator's parents/guardians of the threat and the procedures that will be followed. A threat is viewed as a crisis, and parent permission is not required.

The principal or principal's designee is responsible for collecting background data regarding the details of the reported threat and personal information of the perpetrator (e.g., school behavior, demeanor, life changes, and peer relations). The principal or principal's designee also obtains a copy of the child's schedule, including academic subjects, classroom locations, class times, discipline records, academic grades, past testing/placement, and teachers' names.

Step 2: Screener

The purpose of this step is to gather a sufficient amount of data to reach a preliminary conclusion regarding the reported threat. To accomplish this, the TAT Coordinator receives and reviews the initial data from the principal or principal's designee. The TAT Coordinator begins the screening process that includes an interview with the perpetrator, the person(s) who reported it, and any follow-up interviews that appear warranted (e.g., counselors, teachers, other students). The goal is to obtain the details of the events surrounding the threat, the relationship between perpetrator and victim, as well as personal information about the perpetrator.

Step 3: Preliminary Meeting and Conclusions

This step is intended to allow the principal and the TAT Coordinator the opportunity to review all collected data and make preliminary decisions regarding the seriousness of the threat (e.g., low, moderate, or high).

Step 4: Level II Assessment

A Level II assessment is entertained only if the initial three steps suggest that the threat is at a moderate or high level of risk. It is designed to obtain any and all information that may be helpful in fully assessing the variables that may be contributing to the level of risk posed by the threat. This step includes a full assessment of the child using assessment strategies that are designed to provide important information related to personality, school, and home. Those providing information should include the child's parents/guardians, his/her teachers, and, when applicable, the child himself/herself.

In the event that a Level II assessment is deemed necessary, the principal or principal's designee should again contact the child's parents/guardians and request that they come to the school to provide important family information as part of the assessment. The principal or principal's designee explains the seriousness of the situation to the parents/guardians and fully explains that the child will not be allowed to return to school until the assessment is complete. At the conclusion of the Level II assessment, the principal or principal's designee is also responsible for reconvening the TAT to fully discuss the assessment and to formulate future intervention or treatment efforts. Simultaneously, the child should be closely supervised by parents and/or community safety personnel.

Step 5: Follow-Up TAT Meeting

The purposes of the follow-up TAT meeting are for the TAT Coordinator to provide the team members with the data gathered throughout the Level I and/or Level II assessments and to discuss possible intervention/treatment efforts before meeting with the student and the child's parent(s). Specifically, the team will determine whether the threat can be considered a low-, moderate-, or high-level threat.

Step 6: Final Meeting of the TAT

The purpose of this step is to close the case with agreement among team members as to the level of threat posed by the student and what future actions should be pursued. The principal or principal's designee is responsible for contacting the child's parents/guardians and scheduling a meeting time and place. Once scheduled, both the principal or principal's designee and the TAT Coordinator will meet with the child's parents/guardians. At this meeting, the parents/guardians are informed of the results of the assessment. In addition, the principal explains any suggested further action (e.g., disciplinary actions, psychological treatment/therapy). For moderate- or high-level threats, the principal also contacts any ancillary community services that may support treatment efforts. Service agencies may include law enforcement, mental health facilities, and outside counseling services.

The TAT Coordinator should also contact the intervention assistance team personnel, including the school counselor, at the child's school to assist in the development of a reentry plan. School-based personnel will be responsible for any

debriefing that may be necessary for the school community in response to this incident. Regardless of the level of threat determined, a full report will be submitted to the principal. This report will include narratives of all interviews, the results of any rating scales or tests, and a description of the recommended future actions determined by the TAT.

In summary the threat assessment process is critical to school personnel in this day and time. It is essential for school psychologists to take a leadership role in this process given their expertise in consultation, crisis response/management, and treatment planning. Furthermore, it will serve to determine who actually poses a threat and is in need of specialized services.

See also: School Threats: Legal Aspects; School Violence Prevention; *Tarasoff v. Regents of the University of California*

BIBLIOGRAPHY

Borum, R., Fein, R., Vossekuil, B., & Berglund, J. (1999). Threat assessment: Defining an approach for evaluating risk of targeted violence. *Behavioral Sciences and the Law, 17,* 323–337.

Borum, R., & Reddy, M. (2001). Assessing violence risk in *Tarasoff* situations: A fact based model of inquiry. *Behavioral Sciences and the Law, 19,* 375–385.

Fein, R., Vossekuil, B., & Holden, G. (1995, September). *Threat assessment: An approach to prevent targeted violence.* National Institute of Justice: Research in Action.

O'Toole, M. E. (2000). *The school shooter: A threat assessment perspective.* Quantico, VA: Federal Bureau of Investigation, Critical Incidence Response Group, National Center for the Analysis of Violent Crime.

Tarasoff v. Regents of the University of California, 17 Cal.3d 425, 551 P.2d 334 (1976). United States Department of Education/United States Department of Justice. (2000). Indicators of school crime and safety. Washington, DC: U.S. Government Printing Office.

Additional Readings for Nonprofessionals

Fein, R. & Vossekuil, B. (2002). *Safe schools 4 kids: Working together to stop the violence.* National Threat Assessment Center, United States Secret Service. Available from http://www.safeschools4kids.org

National School Safety Center. (2001, June). *NSSC review of school safety research* Pepperdine, CA: National School Safety Center. Available from www.nssc1.org

Additional Readings for Professionals

Burns, M. K., Dean, V. J., & Jacob-Trimm, S. (2001). Assessment of violence potential among school children: Beyond profiling. *Psychology in the Schools, 38,* 239–247.

Reddy, M., Borum, R., Berglund, J., Vossekuil, B., Fein, R., & Modzeleski, W. (2001). Evaluating risk for targeted violence in schools: Comparing risk assessment, threat assessment, and other approaches. *Psychology in the Schools, 38,* 157–172.

D. Joe Olmi
Dana M. Trahant

Tics

See: Motor Tics; Tourette Syndrome; Vocal Tics

Time-Out

Parents, teachers, school psychologists, and others responsible for children's well-being have a variety of empirically based behavior management techniques from which to choose in an attempt to deal with children's problem behaviors. One of the most frequently used, but misunderstood, of those behavior management techniques is time-out (TO). TO is defined as "a procedure whereby positive reinforcement is not available to an individual for a period of time" (Forehand, 1985, p. 222).

TO is an intervention/treatment best used for behaviors maintained by either attention or tangible reinforcement (Sterling-Turner & Watson, 1999) and should be used in conjunction with positive behavioral techniques designed to teach appropriate behavior (Marlow, Tingstrom, Olmi, & Edwards, 1997; Olmi, Sevier, & Nastasi, 1997). TO has been empirically investigated for over 30 years and during that time has been found to be an effective treatment for a wide array of problem behaviors (e.g., noncompliance, aggression, tantrumming) across a wide range of settings (e.g., homes, schools, residential institutions) with children of a wide variety of functioning levels (Forehand, 1985). Although TO has been shown to be an effective behavioral intervention under a wide array of circumstances, many assume it to be a one-size-fits-all treatment that can be used in any situation for any type of problem behavior. In reality, TO can be a difficult procedure to understand and effectively implement for a variety of reasons including the level of skill necessary for effective implementation, legal and ethical concerns, and the variables included in the effective use of TO.

BASICS OF TIME-OUT IMPLEMENTATION

To effectively enforce a TO procedure and expect positive behavior change as a result, there must be an understanding of (a) basic reinforcement contingencies (Forehand, 1985; Olmi et al., 1997; Shriver & Allen, 1996), (b) different forms of TO (Harris, 1985; Sterling-Turner & Watson, 1999), and (c) procedures involved in TO administration (Harris, 1985; Shriver & Allen, 1996; Wilson & Lyman, 1982).

Reinforcement Contingencies

As noted in the above definition, TO involves separating an individual from opportunities to receive positive reinforcement. This separation can be accomplished either by removing the child from the reinforcing environment (e.g., placing the child in a designated location) or by removing access to preferred materials or activities. Herein lies the major implementation problem with TO. For a period of separation from reinforcement to function as TO, there must be a noticeable difference in the reinforcing contingencies available to the child in the natural environment (time-in [TI]) as compared to those available to the child in TO (Shriver & Allen, 1996). It is imperative that the child is able to easily distinguish between the TI environment, where positive response to behavior is readily available, thereby creating a rich reinforcement schedule, and the TO environment where no opportunities for reinforcement should exist. To briefly summarize, the noticeable differences in reinforcement contingencies should signal the child that positive reinforcement would only be available in the TI environment. Therefore, the greater the differences in reinforcement contingencies between the TI and TO environments the more successful TO will be (Harris, 1985; Sterling-Turner & Watson, 1999).

Although the importance of distinguishing the reinforcement contingencies available in both the TI and TO environments is central to the effective use of TO, problems continue to exist with regard to adjusting the contingencies if TO fails to affect positive behavior change. For this reason Shriver and Allen (1996) constructed a "time-out grid" (p. 68) that can assist those implementing a TO procedure in adjusting the reinforcing contingencies associated with either TI or TO. The authors discuss both high and low reinforcement available in both the TI and TO environments for a total of four resulting combinations. The first possibility and the only combination under which TO will be effective is when there is high reinforcement in the TI environment and low reinforcement in the TO environment. Under these optimal circumstances no changes should be made. The second possibility occurs when both the TI and TO environments are found to be highly reinforcing to the child. In this situation, Shriver and Allen recommend decreasing the available reinforcement in the TO environment. The next possibility deals with the problem of low reinforcement in both the TI and TO environments. Here Shriver and Allen recommend increasing the reinforcement contingencies in the TI environment. Finally, TO may fail to affect positive behavior change because of an absence of TI. In this situation the TO environment may be found to be reinforcing in and of itself.

Forms of TO

Once the reinforcement contingencies available to the child are arranged in the proper manner, a decision needs to be made regarding the type of TO to be implemented. Harris (1985) described five forms of TO and arranged them along a continuum depending on the degree of change from a more reinforcing to a less reinforcing environment.

The first three forms of TO described by Harris (1985) are labeled ignoring, removal of reinforcing stimuli, and contingent observation and are collectively referred to as *nonexclusion TO procedures*. Nonexclusion TO refers to a situation whereby the child is removed from access to reinforcement, but remains in the same general environment to observe others. For example, a child who was misbehaving in music class may be placed in TO in a separate part of the music room while still able to view the remainder of the class behaving appropriately. The least restrictive nonexclusion TO procedure is ignoring, which is simply denying the child access to attention by turning away. The second form of nonexclusion TO, labeled removal of reinforcing stimuli, involves taking away some tangible item that was preferred or reinforcing to the child. The final type of nonexclusion TO is contingent observation, which involves requiring the child to sit on the sidelines of an activity and watch their peers engage in the activity while behaving appropriately.

The next broad category of TO as described by Harris (1985) is *exclusion TO*. Exclusion TO is seen as more restrictive than each of the forms of nonexclusion TO as described above because the child is both removed from access to reinforcement and prohibited from observing the continuing activities. For example, the child misbehaving in music class may be sent to a chair in the music room that faces the corner instead of the remainder of the class. By being placed in such a manner and location the child is now denied positive reinforcement previously available in the music class by not being able to participate with or observe his peers. Of course, this presumes that participation with his peers or inclusion in music class is preferred or reinforcing to the child.

The final general type of TO outlined by Harris (1985) is termed *isolation* and is defined as "total removal from the reinforcing environment" (p. 280). Practically, isolation TO usually refers to removing the child from the room where an activity is ongoing and placing him/her in another room until the completion of TO. For example, the student misbehaving in music class may be sent to a special TO room, such as an empty classroom or other segregated setting for a predetermined amount of time.

Although this type of procedure may produce desired behavior change because of the substantial differences in the reinforcement contingencies available in both the TI and TO environments, there are many legal and ethical concerns that accompany the decision to use isolation TO. Of utmost concern is the safety of the child in TO where there may be opportunities for injury if the child is given little or no supervision during isolation. Second, concerns arise about the amount of instruction missed as a result of completely removing the child from

the instructional environment. A related concern deals with the practical issue of where to conduct isolation TO. With many schools having little or no extra room, it is difficult to imagine that many would be able to devote an entire classroom or other space for the purpose of an isolation TO room. Issues of ethical use, appropriate training of staff, supervision of the child during placement, parent permission for use of such a procedure, and adoption of implementation guidelines make use of isolation TO unlikely, unless under extreme circumstances. Furthermore, in educational settings, use of such a procedure may be less favored as compared to less punitive forms of TO.

TO Procedures and Options

As previously stated, TO may be a complicated intervention to implement because of the parameters involved in its application. TO is much more than simply placing a child in the corner of a classroom (as in education settings) or on the sofa (as in home application). Although previous research has identified several factors involved in TO administration, debate continues as to the essential components necessary in the effective implementation of TO. In addition, some might suggest a standard implementation protocol, whereas others might suggest tailoring the procedure to the individual child. The following is a brief overview of the various parameters of TO that have been investigated.

Verbalized Explanation

TO may or may not be accompanied with a verbal explanation as to why the child is being placed in TO (Forehand, 1985). For example, before sending a child to TO an adult may say, "____, you did not pick up your shoes. TO." According to Harris (1985) few studies indicate whether or not a verbalized reason was given to the child prior to TO. Although specifics for this parameter are scarce, several researchers suggest the use of a brief reason prior to TO (Olmi et al., 1997; Shriver & Allen, 1996; Sterling-Turner & Watson, 1999). Such verbalized reasons should be kept simple and brief so that the child forms an association between their actions and TO (Wilson & Lyman, 1982). Longer explanations may serve to reinforce the child's misbehavior because of the verbal attention provided (Harris, 1985). In support of adapting TO procedures to meet individual characteristics, Wilson and Lyman suggest that the use of a verbalized reason may be more appropriate with children of "higher intelligence or verbal skills" (p. 8) because of the cognitive nature of the instruction.

Warning Prior to TO

A second parameter that may or may not accompany TO is a warning, which is a verbal statement to the child indicating that further display of inappropriate behavior will result in TO. For example, a parent might say, "____, if you take your sister's toy once more you will go to TO." Similar to research regarding the use of a verbalized reason, research with regard to the presence or absence of a warning is scarce because few studies indicate whether a warning was given prior to TO (Harris, 1985; Wilson & Lyman, 1982). Although warnings do allow children one more opportunity to correct their inappropriate behavior before TO is implemented, thereby possibly avoiding punishment, this practice may prove detrimental to the specific behavioral goals. Providing a child with a warning may in fact allow the child to misbehave for an extended period of time and earn more reinforcement for this inappropriate behavior, or use of the warning may place the child in an unsafe situation (e.g., run into the street into oncoming traffic) while awaiting the second delivery of the instruction. Such possible consequences of providing a warning seem to argue against the practice.

Instructional and Physical Implementation

This TO parameter distinguishes between verbally instructing a child to go to TO or with a degree of physical assistance by the adult, assisting the child to TO. The choice of either instructional or physical guidance is usually a function of the amount of resistance the child displays toward TO (Harris, 1985; Wilson & Lyman, 1982). For example, simply instructing a tantrumming toddler to go sit in TO may not work, and the adult may have to physically assist the child to TO. Wilson and Lyman suggest that physical implementation may be more necessary in situations where severely disruptive behavior is present, an exclusionary TO procedure is used, and when the child is physically resistant.

TO Location

As previously discussed, Harris (1985) outlined three general classes of TO procedures that range along a continuum from least intrusive to most intrusive. To briefly review, TO can be implemented by (a) removing the child from the TI environment, but allowing viewing of the ongoing activities (i.e., nonexclusionary); (b) removing the child from the TI environment and prohibiting observation of ongoing activities (i.e., exclusionary); or (c) removing the child from the setting altogether (i.e., isolation). Although each of these procedures has associated benefits, Harris (1985) recommends choosing the least restrictive technique that will effect positive behavior change.

TO Duration

Determining the optimal TO duration can be a difficult task because of problems associated with leaving a child in TO for either too little or too great an amount of time. Some would suggest that if a child remains in TO for too little a time the procedure might lose some of its effectiveness. Conversely, if a child remains in TO for an extended period of time problems arise concerning the loss of instructional time and lack of opportunities to gain positive reinforcement. The main benefit of a shorter TO duration is this opportunity for the child to once again return to the TI environment and potentially gain positive reinforcement for appropriate behavior (Sterling-Turner & Watson, 1999).

Although most TO studies specifically mention duration, the results of previous research concerning an optimal TO duration remain inconclusive. One exception to this inconclusiveness is the finding regarding a sequencing effect concerning shorter and longer TO durations (Harris, 1985; Wilson & Lyman, 1982). Although shorter TO durations are preferable, they are only as effective as longer TO durations when presented prior to the longer durations. Practically, this means that a child should not be sent to TO for 5 minutes followed by a second TO of 1 minute. This example is contrary to the TO duration sequencing effect and may limit the effectiveness of the procedure.

These authors would offer an alternative to the duration debate. Operating within a TO procedure (e.g., removal punishment) is a negative reinforcement procedure (e.g., escape from TO). Duration in TO should not be dictated by time, but rather by the display of appropriate TO behavior (e.g., quiet hands, feet, and mouth). Escape from TO serves to teach the child the behavior that results in escape from the TO condition. But, one must keep in mind that TO is only as effective as TI. In Olmi et al. (1997) TO duration was no more than 3–5 seconds from initial placement to exit from TO.

Release Procedures

Release from TO is another parameter usually involved in a discussion of the most salient TO features. Release from TO is either contingent (e.g., in response to appropriate TO behavior for a period of time) or noncontingent (e.g., contingent on a specified amount of time in TO irrespective of behavior). Olmi et al. (1997) recommend a 3- to 5-second contingent release period after the child displays appropriate TO behavior, whereas Shriver and Allen (1996) caution against the use of behaviorally contingent release because of possible disruption of the surrounding environment and not having the time to await appropriate TO behavior.

In addition to those discussed above, several other TO parameters have received attention in the literature, including (a) intermittent versus continuous administration schedules (Forehand, 1985; Harris, 1985), (b) debriefing following dismissal from TO (Wilson & Lyman, 1982), and (c) a stimulus to signal the onset of TO (Wilson & Lyman, 1982). Similar to each of the parameters discussed previously, there continues to be variability in how these additional features are incorporated into TO.

SUMMARY

TO is an effective behavior management procedure that, when applied correctly and under the proper circumstances (i.e., behavior maintained by either attention or tangible reinforcement), may reduce problem behavior in a variety of situations. To further enhance the probability of positive behavior change, TO should be used in conjunction with positive behavioral techniques. It is imperative to remember that TO is an intervention involving many variables that need to be carefully considered before use. These variables include not only subject characteristics (i.e., individual child characteristics), but procedural considerations as well (i.e., TI, type of TO, and parameters).

See also: Negative Reinforcement; Oppositional Defiant Disorder; Positive Reinforcement; Punishment; Tough Kids

BIBLIOGRAPHY

Forehand, R. (1985). Time-out. In A. S. Bellack & M. Hersen (Eds.), *Dictionary of behavior therapy techniques* (pp. 222–223). New York: Pergamon.

Harris, K. R. (1985). Definitional, parametric, and procedural considerations in timeout interventions research. *Exceptional Children, 51*, 279–288.

Marlow, A. G., Tingstrom, D. H., Olmi, D. J., & Edwards, R. P. (1997). The effects of classroom-based time-in/time-out on compliance rates in children with speech/language disabilities. *Child & Family Behavior Therapy, 19*(2), 1–15.

Olmi, D. J., Sevier, R. C., & Nastasi, D. F. (1997). Time-in/time-out as a response to noncompliance and inappropriate behavior in children with developmental disabilities: Two case studies. *Psychology in the Schools, 34*, 31–39.

Shriver, M. D., & Allen, K. D. (1996). The time-out grid: A guide to effective discipline. *School Psychology Quarterly, 11*, 67–74.

Sterling-Turner, H., & Watson, T. S. (1999). Consultant's guide for the use of time-out in the preschool and elementary school classroom. *Psychology in the Schools, 36*, 135–148.

Wilson, D. R., & Lyman, R. D. (1982). Time-out in the treatment of childhood behavior problems: Implementation and research issues. *Child & Family Behavior Therapy, 4*(1), 5–20.

Additional Reading for Nonprofessionals

Rhode, G., Jensen, W. R., & Reavis, H. D. (1998). *The tough kid book: Practical classroom management strategies.* Longmont, CO: Sopris West.

Additional Readings for Professionals

Brantner, J. P., & Doherty, M. A., (1983). A review of timeout: A conceptual and methodological analysis. In S. Axelrod & J. Apsche (Eds.), *The effects of punishment on human behavior* (pp. 87–132). New York: Academic Press.

O'Dell, S. L., Krug, W. W., Patterson, J. N., & Faustman, W. O. (1980). An assessment of methods for training parents in the use of time-out. *Journal of Behavior Therapy and Experimental Psychiatry, 11*, 21–25.

D. Joe Olmi
Gregory E. Everett

Title IX

Title IX of the Education Amendments of 1972 was signed into law June 23, 1972. The passage of Title IX was part of a larger effort to expand the protection against discrimination in federally funded programs legislated by the Civil Rights Act of 1964. Building on Title VI of the Civil Rights Act's prohibition against discrimination on the basis of race, color, or national origin, Title IX protects students and employees against sex discrimination in educational institutions and programs. Title IX states, "No person in the United States shall, on the basis of sex, be excluded from participation in, be denied the benefits of, or be subjected to discrimination under any education program or activity receiving Federal financial assistance" (Title 20 U.S.C. § 1681, 1972).

Title IX applies to activities in a range of educational settings. In addition to schools, colleges, and universities, Title IX regulates public libraries, museums, and training programs sponsored by organizations receiving federal funds. This protection covers all areas of education, including recruitment and admission, course enrollments, scholarships, financial aid, housing, benefits, services, and athletics. Title IX regulations allow exemptions for institutions and programs that meet specific criteria. The law does not apply to institutions that do not receive federal funds, to religious institutions in which the regulations would violate religious tenets, to historically single-sex schools established prior to Title IX, and to institutions that prepare individuals for service in the United States military or merchant marine. Exceptions to Title IX also apply to programs such as Boy Scouts and Girl Scouts, fraternities, sororities, sex segregation in choirs, sports teams that involve physical contact, and sex education programs.

The passage of Title IX was a landmark effort to remove obstacles that limited the educational opportunities of women and girls at all levels of education. Secondary schools often expelled pregnant students and barred females from enrolling in academic and vocational classes traditionally associated with males. Many colleges and universities held women to higher admission standards, subjected them to stricter behavior codes, and gave men preferential treatment in the award of scholarships and fellowships. Barriers further increased for women seeking entrance to medical and law schools. Enrollment quotas in most medical and law schools allowed women to make up only a small percentage of each entering class (American Association of University Women Legal Advocacy Fund, 2000).

Since 1972, Title IX legislation has allowed women and girls to make remarkable gains in their levels of educational participation and attainment. In 1972, women earned 38 percent of all bachelor's degrees, 9 percent of medical degrees, and 7 percent of law degrees (National Coalition for Women and Girls in Education, 2002). By 1997 the proportion of degrees awarded to women had risen to 56 percent of bachelor's degrees, 41 percent of medical degrees, and 44 percent of law degrees (U.S. Census Bureau, 2001).

Despite Title IX's achievements in addressing multiple forms of sex discrimination, media reports have primarily focused on its impact on athletics. Prior to Title IX, negligible funding and stereotypical assumptions about female athletic ability and interest blocked females from enjoying the numerous benefits of athletic participation. Title IX's requirement of equity in athletic opportunity dramatically increased the number of high school and college female athletes. A comparison of the 1971 and 2001 numbers of female varsity athletes shows an increase of 847 percent for high schools and 403 percent for colleges (National Coalition for Women and Girls in Education, 2002). A very different picture emerges when looking at women's athletic participation by race. The fastest growing women's sports (e.g., soccer, rowing, lacrosse, and golf) are overwhelmingly dominated by white athletes. Equity among women, not just between men and women, remains a challenge in the implementation of Title IX.

Institutions can demonstrate compliance with Title IX in three ways: (1) showing that the percentage of female athletes is approximately proportionate to their numbers in the student body; (2) expanding or adding programs that respond to the interests and abilities of female athletes; or (3) demonstrating that existing programs fully and effectively accommodate the interests and abilities of female athletes. The fact that some universities have chosen to eliminate men's varsity sports such as gymnastics and wrestling to achieve proportionality of male and female athletes has generated considerable criticism. Defenders of Title IX counter that institutions use Title IX as a scapegoat for avoiding the larger issue of how the men's athletics budget is distributed.

Over 30 years after its passage, Title IX continues to highlight the importance of educational institutions in combating sex discrimination. Title IX has broadened women's and girls' educational opportunities and raised public awareness of gender equity issues. In 2003, the most pressing issues for Title IX are controversies over its impact on male athletics and Secretary of Education Rod Paige's proposal to alter how Title IX is interpreted and regulated. The possibility for changes to the Title IX law has generated grass-roots activism among both Title IX supporters and critics. Both groups are lobbying for the courts to revisit Title IX. Whether this will result in strengthening or relaxing the 1972 legislation will likely be decided in the next few years.

See also: Nutrition; Sports

BIBLIOGRAPHY

American Association of University Women Legal Advocacy Fund. (2000). *A license for bias: Sex discrimination, schools, and Title IX*. Washington, DC: Author.

National Coalition for Women and Girls in Education. (2002). *Title IX at 30: Report card on gender equity*. Washington, DC: Author.

Title IX of the Education Amendments, Title 20 U.S.C. § 1681–1688 (1972).

U.S. Census Bureau. (2001). *Census Bureau facts for features*. Retrieved April 29, 2002, from http://www.census.gov/Press-Release/www/2001/cb01ff03.html

Additional Readings for Professionals and Nonprofessionals

National Coalition for Women and Girls in Education. Save Title IX Campaign. Retrieved April 26, 2003, from http://www.savetitleix.com/index.html

The Women's Educational Equity Act (WEEA) Equity Resource Center. Title IX and Education Policy. Retrieved April 26, 2003, from http://www.edc.org/WomensEquity/ resource/title9/index.htm

DIANA MOYER

Tough Kids

Tough kid is a common term used to describe a student who exhibits a set of problematic externalizing behaviors and behavioral deficits. They are *externalizing* because these behaviors affect others external to the student. The term was introduced in a best-selling behavior management book, *The Tough Kid Book: Practical Classroom Management Strategies*, by Rhode, Jenson, and Reavis (1992). However, these students have a host of labels and diagnoses such as behavior disordered, severely emotionally disturbed, attention-deficit/hyperactivity disorder, conduct disordered, oppositional defiant disordered, and many more. The labels and diagnoses have less to do with identifying and designing practical interventions than understanding the tough kid's basic behavioral excesses and deficits.

CHARACTERISTICS

The behavioral excesses of tough kids include noncompliance, arguing, tantrum throwing, property destruction, and rule breaking. All students engage in these excesses to some extent. However, the central characteristic of tough kids is the frequency in or degree to which they engage in these behaviors. Tough kids exhibit a much higher frequency of these excesses, which causes so much difficulty for others. It is these excesses that get tough kids referred for special services.

Of the many behavioral excesses, noncompliance stands out as the "kingpin" behavior of tough kids. It is the axis around which the other behavioral excesses revolve. Noncompliance is simply defined as not following a direction in a reasonable amount of time. Most of the arguing, temper tantrums, rule breaking, and aggression are secondary to avoiding tasks or requests. Tough kids exhibit these aversive behaviors to escape or avoid a request, generally from an adult. This process is called pain control or coercion.

It is a mistake to focus only on the behavioral excesses of tough kids. Although these are the most annoying and disturbing behaviors exhibited by tough kids, there are also significant behavioral deficits. One of the major deficits exhibited by tough kids is their lack of ability to self-manage their behaviors. They are *contingency-governed*, which means the next stimulus in their immediate environment will impulsively control their behavior. They are not like other students who are *rule-governed* and have internalized a set of rules and values, which govern their behaviors. Other common deficits for tough kids include academic deficiencies. The most common academic deficit for tough kids appears to be basic reading skills. Many tough kids simply lack the ability to read at grade level, which affects all other aspects of their educational adjustment. In addition to poor reading ability, tough kids lack basic study skills that allow them to extract, organize, and perform with academic materials. They are commonly disorganized, lose books and assignments, have poor test-taking ability, have difficulty writing and taking notes, and several other critical study skills. Another related academic deficit is the tough kid's poor ability to pay attention and stay on task. The average student is on task 85 percent of the time, during which they actively attend to the teacher and their assigned work. Tough kids are on task about 60 percent of the time. This 20 percent difference between the on-task behavior of the average student and tough kids has a dramatic impact on the tough kid's academic skill development (Rhode et al., 1992).

Social skills deficits are a real problem for tough kids. They simply do not fit in with their peers and are commonly rejected. Social skills can be simply defined as a set of basic skills needed to successfully interact with adults and peers. Tough kids lack these basic skills and are often described as socially immature, pushy, noncooperative, bullies, or always needing control. Frequently, tough kids go through a series of friendships that do not last. They seek younger friends whom they can dominate. Or, as tough kids get older they make friends with other students who have similar behavior problems (Achenbach, 1991).

The behaviors described above are not an inclusive list but a general description because each student is an individual. However, it is important to note the functional interaction of behavioral excesses and deficits. If tough kids are placed in an educational environment in which they do not fit academically and socially, they will revert to their behavioral excesses to escape that environment.

CAUSES AND CONTRIBUTORY FACTORS

There is no one single cause for a student to develop tough kid behavior. Some factors include genetically determined temperament, abuse, parents' poor parenting ability, lack of adult supervision, parental divorce, and many other factors. However, there is one contributory factor that is foremost in the development of tough kid problematic behavior. This process is called coercion or pain control (Patterson, Reid, & Dishion, 1992; Reid, Patterson, & Snyder, 2002). It has been shown to be at the root of noncompliance, arguing, and aggression. For example, in this interaction, a request is made of the student by an adult, who in turn ignores the request, then the adult requests again with emphasis, the student then delays, the adult yells and the student offers excuses or argues, the adult then issues an ultimatum and the student becomes aggressive or tantrums. Approximately 60 percent of the time when a student becomes extremely aversive by arguing, throwing a tantrum, or becoming aggressive, the adult will withdraw the request. The adult is reinforced by a cessation of the student's aversive behavior, and the student is rewarded by the adult's withdrawing the request. Other things are also learned by the student. The faster and more intensely the student can exhibit these aversive behaviors, the faster the adult will withdraw the request or learn not to make it. These "microbursts" of aversive behaviors are actually learned. The adult makes the request and it is like knocking a chip off the student's shoulder, which results in an immediate burst of aversive behaviors. This is a random process that helps maintain these aversive interactions. Utilizing coercive behaviors to avoid compliance leads to poor social skills development, academic underachievement, peer rejection, low self-esteem, depression, association with deviant peers, delinquency, and many more negative outcomes (Patterson et al., 1992). Managing coercion is the key to managing tough kids.

INTERVENTIONS

For tough kids, one of the most important intervention goals is to reduce the coercive cycle and its accompanying aversive behaviors, particularly noncompliance. There are two basic approaches for reducing the coercive cycle and noncompliance. The first and easiest is antecedent control. The second approach, which is more difficult, is to consistently apply consequences for these aversive behaviors.

Antecedent control maximizes the way in which requests and commands are made of tough kids. An antecedent is any behavior that comes just before the problematic behavior and sets the occasion for it to occur. Since requests and commands always precede the student's noncompliance, giving requests and commands correctly greatly reduces misbehavior. The characteristics of a good request or command are

- Use a statement rather than a question format
- Get close to the student (about 3 feet)
- Use a quiet voice
- Look them in their eyes
- Give the student time to comply (about 3 to 5 seconds)
- Make only two requests (do not nag)
- Describe what you want
- Do not be emotional.

It is also very important to socially reward and acknowledge when a student follows your request. Research has shown that requests and commands given in this precision manner can increase compliance by approximately 30 percent (Jesse, 1989).

However, if the student is still noncompliant, it is sometimes necessary to follow through with a mild aversive consequence. These consequences can include response cost (losing something they like), time-out, and think-time procedures (Nelson & Carr, 1996). It is also important to design positive-consequence systems to reinforce compliance, such as mystery motivators, reward spinners, the compliance matrix, and several other procedures (Rhode et al., 1992). Without a positive consequence component, any program is likely to fail. Tough kids generally come from negative backgrounds both at home and school, and they have become immune to punishment when it is used as the primary consequence procedure (Jenson, Olympia, & Farely, in press).

Effective programs for tough kids also use effective interventions that teach skills necessary to remedy the student's deficits. Teaching tough kids to use self-management strategies is a powerful tool, which will help them in less structured and supervised environments. The most effective reading programs for tough kids are direct instruction programs that are phonetically based. Reading skills are critical but study skills are also important. There are several research-tested study skills programs that help students learn to organize and effectively handle academic information. Clearly, social skills programs are also needed for the social adjustment of tough kids. These programs should not be taught in isolation in pull-out groups, but rather taught across the whole day, where social problems provide teaching opportunities for tough kids. If behavioral excesses are reduced and educationally relevant skills taught to remedy deficits, tough kids can become some of the most rewarding kids to work with in the school.

See also: Academic Interventions for Written Language and Grammar; Aggression; Attention-Deficit/Hyperactivity Disorder; Conduct Disorder Oppositional Defiant Disorder; Punishment; Social Skills Study Skills and Test Preparation; Time-Out

BIBLIOGRAPHY

Achenbach, T. M. (1991). *Manual for the Child Behavior Checklist/ 4-18 and 1991 profile.* Burlington: University of Vermont Department of Psychiatry.

Jenson, W. R., Olympia, D., & Farely, M. (in press). Positive psychology and externalizing disorders in a sea of negativity. *Psychology in the Schools.*

Jesse, V. (1989). *Compliance training and generalization effects using a compliance matrix and spinner system.* Unpublished doctoral dissertation, University of Utah, Salt Lake City.

Nelson, J. R., & Carr, B. A. (1996). *The think time strategy for schools.* Longmont, CO: Sopris West.

Patterson, G. R., Reid, J. B., & Dishion G. A. (1992). *Antisocial boys.* Eugene, OR: Castilia.

Reid, J. B., Patterson, G. R., & Snyder, J. J. (2002). *Antisoical behavior in children and adolescents.* Washington, DC: American Psychological Association.

Rhode, G., Jenson, W. R., & Reavis, H. K. (1992). *The tough kid book: Practical classroom management strategies.* Longmont, CO: Sopris West.

Additional Reading for Nonprofessionals

Jenson, W. R., Rhode, G., & Neville-Hepworth, M. (2003). *The tough kid parent book: Practical solutions to tough childhood problems.* Longmont, CO: Sopris West.

Additional Readings for Professionals

Jenson, W. R., Rhode, G., Bowen, J., & Evans, C. (in press). *The tough kid pre-school book: Practical behavior management and developmental solutions.* Longmont, CO: Sopris West.

Jenson, W. R., Rhode, G., Morgan, D. P., & Evan, C. (in press). *The tough kid principal's brief case: Behavior management strategies for the whole school.* Longmont, CO: Sopris West.

Rhode, G., Jenson, W. R., & Morgan, D. P. (2003). *The tough kid new teacher kit: Practical classroom management survival strategies for the new teacher.* Longmont, CO: Sopris West.

Table 1. Practical Definition of a Tough Kid

Behavior Excesses: Too much of a behavior
Noncompliance
Does not do what is requested
Breaks rules
Argues
Makes excuses
Delays
Does the opposite of what is asked
Aggression
Tantrums
Fights
Destroys property
Vandalizes
Sets fires
Teases
Is verbally abusive
Is revengeful
Is cruel to others

(continued)

Table 1. (*Continued*)

    Behavior Deficits: Inability to adequately perform a behavior
Self-management skills
    Cannot delay rewards
    Acts before thinking—impulsive
    Shows little remorse or guilt
    Will not follow rules
    Cannot foresee consequences
Social skills
    Has few friends
    Goes through friends fast
    Noncooperative–bossy
    Does not know how to reward others
    Lacks affection
    Has few problem-solving skills
    Constantly seeks attention
Academic skills
    Generally behind in academics, particularly reading
    Off task
    Fails to finish work
    Poor study skills
    Truant or frequently tardy
    Forgets acquired information easily

WILLIAM R. JENSON
DANIEL E. OLYMPIA
GINGER RHODE

Tourette Syndrome

Tics are sudden, rapid, repetitive, nonrhythmic, stereotyped movements or vocalizations (American Psychiatric Association, 2000). Motor and vocal tics can be classified as simple, which are sudden, brief, meaningless movements or sounds, or complex, which are slower, longer, more purposeful movements or utterances (Evans, King, & Leckman, 1996). Examples of simple motor tics include shoulder shrugging, eye blinking, and neck jerking, and examples of simple vocal tics include sniffing, grunting, or throat clearing. Complex motor tics can include behaviors such as hand gestures, touching, and repeatedly tapping an object. Complex vocal tics can include single words, sentences, or coprolalia (sudden expression of a socially unacceptable word or phrase, such as an obscenity or ethnic slur). Coprolalia occurs in less than 10 percent of individuals with tic disorders (American Psychiatric Association, 2000).

Tourette Syndrome (TS) is a neurobehavioral disorder, which consists of multiple motor and one or more vocal tics. To receive a diagnosis of TS, the onset of tics must occur before the age of 18, the tics must not be due to substance use or a general medical condition, and the associated tics must occur for at least 1 year without a 3-month tic-free period in that year.

Furthermore, the tics must cause a disruption in social, occupational, or other areas of functioning (American Psychiatric Association, 2000).

Although the exact course of TS varies, tics typically begin between the ages of 2 and 13 years, with the mean age of onset being 7 years (Dedmon, 1990). Motor tics usually develop before vocal tics, and often begin with facial tics such as eye blinking (Evans et al., 1996). The first vocal tics that develop are usually simple tics such as grunting or throat clearing. Tics often occur in bouts and can be separated by tic-free periods that can last from minutes to hours. In addition, tics go through a natural waxing and waning cycle and may vary in frequency and severity as a function of different contexts. For instance, children or adults may be able to suppress their tics while at school or work but may exhibit an increase in tic frequency while relaxing in private. For many, tic severity and frequency decreases during late adolescence and into adulthood, and for some, tics greatly diminish in adulthood. Prevalence estimates of TS range from .04 to .05 percent of the population and the syndrome is 3 to 5 times more common among males (American Psychiatric Association, 2000).

COMORBID CONDITIONS

Although the presence of motor and vocal tics constitutes the diagnosis, individuals with TS exhibit higher rates of other disorders, such as attention-deficit/hyperactivity disorder (ADHD), obsessive–compulsive disorder (OCD), depression, and learning disorders. Specifically, research has found that approximately 50 percent of those with TS also have ADHD, and 50 to 90 percent of persons with TS develop obsessive–compulsive behavior although only 30 to 40 percent develop actual OCD (Dedmon, 1990; Evans et al., 1996). Individuals with TS also have a higher likelihood of developing depression (Dedmon, 1990) and exhibit higher rates of learning disorders, particularly in the areas of mathematics and reading (Evans et al., 1996).

Individuals with TS have also been found to experience difficulties in social functioning. Children with TS are perceived as less popular, more withdrawn, and less socially acceptable than those without the disorder (Woods, Friman, & Teng, 2001). These social difficulties appear to continue into adulthood. Adults with TS may be perceived as less socially acceptable, and often experience problems with dating, making and keeping friends, and job discrimination.

ETIOLOGY

Although the etiology of TS remains unclear, research has focused on the genetic, neurobiological, and environmental underpinnings of the disorder. The vulnerability to developing tics and TS appears to be genetic. Research has shown that 50 to 70 percent of individuals with TS have a relative with a tic disorder (Dedmon, 1990). Furthermore, individuals with TS have a 50 percent chance of passing the gene on to their children. Although not all children with the genetic predisposition will have the disorder, since prevalence in males is so much higher than in females, researchers believe that 100 percent of boys with the disposition will have TS, a chronic tic disorder, or obsessive–compulsive disorder with tics.

In terms of neurobiology, there is evidence that particular brain circuits, as well as neurotransmitters, likely contribute to the etiology of tics. Because a variety of behaviors are involved in TS, the brain circuits that involve motor regions, inhibition, and higher cognitive processes, are thought to play a role in TS (Evans et al., 1996). Specifically, research has implicated the cortico–striatal–thalamocortical circuits of the brain in the development of TS. Also, research has focused on the role of the basal ganglia—a part in the brain that is involved with motor activity, attention difficulties, and habit formation—in TS (Jankovic, 2001). In terms of neurotransmitters, the abnormal metabolism of at least one neurotransmitter, dopamine, as well as other neurotransmitters, such as serotonin and norepinephrine, has been implicated in TS.

Relationships between environmental conditions and tics have also been examined. Some have proposed that infectious and autoimmune conditions, such as streptococcal infection, may affect the basal ganglia and be associated with disorders such as TS, OCD, and ADHD (Evans et al., 1996). Another area of focus is on the relationship between stimulant medication and tics, since research has shown that some children who are prescribed stimulants for ADHD develop tics (Dedmon, 1990). Stress also appears to have an impact on tic frequency, with persons with TS exhibiting more tics when under stress (Evans et al., 1996). A number of other environmental variables, such as allergies and diet, have also been implicated in the etiology of tics, but evidence supporting these claims is equivocal (Silva, Munoz, Barickman, & Friedhoff, 1995).

ASSESSMENT

There are no neurological or blood tests to specifically diagnose TS. However, physicians may advise persons with tics to undergo a medical evaluation with neurological testing to rule out other medical conditions that may be contributing to or appearing as the tic disorder. To aid in diagnosis and treatment planning for persons with tics, tic frequency and severity can be assessed in a number of ways including parental and self-report measures and clinician-observer ratings (Leckman, Towbin, Ort, & Cohen, 1988). In addition, direct observation is often utilized in comprehensive assessments. Practitioners should also assess for areas not directly related to tic expression, including attentional and learning disorders, anxiety and mood disorders, and concerns with social functioning.

TREATMENTS

Although there is not a cure for TS, two main types of treatment exist: pharmacotherapy and behavior therapy. In general, the goal in treating tics is not the complete elimination of tics but rather tic reduction (Jankovic, 2001). Along with tic reduction, treatment should focus on educating the patient/client and his/her family about TS, advocating for the patient/client, treating comorbid conditions, and relieving tic-related discomfort or difficulties.

In terms of tic reduction, pharmacotherapy is the most common form of treatment for TS. Neuroleptics, a class of medications that alter the effect of dopamine (the neurotransmitter thought to produce tics) in the brain, have been found to be the most useful in producing tic reduction (Watson, Howell, & Smith, 2001). Examples of neuroleptics include haloperidol (Haldol), pimozide (Orap), clozapine (Clozaril), olanzapine (Zyprexa), and risperidone (Risperdal). Clonidine (Catapres) and guanfacine (Tenex), although not neuroleptics, are also commonly used for tic reduction. Despite the finding that some of these medications produce a 70 to 80 percent reduction in tics, side effects are common, and may include sedation, weight gain, muscle spasms, extrapyramidal Parkinson-like symptoms, tardive dyskinesia, and akathisia (restlessness).

An alternative to pharmacotherapy is behavior therapy. Several types of behavioral interventions have received attention, including massed negative practice, differential reinforcement, contingency management, and habit reversal (Watson et al., 2001). Of these behavioral procedures, habit reversal has been found to be the most effective for tic reduction. Habit reversal is a multicomponent procedure, which centers around engaging in an alternative behavior contingent on the occurrence of behaviors that precede the tic or the tic itself. There are no known adverse side effects of the procedure, and it has been shown to produce substantial reductions in tics.

See also: Attention-Deficit/Hyperactivity Disorder; Depression in Children and Adolescents; Habits; Learning Disabilities; Motor Tics; Obsessive–Compulsive Disorder; Vocal Tics

BIBLIOGRAPHY

American Psychiatric Association. (2000). *Diagnostic and statistical manual of mental disorders* (4th ed., text rev.). Washington, DC: Author.

Dedmon, R. (1990). Tourette syndrome in children: Knowledge and services. *Health and Social Work, 15*, 107–115.

Evans, D. W., King, R. A., & Leckman, J. F. (1996). Tic disorders. In E. J. Mash & R. A. Barkley (Eds.), *Child psychopathology* (pp. 436–454). New York: Guilford.

Jankovic, J. (2001). Tourette's syndrome. *New England Journal of Medicine, 345*, 1184–1192.

Leckman, J. F., Towbin, K. E., Ort, S. I., & Cohen, D. J. (1988). Clinical assessment of tic disorder severity. In D. J. Cohen, R. D. Bruun, & J. F. Leckman (Eds.), *Tourette's syndrome and tic disorders: Clinical understanding and treatment* (pp. 56–78). New York: Wiley.

Silva, R. R., Munoz, D. M., Barickman, J., & Friedhoff, A. J. (1995). Environmental factors and related fluctuations of symptoms in children and adolescents with Tourette's disorder. *Journal of Child Psychology and Psychiatry, 36*, 305–312.

Watson, T. S., Howell, L. A., & Smith, S. L. (2001). Behavioral interventions for tic disorders. In D. W. Woods & R. G. Miltenberger (Eds.), *Tic disorders, trichotillomania, and other repetitive behavior disorders: Behavioral approaches to analysis and treatment* (pp. 53–72). Boston: Kluwer Academic.

Woods, D. W., Friman, P. C., & Teng, E. J. (2001). Physical and social impairment in persons with repetitive behavior disorders. In D. W. Woods & R. G. Miltenberger (Eds.), *Tic disorders, trichotillomania, and other repetitive behavior disorders: Behavioral approaches to analysis and treatment* (pp. 33–52). Boston: Kluwer Academic.

Additional Reading for Nonprofessionals

Shimberg, E. F. (1995). *Living with Tourette's syndrome*. New York: Simon & Schuster.

Additional Readings for Professionals

Leckman, J. F., & Cohen, D. J. (Eds.). (1999). *Tourette's syndrome: Tics, obsessions, compulsions: Developmental psychopathology and clinical care*. New York: Wiley.

Woods, D. W., & Miltenberger, R. G. (Eds.). (2001). *Tic disorders, trichotillomania, and other repetitive behavior disorders: Behavioral approaches to analysis and treatment*. Boston: Kluwer Academic.

DOUGLAS W. WOODS
BROOK A. MARCKS

Transition for Students with Disabilities

The term *transition* is used to describe the complex process encompassing a wide array of support and services that help secondary school age students with disabilities go to work or attend postsecondary training after graduation (Rubin & Roessler, 2001). Transition services are designed to facilitate the movement of students with disabilities from receiving special education services in the schools to receiving vocational rehabilitation services from state/federal agencies (Edmondson & Cain, 2002). In the Individuals with Disabilities Education Act of 1990 (IDEA; Pub. L. No. 102-476), *transition* is defined as "a coordinated set of activities for a student, designed within an outcome-oriented process, which promotes movement from school to post-school activities" (Rubin & Roessler, 2001, p. 304). These activities may include vocational training, postsecondary education, supported employment or other integrated employment services, independent living, continuing education, adult education, other adult services, and community participation. It is recommended that transition services begin as early as age 14 (Edmondson & Cain, 2002) and be based on individual needs, preferences, and interests. Successful transition plans include all services tailored to the individual students' needs to facilitate the move from school to employment or postsecondary training using adult living objectives, including community-based experiences and instruction.

State vocational rehabilitation (VR) agencies have been involved with the transition process since the 1940s, when school-to-work transition programs were developed to assist students with mental retardation in the areas of life- and employment-skills development (Rubin & Roessler, 2001). Vocational rehabilitation was developed to assist people with disabilities throughout the employment process, from the provision of job-readiness skills, advanced training, and job placement (Szymanski & Danek, 1985). Prior to 1973, individuals with mental retardation were served primarily by state agency rehabilitation counselors or private agencies such as the Associations for Retarded Citizens. In the 1960s, the Rehabilitation Services Administration (RSA)—which houses vocational rehabilitation—joined with public school systems in support of transition (Rubin & Roessler, 2001). This partnership resulted in an expansion of transition services to students with mental retardation by both VR and school-based agencies (Szymanski & Danek, 1985). In the 1970s, three laws were passed which had significant effects on the provision of services to adolescents with disabilities: the Vocational Rehabilitation Act of 1973, the Education for all Handicapped Children Act of 1975, and the Rehabilitation Act Amendments of 1976. The passage of this legislation shifted responsibility for preparing adolescents with disabilities for the workforce from the shared VR–school systems partnership directly onto the schools, and state/federal VR agencies were mandated to place priority on providing services to individuals with severe disabilities (Szymanski & Danek, 1985).

In the 1980s, the United States Department of Education was established, housing both the RSA and special education within the Office of Special Education and Rehabilitative Services (OSERS) (Szymanski & Danek, 1985). Since the RSA terminated funding for such cooperative programs as transition services in 1978, special education programs have expanded into transition services. However, special education programs are prevented from hiring counselors to assist in transition services provision because of certification regulations developed prior to 1973. Therefore, school systems must provide transition services but cannot legally recognize rehabilitation counselors within the school system. Currently, school systems cannot provide transition services to their students directly, but must work through external agencies such as VR (Szymanski & Danek, 1985).

As a result of the passage of the Individuals with Disabilities Act of 1990 (IDEA)—originally the Education for all Handicapped Children Act of 1975—grants were established to provide all school-age students with disabilities both free and public education, which includes transition services to assist them in moving from school to adult life (Edmondson & Cain, 2002). Today, an interdisciplinary team, including rehabilitation counselors and professionals who work with the student from special and vocational education, school counseling and school psychology, and school social work, work cooperatively across agencies to provide the student with all services he/she may need postschool. Effective transition services planning must incorporate functional linkages between the school system, rehabilitation agencies, and other adult-services agencies (Elliott, Alberto, Arnold, Taber, & Bryar, 1996). In addition, the team must include the student and at least one of the student's parents. At or around age 14, these students' Individual Education Plans (IEP) must include a statement regarding how their course of study relates to transition goals. Transition goals must be outcome-oriented and should include functional skills curricula across three domains: skills/activities of daily living, personal and social skills, and occupational preparation and guidance (Rubin & Roessler, 2001). Because of the high rate of unemployment and underemployment for youth with disabilities, it is imperative to include academic, independent-living, and work-related goals in the transition plan, to give the student more opportunities for independence postschool. At age 16, the IEP is amended to include statements of needed transition services.

To be successful, transition plans should include both short- and long-term goals that are decided on and agreed upon by the student and the student's family. In each IEP, the transition team must include issues that address all postschool activities and areas in which the student chooses to participate (Edmondson & Cain, 2002). For each activity identified in the IEP, the team must identify what objectives should be written into the plan, what types of instruction will be needed to prepare the student for adult life, and what appropriate community-based experiences are available to further the transition process in which the student may participate. Each activity should result in measurable outcomes and must lead to the end goal of successful employment or independent living. Interagency responsibilities should be identified in the IEP, and a representative of each agency must attend each IEP meeting.

Transition planning is a complex process designed to assist students with disabilities in their movement postschool to adult life successfully. Coordination between school system personnel, rehabilitation personnel, and other involved professionals is imperative for a successful delivery of the transition service plan. Transition planning should start early in the student's academic course, and transition plans must identify measurable goals for employment, independence, social integration, and community opportunities. Plans may include a diverse array of multiagency services designed to help the student reach those goals. Transition professionals should consider each student as an individual, with strengths, interests, and preferences to be satisfied through postschool activities. This coordinated multidisciplinary approach that is tailored to each student's individual needs will help individuals with disabilities live satisfying lives with full participation in society after secondary education.

BIBLIOGRAPHY

Edmondson, C. A., & Cain, H. M. (2002). The spirit of the Individuals with Disabilities Education Act: Collaboration between special education and Vocational Rehabilitation for the transition of students with disabilities. *Journal of Applied Rehabilitation Counseling, 33*, 10–14.

Elliott, N. E., Alberto, P. A., Arnold, S. E., Taber, T. A., & Bryar, M. R. (1996). The role of school district interagency transition committees within an overall collaborative structure. *Journal of Applied Rehabilitation Counseling, 27*, 63–68.

Rubin, S. E., & Roessler, R. T. (2001). *Foundations of the Vocational Rehabilitation process*. Austin, TX: Pro-Ed.

Szymanski, E. M., & Danek, M. M. (1985). School-to-work transition for student with disabilities: Historical, current, and conceptual issues. *Rehabilitation Counseling Bulletin, 29*, 81–89.

Additional Reading for Nonprofessionals

Sax, C. L., Thoma, C. A., & Strully, J. M. S. (Eds.). (2002). *Transition assessment: Wise practices for quality lives*. Baltimore: Brookes.

Additional Readings for Professionals

Wehman, P., Moon, M. S., Everson, J. M., Wood, W., & Barcus, J. M. (1988). *Transition from school to work: New challenges for youth with severe disabilities*. Baltimore: Brookes.

West, M., & Newton, P. (1983). *The transition from school to work*. New York: Nichols.

AMY L. SKINNER

Traumatic Incidents

The term *traumatic* in "traumatic incident" and the term *critical* in "critical incident" are typically regarded as synonymous and there is considerable overlap between them. Nevertheless, no two terms mean exactly the same thing. *Traumatic* and *critical* are derived from different linguistic roots and originated in different contents. The former term, *traumatic*, originated in the treatment of physical wounds and injuries. Medical personnel work in trauma units of hospitals and treat victims of natural disasters (e.g., floods, hurricanes, earthquakes, and avalanches), accidental disasters (e.g., car, train, boat, or airplane accidents; fires; and explosions), and human design, deliberate disasters (e.g., terrorist bombing, hostage taking, shooting, rape, and assault and battery; Kleber & Brom, 1992).

The latter term, *critical*, originated in the treatment of psychic or psychological wounds and injuries. Critical incidents refer to extremely stressful and dangerous events that are out of the range of ordinary human experience. Nonmedical personnel provide what has been called debriefing or brief psychotherapy to people who were exposed to any of the disasters cited above, but especially to the human design disasters. The term was first applied to people who were exposed to distressing incidents in the course of their duties or in their place of employment. Clients for critical incident treatment include workers in the foreign service and military personnel taken hostage outside the United States and exposed to threats, deprivation of food and sleep, torture, and the execution of others; agents of the Federal Bureau of Investigation, local and state police officers, and prison guards who witnessed the shooting or assault upon the person of their colleagues, or who were themselves the agents, targets, or victims of attack; fire prevention personnel exposed to the dangers and the damage inherent in fire fighting; and teachers who witnessed violence on school premises vented against other teachers or students, or who were themselves the targets or victims of violence (Reese, Horn, & Dunning, 1991).

CONCEPTUAL INTEGRATION OF TERMS

Over time, the term *traumatic incident* has become synonymous with *critical incident* for several reasons:

1. There is increasing awareness of the psychic wounds that accompany many, if not most, physical wounds associated with natural, accidental, and especially human design disasters.
2. There has been a proliferation of psychic injuries that occur without any visible psychical injury to the victims.
3. Modern psychiatry, a branch of medicine, initiated the tradition of applying the term *psychic trauma* to severe psychological distress over a century ago, as it attempted to understand the psychological consequences of train collisions and other life-threatening and routine-shattering experiences.

4. Many connotations of the term *critical* make an important contribution to an understanding of *traumatic* incidents, their impact, and treatment. *Critical* is defined in several ways: (a) "fraught with danger" as in critical illness; (b) "arriving at a turning point, with the imminence of a decisive dangerous change"; as a synonym to *crisis*, which is defined as "an unstable, critical point in the development of a condition fraught with peril"; as a synonym to *crucial*, defined as "a significant change that will shape future events." These connotations highlight the possible long-term effects of the traumatic event and imply that there will be dire consequences for the victim until there is immediate and appropriate intervention.
5. Terr (1991) combined the two terms under one heading and clarified the distinction between two categories of adverse experiences that differ in severity of the experience and the concomitant consequences of the experience.

Type I traumas: These are unexpected traumatic incidents of short duration (minutes, hours, or a few days at the most). Examples are assault and battery, rape, and sniper shooting. By this definition, critical or traumatic incidents are Type I traumas. They create vivid memories of the event and often lead to Posttraumatic Stress Disorder (PTSD), symptoms of intrusive ideation and imagery, hyperactive arousal, and avoidance of stimuli reminiscent of the traumatic event.

Type II traumas: These are sustained and repeated stressors of long duration. Examples are long-term physical, sexual, and/or psychological abuse in the home, school, or workplace; long-term imprisonment in one's own country or incarceration in a foreign country under conditions of cruel and inhuman treatment; repeated exposure to life-threatening conditions during months of military combat; and prolonged and repeated torture as a political prisoner. These traumas cannot be termed incidents or events because of their duration and their long-term consequences. They are more likely to lead to an altered view of self and of the world, with accompanying feelings of shame, guilt, and worthlessness. They also lead to longstanding interpersonal problems such as increased detachment from other people, restricted range of emotional expression, and emotional lability (i.e., hypersensitivity to stimuli that leads to a rapid shift from positive feelings such as joy or pleasure to negative feelings such as anger or depression). As a consequence of Type II trauma, people resort to dissociation (trauma-related thoughts and actions are split off from the rest of consciousness and function outside of awareness), the excessive use of addictive substances, and other maladaptive behaviors. These disorders mandate lengthy, intense treatment and have a poorer prognosis for rehabilitation or recovery than the Type I trauma disorders.

TREATMENT OF TRAUMATIC (CRITICAL, TYPE I) INCIDENTS

The experience of American psychiatrists during and following World War I led to the formulation of four principles of short-term intervention following exposure to any traumatic incident of limited duration: immediacy, proximity, expectancy, and community. These principles were used by Israeli psychologists in treating military combat personnel during and after the war in Lebanon (Milgram et al., 1986) and are routinely employed in Western nations.

Immediacy

This principle refers to the time that elapses between exposure to the traumatic incident and the initiation of treatment. Immediacy refers to the initiation of treatment and not to the duration of treatment that will vary as a function of the needs of the affected person and the resources of the therapeutic services. The elapsed time should be as brief as possible. The more time that elapses, the greater the probability that the trauma-related reactions (e.g., hyperarousal, negative emotions, thoughts, memories, and behaviors) will be permanently etched and become symptoms that resist treatment.

Proximity

This principle refers to the setting where treatment is initiated. Treatment should be initiated as close as possible to the setting in which the traumatic incident took place: in the case of combat soldiers during war, a field station several miles behind the lines; in the case of school children involved in a bus accident during a school outing, the school premises soon after the accident. In the case of a rape victim brought to a hospital for examination and treatment, trauma-related treatment should begin in the hospital itself. Immediacy and proximity are usually related. If treatment is initiated at a great distance from the scene of the traumatic incident, it may be unnecessarily delayed. American hostages released after prolonged captivity in Lebanon were flown to Europe, the nearest and most practical place to initiate treatment, or debriefing as it was called.

Expectancy

This principle refers to the expectation of recovery that is imparted by the professional staff to persons exposed to traumatic incidents. They impart their perception by word and by actions. The very term used by the professional staff to designate the injured person—victim, survivor, client, patient, or some other label—says a great deal about their perception of the person, the circumstances of the traumatic incident, and their own therapeutic orientation. Placing a person in a psychiatric ward creates one kind of expectation, talking with the same person in a classroom or an army barrack creates another kind. The setting in which the treatment takes place, the technical terms used by the professional personnel to describe for the person what is bothering him, and the subtle nuances of their behavior affect the person's expectations as to current status and eventual recovery far more than formal statements about diagnosis, prognosis, and a list of prescriptive behaviors.

Community

This principle can be applied in several ways depending on circumstances. Community may refer to a specific community: the squad or company to which the soldier belonged when exposed to the traumatic combat incident, or to the headquarters and the coworkers of the affected police officer, or to the school in which the affected teacher worked or the affected child attended. The traumatic incident generally disrupts the connection of the affected person to this community. One of the goals of treatment is to restore the affected person to the original community. Contact is reestablished by encouraging members of the community to visit the affected person, by making it possible for the latter to make visits to the community setting as soon as possible, and by encouraging the affected person to rejoin the community. Community may also refer to society in general and to work, school, and/or home routines and locales that constituted the life space and activities of the affected person before being exposed to the traumatic incident.

See also: Anxiety; Coping; Posttraumatic Stress Disorder; Stress

BIBLIOGRAPHY

Kleber, R. J., & Brom, D. (1992). *Coping with trauma: Theory, prevention and treatment*. Amsterdam: Swets & Zeitlinger.

Milgram, N. A. (1986). Section III: Treatment of combat stress reactions and post traumatic stress disorders in the war in Lebanon. In N. A. Milgram (Ed.), *Stress and coping time of war: Generalizations from the Israeli experience* (pp. 97–176). New York: Brunner/Mazel.

Reese, J. T., Horn, J. M., & Dunning, C. (Eds.). (1991). *Critical incidents in policing* (rev. ed.). Washington, DC: United States Department of Justice, Federal Bureau of Investigation.

Terr, L. C. (1991). Childhood traumas: An outline and overview. *American Journal of Psychiatry, 148*, 10–20.

Additional Readings for Nonprofessionals and Professionals

Figley, C. R. (Ed.). (1985). *Trauma and its wake: The study and treatment of Post Traumatic Stress Disorder* (Vol. 1). New York: Brunner/Mazel.

Figley, C. R. (Ed.). (1986). *Trauma and its wake: Traumatic stress, theory, research, and intervention* (Vol. 2). New York: Brunner/Mazel.

Freedy, J. R., & Hobfoll, S. E. (Eds.). (1995). *Traumatic stress: From theory to practice*. New York: Plenum.

Herman, J. L. (1992). *Trauma and recovery: The aftermath of violence—from domestic abuse to political terror*. New York: Basic Books.

Wilson, J. P., & Raphael, B. (Eds.). (1993). *International handbook of traumatic stress syndromes*. New York: Plenum.

NOACH MILGRAM

Treatment Acceptability

Treatment acceptability is defined as beliefs of laypersons as to whether the procedures recommended for treatment are suitable, reasonable, and practical for the problem or client. Although there are a number of different treatment acceptability models, the common theme among them is the notion that as the acceptability of treatment increases so does the likelihood of a person implementing that treatment (treatment integrity). Furthermore, it is logical to assume that increased integrity leads to better treatment outcome. The factors that are thought to affect treatment acceptability include (1) the severity of the problem, (2) the amount of time needed to implement the intervention, (3) the type of treatment approach, (4) the cost of the intervention, (5) the side effects of a treatment, (6) the effectiveness of a treatment, (7) treatment integrity, and (8) the level of understanding of the treatment (Reimers, Wacker, & Koeppl, 1987; Witt & Elliott, 1985). Most typically, treatment acceptability is measured using a rating scale such as the *Treatment Evaluation Inventory* (TEI) (Kazdin, 1980), the *Behavioral Intervention Rating Scale* (BIRS) (Von Brock & Elliott, 1987), and the *Children's Intervention Rating Profile* (CIRP) (Witt & Elliott, 1985).

Research has consistently found that acceptability ratings are higher for positive interventions (e.g., positive reinforcement), more severe problems, and interventions requiring less time to implement. Some research has found that providing lectures on different treatments significantly increases acceptability ratings. Furthermore, the use of nontechnical language when describing treatments tends to increase acceptability ratings.

Although the findings mentioned above are consistent across studies, there are a number of concerns that cause one to question the utility of treatment acceptability. First, all studies except one (Cowan & Sheridan, 2003) have used analog situations to assess the factors associated with acceptability. The match between analog situations and real-life situations has not been shown. Second, there is limited research related to how treatment acceptability affects treatment use, integrity, and out-

come. Some studies have shown a modest relationship, whereas others have shown either no relationship or an inverse relationship between ratings of acceptability and treatment integrity. Thus, knowing whether a treatment is rated as acceptable does not seem to predict whether a parent or teacher will implement the treatment.

Research has also begun to investigate treatment acceptability and its relationship to treatment outcome. A study by Wacker and colleagues found that treatment acceptability ratings were generally high *after* the intervention. However, data on treatment acceptability ratings *during* the intervention were not provided. Thus, it is unclear as to whether acceptability scores changed over time and as a function of improvements in child behavior. Further explanation of the relationship between treatment outcomes, compliance, and acceptability is needed.

CONCLUSIONS

The research in the area of treatment acceptability is still unclear as to its impact on treatment compliance and outcome. Theorists have considered acceptability to be a crucial variable in determining compliance with treatment recommendations. The research is clear that acceptability of treatments can be differentiated for college students, parents, children, and teachers. However, the impact of these acceptability ratings on treatment compliance and outcome is still unanswered. The few studies that have addressed this area seem to indicate that compliance results in increases of treatment acceptability when treatment acceptability started out low. The question of what role treatment acceptability plays in treatment compliance still needs to be answered.

See also: Treatment Integrity

BIBLIOGRAPHY

Cowan, R. J., & Sheridan, S. M. (2003). Investigating the acceptability of behavioral interventions in applied conjoint behavioral consultation: Moving from analog conditions to naturalistic settings. *School Psychology Quarterly, 18*, 1–21.

Kazdin, A. E. (1980). Acceptability of time out from reinforcement procedures for disruptive child behavior. *Behavior Therapy, 11*, 329–344.

Reimers, T. M., Wacker, D. P., & Koeppl, G. (1987). Acceptability of behavioral interventions: A review of the literature. *School Psychology Review, 16*, 212–227.

Von Brock, M., & Elliott, S. N. (1987). Influence and treatment effectiveness information on the acceptability of classroom interventions. *Journal of School Psychology, 25*, 131–144.

Witt, J. C., & Elliott, S. N. (1985). Acceptability of classroom intervention strategies. In T. R. Kratochwill (Ed.), *Advances in school psychology* (Vol. 4, pp. 251–288). Mahwah, NJ: Erlbaum.

Additional Reading for Nonprofessionals

Witt, J. C., & Elliott, S. N. (1985). Acceptability of classroom intervention strategies. In T. R. Kratochwill (Ed.), *Advances in school psychology* (Vol. 4, pp. 251–288). Mahwah, NJ: Erlbaum.

Additional Readings for Professionals

Eckert, T. L., & Hintze, J. M. (2000). Behavioral conceptions and applications of acceptability: Issues related to service delivery and research methodology. *School Psychology Quarterly, 15*, 123–148.

Kazdin, A. E. (1977). Assessing the clinical or applied significance of behavior change through social validation. *Behavior Modification, 1*, 427–452.

RACHEL J. VALLELEY

Treatment Integrity

One of the most essential, yet overlooked, aspects of psychological/educational intervention is treatment integrity. Treatment integrity, sometimes referred to as treatment fidelity or procedural integrity, is the degree to which interventions are implemented as they are intended. There are two components of treatment integrity: *consistency* and *accuracy*. Consistency refers to the extent to which the treatment is implemented as a function of the number of times the opportunity exists to apply the treatment. For instance, if a student received direct reading instruction only 2 days out of 5, then the consistency is 40 percent. Accuracy refers to the degree to which the treatment was implemented correctly, regardless of the number of times it was applied. For example, if there are five steps involved in a time-out procedure and a parent only correctly implements an average of three of them, accuracy is 60 percent.

An analogy from the medical field may help to further highlight the importance of treatment integrity and the roles of accuracy and consistency. Consider the case of a young child with a severe poison ivy rash on her right arm. The physician instructed the parents to wash the affected area and place medicated ointment on the rash three times daily to help heal the rash and avoid spreading of the rash to other parts of the body. Diligently, the parents wash her arm three times per day and apply the ointment as prescribed (100 percent consistency), but apply it to the incorrect arm (0 percent accuracy). In this instance, the rash is not going to get better and will probably spread, adding to the child's discomfort. Likewise, the parents may actually wash the correct arm and apply the ointment to the intended location (100 percent accuracy), but they only do it one time per day (33 percent consistency). Again, the rash is not going to heal very quickly and will likely spread to other parts of the child's body.

Although both are important, there is not necessarily a correspondence between accuracy and consistency. That is, there could be high accuracy and low consistency (implementing the procedure correctly but infrequently), low accuracy and high consistency (implementing the procedure incorrectly but frequently), high accuracy and high consistency (implementing the procedure correctly and frequently), and low accuracy and low consistency (implementing the procedure inaccurately and infrequently). The only desirable of these circumstances is when both of the components are high. Therefore, when one refers to treatment integrity, it should be in the context of both accuracy and consistency.

PROBLEMS WITH NOT MONITORING TREATMENT INTEGRITY

Because of the logical relationship between treatment integrity and effectiveness, one would suspect that researchers and clinicians would be diligent in measuring this construct. Sadly, this is not the case, as only about 28 percent of published studies report treatment integrity (Gresham, Gansle, & Noell, 1993; Gresham, Gansle, Noell, Cohen, & Rosenblum, 1993). Furthermore, when treatments fail to work as desired and treatment integrity has not been monitored, one does not know if the treatment lacked sufficient strength or was simply not implemented accurately and/or consistently (Yeaton & Sechrest, 1981). On the other hand, if the treatment was effective and integrity was not monitored, one cannot be certain that the treatment caused changes in the dependent variable and not some extraneous event.

VARIABLES THAT AFFECT TREATMENT INTEGRITY

It is likely that a number of factors affect the integrity of interventions, among them complexity of the intervention, number of different people required to implement treatment, the amount of time and effort required to implement treatments, the motivation of those implementing the intervention, the materials and resources required by the intervention, and the actual and perceived effectiveness of a treatment (Gresham, 1989). Generally speaking, complex, time-consuming, effortful, resource-demanding interventions *decrease* treatment integrity. A high degree of motivation to actually change the behavior by the person(s) who must implement the treatment *increases* integrity.

The relationship between perceived effectiveness and treatments is a bit more tenuous. This link between perceived treatment ratings led to a number of research articles on the purported relationship between acceptability (perceived treatment effectiveness) and integrity (Yeaton & Sechrest, 1981). Although this relationship sounds very logical, there is no research to validate the assumption that when one perceives or rates a treatment to be acceptable, integrity will be improved. In fact, researchers have found that acceptability ratings are actually very poor predictors of subsequent integrity (Sterling-Turner & Watson, 2002). This same group of researchers found that the methods used to train the individuals to implement the intervention were the strongest predictor of integrity, regardless of acceptability ratings (Sterling-Turner, Watson, & Moore, 2002; Sterling-Turner, Watson, Wildmon, Watkins, & Little, 2001).

THE EMPIRICAL RELATIONSHIP BETWEEN INTEGRITY AND EFFECTIVENESS

The exact nature of the relationship between integrity and effectiveness is not completely clear. For instance, Gresham, Gansle, Noell, et al. (1993) reported a median correlation of .54 between treatment integrity and treatment outcome. Similarly, McCurdy and Watson (1999) and Rhymer, Evans-Hampton, McCurdy, and Watson (2002) suggested that integrity levels of 50–75 percent were sufficient for producing rather large changes in behavior. Results from these studies have been very consistent in confirming the necessity of having high, but not total, integrity for affecting behavior change. Another area that is virtually unresearched is the degree to which each of the components of integrity, accuracy, and consistency is functional for producing change. That is, is it more important to be accurate or more important to be consistent, or is there some degree of combination that works best to affect change? These questions have simply not been tested by empirical research.

MEASURING TREATMENT INTEGRITY

How does one measure integrity? Essentially, the same methods that are used for other behaviors can be used to measure integrity. Perhaps the most valid and least inferential way is to *directly observe* implementation of the intervention. The three steps involved when using direct observation of treatment implementation are (1) operationally defining each of the elements of the treatment, (2) recording the occurrence or nonoccurrence of each element, and (3) computing both consistency and accuracy percentages and plotting these data concurrent with changes in the dependent variable. Although this method may be appropriate in some situations (schools, residential treatment facilities), it is much more difficult when parents are the behavior change agents. Although this is probably the most reliable and valid method for measuring integrity, the primary disadvantage is that the person may only implement the treatment with integrity while they are being observed and not at other times (a situation referred to as reactivity).

A second method is to use indirect measures, including permanent products, self-reports, rating scales, and interviews. Among these, permanent product measures are the most preferred. Researchers have begun using permanent products such as outcomes expected as part of the intervention (e.g., number of points earned indicated on a student's behavior chart) to measure integrity. When using this method, there should be a permanent product outcome for each component or step of treatment. The advantages of using permanent products to measure integrity include being time-efficient, having a high degree of reliability and validity, and causing less reactivity than direct observation.

Self-report could be used to measure treatment integrity by having teachers or parents indicate on some type of checklist whether they implemented a particular component of treatment. One advantage of using this method is that the checklist may actually serve as a cue to implement various parts of the treatment (a desired effect). The obvious disadvantage is that self-reports have been shown to be grossly inaccurate in that they overestimate the degree of integrity.

TECHNIQUES TO ENHANCE TREATMENT INTEGRITY

There are three primary means of improving the integrity of treatments: (1) training in the intervention, (2) scripting, and (3) providing performance feedback. With training, the individual is instructed using techniques such as verbal instructions, modeling, and coaching to reach a desired level of performance in implementing each component of treatment. Training has been shown to increase integrity even when acceptability is low (Sterling-Turner, Watson, Wildmon, Watkins, & Little, 2001). Scripting involves providing the behavior change agent with a literal, written script of what to do and say for each component of treatment. Scripting has also been shown to enhance integrity (Ehrhard, Barnett, Lentz, & Stollar, 1996). Finally, performance feedback involves providing feedback based on either direct observation or review of permanent products about integrity. Studies have shown that performance feedback is very effective for enhancing integrity, even when previous integrity was low for the same change agent and same treatment (Martens, Hirallal, & Bradley, 1997).

CONCLUSION

The measurement of treatment integrity is critical in determining if an intervention is effective, why it is or is not effective, and for understanding functional relationships between independent and dependent variables in psychological treatment. It should be a required component of published intervention research, yet it is not. Precision in measuring all variables, not just dependent variables, is necessary if the practice of psychology is to become a more exacting science and not just one of "it was done because the authors said it was done."

See also: Treatment Acceptability

BIBLIOGRAPHY

Ehrhard, K. E., Barnett, D. W., Lentz, F. E., & Stollar, S. A. (1996). Innovative methodology in ecological consultation: Use of scripts to promote treatment acceptability and integrity. *School Psychology Quarterly, 11,* 149–168.

Gresham, F. M. (1989). Assessment of treatment integrity in school consultation and prereferral intervention. *School Psychology Quarterly, 18,* 37–50.

Gresham, F. M., Gansle, K. A., & Noell, G. H. (1993). Treatment integrity in applied behavior analysis with children. *Journal of Applied Behavior Analysis, 26,* 257–264.

Gresham, F. M., Gansle, K. A., Noell, G. H., Cohen, S., & Rosenblum, S. (1993). Treatment integrity of school-based behavioral intervention studies: 1980–1990. *School Psychology Review, 22,* 254–272.

Martens, B. K., Hirallal, A. S., & Bradley, T. A. (1997). A note to teacher: Improving student behavior through goal setting and feedback. *School Psychology Quarterly, 12,* 33–41.

McCurdy, M., & Watson, T. S. (1999, April). *Techniques to strengthen the practice of school-based consultation using direct behavioral consultation.* Paper presented at the 31st annual meeting of the National Association of School Psychologists, Las Vegas.

Rhymer, K. N., Evans-Hampton, T. N., McCurdy, M., & Watson, T. S. (2002). Effects of varying levels of treatment integrity on aggressive toddler behavior. *Special Services in the Schools, 18*(1/2), 75–82.

Sterling-Turner, H. E., & Watson, T. S. (2002). An analog investigation of the relationship between treatment acceptability and treatment integrity. *Journal of Behavioral Education, 11,* 39–50.

Sterling-Turner, H. E., Watson, T. S., & Moore, J. W. (2002). Effects of training on treatment integrity and treatment outcomes in school-based consultation. *School Psychology Quarterly, 17,* 47–77.

Sterling-Turner, H. E., Watson, T. S., Wildmon, M., Watkins, C., & Little, E. (2001). Investigating the empirical relationship between training type and treatment integrity. *School Psychology Quarterly, 16,* 56–67.

Yeaton, W., & Sechrest, L. (1981). Critical dimensions in the choice and maintenance of successful treatments: Strength, integrity, and effectiveness. *Journal of Consulting and Clinical Psychology, 49,* 156–167.

Additional Readings for Professionals and Nonprofessionals

Gresham, F. M., MacMillan, D. L., & Beebe-Frankenberger, M. E. (2000). Treatment integrity in learning disabilities intervention research: Do we really know how treatments are implemented? *Learning Disabilities Research and Practice, 15,* 198–205.

Wickstrom, K. F., Jones, K. M., & LaFleur, L. H. (1998). An analysis of treatment integrity in school-based behavioral consultation. *School Psychology Quarterly, 13,* 141–154.

T. STEUART WATSON

Trichotillomania

Trichotillomania refers to the act of pulling out one's own hair that results in noticeable hair loss (alopecia). Hallopeau, a French physician, first described the condition in 1889. It was not until about 30 years ago, however, that our understanding of this disorder began to progress and has advanced to the point where effective treatments have been identified.

The *Diagnostic and Statistical Manual of Mental Disorders* (4th ed.) (*DSM-IV*) classifies trichotillomania as an Impulse Control Disorder Not Otherwise Classified. The diagnostic criteria for trichotillomania include (a) noticeable hair loss that is the result of one's own pulling, (b) increasing tension right before the pulling occurs or when trying not to engage in the behavior, (c) a sense of satisfaction or tension release after the pulling occurs, (d) the hair pulling is not due to another mental disorder and the hair loss is not explained by a medical condition, and (e) the pulling causes clinically significant social, occupational, academic, or personal distress. In children, especially younger children, it is difficult to determine if there is an increasing sense of tension associated with the pulling as their lack of awareness and cognitive development may interfere with their ability to detect tension and then convey that information in an accurate manner. In addition, the hair pulling rarely causes distress for the younger child; rather, the distress is experienced by their parents or caregivers. For older children, they may directly experience the distress of hair pulling and the concomitant hair loss in the form of teasing from peers and curious looks and questions from strangers. The patchy hair loss sometimes associated with trichotillomania resembles the pattern of hair loss experienced by those undergoing chemotherapy.

CHARACTERISTICS OF THE DISORDER

Most typically, hair is pulled from the scalp, although occasionally hair is pulled from the eyebrows, eyelashes, face, or other parts of the body. In rare instances, hair is pulled from the underarms or genital area. In some cases, children will also pull hair, string, and fabric from objects such as dolls, blankets, and clothes. Some children are aware of their hair pulling and feel a "need" to pull. These are referred to as "focused hair pullers." Other children are not aware of their hair pulling and typically pull while engaging in some type of sedentary activity. These are referred to as "automatic hair pullers."

The prevalence of trichotillomania among children in the general population is unknown. However, data from studies on college-aged adults (e.g., Stanley, Borden, Mouten, & Breckenridge, 1995) and children with disabilities (e.g., Long, Miltenberger, & Rapp, 1999) suggested that the prevalence rate may be about 3–5 percent. It appears that, among children, about an equal number of males and females meet diagnostic criteria for trichotillomania. Studies of adults indicate that females are more likely to meet diagnostic criteria for trichotillomania. It is unclear if the gender differences are due to disparities in help-seeking behavior or the greater ease with which males can disguise hair loss (e.g., shaving face or head).

The average age of onset of hairpulling has ranged from about 10 years of age to 15 years of age, depending upon the particular study. Some children, however, begin pulling hair before they are 1 year old. Those who begin pulling at such a young age usually do so for only a few months and stop without treatment. Young children whose hair pulling continues for more than 6 months are usually more resistant to treatment efforts. Older children who begin pulling typically do so after a stressful event (e.g., death of loved one, illness, hospitalization) or significant change in their environment (e.g., entering college, moving, academic pressure). Children whose pulling was not precipitated by a specific event tend to pull for shorter periods of time and cease pulling without intervention.

Children diagnosed with trichotillomania may also meet diagnostic criteria for other disorders such as affective disorders and disruptive behavior disorders such as ADHD, ODD, and CD (King et al., 1995). In older children and adolescents who pull their hair, there is increased risk of also being diagnosed with generalized anxiety disorder, obsessive–compulsive disorder, depression, and substance abuse disorder (Swedo & Leonard, 1992). It is not unusual for children with trichotillomania to simultaneously engage in a habit such as thumb or finger sucking. Although there is a degree of comorbidity between trichotillomania and other disorders, there is no evidence that hair pulling is "caused" by underlying psychopathology.

After the hair has been extracted from its location on the body, children often manipulate the hair by looking at it, rubbing it between their fingers, rubbing it across their lips and/or tongue, and in some instances ingesting the hair. Ingesting hair is called trichophagia. If enough hair is consumed, a trichobezoar (hairball) could develop in the intestine, a condition that requires immediate medical attention.

ETIOLOGY

Like most other disorders, there is no one specific explanation for all instances of the behavior across all individuals. There are, however, categories of factors that explain the development and maintenance of trichotillomania. The first of these is called operant factors. Operant refers to situations where the consequences of the behavior are responsible for the continuance of the behavior. The most common operant explanations for hair pulling are that the behavior results in reduction of tension or negative affective states (automatic negative reinforcement) or

in sensory arousal in situations where there is low stimulation (automatic positive reinforcement). Each of these explanations is supported by empirical research. The second factor is genetics. Preliminary research suggests a possible genetic mechanism, but this link has not been clearly established. The third factor is biological. Other species are known to engage in behaviors that resemble trichotillomania, thus suggesting some type of basic biological mechanism at work. This explanation is the least supported and has not been well researched.

TREATMENT

Treatments for trichotillomania generally fall into one of two categories: pharmacological or behavioral. The most common class of drugs used to treat trichotillomania is the antidepressants that have antiobsessional effects. Although clomipramine was shown to be effective in one study (Swedo, Leonard, Rapoport, Lenane, Goldberger, & Cheslow, 1989), subsequent investigations have not supported its use nor the use of selective serotonin reuptake inhibitors (SSRIs). Adding neuroleptic medications—pimozide and risperidone—did not enhance the effects of the SSRIs.

The most effective treatment for trichotillomania is habit reversal, a behavioral technique originally described by Azrin and Nunn (1973). Other behavioral techniques, including punishment, function-based treatments, awareness training, cognitive–behavioral therapy, and treatment of covarying habits have all been used quite successfully to treat trichotillomania. An interesting device was designed by Watson and Allen (1993) for a 5-year-old who sucked her thumb just prior to pulling her hair. The thumb splint was placed around her thumb and prevented the thumb from contacting the palate but not from entering her mouth, thus preventing the hypothesized pleasing sensation associated with thumb sucking. When thumb sucking was eliminated, so was hair pulling. Because of the effectiveness of a wide range of behavioral treatments, they should be considered the treatment of choice for trichotillomania.

See also: Motor Tics; Obsessive–Compulsive Disorder; Tourette Syndrome; Vocal Tics

BIBLIOGRAPHY

Azrin, N. H., & Nunn, R. G. (1973). Habit reversal: A method of eliminating nervous habits and tics. *Behaviour Research and Therapy, 11*, 619–628.

King, R. A., Scahill, L., Vitulano, L. A., Schwab-Stone, M., Tercyak, K. P., & Riddle, M. A. (1995). Childhood trichotillomania: Clinical phenomenology, comorbidity, and family genetics. *Journal of the American Academy of Child and Adolescent Psychiatry, 34*, 1451–1459.

Long, E. S., Miltenberger, R. G., & Rapp, J. T. (1999). Simplified habit reversal plus adjunct contingencies in the treatment of thumb sucking and hair pulling in a young child. *Child & Family Behavior Therapy, 21*, 45–58.

Stanley, M. A., Borden, J. W., Mouton, S. G., & Breckenridge, J. K. (1995). Nonclinical hairpulling: Affective correlates and comparison with clinical samples. *Behavior Research and Therapy, 33,* 179–186.

Swedo, S. E., & Leonard, H. L. (1992). Trichotillomania: An obsessive compulsive spectrum disorder? *Psychiatry Clinics of North America, 15,* 777–790.

Swedo, S. E., Leonard, H. L., Rapoport, J. L., Lenane, M. C., Goldberger, B. A., & Cheslow, B. A. (1989). A double-blind comparison of clomipramine and desipramine in the treatment of trichotillomania (hair pulling). *New England Journal of Medicine, 321,* 497–501.

Watson, T. S., & Allen, K. D. (1993). Elimination of thumb-sucking as a treatment for severe trichotillomania. *Journal of the American Academy of Child and Adolescent Psychiatry, 32,* 830–834.

Additional Readings for Professionals and Nonprofessionals

http://www.trich.org 2002 (Trichotillomania Learning Center)

Rodriguez-Srednicki, O., & Srednicki, H. J. (2002). *Trichotillomania: Chronic hair pulling.* Retrieved November 13, 2003, from http://www.naspweb.org/Members_Only_Test/cqextra_tricho.asp

Woods, D. W., & Miltenberger, R. G. (2001). *Tic disorders, trichotillomania, and other repetitive behavior disorders: Behavioral approaches to analysis and treatment.* New York: Kluwer.

T. Steuart Watson
Tonya Sartor Butler

Uu

Under- and Overachievement

Our notion of under- and overachievement often is based on at least two assumptions: (1) that a child's ability to learn can be accurately measured in the first place (generally measured with an intelligence test), and (2) measured ability (an intelligence test score) can be compared to measured achievement to determine whether a child is an under- or an overachiever. For example, a student who scores in the average range on an intelligence test would be expected to score in the average range on an achievement test, presumably because his/her learning rate should be average. Alternately, those students whose achievement exceeds their intelligence test score would be considered overachievers and those students whose achievement scores fall below their intelligence test score (Intelligence Quotient [IQ]) would be considered underachievers.

This simple model of predicting learning has caused people to characterize students as under- and overachievers on the basis of educational assessments. With such labels, there is an implied assumption that a child's achievement or learning rate is stable or consistent. Thus, a child who underachieves would be expected to underachieve across subject areas (e.g., mathematics and reading), environments (e.g., in Mrs. Smith's class and Mrs. Jones's class), instructional approaches (e.g., direct instruction vs. discovery learning), and time (e.g., during the first week of school and during the last week of school). Similarly, an overachiever would be expected to consistently overachieve across all these contexts. Although this conception of under- and overachievement is alluring because of its simplicity and the widespread availability of psychoeducational tests, there are a number of problems with this approach.

ALL CHILDREN DISPLAY UNDER- AND OVERACHIEVEMENT

Instead of thinking categorically about under- and overachievers, it is more useful to consider instances of under- and overachievement. This approach still requires educators and parents to maintain expectations for level of achievement and rate of progress. However, this focus acknowledges that a given student may vary in degree of achievement across situations, context, and time. Furthermore, it allows us to investigate reasons for under- or overachievement rather than leaving us with a label for a student. Labels are essentially useless because it is hard to know what to do about a label.

To illustrate this point consider Ralph, a fourth-grade student. Ralph's IQ is average or typical for a fourth-grade student, but his mathematics achievement shows he is functioning at about the second-grade level. Thus, Ralph could be considered an underachiever. In addition, assessments show that Ralph has not mastered basic addition, subtraction, and multiplication facts. Currently, Ralph is being instructed in fourth-grade-level mathematics and they are working on long division. Because basic addition, subtraction, and multiplication skills are required to accurately perform long division tasks, Ralph continues to demonstrate poor progress in division. Calling Ralph an underachiever may be questionable when the real problem is that he has not mastered the more basic skills that are necessary to perform division problems.

Now assume that Ralph is given remedial instruction that enhances his skills with basic math facts and his mathematics achievement increases rapidly. Let us say he progressed from beginning second-grade level to beginning middle third-grade level in 5 months. As he enhanced his achievement 1.5 levels in only 5 months, Ralph could be now considered an overachiever if we stick to the common assumptions people make. Thus, Ralph could be considered both an underachiever and an overachiever, but neither label provided much useful information. More important, through a little investigation we discovered that (a) his placement in the curriculum did not fit his skill level, (b) he had weaknesses in specific prerequisite skills, and (c) the problem could be solved by adapting instruction to his skill level (Daly, Lentz, & Boyer, 1996).

CAUSES OF UNDERACHIEVEMENT

Because all children display overachievement (learning more than we would expect under the circumstances in the allotted time) and underachievement (learning less than we would expect under the circumstances in the allotted time), it is more productive to identify situational factors that detract from or enhance the child's learning or achievement. Identifying all instances of under- and overachievement requires us to be able to predict how much learning or achievement should occur for an individual child without considering and accurately measuring *all* the variables that affect learning. Although psychological science has identified many variables that influence learning, our science has not advanced to the point where we can precisely predict how much a given child should learn under all learning opportunities and conditions. However, we have identified generally universal instructional strategies that can be used to enhance learning rates or achievement for all students. Granted, not all students need the same strategies or learning opportunities, but the number of strategies that work with all students is relatively small, making them quite useful.

Motivation

What we call achievement is a product of learning, which is a process that requires children to actively engage in tasks that are relevant to the school curriculum. For instance, paying attention, completing homework, studying, and/or working with peers on group projects all qualify as activities that actively engage students. Regardless of the activity, if students choose not to engage in planned activities, they will not learn. One reason students may choose to not engage in planned activities is a lack of motivation for the activity or achieving the result of the activity—motivation. A variety of things can be done to enhance motivation or the probability that students will choose to engage in schoolwork. One might change how students are expected to respond in ways that are more interesting (e.g., using the computer rather than worksheets). The teacher might break long tasks down into multiple brief tasks or reduce the effort required to complete tasks. Teachers could attempt to make instructional activities more interesting (e.g., having students simulate buying items at the school store with play money rather than having them just fill in worksheets on coin com-

binations) or even allow students to choose assignments that interest them.

Students are more likely to engage in academic tasks when rewards for engaging in school tasks (e.g., receiving praise from the teacher and/or parents, getting good grades) are superior to rewards for engaging in other behaviors (e.g., fooling around with a peer, playing with an eraser on the desk). One strategy for increasing motivation for school tasks is to remove rewarding opportunities to engage in nonproductive behaviors. For example, moving a student's desk away from a friend's desk may increase the probability that the student will complete the assignment because opportunities to interact socially are decreased. Other strategies include the quality, immediacy, and rates of reinforcement delivered contingent upon doing and completing schoolwork (Neef & Lutz, 2001).

Inappropriate Placement

When students are not correctly placed in the curriculum, problems arise. For example, if instruction focuses on enhancing skills students have already mastered, then not much learning will occur. Thus, although the student is functioning well academically—indeed their grades may be excellent—they appear to be underachieving because they are not improving rapidly. All students have instances in which this occurs.

When students are provided instruction or assigned learning activities that they cannot perform because they lack prerequisite skills, then students will underachieve regardless of how well instruction is delivered. In these instances, underachievement is not related to how instruction is presented or motivational factors; rather, underachievement is caused by the student being given learning activities that he/she cannot do. In these instances, underachievement can be addressed by either remedying prerequisite skill deficits or providing accommodations so that students can learn despite these skill deficits. To prevent inappropriate placement, educators have often relied on norm-referenced achievement tests. The advantage of such tests is that they provide a broad measure of student achievement. However, they do not measure specific skill development and do not lend themselves to repeated assessment over time (to determine rate of progress). More recently, researchers and educators have begun to develop and implement curriculum-based measurement that gives brief samples of vital skills and allows for repeated assessments over time (Shapiro, 1996). Curriculum-based measurement gives a more precise measure of skill development and mastery, which in turn can lead to more accurate placement within the curriculum. This information allows teachers to know when students can be moved from one objective to the next. Thus, these procedures can enhance achievement by rapidly identifying when to move students to subsequent learning objectives.

Instructional Activities

Assuming that students are placed appropriately and are choosing to engage in assigned work, the next goal is to identify the instructional procedures and academic tasks that cause the greatest increase in achievement. Taking the wrong approach here can be very counterproductive. For instance, some professionals have focused on identifying children's information processing strengths and weaknesses to determine the best methods for instruction and best activities for learning. One might suppose that a student who is a visual learner may achieve more by watching a film as opposed to listening to a history lecture. Although such a conclusion might have strong intuitive appeal, teaching to children's information processing strengths and/or remedying their information processing weaknesses has not proved to be a very useful strategy for enhancing student achievement (Kavale & Forness, 1999; Reschly & Ysseldyke, 2002). On the other hand, instructional methods that are based on a student's current level of skill development have proven quite effective at enhancing learning. A discussion of some of the key strategies follows. There is a very useful website—Interventioncentral (available on the Internet at: http://www.interventioncentral.com/index.shtml)—which has a lot of materials for adapting instruction to students' needs. We highly recommend it when you are concerned about what to do about a student's lack of achievement.

Describe, demonstrate, guided practice, and feedback

When students cannot do a specific academic task, the focus is on instruction. Teachers should demonstrate or describe how to get the answer (i.e., accurate responding) and provide the student with opportunities to practice while prompting them when answers come slowly and reinforcing accurate responding or correcting incorrect answers. Corrective feedback prevents students from learning and practicing inaccurate answers. This feedback can be self-delivered or delivered by teachers, parents, peers, and technology (e.g., computers).

Perfect practice makes perfect

After students can perform a skill with some reasonable degree of accuracy (i.e., students do not make errors), the next step is to help them develop and master the skill. Skill mastery means that the student (a) can perform the skill quickly and with little effort, (b) maintains this ability to respond accurately and quickly over time, and (c) can apply this skill across situations and problems. After students have become reasonably accurate with skills, providing opportunities to practice these skills leads to skill mastery. The practice opportunities are most effective when students engage in high rates of accurate academic responding. In addition, those responses should be varied in order to enhance student's ability to apply newly acquired skills across tasks (Skinner, Fletcher, & Henington, 1996).

Concerns Regarding Overachievement

Concerns regarding students who often overachieve are rarely related to the overachievement itself. In fact, overachievement is likely to go unnoticed by parents and educators. Instead, the concerns are related to how the overachievement affects the development of other skills or interests.

Parent and educators may become concerned when a student's time and energy is so focused on academic achievement that they fail to develop physically, emotionally, or socially. When such a situation occurs, adults must help children schedule their time and become involved in activities that support their development in these other areas without discouraging their interest and motivation to enhance their academic skills. For example, parents might schedule time for activities that help them develop physical and emotional skills, such as participating in soccer. This process is not always easy. Because all people have strengths and weaknesses, some people may consistently choose to engage in activities in which they have had much success and avoid new activities or activities in which they have had less success. Thus, in addition to providing opportunities to engage in these other activities, parents and educators should (a) encourage children to engage in these activities and support them when they do not *overachieve*, (b) teach students to focus on their improvement in activities as opposed to their ability relative to peers, (c) allow students choices among these other activities so that they can develop their own interests, friends, and social skills, (d) model this broad range of behavior by engaging in these other activities, and (e) encourage students to focus more on enjoying the activity itself, as opposed to their development or achievement relative to peers.

See also: Curriculum-Based Measurement; Intelligence Quotient (IQ); Learning Disabilities; Positive Reinforcement

BIBLIOGRAPHY

Daly, E. J., Lentz, F. E., & Boyer, J. (1996). The instructional hierarchy: A conceptual model for understanding the effective components of reading interventions. *School Psychology Quarterly, 11*, 369–386.

Kavale, A. K., & Forness, S. R. (1999). Effectiveness of special education. In C. R. Reynolds & T. B. Gutkin (Eds.), *The handbook of school psychology* (3rd ed., pp. 984–1024). New York: Wiley.

Neef, N. A., & Lutz, M. N. (2001). Assessment of variables affecting choice and application to classroom interventions. *School Psychology Quarterly, 16*, 239–252.

Reschly, D. J., & Ysseldyke, J. E. (2002). Paradigm shift: The past is not the future. In A. Thomas & J. Grimes (Eds.), *Best practices in school psychology IV* (pp. 3–20). Bethesda, MD: National Association of School Psychologists.

Shapiro, E. S. (1996). *Academic skills problems: Direct assessment and intervention* (2nd ed.). New York: Guilford.

Skinner, C. H., Fletcher, P. A., & Henington, C. (1996). Increasing learning trial rates by increasing student response rates: A summary of research. *School Psychology Quarterly, 11*, 313–325.

Additional Readings for Professionals

Howell, K., & Nolet, V. (2000). *Curriculum-based evaluation: Teaching and decision making* (3rd ed.). Atlanta, GA: Wadsworth.

Shinn, M. R., Walker, H. M., & Stoner, G. (2002). *Interventions for achievement and behavior problems II* (2nd ed.). Bethesda, MD: National Association of School Psychologists.

CHRISTOPHER H. SKINNER
EDWARD J. DALY III

Universal Nonverbal Intelligence Test (UNIT)

The *Universal Nonverbal Intelligence Test* (UNIT) (Bracken & McCallum, 1998) is a measure of nonverbal intelligence. It provides a good measure of general intelligence, or *g*, which is considered to represent a pervasive and fundamental cognitive ability (e.g., see Jensen, 1980), and which provides a basis for the development of somewhat unique specialized skills. The ability of the UNIT to assess *g* is a function of the complexity of its six subtests (e.g., the memory subtests require considerable cognitive engagement, rather than simple rote memory). In addition to *g*, the UNIT is designed to provide a unique measure of cognitive organization (i.e., symbolic and nonsymbolic content) and function (memory and reasoning).

GOAL FOR UNIT DEVELOPMENT

Several goals guided the development of the UNIT. The primary goal was to develop a test that would ensure a fair(er) assessment of intelligence for children and adolescents whose cognitive and intellectual abilities cannot be adequately assessed with language-loaded measures or with existing unidimensional nonverbal measures (Bracken & McCallum, 1998). Likely examinees include those who are deaf or have hearing impairments, those from different cultural backgrounds, individuals who have learning/language limitations, those with speech impairments, and those with serious emotional or intellectual limitations. The UNIT can be administered in a (100%) nonverbal format, and was standardized accordingly—the only nonverbal test so developed.

DESCRIPTION OF THE UNIT

The UNIT is designed to assess cognitive functioning via administration of six subtests, bound in two easels; the easels and additional test materials (e.g., blocks, chips) are housed in a vinyl case. The test model adheres to a two-tier conceptualization of intelligence. Examinees are required to use memory or reasoning and one of two organizational strategies (symbolic and nonsymbolic organization) to complete tasks. Three of the six subtests require memory; these subtests are Object Memory (OM), Spatial Memory (Spa M), and Symbolic Memory (Sym M). Similarly, three subjects were developed to assess reasoning; these subjects are Cube Design (CD), Mazes (M), and Analogic Reasoning (AR). Five of the subjects require minor motoric manipulation (i.e., CD, OM, M, Sym M, Spa M), and one requires only a pointing response (AR). With two exceptions (CD, M), the subjects that require motoric manipulation can be adapted to allow for a pointing response only.

As operationalized on the UNIT, symbolic organization strategies require the use of concrete and abstract symbols to conceptualize the environment; these symbols are typically language-related (e.g., labels, words), although symbols may take on any form (e.g., numbers, statistical equations, arrows, signs). Cognitive development enables individuals to internalize symbols as they begin to label, mediate, and, over time, make experiences meaningful. Nonsymbolic strategies require the ability to perceive and make meaningful judgments about the physical relationships within our environment; this ability is relatively symbol-free, and is closer to fluid-like intellectual abilities. Within each of the two fundamental organizational categories (nonsymbolic and symbolic) of the UNIT, problem solution requires either memory or reasoning. The rationale for assessing intelligence using the four strategies operationalized by the UNIT is based on several lines of theory and research. For example, David Wechsler (1939) emphasized the importance of distinguishing between highly symbolic (verbal) versus nonsymbolic (performance) expression. Jensen (1980) provided rationale for a two-tiered hierarchical conceptualization of intelligence consisting of the two subconstructs of memory (Level I) and reasoning (Level II).

The theoretical organization of the UNIT is consistent with a number of newly developed instruments that adopt the Cattell–Horn–Carroll (CHC) Model of cognitive ability

(Woodcock, 1990). According to an analysis presented by McGrew and Flannagan (1998) in their *Intelligence Test Desk Reference*, UNIT subtests assess a number of the CHC Stratum I (visual memory, spatial relations, quantitative reasoning, spatial scanning) and Stratum II abilities (visual processing, fluid intelligence).

ADMINISTRATION AND SCORING OF THE UNIT

Administration and scoring of the UNIT are relatively straightforward. The nonverbal administration requires use of pantomime and gestures and the Manual provides ample directions, including graphics showing how test materials should be arranged. Both a training video and a University Training Guide are available to aid examiners in learning to administer and score the test. A UNIT Compuscore software program is available to aid in scoring and interpretation. The UNIT yields a full-scale intelligence quotient (FSIQ), a composite memory score (Memory Quotient), a composite reasoning score (Reasoning Quotient), a composite symbolic organizational score (Symbolic Quotient), and a nonsymbolic organizational score (NonSymbolic Quotient).

UNIT TECHNICAL PROPERTIES

The UNIT Manual describes a wealth of reliability and validity data. The reliability of a test is its single most important psychometric characteristic because it provides an estimate of the true (systematic) variability; for the UNIT these indices are .91 and above for all three full-scale IQs (i.e., for the two-subtest screener, the four-subtest standard battery, and the six-subtest extended battery). Composite (scale) scores, such as the Reasoning Quotient, range from .86 to .91 for the Standard Battery. As might be expected, subtest reliabilities are lower, ranging from .64 (Mazes) to .91 (Cube Design). Subtests on the Standard Battery range from .79 (Analogic Reasoning) to .91 (Cube Design). In a review of the UNIT, Fives and Flanagan (2002) conclude that the "...effectiveness of the UNIT in this domain is further illustrated by the high levels of internal consistency when the instrument is used for clinical populations typically found in the clinical settings." The UNIT reports consistently high reliabilities for the combined clinical populations taken from the various validity studies (e.g., .92 for the FSIQ). Split-half reliabilities are less impressive, ranging from .58 (Mazes) to .85 (Cube Design); again the subtests in the Standard Battery yield more impressive values, though they range from only .68 (Spatial Memory) to .85 (Cube Design).

Content/construct validity indices reflect the extent to which a test assesses what it is intended to assess. For the UNIT, construct validity was determined in part by examining growth curves. Children become more cognitively sophisticated as they age, and their raw scores should increase with age. *W*-score growth curves maintain the age-dependent relationship between cognitive sophistication and age, and the UNIT Manual shows consistent *W*-score gains on all subtests as a function of age. Additional indices of internal validity were obtained using exploratory and confirmatory factor analyses. These procedures provided support for the overall structure, showing evidence in support of memory and reasoning, and the lower order symbolic and nonsymbolic factors. Multiple goodness-of-fit statistics are provided using the confirmatory procedures. Floor and ceiling data are shown in detail in the Manual and exhibit good properties in general; however, the floor is somewhat problematic for very young (5-year-old) examinees who exhibit limited cognitive abilities, and the Abbreviated Battery is not recommended for cognitively limited 5-year-old examinees for this reason. Item gradients are good, and as Fives and Flanagan (2002) note, care was taken to ensure that correct performance on each item changed the examinee standard score by no more than .33 standard deviation.

Independent reviews have been favorable in the main. Fachting and Bradley-Johnson (in press) conclude their review by noting that the UNIT is a welcome addition to present methods of measuring intellectual functioning in a nonvocal manner. Fives and Flanagan (2002) conclude by noting that the UNIT "...is theoretically driven...psychometrically sound...and appears to be highly useful." Other specific strengths and limitations are pointed out by both sets of reviewers and are summarized in McCallum, Bracken, and Wasserman (2001).

See also: Intelligence Quotient (IQ)

BIBLIOGRAPHY

Bracken, B. A., & McCallum, R. S. (1998). *Universal Nonverbal Intelligence Test*. Itasca, IL: Riverside.

Fachting, A., & Bradley-Johnson, S. (2000). Review of the Universal Nonverbal Intelligence Test. *Psychology in the Schools, 37*, 193–201.

Fives, C., & Flanagan, R. (2002). Review of the Universal Nonverbal Intelligence Test: An advance for evaluating youths with diverse needs. *School Psychology International, 23*, 425–448.

Jensen, A. R. (1980). *Bias in mental testing*. New York: Free Press.

McCallum, R. S., Bracken, B. A., & Wasserman, J. D. (2001). *Essentials of nonverbal assessment*. New York: Wiley.

McGrew, K. S., & Flannagan, D. P. (1998). *The Intelligence Test Desk Reference (ITDR): Gf–Gc cross-battery assessment*. Boston: Allyn & Bacon.

Wechsler, D. (1939). *Measurement of adult intelligence*. Baltimore: Williams & Wilkins.

Woodcock, R. W. (1990). Theoretical foundations of the WJ-R measures of cognitive ability. *Journal of Psychoeducational Assessment, 8*, 231–258.

Additional Reading for Nonprofessionals

Woodrich, D. L. (1997). *Children's psychological testing* (3rd ed.). Baltimore: Brookes.

Additional Readings for Professionals

Gopaul-McNicol, S. A., & Armour-Thomas, E. (2002). *Assessment and culture.* New York: Academic Press.

Kamphaus, R. W. (2001). *Clinical assessment of child and adolescent intelligence* (2nd ed.). Boston: Allyn & Bacon.

McCallum, R. S. (1999). A "baker's dozen" criteria for evaluating fairness in nonverbal testing. *School Psychologist, 40,* 60.

McCallum, R. S. (Ed.). (2003). *Handbook of nonverbal assessment.* New York: Kluwer Academic/Plenum.

Sattler, J. M. (2001). *Assessment of children: Cognitive applications* (4th ed.). San Diego, CA: Author.

R. STEVE MCCALLUM

Vv

Vocal Tics

Vocal tics are sudden, repetitive, stereotyped phonic productions (Leckman, King, & Cohen, 1999). Vocal tics can vary in frequency and severity and are often characterized as simple or complex. Simple tics are sudden, meaningless sounds or noises such as throat clearing, sniffing, whistling, or barking. Complex vocal tics are sudden, more meaningful utterances including the expression of single words or phrases; sudden and meaningless changes in the pitch, emphasis, or volume of speech; coprolalia (involuntary utterances of obscene words); echolalia (repetition of others' words or phrases); and palilalia (repetition of one's own words or phrases).

Vocal tics can be symptomatic of various tic disorders including transient tic disorder, chronic tic disorder, and Tourette Syndrome (TS) (Leckman et al., 1999). Transient tic disorder involves the occurrence of vocal tics nearly every day for more than 4 weeks, but less than 1 year, whereas the intermittent occurrence of vocal tics for more than 1 year, without a tic-free period of at least 3 months indicates a chronic tic disorder. When at least one vocal tic co-occurs with multiple motor tics for more than 1 year without a tic-free period of more than 3 months, a diagnosis of TS may be warranted.

In addition to the actual vocal tics, individuals with a tic disorder may experience premonitory urges, or sensory phenomena such as a tickle, itch, tingle, or pressure on their skin or within their body immediately prior to the tic (Leckman et al., 1999). These sensations temporarily abate after engaging in the tic.

ONSET, PREVALENCE, AND COURSE

Vocal tics develop between 8 and 15 years of age. Vocal tics generally appear after motor tics and simple vocal tics usually precede complex vocal tics. Findley (2001) reported higher rates of TS for boys (4.9 per 10,000) than for girls (3.1 per 10,000) in an adolescent sample.

The frequency, intensity, and complexity of vocal tics vary throughout the course of a day, with periods of waxing and waning over days and weeks (Findley, 2001). In addition, most children who suffer from chronic tics see an increase in symptoms throughout childhood. Tics may decline with the onset of puberty, so that two thirds of those same children have few or no tics by adulthood. New vocal tics may spontaneously develop over the course of the various tic disorders.

ETIOLOGY

Although the exact cause of tic disorders is unknown, Findley (2001) has summarized the three main areas thought to contribute to the development of tics: genetics, neurobiology, and environmental factors. Research on the genetic basis for TS suggests that a family member of a person with TS has a 10 to 11 percent chance of developing TS and about a 15 percent chance of developing chronic tics. In neurobiology, brain areas involved with control of motor function have been linked to movements and repetitive behaviors associated with TS, Attention-Deficit/Hyperactivity Disorder (ADHD), and Obsessive–Compulsive Disorder (OCD). Higher cognitive processes have been theorized to be associated with the premonitory urges seen in TS and OCD, whereas inhibitory brain regions are candidates for the disinhibition found in TS. Also, pharmacological treatments that block the neurochemical dopamine have resulted in improvements in tic symptoms, suggesting that brains of persons with tics have high levels of dopamine activity.

Environmental factors, such as stress and exposure to stimulants, have been linked to an increase in tic frequency, as have fatigue, engaging in social activities, and anticipation of anxiety-provoking events (i.e., waiting for test results; Silva, Munoz, Barickman, & Friedhoff, 1995). A study by Woods et al. (2001) evaluated the effects of having individuals with motor and vocal tics talk about their tics and found that there were significant increases in vocal, but not motor, tics in both of their participants. Therefore, talking about tics may serve as a cue to increase the rate of vocal tics. Perinatal complications and streptococcal infection have also been implicated in development of tics.

COMORBIDITY

Research shows a large overlap between TS and two other disorders (Findley, 2001). Clinical samples of individuals with TS have a 50 to 90 percent comorbidity rate with ADHD and an 11 to 80 percent comorbidity rate with OCD. Likewise, many individuals with TS display obsessive or compulsive behaviors, but do not meet full qualifications for OCD. Other disorders that are commonly comorbid with TS include depression, phobias, and learning disabilities.

ASSESSMENT

Individuals displaying symptoms resembling vocal tics should be evaluated by a medical professional before undergoing psychological evaluation (Carr & Rapp, 2001). Assessment measures for vocal tics include self- or parent-report measures, clinician ratings, or behavioral interviews. Because of the variability in frequency and complexity in distinguishing certain types of vocal tics (coughing or repetitive phrases) from typical behaviors, direct observations by the clinician, caretakers, or videotaping in a natural environment may also be useful. It should be noted that self-monitoring and self-reports may lead to increased awareness of the individual's tics and consequently may reduce their frequency or intensity.

TREATMENT

Pharmacotherapy and behavioral interventions have been demonstrated to be the most efficacious treatments for vocal tics. According to Watson, Howell, and Smith (2001), the most common pharmacological treatments of tic disorders are neuroleptics, which reduce symptoms by blocking the transmission of dopamine. Such medications have been found to reduce tics by 70 to 80 percent when successful. Despite the high rate of reduction, these drugs have numerous potential side effects, including dry mouth, constipation, impotence, muscle spasms, tardive dyskinesia, and seizures. New hybrids of neuroleptics (i.e., olanzapine, clozapine, and risperidone), as well as other medications such as clonidine and guanfacine, are currently being developed that have shown less efficacy in reducing tic symptoms but may not carry the same risk of serious side effects such as tardive dyskinesia and seizures.

The behavioral procedure that has proven to be the most effective nonpharmacological treatment for tic disorders is habit reversal (Azrin & Nunn, 1973). Habit reversal first teaches the individual to be more aware of his or her tics and premonitory urges. Next, the individuals are taught to emit a behavior that will compete with the tic. The competing behavior for vocal tics is typically diaphragmatic breathing for 1 minute contingent on the tic or the premonitory urge. Social support from a caretaker is also employed to remind the individual to use the competing response and praise him/her after its performance. Habit reversal has been found to reduce tics by up to 90 percent (Peterson & Azrin, 1993).

See also: Attention-Deficit/Hyperactivity Disorder; Depression in Children and Adolescents; Habits; Motor Tics; Tourette Syndrome

BIBLIOGRAPHY

Azrin, N. H., & Nunn, R. G. (1973). Habit reversal: A method of eliminating nervous habits and tics. *Behavior Therapy and Research, 11*, 619–628.

Carr, J. E., & Rapp, J. T. (2001). Assessment of repetitive behavior disorders. In D. W. Woods & R. G. Miltenberger (Eds.), *Tic disorders, trichotillomania, and other repetitive behavior disorders: Behavioral approaches to analysis and treatment* (pp. 53–67). New York: Kluwer Academic.

Findley, D. B. (2001). Characteristics of tic disorders. In D. W. Woods & R. G. Miltenberger (Eds.), *Tic disorders, trichotillomania, and other repetitive behavior disorders: Behavioral approaches to analysis and treatment* (pp. 53–67). New York: Kluwer Academic.

Leckman, J. F., King, R. A., & Cohen, D. J. (1999). Tics and tic disorders. In J. F. Leckman & D. J. Cohen (Eds.), *Tourette's syndrome: Tics, obsessions, compulsions: Developmental psychopathology and clinical care* (pp. 23–42). New York: Wiley.

Peterson, A. L., & Azrin, N. H. (1993). Behavioral and pharmacological treatments for Tourette syndrome: A review. *Applied and Preventive Psychology, 2*, 231–242.

Silva, R. R., Munoz, D. M., Barickman, J., & Friedhoff, A. J. (1995). Environmental factors and related fluctuation of symptoms in children and adolescents with Tourette's disorder. *Journal of Child Psychology and Psychiatry, 36,* 305–312.

Watson, T. S., Howell, L. A., & Smith, S. L. (2001). Behavioral interventions for tic disorders. In D. W. Woods & R. G. Miltenberger (Eds.), *Tic disorders, trichotillomania, and other repetitive behavior disorders: Behavioral approaches to analysis and treatment* (pp. 53–67). New York: Kluwer Academic.

Woods, D. W., Watson, T. S., Wolfe, E., Twohig, M. P., & Friman, P. C. (2001). Analyzing the influence of tic-related conversation on vocal and motor tics in children with Tourette's syndrome. *Journal of Applied Behavior Analysis, 34,* 353–356.

Additional Readings for Professionals

Leckman, J. F., & Cohen, D. J. (Eds.). *Tourette's syndrome: Tics, obsessions, compulsions. Developmental psychopathology and clinical care.* New York: Wiley.

Woods, D. W., & Miltenberger, R. G. (Eds.). (2001). *Tic disorders, trichotillomania, and other repetitive behavior disorders: Behavioral approaches to analysis and treatment.* New York: Kluwer Academic.

Douglas W. Woods
Chad T. Wetterneck

Ww

Watson, John B.

John Broadus Watson was born in 1878 on a farm a few miles from Greenville, South Carolina. After a master's degree at Furman University in Greenville in 1899, Watson became the youngest recipient of a Ph.D. at the University of Chicago. In 1908, the chance of a lifetime came when he was offered a professorship and department chairmanship at Johns Hopkins, which he gladly accepted.

FOUNDER OF BEHAVIORISM

Until 1915, his research was restricted to animal behavior, but after that time his interest centered on child development. Although Watson often pointed out that he was not the founder of behaviorism, it is certain that he was its most vocal and effective advocate. He argued that the analysis of human consciousness, which had almost exclusively occupied psychologists, was misguided and an extremely damaging process. He argued that a science of behavior could aid in the raising of our children and eventually lead to a world "fit for human habitation."

WHAT IS BEHAVIORISM?

In 1913 Watson published "Psychology as the behaviorist views it," a paper that blasted the method of introspection, or verbal descriptions of conscious experience, practiced by Edward Titchener and other so-called structuralists. He charged that the psychology of the period was a waste of time and that

if it were continued we would still be arguing over whether auditory sensations were extended in space 200 years hence. In 1928, Watson noted that consciousness has never been seen, smelled, nor tasted, nor does it take part in any human reactions. If it is irrelevant to what we actually *do*, why devote all of our time to studying it?

He was not denying that we see, hear, smell, hope, and remember, but to him these are activities, behaviors, or things that we do. As behaviorists, we study what people do, not what they experience. Watson was extremely interested in emotion but, in general, as long as people react to a red traffic light in the same way, he didn't care what each of them experienced as "red."

LOOK TO THE ENVIRONMENT, NOT HEREDITY

Watson wrote that we are "what we come with and what we have been through," and what we go through is by far the more important factor, at least as far as psychology is concerned. Through life we are constantly adjusting—adjustment occurring when our actions remove a source of stimulation. We adjust continually while in the womb and we do not stop until we make the final adjustment, death.

He argued that the goal for psychology should be to predict the response, given the stimulus, and to discover the stimulus, given the response. What is the effect of different methods of teaching a child to read? What is the effect of hugging or of spanking? Only research can answer such questions. He also classified our behavior into three kinds, manual, verbal, and visceral (moving, speaking, and feeling emotion), all of which occur to some extent every instant of our lives. At any moment in our lives, all three systems are active, although one may be overshadowing another.

FORGET MEMORY

As far as memory goes, Watson denied its existence, at least as a conception of storage and retrieval of memories. He felt that too much emphasis is placed on verbal memory, the ability to "recall" and recite words and lists and to produce verbal descriptions of past events—memory if far more than that. As for thinking, he believed it is part of what we do in the process of adjustment. Also when Watson denied mind, consciousness, and imagery, he was not denying experience in general, rather he was merely denying the existence of mind, thoughts, images, and the like as actual things that constitute mental content.

HOW FEARS ARE LEARNED AND UNLEARNED

Watson (1930) proposed that the belief in instinct and traits—the "gifts that are passed from generation to generation"—reflects only our desire to live forever, a desire that is fulfilled when we see our characteristics, both physical and "mental," in our children. Watson carefully observed the development of hundreds of infants and concluded that we do come with a large set of instinctive reactions, but that they are much more elementary than is usually supposed. We have instinctive fears that appear in infancy and are independent of environment. During our lifetime, new stimuli become attached to those producing the original instinctive positive or negative reactions and we live a life of attractions, aversions, and mixtures of attraction/aversion for reasons that elude us.

Watson postulated that there are three basic emotions: the X, Y, and Z reactions, corresponding to fear, rage, and love. Soon after birth, the infant shows the innate fear reaction. Such a reaction is reliably produced by a loud noise or loss of support, but nothing else, except inflicted pain. Watson briefly experimented on an infant by the name of Albert B. "Little Albert" showed only curiosity when presented with a white rat. As he reached for it, a hammer nearby but behind him and out of sight struck a long steel bar. He jumped violently, but did not cry. After weeks past, the loud noise and the rat were paired six more times—finally, Albert cried. The sight of the rat alone sent him crying and crawling away very rapidly. Albert had acquired a new fear. The work done with Albert appeared in many textbooks soon after the experiment was completed, and only Pavlov's basic salivary conditioning in dogs has been mentioned more often.

Watson used the method of reconditioning as an effective way to remove certain fears. Reconditioning aims to connect a new reaction to the feared object, replacing the existing fear response. This was accomplished by presenting the feared object in such a way that it provoked no fear reaction. Although Watson failed to properly publicize what he had done, decades later Joseph Wolpe (1958) made it popular with his systematic desensitization.

Soon Watson's writing diminished and after being away from academics for a long period of time, he found he had nothing more to say. An adulterous affair and divorce in 1920 led to his being shunned by the entire academic community and he spent many years in advertising. Watson was belatedly honored by the American Psychological Association, which awarded him its gold metal in 1957. The award read that he had "initiated a revolution in psychological thought." He backed out of accepting the award publicly and later died in 1958 at the age of 80.

See also: Pavlov, Ivan; Personality Theory: Operant; Skinner, B. F.

BIBLIOGRAPHY

Watson, J. B. (1913). Psychology as the behaviorist views it. *Psychological Review, 20,* 158–177.
Watson, J. B. (1928). *The ways of behaviorism.* New York: Harper.
Watson, J. B. (1930). *Behaviorism* (3rd ed.). New York: Norton.
Wolpe, J. (1958). *Psychotherapy by reciprocal inhibition.* Stanford, CA: Stanford University Press.

Additional Reading for Nonprofessionals

Buckley, K. W. (1989). *Mechanical man: John B. Watson and the beginnings of Behaviorism.* New York: Guilford.

Additional Reading for Professionals

Malone, J. C. (1991). *Theories of learning: A historical approach.* Belmont, CA: Wadsworth.

JOHN C. MALONE
CANDICE N. CARPENTER

Wechsler Adult Intelligence Scale—Third Edition (WAIS-III)

Introduced in 1939, the *Wechsler–Bellevue Intelligence Scale, Form 1* (Wechsler, 1939), was the original version of what is now known as the *Wechsler Adult Intelligence Scale* (WAIS) (Wechsler, 1955). Now on its third revision, the WAIS-III (Wechsler, 1997) continues the tradition of the Wechsler scales. The WAIS-III is an individually administered test of intelligence designed for adults between the ages of 16 through 89. Individual testing with the WAIS-III takes more than an hour, with a range in administration time of about 65 to 95 minutes. Two other Wechsler scales of intelligence for different age levels include the *Wechsler Intelligence Scale for Children—Fourth Edition* (WISC-IV) (Wechsler, 2003) and the *Wechsler Preschool and Primary Scale of Intelligence—Third Edition* (WPPSI-III) (Wechsler, 2002).

DESCRIPTION OF SCALES

The WAIS-III contains 14 subtests that are grouped into four composite scores, referred to as Index Scores. These Index Scores are grouped into the Verbal Scale and the Performance Scale, which combine to provide a global measure of general intellectual functioning, called the Full Scale Intelligence Quotient (FSIQ). Of these 14 subtests, 3 are considered supplemental and can be used to substitute if certain subtests are spoiled. Supplemental subtests include Letter-Number Sequencing, Symbol Search, and Object Assembly.

The Verbal Scale is composed of the Verbal Comprehension Index (VCI) and the Working Memory Index (WMI). The VCI measures verbal-related knowledge and understanding obtained both through formal and informal education as well as reflecting the application of verbal skills to new situations and reasoning. VCI subtests include Vocabulary, Similarities, and Information.

The Working Memory Index measures the ability to sustain attention, concentrate, and exert mental control. This index reflects the ability to hold information within the working memory in order to perform mental manipulations or calculations on the information. Subtests within the WMI include Arithmetic, Digit Span, and Letter–Number Sequencing.

The Performance Scale is composed of the Perceptual Organizational Index (POI) and the Processing Speed Index (PSI). The POI measures the ability to interpret and organize visually perceived material within a time limit. Ability to reason nonverbally, giving attention to detail, and visual–motor integration are included in this index. The POI includes the subtests Block Design, Matrix Reasoning, and Picture Completion.

The Processing Speed Index measures the ability to process visually perceived information quickly. Rapid eye–hand coordination and concentration are important components as reflected in both mental and psychomotor performance. Subtests in this Index include Digit Symbol-Coding and Symbol Search.

SCORE INTERPRETATION

Intelligence tests report scores as standard scores. These scores are based on score distributions that would occur if a large group of randomly selected people were measured or tested by this instrument. The scores taken from the general population are distributed on what is called a normal distribution. This normal distribution creates a bell-shaped curve, with 68% of the population falling within the average range. Therefore, when an individual takes the WAIS-III, his/her performance is compared to the rest of the general population.

Although standardized tests are technically sophisticated, they do contain measurement error. For example, if we gave the same person the test several times, the scores would slightly vary. Therefore, the standard scores an individual receives represent an approximation of that individual's "true" score. To give an estimation of the true score, the standard error of measurement (*SEM*) is used to give a range of scores wherein the individual's true score is likely to fall. This range of scores is sometimes referred to as the confidence interval. For example, the *SEM* of the Verbal Scale on the WISC-III is ±4. Therefore, if an individual achieves a score of 100, ninety percent of the time his/her scores would fall between 96 and 104.

Fifty percent of the population falls in the Average range on the WAIS-III. Average scores on the WAIS-III are between 90 and 109. High Average scores fall between 110 and 119, Superior scores fall between 120 and 129, and Very Superior scores are considered 130 and above. Low Average scores fall between 80 and 89, Borderline scores fall between 70 and 79, and Extremely Low scores are considered 69 and below (Wechsler, 1997).

Standard scores are also given for each subtest on the WAIS-III. These standard scores are called Scaled Scores and are based on a mean score of 10 and a standard deviation of 3. Therefore, scores between 7 and 13 would be considered an average score on any given subtest. Scaled Scores below 7 are considered to be below average and Scaled Scores above 13 are considered to be above average.

PURPOSES OF THE WAIS-III

Instruments assessing intellectual ability are used for a number of purposes. The WAIS-III is used as a psychoeducational test for secondary and postsecondary school planning and placement. Along with other types of assessments (e.g., achievement tests, interviews, and behavioral observations), tests of intelligence are often used as a core test for assessing learning disabilities. The WAIS-III is also used in diagnosing mental retardation, determining exceptionality or giftedness, and diagnosing neuropsychological impairments. In addition, tests that assess intellectual functioning are also used to predict future academic achievement.

See also: Gifted and Talented; Intelligence Quotient (IQ); Wechsler Intelligence Scale for Children—Fourth Edition (WISC-IV); Wechsler Preschool and Primary Scale of Intelligence—Third Edition (WPPSI-III)

BIBLIOGRAPHY

Wechsler, D. (1939). *The measurement of adult intelligence.* Baltimore: Williams & Wilkins.

Wechsler, D. (1955). *Manual for the Wechsler Adult Intelligence Scale.* New York: The Psychological Corporation.

Wechsler, D. (1997). *Manual for the Wechsler Memory Scale—Third Edition.* San Antonio, TX: The Psychological Corporation.

Wechsler, D. (1997). *Wechsler Adult Intelligence Scale—Third Edition.* San Antonio, TX: The Psychological Corporation.

Wechsler, D. (2002). *Wechsler Preschool and Primary Scale of Intelligence—Third Edition.* San Antonio, TX: The Psychological Corporation.

Wechsler, D. (2003). *Wechsler Intelligence Scale for Children—Fourth Edition.* San Antonio, TX: The Psychological Corporation.

Additional Reading for Nonprofessionals

Zenderland, L. (1998). *Measuring minds—Henry Herbert Goddard and the origins of American intelligence testing.* New York: Cambridge University Press.

Additional Readings for Professionals

Anastasi, A., & Urbina, S. (1997). *Psychological testing* (7th ed.). Upper Saddle River, NJ: Prentice–Hall.

Sattler, J. M. (2001). *Assessment of children—Cognitive applications.* San Diego, CA: Author.

JESSICA D. ALLIN
SHERRY K. BAIN

Wechsler Individual Achievement Test

The *Wechsler Individual Achievement Test* (WIAT), published by the Psychological Corporation in 1992, is a comprehensive, individually administered battery used to assess a variety of academic abilities in children in grades kindergarten through 12th. This instrument, which assesses ability on eight subtests, is directly linked to the *Wechsler Intelligence Scale for Children—Third Edition* (WISC-III), *Wechsler Preschool and Primary Intelligence Scale for Children—Revised* (WPPSI-R), and the *Wechsler Adult Intelligence Scale—Revised* (WAIS-R). Individuals 5 through 19 years of age were administered both the achievement and the above-mentioned intelligence tests to strengthen the diagnostic ability of the tests (Psychological Corporation, 1992).

The WIAT assesses ability in all of the areas identified for learning disabilities specified by the U.S. Department of Education (i.e., oral expression, listening comprehension, written expression, basic reading skill, reading comprehension, mathematics calculation, mathematics reasoning). The subtests are variously combined to yield a Reading Composite, Mathematics Composite, Language Composite, and Writing Composite. All of the composites are combined to yield a Total Composite. The Basic Reading, Mathematics Reasoning, and Spelling subtests combine to yield a Screener Composite. Each subtest yields a Standard Score (Mean = 100, SD = 15), Percentile Rank, Equivalent Score, Normal Curve Equivalent, and Stanine. The Standard Score, Percentile Rank, and Equivalent Scores can be computed by age or by grade.

The manual indicates that test administration time varies by the age of the child. Younger children (e.g., kindergarten to second grade) require 30–50 minutes to complete the battery; for Grades 3–12, administration time is estimated to be 55 to 60 minutes, with extra time required for the Written Expression subtest. The Screener requires approximately 10 to 18 minutes. Administration should occur in the sequence the subtests are presented in the Stimulus Booklet. Scoring is straightforward and the materials are easy to use. Intraindividual comparisons across subtests are also available, with a table providing frequency of differences in the norm sample available in the manual.

The norm sample, based on the 1988 U.S. census data, consisted of 13 age groups of children from 5 to 19 years of age. Slightly more girls than boys were in the sample, with proportions of white, black, Hispanic, and other ethnic groups based on the census figures. Four geographic regions were represented and parent education levels were tracked.

The manual presents a variety of information to support the validity of the WIAT. A multitrait–multimethod study comparing scores on the WIAT with those on the Iowa Tests of Basic Skills, California Achievement Tests, and Stanford Achievement Test indicates correlations ranging from .69 to .77 on the composite scales (Psychological Corporation, 1992). Other comparisons were made with such achievement tests as the Kaufman Test of Educational Achievement, Wide Range Achievement Tests, Woodcock–Johnson Psycho-Educational Battery, Differential Ability Scales, and Peabody Picture Vocabulary Test, with correlations ranging from .68 to .87. Correlations were highest in Spelling.

The WIAT allows basic skill analysis, with clear identification of skills assessed. The manual provides tables to indicate approximate grade level for achievement of each skill in the areas of spelling, mathematics, and reading. In Oral Expression, items are grouped to assist in identifying specific skills required to complete the task. The manual provides comprehensive assistance in the scoring of this subtest. Comprehensive assistance for various discrepancy analyses is also presented in the manual, and many consumers may find this information very useful.

See also: Curriculum-Based Measurement; Wide Range Achievement Test—3 (WR AT-3)

BIBLIOGRAPHY

Psychological Corporation. (1992). *Wechsler Individual Achievement Test manual.* San Antonio, TX: The Psychological Corporation.

Additional Readings for Nonprofessionals

Grissmer, D., Flanagan, A., Williamson, S., & Kawata, J. (2001). *Improving student achievement: What state NAEP test scores tell us.* Santa Monica, CA: Rand.

Lyman, H. B. (1997). *Test scores and what they mean.* Boston: Allyn & Bacon.

Additional Readings for Professionals

Flanagan, D. P., Ortiz, S. O., Alfonso, V. C., & Mascolo, J. T. (2002). *The Achievement Test Desk Reference (ATDR): Comprehensive assessment and learning disabilities.* Boston: Allyn & Bacon.

Sattler, J. M. (2001). *Assessment of children: Cognitive applications* (4th ed.). San Diego, CA: Author.

CARLEN HENINGTON

Wechsler Intelligence Scale for Children—Fourth Edition (WISC-IV)

Individually administered intelligence tests are typically given only to children who have serious academic or behavioral problems, or who are suspected of being intellectually gifted. One such test is the *Wechsler Intelligence Scale for Children—Fourth Edition* (WISC-IV) (Wechsler, 2003). One of three age-related intelligence scales originally developed by David Wechsler, the WISC-IV is the most recently revised version for children aged 6 years 0 months to 16 years 11 months. Two other Wechsler scales of intelligence for different age levels are the *Wechsler Preschool and Primary Scale of Intelligence—Third Edition* (WPPSI-III) (Wechsler, 2002) for children approximately 2.5 to 7 years old, and the *Wechsler Adult Intelligence Scale—Third Edition* (WAIS-III) (Wechsler, 1997) for older adolescents and adults aged approximately 16 years and older.

Wechsler began developing these intelligence scales in the 1930s, naming his first scale the *Wechsler–Bellevue Intelligence Scale* (Wechsler, 1939). His original scale was actually an adaptation of 11 subscales from other tests, which Wechsler considered suitable contributing elements for an assessment of general mental abilities (Sattler, 2001). The current version for children, the WISC-IV, follows the original *Wechsler Intelligence Scale for Children* (Wechsler, 1949) and two revisions, the *Wechsler Intelligence Scale for Children—Revised* (Wechsler, 1974), and the *Wechsler Intelligence Scale for Children—Third Edition* (WISC-III) (Wechsler, 1991). Revisions of the test generally focus on updating test items, collecting new normative data, and reducing test bias based on gender, ethnic, or racial status.

The WISC-IV provides a global measure of general intellectual functioning, called the Full Scale Intelligence Quotient (FSIQ), and four composite scores, referred to as Index Scores. Previous editions of the test focused on two additional global scores, the Verbal Intelligence Quotient (VIQ) and the Performance Intelligence Quotient (PIQ), with four Index Scores introduced with the publication of the WISC-III. The current version relies on the use of the FSIQ and a revision of the four Index Scores, based upon theory, clinical research, and statistical analysis.

Individual testing with the WISC-IV generally takes more than an hour. The child is administered 10 or more subtests by a trained examiner. Subtest tasks are generally designed to maintain the child's interest. Some tasks involve timing, and extra points are given for quick completion. Several subtests require manipulation of materials, such as blocks or puzzles. Others require oral responses to questions. Reading skills are not evaluated on this test. However, arithmetic skills may be explored in one of the supplemental subtests.

INDEX SCORES AND SUBTESTS

The four Index Score areas are labeled Verbal Comprehension Index (VCI), the Perceptual Reasoning Index (PRI), the Working Memory Index (WMI), and the Processing Speed Index (PSI). Measurement for each index includes two to three subtests, with supplemental subtests available for administration under each index category.

The Verbal Comprehension Index consists of core subtests titled Similarities, Vocabulary, and Comprehension. Items are administered by asking the child to state similarities between concepts, define words, or provide oral solutions to questions involving general principles or social situations, respectively. The child's responses are written by the examiner on the record form, and the accuracy and quality of responses are scored. Two optional subtests, Information and Word Reasoning, provide supplemental data. The Information subtest requires the child to answer questions covering topics of general knowledge; the Word Reasoning subtest requires the child to identify a common concept when a series of clues are supplied.

The Perceptual Reasoning Index includes three core subtests: Block Design, Picture Concepts, and Matrix Reasoning. Respective to each subtest, tasks involve arranging blocks to match presented designs, identifying common characteristics among pictured items, and choosing correct choices when presented with pictures or designs representing analogous relationships. A supplemental subtest, Picture Completion, requires the child to look at an incomplete picture and point to, or name, the missing part.

The Working Memory Index includes two core subtests: Digit Span and Letter–Number Sequencing. Digit Span requires the child to repeat a series of numbers following the examiner's oral presentation. Letter–Number Sequencing requires the child to recall and reorder a series of letters and numbers according to rules involving ascending values and alphabetical sequencing. One supplemental subtest, Arithmetic, consists of math-related problems presented orally to the child.

The Processing Speed Index consists of two core subtests, Coding and Symbol Search, and one supplemental subtest, Cancellation. Each subtest involves the presentation of worksheets. In Coding, the child copies symbols that are associated with specific geometric forms. In Symbol Search, the child scans groups of symbols to identify if specific target symbols are present. In Cancellation, the child marks out target items pictured among multiple arranged items. Each of these subtests is timed.

WHAT DO THE SCORES MEAN?

Intelligence tests, or tests of cognitive ability, usually report scores in terms of some type of standardized score. Standardized scores, or standard scores, are based on score distributions that would be produced if a large group of people randomly drawn from the general population were measured or tested. These acquired scores produce a classic bell-shaped curve when plotted on a graph. When a standard score is calculated for any child taking the test, his/her performance compared with the general population can be estimated. For the WISC-IV, standard scores for the FSIQ and the four Index Scores are based upon a scale with a mean of 100 and a standard deviation of 15.

The standard score a child achieves at each test administration is an estimate of his/her functioning level. There is a standard error of measurement (*SEM*), which provides a band of error around the score telling the examiner, parents, and teacher the range of scores that the child's true score would be expected to fall within if we could test the child numerous times. In the case of the WISC-IV, the *SEM* for the FSIQ and the Index Scores is reported as 3. With an acquired FSIQ score of 100, sixty-eight percent of the time a child's true score would be expected to fall between 97 and 103. Furthermore, 95 percent of the time, the child's true FSIQ score would be expected to fall within 6 points (2 times the *SEM*) of the acquired score, from 94 to 106. Acquired scores should never be considered fixed scores but should be interpreted using the range of scores calculated on the basis of the *SEM*.

If a child scores 100 (plus or minus 6) on the WISC-IV FSIQ, the score is interpreted to mean the child performs at the mean or average level (50th percentile) compared with other children his/her age. If a child scores 85 or below on the WISC-IV FSIQ, this means that he/she scored at or below 1 standard deviation below the mean. A standard score of 85 falls at approximately the 16th percentile (not to be confused with percentage correct scores). A child scoring 115 or above on the WISC-IV FSIQ falls at or above 1 standard deviation above the mean (the 84th percentile). Standard scores from 86 to 114 would be interpreted as falling within the average level of the general population, with the high end of this range described as High Average and the low end of the range described as Low Average. Scores falling at 120 to 129 are described as Superior. A score of 130 or above is described as Very Superior. Scores falling within 70 to 79 are described as Borderline, and scores of 69 or below as Extremely Low (Wechsler, 2003).

The subtests of the WISC-IV also produce standardized scores; in this case they are labeled Scaled Scores. Subtest Scaled Scores have a mean score of 10, with a standard deviation of 3. Children who acquire Scaled Scores between 7 and 13 on a subtest are generally interpreted as having performed at an average level. Children whose Scaled Scores fall below 7 are interpreted as performing below the average level of children that age, and those whose Scaled Scores fall above 13 are interpreted as performing above the average level.

WHO GETS TESTED?

Individually administered tests of intelligence or cognitive ability are not generally given to children who are working within the average range academically, although children within the average range of intelligence are always included in the sample that makes up the standardization group. Tests such as the WISC-IV are administered to aid in the diagnosis of children falling at the two extremes of mental ability, including children referred for assessment of giftedness or mild to moderate mental retardation. The WISC-IV or other intelligence tests are also used to evaluate children who are seriously lagging behind academically and are suspected of having learning disabilities. Intelligence tests are typically included in assessment batteries for children with emotional or behavioral problems, or with attention-deficit/hyperactivity disorder. A test such as the WISC-IV would generally not be given without considerable adaptation to children with physical impairments such as visual, hearing, or motor disabilities. If administered under such circumstances, results need to be reported and interpreted with caution if standardized procedures were not followed.

Individualized intelligence tests are generally predictive of future academic achievement. This is one of the values of their usage, besides aiding in diagnosis of academic-related disorders. However, intelligence tests have not been found particularly useful in generating direct recommendations for specific classroom remediation or recommendations. For this purpose, other types of assessment would be more appropriate. For example, classroom-based recommendations might be developed following observations of the child in the school setting, behavioral checklists, examination of his/her school products, and curriculum-based assessment. Any assessment of a child having academic or emotional/behavioral problems should be based upon a battery of appropriate tests, not just on an intelligence test.

See also: Intelligence Quotient (IQ); Wechsler Adult Intelligence Scale—Third Edition (WAIS-III); Wechsler Preschool and Primary Scale of Intelligence—Third Edition (WPPSI-III)

BIBLIOGRAPHY

Wechsler, D. (1949). *Wechsler Intelligence Scale for Children.* New York: The Psychological Corporation.

Wechsler, D. (1974). *Wechsler Intelligence Scale for Children—Revised.* San Antonio, TX: The Psychological Corporation.

Wechsler, D. (1997). *Wechsler Adult Intelligence Scale—Third Edition.* San Antonio, TX: The Psychological Corporation.

Wechsler, D. (2002). *Wechsler Preschool and Primary Scale of Intelligence—Third Edition.* San Antonio, TX: The Psychological Corporation.

Wechsler, D. (2003). *Wechsler Intelligence Scale for Children—Fourth Edition.* San Antonio, TX: The Psychological Corporation.

Additional Readings for Nonprofessionals

Glover, J. A. (1979). *A parent's guide to intelligence testing—How to help your children's intellectual development.* Chicago: Nelson Hall.

Zenderland, L. (1998). *Measuring minds—Henry Herbert Goddard and the origins of American intelligence testing.* New York: Cambridge University Press.

Additional Reading for Professionals

Sattler, J. M. (2001). *Assessment of children—Cognitive applications.* San Diego, CA: Author.

SHERRY K. BAIN

Wechsler Preschool and Primary Scale of Intelligence—Third Edition (WPPSI-III)

Binet and Simon published the first intelligence test in 1905. There have been several intelligence tests published since that time, but the primary purpose of this type of assessment remains the same. Individually administered intelligence tests are designed to assess individuals who exhibit academic or behavior problems, and to assess individuals who may be intellectually gifted. The *Wechsler Preschool and Primary Scale of Intelligence—Third Edition* (WPPSI-III) (Wechsler, 2002) is an individually administered intelligence test designed for children ranging from 2 years 6 months to 7 years 3 months. Administration time for the WPPSI-III varies with the age of the child and the number of subtests given. Administration time typically varies from 30 minutes to 1 hour. The WPPSI-III is one of the three Wechsler age-based intelligence tests. The *Wechsler Intelligence Scale for Children—Fourth Edition* (Wechsler, 2003) and the *Wechsler Adult Intelligence Scale—Third Edition* (Wechsler, 1997) are designed for individuals 6 years to 16 years 11 months and 17 years and older, respectively.

The WPPSI-III is comprised of 14 subtests (7 Verbal Subtests, 5 Performance Subtests, and 2 Processing Speed Subtests). For children aged 2 years 6 months to 3 years 11 months, there are four core subtests required to compute the Full Scale Intelligence Quotient (FSIQ) (i.e., Receptive Vocabulary, Information, Block Design, and Object Assembly). The FSIQ is considered a global measure of intellectual function. For children aged 4 years to 7 years 3 months, there are seven core subtests required to compute the FSIQ (i.e., Information, Vocabulary, Word Reasoning, Block Design, Matrix Reasoning, Picture Concepts, and Coding).

The Verbal IQ (VIQ) involves measuring skills that are language-related. The child is typically asked questions by the examiner and has to respond orally. The VIQ comprises the Information and Receptive Vocabulary subtests for children aged 2 years 6 months to 3 years 11 months. For children aged 4 years to 7 years 3 months, the VIQ consists of the Information, Vocabulary, and Word Reasoning subtests.

The Performance IQ (PIQ) consists of subtests that involve manipulation of objects such as blocks or puzzles, or solution of visually presented problems such as finding the missing element in a picture or selecting the final element of a pattern or matrix. For children aged 2 years 6 months to 3 years 11 months, the PIQ consists of two core subtests: Block Design and Object Assembly. The core PIQ subtests for children aged 4 years to 7 years 3 months are Block Design, Matrix Reasoning, and Picture Concepts.

Supplemental and optional subtests are used to derive additional composite scores such as the General Language Composite (GLC) and the Processing Speed Quotient (PSQ). The GLC is derived from the Receptive Vocabulary and Picture Naming subtests for both age groups. The PSQ is only derived for students aged 4 years to 7 years 3 months. The PSQ is comprised of five subtests: Symbol Search, Comprehension, Picture Completion, Similarities, and Object Assembly.

Supplemental subtests provide a broader representation of intellectual and cognitive functioning when added to the core subtests. They can also be used to substitute for core subtests, if the need arises. The supplemental subtest for children aged 2 years 6 months to 3 years 11 months is Picture Naming. Supplemental subtests for ages 4 years to 7 years 3 months are Symbol Search, Comprehension, Picture Completion, Similarities, and Object Assembly. Optional subtests are used only to compute optional scores and cannot be used as a substitute for a core subtest. There are two optional subtests, Receptive Vocabulary and Picture Naming, for children aged 4 years to 7 years 3 months. A brief description of the subtests follows.

UNDERSTANDING THE SCORES

Intelligence tests typically report scores in terms of a standardized or standard score. Conversion of raw scores into standard scores allows for score comparisons within the WPPSI-III and between the WPPSI-III and other related measures. The WPPSI-III uses two types of age-corrected standard scores: scaled and composite scores. These scores allow for comparison of a child's performance to that of other children of the same age. Subtest scaled scores have a mean of 10 and a standard deviation of 3. Composite scores (i.e., FSIQ, VIQ, PIQ, PSQ, and GLC) are based on sums of clustered subtest scaled scores. These scores are scaled with a mean of 100 and a standard deviation of 15.

With any type of assessment, there will always be some degree of error. The Standard Error of Measurement (*SEM*) allows this error to be taken into consideration. A child's score on the WPPSI-III is only an estimate of the child's true score. The *SEM* is used to provide a confidence interval, which is a range of scores in which the child's true score is likely to fall if the child took the test several times. For example, if a 6-year-old child attained an FSIQ score of 106 on the WPPSI-III, with a confidence level of 95%, the examiner could say that the child's true score falls within the range of 100 to 112.

The WPPSI-III, like many clinical instruments used to assess intelligence, also provides age-based percentile rank scores. Percentile ranks provide an easily interpreted means of comparing a child's performance to others of the same age. For example, if a child receives an FSIQ score of 100 (plus or minus 6) the percentile rank would be 50, indicating that the child's score is equal to or better than 50% of his/her same-age peers.

The WPPSI-III also provides descriptive classification of FSIQ composite scores. FSIQ scores of 130 or above are considered Very Superior. FSIQ scores of 120 to 129 are considered in the Superior Range. FSIQ scores between 110 and 119 are classified as High Average. Scores of 90–109 are considered Average. Scores ranging from 80–89 are considered Low Average. Scores ranging from 70 to 79 are classified as Borderline. Scores at or below 69 are considered Extremely Low.

USING SCORES DERIVED FROM INTELLIGENCE TESTS

Scores from individualized intelligence tests can often be used to predict the student's future level of academic achievement. Scores are also used to aid in the diagnosis of various academically related disorders such as learning disability or mental retardation. Results from individualized intelligence tests are typically not used alone. Other important information such as achievement tests for school-aged children, direct observation, parent interviews, student interviews, and teacher interviews are often used along with IQ scores when making decisions concerning a child.

See also: Intelligence Quotient (IQ); Wechsler Adult Intelligence Scale—Third Edition (WAIS-III); Wechsler Intelligence Scale for Children—Fourth Edition (WISC-IV)

BIBLIOGRAPHY

Wechsler, D. (1997). *Wechsler Adult Intelligence Scale—Third Edition*. San Antonio, TX: The Psychological Corporation.
Wechsler, D. (2002). *Wechsler Preschool and Primary Scale of Intelligence—Third Edition*. San Antonio, TX: The Psychological Corporation.
Wechsler, D. (2003). *Wechsler Intelligence Scale for Children—Fourth Edition*. San Antonio, TX: The Psychological Corporation.

Additional Readings for Nonprofessionals

Glover, J. A. (1979). *A parent's guide to intelligence testing—How to help your children's intellectual development*. Chicago: Nelson Hall.
Zenderland, L. (1998). *Measuring minds—Henry Herbert Goddard and the origins of American intelligence testing*. New York: Cambridge University Press.

Additional Reading for Professionals

Sattler, J. M. (2001). *Assessment of children—Cognitive applications*. San Diego, CA: Author.

ANDREA D. HALE
SHERRY K. BAIN

Wide Range Achievement Test—3 (WRAT-3)

The *Wide Range Achievement Test* was originally developed nearly 60 years ago by Dr. Joseph Jastak at Columbia University. The test was developed at about the same time as the

Wechsler–Bellevue Scales, which were being developed by Dr. David Wechsler. In accordance with Wechsler's belief that cognitive functioning is multifaceted, the WRAT was intended to add the dimensions of word recognition, spelling, and mathematical computation to Wechsler's scales.

The WRAT-3, printed in 1993, is the most recent restandardization effort of this longstanding achievement measure. This standardization involved a stratified sampling with almost 5,000 people from across the United States. This instrument uses the Rasch model, identification of the difficulty level of each score on an interval scale, for item analysis and scaling (Wilkinson, 1993). The WRAT assesses three areas: Reading—letter recognition/naming and word pronunciation when presented individually; Spelling—writing names, letters, and words from dictation; and Arithmetic—counting, reading number symbols, solving oral problems, and written computations. Intended to be used with individuals from 5 to 75 years, this instrument purports to provide a reliable measurement of basic academic functioning needed for successful learning. This instrument does not examine reading comprehension; rather it emphasizes reading mechanics. This focus on reading mechanics minimizes the need for the individual to also have the ability to read and define a particular word. Generally, this test is administered individually; however, the arithmetic and spelling subtests can be administered in small groups with young individuals and in larger groups with older individuals.

Using age norms, the WRAT provides Standard Scores (Mean = 100, SD = 15), Absolute Scores, grade scores, percentiles, and normal curve equivalents. The Absolute Score (Mean = 500) allows a comparison of each subtest across a continuum (i.e., without regard for grade or age) of ability. The test developers offer this score primarily as a method for developing local norms.

Analysis of errors, although not a formal component of the instrument, can be conducted by examining responses for error patterns. Often this analysis is facilitated through the observation of different types of mistakes. Administration time ranges from 15 to 30 minutes. The instrument has two alternative test forms (BLUE and TAN) that can be used separately or as pre- and posttest forms. The two forms can be combined to yield a more reliable estimate of functioning. Subtests can be administered in any order.

The norm sample used in the most recent version of this instrument contains 23 age groups, with regional representation from four areas of the United States. There were slightly more boys than girls through age 20 (reflecting national ratios) and representation of ethnicity (white, black, Hispanic, and other) and parental occupation reflected the 1990 U.S. Census numbers.

Because this instrument is brief and covers basic academic functioning, with a minimum of items for each skill assessed, it is easy to administer and score. The WRAT is best used as a research instrument rather than to determine eligibility for services. It may also serve as a screener to determine the need for more comprehensive assessment.

See also: Curriculum-Based Measurement; Wechsler Individual Achievement Test

BIBLIOGRAPHY

Wilkinson, G. S. (1993). *Wide Range Achievement Test administration manual, 1993 ed.* Wilmington, DE: Wide Range, Inc.

Additional Readings for Nonprofessionals

Grissmer, D., Flanagan, A., Williamson, S., & Kawata, J. (2001). *Improving student achievement: What state NAEP test scores tell us.* Santa Monica, CA: Rand.
Lyman, H. B. (1997). *Test scores and what they mean.* Boston: Allyn & Bacon.

Additional Readings for Professionals

Flanagan, D. P., Ortiz, S. O., Alfonso, V. C., & Mascolo, J. T. (2002). *The Achievement Test Desk Reference (ATDR): Comprehensive assessment and learning disabilities.* Boston: Allyn & Bacon.
Sattler, J. M. (2001). *Assessment of children: Cognitive applications* (4th ed.). San Diego, CA: Author.

CARLEN HENINGTON

Witmer, Lightner

Lightner Witmer, the founder of the field of clinical psychology, was called a pioneer of school psychology by many (e.g., Fagan, 1996). Born in 1867, Witmer grew up in Pennsylvania and after high school attended undergraduate school at the University of Pennsylvania, where he was valedictorian of his class. He later went to graduate school, where he took some law classes but finally decided to study the relatively new topic of psychology (at the University of Pennsylvania) under James Cattell. After Cattell left for a position at Columbia University, Witmer opted to complete his dissertation under the supervision of Wilhelm Wundt in Leipzig, Germany, where he conducted his research in the Leipzig Psychology Laboratory (McReynolds, 1997).

In 1896, after his work in Germany, Witmer founded the first applied psychology clinic at the University of Pennsylvania. At this clinic, many of Witmer's first cases were children with academic or other school problems. Witmer developed programs to help them become more successful at school. Witmer also taught graduate courses on special methods that could be used to treat children with academic difficulties.

Prior to this point, little psychological research included the application of psychology to human problems. Witmer was the first to teach classes regarding the applied techniques of psychology. Witmer also was one of the early members of the American Psychological Association (APA).

Witmer received a grant that helped start the first clinical psychology journal, *The Clinical Psychologist*. Psychological clinics at other universities were founded throughout the United States by Witmer, and some of his former students directed these new clinics. Witmer developed two psychological tests, the Witmer Formboard and the Witmer Cylinders, which were used extensively in the psychological clinic at the University of Pennsylvania. Normative data were collected for these tests and the Witmer Formboard test was considered one of the best formboard tests of the time (McReynolds, 1997).

Throughout the rest of his career, Witmer continued to link psychology to educational settings and practices. During Witmer's early years with the psychology clinic and throughout his professional career, his conceptualization of the clinic included teaching applied skills not only to his graduate students studying psychology but also to students majoring in education (McReynolds, 1997). Many of the early internships for clinical psychology students were in school settings and many of Witmer's clients were referred by school teachers and administrators (Fagan, 1996). A number of Witmer's graduate students in psychology took psychologist positions in school settings. For 50 years, Witmer served as a consultant at special schools for children with developmental disabilities, including the Pennsylvania Training School for Feeble-Minded Children. Witmer also consulted at a Home School in Philadelphia and at the Haddonfield Training School for the Mentally Deficient and Peculiarly Backward in New Jersey. Witmer was one of the first psychologists to serve as a consultant rather than work for an agency (McReynolds, 1997).

Later, Witmer opened his own school for children with developmental and behavioral difficulties. One of his goals for this new residential facility was to provide a home-like 24-hour therapeutic environment to children who might otherwise be institutionalized. Witmer's work in schools and with school-aged children is similar to the role of school psychologists today.

Although Witmer is considered a pioneer of school psychology and a large number of his clients were children with school problems, he believed that clinical psychology should not be limited to children with academic and behavior problems and that clinical psychology should be used whenever assessment or treatment of a child or adult is conducted (McReynolds, 1997).

Lightner Witmer was clearly considered a founder of clinical psychology and a pioneer in school psychology. School psychology does not appear to have a specific founder but has evolved into a recognized profession after many years of psychol-

ogists' fulfilling the psychological needs of children in school settings (McReynolds, 1997). Although Witmer's ideas about clinical psychology were broad, the majority of his work in clinical psychology could be considered very similar to the work of a school psychologist (Fagan, 1996).

Since 1973, the American Psychological Association's Division 16 (School Psychology Division) has annually awarded the Lightner Witmer Award to outstanding school psychologists who have contributed significantly to the research field of school psychology early in their careers (McReynolds, 1997).

See also: American Psychological Association—Division 16; Lightner Witmer Award

BIBLIOGRAPHY

Fagan, T. K. (1996). Witmer's contributions to school psychological services. *American Psychologist, 51*, 241–243.
McReynolds, P. (1997). *Lightner Witmer: His life and times.* Washington, DC: American Psychological Association.

Additional Readings for Nonprofessionals

Fagan, T. K., & Wise, P. S. (1994). *School psychology: Past, present, and future.* White Plains, NY: Longman.
Routh, D. K. (1996). Lightner Witmer and the first 100 years of clinical psychology. *American Psychologist, 51*, 244–247.

Additional Readings for Professionals

McReynolds, P. (1987). Lightner Witmer: Little-known founder of clinical psychology. *American Psychologist, 43*, 849–858.
Witmer, L. (1907/1996). Clinical psychology. *The Psychological Clinic, 1*, 1–9.

KAREN I. DITTMER-MCMAHON

Woodcock–Johnson III Tests of Achievement

The *Woodcock–Johnson III* (Woodcock, McGrew, & Mather, 2001) comprises two published norm-referenced standardized assessment instruments: Tests of Cognitive Abilities (WJ III COG) and Achievement (WJ III ACH). The test instruments are individually administered by persons with training in standardized assessment and evaluation. The WJ III ACH includes 22 subtests that are organized into a standard battery (12 subtests) and an extended battery (10 subtests) and are used to assess individuals across six curriculum areas: Reading, Oral Language, Mathematics, Written Language, Knowledge, and Supplemental.

The WJ III ACH is the third and most recent revision of the instrument that was originally published in 1977. Some of the major differences of the WJ III ACH are (a) new subtests, (b) computerized scoring that replaced hand scoring (no precise hand scoring option is available), (c) new achievement clusters, (d) improved measurements of reading performance, (e) addition of analogy items, (f) condensed assessments of science, (g) condensed Academic Knowledge subtest, and (h) oral language ability/achievement discrepancies (Blackwell, 2001; Mather & Woodcock, 2001).

ADMINISTRATION AND SCORING

The WJ III ACH tests should be administered by those with specialized training in assessment and psychoeducational diagnostic decision making, including school psychologists, psychometrists, and specially trained education staff. The WJ III administrator's manual states that the test administrator "needs thorough knowledge of the exact administration and scoring procedures and an understanding of the importance to adhering to these standardized procedures" (Mather & Woodcock, 2001, p. 8). The individual responsible for interpreting the test "requires a higher degree of knowledge and experience than is required for administering and scoring the test. Graduate-level training in educational assessment and a background in diagnostic decision making is recommended" (Mather & Woodcock, 2001, p. 8). Those who administer and report assessment outcomes should be aware of the reliability and validity characteristics and how they might be influenced by assessment conditions and the characteristics of the individual being assessed. The relevant characteristics of individuals with impairments (motor, hearing, vision) or psychological diagnoses (attention-deficit disorder, autism, schizophrenia) should be considered when interpreting assessment outcomes.

The WJ III ACH is organized in two easels: standard battery (12 subtests) and extended battery (10 subtests). The administration of the extended battery is optional. The tests are administered orally (sometimes with a taped presentation) and/or visually, with either timed or untimed formats. The administrator places the record form out of the examinee's view by placing it behind the standing easel. Each test, with the exception of the timed tests, requires the administrator to establish and follow subtest-specific basal and ceiling rules (Mather & Woodcock, 2001; McGrew & Woodcock, 2001a). The basal is the minimum level of accurate performance within a subtest, and the ceiling is the maximum level of accurate performance. These assessment outcomes are used to estimate an individual's general level of achievement.

Test administration takes approximately 60 to 70 minutes for an experienced examiner. However, very young subjects or individuals with unique characteristics may require additional time. The tests should be administered in the order in which they appear in the book. The starting points for each subtest are indicated on the first page of the subtest in the test book. All scoring and administration procedures are listed in the Examiner's Manual (Mather & Woodcock, 2001). When scores are reported, they should always be reported and interpreted with the standard error of measurement (American Educational Research Association, American Psychological Association, & National Council on Measurement in Education, 1999). Scoring is discussed in greater detail below.

WJ III ACH outcomes can be reported as raw scores, grade equivalents, age equivalents, relative proficiency index (to define the instructional zone), or standard scores. The standard error of measurement should be reported with the point estimates of the scaled score. Thus, a standard score of 95 should be reported with a confidence band (or confidence interval). For example, a reported outcome might read, "At the time of assessment, Sheniqua's performance on the WJ III reading and writing ability subscale was equivalent to a standard score value of 105 ±7. Her performance places her within the average range at or about the 53rd percentile."

The standard score distribution is the most common, with an average of 100 and a standard deviation of 15. Based on the distribution of standard scores, 68% of individuals will evidence outcomes between 85 and 115; 95% of individuals will evidence outcomes between 70 and 130. Qualitative descriptions of standard score outcomes include the following: very low (below 70), low (70 to 79), low average (80 to 89), average (90 to 110), above average (111 to 120), superior (121 to 130), and very superior (above 130). Standard scores are often reported with percentile values. Percentile values estimate the relative rank order of the examinee. For example, an examinee whose WJ III outcome score approximates the 53rd percentile has performed above approximately 52% of students and below 46% of students. This performance is well within the average range.

THEORETICAL FOUNDATION

The WJ III has a strong theoretical foundation in the Cattell–Horn–Carroll (CHC) theory (Mather & Woodcock, 2001; McGrew & Woodcock, 2001a). CHC theory, or Gf–Gc theory, suggests that intelligence is composed of fluid (Gf) and crystallized (Gc) intellectual abilities, which combine for an overall estimate of general intellectual functioning (GIA). Gf is an estimate of an individual's ability to process and manipulate information, and Gc is an estimate of an individual's ability to store and retrieve information (Woodcock, 1998). The CHC theory of cognitive abilities was a theoretical foundation in the development of the test and is used to interpret assessment outcomes derived from the WJ III COG and WJ III ACH. Of the total, WJ III ACH contains tests designed to estimate achievement and cognitive abilities related to quantitative knowledge (Gq), reading–writing ability (Grw), comprehension knowledge (Gc), and auditory processing (Ga).

RELIABILITY AND VALIDITY

Test reliability is the consistency of measurement outcomes across time, as evidenced by minimal measurement error (American Educational Research Association et al., 1999; Blackwell, 2001; McGrew & Woodcock, 2001). More precise test scores have smaller standard errors of measurement than less precise test scores. The reliability of all the tests with the exception of the timed tests and the multiple-point scoring tests was measured using the split-half reliability procedure. Rasch analysis procedures, which provide a "unique estimate of the standard error of measurement of the ability score associated with each raw score for every person in the norm sample" (McGrew & Woodcock, 2001, p. 36), were used to calculate the other tests. For most tests, the median reliability coefficient is in the .80 range or higher (Blackwell, 2001).

Test validity refers to the level at which the use and interpretation of the test is supported by evidence and theory (American Educational Research Association et al., 1999; Blackwell, 2001; McGrew & Woodcock, 2001). Three types of validity scores are provided: content, construct, and concurrent. The authors provide a broad variety of evidence to support content and construct validity. The WJ III ACH measures achievement in the areas of reading, mathematics, written language, oral language, and curricular knowledge. Teachers and psychologists contributed the items on the test, and reviewers examined the items on the test for bias and sensitivity (McGrew & Woodcock, 2001). Concurrent validity was measured across different age levels and across a wide selection of other achievement tests. Correlations with these tests fall within the moderate to high range, suggesting that the WJ III ACH measures skills similar to those measured by the other tests (Blackwell, 2001). Correlations were computed between the WJ III ACH and the Wechsler Individual Achievement Test (WIAT), which resulted in a correlation of .65. Also, the WJ III ACH total achievement score and the Kaufman Test of Educational Achievement have a correlation of .79 (McGrew & Woodcock, 2001).

See also: *Gf–Gc* Theory of Intelligence

BIBLIOGRAPHY

American Educational Research Association, American Psychological Association, & National Council on Measurement in Education. (1999). *Standards for educational and psychological testing.* Washington, DC: American Educational and Psychological Research Association.

Blackwell, T. L. (2001). Test review. *Counseling Bulletin, 44,* 323–235.

Mather, N., & Woodcock, R. W. (2001). Examiners manual: Standard and extended batteries, *Woodcock–Johnson III Tests of Achievement.* Itasca, IL: Riverside.

McGrew, K. S., & Woodcock, R. W. (2001a). *Technical manual, Woodcock–Johnson III.* Itasca, IL: Riverside.

McGrew, K. S., & Woodcock, R. W. (2001b). *Technical manual, Woodcock–Johnson III Tests of Achievement.* Itasca, IL: Riverside.

Woodcock, R. W. (1998). Extending the *Gf–Gc* theory into practice. In J. J. McArdle & R. W. Woodcock (Eds.), *Human cognitive abilities in theory and practice.* Mahwah, NJ: Erlbaum.

Woodcock, R. W., McGrew, K. S., & Mather, N. (2001). *Woodcock–Johnson III.* Itasca, IL: Riverside.

Additional Readings for Professionals

Evans, J. E., Floyd, R. G., McGrew, K. S., & Leforgee, M. H. (2001). The relations between measures of Cattell–Horn–Carroll (CHC) cognitive abilities and reading achievement during childhood and adolescence. *School Psychology Review, 31,* 246–262.

Flanagan, D. P., Genshaft, J. L., & Harrison, P. L. (Eds.). (1997). *Contemporary intellectual assessment: Theories, tests, and issues.* New York: Guilford.

Flanagan, D. P., & Ortiz, S. O. (2002). Best practices in intellectual assessment: Future directions. In A. Thomas & J. Grimes (Eds.), *Best practices in school psychology IV* (Vol. 2, pp. 1351–1373). Bethesda, MD: National Association of School Psychologists.

Reschly, D. J., & Grimes, J. P. (2002). Best practices in intellectual assessment. In A. Thomas & J. Grimes (Eds.), *Best practices in school psychology IV* (Vol. 1, pp. 3–20). Bethesda, MD: National Association of School Psychologists.

Salvia, J., & Ysseldyke, J. E. (1995). *Assessment.* Boston: Houghton Mifflin.

THEODORE A. CHRIST
JENNIFER L. RICE

Writing (Written Language)

CURRICULUM-BASED MEASUREMENT

Curriculum-based measurement (CBM) is a progress monitoring procedure that allows educators to repeatedly assess a child's academic performance. CBM utilizes materials based on the curriculum in which the child is currently being taught and, therefore, offers a direct evaluation of skills that the student has been expected to acquire in the classroom. Using curriculum-based measurement procedures has several advantages over norm-referenced measures owing to the possibility of multiple probe development, ease and brevity of administration, and the potential for progress monitoring (Shapiro, 1996; Shinn, 1989). Writing probes can be easily developed by a teacher or school psychologist, and an unlimited number of probes can be developed.

One disadvantage to using curriculum-based measurement of writing is the lack of available norms and paucity of information regarding typical student writing. One option for correcting this problem is to construct a norming sample in a student's school district or classroom. Shapiro (1996) suggests administering written expression probes to 5 to 10 other students in the same grade who are identified by their teacher as average or typical writers. The mean or median of these scores can serve as an average score by which to compare other students' writing performance. In addition, writing probes can be administered to an entire class to determine class norms and to screen for writing deficits.

Psychometric Properties of CBM

The technical adequacy for the CBM of written expression has been thoroughly examined (Deno, Marston, & Mirkin, 1982). To determine the most useful criteria that would discriminate "good" writers from "poor" writers, six outcome measures (e.g., number of words written, number of words spelled correctly, number of correct letter sequences, number of mature word choices, number of large words written, and Hunt's average *t*-unit length) were correlated with three criterion measures (e.g., Test of Written Language, the Developmental Sentence Scoring System, and the Stanford Achievement Test—Language). Results indicated that total words written, words spelled correctly, correct letter sequences, and mature words were highly correlated with the criterion measures. Therefore, many psychologists and researchers now use these three criteria to examine written language probes.

CBM can be used to differentiate between typical learners and students with learning disabilities, which indicates a possible use for CBM in educational decisions related to the delivery of special education services. There has been much criticism directed at norm-referenced testing owing to the lack of information provided by these tests that would assist with instructional decision making. The CBM was developed to address this concern, and its use in identifying specific areas of skill remediation is gaining support.

Reliability estimates for total words written, words spelled correctly, and correct letter sequences in written expression have been found to be moderately to highly reliable (see Shinn, 1989, for a review). Some concerns with the research on the reliability of CBM include the homogeneity of the participating groups and a lack of data on standard errors of measurement. With these concerns in mind, the data do support the reliability of CBM for all subject areas, with written expression estimates lower than in any other area. The fact that reliability estimates are lower for written expression may be due to the complexity of the writing process and the numerous skills that are required to produce a written product.

Assessment and Scoring Procedures

Shinn (1989) and Shapiro (1996) have standardized the procedures for the administration of CBM of written expression. This administration can occur in group or individual format and students are instructed to write a story based upon a story starter (see below for examples of story starters). Instructions defined by Shinn (1989) include the following steps:

Say to the student: "I want you to write a story. I am going to read a sentence to you first, and then I want you to write a short story about what happens. You will have 1 minute to think about the story you will write and then have 3 minutes to write it. Do your best work. If you don't know how to spell a word, you should guess. Are there any questions? For the next minute, think about... [insert story starter]." After 1 minute is up, say "Start writing." After 3 minutes are up, say "Stop and put your pencil down."

Typical scoring procedures for written expression probes include four options: (a) total words written, (b) words spelled correctly, (c) total letters written, and (d) correct word sequences. Total Words Written includes a count of all words that are written, including misspelled words, proper names, and nouns, but excludes written numbers. Words Spelled Correctly includes all correctly spelled words that are recognizable in the English language disregarding the intent of the word in the story. Total Letters Written includes all of the letters of the words that met the criterion for total words written. Correct Word Sequences considers two words written side by side that are spelled correctly and are grammatically correct, excluding numbers. In addition, educators can examine written language probes for grammatical errors and deletions, such as capitalization, punctuation, and use of adjectives and adverbs.

Story starters used in written language probes can be developed on any topic area. The goal of the story starter is to provide a student (or groups of students) with an idea for a short story. The probes can be fanciful (i.e., "The best thing about a talking dog is ... ") or reality-based (i.e., "When I grow up I would like to be ... ").

See also: Academic Interventions for Written Language and Grammar; Written Language Learning Disabilities

BIBLIOGRAPHY

Deno, S. L., Marston, D., & Mirkin, P. K. (1982). Valid measurement procedures for continuous evaluation of written expression. *Exceptional Children, 48,* 368–371.

Shapiro, E. S. (1996). *Academic skills problems: Direct assessment and intervention.* New York: Guilford.

Shinn, M. R. (1989). *Curriculum-based measurement: Assessing special children.* New York: Guilford.

Additional Reading for Nonprofessionals

Rathvon, N. (1999). *Effective school interventions: Strategies for enhancing academic and social competence.* New York: Guilford.

Additional Readings for Professionals

Daly, E. J., & Murdoch, A. (2000). Direct observation in the assessment of academic skills problems. In E. S. Shapiro & T. R. Kratochwill (Eds.), *Behavioral assessment in schools: Theory, research, and clinical foundations* (pp. 46–77). New York: Guilford.

Fuchs, L. S., & Fuchs, D. (2001). Analogue assessment of academic skills: Curriculum-based measurement and performance assessment. In E. S. Shapiro & T. R. Kratochwill (Eds.), *Behavioral assessment in schools: Theory, research, and clinical foundations* (pp. 168–201). New York: Guilford.

MERILEE McCURDY

Written Language Learning Disabilities

Written language is divided among the components of written expression, spelling, and handwriting. It is characterized as being the most sophisticated and complex of all the parts of the language system (Lerner, 2003). Writing involves the integration of the previously learned skills of listening, speaking, and reading. The activity of writing requires mental conceptualization, thought organization, and the physical transference of thoughts to paper via handwriting or word processing. With these skill areas in mind, it is not difficult to understand why many students with learning disabilities have problems acquiring written language abilities, and that these problems often persist into adulthood (Troia, Graham, & Harris, 1999; Vogel, 1998).

WRITTEN EXPRESSION

Individuals with learning disabilities often lack many of the prerequisite skills needed for successful written expression. These skills include abilities in spoken language, reading, spelling, handwriting, knowledge of rules of grammar, and cognitive approaches to organizing and planning for writing. Thus, the written products of individuals with learning disabilities tend to be short, to lack organization and continuity, and to contain "atomized," random thoughts rather than rich and thoroughly developed themes. Their writing also tends to be replete with incomplete and run-on sentences, *nonstandard verb and pronoun forms,* and *other problems with the conventions of standard written English.*

EMOTIONAL SUPPORT AND MOTIVATION

In order to alleviate their typical anxieties toward writing, individuals with disabilities need emotional support, encouragement, and motivation. Parents and writing teachers can help students gain confidence by finding some aspect of the students' writing to praise. They can build confidence by allowing beginning writers the opportunity to explore ideas without undue concern about the mechanics of punctuation, spelling, and grammar. Once students have begun to develop ideas with some organization and specificity, the need for standard forms can be introduced. Only in the editing/proofreading stage of the writing process should the students be asked to concentrate on mechanics. Students can thus focus on planning and developing their ideas without the fear of "making mistakes." During editing and revising, they can be taught the use of standard forms.

Motivation can be fostered in a number of ways. One way is to provide activities with real-world connection or application. If the content of the writing is important to the student, then he/she will be more motivated to communicate that content in writing to others. For example, students writing a booklet for publication about their school or community history will work hard to make the writing clear and correct. Or, making a young sports fan write a letter to his/her favorite athlete can promote usage of proper grammar and syntax.

STRATEGIES TO IMPROVE WRITTEN LANGUAGE SKILLS

To assist students with learning disabilities in acquiring writing skills, it has been suggested that they be provided purposeful writing tasks, with techniques to help promote structure and organization (Graham, Harris, & Larsen, 2001). It is also important to nurture the students' confidence. Thus, parents and teachers of students with learning disabilities need to provide activities that the students can master, slowly adding more challenging tasks as the students acquire the prerequisite skills. The following teaching strategies have been shown effective for improving the written language skills of students with disabilities and to help the students become more competent and confident writers.

Writing Conversations

An effective method for engaging students in writing is to design a written conversation in which two students, or a student and a teacher, or a child and a parent, sit near each other and engage in "conversation." However, this conversation can only be written, not spoken. Thus, the two communicators give each other written rather than oral messages. Writing conversations help stimulate students with learning disabilities to record their thoughts on paper.

Personal Journals

Students practice their writing skills by recording day-to-day accounts of events in their lives and their feelings about those events in their personal journals. A composition notebook can serve as a journal wherein daily entries are written. Teachers may expand on the autobiographical nature of the journals by providing thought-provoking statements, to which students respond with journal entries. Although reviewed by teachers, journal writing typically is free writing with no rules or format. As such, students can explore their own thoughts and experiment with their own writing styles without fear of criticism.

Writing Portfolios

Slightly more sophisticated than the personal journal is the writing portfolio. It may contain some selections from the personal journal but will also contain other pieces of writing. The teacher may assign a certain number of required entries for the portfolio, allowing the student to choose which selections to include within specified time frames. The portfolio becomes the selective record of the student's writing over time. Indicative of the student's growth as a writer, it also provides a type of publication that can be shared with parents, classmates, and the school community. The physical product itself can instill pride in both the student and his/her parents.

Models

To enable students to move from the tendency to write random, disorganized thoughts, teachers can use models that demonstrate well-developed and organized writing contrasted with examples of writing that lacks these qualities. Using student writing (always anonymous and never from the same class) for the model examples helps the students to relate to the pieces and prevents the intimidating result that professional writing can produce. In addition to providing a structure that students can emulate, student models can stimulate thought.

Process Writing

Students should be taught that writing is a process with several stages; thus writing assignments need to reflect these stages. Writing must be planned with significant time devoted to arriving at an idea, deriving a thesis, and organizing the content. During the planning process, students can organize their ideas with traditional outlines, tree outlines, graphic organizers,

or with some personal strategy that enables them to represent the structure of their writing. Students next write the initial drafts of their papers followed by editing and revising. Several drafts may be needed before reaching the final proofreading stage. An essay assignment can be a daunting task, especially for individuals with disabilities. Dividing the task into smaller assignments makes it much more doable, and enables the students to concentrate on one aspect of the assignment at a time.

Cooperative Learning

Cooperative learning can be used to enhance the process writing approach. Students can be divided into groups of three or four that not only provide a real audience but valuable feedback on the effectiveness of the writing. In their peer response groups, students evaluate the content and organization of papers during the rough draft stage. Each student in the group reads his/her paper aloud while group members write comments on various aspects of the content and the overall effectiveness of the paper. The members give their written responses to the reader for consideration as he/she revises the paper.

Another cooperative learning strategy that has produced good results for basic writers is cooperative editing. With this method, students are randomly placed into groups to edit student papers (not from their own class) that contain nonstandard grammatical errors. Students are instructed to find the errors, correct them, and supply the appropriate rules. To facilitate the process, they can use error sheets and grammar books. Students must work together, arrive at consensus, and turn in one corrected paper from the group. This method has produced significant improvements in students' own written grammar in basic writing classes (Minchew & Amos, 2000).

Use of Technology

At school and at home, access to PC-based word processing programs can greatly aid students' attempts at written expression. Use of software that checks spelling and grammar can assist the student in developing a more acceptable written product. Students can edit without the tedium of recopying and thus may make more revisions. Word processing combined with instruction in revision has been shown to produce substantive revisions in students with learning disabilities (MacArthur, 1996).

Publishing Student Writing

Teachers of students with learning disabilities can generate enthusiasm among their students by devising writing assignments that are real. Projects that will eventually result in publication assume real-world significance. Students may be asked to produce a class newsletter, to edit a booklet of class essays, or to write a letter to the school or community newspaper in response to a local issue. Teachers can also coordinate with other teachers on collaborative projects. For example, students in an English class can write advertisements for a plant sale hosted by the horticulture class or edit a book of recipes developed by the home economics class. A simple, but effective, type of publication is the display of student products on the bulletin board.

Writing, like reading and mathematics, requires much practice for skill mastery. Students with learning disabilities, because of their characteristic struggles with the writing process, need more, not fewer, opportunities to hone their skills. They need strong and frequent emotional support and encouragement. They also need time and the patience of the parents and teachers who work with them.

See also: Academic Interventions for Written Language and Grammar; Curriculum-Based Measurement

BIBLIOGRAPHY

Graham, S., Harris, K. R., & Larsen, L. (2001). Prevention and intervention of writing difficulties for students with learning disabilities. *Learning Disabilities Research & Practice, 16,* 74–84.

Lerner, J. (2003). *Learning disabilities: Theories, diagnosis, and teaching strategies* (9th ed.). Boston: Houghton Mifflin.

MacArthur, C. A. (1996). Using technology to enhance the writing processes of students with learning disabilities. *Journal of Learning Disabilities, 29,* 344–354.

Minchew, S. S., & Amos, N. G. (2000). Cooperative editing: An effective strategy for error reduction in remedial freshman composition. *Research in the Schools, 7,* 43–52.

Troia, G., Graham, S., & Harris, K. R. (1999). Teaching students with learning disabilities to mindfully plan when writing. *Exceptional Children, 65,* 235–252.

Vogel, S. A. (1998). Adults with learning disabilities. In S. A. Vogel & S. Reder (Eds.), *Learning disabilities, literacy, and adult education* (pp. 5–8). Baltimore: Brookes.

Additional Reading for Nonprofessionals

Richards, R. G., & Richards, E. I. (2000). *Eli, the boy who hated to write: Understanding dysgraphia.* Riverside, CA: RET Center Press.

Additional Readings for Professionals

Harris, K. R., & Graham, S. (1997). *Making the writing process work: Strategies for composition and self-regulation.* Cambridge, MA: Brookline.

Hillocks, G. (1986). *Research on written composition.* Urbana, IL: National Conference on Research in English.

G. Franklin Elrod
Sue S. Minchew

Contributors

K. Angeleque Akin-Little, Benerd School of Education, University of the Pacific, 3601 Pacific Ave. Stockton, CA 95211

Candice A. Alfano, Maryland Center for Anxiety Disorders, Department of Psychology, University of Maryland, College Park, MD 20742

Keith D. Allen, University of Nebraska Medical Center, Munroe-Meyer Institute, 985450 Nebraska Medical Center, Omaha, NE 68198-5450

Jessica D. Allin, Department of Educational Psychology and Counseling, University of Tennessee, Claxton A525, Knoxville, TN 37996-3452

Cynthia M. Anderson, Ph.D., Department of Psychology, Behavior Analysis Program, West Virginia University, P.O. Box 6040, Morgantown, WV 26506

Maria E. A. Armento, Department of Psychology, University of Tennessee, Knoxville, TN 37996-0900

Kevin J. Armstrong, Department of Psychology, Mississippi State University, P.O. Box 6161, Mississippi State, MS 39762

Sherry K. Bain, Department of Educational Psychology and Counseling, University of Tennessee, Claxton A525, Knoxville, TN 37996-3452

Candice Barr, Department of Counseling, Educational Psychology, and Special Education, School Psychology Program, Mississippi State University, P.O. Box 9727, Mississippi State, MS 39762

Anjali Barretto, Department of Special Education, Gonzaga University, Spokane, WA 99258-0015

Laura M. Baylot, Department of Counseling, Educational Psychology, and Special Education, School Psychology Program, Mississippi State University, P.O. Box 9727, Mississippi State, MS 39762

Andrea M. Begotka, University of Wisconsin—Milwaukee, 358 Pearse Hall, Milwaukee, WI 53201

Deborah C. Beidel, Department of Psychology, Maryland Center for Anxiety Disorders, University of Maryland, College Park, MD 20742

Phillip J. Belfiore, Education Division, Mercyhurst College, Erie, PA 16546

Sherry Mee Bell, Department of Theory and Practice in Teacher Education, University of Tennessee, Claxton Complex A414, Knoxville, TN 37996-3442

Kimberly D. Bellipanni, Department of Psychology, University of Southern Mississippi, P.O. Box 5025, Hattiesburg, MS 39406

Mike Bonner, Department of Psychology, University of Nebraska at Omaha, 6001 Dodge Street, Omaha, NE 68182-0274

Kathryn M. Benes, Clinical Program, Catholic Social Services, 8101 "O" Street, Suite S-111, Lincoln, NE 68510

Sara E. Bolt, 350 Elliott Hall, 75 East River Rd., Minneapolis, MN 55455

Greg G. Brannigan, University of Missouri—St. Louis, St. Louis, MO 63121

Melissa A. Bray, School Psychology Program, University of Connecticut, Storrs, CT 06269-2064

Jacqueline Beine Brown, Department of Psychology, University of Southern Mississippi, P.O. Box 5025, Hattiesburg, MS 39406

Rachel Brown-Chidsey, School Psychology Program, University of Southern Maine, 400 Bailey Hall, Gorham, ME 04038

Tonya Sartor Butler, Girls and Boys Town, 13606 Flanagan Blvd, Youth Care Building, BoysTown, NE 68010

Candice N. Carpenter, Department of Psychology, University of Tennessee, Knoxville, TN 37996-0900

Craig S. Cashwell, Department of Counseling and Educational Development, School of Education, University of North Carolina—Greensboro, P.O. Box 6171, Greensboro, NC 27402

Tammy H. Cashwell, Department of Counseling and Educational Development, School of Education, University of North Carolina—Greensboro, P.O. Box 6171, Greensboro, NC 27402

Gary L. Cates, Psychology Department, 1433 Physical Sciences Building, Eastern Illinois University, Charleston, IL 61920

Emile Catignani, Department of Sport and Leisure Studies, University of Tennessee, 1914 Andy Holt Ave., Knoxville, TN 37996-2700

Karla Carmichael, Program in Counselor Education, University of Alabama, P.O. Box 0231, Tuscaloosa, AL 35487

Theodore J. Christ, Department of Psychology, University of Southern Mississippi, P.O. Box 5025, Hattiesburg, MS 39406

Kent Coffey, Department of Counseling, Educational Psychology, and Special Education, Mississippi State University, P.O. Box 9705, Mississippi State, MS 39762

Mark S. Cotter, Ed.D., College of Education, Health, and Human Sciences, University of Tennessee, 317 Claxton Complex, Knoxville, TN 37996

David B. Creel, Pennington Biomedical Research Center, Louisiana State University, 6400 Perkins Rd., Baton Rouge, LA 70808

Edward J. Daly III, School Psychology Program, University of Nebraska—Lincoln, 234 Teachers College Hall, Lincoln, NE 68508

L. Scott Decker, University of Missouri—St. Louis, St. Louis, MO 63121

K. Mark Derby, Gonzaga University, 502 E. Boone Ave., A.D. Box 0025, Spokane, WA 99258

Sandy D. Devlin, Department of Counseling, Educational Psychology, and Special Education, Mississippi State University, P.O. Box 9705, Mississippi State, MS 39762

Denise M. DeZolt, Walden University, 155 Fifth Avenue South, Minneapolis, MN 55401

Joel F. Diambra, Department of Educational Psychology and Counseling, University of Tennessee, 449 Claxton Complex, Knoxville, TN 37996-3452

Karen L. Dittmer-McMahon, Children's Hospital, Omaha, Children's Family Support Center, 8200 Dodge St., Omaha, NE 68114-4113

R. Anthony Doggett, Department of Counseling, Educational Psychology, and Special Education, School Psychology Program, Mississippi State University, P.O. Box 9727, Mississippi State, MS 39762

Theresa A. Doggett, Starkville Public Schools, Starkville, MS 39759

Shannon E. Dowd, School Psychology Program, University of Nebraska—Lincoln, 234 Teachers College Hall, Lincoln, NE 68508

Melanie DuBard, Department of Psychology, University of Southern Mississippi, P.O. Box 5025, Hattiesburg, MS 39406

George J. DuPaul, College of Education, Lehigh University, 111 Research Drive, Bethlehem, PA 18015

Tanya L. Eckert, Department of Psychology, 430 Huntington Hall, Syracuse University, Syracuse, NY 13244

Ron P. Edwards, Department of Psychology, University of Southern Mississippi, Southern Station, P.O. Box 5025, Hattiesburg, MS 39406

G. Franklin Elrod, Department of Counseling, Educational Psychology, and Special Education, Mississippi State University, P.O. Box 9727, Mississippi State, MS 39762

William P. Erchul, Department of Psychology, North Carolina State University, Poe 640, P.O. Box 7801, Raleigh, NC 27695

Gregory E. Everett, Department of Psychology, University of Southern Mississippi, Southern Station, P.O. Box 5025, Hatticsburg, MS 39406

Terry S. Falcomata, Department of School Psychology, University of Iowa, 361 Lindquist, Iowa City, IA 52242-1569

Daniel Fasko, Jr., Division of Educational Foundations and Inquiry, Bowling Green State University, 550 Education Bldg., Bowling Green, OH 43403-0251

Catherine A. Fiorello, School Psychology Program, Temple University, 1301 Cecil B. Moore Ave. RA-260, Philadelphia, PA 19122-6091

Leslee A. Fisher, University of Tennessee, 336 HPER Building, 1914 Andy Holt Ave., Knoxville, TN 37996-2700

Leanne M. Fitzgerald, Centre for Addiction and Mental Health, Queen Street Site, Toronto, Ontario, Canada M6J 1H4

Dawn P. Flanagan, St. John's University, 8000 Utopia Parkway, Jamaica, NY 11439

Michael C. Forcade, Past Chair, NASP Ethics Committee, Hamilton County Educational Service Center, 11083 Hamilton Ave., Cincinnati, OH 45232

Nancy Foster, Girls and Boys Town, 13603 Flanagan Blvd., Boys Town, NE 68010

Jennifer T. Freeland, School of Education, Department of Educational and School Psychology, Indiana State University, Terre Haute, IN 47809

Patrick C. Friman, Girls and Boys Town, 13603 Flanagan Blvd., Boys Town, NE 68010

Michael J. Furlong, Gevirtz Graduate School of Education, Center for School-Based Youth Development, University of California—Santa Barbara, Santa Barbara, CA 93106

Paul E. Garfinkel, President and CEO, Centre for Addiction and Mental Health, Queen Street Site, Toronto, Ontario, Canada M6J 1H4

Arnold P. Goldstein, Department of Psychology, Syracuse University, 430 Huntington Hall, Syracuse, NY 13244

Andrea D. Hale, Department of Educational Psychology and Counseling, University of Tennessee, Claxton A525, Knoxville, TN 37996-3452

Justin Hall, Department of Psychology, University of Tennessee, Knoxville, TN 37996-0900

Kimberly R. Hall, Department of Counseling, Educational Psychology, and Special Education, Mississippi State University, P.O. Box 9727, Mississippi State, MS 39762

Michael L. Handwerk, Father Flanagan's Boys Home, Girls and Boys Town, 13603 Flanagan Blvd., Boys Town, NE 68010

Patti L. Harrison, School Psychology Program, University of Alabama, Tuscaloosa, AL 35487

Jesse Hartley, Department of Psychology, Mississippi State University, P.O. Box 6161, Mississippi State MS 39762

Carlen Henington, Department of Counseling, Educational Psychology, and Special Education, School Psychology Program, Mississippi State University, P.O. Box 9727, Mississippi State, MS 39762

Mary A. Hermann, Department of Counseling, Educational Psychology, and Special Education, Mississippi State University, P.O. Box 9727, Mississippi State, MS 39762

W. Jeff Hinton, Department of Counseling, Educational Psychology, and Special Education, Mississippi State University, P.O. Box 9727, Mississippi State, MS 39762

John M. Hintze, School Psychology Program, University of Massachusetts at Amherst, 362 Hills South, Amherst, MA 01003

Nicholas E. Hoda, School Psychology Program, Mississippi State University, P.O. Box 9727, Mississippi State, MS 39762

Sacky Holdiness, Department of Counseling, Educational Psychology, and Special Education, Mississippi State University, P.O. Box 9727, Mississippi State, MS 39762

Chris Horton, Department of Counseling, Educational Psychology, and Special Education, Mississippi State University, P.O. Box 9727, Mississippi State, MS 39762

Duane M. Isava, School Psychology Program, 5208 University of Oregon, Eugene, OR 97403-5208

William R. Jenson, University of Utah, 1705 East Campus Center Drive, MBH 327, Salt Lake City, UT 84114

Shane R. Jimerson, Gevirtz Graduate School of Education, Counseling, Clinical, and School Psychology, Child and Adolescent Development, University of California—Santa Barbara, 2208 Phelps Hall, Santa Barbara, CA 93106-9490

Christopher A. Kearney, Department of Psychology, University of Nevada, Las Vegas, 4505 Maryland Parkway, Las Vegas, NV 89154-5030

Thomas J. Kehle, School Psychology Program, University of Connecticut, Storrs, CT 06269-2064

Lori Kruger, University of Nebraska Medical Center, Munroe-Meyer Institute, 985450 Nebraska Medical Center, Omaha, NE 68198-5450

Anisha Kurian-Philip, Temple University, 14 Bromley Place, Bloomfield, NJ 07003

Nigel O. Lay, Department of Psychology, University of Tennessee, Knoxville, TN 37996-0900

Lakisha Lewis, University of Nebraska Medical Center, Munroe-Meyer Institute, 985450 Nebraska Medical Center, Omaha, NE 68198-5450

Stephen G. Little, Benerd School of Education, University of the Pacific, 3601 Pacific Ave., Stockton, CA 95211

Kristi S. Lorah, College of Education, Lehigh University, 111 Research Drive, Bethlehem, PA 18015

John R. Lutzker, Division of Violence Prevention, Prevention Development and Evaluation Branch, National Center for Injury Prevention and Control, Centers for Disease Control and Prevention, 4770 Buford Highway, NE, Mailstop K60, Atlanta, GA 30341

Elizabeth A. Lyons, Department of Psychology, University of Southern Mississippi, P.O. Box 5025, Hattiesburg, MS 39406

John C. Malone, Department of Psychology, University of Tennessee, Knoxville, TN 37996-0900

Brook A. Marcks, Department of Psychology, University of Wisconsin—Milwaukee, P.O. Box 413, Milwaukee, WI 53201

Emma Martin, University of Oregon, Eugine, OR 97903

Elizabeth McCallum, School Psychology Program, University of Tennessee, 527 Claxton Addition, Knoxville, TN 37919

R. Steve McCallum, Department of Educational Psychology and Counseling, University of Tennessee, Claxton Complex A526, Knoxville, TN 37996-3452

Nancy G. McCarley, Department of Psychology, Mississippi State University, P.O. Box 6161, Mississippi State, MS 39762

Dalene M. McCloskey, 15815 N. 43rd Street, Phoenix, AZ 85032

Stephanie H. McConaughy, Department of Psychiatry, University of Vermont, 1 South Prospect Street, Burlington, VT 05401-3454

Merilee McCurdy, School Psychology Program, University of Nebraska—Lincoln, 234 Teachers College Hall, Lincoln, NE

Aimee T. McGeorge, Department of Psychology, University of Southern Mississippi, P.O. Box 5025, Hattiesburg, MS 39406

T. F. McLaughlin, Department of Special Education, Gonzaga University, Spokane, WA 99258-0015

Kenneth W. Merrell, Ph.D., School Psychology Program, 5208 University of Oregon, Eugene, OR 97403-5208

Noach Milgram, Professor Emeritus, Tel Aviv University, Dean, Faculty of Social Sciences & Humanities, College of Judea & Samaria, Ariel 44837 Israel, P.O. Box 157, Kochav Yair 44864 Israel

David N. Miller, Centennial School of Lehigh University, 2196 Avenue C, LVIP #1, Bethlehem, PA 18017

Raymond G. Miltenberger, Department of Psychology, North Dakota State University, Fargo, ND 58105

Sue S. Minchew, Office of the Dean, College of Education, Mississippi State University, P.O. Box 9727, Mississippi State, MS 39762

Diana Moyer, Department of Instructional Technology and Educational Studies, University of Tennessee, 338 HPER Bldg., Knoxville, TN 37996-2700

Michael M. Mueller, Director, School Consultation Services and Center for Applied Research, May South, 1770 The Exchange, Suite 140, Atlanta, GA 30339

Christine E. Neddenriep, University of Nebraska—Omaha, 16901 Oakmont Drive, #17, Omaha, NE 68136

D. Joe Olmi, Department of Psychology, University of Southern Mississippi, P.O. Box 5025, Hattiesburg, MS 39406

Daniel E. Olympia, University of Utah, 1705 East Campus Center Drive, MBH 327, Salt Lake City, UT 84114

Samuel O. Ortiz, St. John's University, 8000 Utopia Parkway, Jamaica, NY 11439

Charles D. Palmer, Department of Counseling, Educational Psychology, and Special Education, Mississippi State University, P.O. Box 9727, Mississippi State, MS 39762

Stephanie Paulos, Department of Educational Psychology, University of Texas—Austin, 1 University Station, D5800, Austin, TX 78712-0383

Jodi Polaha, University of Nebraska Medical Center, Munroe-Meyer Institute, 985450 Nebraska Medical Center, Omaha, NE 68198-5450

Scott Poland, Director of Psychological Services, Cypress-Fairbanks ISD, 14103 Reo St., Houston, TX 77040

Joseph Prus, Department of Psychology, Winthrop University, Rock Hill, SC 29733

John Rapp, Texana MHMR Behavior Treatment and Training Center, 5901 Long Drive, Suite 312, Houston, TX

Amy M. Rees, Lewis & Clark College, Graduate School of Education, 0615 S.W. Palatine Hill Road, Portland, OR 97219

Jennifer A. Renn, Indiana State University, School of Education Department of Educational and School Psychology, Terre Haute, IN 47809

Ginger Rhode, Davis County School District, Farmington, UT

Cynthia A. Riccio, Department of Educational Psychology, Texas A&M University, TAMU MS 4225, College Station, TX 77843-4225

Jennifer L. Rice, Department of Psychology, University of Southern Mississippi, P.O. Box 5025, Hattiesburg, MS 39406

Dannell S. Roberts, University of Southern Mississippi, P.O. Box 7585, Hattiesburg, MS 39406

Gabrielle Roberts, Department of Educational Psychology, University of Texas—Austin, 1 University Station, D5800, Austin, TX 78712-0383

Daniel R. Robinson, Department of Educational Psychology, University of Texas—Austin, 1 University Station, D5800, Austin, TX 78712-0383

Sheri L. Robinson, Department of Educational Psychology, University of Texas—Austin, 1 University Station, D5800, Austin, TX 78712-0383

Melissa L. Rosenblatt, Department of Psychology, Syracuse University, 430 Huntington Hall, Syracuse, NY 13244

Blair D. Rosenthal, Department of Psychology, Syracuse University, 430 Huntington Hall, Syracuse, NY 13244

Amy E. Rzeznikiewicz, Pennington Biomedical Research Center, Louisiana State University, 6400 Perkins Road, Baton Rouge, LA 70808

Dorothy Scattone, Department of Child Development, University of Mississippi Medical Center, Jackson, MS

G. Thomas Schanding, Jr., Department of Psychology, University of Southern Mississippi, P.O. Box 5025, Hattiesburg, MS 39406

Melissa D. Scoggins, Department of Psychology, University of Southern Mississippi, P.O. Box 5025, Hattiesburg, MS 39406

Anitra Shelton, Department of Counseling, Educational Psychology, and Special Education, School Psychology Program, Mississippi State University, P.O. Box 9727, Mississippi State, MS 39762

Carl Sheperis, Department of Counseling, Educational Psychology, and Special Education, Mississippi State University, P.O. Box 9727, Mississippi State, MS 39762

Shelly F. Sheperis, Department of Counseling, Educational Psychology, and Special Education, Mississippi State University, P.O. Box 9727, Mississippi State, MS 39762

Susan M. Sheridan, School Psychology Program, University of Nebraska, 234 Teachers College Hall, Lincoln, NE 68508

Mark D. Shriver, University of Nebraska Medical Center, Munroe-Meyer Institute, 985450 Nebraska Medical Center, Omaha, NE 68198-5450

Amy L. Skinner, Rehabilitation Counselor Education, University of Tennessee, A207 Claxton Complex, Knoxville, TN 37996-3452

Lori Chambers Slay, Department of Counseling, Educational Psychology, and Special Education, School Psychology Program, Mississippi State University, Starkville, MS 39762

Stephen W. Smith, Department of Special Education, University of Florida, G315 Norman Hall, Gainesville, FL 32611

Alicia Soliz, Gevirtz Graduate School of Education, Center for School-Based Youth Development, University of California—Santa Barbara, Santa Barbara, CA 93106

Samuel Y. Song, School Psychology Program, University of Nebraska—Lincoln, 114 Teachers College Hall, Lincoln, NE 68508

Charles L. Spirrison, Department of Psychology, Mississippi State University, P.O. Box 6161, Mississippi State, MS 39762

Mark W. Steege, School Psychology Program, University of Southern Maine, 400 Bailey Hall, Gorham, ME 04038

Heather E. Sterling-Turner, Department of Psychology, University of Southern Mississippi, P.O. Box 5025, Hattiesburg, MS 39406

Jeannine R. Studer, Department of Educational Psychology and Counseling, School Counseling Program, University of Tennessee, 438 Claxton Complex, Knoxville, TN 37922

George Sugai, College of Education, Department of Special Education, University of Oregon, Eugene, OR 97403

Sara E. Sytsma-Jordan, Department of Psychology, University of Southern Mississippi, P.O. Box 5025, Hattiesburg, MS 39406

Mark Thomas, Mississippi State University, P.O. Box 802, Mississippi State, MS 39762

Daniel H. Tingstrom, Department of Psychology, University of Southern Mississippi, P.O. Box 5025, Hattiesburg, MS 39406

Tary J. Tobin, College of Education, University of Oregon, Eugene, OR 97403

Dana M. Trahant, Department of Psychology, University of Southern Mississippi, P.O. Box 5025, Hattiesburg, MS 39406

Oanh Tran, Gevirtz Graduate School of Education, Center for School-Based Youth Development, University of California—Santa Barbara, Santa Barbara, CA 93106

Michael Twohig, Department of Psychology/298, University of Nevada, Reno, Reno, NV 89557

Linda Anne Valle, Division of Violence Prevention, Prevention Development and Evaluation Branch, National Center for Injury Prevention and Control, Centers for Disease Control and Prevention, 4770 Buford Highway, NE, Mailstop K60, Atlanta, GA 30341

José A. Villalba, Department of Counseling and Educational Development, University of North Carolina—Greensboro, 228 Curry Building, P.O. Box 6170, Greensboro, NC 27402

Rachel J. Valleley, University of Nebraska Medical Center, Munroe-Meyer Institute, 985450 Nebraska Medical Center, Omaha, NE 68198-5450

Timothy R. Vollmer, Psychology Department, University of Florida, Gainesville, Florida 32611

Penny Ward, Department of Counseling, Educational Psychology, and Special Education, School Psychology Program, Mississippi State University, Mississippi State, P.O. Box 9727, MS 39762

Tara S. Wass, Department of Child and Family Studies, University of Tennessee, 2155 S. Cumberland Ave., Knoxville, TN 37996

Adam D. Weaver, University of Nebraska Medical Center, Munroe-Meyer Institute, 985450 Nebraska Medical Center, Omaha, NE 68198-5450

Kimberly P. Weber, Department of Special Education, Gonzaga University, Spokane, WA 99258-0015

Chad T. Wetterneck, University of Wisconsin—Milwaukee, 358 Pearse Hall, Milwaukee, WI 53201

Vernon Wiehe, Buckhorn Professor of Child Welfare, College of Social Work, University of Kentucky, Lexington, KY 40506

Susan M. Wilczynski, Munroe-Meyer Institute, 985450 Nebraska Medical Center, Omaha, NE 68198-5450

Donald A. Williamson, Pennington Biomedical Research Center, Louisiana State University, 6400 Perkins Road, Baton Rouge, LA 70808

Douglas W. Woods, University of Wisconsin—Milwaukee, 213 Garland Hall, Milwaukee, WI 53201

Elizabeth M. Young, Department of Nutrition, University of Tennessee, 1215 Cumberland Ave., 213A Jessie Harris Building, Knoxville, TN 37996

J. Scott Young, Department of Counselor Education, Educational Psychology, and Special Education, PO Box 9727, Mississippi State, MS 39762

James E. Ysseldyke, Educational Psychology, University of Minnesota, 204 Burton Hall, 178 Pillsbury Drive SE, Minneapolis, MN 55455-0211

Uu

Under- and Overachievement

Our notion of under- and overachievement often is based on at least two assumptions: (1) that a child's ability to learn can be accurately measured in the first place (generally measured with an intelligence test), and (2) measured ability (an intelligence test score) can be compared to measured achievement to determine whether a child is an under- or an overachiever. For example, a student who scores in the average range on an intelligence test would be expected to score in the average range on an achievement test, presumably because his/her learning rate should be average. Alternately, those students whose achievement exceeds their intelligence test score would be considered overachievers and those students whose achievement scores fall below their intelligence test score (Intelligence Quotient [IQ]) would be considered underachievers.

This simple model of predicting learning has caused people to characterize students as under- and overachievers on the basis of educational assessments. With such labels, there is an implied assumption that a child's achievement or learning rate is stable or consistent. Thus, a child who underachieves would be expected to underachieve across subject areas (e.g., mathematics and reading), environments (e.g., in Mrs. Smith's class and Mrs. Jones's class), instructional approaches (e.g., direct instruction vs. discovery learning), and time (e.g., during the first week of school and during the last week of school). Similarly, an overachiever would be expected to consistently overachieve across all these contexts. Although this conception of under- and overachievement is alluring because of its simplicity and the widespread availability of psychoeducational tests, there are a number of problems with this approach.

ALL CHILDREN DISPLAY UNDER- AND OVERACHIEVEMENT

Instead of thinking categorically about under- and overachiev*ers*, it is more useful to consider instances of under- and overachiev*ement*. This approach still requires educators and parents to maintain expectations for level of achievement and rate of progress. However, this focus acknowledges that a given student may vary in degree of achievement across situations, context, and time. Furthermore, it allows us to investigate reasons for under- or overachievement rather than leaving us with a label for a student. Labels are essentially useless because it is hard to know what to do about a label.

To illustrate this point consider Ralph, a fourth-grade student. Ralph's IQ is average or typical for a fourth-grade student, but his mathematics achievement shows he is functioning at about the second-grade level. Thus, Ralph could be considered an underachiever. In addition, assessments show that Ralph has not mastered basic addition, subtraction, and multiplication facts. Currently, Ralph is being instructed in fourth-grade-level mathematics and they are working on long division. Because basic addition, subtraction, and multiplication skills are required to accurately perform long division tasks, Ralph continues to demonstrate poor progress in division. Calling Ralph an underachiever may be questionable when the real problem is that he has not mastered the more basic skills that are necessary to perform division problems.

Now assume that Ralph is given remedial instruction that enhances his skills with basic math facts and his mathematics achievement increases rapidly. Let us say he progressed from beginning second-grade level to beginning middle third-grade level in 5 months. As he enhanced his achievement 1.5 levels in only 5 months, Ralph could be now considered an overachiever if we stick to the common assumptions people make. Thus, Ralph could be considered both an underachiever and an overachiever, but neither label provided much useful information. More important, through a little investigation we discovered that (a) his placement in the curriculum did not fit his skill level, (b) he had weaknesses in specific prerequisite skills, and (c) the problem could be solved by adapting instruction to his skill level (Daly, Lentz, & Boyer, 1996).

CAUSES OF UNDERACHIEVEMENT

Because all children display overachievement (learning more than we would expect under the circumstances in the allotted time) and underachievement (learning less than we would expect under the circumstances in the allotted time), it is more productive to identify situational factors that detract from or enhance the child's learning or achievement. Identifying all instances of under- and overachievement requires us to be able to predict how much learning or achievement should occur for an individual child without considering and accurately measuring *all* the variables that affect learning. Although psychological science has identified many variables that influence learning, our science has not advanced to the point where we can precisely predict how much a given child should learn under all learning opportunities and conditions. However, we have identified generally universal instructional strategies that can be used to enhance learning rates or achievement for all students. Granted, not all students need the same strategies or learning opportunities, but the number of strategies that work with all students is relatively small, making them quite useful.

Motivation

What we call achievement is a product of learning, which is a process that requires children to actively engage in tasks that are relevant to the school curriculum. For instance, paying attention, completing homework, studying, and/or working with peers on group projects all qualify as activities that actively engage students. Regardless of the activity, if students choose not to engage in planned activities, they will not learn. One reason students may choose to not engage in planned activities is a lack of motivation for the activity or achieving the result of the activity—motivation. A variety of things can be done to enhance motivation or the probability that students will choose to engage in schoolwork. One might change how students are expected to respond in ways that are more interesting (e.g., using the computer rather than worksheets). The teacher might break long tasks down into multiple brief tasks or reduce the effort required to complete tasks. Teachers could attempt to make instructional activities more interesting (e.g., having students simulate buying items at the school store with play money rather than having them just fill in worksheets on coin com-

binations) or even allow students to choose assignments that interest them.

Students are more likely to engage in academic tasks when rewards for engaging in school tasks (e.g., receiving praise from the teacher and/or parents, getting good grades) are superior to rewards for engaging in other behaviors (e.g., fooling around with a peer, playing with an eraser on the desk). One strategy for increasing motivation for school tasks is to remove rewarding opportunities to engage in nonproductive behaviors. For example, moving a student's desk away from a friend's desk may increase the probability that the student will complete the assignment because opportunities to interact socially are decreased. Other strategies include the quality, immediacy, and rates of reinforcement delivered contingent upon doing and completing schoolwork (Neef & Lutz, 2001).

Inappropriate Placement

When students are not correctly placed in the curriculum, problems arise. For example, if instruction focuses on enhancing skills students have already mastered, then not much learning will occur. Thus, although the student is functioning well academically—indeed their grades may be excellent—they appear to be underachieving because they are not improving rapidly. All students have instances in which this occurs.

When students are provided instruction or assigned learning activities that they cannot perform because they lack prerequisite skills, then students will underachieve regardless of how well instruction is delivered. In these instances, underachievement is not related to how instruction is presented or motivational factors; rather, underachievement is caused by the student being given learning activities that he/she cannot do. In these instances, underachievement can be addressed by either remedying prerequisite skill deficits or providing accommodations so that students can learn despite these skill deficits. To prevent inappropriate placement, educators have often relied on norm-referenced achievement tests. The advantage of such tests is that they provide a broad measure of student achievement. However, they do not measure specific skill development and do not lend themselves to repeated assessment over time (to determine rate of progress). More recently, researchers and educators have begun to develop and implement curriculum-based measurement that gives brief samples of vital skills and allows for repeated assessments over time (Shapiro, 1996). Curriculum-based measurement gives a more precise measure of skill development and mastery, which in turn can lead to more accurate placement within the curriculum. This information allows teachers to know when students can be moved from one objective to the next. Thus, these procedures can enhance achievement by rapidly identifying when to move students to subsequent learning objectives.